The Postmodern Art of Imants Tillers

Commissioning Editor
Maurice Owen

Acknowledgements

Professor Nicholas Zurbrugg was my close friend and mentor whose scholarly guidance informed this text from its incipience almost to completion. I am deeply saddened by the fact that he did not live to see the final published version. Nicholas' colleague Professor Gen Doy was able to help me finish this project in his absence. Gen also enabled me to adjust my perspective from one located in Australia to one situated in the UK. Her incisive insights have added a great deal to this text. Comments by Urszula Szulakowska, Ian McLaren and Jan Birksted are also highly valued. Many thanks to Angela Lautenschlager who went through the final drafts with a fine tooth comb and a more sensitive feeling for the English language than my own. Her suggestions have made this text significantly more readable. Graham Bartlett also kindly cast his eagle eye across the first gallery proof. Thanks too to Marah Braye who applied her extremely keen typographical gaze to the final galley proof. The mistakes never seem to end. And lastly thanks to Imants and Jennifer for their help throughout this long project and to Professor Maurice Owen who made this publication possible.

The Postmodern Art of Imants Tillers

Appropriation *en abyme*, 1971–2001

Graham Coulter-Smith

Fine Art Research Centre, Southampton Institute & Paul Holberton publishing

First produced 2002 by the Fine Art Research Centre, FMAS, Southampton Institute, East Park Terrace, Southampton, SO14 0RE, United Kingdom; in association with Paul Holberton publishing, 37 Snowfields, London, SE1 3SU. books@paul-holberton.demon.co.uk

ISBN 1 874011 49 4

A full CIP record for this book is available from the British Library

Design and Production: CFAR

Printed by Hobbs the Printers
Brunel Road, Totton, Hampshire, United Kingdom

In Memory of Nicholas Zurbrugg
1947–2001

CONTENTS

CONTEXTUALISING TILLERS AND EVALUATING HIS CONTRIBUTION

In a recent history of Australian art—*Art in Australia: From Colonisation to Postmodernism*—Christopher Allen was able to note that 'The most important and representative of postmodern artists in Australia is Imants Tillers …' (Allen 1997: 194). Allen's observation stems from the current association of the term 'postmodern art' with the strategy of appropriation that came into prominence in the late twentieth century. The New York school of appropriation played a pivotal role in this movement with leading artists such as Cindy Sherman, Barbara Kruger, Sherrie Levine, David Salle, Hans Haacke and Jeff Koons. Apart from Levine and Mike Bidlo, the New York school is primarily characterised by the deconstructive appropriation of mass media imagery. In contrast, Tillers' strategy transgresses traditional concepts of authorship via the appropriation of the work of other artists.

His major contribution to postmodern art is a monumental project that will be referred to here, for reasons that will become apparent, as his Canvasboard System. It consists of hundreds of large-scale paintings constructed in a modular fashion using pre-primed canvasboards of the type used mostly by amateur artists. Each panel is stamped on the back with a consecutive number, like the pages of a book, and attached to gallery walls in gridded arrays. The list of

Installation view of the retrospective exhibition, Towards Infinity: Works by Imants Tillers at MARCO, Museum of Contemporary Art, Monterrey, Mexico, September 1999–January 2000.

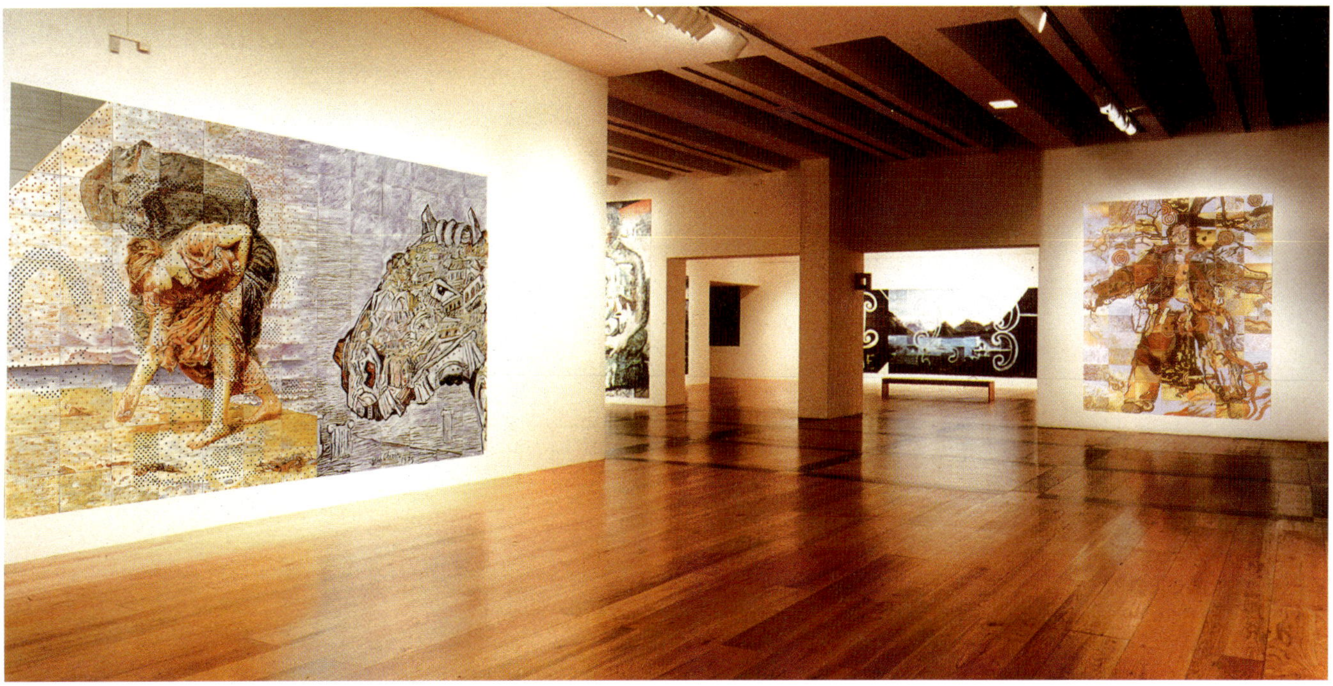

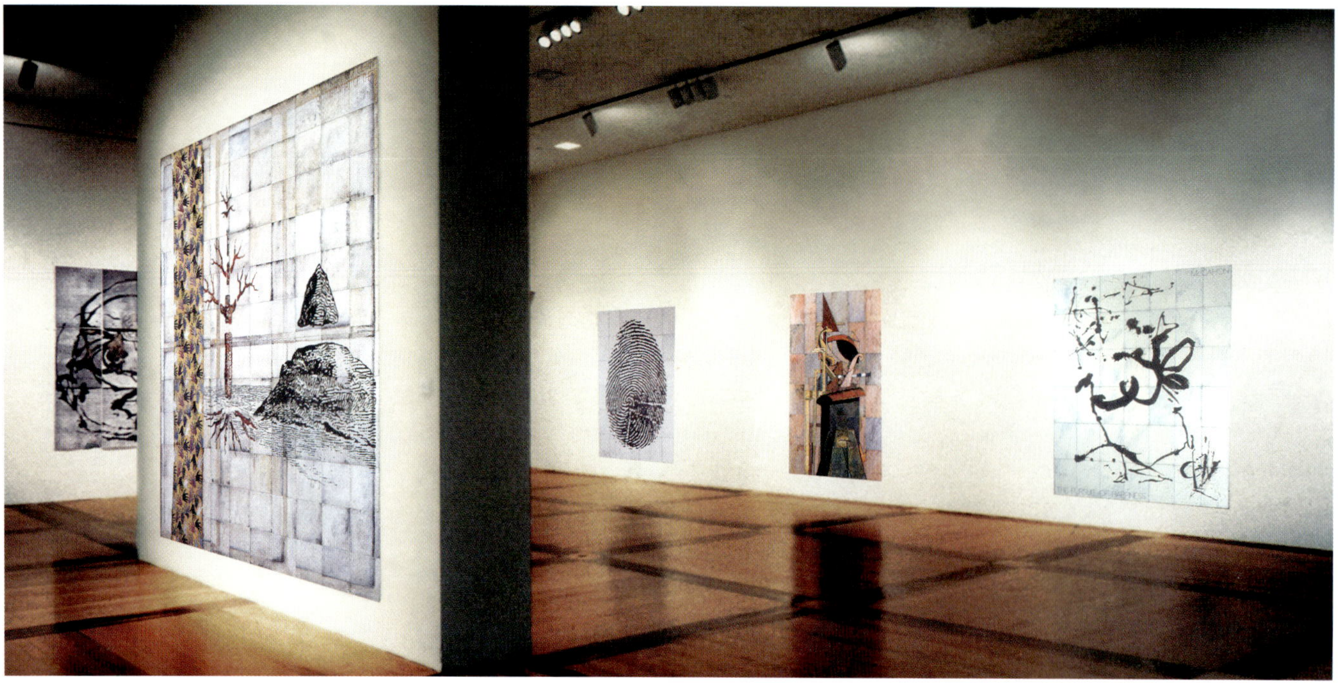

Installation view of the retrospective exhibition, Towards Infinity: Works by Imants Tillers at MARCO, Museum of Contemporary Art, Monterrey, Mexico, September 1999–January 2000.

Tillers' appropriational sources runs into the hundreds but his key sources are: Giorgio de Chirico, Georg Baselitz, Shusaku Arakawa, Robert Barry, Joseph Beuys, Sigmar Polke, modern Aboriginal Papunya painting (which has now grown into collaborations with Michael Nelson Jagamara),[1] and the powerful conceptual-religious art of the New Zealand painter Colin McCahon. The Canvasboard System was initiated in 1981-83 and continues today.

This critical account of Tillers' theory and practice will span three decades from 1971-2001. The crux of the analysis will be a demonstration that Tillers' Canvasboard System evolved out of major works produced in the 1970s such as *Moments of Inertia*, 1972-73; *Conversations with the Bride*, 1974-75; *Untitled*, 1978; and *One Painting, Cleaving*, 1980-81. It will be shown that *Conversations with the Bride* and *Untitled*, 1978, are especially successful and innovative works that provided Tillers with a solid foundation for his Canvasboard System. The detailed analysis of these works provided here plus their location within the context of developments in avant-gardist art in the late twentieth century will demonstrate that Tillers' Canvasboard System is informed by an approach to appropriation that is as sophisticated as, but also significantly different from, that evident in the New York school of appropriation.

It will be argued that Tillers' appropriational strategy is, paradoxically, highly original. His unique mode of deconstructive authorial appropriation was informed by a scientific poetics when American and European artists were oriented towards a deconstructive appropriation of mass media imagery. Yet, at the same time Tillers' work can be understood from the standpoint of key interpretations of appropriationism, in particular, Craig Owens and Rosalind Krauss' pioneering applications of poststructuralist theory to the analysis of art in the age of photo-mediated representation.

In 'Photography *en abyme*' (1978) Owens applied Jacques Derrida's concept of deconstruction to visual art using the literary theorist Lucien Dällenbach's analysis of a self-reflexive, Russian doll-like narrative structure he refers to as *mise en abyme*. In his essay Owens describes the specular logic of the *mise en abyme* as: '"when one can read a book within a book, an origin within the origin, a center within the center" and … a photograph within a photograph …' (Owens 1978: 77). Owens did not apply his interpretation to appropriationism but Krauss used a very similar approach in her early analysis of Cindy Sherman's appropriationist Untitled Film Stills series (Krauss 1984a). It will be argued that what will be referred to here as the 'Owens-Krauss interpretation' provides a valuable basis for understanding Tillers' application of authorial appropriation in combination with self-reflexivity and paradox evident in his work from *Conversations with the Bride,* 1974-75, to his most recent canvasboard paintings.

Krauss' analysis of Sherman's work emphasises her deconstruction of the concept of authorship, and it will be argued that Tillers' extensive appropriations of the work of other artists has, at least from 1978, been informed

Installation view of the retrospective exhibition, Towards Infinity: Works by Imants Tillers at MARCO, Museum of Contemporary Art, Monterrey, Mexico, September 1999–January 2000.

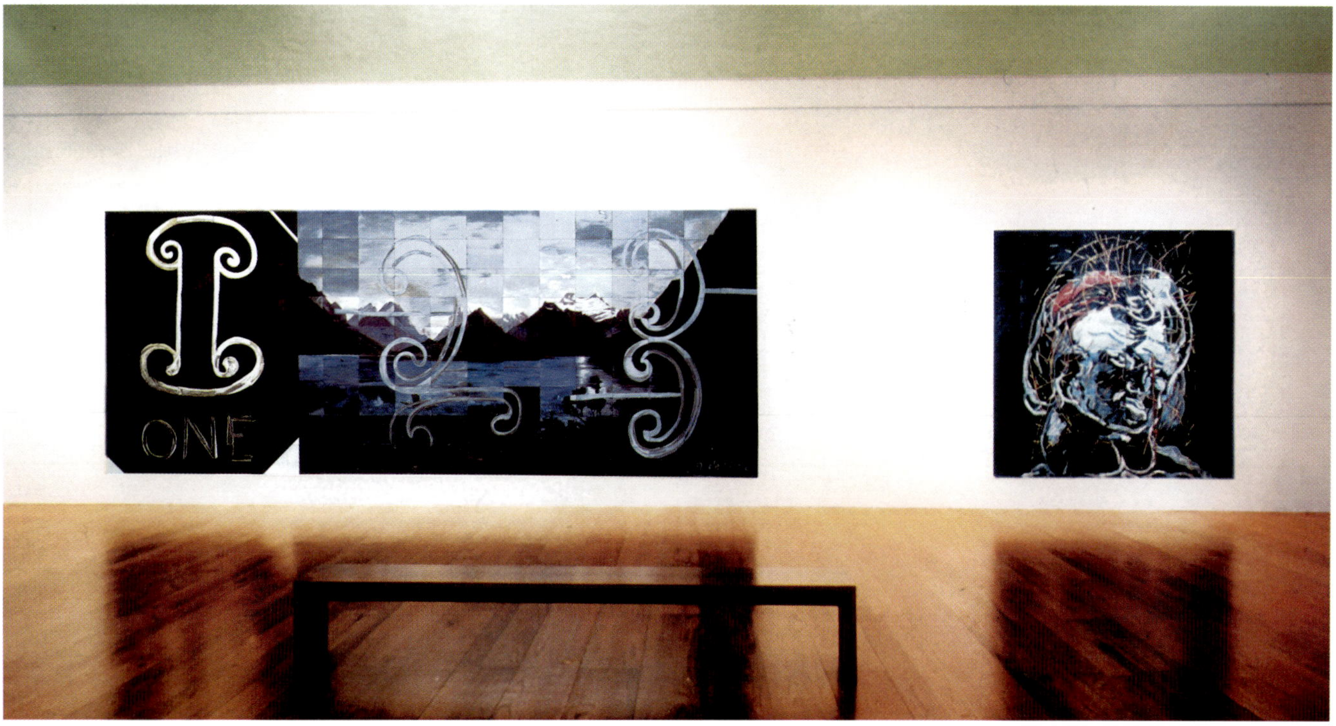

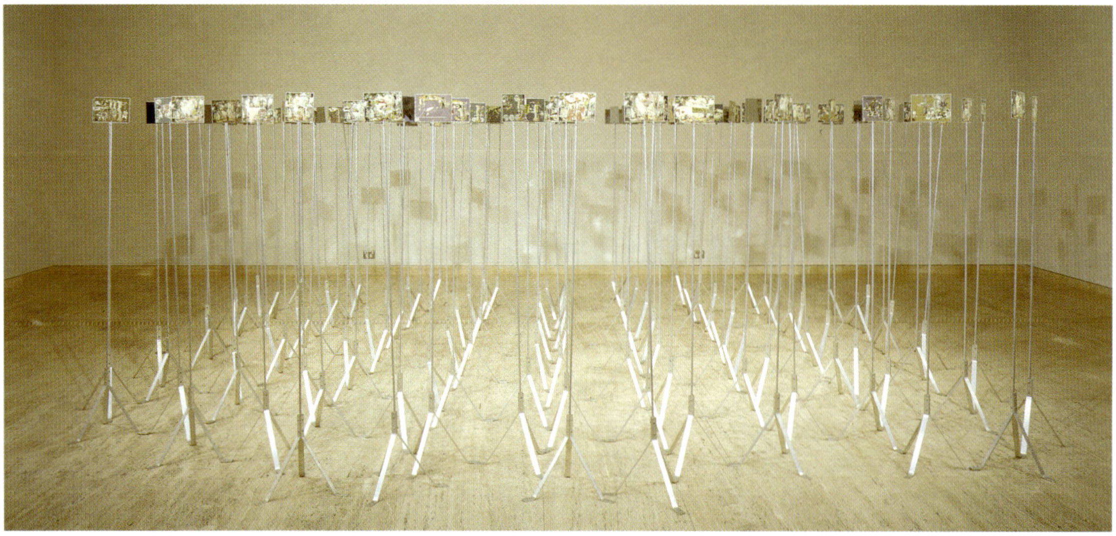

by an awareness that his authorial self is, metaphorically, 'invisible'. *Untitled*, 1978, plays a pivotal role in this respect due to the fact that it is a particularly radical appropriation of the Australian landscape painter Hans Heysen's *Summer*, 1909. The viewer is alerted to Tillers' problematisation of authorship in this work by the fact that it consists of two virtually identical paintings. To make these 'paintings' Tillers used the Neco process, sending reproductions of *Summer* to be scanned into a computer that controlled a colour paint-jet apparatus. The fact that *Untitled*, 1978, consists of photomechanical reproductions of photomechanical reproductions leads the question of its authorship into the paradoxical space of the *mise en abyme*. And this authorial infinite regress becomes intensified each time *Untitled*, 1978, is in turn reproduced. It will be shown that the authorial *mise en abyme* of *Untitled*, 1978, was inspired by Tillers' introduction to Kurt Gödel's proof that self-reflexive paradox is an intrinsic feature of mathematical logic. As far as I am aware no other artists used the Neco process as early as 1978 or Gödel's Proof, let alone both.

TOP: Imants Tillers, *Conversations with the Bride,* 1974–75. (see also opposite top). BOTTOM: Left and right hand panels of *Untitled,* 1978. From digitally restored surviving photographs, showing the different colour casts evident in the photomechancial reproductions used by Tillers as his source material (see also opposite bottom).

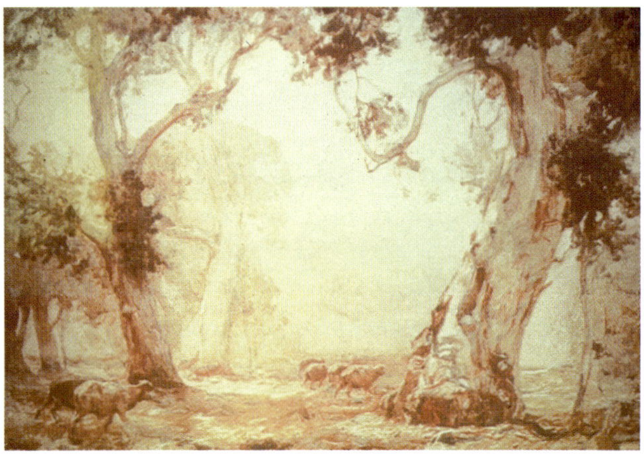

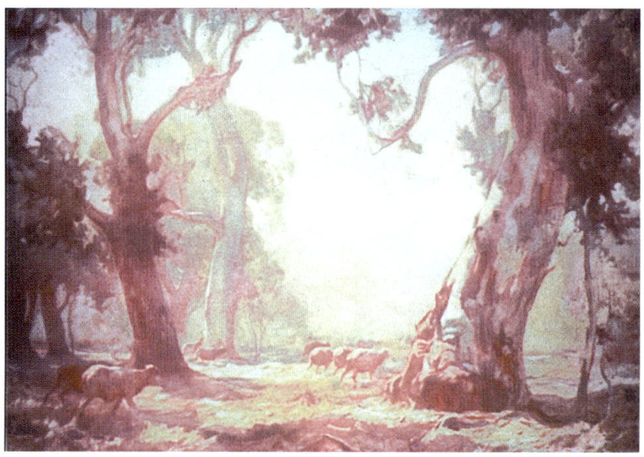

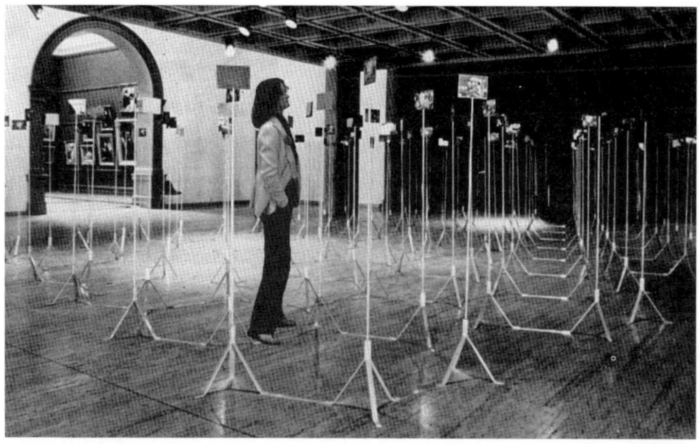

Tillers' initial excursion into the appropriation of fine art imagery is similarly concerned with creating aesthetic complexity via authorial appropriation. In *Conversations with the Bride*, 1974-75, he created an image maze comprised primarily of juxtapositions of Heysen's *Summer* with elements appropriated from Marcel Duchamp's *The Bride Stripped Bare by her Bachelors, Even*, 1915-23, also known as *The Large Glass*. To view the work the spectator must enter what Tillers calls the 'image matrix' which is also a mirror maze because each image has a mirrored back that generates random 'couplings' between the images as the spectator moves through the installation.

Conversations with the Bride can be understood as a prototype for Tillers' Canvasboard System because it is composed of a large number of discrete images that are interconnected in a nonlinear fashion. Although the Canvasboard System is considerably larger, consisting of hundreds of large paintings these individual works should be understood as interconnected in a manner Tillers refers to as 'one painting', with the qualification that this 'one painting' is 'cloven' thereby allowing innumerable intra- and intertextual 'couplings'.

TOP: Imants Tillers, *Conversations with the Bride,* 1974–75. 112 images, gouache and Resene Imperite acrylic-epoxy on chrome plated aluminium with mirrored backs mounted on aluminium stands. Each image 8.5 x 11.8 cm, stand height 163 cm, space between stands 75 cm. Collection: Art Gallery of New South Wales, Sydney. Spectator digitally inserted. BOTTOM: Imants Tillers, *Untitled*, 1978. On display at National Gallery of Australia, Canberra March 1984. Neco digital paint-jet print on canvas. Two parts each 163.9 x 185.5 cm. Collection: was in National Gallery of Australia, Canberra until lost or accidently destroyed.

And the more Tillers appropriates, the more he becomes appropriated by his appropriations. In the 1990s he came to the point when even his attempts to 'speak' about his Latvian family background, in his monumental Diaspora Trilogy (page 180), made use of the 'voice' of another (the New Zealand artist Colin McCahon). After almost thirty years of appropriating the work of other artists Tillers acknowledges that he has become encompassed and subsumed by the web of intra- and intertextual resonances he has woven.

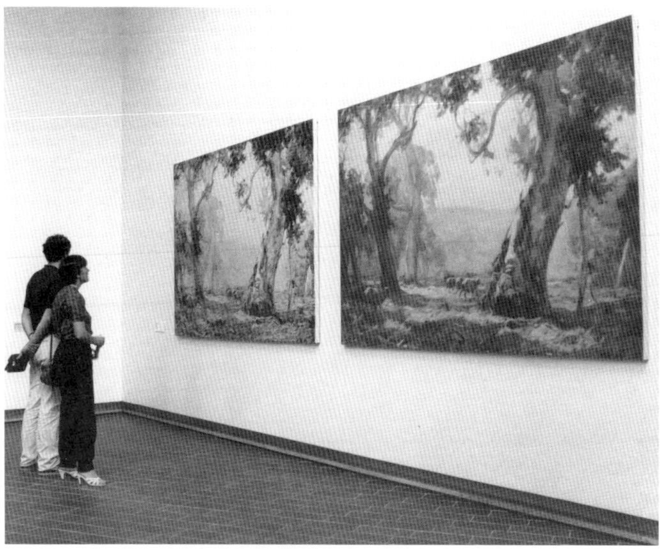

During the 1990s he described his Canvasboard System as 'self-organising' a notion that can be traced back to 1972-73 when he produced a scholarly analysis of holistic systems theory and its relationship to avant-gardist art of the 1960s—such as land and environmental art, and minimal and conceptual art. At that time Tillers' concern with systems was shared by many other artists, and he was particularly inspired by the American art theorist Jack Burnham's 'systems esthetics' approach to the interpretation of avant-gardist art of the 1960s (Burnham 1968).

One of the most important outcomes of an understanding of Tillers' holistic systems aesthetics lies in the observation that his initial turn to the appropriation of fine art imagery in 1974-75 should be understood as the appropriation of 'readymade' 'art information' that is subjected to a 'non-linear' system of 'information processing'. When one acknowledges this one also realises the originality of Tillers' mode of appropriation and the fact that it cannot be limited to the genres of appropriationism that emerged in the 1980s

THREE PHASES IN THE EVOLUTION OF POSTMODERN ART, THREE PERIODS IN TILLERS' OEUVRE

An appreciation of this fact emerges when one places Tillers' oeuvre in context. Indeed the contextualisation of Tillers provided in this analysis will show that his concern with holistic systems should be located in three interrelated phases in the evolution of postmodern art in the late twentieth century. The first phase concerns the radical avant-gardist movements of the 1960s such as minimal, conceptual, environmental and performance art. The period in which this mosaic of movements arose will be referred to here using the Australian art theorist Donald Brook's portmanteau term 'post-object art'. It is in this phase that a general concern with systems became prominent. The second phase is characterised by the increased use of photography by conceptual artists in the 1970s. I have coined the term 'photo-conceptualism' to refer to this movement. It will be argued that photo-conceptual art of the 1970s provides a bridge between post-object art of the 1960s and the rise of appropriationism in the late 1970s and 1980s. It will also be shown that Tillers' development in the 1970s displays significant parallels with two key contributors to the discourse of photo-conceptual art, Hans Haacke and Victor Burgin. This is evident in two aspects of Haacke and Burgin's work: firstly, their combination of a conceptualist concern with systems with a use of photomedia; and, secondly, in their evolution from photo-conceptualism into appropriationism, which becomes a third phase in the evolution of postmodern art in the late twentieth century.

Tillers followed a similar path but with important differences. Whereas Haacke and Burgin evolved from photo-conceptualism towards the deconstructive appropriation of mass media imagery, Tillers appropriated fine art imagery in an authorially deconstructive manner. Furthermore, whereas Haacke and Burgin's turn towards appropriation was accompanied by a relinquishment of their minimal-conceptualist concern with systems, Tillers' turn to appropriation continued the elaboration of his systems aesthetic. However, Tillers' approach to systems in his appropriational works became less informed by the post-object discourse of minimal-conceptualism and more by his increasingly sophisticated scientific poetics.

Tillers' scientific poetics began with his extension of Burnham's systems aesthetics into a *holistic* systems aesthetics based on Ludwig von Bertalanffy's mathematical descriptions of biological systems (von Bertalanffy 1950) and Ian McHarg's ecopolitical design theory (McHarg 1969). This became elaborated by his interpretation of Marcel Duchamp's involvement with the non-Euclidean conception of a fourth spatial dimension in *Conversations with the Bride*, 1974-75, and later by his introduction to Kurt Gödel's Incompleteness Theorem in 1978. It will be argued that Tillers' visual-poetic interpretation of scientific ideas has played a crucial role in allowing him to develop a unique approach to deconstructive authorial appropriation.

THE AUSTRALIAN CONTEXT

Tillers' first direct contact with avant-gardist art came in 1969 when he volunteered to assist Christo and Jeanne-Claude construct *Little Bay Wrap Up* in Sydney. Tillers described this work as 'one million square feet of coastline ... wrapped up with a cream colored Sarlon plastic and fixed with orange polypropylene rope' (Tillers 1973a: Appendix A 22). At the time he was an undergraduate pursuing an Honours degree in architecture at the University of Sydney. The fact that this was a BSc rather than a BA helps explain his ability to grasp scientific and mathematical ideas. But the fact that he was also able to apply such ideas to art stems from the cultural context in which he was located.

Tillers' contact with Christo and Jeanne-Claude in 1969 coincided with a burgeoning enthusiasm for radical avant-gardism in Sydney and Melbourne. Instances of this development include the Central Street Gallery in Sydney, Ian Burn's addition of an Australian arm to the Art & Language group, the elegant and sophisticated minimal art of Robert Hunter, the site-related sculpture of Nigel Lendon and Ti Parks and the wry humour of Aleks Danko's conceptual sculpture. A small, but informed and talented, coterie of Australian avant-gardist artists was supported by the art historian Terry Smith and art theorist Donald Brook both of whom were committed to avant-gardist art, Smith from a broadly Marxian standpoint and Brook from a position informed by the philosophy of art.

Australia's involvement in 1960s avant-gardism began in the late 1960s and developed in the 1970s and, accordingly, was somewhat delayed—a phenomeenon that reflects its unique, antipodean isolation, an English-speaking population located ten thousand miles away from New York and London. The antipodean situation is very relevant to Tillers' artistic development as it helps explain his turn to appropriation, and the originality of his approach, as will be shown later.

THE PROVINCIALISM PROBLEM

In 1974 a landmark essay on Australian art by Terry Smith was published entitled 'The Provincialism Problem' (Smith 1974). Smith's essay is important here as it had a crucial part to play in turning Tillers towards his strategy of appropriation in his second major work *Conversations with the Bride*,

1974-75. Smith's essay is a trenchant critique of Australian art that in retrospect can be understood as a provocation, an attempt to force Australian artists to realise the need for a 'world class' avant-gardist culture. Smith defines provincialism as 'an attitude of subservience to an externally imposed hierarchy of cultural values' (Smith 1974: 54) and suggests that Australian artists mimic the models set by the cultural centre: 'like a succession of faithful echoes, always open to replenishment at the sound of a new call from the other side of the divide' (Smith 1974: 55).

Smith's analysis of antipodean provincialism is scathing but at the same time extremely pertinent and strangely stimulating, as if being so radically isolated possesses an element of advantage. Certainly it will be argued here that Tillers responded forcefully to Smith's provocation by creating a means whereby provincialist mimicry could be transmuted into originality. Moreover, he did this in 1974-75, preempting the turn towards appropriation by his colleagues in the cultural centre of New York.

Ten years after reading 'The Provincialism Problem' Tillers paid homage to Smith via an essay 'In Perpetual Mourning' which contains extensive quotations from 'The Provincialism Problem' but, instead of accepting Smith's analysis of the antipodean predicament as an inescapable 'bind', Tillers interprets it as an advantage:

> Today, in 1984, we place our hope in what the English critic John Roberts has termed 'the re-emergence of a strong urban based art, oriented towards mimicry and deconstruction of the codes and signs of consumerism'. These sentiments invite us to exaggerate our natural tendencies towards mimicry, to emphasise rather than hide our provincialism, even to bathe ostentatiously in it. For once the call from the other side of the world is congruent with our real cultural condition. (Tillers 1984: 23)

In 1984 the 'call from the other side of the world' was to appropriate. But it is interesting that Tillers notes that this call to appropriation focused on the 'deconstruction of the codes and signs of consumerism' because, as has been noted, that was not Tillers' strategy—he appropriated the codes and signs of Euro-American fine art.

THE ORIGINALITY OF AUSTRALIAN APPROPRIATIONISM

Tillers' focus on the appropriation of Euro-American art is also apparent in the work of other major Australian artists associated with 'postmodern' appropriation in the 1980s, in particular: Gordon Bennett, Janet Burchill and Jennifer McCamley, Juan Davila, Lindy Lee, John Nixon, Julie Rrap, Dick Watkins and John Young. There were more Australian artists appropriating fine art in the 1980s than was the case in New York or London. Perhaps, as in the case of Tillers, this was due to the challenge of Smith's provocative definition of provincialism in terms of mimicry. Another interpretation, which also has relevance to Tillers, is that Australian appropriations of European and American fine art can be read as a postcolonial deconstruction of a cultural hegemony. As far as I am aware nobody has pointed to the fact that this aspect of Australian appropriation constitutes an alternative approach to the deconstruction of mass media predominant in the New York school of appropriationism.[2]

The number of New York artists who appropriated fine art is minimal in comparison to Australia. One can cite Sherrie Levine's series of appropriations of the works of 'master photographers' and Mike Bidlo's post-popist appropriations, but for the most part non-Australian artists such as Sherman, Kruger, Burgin, Haacke, Salle and Koons appropriated material from mass media sources.

But even in the Australian context, Tillers' appropriation of fine art sources is outstanding due to the fact that he began so early and produced an elegant and sophisticated scientific aesthetic that continues to grow into the 2000s in a manner that he describes as a 'self-organising system'. Although this notion cascades back to the very beginnings of Tillers' theory and practice, the sophistication of his scientific poetics is evident in the fact that it remains progressive, in the sense of resonating with current concerns evident in chaos and complexity theory, and explorations of 'artificial life'. Clearly Tillers' turn to appropriation cannot be reduced to his contact with Smith's 'The Provincialist Problem', for although Smith offered a powerful provocation to Australian artists he did not provide effective answers to the problem he articulated, whereas Tillers did. In order to understand how Tillers answered Smith's provocation one has to return to his earliest theory and practice. The analysis of Tillers' theory and practice provided here will explore the connections between his early and later work that will establish the uniqueness and sophistication of his contribution to post-object, photo-conceptual and appropriationist art.

THE STRUCTURE OF THE TEXT

Earlier in this introduction it was noted that three interrelated evolutionary phases of postmodern art in the late twentieth century will be delineated in this study: post-object art, photo-conceptualism, and appropriationism. The first three chapters in Part One will focus primarily on these three phases with a view to describing the contexts in which Tillers' theory and practice developed. The focus in these chapters will be upon delineating each of the three contexts and their direct influences on Tillers rather than evaluating his individual contribution. The fourth chapter in Part One will examine the body of commentary on Tillers' work across these three phases.

In addition, in Part One I will argue that the three interrelated phases delineated here can assist in understanding postmodern art as a broad set of interacting discourses and practices. It will be acknowledged that the theories of Douglas Crimp, Benjamin Buchloh, Hal Foster, Rosalind Krauss and Craig Owens that emerged in the late 1970s and early 1980s played a major role in defining the concept of postmodern art and the strategy of appropriation. However, it will be argued that Jack Burnham's systems aesthetic provides another important frame of reference, when its influence on Tillers is considered.

After the direct influences on Tillers' theory and practice have been determined in Part One, the remaining three parts will focus on evaluating the originality of his contribution within each of the three evolutionary phases. In Part Two and Part Three it will be shown that Tillers' elaboration of Burnham's systems aesthetic into a holistic systems aesthetic requires that his use of appropriation in *Conversations with the Bride*, 1974-75, and *Untitled*, 1978, be understood in terms of a Burnhamian strategy of 'processing' readymade 'art information', or as a mode of information processing within the 'art system'.

In Part Four it will be proposed that the Burnhamian aspect of Tillers' mode of appropriation extends into his Canvasboard System in a manner that demands an expansion of our understanding of the strategy of appropriation. Tillers' continuing concern with systems indicates that the ideas informing the strategy of appropriation are not limited to the international style that dominated art in the 1980s but can be traced back into the ideas and practices motivating post-object and photo-conceptual art in the 1960s and 1970s. Indeed the following examination will stretch further back into the history of avant-gardist art when the influence of Marcel Duchamp on Tillers' theory and practice is investigated.

Principally, the following analysis will demonstrate that the strategy of appropriation possesses a broader spread of historical roots than have been previously considered. And it is within this broader discourse that Tillers' achievements will be evaluated.

1

POST-OBJECT ART OF THE 1960s AND EARLY 1970s

Tillers' theory and practice of the period 1972-73 was influenced by the complex of avant-gardist movements that arose in the 1960s including: minimal art, land art, performance art and conceptual art. Major figures in these movements who influenced Tillers include: Carl Andre, Donald Judd and Frank Stella, Richard Long, Dennis Oppenheim, Joseph Kosuth, Robert Barry, and Hans Haacke. A very precise picture of the influences on Tillers is provided by his first major writing, a scholarly study given the ironic title 'The Beginner's Guide to Oil Painting'. As this key text is an unpublished dissertation and references to it appear throughout this study it has been appended here (Tillers 1973a: Appendix A).[3] The avant-gardist art movements of the 1960s developed out of a common cultural-historical context, and specific ideological and rhetorical features can be identified across these movements. At least four interrelated key generic principles motivating avant-gardist art of the 1960s can be identified: a desire to relate art to discourses and environments external to art, in particular science, social systems, environment, and ecosystems; a move away from the traditional conception of the aesthetic object; an interest in systems and the concept of art as information; and a deconstruction of the preeminence of the artist as creator. All four features are relevant to Tillers' understanding of how notions of systems relate to minimal, conceptual and environmental art and his belief that systems should attain greater importance than the individual artist.

DONALD BROOK'S PORTMANTEAU TERM: 'POST-OBJECT ART'

British and American literature on avant-gardist art of the 1960s tends to refer to this period by using the names of specific movements such as: 'minimal art', 'land art', 'performance art' and 'conceptual art'. Nevertheless, it would be useful to have a portmanteau term that reflects the common concerns evident across this mosaic of movements. As noted in the Introduction, such a term was coined by the Australian art theorist Donald Brook in 'Flight from the Object' (Brook 1970).[4] Brook's term was quickly picked up by his colleague, the art historian Terry Smith. In his catalogue essay for the Situation Now exhibition 1971, Smith elaborated Brook's concept of 'post-object art' by listing the radical avant-gardist movements of the 1960s to which the term could be applied:

> Post-object art is tremendously various. … It ranges through scatter pieces, buried sculpture, earth art, ecological art, systems art, process art, body sculpture, mail art, auto-destructive art, language art, and many more. (in Taylor 1984: 27 [orig. 1971])

Brook's term 'post-object art' is metonymic as it uses a generic feature apparent across most of the radical avant-gardist movements of the 1960s to designate all of these movements. Brook described this generic feature as a 'flight from the object' meaning a move away from the traditional notion of the work of art as a precious object. This 'flight' is manifested in work that escapes the confines of the museum such as land art and performance art or 'happenings', and it is especially evident in conceptual art. The latter meticulously avoided any use of traditional art materials preferring what was referred to by Jack Burnham (Burnham 1968) and Harold Szeeman (in ICA and Philip Morris 1969) as 'information' in the form of written text, or photographic documentation.

In 'The Beginner's Guide to Oil Painting' Tillers refers to the move away from the traditional art object when he quotes a passage from the catalogue essay for the exhibition When Attitudes Become Form (Works-Concepts-Process-Situations-Information) where Harold Szeeman notes: 'the artists represented in this exhibition are in no way object-makers. On the contrary they aspire to freedom from the object.' (in Tillers 1973a: Appendix A 16). The subtitle of the exhibition also reinforces a move away from the object in its references to 'concepts', 'process' and 'information'. Most importantly, it is the connection between the desire to move away from the aesthetic object towards a condition of art as information that is particularly relevant to Tillers. In 'The Beginner's Guide to Oil Painting' Tillers makes a clear link between the move away from the object and the concept of information when he writes:

> The recognition that art is really concerned with information processing and not necessarily working from data in the form of objects was confirmed by the emergence of conceptual art. Sol LeWitt has stated 'since no form is intrinsically superior to another, the artist may use any form, from an expression of words (written or spoken) to physical reality, equally.' (Tillers 1973a: Appendix A 25)

Later in this chapter it will be shown that Tillers' concern with the evolution of art away from the aesthetic object and towards a condition of information is indebted to Burnham's interpretation of post-object art in terms of information theory and systems aesthetics. It will also be noted that Tillers provides a substantive theoretical elaboration of Burnham's systems aesthetics in 'The Beginner's Guide to Oil Painting' (Tillers

1973a: Appendix A), and successfully translated his ideas into artistic practice in his first major work of art *Moments of Inertia*, 1972-73. In the latter he used the visual rhetoric of minimalist seriality as the basis for his initial realisation of a systemic art work. Moreover, in the more detailed examination of Tillers' theory and practice that follows Part One, it will be shown that he subjected minimalist linear seriality to a sophisticated mode of 'information processing' that led into the self-referential and nonlinear logic of the *mise en abyme*.

AUSTRALIAN POST-OBJECT ART

Although post-object art in America and Europe began in the early 1960s it did not impact on Australian art until the late 1960s and early 1970s. The delay is due to the geographical isolation of Australia and its relatively small population (12.66 million in 1970). The Australian artists who embraced the post-object genre include: Mike Parr, Jill Orr, Joan Grounds, Aleks Danko, Tim Johnson, John Armstrong, Nigel Lendon, Clive Murray-White, the Optronic Kinetics group, Ti Parks, and Imants Tillers. Ian Burn should also be mentioned as he was an active member of the conceptual art movement in New York during the 1970s. It is significant to note that Burn felt it necessary to leave Australia for New York in order to pursue his career as an avant-gardist artist.

In his landmark essay 'The Provincialism Problem' strategically published in the New York art periodical *Artforum* in 1974 Terry Smith makes it clear that in the latter part of the 1960s and in the 1970s Australian avant-gardist art was primarily dependent on the cultural hothouse of New York. Smith observes:

> New York remains the metropolitan center for the visual arts, to which artists living in the rest of America, in Holland, Germany, Brazil, England, France, Japan, Australia, etc. stand in a provincial relationship. They are making art indistinguishable from that of the majority of New York artists, but their art needs to funnel through New York before it has a chance to significantly 'change the culture', even the culture back home. (Smith 1974: 56)

One of the first instances of the influence of New York on Australian art is apparent in the group of artists associated with the Central Street Gallery in Sydney in the second half of the 1960s. They followed the 'post-painterly', 'hard-edge', 'colour field' style pioneered by the New York artists Kenneth Noland and Barnett Newman a decade earlier in the second half of the 1950s. The time lag became attenuated when high quality art journals such as *Artforum* and the London based *Studio International* began to focus on radical avant-gardist art of 1960s and the first half of the 1970s. *Artforum* was both Tillers' main source for information about American post-object art and the target vehicle for Smith's essay 'The Provincialism Problem'. The focus of Australian avant-gardist art on New York flowed through into the 1980s when New York became the centre for the genre of postmodern appropriation.

The Australian focus on New York can be traced back to the Central Street artists who initiated the strategy of deliberately engaging with a dominant American style in order to gain an international profile. But by 1970 the style adopted by the Central Street artists was considered passé by the new generation of American artists. Ian Burn, Nigel Lendon, Charles Merewether and Ann Stephen note that in 1970 Terry Smith described the Central Street artists as 'a provincial branch of an international style' having 'to this stage, nothing peculiarly Australian in its make-up' (in Burn et al. 1988: 107). Although Smith recognised the desire for international recognition that motivated the Central Street artists he saw them as incapable of achieving their goal. Burn, Lendon, Merewether and Stephen quote the following statement by Smith:

> It has now clearly reached a point where ... the success of the attempt to establish an avant-garde situation is (to put it generously) very much in the balance ... The effort to lift their art into an international context has, as regards the quality of the work, not succeeded, but has begun to succeed in drawing international attention to local art. (in Burn et al. 1988: 107 [orig. 1970])

In spite of Smith's reservations it is clear that he understands that 'the attempt to establish an avant-garde' in Australia was a primary objective in the late 1960s and early 1970s. Later it will be argued that Smith's provocative essay, 'The Provincialism Problem', can be understood as a challenge to Australian artists to 'lift their art into the international context'; and it will be argued that Tillers accepted, and answered that challenge.

The first exhibition of Australian post-object art The Situation Now was curated by Terry Smith and took place in 1971.[5] Smith's catalogue essay is interesting as it provides insight into the understanding of post-object art in Australia in the early 1970s. Smith points out that painting is becoming 'less practiced by artists' (in Taylor 1984: 26) and emphasised the growth of what he refers to as 'open-form sculpture'. Smith explains that open-form sculpture consists of:

> not objects with a core, nor even physical elements arranged coherently, but rather dispersed, thrown, placed, laid elements, disposed in real space. This kind of sculpture invokes in its perceptor a participatory

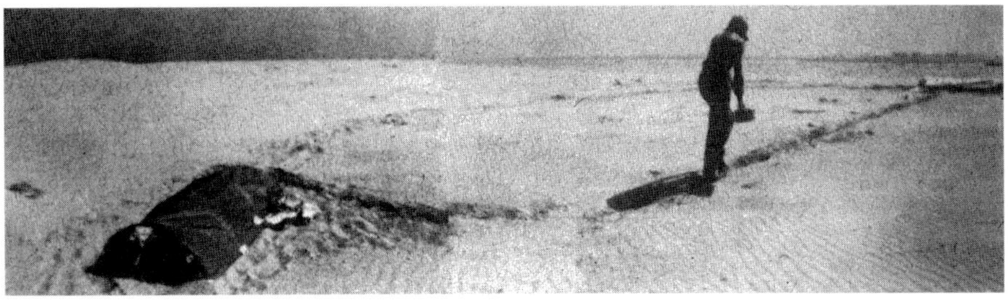

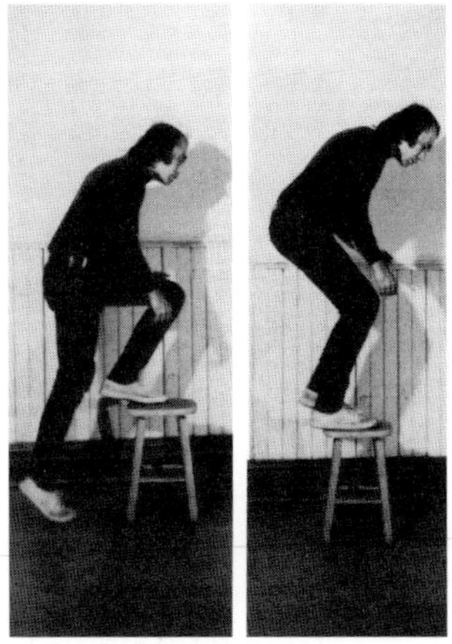

LEFT: Imants Tillers, *Enclosure,* performance, Sydney beach, Mildura Sculpture Triennial, 1973. Photograph: Alec Tzannes. Collection: the artist. RIGHT: Vito Acconci, *Step Piece,* 1970.

> sense of himself as a physical body functioning in a space continuous with that of the sculpture. (in Taylor 1984: 26 [orig. 1971])

Later in this chapter it will be shown that Smith's concept of open-form sculpture was most probably influenced by the aesthetics of minimal art, which is relevant here because Tillers' first major work *Moments of Inertia* was based on minimalist premises, and can be described very appropriately as an example of 'open-form sculpture'. Additionally, it will be suggested that the notion of open-form sculpture is elaborated into what might be described as an 'open-form painting' in his second major work *Conversations with the Bride*, 1974-75.

During the 1970s the bulk of Australian post-object art was primarily focused on two main areas; firstly, open-form sculpture (Aleks Danko, John Armstrong, Bill Gregory, Nigel Lendon, Ti Parks, Imants Tillers) and secondly performance art (Mike Parr, Peter Kennedy, Jill Orr, Aleks Danko). The varieties of performance art in Australia in the 1970s have been treated by Ann Marsh in *Body and Self: Performance Art in Australia 1969-92* (Marsh 1993). Tillers' desultory excursions into this genre are not outstanding. His most substantial performance piece is *Enclosure* 1973, part of which is reproduced above left. *Enclosure* consisted of two low-profile tents set up on a beach. Marsh describes the event as follows:

> Tillers mapped out an area on the beach in Sydney and placed two tents on the perimeter of a circle. He then proceeded to dig out the mirror-image of one tent (producing a tent-shaped hole in the ground inside the structure) and fill the other tent on the opposite side of the circle with sand extracted from the first. (Marsh 1993: 56)

In retrospect *Enclosure* seems derivative of American post-object art in a manner that contrasts with his highly innovative approach in *Moments of Inertia,* 1972-73. In *Enclosure* Tillers uses the subgenre of systematic performances evident in the work of artists such as Vito Acconci. A photographic record of Acconci's *Step Piece*, 1970 is reproduced above right. True to the spirit of post-objectness Acconci's typed descrip-

Date		Duration
Feb.	1	3 min. 20 sec.
	2	3 min. 40 sec.
	3	3 min. 8 sec.
	4	3 min. 12 sec.
	5	3 min. 20 sec.
	6	3 min. 16 sec.
	7	6 min. 36 sec.
	8	8 min. 0 sec.
	9	8 min. 48 sec.
	10	3 min. 52 sec.
	11	9 min. 8 sec.
	12	9 min. 0 sec.
	13	10 min. 12 sec.
	14	10 min. 44 sec.
	15	11 min. 12 sec.
	16	11 min. 40 sec.
	17	13 min. 20 sec.
	18	13 min. 48 sec.
	19	14 min. 40 sec.
	20	14 min. 52 sec.
	21	15 min. 40 sec.
	22	17 min. 24 sec.
	23	18 min. 8 sec.
	24	19 min. 12 sec.
	25	20 min. 36 sec.
	26	21 min. 16 sec.
	27	21 min. 48 sec.
	28	23 min. 0 sec.

Project: An eighteen-inch stool is set up in my apartment and used as a step. Each morning, during the designated months, I step up and down the stool at the rate of thirty steps a minute; each morning, the activity lasts as long as I can perform it without stopping.

tion of *Step Piece* (above) is considered as part of the work, as is his detailed account of his actions reproduced right. The systematic approach to performance art evident in *Step Piece* is echoed in *Enclosure.* But although *Enclosure* is systematic it pales in comparison with the complexity, sophistication and originality evident in Tillers' articulation of his holistic systems aesthetic in his first major work *Moments of Inertia*, 1972-73, part of which is illustrated below. The reproduction shows *Moments of Inertia: Still Life 2* as exhibited in the Art Gallery of South Australia in 1974. It fits Smith's definition of open-form sculpture as 'objects thrown rather than ordered'. There are objects on the wall, and leaning against the left hand wall and in the centre of the room there is a large cabinet which was especially constructed to house the objects that comprise *Moments of Inertia: Still Life 2.*

OBJECT AND IDEA

Tillers exhibited *Moments of Inertia: Still Life 2* in the second major exhibition of Australian post-object art: Object and Idea. The latter took place at the National Gallery of Victoria in 1973. In company with Tillers, other aspiring post-object artists were: John Armstrong, Anthony Coleing, Aleksander Danko, Nigel Lendon, and Ti Parks. Parks and Tillers exhibited open-form sculpture whereas Armstrong exhibited what might be called conceptual or allegorical sculpture somewhat similar to surrealist objects. For example, Armstrong's *Fur Tap*, 1972, is a water tap with a fur tail as its pipe. Similar work was apparent in America during the 1960s, one could cite the early work of Robert Morris and the work of Stephen Kaltenbach. Aleks Danko was the only artist to engage in performance art for this exhibition,

TOP LEFT AND RIGHT: Text components from Vito Acconci, *Step Piece*, 1970. BOTTOM: *Moments of Inertia: Still Life 2*, 1972–73. Installation view of the Link Exhibition in the Art Gallery of South Australia, Adelaide, in 1974.

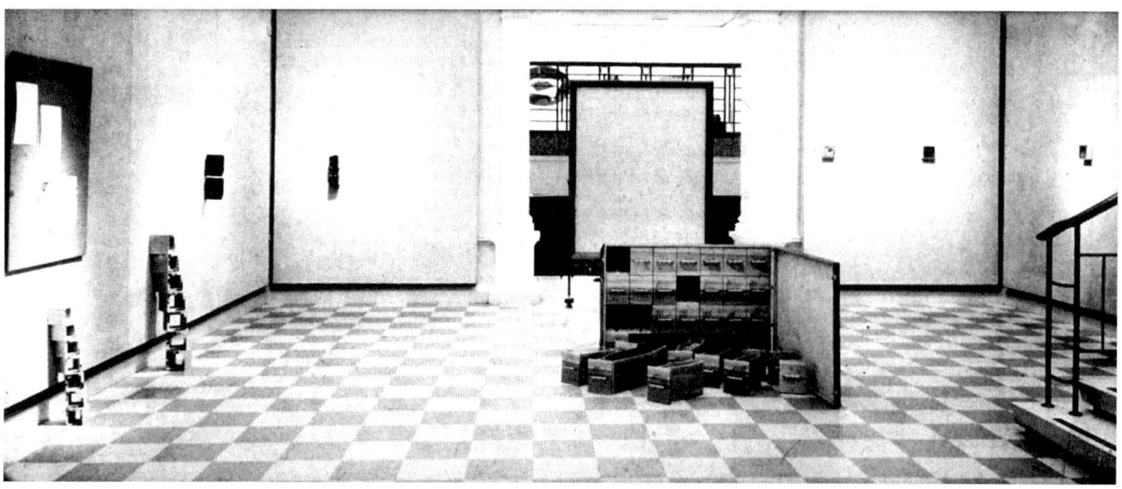

but at that time he was also producing conceptual sculptures not unlike those of Armstrong. The title of the exhibition 'Object and Idea' deserves some attention as it suggests that although the works in the exhibition are objects they are, in some crucial manner, informed by ideas and are thereby associated with the emergence of conceptual art in the latter part of the 1960s.

ART AS AN ACTIVITY 'CONTINUOUS WITH LIFE'

Apart from a move away from the traditional art object many of the radical art movements of the 1960s were also informed by a desire to relate art to society and the environment. Manifestations of this particular tendency include: the use of mass-reproduced imagery in pop art, the interaction with the exhibition space and the viewer in minimal art, the interaction with the natural environment in land art and ecological art, and the phenomenon of 'happenings' that brought art into public spaces. The desire to relate art to life was also an important strand informing the theory of post-object art in Australia during the 1970s. For instance in the catalogue essay for The Situation Now (1971) Terry Smith stated: 'The only major idea shared by all post-object artists … is that art is an activity continuous with life, not a special sort of activity separate from life.' (in Taylor 1984: 27). Significantly, Donald Brook also deployed the same phrase 'art is … continuous with life' in the context of an article on Tillers in *Art and Australia* (Brook 1975: 59). He suggested it was unlikely that Tillers' avant-gardist systems approach would become aestheticised, explaining:

> There is very little danger of this if one takes into account the general international scene, nor any reason why Australian artists should relapse into 'modernism' after breaking through to the recognition that artistic perception, like any other sort, is not a matter of sensation-having but of information-getting, that art is ideologically continuous with life. (Brook 1975: 59)

It is also interesting to note that Brook's disparagement of 'modernism' indicates that a seminal notion of what is now referred to as 'postmodern art' is evident in the post-object period.

The principle of bringing art into life is apparent in Tillers' first major work *Moments of Inertia,* 1972-73. Tillers wanted to create an interaction between the work and what he referred to, after Burnham, as the 'art system'. A primary instance of this is the fact that he held a special viewing of *Moments of Inertia* to which the critics Donald Brook and Daniel Thomas were invited. Both were asked to write reviews of the work which were subsequently incorporated into it (the texts are inserted into the cabinet that stores the objects making up *Moments of Inertia: Still Life 2*). In 'The Beginner's Guide to Oil Painting' Tillers explains:

> A systems approach reveals the interrelationship of dealers, galleries, collectors, artists and both their works and the software extensions of their works (i.e. in magazines, books, etc.). Such an approach shows that each component [of the art system] has an effect on the total art information produced and that more frequently writers, critics and historians rather than artists generate actual art information. (Tillers 1973a: Appendix A 27)

By accepting that art critics are an integral part of the work of art Tillers moves away from traditional notions of the work of art that stress the primary role played by the 'genius' of the artist-creator.

TILLERS' HOLISTIC SYSTEMS AESTHETIC

Tillers' emphasis upon the supersession of the centrality of the artist-creator stems from the influence of Burnham's 'systems esthetics' outlined in his article of the same title (Burnham 1968), but the majority of Tillers' references to Burnham in 'The Beginner's Guide to Oil Painting' (Tillers 1973a: Appendix A) are to another article, 'Real Time Systems' (Burnham 1969). Burnham's use of the term 'real-time' relates in part to its application in computer terminology.[6] This reading is supported by other Burnhamian terms noted by Tillers including: 'information', 'information processing', 'programming', and 'meta-programming'. The influence of Burnham's cybernetic systems aesthetics on Tillers is evident in a section of 'The Beginner's Guide to Oil Painting' entitled 'The Art System' where Tillers quotes Burnham stating: 'Programming the art system involves some of the same features found in human brains and large computer systems.' (in Tillers 1973a: Appendix A 18). Tillers elaborates, noting that for Burnham:

> artists are the equivalent in their position in the system to that of programs and subroutines in a computer, i.e. they prepare new codes and analyse data in making works of art. (Tillers 1973a: Appendix A 18)

Indeed, Tillers intensifies Burnham's initial analogy to the extent of claiming that artists merely produce 'raw data':

> In a sense the artist produces the raw data and critics, magazines, galleries, museums, collectors and historians all exist to create information out of the unprocessed art data. … the institutions which process art data are as important components of the system as the producer of data. (Tillers 1973a: Appendix A 18)

Tillers' statement points to a shift from the traditional concept of the transcendental role of the artist-creator towards one that conceives the artist as immanent within the systems in which he or she operates. As this analysis develops it will become apparent that such ideas provide a foundation for Tillers' questioning of the primacy of authorship in his photo-conceptual art of the 1970s and his Canvasboard System.

NEGENTROPY AND CREATION IN THE ABSENCE OF A CREATOR

In the more detailed examination of 'The Beginner's Guide to Oil Painting' in Chapter Five it will be shown that Tillers formulated a substantive elaboration of Burnham's aesthetic especially evident in his research into the 'holistic' dimension of systems. The sources for Tillers' contribution were the biologist and mathematician Ludwig von Bertalanffy's General Systems Theory, and Ian McHarg's ecological and ecopolitical theory of design. The result of Tillers' elaboration of Burnham's 'systems esthetic' will be referred to here as his 'holistic systems aesthetic' and its most central notion is that of 'negentropy'. As negentropy is such a crucial component of Tillers' seminal theory, a brief account of it will be provided here.

One of the principal sources cited by Tillers is 'The Theory of Open Systems in Physics and Biology' (von Bertalanffy 1950). In this work von Bertalanffy sought a mathematical description of the systems found in the biological domain. To this end he made a distinction between 'open' and 'closed' systems. The adjective 'open' referred to biological systems whereas 'closed' referred to the systems described by classical physics. Von Bertalanffy points out that a fundamental difference between the two species of systems is that closed systems evolve entropically whereas biological systems evolve negentropically. In physics the concept of entropy predicts that closed systems dissipate energy until the point where all their energy is spent and order collapses into disorder. In contrast as 'open', biological, systems evolve they actually increase their level of organisation and develop more complex structures, which can be described in terms of negative entropy, or negentropy. Moreover, open systems evolve in a manner that can be characterised as 'self-organising'. For Tillers negentropy has crucial poetic importance due to the fact that it entails creation in the absence of a creator—an idea that is perhaps even more mysterious than that of a divine 'god-like' creator. The influence of Burnham's systems theory and the notion of negentropy is particularly apparent in Tillers' observations on leading post-object artists in 'The Beginner's Guide to Oil Painting'.

TILLERS' OBSERVATIONS ON SELECTED POST-OBJECT ARTISTS

An examination of 'The Beginner's Guide to Oil Painting' (Tillers 1973a: Appendix A) reveals that the majority of artists who influenced Tillers were Americans: for example: Hans Haacke, Dennis Oppenheim, Douglas Huebler, Robert Barry, and Joseph Kosuth. For Tillers these artists created radical forms of art that broke down the boundary between art and everyday life, moved away from the traditional concept of the art object, and the ascendancy of the artist-creator. These three points are reinforced again and again in Tillers' discussion of these artists. But most importantly, he emphasises what he understands as the supersession of the traditional artist-creator by 'systems'.

DOUGLAS HUEBLER

Tillers provides an example of what could be referred to as 'mail art' when he examines Douglas Huebler's interaction with the U.S. postal system in a work entitled *Duration Piece 9*. The work consists of a 1 x 1 x ¾ inch plastic box which was enclosed within a larger cardboard container and sent by registered mail to an address in California. On being returned as undeliverable it was left altogether intact, enclosed in a slightly larger container and sent to Utah. When it was returned again Huebler continued the same process, selecting addresses which formed a line joining the east and west coasts of the United States.

Commenting on this work Tillers notes that 'Huebler's awareness of systems is quite substantial—he is drawing attention to the existence of various energy systems in the world that can be "plugged into".' (Tillers 1973a: Appendix A 25). Tillers concludes:

> It is significant that Huebler does not produce any art data, he selects a system already in the world (the U.S. postal service) and turns this data into art information (by simply posting a package in the mail). (Tillers 1973a: Appendix A 25)

Tillers' commentary is interesting as he focuses on all three generic principles outlined at the beginning of this chapter. Firstly, he points to the lack of an art object ('art data'); secondly, he points to the backgrounding of the artist as creator and the foregrounding of 'systems'; and thirdly, he provides an example of an artist interacting with the world outside the museum.

ROBERT BARRY

Another interaction with quite different systems already present in the environment is evident in Tillers' examination of an exhibition of radio waves by the conceptualist Robert Barry. The latter's 1968 exhibition consisted of three radio carrier waves, which is to say unmodulated waves that contain no information. In his analysis of this work Tillers notes: 'again there is no data presented as such by Barry—the things used as his data exist in the real world—he merely selects them for art processing' (Tillers 1973a: Appendix A 25). As in his analysis of Huebler Tillers identifies the presence of the three salient features outlined above: there is no art object in the traditional sense; there is an interaction with 'the real world'; and the artist as creator is backgrounded by his use of systems or phenomena already in existence.

HANS HAACKE

Tillers also addresses what might be termed an ecological work by Hans Haacke entitled *The Spray of Ithaca Falls, freezing and melting on rope, February 8, 9, 10 … 1969*. In this work a nylon rope was wrapped in screening and suspended across the falls in winter. The freezing and melting of the rope depended on environmental conditions. Flowing water and freezing cycles quickly built a snow and ice configuration over a four day period. In his analysis of this work Tillers points out that: 'Haacke reveal[s] his decision to allow natural entities to organise themselves' (Tillers 1973a: Appendix A 23). What is striking about Tillers' observation is that he focuses on the way in which the natural processes displace the traditional role of the artist as primary creator.

DENNIS OPPENHEIM

Tillers uncovers similar concerns in a work by Oppenheim where the artist interacted with the agriculture system. In July 1968 Oppenheim directed the harvest of a 300 x 900 foot oat field. Cutting, gathering, baling and trucking of bales were documented photographically. A portion of the crop was to be selected by the artist and sold in twenty-five pound sacks. Tillers' comments on this work are similar to those on Haacke, when he observes that:

> The significance of this project is that Oppenheim is using the untapped energy and information network of the day-to-day environment with a minimum of reorganisation. (Tillers 1973a: Appendix A 24)

As in his analysis of Haacke Tillers points to a foregrounding of the systems the artist interacts with over and above any contribution made by the artist. And, as in the case of *The Spray of Ithaca Falls …*, the nature of the product does not fit the traditional concept of an aesthetic object.

In each instance Tillers promotes the use of natural, self-organising systems and demotes the role of the artist or aesthetic object. He praises Robert Barry for merely selecting objects for 'art processing' (Tillers 1973a: Appendix A 25); lauds Hans Haacke for allowing 'natural entities to organise themselves' (Tillers 1973a: Appendix A 23); commends Douglas Huebler for 'not producing data' and 'selecting a system already in the world' (Tillers 1973a: Appendix A 25); and compliments Dennis Oppenheim for using a 'day-to-day environment' with a 'minimum of reorganisation' (Tillers 1973a: Appendix A 24). The analysis of Tillers' oeuvre in Parts 2-4 will show that his dedication to the supersession of the artist-creator by self-organising systems became an enduring, and increasingly elaborated, facet of his work from his first major work *Moments of Inertia*, 1972-73, to his Canvasboard System which began in the early 1980s and continues into the present.

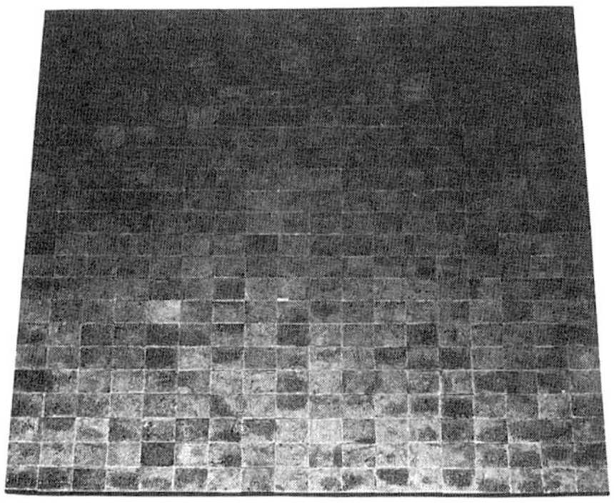

THE DUCHAMPIAN READYMADE

Another important point is that Tillers' attraction to works in which the artist uses a phenomenon that was already in existence is reminiscent of the Duchampian readymade. Indeed Tillers himself makes this connection in his discussion of Oppenheim's oat field when after observing that the work involved a 'minimum of reorganisation' of the agricultural environment he adds: it is a 'ready made' process taken from the real environment (Tillers 1973a: Appendix A 24).

The association of the term 'ready made' with the concept of an artist using a 'day-to-day environment with a minimum of reorganisation' is significant as it links Tillers' reference to the 'ready made' with his examination of works by Haacke, Huebler, and Barry. It can be suggested that Tillers is, at least implicitly, indicating that in post-object art of the 1960s the Duchampian readymade is elaborated by moving away from 'found objects' to what might be referred to as 'found systems'. Tillers' subsequent homage to Duchamp, *Conversations with the Bride*, 1974-75, reinforces the importance of taking into account Tillers' seminal understanding of the Duchampian readymade.

TOP: Carl Andre, *Brooklyn Field*, 1966. Alnico magnets; 356 units, each 2.5 x 3 cm; overall dimension 55.9 x 55.9 cm. Private collection, Elko, Belgium. BOTTOM: Carl Andre, *Equivalent VIII*, 1966. Sand-lime bricks, 12.7 x 68.6 x 229.2 cm. Collection: Tate Gallery, London.

MINIMALIST SERIALITY AND *MOMENTS OF INERTIA*, 1972–73

At the same time Tillers was writing 'The Beginner's Guide to Oil Painting' he was working on his first major work *Moments of Inertia*, 1972-73. The innovative manner in which he was able to articulate his notions of holism and negentropy in *Moments of Inertia* will be dealt with in detail in Chapter Six. The primary focus of this chapter will be on the direct influences of post-object art on Tillers' early theory and practice rather than on his contribution to the discourse of post-object art.

The primary influence on *Moments of Inertia* stems from minimal art and the present examination will focus on two major aspects of this influence: firstly, minimal art's dissolution of the barrier between artwork and viewer; and, secondly, Tillers' use of the 'systematic' rhetoric of minimalist seriality. The first point is evidenced in 'The Beginner's Guide to Oil Painting' when Tillers makes a connection between minimal art and a move away from the centrality of the author, observing that minimal art tends to intensify the role of the viewer. He notes that minimal art is informed by a 'phenomenological' frame of reference:

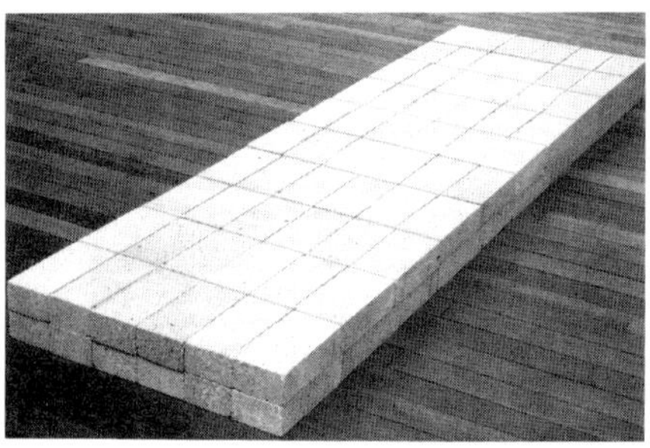

> based on the philosophical idea that experience through our senses is the only reality—in other words that experience has to be dealt with directly. Thus the object and perceiver are both conceived as necessary constituents of a specific situation. (Tillers 1973a: Appendix A 21)

The relationship between minimalist seriality and Tillers' Burnhamian understanding of systems is evident when he notes that 'the beginnings of a systems-oriented aesthetic seems to appear in Minimal Art' (Tillers 1973a: Appendix A 21). 'The Beginner's Guide to Oil Painting' is also useful as a record of the individual minimalist artists who interested Tillers most at the time he was working on *Moments of Inertia*. For example Tillers focuses on the work of Carl Andre observing:

> Carl Andre's works are typically within a strict self-imposed modular system. He uses convenient commercially available objects, like bricks, styrofoam planks, ceramic magnets, cement blocks and wooden beams. (Tillers 1973a: Appendix A 21)

Significantly, Tillers focuses on the systematic aspect of Andre's work apparent in his use of 'a strict self-imposed modular system'. His comments on Andre are particularly important because of all the minimal artists Andre has had the greatest impact on Tillers' use of a minimalist rhetoric. The illustrations on the facing page are of Carl Andre's *Brooklyn Field*, 1966, (top) and *Equivalent VIII*, 1966, (bottom):

Andre's floorpieces substantiate Tillers' reference to Andre's use of a 'strict self-imposed modular system'. *Brooklyn Field* is made up of magnetic tiles and *Equivalent VIII* is constructed of bricks, both of which support Tillers' observation that Andre 'uses convenient commercially available objects, like bricks, styrofoam planks, ceramic magnets, cement blocks and wooden beams'. Tillers' description of Andre's work in terms of a 'strict ... modular system' also points to one of the key generic features of minimalist art currently referred to as 'seriality'. In the case of Andre's rug-like floor sculptures seriality is evident in his use of the extremely simple and systematic rhetoric of the grid. The grid has played an important role in the work of other minimalist artists, notably Agnes Martin and Sol LeWitt.

Andre's 'rugs' possess another salient feature of minimal art: the dissolution of the traditional barrier between the sculptural object, its environment and the spectator that characterises traditional sculpture mounted on pedestals. His rugs enable an intimate relationship with the space in which they are exhibited and although it is not generally permitted by art galleries, Andre's original intention was to allow the public to walk on his works.[7]

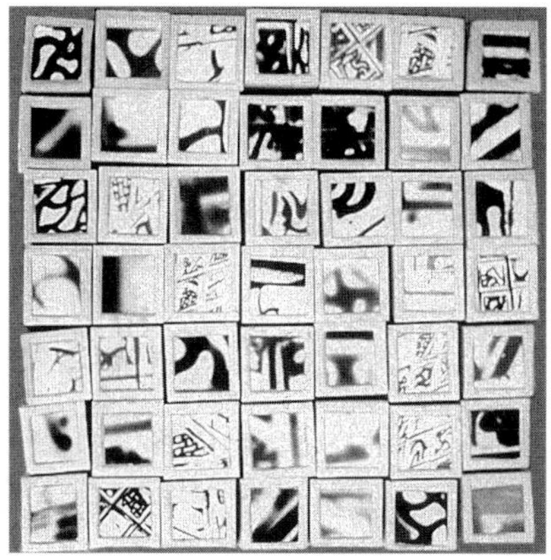

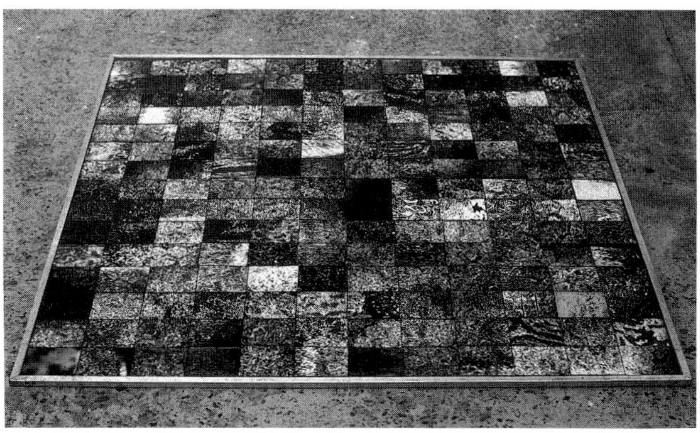

TOP: Imants Tillers, One of 7 Floorpiece objects from *Moments of Inertia: Still Life 2*, 1972–73. Ceramic tiles with photographic images applied. 49 units, each 1.7 x 1.7 cm; overall dimension 12 x 12 cm. Collection: National Gallery of Australia, Canberra. BOTTOM: Imants Tillers, *Permutant*, 1971. 180 wooden tiles with photographic images applied, 122 x 122 cm. Collection the artist.

TRACING ANDRE'S INFLUENCE ON TILLERS' OEUVRE

The influence of Andre's gridded rug sculptures on *Moments of Inertia* is apparent in what Tillers referred to as a 'Floorpiece' object illustrated above right. But Andre's influence can be traced back to Tillers' very early work, *Permutant,* 1971, illustrated below right. *Permutant* consists of a gridded array of tiles laid out on the floor. The

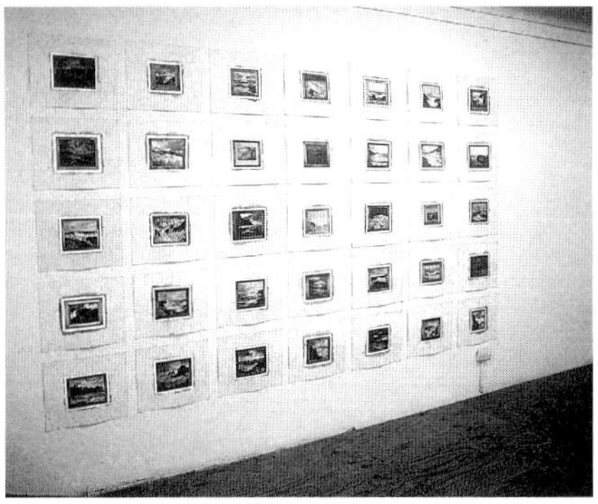

influence of Andre's grid is not only manifested in a very early work such as *Permutant* but is also a theme that can be traced throughout Tillers' oeuvre. It is evident in the gridded array of images that make up *Conversations with the Bride,* 1974-75, illustrated below left. *52 Displacements (Of Image, Of Time, Of Water, Of Feeling, One Year's Work)*, 1979-80, illustrated top left, also displays a gridded array. And the influence of Andre extends into Tillers' modular canvasboard paintings. One of the earliest works in Tillers' Canvasboard System, *Settlement at Papunya,* 1983, is illustrated below right. The installation view shows Tillers graphically portraying the influence of Andre on his canvasboard strategy by placing a very Andresque gridded 'rug' in front of the wall-mounted modular canvasboard array.

Andre's influence on Tillers' work became known in the latter part of the 1980s when Tillers was working on his Canvasboard System. It was first reported by Terence Maloon (Maloon 1986-87). And in 1988 Tillers underscored this aspect of his work in an interview with his partner Jennifer Slatyer (Slatyer and Tillers 1988) published on the occasion of his one-person exhibition at the ICA (Institute of Contemporary Arts), London. In the interview Slatyer comments: 'artists such as Carl Andre who were influential on your work in the early 70s have continued to influence you despite their exit from the centre stage' (Slatyer and Tillers 1988: 2). Tillers responds:

> It was Andre's idea of making works from mass produced 'democratic' industrial materials that led me to adopt canvasboards as the material support for my paintings in the first place. Canvasboards are of course, mass produced for amateur painters. (Slatyer and Tillers 1988: 2)

TOP: Detail of the painted component of *52 Displacements (Of Image, Of Time, Of Water, Of Feeling, One Year's Work)*, 1979–80. 52 parts gouache on canvas and 52 parts framed texts. Each canvas 34.4 x 42.5 cm; each framed text of varying dimensions. Various private and public collections. BOTTOM LEFT: *Conversations with the Bride*, 1974–75. 112 images, gouache and Resene Imperite acrylic-epoxy on chrome plated aluminium with mirrored backs mounted on aluminium stands. Each image 8.5 x 11.8 cm, stand height 163 cm, space between stands 75 cm. Collection: Art Gallery of New South Wales, Sydney. BOTTOM RIGHT: Imants Tillers, *Settlement at Papunya,* 1983. Installation view, PS 1, New York, 1984. Synthetic polymer paint on 100 canvasboards, Nos. 1655–1754, 254 x 380 cm. Collection: the artist.

Although the reference to the Andresque grid can be traced throughout Tillers' work in the period 1971-2001 it is *Moments of Inertia* and its parallel text, 'The Beginner's Guide to Oil Painting' that provide the best introduction

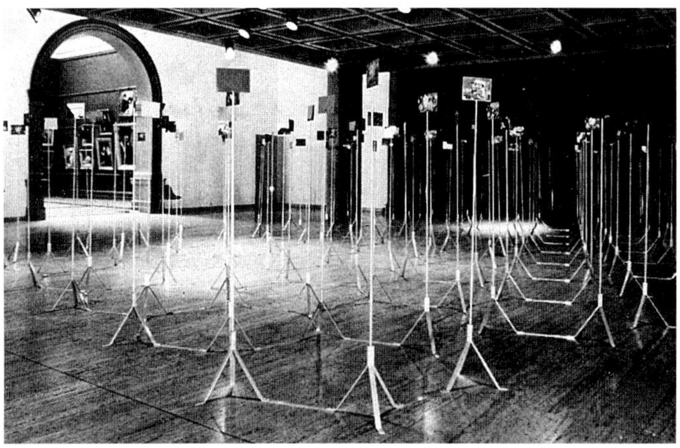

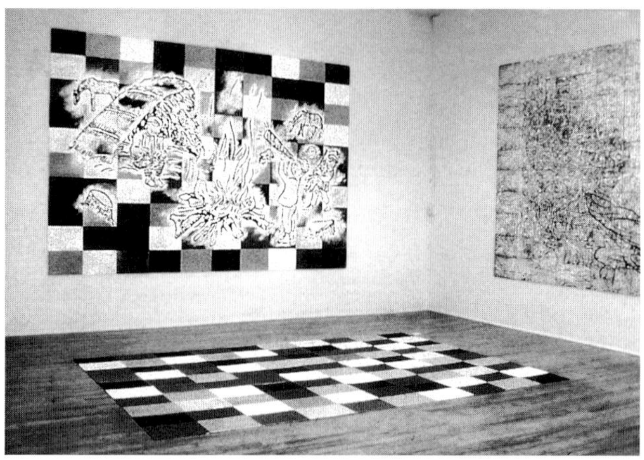

to Tillers' understanding and artistic application of minimalism. *Moments of Inertia* consists of two parts: *Still Life 1* and *Still Life 2*. The brief account here, and the more detailed analysis in Chapter Six, will focus on the latter, as *Still Life 1*, which came after *Still Life 2*, is incomplete. *Moments of Inertia: Still Life 2* consists of four basic object 'types' which are 'processed' to produce a series of seven analogues that create twenty-eight objects in total. Examples of the four basic 'object types' are reproduced below. The objects, from left to right, were referred to by Tillers as 'Floorpiece', 'Wallpiece', 'Box' (paired) and 'Frame' respectively. The formal nature of these objects can be directly related to works by minimal artists. The influence of Andre's 'rugs' on the Floorpiece has already been noted, another direct influence stems from the work of another leading minimalist sculptor Donald Judd. Two typical examples of his work are illustrated on the following page. Both works are entitled, *Untitled*, 1966. The vertical work consists of a serial array of industrially produced and finished galvanised iron boxes bolted onto a gallery wall. The horizontal piece consists of stainless steel and amber perspex boxes also bolted onto a gallery wall. Attaching the boxes onto the wall effectively makes the wall a part of the work and vice versa. As with Andre's rugs this creates an intimate relationship between the work and its environment thereby dissolving traditional barriers between the viewer and the work. Frances Colpitt's analysis of minimal art discusses such issues in terms of 'the vanishing base', or pedestal. She notes:

> According to Jack Burnham, the base functions primarily to support, to distance and dignify, and to isolate the work above it. It physically elevates the sculpture, thereby severing the work of art's contact with the ground. Thus sculpture becomes a thing apart, not sharing the spectator's space, but creating its own space, often delimited by the circumference of the plinth. The experience of a sculpture which stands on the floor without the interference of a base is more direct and immediate. Here, confrontation takes place between spectator and object on equal terms. (Colpitt 1993: 35)

LEFT TO RIGHT: Floorpiece, Wallpiece, Boxes, and Frame objects from *Moments of Inertia: Still Life 2*, 1972–73. Wood, ceramic, acrylic paint, photographic film. Floorpiece 12 x 12 cm; Wallpiece 12 x 12 cm. Boxes 2 parts each 12 cm^3; Frame, 84 x 12 x 12 cm. Collection: National Gallery of Australia, Canberra.

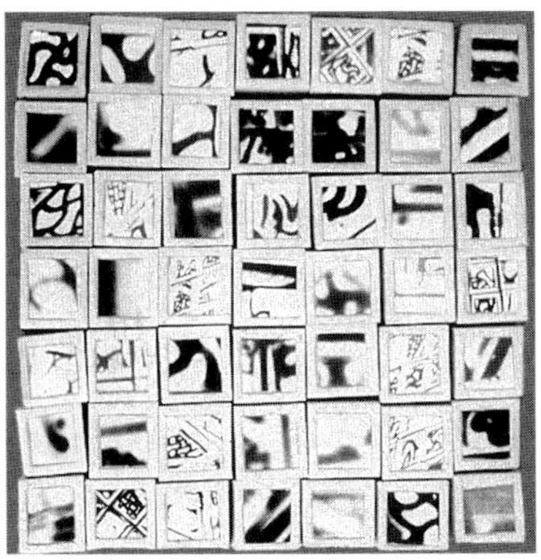

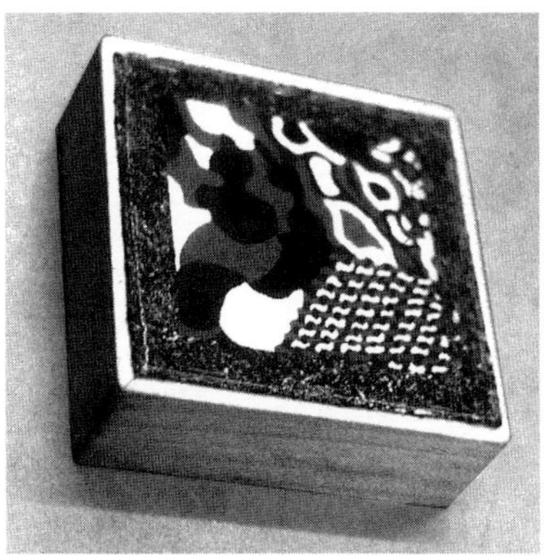

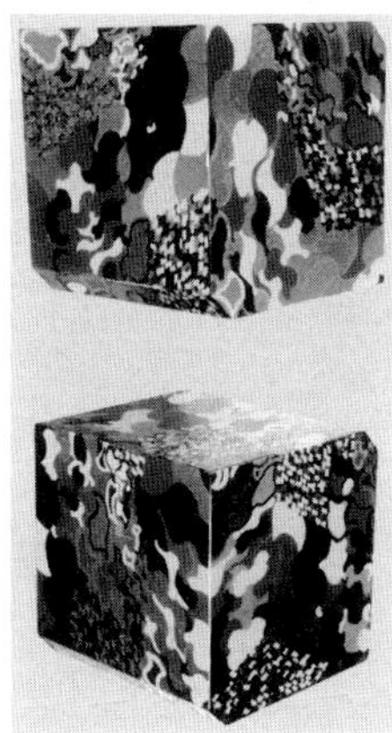

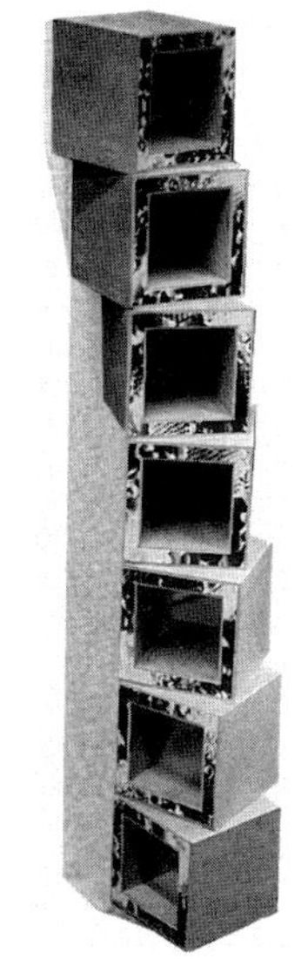

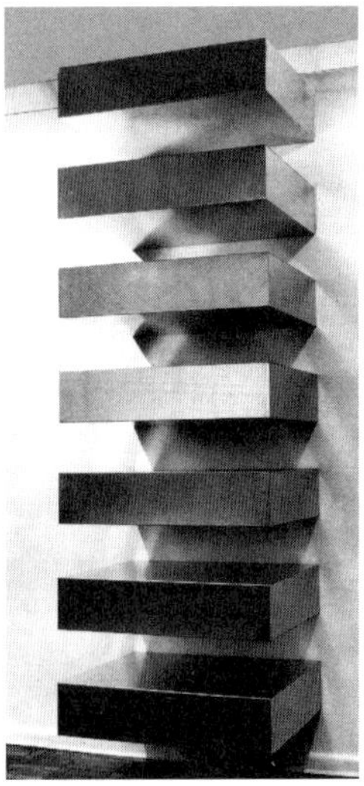

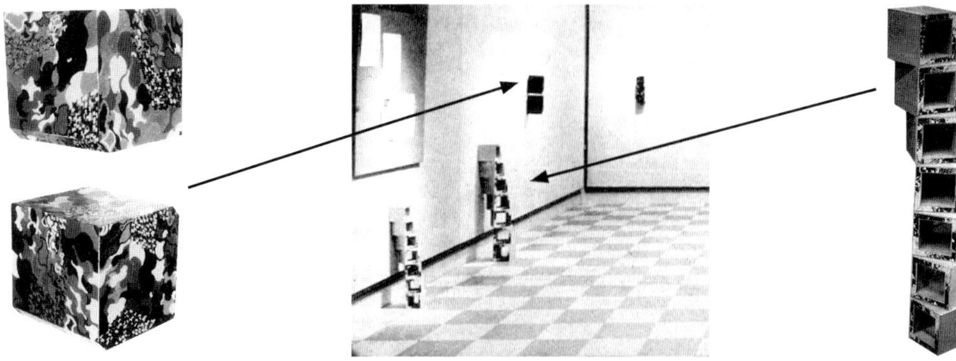

TOP LEFT TO RIGHT: Donald Judd, *Untitled,* 1966. Galvanised iron; 7 units, 23 x 101 x 78.7 cm. Imants Tillers, two Box objects from *Moments of Inertia: Still Life 2.* Detail of installation of Moments of Inertia: Still Life 2. Frame object from *Moments of Inertia: Still Life 2.* BOTTOM: Donald Judd, *Untitled,* 1966. Stainless steel, amber Plexiglas; 4 units, each 86 x 86 x 86 cm.

In 'The Beginner's Guide to Oil Painting' Tillers focuses on Judd's systematic approach to creating a work of art, observing that Judd would prepare his work by compiling a '"list structure" i.e. all the enumerated properties needed to physically build the object' (Tillers 1973a: Appendix A 21). Tillers' comments on Judd immediately precede his description of Andre's work as 'strict self-imposed modular system' (Tillers 1973a: Appendix A 21). Accordingly, in both cases Tillers' primary point of interest lies in the systematic aspect of these artists' work.

The influence of Judd's work on *Moments of Inertia* is evident in two of the objects making up *Still Life 2*: the 'Box' and the 'Frame'. Above left is a typical box-like sculpture by Donald Judd. To the right of this is a depiction of a pair of Tillers' Box objects with a pointer indicating how they are mounted on the wall when installed. The fact that Tillers mounted such sculptural objects on the wall one on top of the other indicates a direct reference to Judd.

To the right of the installation view there is an illustration of one of Tillers' Frame objects with a pointer showing that it is exhibited leaning against the wall and floor—an arrangement that echoes the way in which minimal sculpture integrates itself with its environment. Tillers' Frame objects also bear a significant resemblance to Judd's vertical box sculptures in their serial repetition of box-like shapes; but Tillers has modified this influence by introducing a systematic rotation of the open box-like shapes.

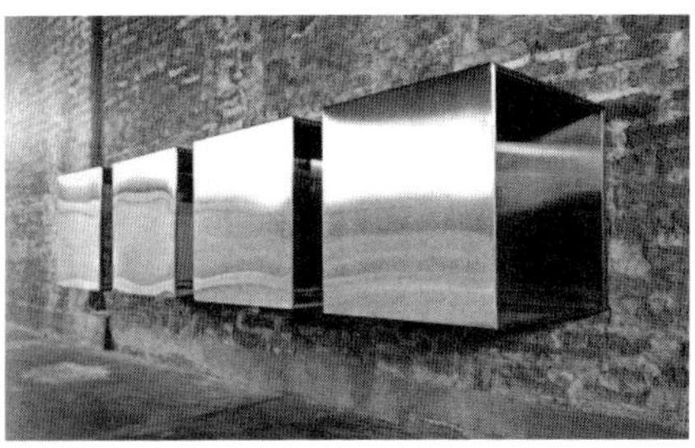

The last object type used by Tillers in *Moments of Inertia*, his 'Wallpiece', also indicates a direct minimalist influence. Tillers' Wallpiece, reproduced opposite top right, can be compared, at least in one aspect, to the minimalist paintings of Frank Stella. Two works by Stella are reproduced opposite top left. They are his Aluminium Paintings exhibited at the Leo Castelli Gallery in New York in 1960. The pointer shows that, like Stella's paintings, Tillers' Wallpiece is mounted on the wall but juts out in a sculptural manner. This is an important point of comparison as Frances Colpitt observes that Stella's minimalist 'sculptural' paintings

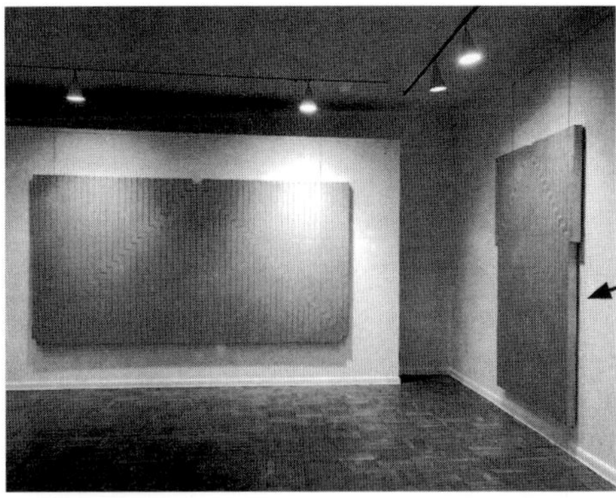

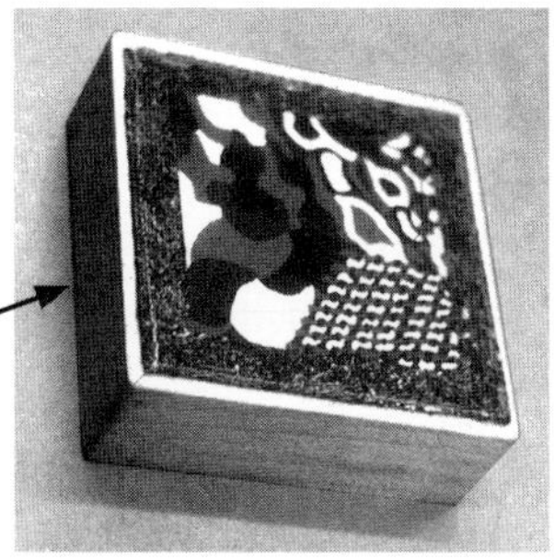

LEFT: Frank Stella, Aluminium Paintings, 1960. Aluminium paint on canvas. Leo Castelli Gallery, New York. Installation view. RIGHT: Imants Tillers, Wallpiece from *Moments of Inertia: Still Life 2*, 1972–73. Acrylic paint on canvas and wood, 12 x 12 cm.

pioneered a transgression of the generic boundaries between painting and sculpture:

> By eliminating relationships within the picture itself, relationships are (must be) established between painting and its surroundings. Thus painting appears to deal with sculptural issues, like shape and placement. Stella's paintings were the first to propose this … (Colpitt 1993: 33)

Although it is apparent that the four basic objects—Floorpiece, Frame, Box and Wallpiece—that make up *Moments of Inertia* contain references to minimal art, the originality of *Moments of Inertia* lies in Tillers' transgressive interpretation of the linear geometric formalism that is a primary characteristic of minimal art. The most important instance of this is his inscription of all the objects making up *Moments of Inertia* with the complex pattern he referred to as the 'image structure type' (Tillers 1972) and, later, as the 'image structure' (Contemporary Art Society 1974). The image structure is a highly important feature as it allowed Tillers to effectively deconstruct minimalist linear formalism in a manner sophisticated enough to provide a solid foundation for his more mature works, notably *Conversations with the Bride*, 1974-75, and *Untitled*, 1978. These works in turn form the foundation for Tillers' major work, his Canvasboard System which began in 1981 and continues, with significant variations, to the present (2002).

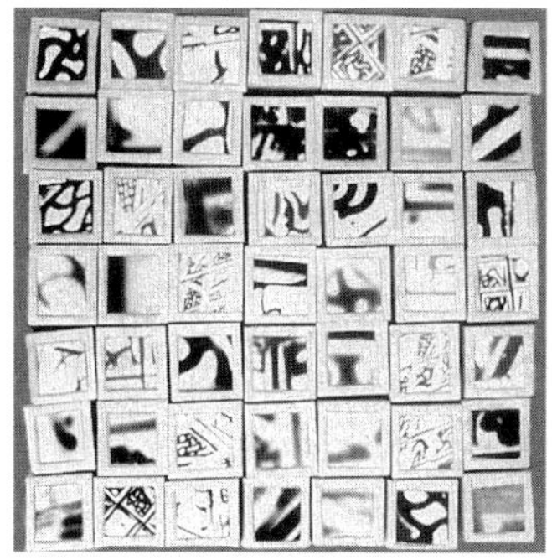

CENTRE: Floorpiece object from *Moments of Inertia: Still Life 2*, 1972–73. 49 ceramic tiles with photographic images applied. BOTTOM: *Permutant*, 1971. 180 wooden tiles with photographic images applied.

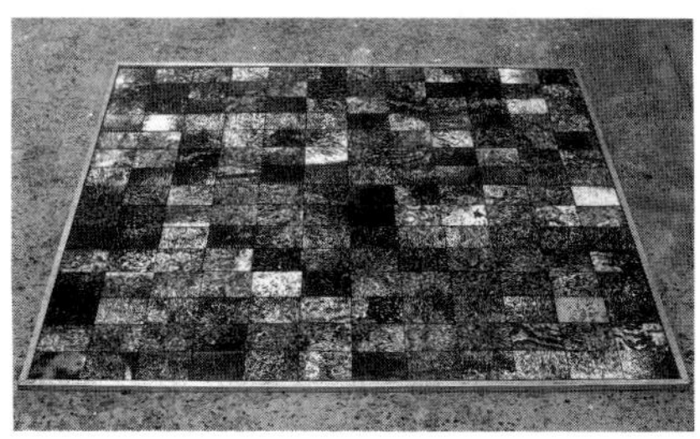

TILLERS' TRANSGRESSION OF MINIMALIST ABSTRACTION

Returning to Tillers' initial quotations of Andre's grid in *Permutant*, 1971, and the Floorpiece objects from *Moments of Inertia* (both illustrated right), it can be noted that these instances are so close to Andre's rugs that they could be considered as a direct appropriation. But this observation is contradicted by the fact that Tillers applied photographic images to each of the tiles making up Permutant and to the tiles making up the Floorpieces in *Moments of Inertia*. These images are evident in the detail of *Permutant*

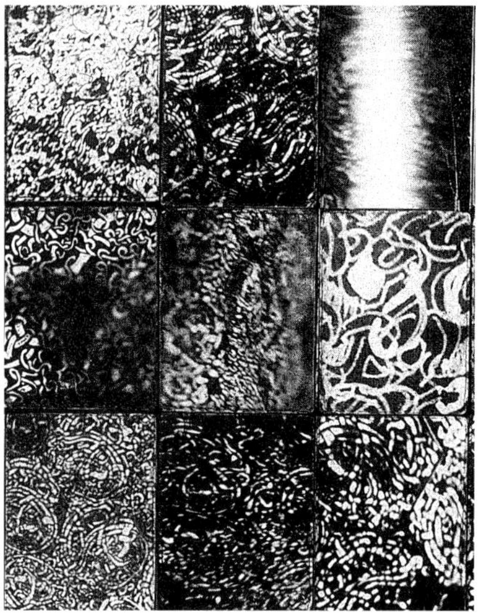

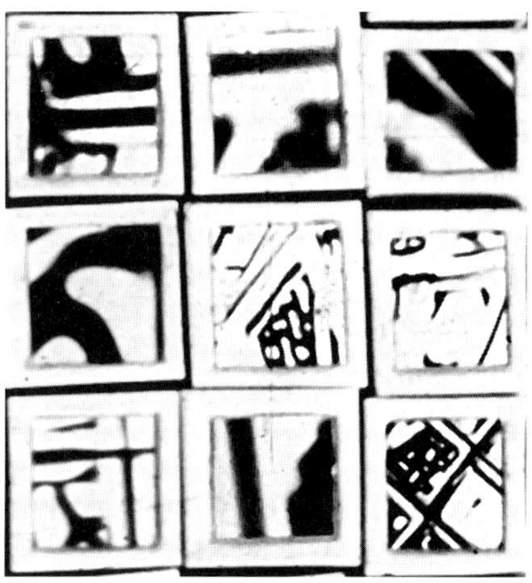

TOP: Detail of *Permutant*.
BOTTOM: Detail of a Floorpiece from *Moments of Inertia: Still Life 2*, 1972–73.

reproduced top left, and the detail of a Floorpiece bottom left. Tillers created the images applied to *Permutant* by taking photographs of a drawing he made of a complex Celtic-like pattern. The photographs of this art work were permutated by means of rotation, focusing in and out, and moving the camera nearer or further from the drawing. The examination of Tillers' understanding of minimal art provided here should be sufficient to indicate that he would have been well aware that applying an image to the minimalistic grid was a transgression of the geometric abstraction that is a key generic feature of minimal art. Moreover the image is highly complex and directly related to Tillers' interest in von Bertalanffy's attempts to create mathematical descriptions of biological systems.

Tillers used the technique he had developed for *Permutant* in *Moments of Inertia*. He attached permutated photographic images, in this case taken from a drawing of his image structure, to the tiles making up his Floorpieces. In Chapter Six it will be argued that Tillers' image structure is the most successful aspect of *Moments of Inertia*. More than any other device it allowed him to deconstruct the linearity of minimalist serialism and produce a self-referential, holistic-like complexity. It will also be argued that Tillers' deconstruction of minimalist linearity via his image structure should be understood in terms of the influence of Burnham's concept of art as 'information processing'. Most importantly, Tillers' development of his image structure laid a foundation for his increasingly elaborate and sophisticated articulations of the self-reflexive and deconstructive rhetoric of the *mise en abyme*.

This chapter has shown that Tillers' first major work *Moments of Inertia* can be located in the context of post-object art, and contains direct references to American minimal art. It has also been pointed out that *Moments of Inertia* is not simply influenced by minimal art; it is marked by Tillers' transformation of the linear geometry of minimalism into a formal vocabulary that expresses his understanding of holistic—in particular, biological and ecological—systems. A detailed examination of this aspect of *Moments of Inertia* will be provided in chapters Five and Six. Chapter Two will continue to explore the contextual influences pertinent to Tillers' artistic evolution.

2

PHOTO-CONCEPTUALIST ART OF THE 1970s

This chapter will continue to explore the influences on Tillers' work, focusing on his position within a genre that will be defined and referred to as 'photo-conceptual art'. During the 1970s Tillers produced two outstanding works that built on his experimental articulation of his holistic systems aesthetics in *Moments of Inertia*. These works are: *Conversations with the Bride*, 1974-75, and *Untitled*, 1978. Both are remarkably innovative works that constitute not only a valuable contribution to the discourse of photo-conceptual art but also a solid foundation for Tillers' Canvasboard System.

Defining the genre I am referring to as 'photo-conceptualism' is important as it provides a means for contextualising *Conversations with the Bride* and *Untitled*, 1978. If these works are examined without contextualisation their sophistication and originality are difficult to explain. Locating Tillers within the discourse of photo-conceptualism is also important because photo-conceptualism provides a bridge between post-object art and appropriationism. The following analysis will use the artistic development of Hans Haacke, Victor Burgin and Imants Tillers to demonstrate lines of evolution from photo-conceptualism into appropriationism. It will be shown that Haacke and Burgin follow very similar pathways whereas Tillers takes an alternative but parallel route.

FROM PHOTO-CONCEPTUALISM TO APPROPRIATIONISM

Like Tillers, Haacke and Burgin's work in the early 1970s exhibits a minimal-conceptualist concern with systems. But in the latter part of the 1970s both Haacke and Burgin relinquish their concern with systems in the course of their evolution from a post-object mode of photo-conceptualism into a proto-appropriationist mode. The latter is characterised by its deconstructive appropriation of mass media imagery employing photography in a manner that emulates the mass media. It will be established that Tillers' photo-conceptual work also evolves towards a proto-appropriationist mode; but,

THE EVOLUTION OF PHOTO-CONCEPTUAL ART INTO APPROPRIATIONISM

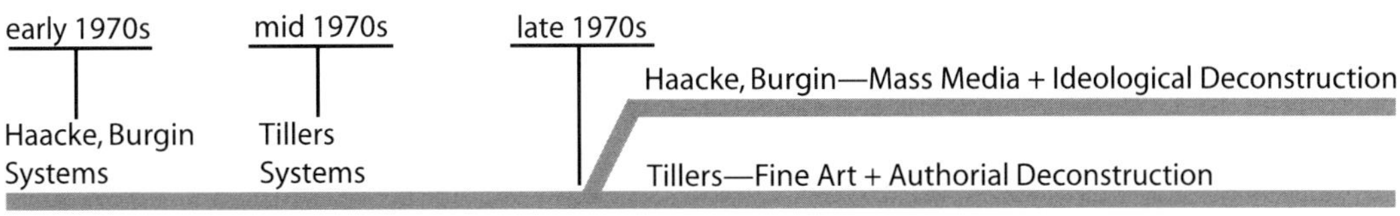

unlike Burgin and Haacke, Tillers continues to pursue a systems aesthetic and its concomitant concern with the relationship between art and science.

The diagram on page 29 shows lines of evolution for Tillers, Haacke and Burgin. In the early part of the 1970s Haacke and Burgin were involved in a mode of photo-conceptual art that continued a minimal-conceptualist concern with systems, be they social systems, as in the case of Haacke, or semiological systems, as in the case of Burgin. By the mid-1970s Tillers was also producing photo-conceptual art that was informed by his artistic interpretation of both minimal-conceptualism and scientific holistic systems theory. In addition, Tillers had turned to the appropriation of 'readymade' 'art information'. Haacke and Burgin's photo-conceptual art also evolved into a strategy of appropriation, but their source material was mass media imagery. Moreover, whereas Haacke and Burgin focused on the deconstruction of mass media ideology, by 1978 Tillers' use of appropriation had evolved into a deconstruction of authorship. It should be noted at this point that this development in Tillers' work can be traced back to his discussion of specific works of art from the 1960s including Haacke's *The Spray of Ithaca Falls ...*, 1969, where Tillers argued that there was a movement away from the centrality of the artist towards a foregrounding of 'systems' (Tillers 1973a: Appendix A 23-25). What follows is a stylistic-generic analysis demonstrating the ways in which photo-conceptualism of the 1970s evolved out of conceptual art and into deconstructive appropriation.

LEFT: Joseph Kosuth, *Titled (Art as Idea as Idea, Nothing)*, 1967. Photostat mounted on cardboard, 120.7 x 120.7 cm. The Panza Collection. © Artists Rights Society (ARS), New York. DACS, London. RIGHT: Lawrence Weiner, *A Stake Set*, 1969. Language and the materials referred to site specific, dimensions variable. Guggenheim Museum, New York. Panza Collection, Gift. 92.4182. © Artists Rights Society (ARS), New York. DACS, London.

THE ORIGINS OF PHOTO-CONCEPTUAL ART

Conceptual art emerged as a major genre of post-object art in the latter part of the 1960s. Tony Godfrey observes that the term 'conceptual art' 'first came into general use around 1967' and 'reached both its apogee and its crisis in the years 1966-72' (Godfrey 1998). And writing in the early 1980s Lucy Lippard noted: 'today's activist art has its roots in the later sixties ... primarily in mini-

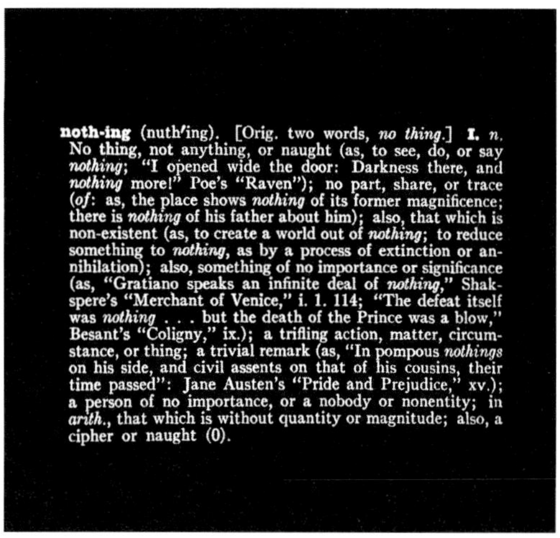

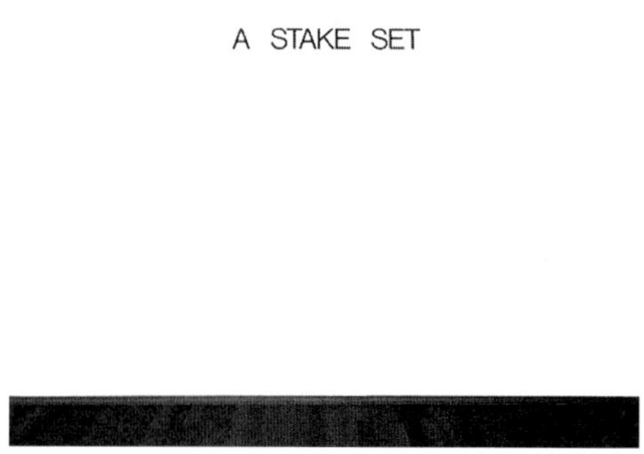

mal and conceptual art' (Lippard 1984: 350). In its early phase conceptual art is typified by the work of artists such as Joseph Kosuth and Lawrence Weiner, who made use of verbal text in a manner that can be understood in the context of the general movement in post-object art away from the traditional art object. Typical works by Kosuth and Weiner produced in the late 1960s are illustrated on the previous page. The Kosuth is in the form of a large scale photostat, which is significant when considering the role of photography in conceptual art. The fact that it is black and white and square indicates the influence of minimalism. Yet conceptual art differs from minimal art due to the fact that the introduction of text marks a radical departure from the abstractionism that is a key generic feature of minimal art. The Weiner would be painted directly onto a gallery wall following the convention established by minimal art to create a relationship between the work and its exhibition space; and, as in the case of Kosuth, Weiner relinquishes minimalist abstraction via his use of text. The move away from the abstraction of minimal art initiated by the introduction of the discursive dimension of text was reinforced in the early 1970s by the incorporation of photographic imagery. As was noted in the discussion of Tillers' application of his image structure onto minimalistic forms in the previous chapter, the image is especially antithetical to the abstractionist aesthetics of minimal art. The introduction of photographic imagery can be discerned in the installation view of the Information exhibition at the Museum of Modern Art, New York, reproduced below left with a detail to the right.

The importance of this exhibition is noted by Irving Sandler who comments: 'with its 1970 exhibition, *Information,* the Museum of Modern Art put its establishment stamp of approval on conceptual art' (Sandler 1996: 7). The use of photographic imagery in the exhibition is apparent in the large scale reproduction of what appears to be a page from a newspaper in the right hand half of the installation view. Photographic imagery is also evident in the left hand portion of the installation view which shows a gridded array of images, a detail of this is shown to the right of the installation view.

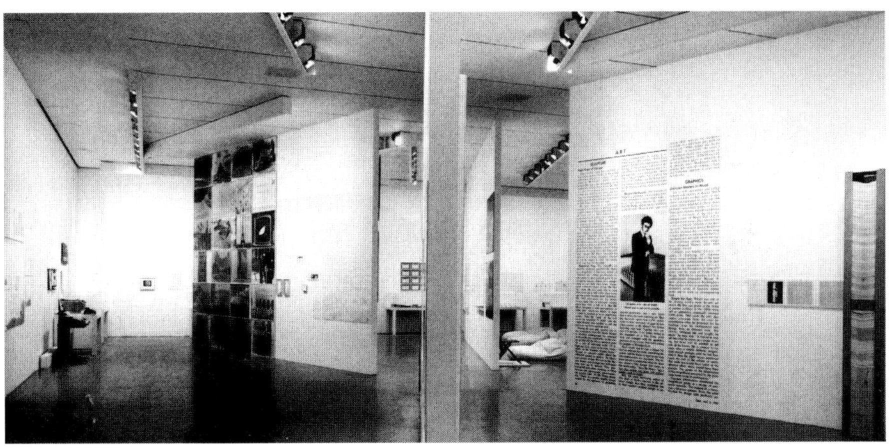

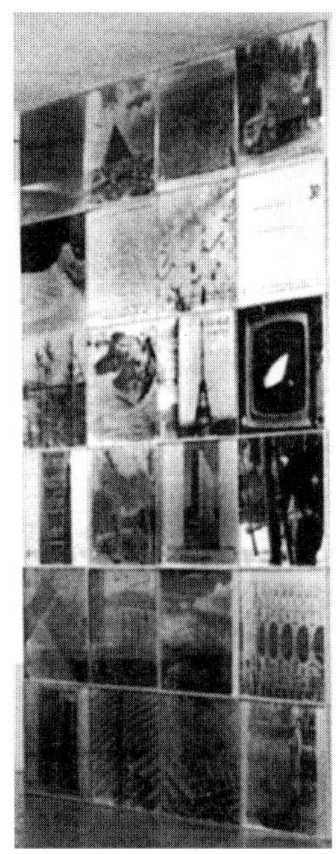

LEFT: Information, Museum of Modern Art, New York, 2 July–20 September 1970.[8] Photo © 1995 The Museum of Modern Art, New York. RIGHT: Detail.

PHOTO-DOCUMENTATION, MINIMALISM AND PHOTO-CONCEPTUALISM

The use of photography by conceptual art can be traced back to the role played by photo-documentation in post-object art movements that arose prior to conceptual art, in particular land and performance art. In his recent examination of land art and environmental art Jeffrey Kastner reports that 'Artists found alternatives to the gallery or museum by co-opting other urban building types or by working in the open air.' He elaborates, noting that in 1969 Barbara Rose wrote that: 'A dissatisfaction with the current social and political system results in an unwillingness to produce commodities which gratify and perpetuate that system.' (in Kastner and Wallis 1998: 13). The problem with making work outside of the gallery system was that it was in many instances ephemeral and, or, inaccessible. In spite of this, sufficient evidence of the movement is extant to serve as illustrations for art historical studies such as Kastner's. This is made possible by the fact that most land and environmental artists used photography to document their work. Although this photo-documentation, somewhat ironically, facilitated an assimilation of such radical forms back into the museum, at least it did so in a form that can be described as 'information' as opposed to being in the form of precious *objets d'art*.

TILLERS ON CHRISTO AND PHOTO-DOCUMENTATION

Tillers' analyses of 1960s avant-gardism indicate his awareness of the salient role played by photo-documentation. As has been noted, he had first hand experience of this phenomenon as early as 1969 when he helped Christo and Jeanne-Claude construct his *Little Bay Wrap Up* which he described as 'one million square feet of coastline ... wrapped up with a cream colored Sarlon plastic and fixed with orange polypropylene rope' (Tillers 1973a: Appendix A 22). But his comments regarding the role played by photo-documentation are particularly interesting when he observes:

> The coastline remained packaged for a few weeks and once the plastic coating was removed there was no evidence at all on the actual site of the event having taken place. ... Thus the work itself is only obtainable through a photographic record. (Tillers 1973a: Appendix A 22)

LEFT: Edward Ruscha, *Every Building on the Sunset Strip,* 1966. Installation view, '18 Paris IV', 66 rue Mouffetard, Paris, April 1970. Organised by Michel Claura. Photo courtesy The Siegelaub Collection and Archives. CENTRE: Robert Barry *One Billion Dots,* 1971. Twenty-five volumes. Photograph courtesy The Getty Centre for the History of Art and the Humanities, Santa Monica, California. RIGHT: On Kawara, *One Million Years,* 1969, Index card from catalogue for '557, 087'.

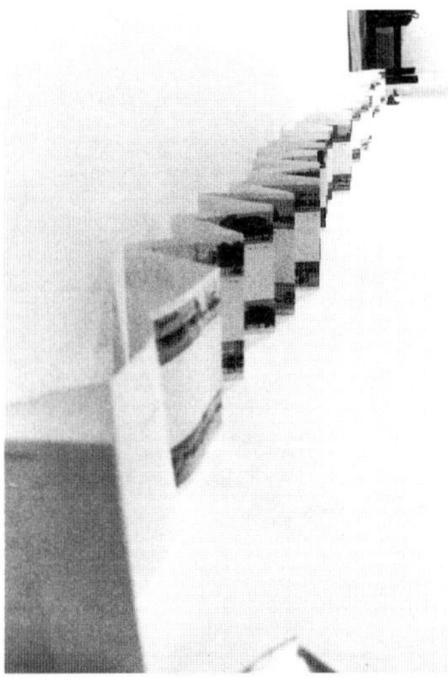

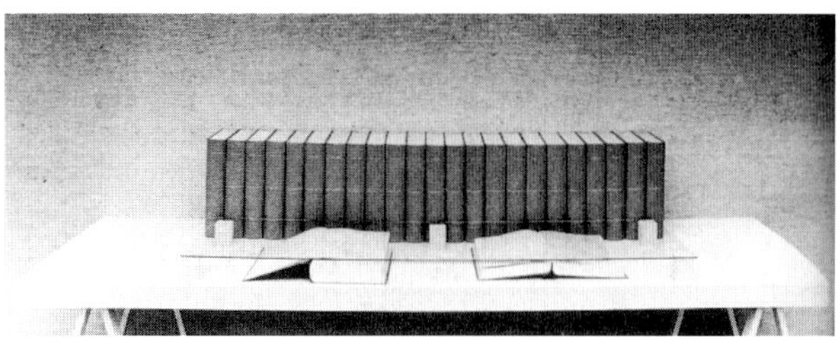

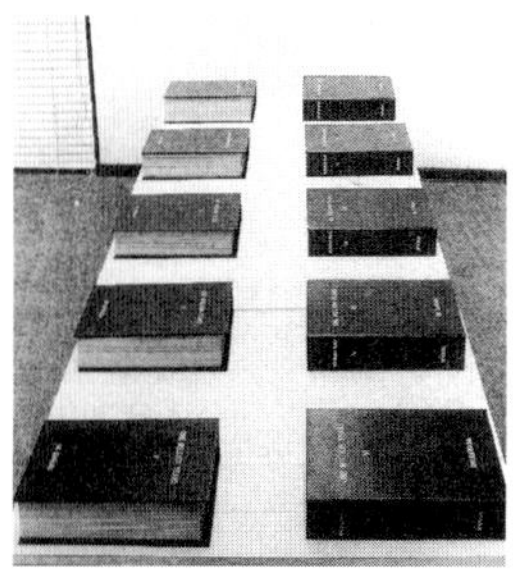

It is the last sentence that points to the critical role played by photo-documentation, and to the fact that Tillers' involvement with Christo and Jeanne-Claude's project made him aware of this role at a very early stage in his development as an avant-gardist artist. In his recent study of conceptual art Tony Godfrey points to the connection between the role of photography as photo-document in post-object art and its subsequent application in conceptual art when he notes:

> The initial role of photography in Conceptual art was to document actions or phenomena. ... The naive view that underlies much early photography by Conceptual artists was that the camera was an 'opinion-less copying device', as the curator Donald Karshan put it in 1970. It was a way of pointing at or indexing something in the world. (Godfrey 1998: 303, 306)

Godfrey's analysis is even more illuminating when he notes:

> Conceptual art has had the widest possible effect on how photography is used in art, because it does not take the medium as a given, but as something whose mechanisms and use have to be analysed. (Godfrey 1998: 301)

Godfrey's comments are valuable as they help explain how the use of photography in conceptual art evolves from the condition of photo-documentation into something more self-reflexive and self-critical.

Benjamin Buchloh points to another distinction between a discursive and non-discursive application of photography in conceptual art in his essay 'From the Aesthetic of Administration to Institutional Critique (Some Aspects of Conceptual Art 1962-1969)'. Buchloh analyses the role played by minimalist serialism in conceptual art in terms of an 'aesthetic of administration' which he defines as occurring when 'an arbitrary abstract principle of pure quantification replaces traditional principles of pictorial or sculptural organization and/or compositional relational order' (Buchloh 1989: 46). He cites a list of works that include: Edward Ruscha's photographic fold-out panorama entitled *Twenty Six Gasoline Stations*; Robert Barry's *One Billion Dots*, On Kawara's *One Million Years*, and Douglas Huebler's life-long project to photo-document everyone alive entitled *Variable Piece* (Buchloh 1989: 45-46). These works are reproduced below on this and the facing page (in the case of Ruscha a similar work has been illustrated). Each case displays a rhetoric of seriality that can be traced

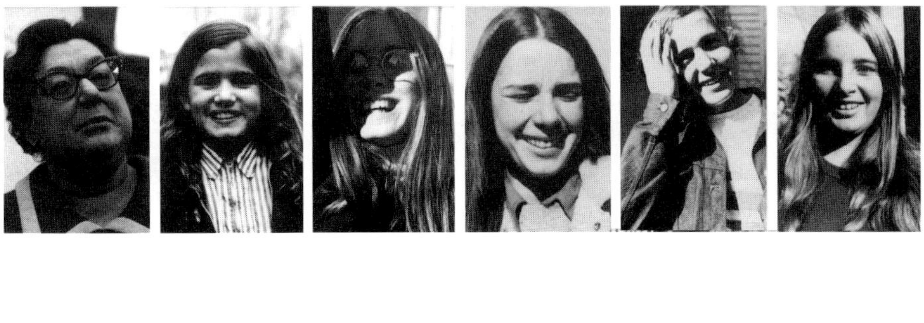

Douglas Huebler, Details from *Variable Piece #34,* 1970. An accompanying typewritten text reads 'During November, 1970 forty people were photographed at the instant exactly after the photographer said, "You have a beautiful face."' © Artists Rights Society (ARS), New York.

back to minimal art, such as the works by Andre and Judd examined in the previous chapter. It is this minimalist formalism that informs Buchloh's concept of 'an arbitrary abstract principle of pure quantification' replacing 'traditional principles of pictorial or sculptural organization and/or compositional relational order'. Significantly the term 'relational' was used by one of the pioneers of minimal art, Frank Stella, to differentiate minimal art from European geometric abstraction:

> European geometric painters ... strive for what I call relational painting. The basis of their whole idea is balance. You do something in one corner and you balance it with something in the other corner. Now the 'new painting' is being characterized as symmetrical. ... It's nonrelational. (in Batcock 1968: 149)

It is also noteworthy that the visual examples cited by Buchloh mix textual and photographic modes of conceptual art. However, Buchloh's analysis reveals that he believes that it is only when the text is able to generate socially relevant meaning that it transcends minimalist formalism.

Buchloh goes on to contrast the implicitly minimalist rhetoric of 'pure quantification' informing the photo-conceptual work of Ruscha and Huebler with a pioneering instance of the combination of text and photography in Dan Graham's *Homes for America*. Interestingly, Graham's piece is not only photo-conceptual but entirely informational due to the fact that it exists primarily as an article published in *Arts Magazine* in December 1966. One page from Graham's work is illustrated below left, on the right are details of his photographs, text and his systematic, serialistic analysis of the mass produced housing he had photographed for the piece. Buchloh points out that Graham's

LEFT: Page from Dan Graham, *Homes for America*, 1966–67. Written and printed texts and black and white and colour photographs mounted on illustration board. Two panels. Each 101.6 x 76.2 cm. Daled Collection, Brussels, Photograph: Paula Goldman. RIGHT: Details from *Homes for America*.

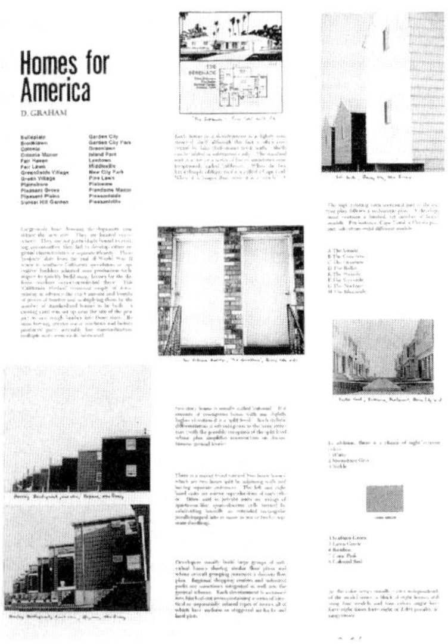
Homes for America

D. GRAHAM

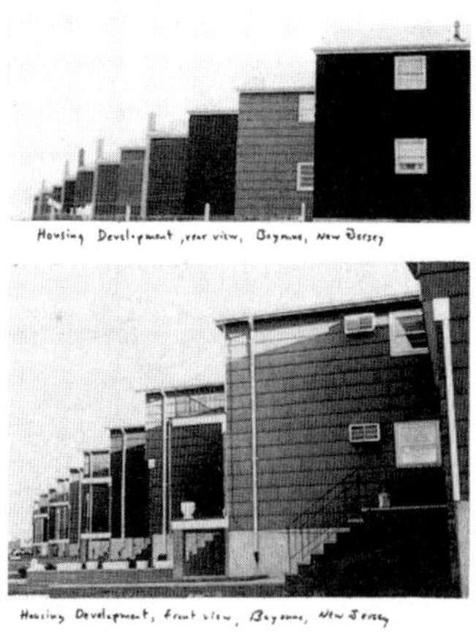

Each block of houses is a self-contained sequence – there is no development – selected from the possible acceptable arrangements. As an example, if a section was to contain eight houses of which four model types were to be used, any of these permutational possibilities could be used:

AABBCCDD	ABCDABCD
AABBDDCC	ABDCABDC
AACCBBDD	ACBDACBD
AACCDDBB	ACDBACDB
AADDCCBB	ADBCADBC
AADDBBCC	ADCBADCB
BBAADDCC	BACDBACD
BBCCAADD	BCADBCAD
BBCCDDAA	BCDABCDA
BBDDAACC	BDACBDAC
BBDDCCAA	BDCABDCA
CCAABBDD	CABDCABD
CCAADDBB	CADBCADB
CCBBDDAA	CBADCBAD
CCBBAADD	CBDACBDA
CCDDAABB	CDABCDAB
CCDDBBAA	CDBACDBA
DDAABBCC	DACBDACB
DDAACCBB	DABCDABC
DDBBAACC	DBACDBAC
DDBBCCAA	DBCADBCA
DDCCAABB	DCABDCAB
DDCCBBAA	DCBADCBA

Homes for America displays a discursive use of photography that communicates a socially relevant message:

> The Minimalists' detachment from any representation of contemporary social experience … resulted from their attempts to construct models of visual meaning and experience which juxtaposed a reductivist formal strategy to a structural and a phenomenological model of perception.
>
> Graham's work, by contrast, argued for an analysis of (visual) meaning which defined signs as both structurally constituted within the relations of a language system as well as grounded in the referent of social and political experience. (Buchloh 1982: 46)

It appears that Buchloh understands Graham's work as socially relevant because of the fact that its juxtaposition of photo-documents and text has reference to the praxis of everyday life. According to Buchloh's analysis a mode of photo-conceptual art dominated by minimalist seriality, such as that of Ruscha and Huebler, is less significant than a mode that opens up the discursive potential of integrating text and photographic images. Buchloh's analysis is useful here as the discursive dimension offered by the juxtaposition of photographic image and text laid the basis for the genre of deconstructive appropriation that characterises much appropriationism of the 1980s. It is also crucially relevant to the evolution of the photo-conceptual work of Haacke and Burgin.

HANS HAACKE AND VICTOR BURGIN

The image reproduced below left, is an installation view of Hans Haacke's *Shapolsky et al. Manhattan Real Estate Holdings: A Real-Time System, As of 1 May 1971*, 1971; a detail is reproduced below right. Like Graham's *Homes for America* this work makes use of photo-documents accompanied by text. It is significant that, like other examples of photo-conceptualism, the installation of Haacke's work continues to utilise a rhetoric of minimalist seriality, however, this serial formalism is accompanied by a discursive dimension.

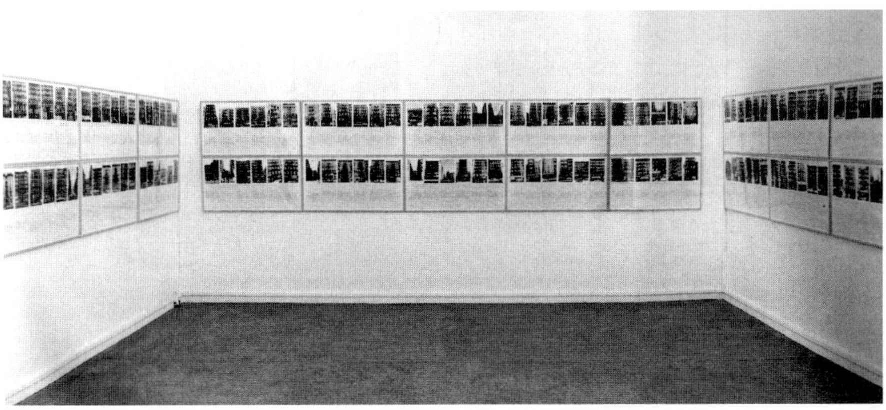

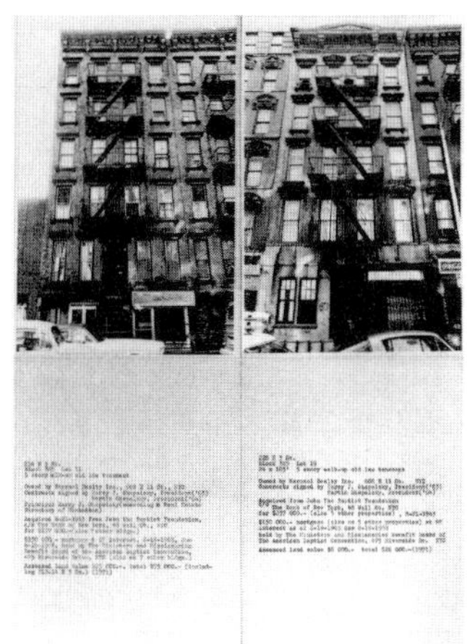

LEFT: Hans Haacke's *Shapolsky et al. Manhattan Real Estate Holdings: A Real-Time System, As of 1 May 1971*, 1971. Two maps, 142 black and white photographs with typewritten data sheets framed in 23 sets of 6 per frame, 6 charts, and explanatory panel (edition of 2). Maps: each 61 x 50.8 cm; photographs and data sheets: each 50.8 x 19.1 cm; charts: each 61 x 25.4 cm; panel 61 x 50.8 cm. Collection the artist. Installation view, Venice Biennale, 1978. Photo courtesy the artist and John Weber Gallery, New York. RIGHT: detail.

Shapolsky et al. ... consists of photographs of real estate in New York accompanied by text displaying information Haacke collated from the public records of the County Clerk's office. The information consisted of details of the owners, previous owners, landlords, mortgages and other business transactions. Tillers refers to *Shapolsky et al. ...* in 'The Beginner's Guide to Oil Painting' quoting a press release by Haacke from 3 April, 1971 which states:

> The works contain no evaluative comment. One set of holdings are mainly slum located properties owned by a group of people related by family and business ties. The other system is extensive real estate interests owned largely in commercial interests, held by two partners. (in Tillers 1973a: Appendix A 26)

Tillers appears impressed by the fact that even in the absence of 'evaluative comment' the exhibition was cancelled by the Director of the Guggenheim Museum 'because Haacke's work in correlating physical decay with specific financial transactions seemed to be too politically loaded' (Tillers 1973a: Appendix A 26). But what is especially important to this analysis is the fact that Tillers' focus on Haacke's statement that his photo-texts 'contain no evaluative comment' relates to a post-object concern for a diminution in the role of the artist in favour of a foregrounding of systems, in this case exploitative financial and real estate systems. Parallels between Haacke's concern with system and that of Tillers are especially evident in the sub-title of the Shapolsky work '*A Real-Time System, As of 1 May 1971*'. Haacke's use of the phrase 'real-time system' relates directly to Tillers' references to Jack Burnham's analyses of post-object art in terms of 'real-time systems' in 'The Beginner's Guide to Oil Painting' (Tillers 1973a: Appendix A 8, 19 ff.). In addition, it can also be noted that the term 'real-time' refers to the context of computer science and 'information processing' indicating that, like Tillers, Haacke was still interested in the scientific notion of systems in the early phase of his photo-conceptualist period.

Another salient example of photo-conceptualist art that corresponds with Tillers' concern with systems is illustrated below. It is Victor Burgin's

RIGHT: installation view, Victor Burgin *Performative/Narrative*, 1971. Black and white photographs and printed text in sixteen parts. Each 45.7 x 86.4 cm. LEFT: detail. Courtesy the artist, John Weber Gallery, New York, and Galerie Liliane & Michel Durand-Dessert, Paris. © DACS, London.

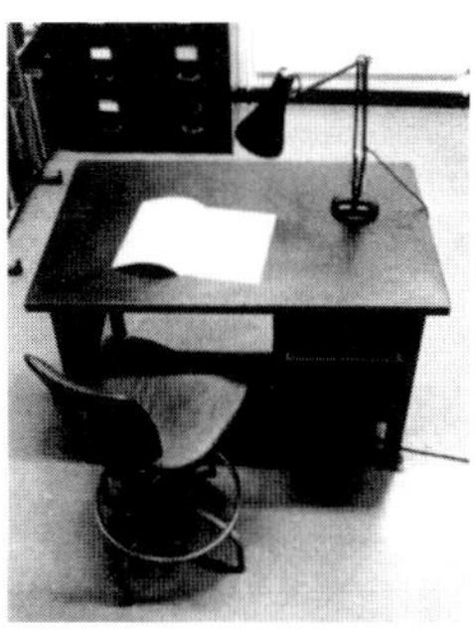

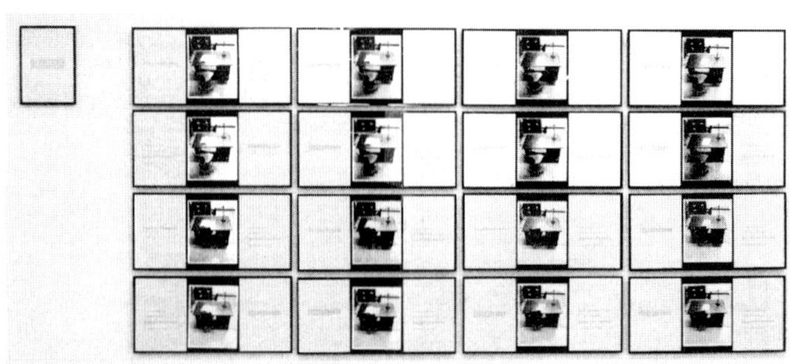

Performative/Narrative, 1971. Like Haacke's piece this work combines photographs with text using an implicitly minimalistic serialism for its formal display. A detail of one of the photographs used in the series is reproduced to the left of the installation view. At first sight the photographic image appears to remain the same throughout the set of images but in fact it is what Ann Rorimer describes as:

> a series of different photographs of permutations of binary states of the same object: a desk (drawer open or closed), a chair (under the desk or away from it), a reading lamp (on or off), and a file folder (open or closed). A series of binary digits (e.g., 0101) appears in each section of the work and reflects the changed state of the objects photographed. (in Goldstein and Rorimer 1995: 94)

Two parallel texts accompany the photographs, one provides a narrative dimension describing events that might have taken place in the office. The other text uses terms from Boolean algebra which describes binary logic in terms of operators such as 'and/or' and 'and/not'.[9] Rorimer notes that:

> the final sequence of numbers, "0000," corresponds to propositions that begin "not…, not..., not…, not…"). This sequence asks viewers to consider all the criteria upon which their knowledge is based. (in Goldstein and Rorimer 1995: 94)

Binary logic lies at the heart of cybernetic information processing and, like Haacke's reference to 'real time systems', can be related to Burnham's analysis of post-object art in terms of a cybernetic conception of systems. This con-

LEFT: ***Conversations with the Bride,*** **1974–75. 112 images, gouache and Resene Imperite acrylic-epoxy on chrome plated aluminium with mirrored backs mounted on aluminium stands. Each image 8.5 x 11.8 cm, stand height 163 cm, space between stands 75 cm. Collection: Art Gallery of New South Wales, Sydney. Spectator digitally inserted. RIGHT: Detail.**

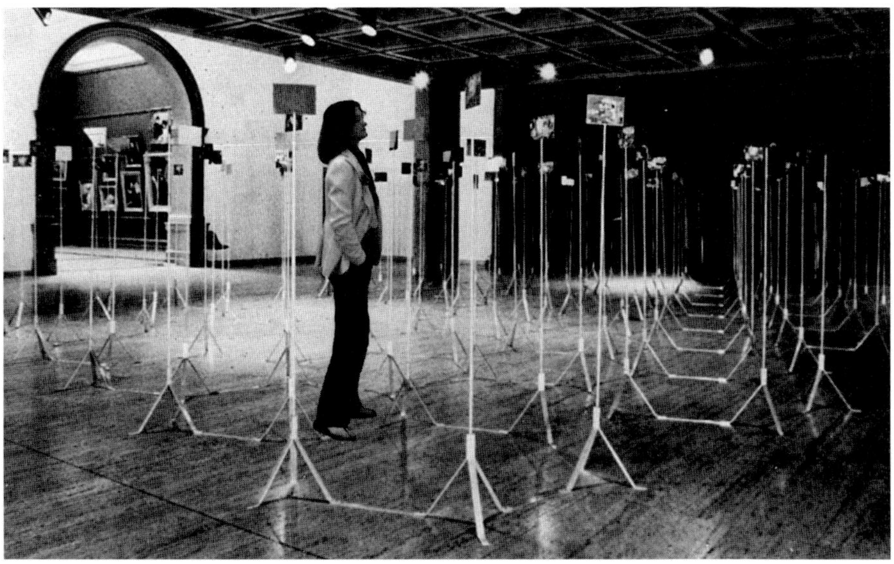

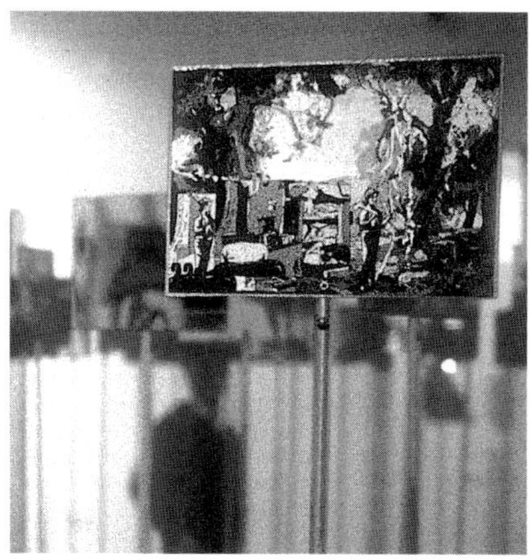

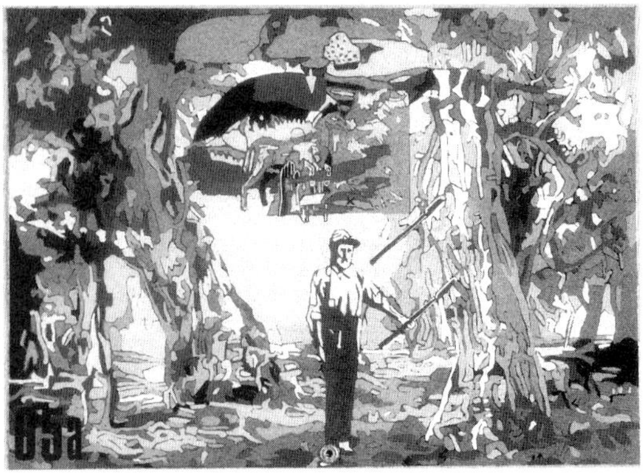
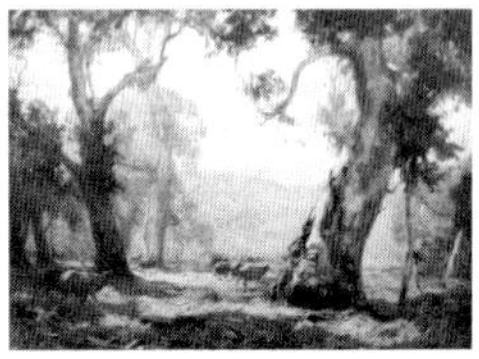
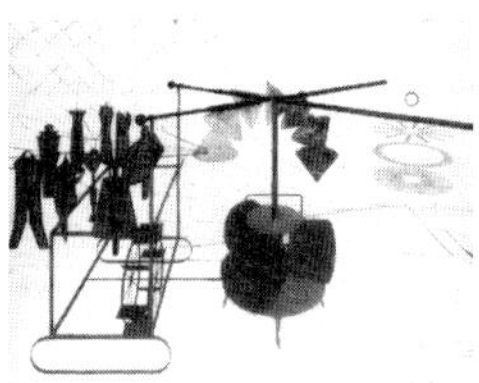
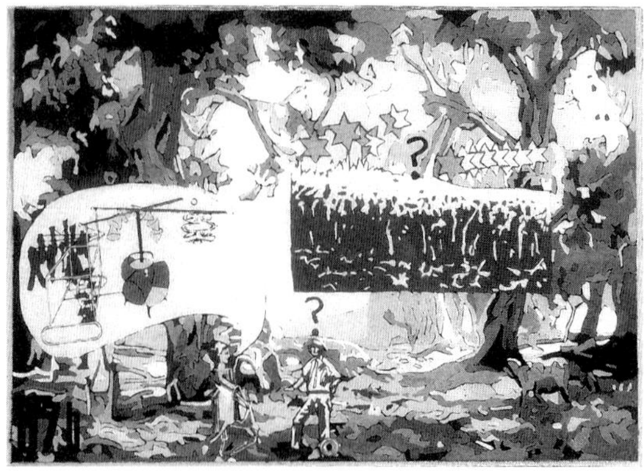

LEFT: Panel 05a, *Conversations with the Bride.* CENTRE TOP: Hans Heysen's *Summer*, 1909. CENTRE BOTTOM: detail from Marcel Duchamp's *The Large Glass.* RIGHT: Panel 07b, *Conversations with the Bride.*

nection also indicates a significant parallel between Burgin's approach, as evidenced in *Performative/Narrative*, and Tillers' systems aesthetics.

TILLERS' PHOTO-CONCEPTUAL WORK

Tillers' first major photo-conceptualist work is *Conversations with the Bride*, 1974-75, this is illustrated as an installation view and detail on page 37. Like Burgin and Haacke's work *Conversations with the Bride* can be located within the genre of photo-conceptualism as the images perched on the 112 stands were appropriated by Tillers from photomechanical reproductions of works of art. The images reproduced above left and right are two of the 112 images that make up *Conversations with the Bride*. In the middle are the two principal sources that Tillers appropriated from photomechanical reproductions. Top centre is the Australian artist Hans Heysen's *Summer*, 1909, and centre bottom is a detail from Marcel Duchamp's *The Large Glass*, 1915-23. Tillers' appropriation of Heysen's *Summer* formed the background for most of the 112 images making up *Conversations with the Bride*. This is particularly apparent in panel 05a from *Conversations with the Bride* reproduced above left. It can also be noted that Tillers mirror inverts his appropriation. The rationale for this will be examined in Chapter Seven. Turning to the detail from Duchamp's *The Large Glass* it can be seen that it appears on the left hand side of panel 07b (reproduced above right).

Tillers' diagram of the systematic layout of *Conversations with the Bride* in *A Companion to Conversations with the Bride* (Tillers 1978a: Table No. 5/1).

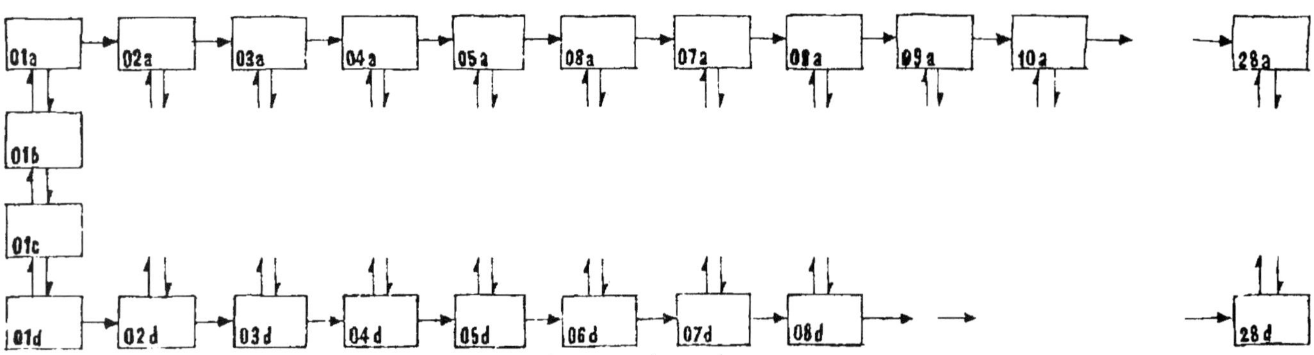

Like *Moments of Inertia*, 1972-73, *Conversations with the Bride*, 1974-75, possesses minimalistic features. One of the most obvious of these is Tillers' use of a gridded array. Another minimalistic feature of the work is its radical involvement of the spectator. In order to see the work the viewer must enter and walk within the image array. Tillers' concern with systems is graphically depicted in his diagrammatic representation of the gridded layout of *Conversations with the Bride*, 1974-75, shown below opposite. Tillers' diagram shows that *Conversations with the Bride* consists of a grid of four rows the systematic nature of which Tillers has reinforced by indexing each of the 112 images with an alphanumeric label. The labelling system runs across twenty-eight rows that run 01a-28a; and four columns, which run 01a, 01b, 01c, 01d through to 28a, 28b, 28c, 28d. Tillers' concern with systems can be compared with Burgin's systematic approach in Performative/Narrative and Haacke's exploration of 'real-time systems' in *Shapolsky et al. Manhattan Real Estate Holdings: A Real-Time System, As of 1 May 1971*, 1971.

To summarise, *Conversations with the Bride* possesses both a photo-mediated dimension and a use of minimalist seriality. These two key features indicate that Tillers was following a line of evolution that displays significant parallels with that evident in the work of Burgin and Haacke. Yet, as early as *Conversations with the Bride,* 1974-75, Tillers takes a different route by appropriating and montaging fine art imagery. Another important difference concerns Tillers' formulation of an elegant poetic articulation of his concern with systems via the development of various specular devices in *Conversations with the Bride* that build on his self-reflexive image structure in *Moments of Inertia*. The sophistication of this aspect of *Conversations with the Bride* will be outlined further in the following chapter which will explore the relationship of this facet of *Conversations with the Bride* with Craig Owens' pio-

RIGHT: Panel from Hans Haacke, *A Breed Apart,* 1978. Photographs on masonite (three with Jaguar images in colour). Seven Panels, each 91 x 91 cm. Framed under glass. First exhibited in one-person exhibition at the Museum of Modern Art, Oxford, 18 November–24 December, 1978. Collection: the artist.
LEFT TOP: Installation view.
LEFT BOTTOM: Detail of text from image reproduced on right.

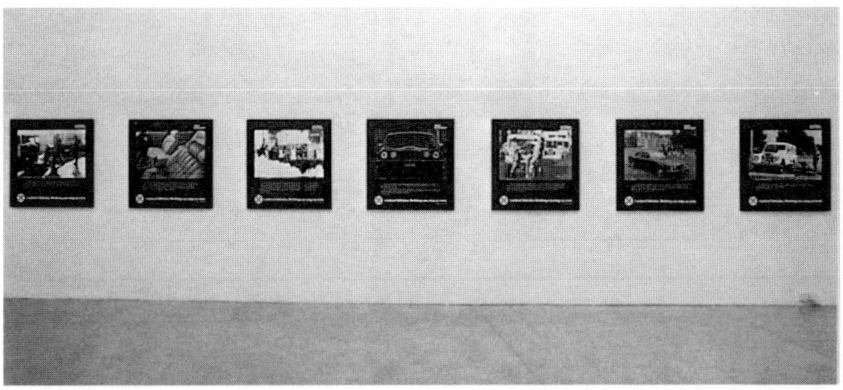

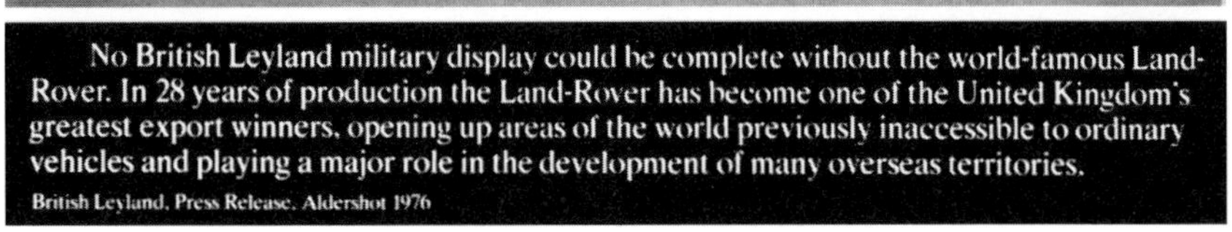

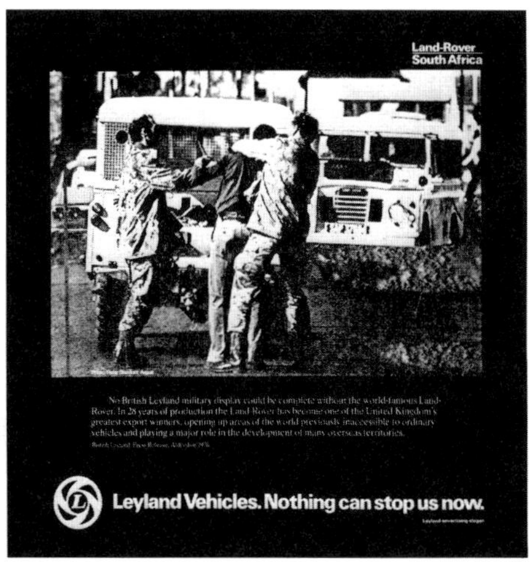

neering development of a poststructuralist aesthetic informed by the specular rhetoric of the *mise en abyme*.

HAACKE, BURGIN AND THE EVOLUTION OF PHOTO-CONCEPTUALISM INTO APPROPRIATIONISM

Haacke and Burgin are important not only as paradigmatic examples of the genre of photo-conceptualism but also as prototypical instances of the way in which photo-conceptualism provided an evolutionary link between post-object art of the 1960s and appropriationism of the 1980s. For example in 1978 Haacke produced *A Breed Apart* (illustrated bottom left page 39 with a detail) consisting of a series of images with texts appropriated from British Leyland advertisements. In the detail the advertising copy has been left unchanged but the image has been substituted with a newspaper photograph of South African police arresting a black person against a background of British Leyland Land Rover vehicles. In other panels the image has been left unchanged and the advertising copy has been rewritten by Haacke using information concerning British Leyland's activities in South Africa uncovered from research into company records in a manner that follows on from the methodology he used for *Shapolsky et al* ....

Although, *A Breed Apart* bears similarities to *Shapolsky et al.* ... it also possesses important differences that indicate the evolution of a new genre. There are two salient similarities: it uses the medium of photography, and it is based on research into business dealings making it socio-critical in the manner of *Shapolsky et al.* .... The critical difference is that it appropriates the rhetoric of the mass media rather than a minimal-conceptualist rhetoric. Haacke uses colour photography in three of the panels and a typographical style similar to that in the original advertisement, which can be contrasted with the minimalist rhetoric of earlier photo-conceptual art apparent in the use of typewritten text together with black and white photography.

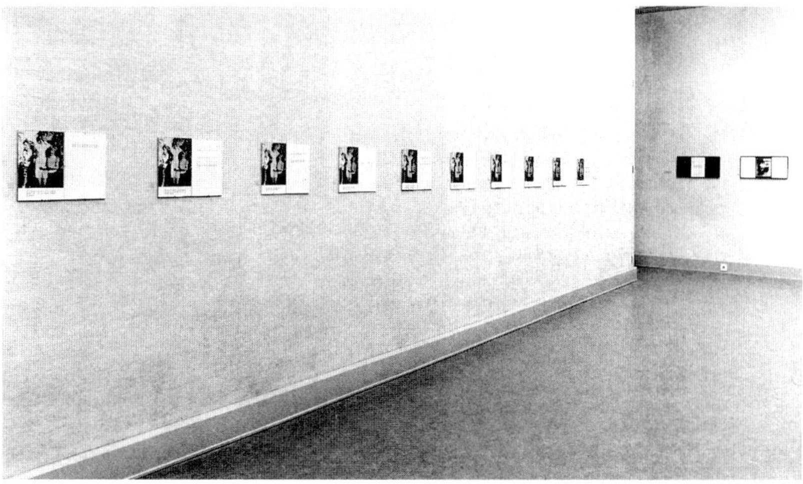

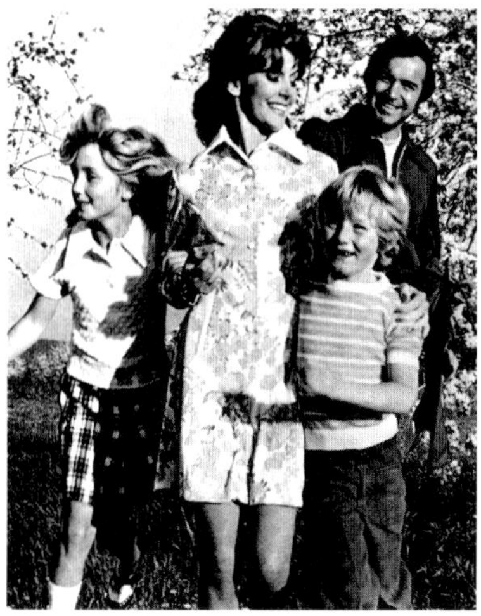

LEFT: Victor Burgin, *VI*, 1973. Offset lithography and printed text in ten parts. Each 45.7 x 86.4 cm. Courtesy the artist, John Weber Gallery, New York, and Galerie Liliane & Michel Durand-Dessert, Paris. RIGHT: detail.

A similar line of evolution can be discerned in Burgin's work in the 1970s. After *Performative/Narrative* Burgin produced *VI*, 1973, illustrated below opposite. *VI* is important because it marks a turn towards the kind of socio-critical concern apparent in Haacke's work. *VI* consists of a minimalist-like serial array of images accompanied by a text. The photograph used is shown as a detail to the right of the installation view. Ann Rorimer comments:

> *VI* marks another step in his [Burgin's] thinking. Here, the same photograph is repeated in tandem with a changing text. *VI* includes more explicitly socially-oriented subject-matter than *Performative/Narrative*. The photograph, taken from a British mail-order catalogue, presents an 'image' of a typical British nuclear family. The captions under each photograph, written by Burgin, and the accompanying individual statements deal directly with dominant social values and beliefs in order to question, if not completely undermine, the seemingly straightforward nature of the photographs. (in Goldstein and Rorimer 1995: 94)

Like Haacke's, Burgin's work begins to follow a socio-critical line of evolution that eventually leads to a deconstructive appropriation of the visual rhetoric of the mass media, as is evident in *Zoo 78*, 1978-79, illustrated in part below. *Zoo 78* consists of two black and white photographic images, one appropriated from a magazine the other a photograph of Berlin's central urban section called 'Zoo' (*Zoologischer Garten*). The appropriated magazine image has been reproduced below left. The image shows both the front and back views of a naked woman by means of the large mirror evident in the background. As

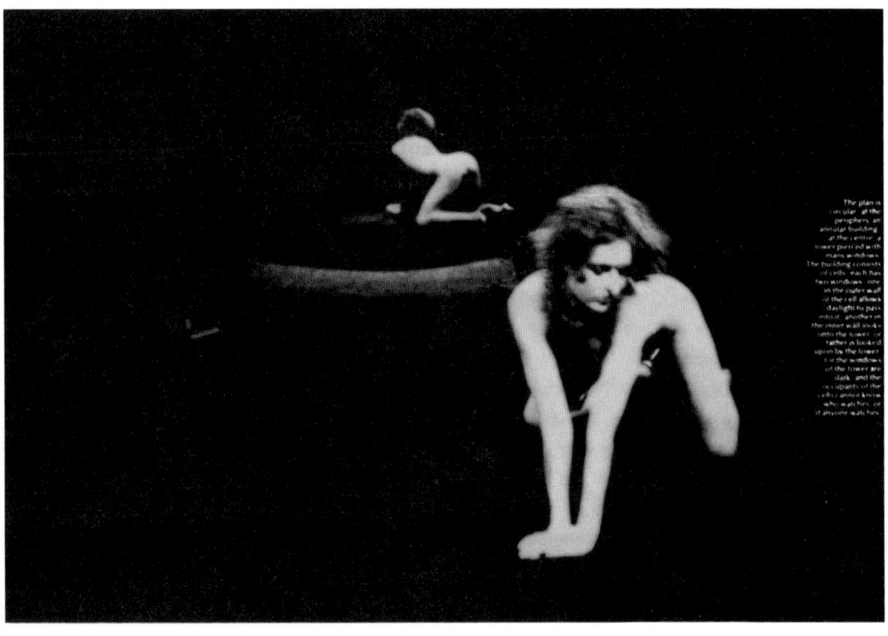

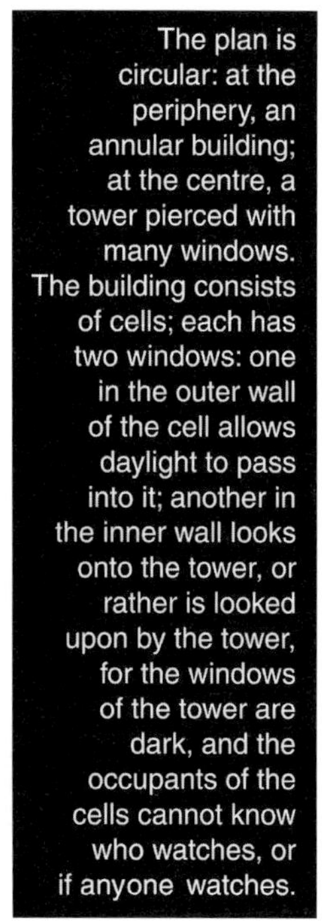

LEFT: Detail (one image of two) from Victor Burgin, *Zoo 78*, 1978–79. Black and white photograph on board, 73.7 x 97.5 cm. RIGHT: Detail of text.

in *VI* Burgin appends a text to this image. The text, reproduced to the right of the image, is taken from Michel Foucault's *Discipline and Punish*, (Foucault 1977) and is a description of Jeremy Bentham's design for a panopticon, a prison with a central observation tower looking onto a circular array of cells with bars that allow the warden to see into every cell.

As in Haacke's *A Breed Apart,* Burgin's *Zoo 78* falls more into the category of deconstructive appropriationism than into that of photo-conceptualism. Like *A Breed Apart* Burgin's *Zoo 78* does not employ a minimalist rhetoric: instead of being a photo-document the image is directly appropriated from the mass media; and instead of using typewritten text Burgin uses the typographical style of the original mass media production.

Both Haacke and Burgin appropriate the rhetoric of mass media in the form of a glossy photographic style together with attractive typographical design. As this rhetoric is quite different from the purism of the minimalist-conceptualist aesthetics informing earlier modes of photo-conceptualism, it signals the emergence of a new genre. This is reinforced by the way in which both Haacke and Burgin rewrite the texts associated with the mass media imagery in order to deconstruct the original ideological message.

LEFT: Hans Heysen, *Summer,* 1909. Watercolour, 56.5 x 78.4 cm. Collection: Art Gallery of New South Wales. RIGHT: Imants Tillers, *Untitled*, 1978. Neco digital paint-jet print on canvas. Two parts each 163.9 x 185.5 cm. Collection: in National Gallery of Australia, Canberra until lost or accidently destroyed.

TILLERS AND AUTHORIAL DECONSTRUCTION

Although Tillers appropriates fine art, his work is also marked by a deconstructive approach. In the case of *Untitled*, 1978, the focus is on a deconstruction of authorship which, it will be argued, laid an important foundation for his Canvasboard System. *Untitled*, 1978, is reproduced below together with its appropriational source Heysen's *Summer*, 1909. The simplicity of *Untitled*, 1978, belies the fact that Tillers made use of a highly sophisticated means of pho-

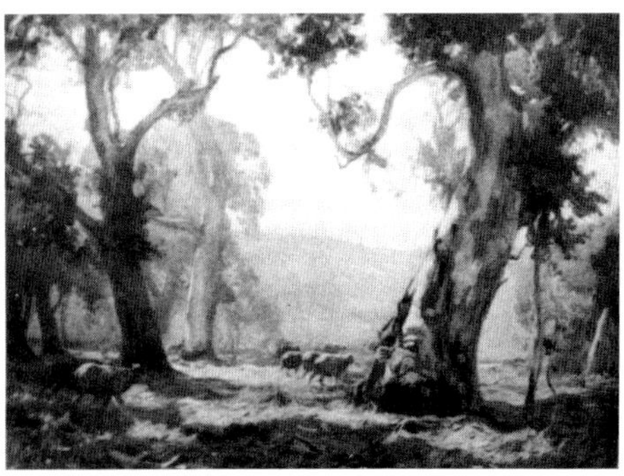

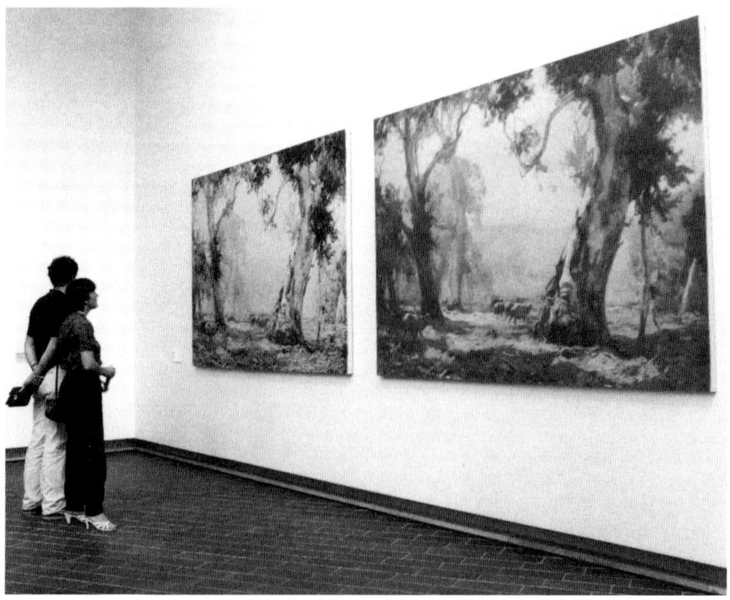

tomechanical reproduction. Whereas in *Conversations with the Bride* Tillers painted his appropriations from photomechanical reproductions of *Summer* and *The Large Glass,* for *Untitled*, 1978, Tillers sent two different reproductions of *Summer* to a factory that used the then technologically advanced Neco process of photomechanical reproduction. As noted in the Introduction, Neco consists of a computer controlled paint-jet system that can create large-scale images on virtually any surface, usually for commercial purposes. The factory scanned the two reproductions of *Summer* into a computer and the computer-controlled paint-jets created the two mural-sized reproductions shown in the illustration. The support specified by Tillers was two large stretched canvases. The work is most definitely photographic, yet at the same time it is a painting on canvas. Three features of this work make it profoundly paradoxical: firstly, it is a radical instance of authorial appropriation posing the problem as to whether it is by Heysen, Tillers, or a meta-author 'Heysen-Tillers'; secondly, it is a painting that is also a photograph; and, thirdly, it is a photomechanical reproduction of a photomechanical reproduction, a characteristic that evokes the paradoxical logic of the *mise en abyme* that will be outlined in the following chapter.

In Chapter Eight it will be shown that *Untitled,* 1978, is based on Tillers' understanding, and poetic interpretation, of Kurt Gödel's Incompleteness Theorem. Gödel's Theorem has a significant place in the history of science as it proved that paradox could not be excluded from mathematical logic. It will be demonstrated that Tillers' understanding of Gödel's Theorem allowed him to create a pioneering instance of authorially deconstructive appropriation—a mode of appropriation which it will be argued is as significant as the genre of ideologically deconstructive appropriation that dominated avant-gardist art of the 1980s.

The analysis of the coherence and sophistication of Tillers' theory and practice in *Conversations with the Bride* and *Untitled* in Chapters Seven and Eight constitutes the crux of this text, and provides a foundation for understanding the originality of Tillers' contribution to the discourse of appropriationism. While both works were produced in the matrix of photo-conceptual art of the 1970s they both preempt important features of deconstructive appropriationism of the 1980s and hence will also be discussed in the following chapter which will outline Tillers' relationship to this context.

3

DECONSTRUCTIVE APPROPRIATIONISM

In the 1980s deconstructive appropriationism evolved into an international style of avant-gardist art and it was within this period that Tillers attained an international reputation based on his Canvasboard System: an integrated series of works based on consecutively numbered or indexed canvasboard modules. Tillers began to experiment with canvasboards in late 1981 producing numerous pencil drawings of imagery appropriated from sources such as Giorgio de Chirico and Latvian childrens' books belonging to his parents.[10] These early canvasboard works were given the generic title *Suppressed Imagery*, a set of which is reproduced below left. From the beginning Tillers systematically indexed each canvasboard with a rubber-stamped number: a procedure that can be traced back to his minimalist-conceptualist inspired numbering systems in *Moments of Inertia* and *Conversations with the Bride*. In 1982 Tillers made the leap from images inscribed onto individual canvasboards to creating a large-scale image on a gridded array of canvasboards. The first such work is *The Field*, illustrated below right.

Tillers' use of charcoal as the medium for *The Field* indicates its prototypical status.[11] By 1983 his Canvasboard System crystallised into a powerful artistic strategy when he acquired sufficient confidence in his new method to begin the production of large scale paintings. The modularity of Tillers' canvasboard grids is a powerful and original approach to painting, facilitating the production of very large works with a minimum of means. Indeed the technique is so successful that it has become a hallmark of his style. Typical works from 1983 such as *Spirit of Place* and *The Great Metaphysical Interior* are reproduced on the following pages. Both works measure 254 x 648 cm (8

LEFT: *Suppressed Imagery,* 1981. Pencil on 49 canvasboards Nos. 1–49, 178 x 267 cm. Private collection, Melbourne. RIGHT: *The Field,* 1982. Charcoal on 100 canvasboards, Nos. 196–295, 254 x 380 cm. Collection: National Gallery of Victoria, Melbourne.

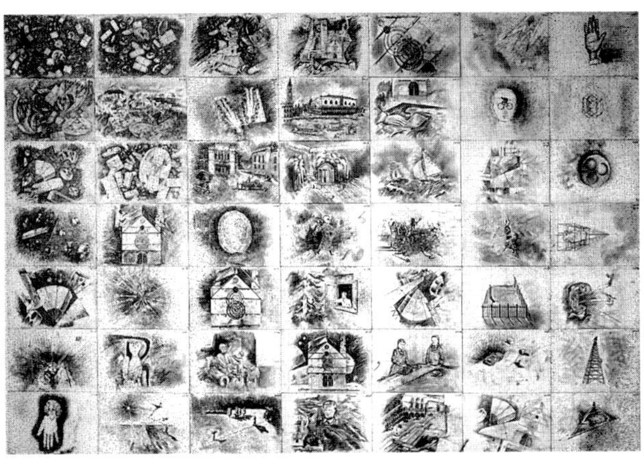

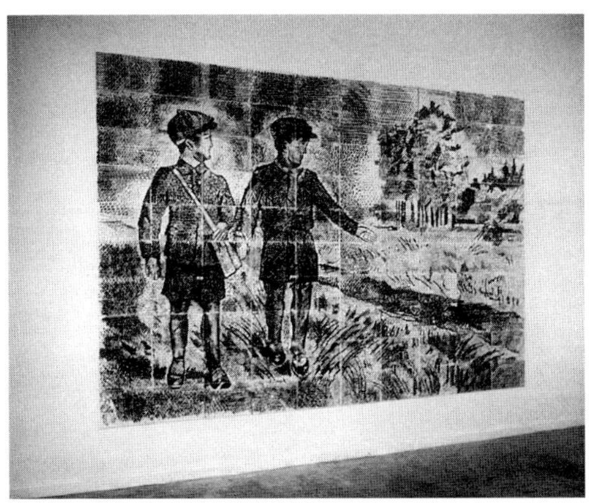

x 21.26 feet) exhibiting the capacity of small-scale canvasboard modules to create impressive large-scale paintings. In 1986 Tillers was able to use the scale of his modular paintings to make a major statement at the Venice Biennale. By 1991 he had produced approximately three hundred modular, intertextual paintings made up of approximately thirty thousand canvasboard panels. By late 2001 his Canvasboard System had reached almost seven hundred paintings and over fifty thousand panels. These quantitative observations are insignificant in themselves, they only become meaningful when it is realised that the Canvasboard System is an integrated whole driven by a sophisticated theory and practice that arose out of the most original features of Tillers' theory and practice in the 1970s. The significance of its contribution to the discourse of deconstructive appropriation is difficult to prove without showing how it evolved out of Tillers' earlier works. Nonetheless, it can be noted that the Canvasboard System is a uniquely sustained, integrated and theoretically sophisticated appropriationist project.

Moreover, it is by no means fully understandable in the context of the international style of appropriationism that dominated avant-gardist art of the 1980s. This will be proven by demonstrating that it arose out of Tillers' earlier theory and practice rather than being primarily influenced by Euro-American appropriationism. What emerged from Tillers' unique development is an appropriationist project that is not only epic in scale but is based on the appropriation of fine art imagery. These last two points are important because there are relatively few instances of sustained authorial deconstruction outside Australia.

As in previous chapters in this introductory section, the task of proving the originality of Tillers' contribution will be undertaken in the main body of the text. This chapter will concentrate on locating Tillers' mode of appropria-

Imants Tillers, *The Great Metaphysical Interior*, 1983. Synthetic polymer paint on 170 canvasboards, 254 x 648 cm.

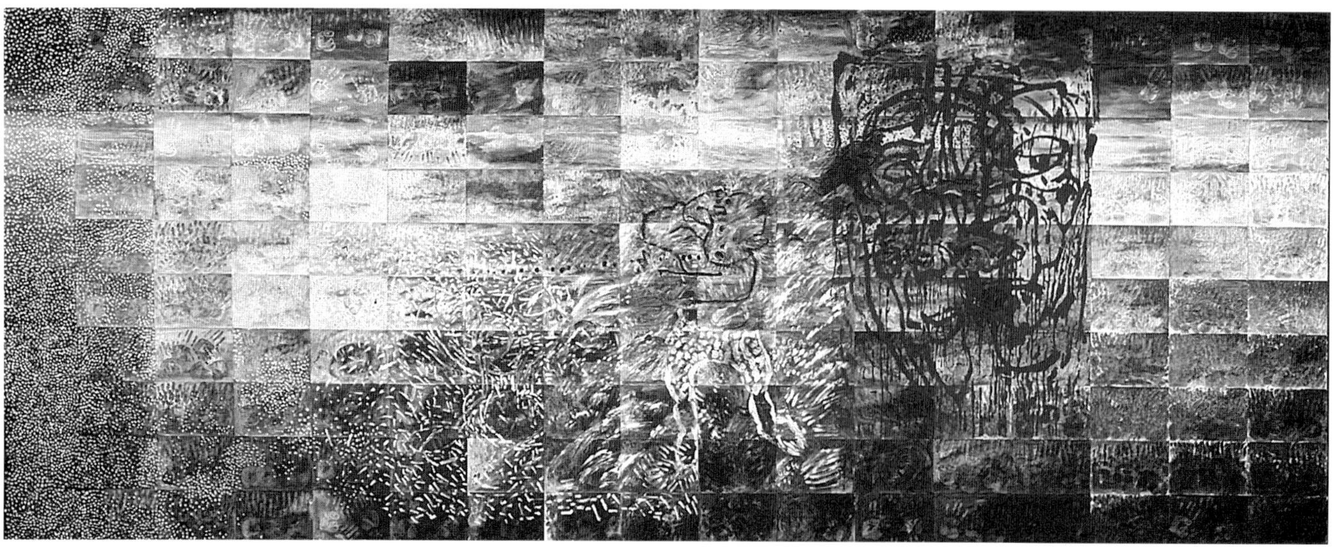

tionism within the international discourse of appropriationism that dominated avant-gardist art during the 1980s. A detailed examination of the originality of Tillers' Canvasboard System will be provided in Part Four.

The discourse of appropriationism began its seminal development in the late 1970s in New York. By the early 1980s New York art theorists such as Benjamin Buchloh, Hal Foster, Craig Owens and Rosalind Krauss began to create coherent theoretical frameworks for the phenomenon. In this chapter it will be shown that these key frameworks can be divided into two (sometimes overlapping) categories which will be referred to as 'ideological' and 'authorial' deconstruction respectively. Although aspects of Tillers' work can be understood in terms of 'ideological deconstruction' it will be argued that the Owens-Krauss interpretation of appropriationism as authorial deconstruction is especially valuable as a means of understanding the more sophisticated features of Tillers' theory and practice.

WHY '*DECONSTRUCTIVE* APPROPRIATIONISM'?

Before examining such theories it is necessary to explain why the term 'deconstructive appropriationism' is employed here. In the late 1970s and early 1980s various theoretical labels were applied to the newly evolved movement including: 'postmodern' (Crimp 1984), 'deconstruction' (Owens 1978; Buchloh 1982), and 'appropriation' (Buchloh 1982). The term 'postmodern' is problematic as it has a very broad usage covering many fields of cultural activity. Accordingly, it will be argued that it is not especially suitable as a label for a specific artistic style or genre.

Douglas Crimp was one of the first art theorists to use the term 'postmodern' in the context of commentary on the emerging genre. In autumn 1977 he organised Pictures, an exhibition of the work of Troy Brauntuch, Jack Gold-

Imants Tillers, *Spirit of Place,* 1983. Synthetic polymer paint on 170 canvasboards, Nos. 1078–1247, 254 x 648 cm. Private collection, Sydney. Photograph: Fenn Hinchcliffe.

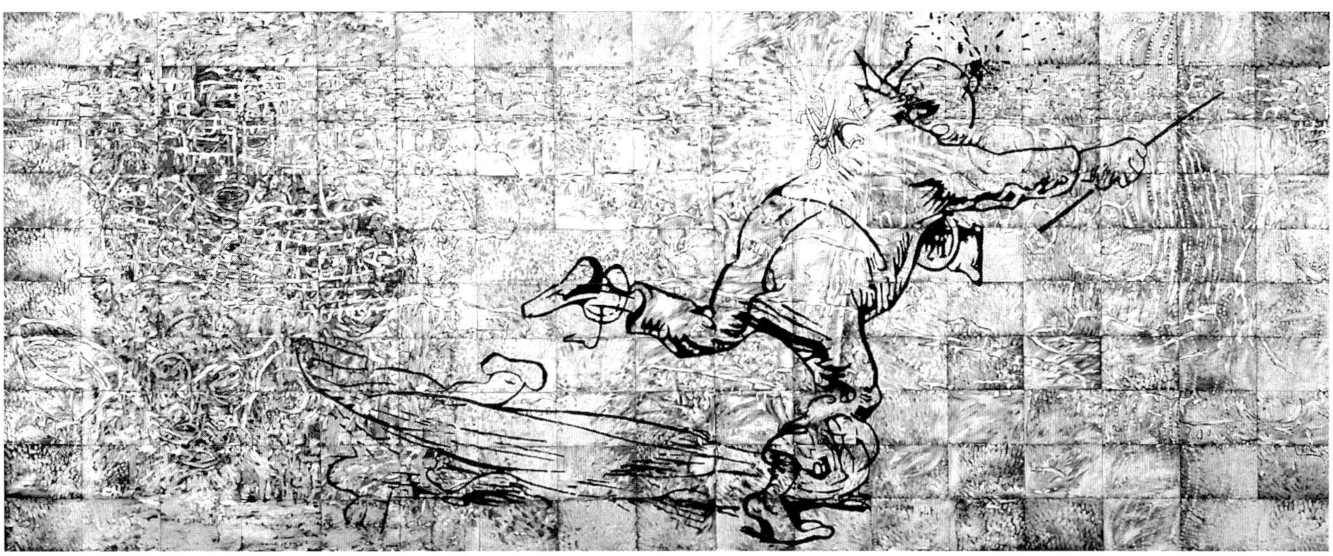

stein, Sherrie Levine, Robert Longo, and Philip Smith for Artists Space in New York City (Crimp 1984: 175). A revised version of Crimp's catalogue essay for this exhibition was published in 1984 in an anthology edited by Brian Wallis (Wallis 1984). In his commentary Crimp uses the term 'postmodernist' to describe the work in the exhibition stating that it is 'useful to consider recent work as having effected a break with modernism and therefore as postmodernist' (Crimp 1984: 186). Images by the Pictures artists accompany the reprint in the Wallis anthology and some of these are reproduced below.

Crimp reports that the exhibition was in the 'fall of 1977' (Crimp 1984: 175). Consequently, of the images that illustrate the revised edition of Crimp's catalogue essay in the Wallis anthology the works by Levine and Longo could not have been in the original exhibition because they are dated 1978. Nevertheless, they do serve to indicate the kind of work that made up the show.

One of the most obvious generic features of these works is that they all use photography or cinematography. Intriguingly, Crimp studiously avoids this outstanding common feature asserting that 'the new work is not confined to any particular medium; instead, it makes use of photography, film, performance, as well as traditional modes of painting, drawing, and sculpture' (Crimp 1984: 175). Indeed Crimp goes so far as to underscore his denial when he asserts:

> Simply to enumerate a list of mediums to which 'painters' and 'sculptors' have increasingly turned—film, photography, video, performance—will not locate them precisely, since it is not merely a question of shifting from the conventions of one medium to those of another. (Crimp 1984: 176)

Crimp's reluctance to accept the obviously photomediated nature of the 'Pictures' artists—Levine, Goldstein, Longo and Brauntuch—can be explained by examining his use of the term 'postmodern' in association with these works. Crimp's painstaking attempts to avoid using photomedia as a defining feature make sense if his use of the concept of postmodern art is understood as an attempt to delineate a broad-based shift in avant-gardist art rather than the specific generic characteristics of the work in his exhibition.

LEFT TO RIGHT: Troy Brauntuch, detail from a photographic installation showing a photograph from the memoirs of Albert Speer where it was captioned 'Hitler asleep in his Mercedes, 1934'; Sherrie Levine, *Untitled*, 1978; Jack Goldstein, Frame shots from *Shane*, 1975,16 mm colour film, 3 minutes.

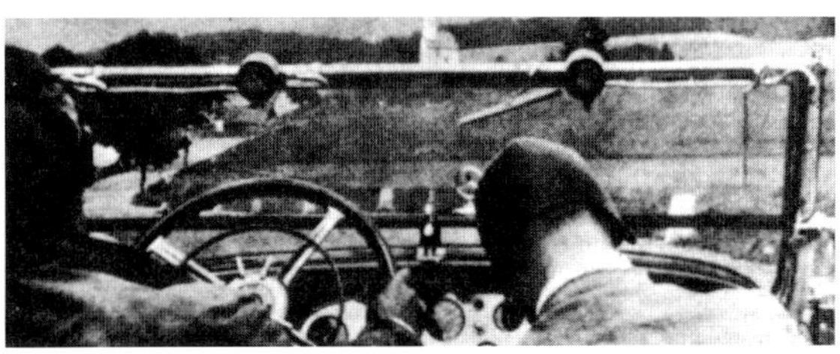
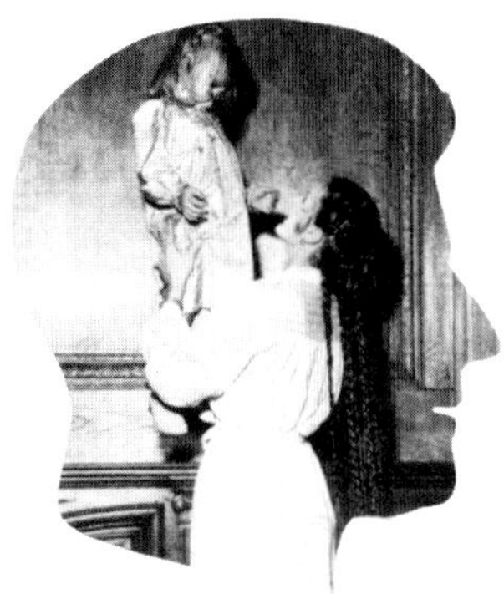
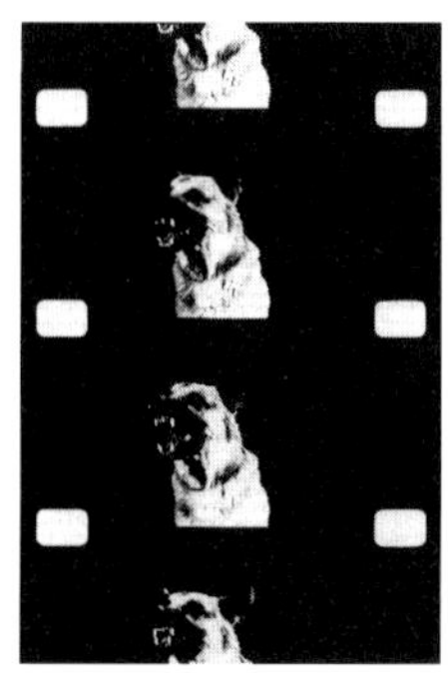

Indeed, it is apparent that Crimp's essay does attempt to address a much broader spectrum of avant-gardist art than that of the photomediated appropriationism of his 'Pictures' artists. This is indicated when he refers to the art theorist Michael Fried's 'famous attack against minimal sculpture, written in 1967' (Crimp 1984: 175). Crimp reports that Fried 'predicted the demise of art as we then knew it, that is, the art of *modernist* abstract painting and sculpture' (Crimp 1984: 175) [emphasis added]. Accordingly, Crimp, after Fried, links 'modernism' with 'abstract painting and sculpture'. Thus, in the context of his essay, Crimp's use of the term 'pictures' becomes implicated with his use of the term 'postmodern'.

As Crimp continues his analysis of Fried it becomes apparent that Crimp's notion of 'pictures' also corresponds with Fried's use of the term 'theatre'. Crimp reports that Fried asserted that 'Art degenerates as it approaches the condition of theater,' (in Crimp 1984: 175-76). He also notes that Fried defined 'theatre' in this context as 'what lies *between* the arts' (in Crimp 1984: 176). It is evident that Crimp effectively accepts Fried's analysis with the exception that whereas Fried understood the 'theatrical' as a degeneration Crimp sees it as evolutionary, observing:

> over the past decade [the 1970s] we have witnessed a radical break with that modernist tradition, effected precisely by a preoccupation with the 'theatrical.' The work that has laid most serious claim to our attention throughout the seventies *has* been situated between, or outside the individual arts, with the result that the integrity of the various mediums—those categories the exploration of whose essences and limits constituted the very project of modernism—has dispersed into meaninglessness. (Crimp 1984: 176)

It appears that Crimp's reluctance to define the kind of work he exhibited in Pictures as photographic or photomediated stems from the fact that his use of the term 'postmodern' is not restricted to a particular genre or style. Instead it describes a paradigm shift in art away from a Friedian valorisation of modernist abstraction towards the reintroduction of imagery in the broadest sense of the term.

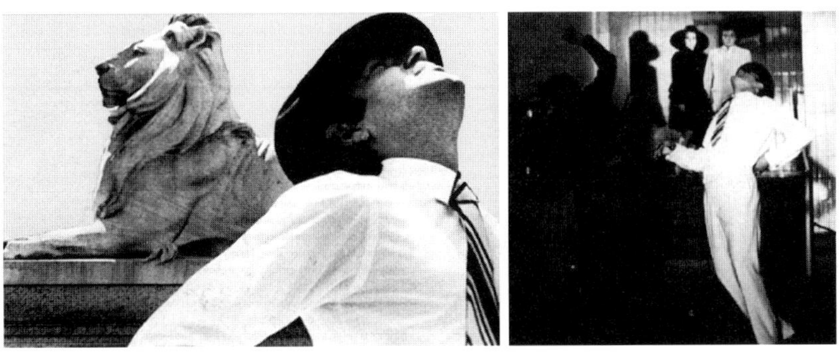

LEFT: Robert Longo, Still from film *Sound Distance of a Good Man*, 1978. 8 mm black and white film, 15 minutes. RIGHT: Still from Werner Fassbinder, *The American Soldier*, 1970.

Crimp's reconstruction of Fried makes sense within the context of this analysis of Tillers' work because, although *Untitled*, 1978, is entirely photomechanical, his Canvasboard System uses painting as its medium, albeit mediated by appropriations from photomechanical reproductions in books and magazines. Crimp's attempt to avoid the closure of defining the newly emerging work as photographic also reinforces the attempt in this analysis to locate appropriationism within a broad evolutionary context that can be traced from post-object art of the 1960s through photo-conceptualism and beyond appropriationism of the 1980s into genres that as yet remain undefined.[12] Finally, it can be argued that Crimp's reluctance to restrict the term 'postmodern' to the photographic and cinematographic nature of the art in his Pictures exhibition indicates that his use of the term has a broader frame of reference than the genre of photomediated appropriation that burgeoned into an international style in the 1980s. This analysis will follow Crimp's lead and avoid reducing the term 'postmodern' to the strategy of appropriation. As was noted in the Introduction, the suggestion here is that the term 'postmodern art' be used as an open-ended concept referring the evolution of deconstructive avant-gardism in the second half of the twentieth century and into the new millennium.

The term 'appropriation' seems more apt as a stylistic label than 'postmodern' because it is more specific to the instances of photomediated art that emerged in the late 1970s and 1980s. Significantly, Crimp's seminal analysis of the emerging genre focuses on appropriation by pointing to instances of 'quotation', as is apparent when he observes: Robert Longo 'quoted from a newspaper reproduction of a fragment of a film still taken from *The American Soldier,* 1970, a film by Rainer Werner Fassbinder' (Crimp 1984: 183); and describes Cindy Sherman's Untitled Film Stills series (not included in the Pictures exhibition), as 'like quotations from the sequence of frames that constitutes the narrative flow of film' (Crimp 1984: 181). The fact that both references to 'quotation' in Crimp's essay involve film, underscores the manner in which such appropriation in the late 1970s and 1980s is characteristically photomediated—in spite of Crimp's reluctance to acknowledge this feature of the work.

Appropriation is certainly a crucial feature of the new style but the appropriation of mass media imagery was also a central feature of pop art in the 1960s. Accordingly, the term 'deconstructive' is a useful modifier as it describes the originality of the approach to appropriated imagery apparent in avant-gardist art of the late 1970s and 1980s.

Significantly, the term 'deconstruction' played a crucial role in the pioneering theoretical analyses of appropriationist art by a group of New York art theorists most of whom, like Crimp, were associated with the intellectual avant-gardist art journal *October*. These theorists can be classified into two major categories. The first stems from Marxian theory of avant-gardism and concentrates on artists who use appropriation to deconstruct the ideology of consumerism. The second is based on poststructuralist theory and focuses mainly on the use of appropriation to deconstruct the traditional notion of authorship. Principal theorists belonging to the first tendency include Benjamin Buchloh and Hal Foster; key theorists associated with the second include Craig Owens and Rosalind Krauss.

It should be noted here that Tillers was not *directly* influenced by either frame of reference. His line of evolution is quite different, being based on his sophisticated understanding and poetic interpretation of scientific theory, and his thorough understanding of avant-gardist art movements. It can also be noted that even the New York based artists who were subjected to such theoretical analyses cannot be said to have been influenced by such theories. By definition the critical analyses of the first wave of appropriationist art came after the work had been produced.

Accordingly, the theoretical frameworks used to analyse appropriationism in the early 1980s can be understood as parallel texts that have no direct input into the production of early appropriationist art. Yet these parallel texts are extremely important because they provide highly coherent and theoretically sophisticated conceptual frameworks for understanding appropriationism. Moreover, the poststructuralist interpretations of photomediated art and appropriation pioneered by Krauss and Owens are especially valuable to this analysis, as pivotal features of their interpretations possess substantive resonances with the theory and practice Tillers was developing in the course of his production of *Untitled*, 1978: a work that provided a crucial foundation for his Canvasboard System.

But Buchloh and Foster's analyses of appropriation in terms of the deconstruction of codes are also very relevant, because they provide a valuable connection between appropriationism and the concern with systems and information evident in post-object and photo-conceptual art. This is especially apparent in Foster's use of the term 'recoding' to refer to the deconstruction of ideologically encoded mass media information.

IDEOLOGICAL DECONSTRUCTION

BENJAMIN BUCHLOH

One of the first paradigmatic interpretations of deconstructive appropriation was published in 1982 by the New York art theorist Benjamin Buchloh. Buchloh began by identifying a 'paradigmatic shift' originating in the late 1970s in New York (Buchloh 1982). He lists the names of the artists he considers part of this shift: Dara Birnbaum, Jenny Holzer, Barbara Kruger, Louise Lawler, Sherrie Levine, and Martha Rosler. Of these artists, Holzer, Kruger, Levine and Lawler, were to become leading figures in the New York school of deconstructive appropriationism. Buchloh explains that in the work of these artists:

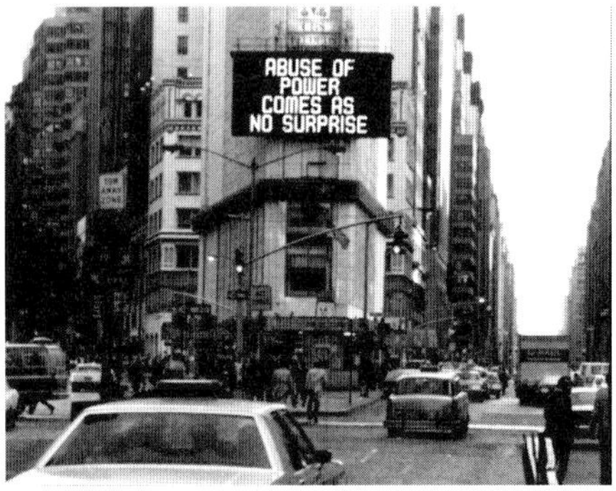

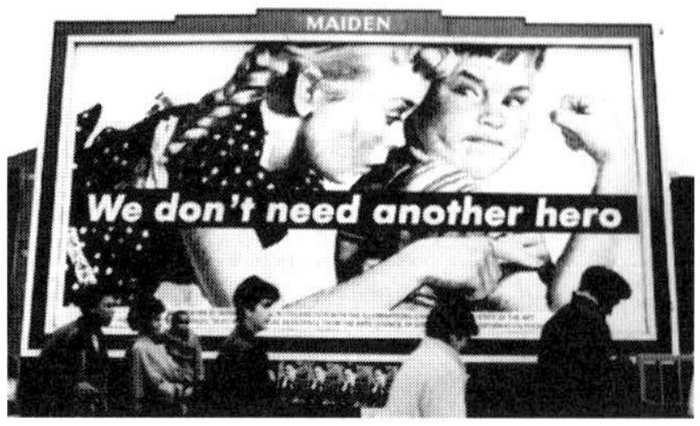

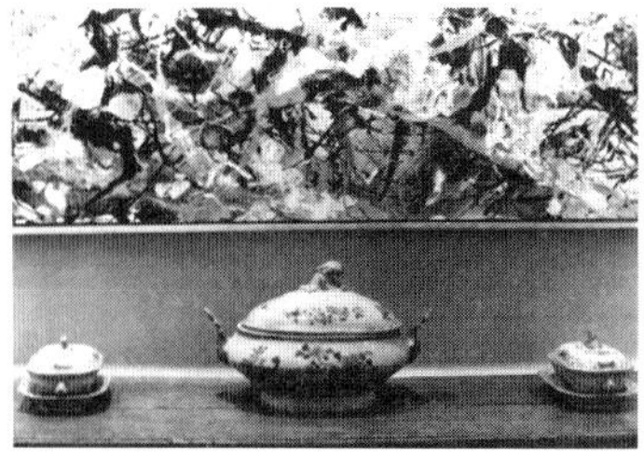

LEFT: Jenny Holzer, *Times Square*, 1982. CENTRE: Barbara Kruger, *Untitled (Another Hero)*, 1985. RIGHT: Louise Lawler, *Pollock and Tureen*, 1984.

> the languages of television, advertising, and photography, and the ideology of everyday life, were subjected to formal and linguistic operations that essentially followed Roland Barthes' model of a secondary mythification that deconstructs ideology. (Buchloh 1982: 48)

Representative samples of work by some of the artists mentioned by Buchloh are reproduced above. It can be seen that Holzer has used the mass media device of an electronic notice board in New York's Times Square to broadcast aphoristic statements such as those in her *Truisms* of the late 1970s and early 1980s. Kruger has appropriated mass media imagery and juxtaposed it with 'punk chic' typography; and Lawler has photographed a work by Jackson Pollock in the domestic setting of the wealthy New York collectors Mr and Mrs Burton Tremaine. Lawler uses a rhetoric of colour photography one might expect to find in the homes section of magazines such as *Vogue* and *Harpers Bazaar*. Holzer uses an electronic billboard usually used for news and advertising, and Kruger transposes the language of graphic design into the realm of art. In each case the artist uses the techniques and technologies of the mass media to infiltrate and deconstruct the ideological messages typically broadcast by such media. It is apparent that these artists are operating in a mode of appropriation very similar to that evident in the work of Victor Burgin and Hans Haacke examined in Chapter Two.

Buchloh contributed to the new genre by providing a coherent theoretical foundation for the interpretation of deconstructive appropriation using an early classic text by Roland Barthes, *Mythologies*, (Barthes 1973) originally published in 1957. Buchloh notes:

> In *Mythologies*, 1957, Roland Barthes deconstructed … contemporary myths as designed objects of consumption and advertising. In certain respects this can still be considered as *the original model for the deconstructive approach of the criticism of ideology* as it has been developed in the work of the artists analyzed here. (Buchloh 1982: 60) [emphasis added]

Buchloh describes the process occurring in the appropriationist works of artists such as Kruger, Holzer and Lawler as a 'deconstructive approach of the criticism of ideology'. His description is borne out by the artists' work: Lawler appropriates a glossy magazine style of photography to underscore the complicity of fine art with the disparity between the very wealthy and the very poor at home as well as abroad. Kruger's juxtaposition of appropriated image with a modish typographical style serves to convey a feminist message that challenges the stereotypical representation of women in the mass media. Holzer's appropriated clichés can be read as a commentary on the banality of mass media messages. In *Art Since 1960* Michael Archer reports that Holzer's *Truisms,* 'short statements with a strong impact but ambiguous meaning':

> were fly-posted, stuck up in telephone booths and printed on T-shirts: 'Protect me from what I want', 'Lack of charisma can be fatal'. As the decade progressed, she moved into more officially sanctioned public communication sites, putting her art on illuminated advertising boards in places such as Times Square or Piccadilly Circus. (Archer 1997: 180)

It is interesting to note that Kruger has also utilised billboards, as illustrated opposite. The use of this strategy by two major New York artists provides strong evidence that deconstructive appropriation is a continuation of the post-object concern with making art socially relevant. This both reinforces Buchloh's definition of such art as a 'deconstructive … criticism of ideology' and indicates that this strategy is located in a broader avant-gardist discourse than appropriationist art of the 1980s.

HAL FOSTER

Another major New York theorist of deconstructive appropriation, Hal Foster, followed Buchloh's use of Barthes' *Mythologies* as the basis for a theoretical explication of appropriationism. By the mid-1980s Foster had published two important texts concerning the issue of postmodernism: *The Anti-Aesthetic: Essays on Postmodern Culture* (Foster 1983) which he edited, and a collection of his essays *Recodings: Art, Spectacle, Cultural Politics* (Foster 1985).

In *Recodings* the strategy of appropriation is likened by Foster to Barthes' notion that myth is best deconstructed by counter-myth—in Buchloh's terms 'secondary mythification'. In other words, the politically incorrect mass media ideology or belief system is substituted with a politically correct message. Foster cites Barthes:

> Truth to tell, the best weapon against myth is perhaps to mythify it in its turn, and to produce an *artificial myth*: and this reconstituted myth will in fact be a mythology … (in Foster 1985: 169)

Foster observes that this process of 'myth robbery' 'is the political motive of much image appropriation in recent art (at least when it pretends to critique)' (Foster 1985: 169). He explains:

> Basically, in art, 'myth-robbery' seeks to restore the original sign for its social context *or* to *break apart the abstracted, mythical sign and to reinscribe it in a countermythical system.* (Foster 1985: 169-70) [the second instance of italics has been added for emphasis]

In the contexts of Barthes' *Mythologies* the notion of a 'countermythical system' can be understood as a 'counter-ideological system'. Accordingly, Foster can be understood as stating that the original 'politically incorrect' signs are 'broken apart' and then 'recoded' with a politically correct message. Thus, Foster's analysis of appropriation is very similar to that provided by Buchloh, both in its description of the technique and in its emphasis upon the superimposition of a politically correct message onto the 'broken' or 'emptied out' appropriated signifiers.

SUMMARY

Buchloh and Foster's pioneering analyses provide substantial and sophisticated interpretations of appropriation. These analyses are especially useful as a means of delineating a specific genre, or subgenre, of appropriationism that will be referred to here, after Buchloh, as 'ideologically deconstructive'. This subgenre is marked by its appropriation of mass media imagery using the very media of mass media to deconstruct the ideologies of consumerism and gender stereotyping promulgated by this apparatus.

Another important aspect of Buchloh and Fosters' analyses is that they indicate an evolutionary link between the semiotic notions of deconstructing signs and 'recoding' (Foster 1985) and the notion of codes, systems, and information associated with post-object art of the 1960s and photo-conceptual art of the 1970s (see diagram below).

Tillers' mode of appropriation is very different to that of mass media appropriationists because he focused on the appropriation of fine art imagery. Yet the concept of encoding has informed Tillers' thinking throughout his oeuvre. In this respect the connection between the 1960s and 1970s contained in Buchloh and Foster's analyses of appropriation provide a useful means of understanding how Tillers could have followed a different course to his American colleagues yet arrive at a similar destination.

In addition, there are ideological dimensions to Tillers' work particularly apparent in his use of the capacity for montage in his modular Canvasboard System to intersect and confront the hegemony of European and Ameri-

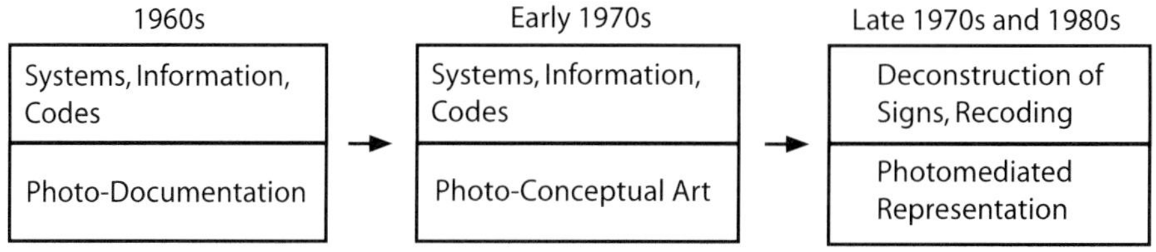

can art with equally powerful antipodean sources, in particular imagery from modern Aboriginal Papunya paintings and the complex and profound conceptual expressionism of the New Zealand painter Colin McCahon. On balance, however, it will be argued here that the crux of Tillers' Canvasboard System and its basis in remarkable works of the 1970s such as *Conversations with the Bride* and *Untitled*, 1978, has greater resonance with the poststructuralist interpretation of appropriationism pioneered by Rosalind Krauss and Craig Owens.

AUTHORIAL DECONSTRUCTION: THE OWENS-KRAUSS INTERPRETATION

What will be referred to here as the 'Owens-Krauss interpretation' is based on two distinctive contributions to the application of poststructuralist theory to avant-gardist art. The first is evident in Craig Owens' pioneering interpretation of Jacques Derrida's concept of 'deconstruction' in 'Photography *en abyme'* (Owens 1978). The second is apparent in Rosalind Krauss' innovative poststructuralist interpretation of Cindy Sherman's strategy of appropriation (Krauss 1984a). In 'Photography *en abyme'* Owens succeeds in focusing on a visual metaphor for Derrida's concept of deconstruction, using the literary theorist Lucien Dällenbach's analysis of the complex rhetorical figure he calls the *mise en abyme*. Unfortunately, Owens did not go on to apply this powerful metaphor directly to an analysis of deconstructive authorial appropriation. Fortunately, Krauss seems to have made use of Owens' groundwork in her early analysis of Sherman.

Krauss' interpretation of Sherman together with Owens' valuable focus on the *mise en abyme* are crucially important to this analysis of Tillers' oeuvre for three reasons: firstly, it will be shown that the rhetoric of the *mise en abyme* plays a critical role in Tillers' theory and practice; secondly, authorial deconstruction also plays an essential part in Tillers' theory and practice; and, thirdly, Tillers arrived at these artistic solutions without any knowledge of the Owens-Krauss interpretation of appropriationism. Accordingly, the Owens-Krauss interpretation not only assists an understanding of Tillers' theory and practice but also serves to underscore the originality and sophistication of his contribution.

CRAIG OWENS AND 'PHOTOGRAPHY *EN ABYME'*

In *Of Grammatology* (Derrida 1976) [originally published in 1967 as *De la Grammatologie*] Derrida uses a particularly *visual* metaphor to describe the 'limitlessness' of a text. It would appear that the *October* critic Craig Owens was one of the first English-speaking art theorists to comprehend the applicability of Derrida's *imagery* to the interpretation of visual art. In his essay 'Photography *en abyme'* published in *October* in 1978 Owens points to Derrida's use of a specular metaphor to describe the 'limitlessness' of a text, or more precisely, any representational system. Owens

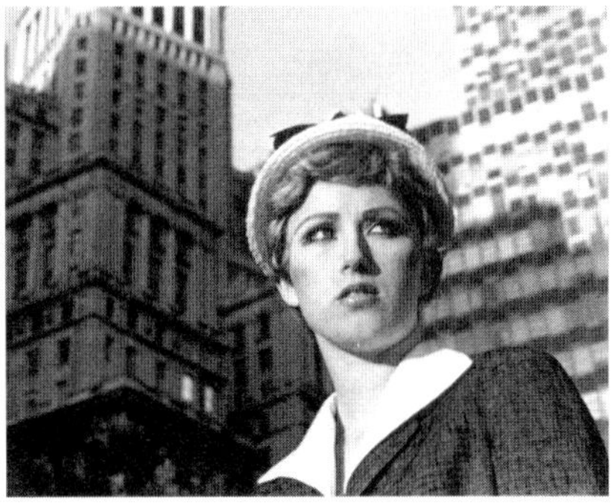

cites Derrida's fundamental deconstructive proposition that representation can never faithfully reflect a concrete immutable truth as it is a process inherently prone to infinite self-reflection or self-referentiality. In particular, Owens focuses on Derrida's use of the metaphor of an 'abyss' to describe the effect of infinite self-reflection or self-referentiality. Owens cites the following passage from *Of Grammatology*:

> An entire theory of the structural necessity of the abyss will be gradually constituted in our reading: the indefinite process of supplementarity has always already infiltrated presence, always already inscribed there the space of repetition and the splitting of the self. Representation in the abyss of presence is not an accident of presence; the desire of presence is, on the contrary, born from the abyss (the indefinite multiplication) of representation, from the representation of representation, etc. (in Owens 1978: 77; Derrida 1976: 163)

TOP: Cindy Sherman, *Untitled Film Still #21*. 1978. Black and white photograph, 18.8 x 23.8 cm. The Museum of Modern Art, New York. BOTTOM: Cindy Sherman, *Untitled Film Still, #15*, 1978. Black and white photograph, 23.5 x 18.9 cm. Guggenheim Museum, New York. © Cindy Sherman and Metro Pictures.

Derrida's reference to the abyss-like representation of representation recalls Tillers' photomechanical reproduction of photomechanical reproduction in *Untitled*, 1978. It will also be shown that the anti-authoriality of *Untitled*, 1978, is echoed in the phrase 'the splitting of the self' and in the connection Derrida establishes between 'presence' [in the sense of the 'presence of self-consciousness'][13] and 'the abyss'. Owens comments on the passage noting:

> For Derrida, the *mise en abyme* describes a fundamental operation of the text—it is synonymous with textuality. ... The Derridean abyss—'when one can read a book within a book, an origin within the origin, a center within the center' and, we might add, a photograph within a photograph—underlies the techniques of deconstructive reading, which describes, among other things, the way in which representation is staged within the text. (Owens 1978: 77)

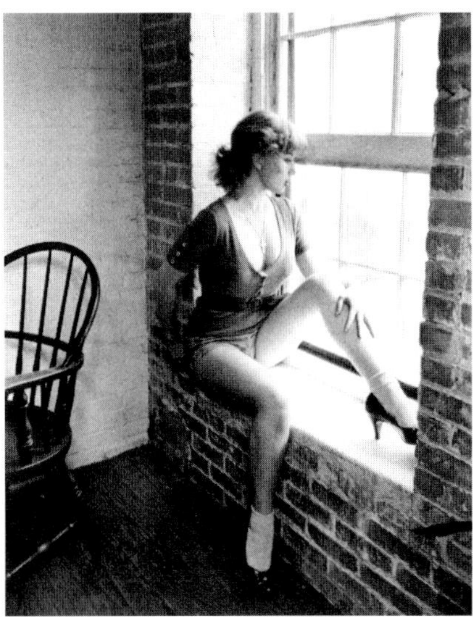

Owens elaborates on Derrida's concept of a semiotic abyss using the notion of *'mise en abyme'*, borrowed from Dällenbach's *Le récit speculaire: essai sur la mise en abyme* (*The Specular Narrative: Essay on the mise en abyme*). As Ross Chambers points out, Dällenbach puts forward the theory that a narrative can function with a variety of devices of 'textual mirroring' (Chambers 1984: 33) or self-referentiality. The latter is evident in the above passage when Owens quotes Dällenbach 'when one can read a book within a book, an origin within the origin, a center within the center'. Owens sets out to show that the same kind of self-referentiality can occur in images, in particular, photographic images.

Owens' pioneering application of Derrida's concept of deconstruction to visual art is an important seminal event in the evolution of a poststructuralist approach to avant-gardist art theory; but it was his colleague, Krauss, who applied such ideas to the analysis of deconstructive appropriation.

ROSALIND KRAUSS' ANALYSIS OF CINDY SHERMAN

The first instance of Krauss' analysis of Sherman appears in 'Note on Photography and the Simulacral' (Krauss 1984a) which includes an analysis of Sherman's Untitled Film Stills series and related work. Two images from the series are reproduced opposite. In her Untitled Film Stills series Sherman used her photographic studio to create *tableaux vivants* based on film stills in which she recreated the *mise en scène* and made, and dressed, herself up to look like the character in a still. Finally Sherman photographed herself.

In Krauss' analysis Sherman's images are characterised as self-reflections which fail to represent an original self. It is significant that Krauss chooses a subject that is intimately concerned with authorial deconstruction. She describes Sherman's work as 'a concatenation of stereotypes' and notes: 'the images reproduce what is already a reproduction' (Krauss 1984a: 59). Her observation that Sherman's works are effectively a reproduction of a reproduction is very similar to Owens' interpretation of Derridean deconstruction in terms of Dällenbach's notion of the self-referential text (Owens 1978: 77). Thus, importantly, the authorial deconstruction that is such an innate facet of Sherman's Untitled Film Stills series is connected with an implicitly Derridean conception of the 'abyss' latent in all forms of representation. The 'abyssmal' 'representation of representation' becomes more closely entwined with the issue of authoriality when Krauss notes:

> If Sherman were photographing a model who was not herself, then her work would be a continuation of this notion of the artist as a consciousness which is both anterior to and distinct from it, a consciousness that knows the world by judging it. (Krauss 1984a: 59-62)

Krauss' point is that it is crucial that the author is immanent in the text she reproduces, not transcendent over it.[14] This differs from the notion of 'the artist as a consciousness which is both anterior to and distinct from it, a consciousness that knows the world by judging it'. Krauss' analysis of Sherman's 'self-portraits' points to an 'endless' series of representations of representations of the 'self'—a process that relates well to both the Derridean notion of an 'abyss' of self-referentiality and to Tillers' deconstruction of authorship via the mirror maze of *Conversations with the Bride* and the Gödelian undecidabilty of *Untitled*, 1978.

As Krauss' analysis continues, her implicit reference to the Derridean framework initially outlined by Owens becomes more pronounced, as is apparent when she employs specular metaphors to elaborate her suggestion that in Sherman's work there is a 'total collapse of difference' (Krauss 1984a: 59-62). A distinctly Owensian specular metaphor emerges in Krauss' analysis when she elaborates on the image of Plato's cave in a discussion of the 'simulacrum' as a 'false copy':

> the false copy is a paradox ... The false copy takes the idea of difference or nonresemblance and internalises it ... a labyrinth is erected, a hall of mirrors, (Krauss 1984a: 62)

Like Owens, Krauss employs implicitly Derridean specular metaphors to express a condition of authorial deconstruction. Furthermore, these metaphors follow on from Krauss' earlier comment that Sherman's images 'reproduce what is already a reproduction ...' (Krauss 1984a: 59).

Krauss' analysis succeeds in bringing together two crucial components of Derridean deconstruction: the specular metaphor of an abyss of self-reflection pointed out by Owens, and the connotations that make Derridean deconstruction a deconstruction of traditional conceptions of authorship. It is this conjunction that makes her analysis of Sherman an especially elegant example of the post-structuralist interpretation of a mode of appropriation defined as authorially deconstructive.

MISE EN ABYME AND AUTHORIAL DECONSTRUCTION IN TILLERS' WORK

The main body of this text will demonstrate that a specular rhetoric of *mise en abyme* can be traced from *Moments of Inertia* through *Conversations with the Bride, Untitled, 1978,* and into the Canvasboard System. Moreover, it will also be shown that as early as 1978, in *Untitled*, Tillers was able to use the *mise en abyme* of the photomechanical reproduction of photomechanical reproduction to create a sophisticated mode of authorially deconstructive appropriation that laid a firm foundation for his development of the Canvasboard System in the 1980s. The following is a synoptic account of the evolution of a rhetoric of specularity and *mise en abyme* and its development into a mode of authorially deconstructive appropriation in *Untitled*, 1978, and its culmination in the mammoth project of authorially deconstructive appropriation that is Tillers' Canvasboard System. The more detailed examination of this crucial aspect of Tillers' work forms the core of this analysis in Chapters Five to Nine.

Panel 24d from *Conversations with the Bride*, 1974–75. Gouache and Resene Imperite acrylic-epoxy on chrome plated aluminium with mirrored backs, 8.5 x 11.8 cm

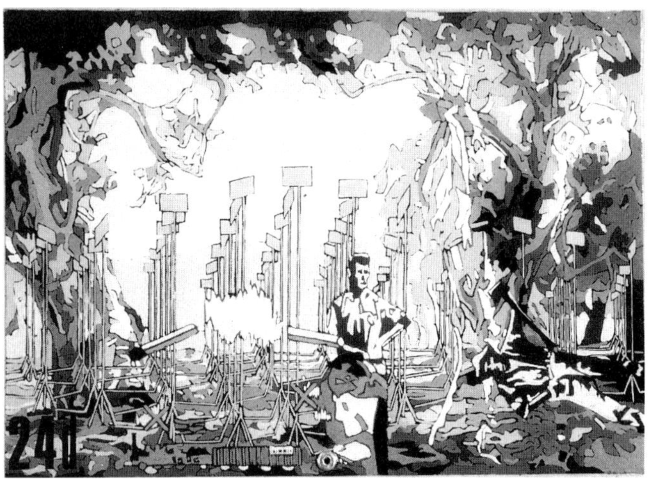

Tillers' affinity for the deconstruction of authorship can be traced back to his analyses of key examples of

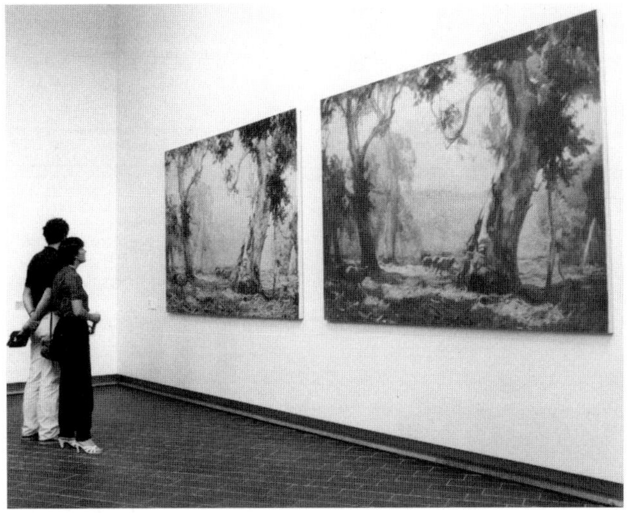

Imants Tillers, *Untitled,* 1978. Neco digital paint-jet print on canvas. Two parts each 163.9 x 185.5 cm. Collection: National Gallery of Australia, Canberra until lost or accidentally destroyed.

avant-gardist art of the 1960s in 'The Beginner's Guide to Oil Painting'. There he showed a strong bias towards art that undermined the traditional primacy of the artist-creator in favour of processes and systems, praising Haacke, Oppenheim, Huebler, and Barry for selecting 'readymade' 'systems' that were able to, more or less, 'organise themselves' (Tillers 1973a: Appendix A 23-25). But Tillers' anti-authorial stance did not intersect with appropriation and evolve into a sophisticated and sustained specular poetics until 1974-75 when he created *Conversations with the Bride*.

Tillers' use of specularity permeates *Conversations with the Bride*. It is evident in the fact that each of the 112 images has a mirrored back; in the fact that Tillers' appropriations of Hans Heysen's *Summer* as the background for most of the images is mirror-inverted; and it is apparent in panel 24d reproduced below opposite. In this image the entire 'matrix' of 112 images on their stands is shown embedded in one of the 112 images.[15] The point of this observation is that in *Conversations with the Bride* Tillers' specular poetics entered into the complexity, paradox and self-reflexivity associated with the logic of the *mise en abyme*. In fact it will be shown that a rhetoric of the *mise en abyme* is a constant feature evident throughout his oeuvre. Moreover, the analysis of Tillers' initial development of a self-reflexive poetics in *Moments of Inertia* will demonstrate that it developed through his interest in science, in other words by an entirely different route than that apparent in the analyses of Owens and Krauss.

The sophistication of Tillers' specular poetics is underscored by what is arguably his single most elegant and sophisticated work: *Untitled*, 1978, reproduced above right. In this work Tillers deploys a creative conflation of his specular poetics and its capacity for *mise en abyme* into a radical problematising of authorship via photomechanically mediated appropriation. As has been noted, *Untitled,* 1978, was produced using the then cutting-edge Neco reprographic technology. As far as this author is aware no other artist had used this process at that time.

Although *Untitled,* 1978, consists of painting on canvas the doubling of the same image alerts the viewer to the fact that the work problematises the concept of an original work of art. It can be noted that the doubling also echoes Tillers' specular rhetoric in *Conversations with the Bride*. Tillers had used authorial appropriation three years previously in *Conversations with the Bride*, 1974-75 but *Untitled,* 1978, is much more radical because it is such a direct appropriation, bordering on plagiarism. In this respect *Untitled*, 1978, can be compared with the work of Sherrie Levine, one of the leading pioneers of New York appropriationism.

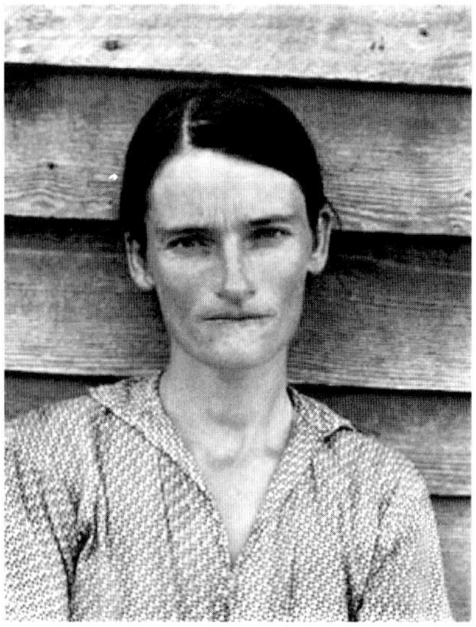

TILLERS AND SHERRIE LEVINE'S DECONSTRUCTIVE AUTHORIAL APPROPRIATION

In 1981 Levine produced a series of works in which she made extremely direct appropriations of works of art. In this sense she provides an instance of a variant of New York appropriationism that parallels Tillers' strategy of appropriating fine art imagery. Levine's strategy was to photograph reproductions of the work of 'master' photographers and reproduce her photographs as her own work with titles beginning: 'After …' followed by the name of the artist appropriated, a strategy evident in the two examples reproduced left. Interestingly, both Owens and Krauss commented on this series of works; possibly because, like Tillers' work, Levine's appropriation of fine art imagery provides a salient instance of authorial deconstruction. In Owens' analysis of Levine's photographic appropriations he notes:

> When Levine wants an image of nature, she does not produce one herself but appropriates another image, and this she does in order to expose the degree to which 'nature' is always already implicated in a system of cultural values to which it assigns a specific, culturally determined position. (Owens 1984: 223)

TOP: Sherrie Levine, *After Walker Evans* (After Walker Evans' portrait of Allie May Burroughs), 1981. Metropolitan Museum of Art, New York.
BOTTOM: Sherrie Levine, *After Eliot Porter*, 1981. Colour photograph, 25.5 x 20.3 cm.

Owens' claim that the representation of nature is 'always already implicated in a system of cultural values' is reinforced by Krauss' comments on Levine in 'The Originality of the Avant-Garde: A Postmodern Repetition' (Krauss 1984b [orig. 1981]) where she describes Levine's work as follows:

> Levine's medium is the pirated print, as in the series of photographs she made by taking images by Edward Weston of his young son Neil and simply rephotographing them, in violation of Weston's copyright. (Krauss 1984b: 27)

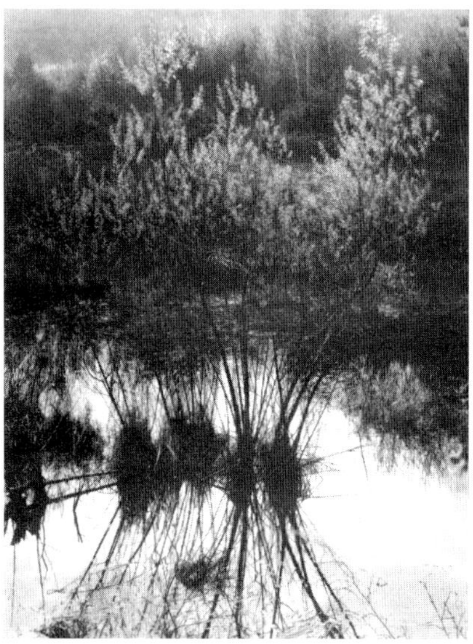

Krauss argues that Levine's apparently audacious act of appropriation is mitigated by the fact that Weston's work is not simply a unique imprint of nature: 'as has been pointed out about Weston's "originals", these are already taken from models provided by others; they are given in that long series of Greek *kouroi* by which the nude male torso has long ago been processed and multiplied within our culture'. Krauss reinforces her point by recourse to the semiotic theory of Roland Barthes, she quotes Barthes' statement:

> To depict is to … refer not from a language to a referent but from one code to another. Thus realism consists not in copying the real but in copying a (depicted) copy … . Through secondary mimesis [realism] copies what is already a copy. (Krauss 1984b: 27)

The crucial point that Krauss makes, after Barthes, is that Weston's photography is not simply 'copying the real' but is instead 'recoding' the real.

Krauss' analysis is especially interesting in the context of the fact that Tillers' use of appropriation will be shown to stem from the influence of Jack Burnham's description of post-object art as 'information processing'.[16] Moreover, it will be demonstrated that his articulation of this concept into art practice from *Moments of Inertia* onwards is based on the production of 'encoded' 'copies'. But this more detailed aspect of Tillers' evolution will be left to the main body of the analysis.

Both Owens and Krauss make the point that the original is as much a copy as is Levine's appropriation. It is a sophisticated theoretical point and it is interesting that Tillers' work fits so neatly into this frame of reference in spite of the fact that he arrived at his Canvasboard System by an entirely different route to the poststructuralist semiotics that informs both Owens and Krauss' analyses of New York appropriationism.

The difference in Tillers' approach to authorial deconstruction in *Untitled*, 1978, is apparent in two published texts associated with this work. The first is in the form of a 'dialogue' in which the budding art theorist Michael Scullion introduced Tillers to Kurt Gödel's Incompleteness Theorem (Scullion and Tillers 1978). The second text is Tillers' artist's book *Three Facts*, published in 1981 (Tillers 1981a). In *Three Facts* Tillers reproduced parts of the 1978 'dialogue' together with some afterthoughts; for example when discussing *Untitled*, 1978, he notes:

> With this ingenious *Japanese* process, [Neco] it was possible for Tillers to produce his own version of *'Summer'* which, when reproduced, was *indistinguishable* from the reproduction of Heysen's original. (Tillers 1981a: 38, §2.5)

In this passage it is evident that Tillers is aware that his use of photomechanically mediated appropriation leads to a radical dislocation of authorship staged in the domain of photomechanical reproduction. It has been noted that *Untitled*, 1978, is a photomechanical reproduction of a photomechanical reproduction but Tillers' comments point to the fact that when *Untitled*, 1978, is reproduced in a book or periodical the *mise en abyme* becomes even deeper. One is reminded of Krauss' commentary on Sherman where she observes: 'the false copy is a paradox … The false copy takes the idea of difference or nonresemblance and internalises it … a labyrinth is erected, a hall of mirrors …' (Krauss 1984a: 62). Traditional notions concerning the originality and uniqueness of the work of art, and the artist are engulfed by paradox. In retrospect, what is especially interesting about this aspect of *Untitled*, 1978, is that the theoretical framework for Tillers' appreciation of an authorial *mise en abyme* lies in his understanding of Gödel's Theorem which, in the context of art theory and practice, is significantly unique and original.

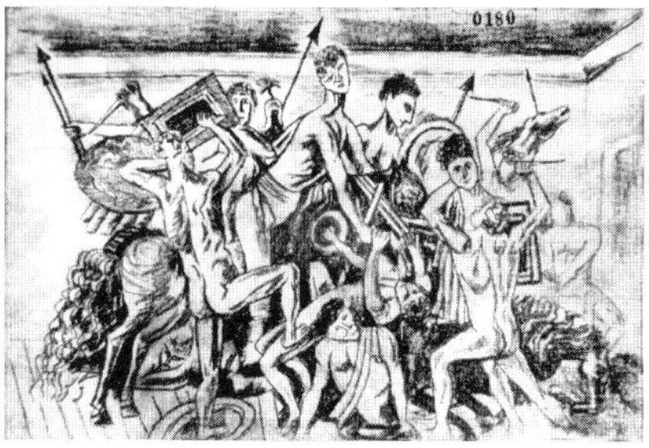

TILLERS' CANVASBOARD SYSTEM

It will be argued that *Untitled*, 1978, together with *Conversations with the Bride*, 1974-75, laid a solid foundation for the appropriationist strategy Tillers developed in the early 1980s. By 1983 he had formulated the method of creating modular paintings made up of minimalistic gridded arrays of canvasboards that he continues to use today. But it should be noted that this strategy of applying images to minimalistic gridded arrays has been shown to be apparent in Tillers' work as far back as *Permutant*, 1971, in which Tillers applied Celtic-like designs to an Andresque gridded 'rug' sculpture.

It was suggested in Chapter One that Tillers' introduction of complex image material into a minimalistic grid can be understood as a deconstruction of the abstraction that is one of the key generic rules of minimal art. In Chapter Two it was noted that Tillers intensified the pictorial dimension of his work via his appropriation of photomechanically reproduced imagery in *Conversations with the Bride* and *Untitled*, 1978. The Canvasboard System can be understood as the culmination of this particular feature of Tillers' work as it allowed him to introduce a manifold of appropriated fine art sources including: Shusaku Arakawa; On Kawara; Giorgio de Chirico, Georg Baselitz, Anselm Kiefer, Robert Barry, Sigmar Polke, Jackson Pollock, Joseph Beuys, Sandro Chia; all of which are interrelated with Tillers' principal antipodean sources, Papunya painting and the work of the New Zealand artist Colin McCahon.

BOTTOM: Imants Tillers, *Pataphysical Man*, 1984. Acrylic paint, charcoal, pencil on 168 canvasboards, Nos. 2466–2633, 304.8 x 530.9 cm. Collection: Art Gallery of New South Wales, Sydney. Photograph: Fenn Hinchcliffe. TOP: Detail of the panel under the chin of the reclining figure.

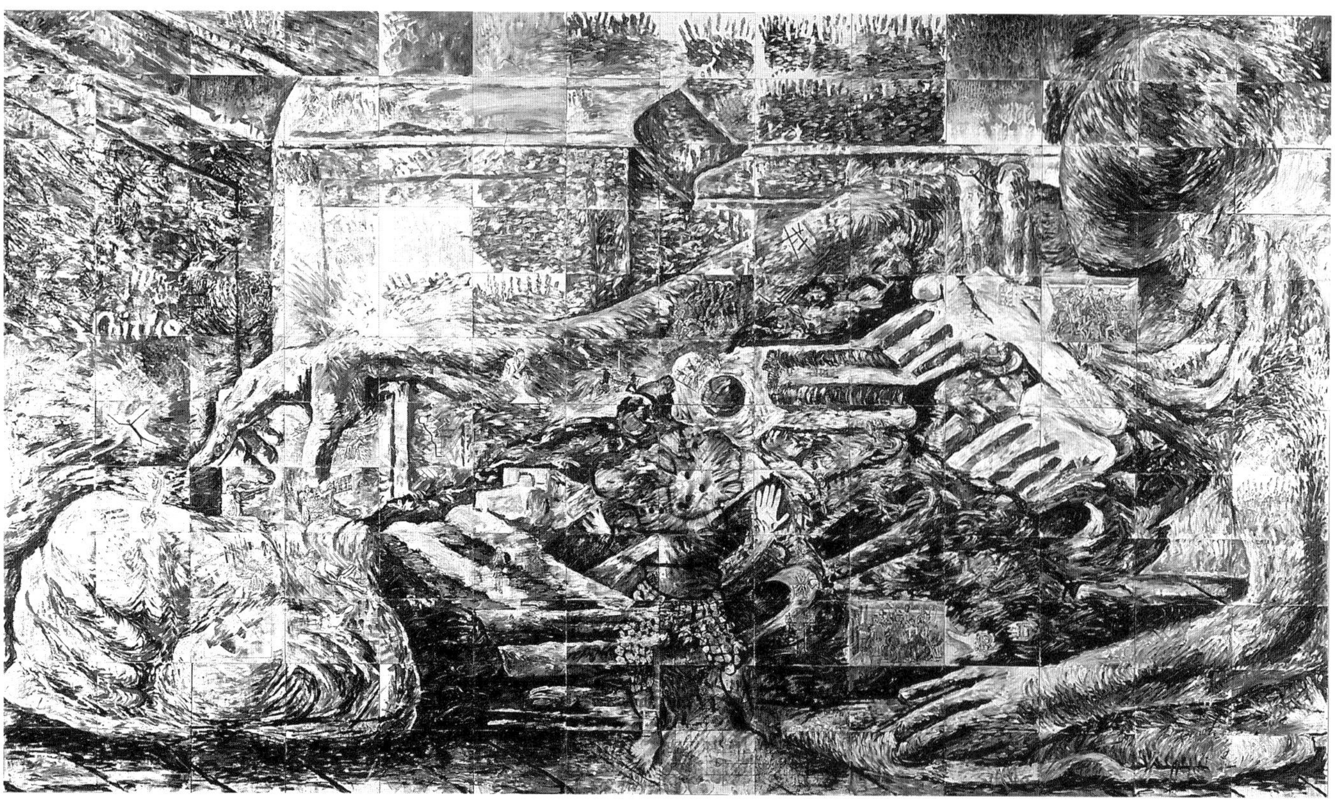

The complexity of Tillers' canvasboard strategy is apparent in its early stages in works such as *Pataphysical Man*, 1984, reproduced below opposite. *Pataphysical Man* is at first glance simply an appropriation of a work by Giorgio de Chirico, but on closer inspection the imagery becomes more complex. The top centre of the painting consists of handprints that echo ancient Aboriginal rock painting; in the bottom centre there is a cartoon boy-bear taken from Latvian illustrated childrens' books; and under the chin of the reclining figure there is a single canvasboard appropriation of a work by Giorgio de Chirico that Tillers created when he began his experiments with canvasboards in 1981 (see opposite top for detail). The embedding of a de Chirico within a de Chirico is indicative of Tillers' continuing use of a rhetoric of the *mise en abyme* and the suitability of his modular painting strategy to such rhetorical devices.

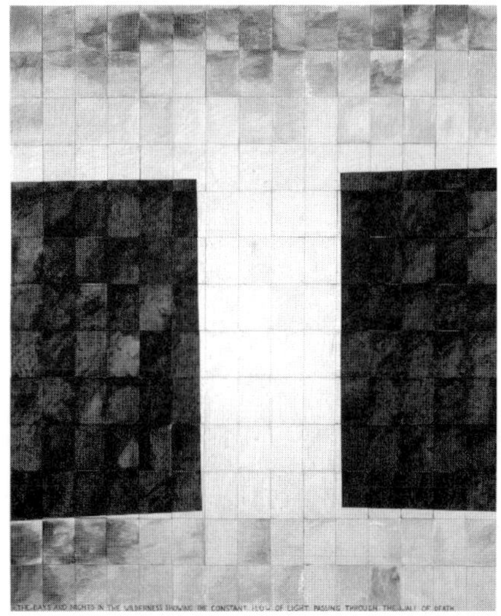

The relationship between *Untitled* 1978 and his canvasboard works of the 1980s was intimated in 1994 when Tillers observed that after he had appropriated another artist's work into his Canvasboard System and then happened to see the original reproduced in a magazine or book: 'it would be like a virtual version of my own work. It would have that same effect on me personally.' (in Coulter-Smith 1994: n.p.). As in the quotation from *Three Facts* cited above, Tillers points to a dislocation of authorship occurring in the domain of photomechanical reproduction. Once more he argues that the appropriated work ceases to appear to be that of another artist and seems to be his own.

TOP: Imants Tillers, *The Letter I*, 1988. Oilstick, gouache and synthetic polymer paint on 195 canvasboards, Nos. 17438–17632, 231 x 190.5 cm. Private Collection. Photograph: Fenn Hinchliffe. BOTTOM: Imants Tillers, *The Letter T*, 1988. Oilstick, gouache, and synthetic polymer paint on 221 canvasboards, Nos. 18579–18799, 231 x 215.9 cm. Photograph: Fenn Hinchliffe

In *Conversations with the Bride,* 1974-75, and *Untitled* 1978, Tillers focused on Heysen's *Summer*. When confronted by the burgeoning discourse of appropriationism in the early 1980s he altered his strategy. He decided to continue to juxtapose antipodean art with Euro-American avant-gardism, but instead of using Heysen he sought out more contemporary modes of antipodean art that could confidently confront European and American avant-gardism within the intertextual arena that is the Canvasboard System.

The first powerful antipodean art Tillers chose was modern Aboriginal art, a 'despiritualised' mode of art that originated in the early 1970s in the Papunya settlement in the Great Western Desert. In the mid-1980s he was severely criticised for appropriating even this modern mode of Aboriginal art and turned to another powerful antipodean artist, the New Zealander Colin McCahon. It is in his use of McCahon's work that the anti-authoriality of Tillers' Canvasboard System becomes especially pronounced, as will be shown in the following chapter.

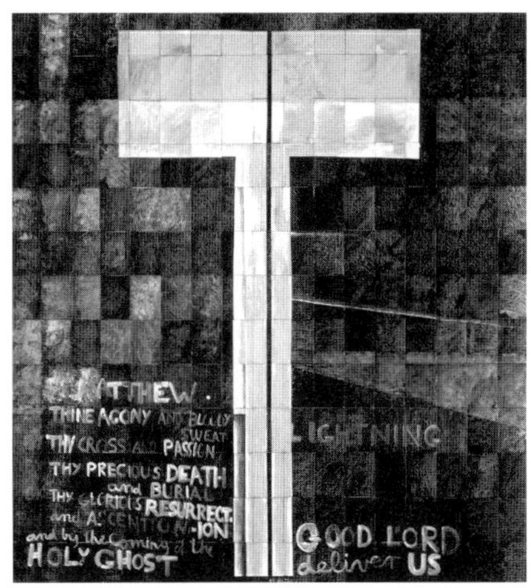

Tillers' works *The Letter I* and *The Letter T*, both dated 1988, are reproduced right and McCahon's originals are reproduced on page 65. Like McCahon's originals, Tillers' appropriation of these initials are large in scale. *The Letter I*, and *The Letter T* consist of grids of 195 and 247 canvasboards respectively. But Tillers' most impressive treatment of these signifi-

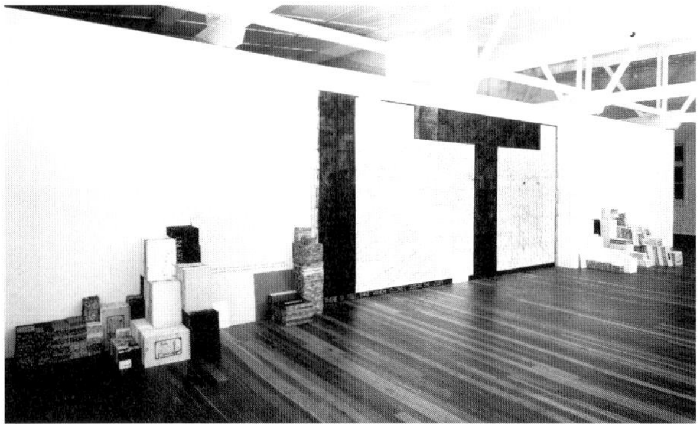

Imants Tillers, ***The Bridge of Reversible Destiny,*** **1990. 7445 panels (mounted and unmounted). Vitreous enamel on steel; gouache, synthetic polymer paint, oilstick on plywood; oilstick, gouache, on canvasboards; blank canvasboards. Panels executed between December 1981 and March 1990, Nos. 21892–29336, 1180 x 279 x 140 cm. Installation at Yuill/Crowley Gallery, Sydney. Photograph: Paul Green.**

ers is evident in his monumental canvasboard work *The Bridge of Reversible Destiny*, 1990, reproduced left. This work is an installation consisting of a large mounted canvasboard painting and massed stacks of unmounted canvasboard paintings. It is obvious that the gigantic 'IT' dominating *The Bridge of Reversible Destiny* can be read as a somewhat ostentatious statement of authorship on Tillers' part. But this presumption is undermined by the fact that Tillers appropriated these signifiers from the work of another artist.

It is obvious that Tillers' appropriation of the McCahonian 'I' and 'IT' motifs relates to his strategy of deconstructive authorial appropriation. What is particularly interesting, however, is that Tillers' self–deconstructive appropriation of such motifs can be explained in terms of the sophisticated and precocious theory and practice associated with *Untitled*, 1978. The main body of this text will examine how the motivation behind Tillers' appropriation of the 'I' and 'T' motifs from McCahon can be traced back to the published 'dialogue' between Michael Scullion and Tillers (Scullion and Tillers 1978) in which Scullion introduces Tillers to Gödel's Incompleteness Theorem.

PERIODISING THE CANVASBOARD SYSTEM

The Canvasboard System began in 1981 with the *Suppressed Imagery* series and in Part Four this analysis will trace its development up to late 2001. There appear to be three phases to the Canvasboard System during the period 1981-2001. The first runs its course with the international style of appropriationism that dominated the 1980s and ends in 1991. The second phase begins in 1992 with Tillers' Diaspora Trilogy which appears to take on a biographical turn, relating to his parents' experiences during the Second World War. Despite this injection of personal subject matter, evidence will be provided to show that the Diaspora Trilogy remains authorially deconstructive due to the fact that Tillers is only able to tell the story of his Latvian heritage via the voices of other artists, most notably Colin McCahon. The third phase is marked by Tillers moving from Sydney to the country town of Cooma in New South Wales. Again Tillers' references to his new locale suggest an 'autobiographical' turn but evidence will be provided to show that, once more, Tillers employs 'autobiography' in a paradoxical and deconstructive mode.

The examination of the three phases of the Canvasboard System will conclude that authorial deconstruction is one of the most important features of the System, as shown by the way in which Tillers' increasing insertion of 'personal' references into his most recent works becomes assimilated into the *abyme*-like intra- and inter-textuality of an ever-expanding image system, which Tillers admits is increasingly out of his control.

Interviewed in January 2001 Tillers emphasised the fact that his biological or ecological concept of 'self-organising systems' has actually become increasingly important to an understanding of his canvasboard works:

> The idea of self-organising systems becomes more relevant the more the Canvasboard System grows. Of course, it is not actually a self-organising system, but it is heading in that direction. What is already there influences what one can add to the series. So what I am doing now [2001] is less of a random process than it was in the 1980s because there is a sufficient density of references and connections to determine what comes next. (in Coulter-Smith 2001: n.p.)

The fact that Tillers' thinking in 2001 can be traced back to his sophisticated analysis of post-object art in terms of holistic systems theory in 'The Beginner's Guide to Oil Painting' (Tillers 1973a: Appendix A) is evidence of the strength and uniqueness of his holistic systems aesthetic and of his capacity to articulate this aesthetic via sophisticated modes of visual rhetoric including: specularity, *mise en abyme*, the photomechanical reproduction of a photomechanical reproduction, and his post-minimalistic modular approach to painting.

Despite the fact that the dominance of appropriationism waned in the 1990s Tillers' work continues to evolve; one of the fundamental reasons being that it never was entirely dependent on the international style of appropriationism. Tillers evolved along his own parallel yet independent route. For example, he continued to elaborate a systems approach when artists such as the New York appropriationists and the British artist Victor Burgin were turning towards the deconstruction of mass media. In this sense Tillers' antipodean isolation was, in retrospect, an advantage.

The following chapter will trace the reception of Tillers' work from *Moments of Inertia* to his Diaspora Trilogy, 1992-94, and will be the final chapter in the introductory section. Part Two will deal with Tillers' development of his holistic systems theory in 'The Beginner's Guide to Oil Painting' and his formulation of a prototypical rhetoric of *mise en abyme* in *Moments of Inertia*. Part Three is the core of the thesis presented here, as it provides a detailed analysis of the sophisticated specular rhetoric Tillers developed in *Conversations with the Bride* and his sophisticated articulation of deconstructive authorial appropriation in *Untitled*, 1978. Finally, Part Four will show how works such as *Conversations with the Bride* and *Untitled*, 1978, provided a substantial foundation for the Canvasboard System. It will also be established that Tillers has been able to sustain the complexity of his appropriational System throughout the 1990s and 2000s by means of paradoxical injections of personal subject matter into what is fundamentally an authorially deconstructive project.

TOP: Colin McCahon, *Untitled (The days and nights in the wilderness showing the constant flow of light passing through the wall of death)*, 1971. Acrylic on unstretched canvas, 234.5 x 184 cm. Collection: Auckland City Art Gallery, on loan from the estate of Colin McCahon. BOTTOM: Colin McCahon, *St. Mathew: Lightning*, 1979. Acrylic on canvas, 268 x 217 cm. Collection: the estate of Colin McCahon.

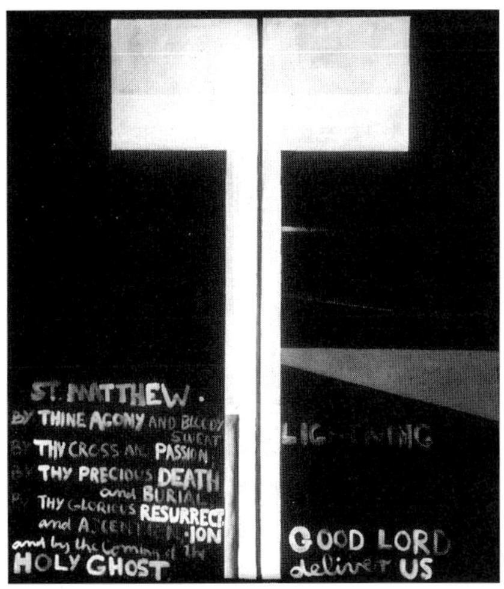

4

THE CRITICAL RECEPTION OF TILLERS' WORK 1971–2001

The critical reception of Tillers' work can be divided into the three periods outlined in the introductory chapters. The first stage concerns Tillers' earliest work *Moments of Inertia*, 1972-73 and his less important performance piece *Enclosure*, 1973. The second stage covers his major works of the 1970s *Conversations with the Bride*, 1974-75; *Untitled*, 1978; and *52 Displacements (Of Image, Of Time, Of Water, Of Feeling, One Year's Work)*, 1979-80. The third stage concerns the transitional work *One Painting, Cleaving,* 1980-81 and his Canvasboard System, which in turn can be broken into three phases: the initial phase 1982-91; the second phase 1992-96 characterised mainly by his 'biographical' Diaspora Trilogy; and the third phase marked by the works Tillers has produced since moving from Sydney to the country town of Cooma in 1997.

In the first stage, 1973-75, critical commentary recognised that *Moments of Inertia* is a major work. Yet, *Moments of Inertia* was difficult to decipher, even by one of the most informed Australian art theorists of the time, because in this work Tillers began to use a formal methodology that entailed a radical deconstruction of minimalist linearity and the generation of considerable negentropic-like complexity. Significantly, while hailing *Moments of Inertia* as a major work, the major commentator on Tillers' very early work, Donald Brook, does not attempt an analysis but instead focuses on the much less original work *Enclosure,* 1973. The reason for this appears to be that *Enclosure* uses an identifiable rhetoric, derived from the discourse of minimal-conceptual performance art of the late 1960s and early 1970s.

It will be argued here that the crux of the problem facing even informed commentators such as Brook was that they were unable to establish parallels between the ideas in Tillers' theoretical writings and his art practice.[17] This problem is not restricted to Brook, it marks the reception of Tillers throughout the period treated in this text—1971-2001. Importantly, linking Tillers' theory and practice is also a necessary basis for the identification of originality of Tillers' contribution to avant-gardist art.

What was to become an enduring lack of understanding of Tillers' early work begins with Donald Brook, in spite of the fact that Brook was probably the best commentator that Tillers could have had in the early 1970s. Brook was a major Australian theorist of 1960s avant-gardism as is evident in the fact that he formulated the useful umbrella term 'post-object art' that is employed in this text. Brook was deeply involved in the theory and practice of post-object art and well qualified to make observations on this genre. The problem facing Brook was that the relationship between the holistic systems aesthetic Tillers outlines in 'The Beginner's Guide to Oil Painting' and his formal strategy in *Moments of Inertia* is extremely difficult to identify and articulate. 'The Beginner's Guide to Oil Painting' is a complex but coherent text. *Moments of Inertia,* on the other hand, is complex but not entirely consistent. In Chapter Six it will be shown that the first part of *Moments of Inertia: Still Life 2* is very coherent, but in the second part *Still Life 1* Tillers' attempts to create negentropic-like complexity begin to flounder. The super-complex and incomplete second stage of *Moments of Inertia: Still Life 1* is an experimental 'work in progress' deliberately left in an incomplete condition and in consequence very difficult to unravel, even now. This is apparent in the fact that even the intensive examination of *Moments of Inertia* provided here, in Chapter Six, focuses on *Still Life 2* and provides only a relatively cursory attempt to analyse *Still Life 1.* Indeed, even Tillers had difficulties recalling some of the more intricate aspects of *Still Life 1* when interviewed in 1991 (Coulter-Smith 1991). The difficulty of the task would have been considerably amplified for Brook writing in 1973 and 1975 without the benefit of historical distance. Accordingly, it is not surprising that he was unable to identify the interplay between *Moments of Inertia* and 'The Beginner's Guide to Oil Painting'.

As the connection between 'The Beginner's Guide to Oil Painting' and *Moments of Inertia* was indecipherable, both works fell into obscurity. After its initial exhibition in the early 1970s *Moments of Inertia* was not exhibited again until 1996 in an exhibition curated by Mary Eagle at the National Gallery of Australia, Canberra. The descent of 'The Beginner's Guide to Oil Painting' into obscurity was assisted by the fact that it existed only as an unpublished BSc (Architecture) Honours dissertation (for which Tillers received first class Honours and the distinction of being awarded the University of Sydney medal).

In retrospect, it can be noted that the 'disappearance' of these two major works created a fundamental problem for the reception of Tillers. Without an understanding of 'The Beginner's Guide to Oil Painting' it is difficult to grasp the evolution of Tillers' theoretical framework in the body of his writings that follow.[18] Accordingly, during the 1970s and 1980s, it became increasingly difficult for commentators to relate Tillers' writings to his work. It is only in an art historical analysis such as this that the opportunity arises to return to the relationship between 'The Beginner's Guide to Oil Painting' and *Moments of Inertia* that provides the master key to understanding Tillers' holistic systems theory, and the way it is articulated in practice in *Moments of Inertia*. When this association is made then one has a solid basis for understanding the relationship between Tillers' theory and practice throughout the period covered by this text: 1971-2001. Finally, and most importantly, *it is in this relationship between Tillers' theory and practice that his originality lies* and it is this originality which is hardest to define.

In the second phase of Tillers' reception—1975-1980—commentators such as Robin Coombes and Peter Myers were able to, quite accurately, label Tillers as a 'conceptual artist' and analyse his work accordingly. What they were less able to do was identify the way in which Tillers' theory and practice went above and beyond the generic rules of the international discourse of conceptual art. Similarly, in the first phase of Tillers' Canvasboard System, 1982-1991, major Australian art critics such as Terry Smith and Terence Maloon were able to analyse Tillers' work in terms of the then dominant discourse of appropriationism, but neither was able to point to Tillers' original contribution to that discourse.

Such observations do not seek to identify the weakness of the body of literature on Tillers examined here. The principal writings on Tillers' work dealt with in this chapter are all produced by informed commentators. However, the following analysis will indicate that contemporaneous commentary on Tillers' work tends to have the function of locating his work within the dominant discourses of the time rather than demonstrating the originality of his contribution.

THE POST-OBJECT PERIOD

DONALD BROOK

The first commentary on Tillers' work appeared as a newspaper review in the *Nation Review* and was written by the progressive Sydney critic and academic Donald Brook (Brook 1973). Brook's positive approach towards Tillers' avant-gardist theory and practice stems from his predilection for intellectual art, in particular conceptual art, which was influential in avant-gardist circles in Australia in the early 1970s. Brook reviewed Tillers' first major work *Moments of Inertia: Still Life 2*, 1972-73, reproduced below. *Moments of Inertia,* 1972-73, represents Tillers' first practical application of the holistic sys-

Imants Tillers, *Moments of Inertia: Still Life 2*, 1972–73. Installation view of the Link Exhibition in the Art Gallery of South Australia, Adelaide in 1974.[19]

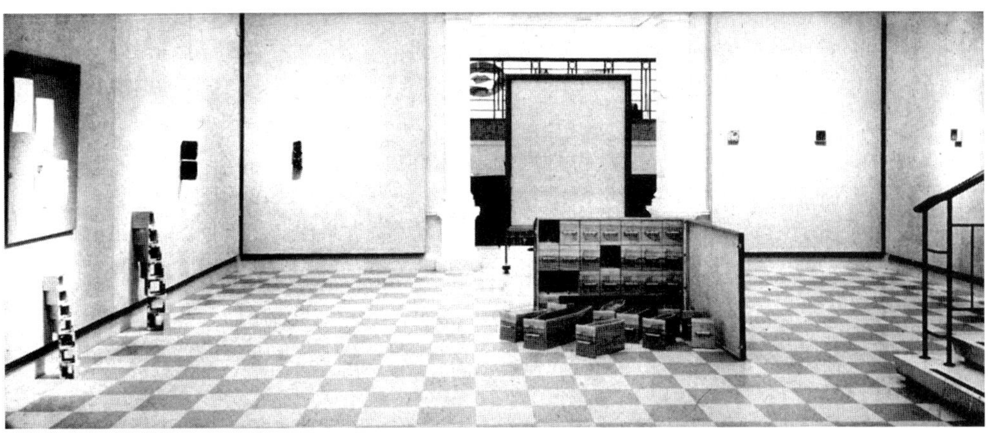

tems theory he develops in 'The Beginner's Guide to Oil Painting' (Tillers 1973a: Appendix A). Brook had access to this unpublished text, however, he frankly admitted that he did not 'fully understand' *Moments of Inertia*, stating:

> Although I doubt that I fully understand it yet, the judgment has clearly formed in my mind that Imants Tillers has made a truly excellent and important work of art that will one day be indispensable to history books and give pleasure to generations. ... It is one of the most intelligent and resolute works of imagination that I have seen in years, in Australia or anywhere else. (Brook 1973)

Brook's enthusiastic comments effectively measure Tillers' *Moments of Inertia* against the many other works of post-object art in Australia and overseas of which Brook would have been aware.

In 1975 Brook was sufficiently interested in Tillers' work to write an article in the major Australian art journal *Art and Australia* (Brook 1975). It is in this article that Brook focused on what is, in retrospect, one of Tillers' more minor works, his 'conceptual' performance piece *Enclosure,* 1973. Although Brook had described *Moments of Inertia* as a 'truly excellent and important work of art' in 1973, in his more detailed analysis of Tillers in 1975 he makes only a passing comment on this major work and its even more revolutionary successor *Conversations with the Bride*, 1974-75. Brook dismisses these two major works of Tillers' early period stating that they 'have had material published' (Brook 1975). Contrary to Brook's claim, however, there were no significant critical analyses of these two highly important works at that time.

THE PHOTO-CONCEPTUAL PERIOD

ART IN THE AGE OF MECHANICAL REPRODUCTION

The next stage of the reception of Tillers' practice concerns his photo-conceptual works: *Conversations with the Bride*, 1974-75; *Untitled*, 1978; *52 Displacements (Of Image, Of Time, Of Water, Of Feeling, One Year's Work)*, 1979-80; and *One Painting, Cleaving,* 1980-81. The reception of Tillers during this period is useful for this analysis because it provides a record of the art theoretical influences manifest in avant-gardist circles in Australia in the late 1970s and early 1980s. In 1978 Tillers produced *Untitled*. It has been noted that this work is based on the photomechanical reproduction of photomechanical reproductions and authorial deconstruction. In retrospect *Untitled*, 1978, is a perfect subject for interpretation via the theoretical framework provided by Walter Benjamin in his landmark essay, 'The Work of Art in the Age of Mechanical Reproduction' (Benjamin 1973). Although originally published in German in 1936 it was not published in English until 1970 and accordingly its influence on art theory in the English speaking world was delayed. As will be shown, Benjamin's essay played a pivotal role in theorising the strategy of photomediated appropriation in the 1980s. Key ideas in Benjamin's essay regarding the supersession of traditional art media by photomedia and the loss of the 'aura' of the unique original through the capacity of photomedia for mass reproduction are extremely relevant to an understanding of the implications of a work such as *Untitled*, 1978. Nevertheless, the evidence provided by the early reception of Tillers' photo-conceptual work indicates that despite tantalising references to art in relation to photography and photomechanical reproduction there are no references to Benjamin's key text.

Another problem facing the second phase of commentary on Tillers is the apparent lack of awareness of the seminal development of deconstructive appropriation in New York in the late 1970s. Evidence of this lacuna in the reception of Tillers' work in this period is valuable as it supports the opinion of this analysis that Tillers was also unaware of such developments in New York at that time. Although he visited New York in 1979 he claims that he did not come into contact with any examples of New York appropriationism. He reports that his main business was to visit the Nicholas Roerich museum and meet Christo and Jeanne-Claude.[20] Indeed, even if Tillers had come into contact with seminal New York appropriationism during that visit, it does not explain the fact that in the previous year he was able to produce *Untitled*, 1978, which appears, in retrospect, to be a precociously paradigmatic example of deconstructive authorial appropriation.

ROBIN COOMBES

After Brook's *Art and Australia* article there is no significant criticism of Tillers' work until the late 1970s. In 1979 Robin Coombes, a British artist then resident in Sydney, wrote a short piece on *Untitled*, 1978, in the catalogue for the third Biennale of Sydney (Coombes 1979). Appropriately, Coombes noted that *Untitled,* 1978, 'bears comparison with the best of European and American researches most usually defined as Conceptual' (Coombes 1979: n.p.). Although his location of *Untitled*, 1978, in the genre of conceptual art is accurate, like Brook, Coombes is unable to make any substantive correlation between Tillers' writings and his practice. As in the case of Brook, this can be explained by pointing out that writing a short catalogue essay on an artist does not usually demand an intensive study of an artist's theory and practice. It is understandable, for example, that Coombes would not have familiarised himself with Tillers' body of theoretical writings, which by 1979 was quite considerable.[21] Commenting on *Untitled*, 1978 Coombes remarks:

> The real quality, I feel, rests in Tillers' ability to demonstrate a sense of irony which is used both to question the nature of painting and mechanical reproductive processes. (Coombes 1979: n.p.)

Reading this passage over twenty years later, its most notable aspect lies in Coombes' use of the phrase 'mechanical reproductive processes'. This phrase suggests that he may have had some awareness of the title of Benjamin's 'The Work of Art in the Age of Mechanical Reproduction' (Benjamin 1973). On the other hand two pieces of evidence indicate that Coombes either had no, or very little, knowledge of Benjamin's theory. Firstly, he uses the term 'mechanical reproductive processes' which sounds awkward when juxtaposed with the smoother, Benjaminian phrase 'mechanical reproduction'. Secondly, Coombes' use of the phrase 'mechanical reproductive processes' represents the full extent of his articulation of this dimension of *Untitled,* 1978. As *Untitled*, 1978, is a paradigmatic instance of the interaction of art and photomechanical reproduction it seems reasonable to assume that if Coombes had any familiarity whatsoever with Benjamin's essay he would surely have been able to elaborate upon the concept of 'mechanically reproductive processes' with at least one of the many notions offered in Benjamin's fertile essay.

Indeed Benjamin's Work of Art essay has played a crucial role in the art theoretical analyses of the turn of avant-gardist art towards photography apparent in art of the 1970s and 1980s. The importance of Benjamin's text is noted by Irving Sandler in *Art of the Postmodern Era: From the Late 1960s to the Early 1990s*. Focusing on the *October* critics whose importance to the discourse of deconstructive appropriation was outlined in Chapter Three, Sandler observes:

> In their thinking about photography and film, the contributors to *October* were greatly influenced by a 1936 essay, "Art in the Age of Mechanical Reproduction," by Walter Benjamin. As Crimp stated, his "classic essay on mechanical reproduction has become central to critical theories of contemporary visual culture." So important was Benjamin's thinking to the editors of *October* that they devoted the winter 1985 issue to an English translation of his "Moscow Diary." (Sandler 1996: 346)

Sandler emphasises his appreciation of the *October* theorists' recognition of the importance of Benjamin by providing a synopsis of Benjamin's essay in the course of which he notes that 'Benjamin believed that the modern age was distinguished by two developments: the rise of mass society and a technological revolution, namely photomechanical reproduction.' (Sandler 1996: 346).

The applicability of Benjamin's sophisticated analysis of photo-mechanical reproduction to an interpretation of Tillers' photomechanical painting *Untitled*, 1978, is so obvious that its absence from commentary on that work is a salient marker that helps indicate precisely when the Australian avant-garde, including Tillers, became aware of developments in New York. The first explicit reference to Benjamin's Work of Art essay in the reception of Tillers' work occurred in January 1981 in the context of the New York art critic Suzi Gablik's article 'Report from Australia' published simultaneously in *Art in America* and *Art and Australia* (Gablik 1981b, 1981a).

PETER MYERS

In 1980 Tillers appeared in a one-person-show, Survey 13, part of a series of exhibitions at the National Gallery of Victoria, Melbourne. The exhibition was coordinated by Robert Lindsay and a catalogue essay was written by the architect Peter Myers (Myers 1980).[22] Although it is a gatefold catalogue, only six pages long, Myers' essay is substantial (approximately two thousand words). It is also very perceptive, but reveals the same lack of awareness of the link between Tillers' theory and his practice evident in the writings of Brook and Coombes.

Another, salient feature of Myers' analysis is the fact that although he makes direct reference to the role played by photomedia in Tillers' work he shows no awareness of Benjamin's Work of Art essay. Like Brook and Coombes, Myers accurately classifies Tillers according to the framework of conceptual art. In addition, like Brook, Myers had some familiarity with Tillers' writings. But like Brook he was, understandably, unable to establish a relationship between Tillers' theory and practice.

The subject of Myers' text is *Conversations with the Bride*, 1974-75, and *52 Displacements (Of Image, Of Time, Of Water, Of Feeling, One Year's Work)*, 1979-80. Of the two works *Conversations with the Bride* is by far the more complex and innovative work. Yet, as in the case of Brook, Myers turns to the less innovative work. Again the most likely reason for this stems from the fact that Myers had not read Tillers' writings associated with *Conversations with the Bride* of which there are three (Tillers 1975, 1978a, 1978b). Myers refers to *Conversations with the Bride* as a 'complex synthesis of high art and vernacular images' (Myers 1980: n.p.) where 'high art' seems to refer to Tillers' appropriation of imagery from Duchamp's *The Large Glass* (1915-23) and the 'vernacular' appears to refer to Heysen's *Summer,* conceived of as 'provincial'. Myers analysis of *Conversations with the Bride* does penetrate further when he notes that this 'complex' work is 'far more accessible' when understood in terms of 'random encounters' (Myers 1980: n.p.) but, in a manner reminiscent of Brook, Myers veers away from this complex work towards the simpler and less

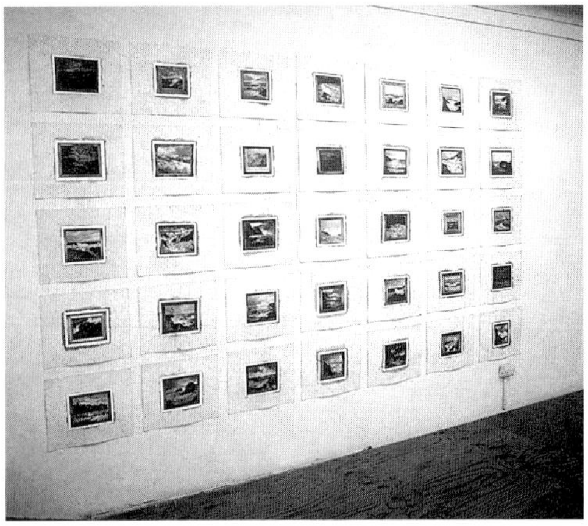

innovative *52 Displacements (Of Image, Of Time, Of Water, Of Feeling, One Year's Work)* which consists primarily of a gridded array of fifty-two paintings of seascapes appropriated from a 'beginner's guide'-type book for amateur painters (see top left). When exhibited this image array is accompanied by 52 framed texts, in the genre of conceptual art (not illustrated). Tillers set himself the task of meticulously copying one image from the book of seascapes each week for a year. A detail of one of the canvases is reproduced centre left. The parodic aspect of this work is manifested by Tillers' inclusion of painted gilded frames which reproduce the frames illustrated in the source book. The image reproduced bottom left is from Susan Hiller's systematic collection of seaside postcards entitled *Dedicated to the Unknown Artists*, 1972-76, which partly inspired Tillers to produce *52 Displacements (Of Image, Of Time, Of Water, Of Feeling, One Year's Work)*.

TOP: Detail of painted component of *52 Displacements (Of Image, Of Time, Of Water, Of Feeling, One Year's Work)*, 1979–80. 52 parts gouache on canvas and 52 parts framed texts. Each canvas 34.4 x 42.5 cm; each framed text of varying dimensions. Installation at the Institute of Modern Art, Brisbane. Photograph: John Nixon. Various private and public collections. CENTRE: Detail of one panel from painted component of *52 Displacements*. BOTTOM: Detail from Susan Hiller, *Dedicated to the Unknown Artists*, 1972–76. One of 14 panels, each panel 66 x 104.8 cm. Collection of the artist.

Myers' analysis of *52 Displacements ...* focuses on the issue of provincialism, as is apparent when he points to a correspondence between *52 Displacements ...* and Tillers' previous use of Heysen's *Summer* in *Conversations with the Bride* (1974), observing:

> Similarly in his adoption of Hans Heysen's revered watercolour, *Summer*, one of Australia's most admired paintings, ...Tillers confirms the inevitability of the photographic process producing further thematic variations on a perennial favourite. Each reproduction is, in fact, a further variation. (Myers 1980: n.p.)

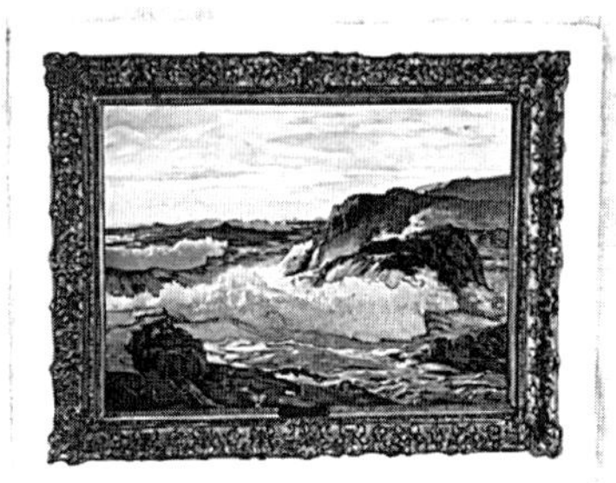

What is especially interesting about Myers' comments is that he seems so positively disposed towards Tillers' precocious appropriation of other artists' work. In spite of the fact that Myers was unaware of Benjamin's Work of Art essay or Tillers' body of writings his observations are extremely keen. Instead of criticising Tillers for his photomediated appropriation of other artists' work Myers makes the interesting observation that each reproduction is a 'variation', a notion that suggests creativity. The sophistication of Myers' appreciation of the role that photomediated reproduction could play in the domain of fine art is especially evident when he notes that:

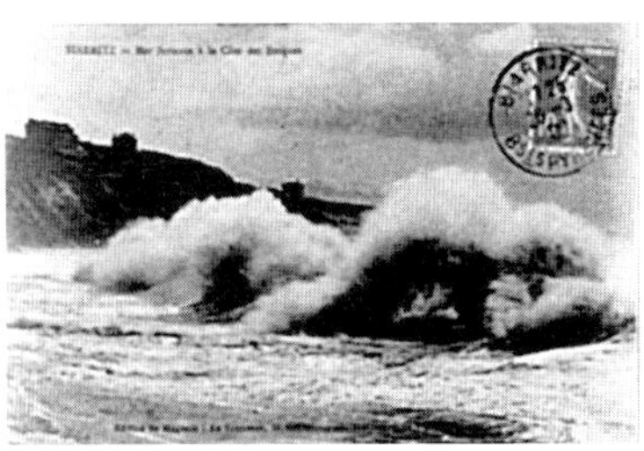

> It is common knowledge that New York minimal artists make separate, small, tonally adjusted ('photo-ready') versions of their huge canvases for magazine reproduction; the trick is you cannot tell the difference until you have a similar image of the *original* work. We have always accepted the veracity of photographic reproductions as innocent facsimiles yet here is Tillers proposing that they are utterly and inexorably unique. (Myers 1980: n.p.)

Myers ascribes the notion that the facsimiles 'are utterly and inexorably unique' to Tillers. Indeed, Tillers used exactly the same words a year later in his artist's book *Three Facts* (Tillers 1981a). The statement that Tillers' 'facsimiles' are 'utterly and inexorably unique' is, in rhetorical terms, a paradox and paradox will be shown to be crucial to an understanding of Tillers' pivotal work *Untitled*, 1978.

Myers' analysis of Tillers' work is notable for its intelligent handling of what is in retrospect the crux of Tillers' work of the 1970s, the intersection of the discourses of photo-conceptualism and appropriation. In addition, Myers' analysis is also interesting because there is no hint of an awareness of Benjamin's landmark analysis of the relationship of art and photomedia in his Work of Art essay. As with the analysis of Coombes' text this suggests the absence of any awareness of the Work of Art essay in Australian avant-gardist art circles even in 1980. An observation that supports the contention that Tillers produced *Untitled*, 1978, independently of any contact with seminal New York appropriationism.

THE DAWNING DISCOURSE OF APPROPRIATIONISM

SUZI GABLIK

Towards the end of 1980 the American art critic Suzi Gablik visited various Australian artists including Tillers. Visiting Tillers' studio she witnessed him working on one of his palimpsestic *One Painting, Cleaving* works, which are based on a misregistered colour reproduction of the Basilica of St. Francis of Assisi Tillers found on a postcard.[23] On her return to New York Gablik published an article on Australian contemporary art in the January 1981 issue of *Art in America* (Gablik 1981a).[24] In her survey she mentions Tillers' debt to Duchamp—evident in his homage to Duchamp, *Conversations with the Bride*, 1974-75. More importantly, it is in her analysis of Tillers that she introduces Walter Benjamin's 'The Work of Art in the Age of Mechanical Reproduction' in the following manner:

> If, as Walter Benjamin says, that which decays in the age of mechanical reproduction is the 'aura' of the work of art, then Tillers' effort must be seen as reclaiming for the mechanical reproduction a unique existence and endowing it with the 'aura' of the original. His elaborate networks of duplications, multiplications and hand-painted reproductions rely on visual analogies and isomorphic relationships that are continually testing what the eye perceives. (Gablik 1981a: 37)

Gablik's comments provide the first indication of the relevance of Benjamin's landmark essay to the interpretation of Tillers' photo-conceptual works.[25]

BERNICE MURPHY

Gablik's lead was soon followed up. Tillers appeared in the 1981 Australian Perspecta exhibition (May-June),[26] and Bernice Murphy, an eminent Australian curator of contemporary art, wrote a short but significant review for the catalogue. Her text is accompanied by an illustration of *52 Displacements (Of Image, Of Time, Of Water, Of Feeling, One Year's Work)*, 1979-80, and *One Painting, Cleaving: A painting which exists for one second*, 1980.[27]

Like Myers, Murphy brought up the issue of the photographic reproduction of works of art. Moreover, she obviously benefited from Gablik's contribution to the literature on Tillers as her essay provides evidence of a more thorough reading of 'The Work of Art in the Age of Mechanical Reproduction' than is indicated in Gablik's analysis of Tillers. Indeed, Murphy's analysis is almost exclusively informed by a Benjaminian perspective, enabling her to provide a much more concise and comprehensive analysis of Tillers' relationship to the increasing role played by photomedia in conceptual art of the 1970s and its evolution into appropriationism of the late 1970s and 1980s. Yet, it is important to note that even this theoretically sophisticated analysis of Tillers' work suffers from a lack of awareness of Tillers' theoretical writings. In her analysis Murphy begins by noting that:

> the mechanical generation, translation and proliferation of images is now so ubiquitous that it entirely surrounds and invades the domain of 'art' imagery, rather than running parallel or ancillary to it. (Murphy 1981: 135)

In this passage, Murphy locks into the heart of Benjamin's argument which is that photomedia would eventually supersede traditional, pre-industrial, forms of art. She provides another precise articulation of Benjamin's position when she states that the 'unique identity of art objects [is] broadly subverted by reproductive processes'.[28] She applies her sophisticated understanding of the Benjaminian framework to an analysis of Tillers' work observing:

> Tillers makes sophisticated works that call attention conceptually to the radically transformed environment within which questions of the making and communication of visual images must now be framed. (Murphy 1981: 135)

In the context of Murphy's obvious familiarity with Benjamin's Work of Art essay her phrase a 'radically transformed environment' can be compared to Benjamin's statement that 'by making many reproductions it [photo-technology] substitutes a plurality of copies for a unique existence' and thereby leads to 'a tremendous shattering of tradition' (Benjamin 1973: 215). In addition, Benjamin's reference to 'a plurality of copies' is reflected in Murphy's earlier reference to 'a proliferation of images'.

Murphy's analysis provided Tillers' photo-conceptualist work with the long-awaited, sophisticated art theoretical framework it deserved. Yet, in spite of the considerable sophistication of Murphy's analysis it still suffers from a lack of awareness of Tillers' own, by then quite unique, theoretical framework. Although, Murphy's understanding of Benjamin enabled her to accurately locate Tillers within the evolution of photomediated art, in common with other writers, she was unable to point to the more unique and original aspects of Tillers' theory and practice.

PAUL TAYLOR

Gablik's introduction of Benjamin's contemplations concerning art in the age of mechanical reproduction and Murphy's elaboration upon the Benjaminian theme were precursors for a flood of postmodern art theory informed by Frankfurt School Marxist aesthetics and French post-structuralism. Its main effect was on the major cultural centres in Australia—Sydney and Melbourne.

The debut of the Australian appropriationists took place in 1982 on the occasion of an exhibition curated by Paul Taylor at the National Gallery of Victoria, Melbourne. At that time Taylor was a young, precocious art writer and founder of the first 'postmodern' Australian art magazine, *Art & Text* (first published in Autumn 1981). Taylor entitled his exhibition Popism and his catalogue essay is extraordinary for its exhaustive list of then new theoretical ideas and their authoritative sources. For example he cites Roland Barthes, Jean Baudrillard, Jacques Lacan, Gilles Deleuze and Félix Guattari, and, of course, Walter Benjamin. He also sprinkled his text with philosophical and aesthetic concepts derived from these 'new, mainly French, theorists'. Some of the terms he introduced include: 'palimpsest'; 'erasure', 'surface', 're-presentation', 'supplement', 'anti-humanism', and 'allegory' (Taylor 1982).

For the exhibition Tillers entered *52 Displacements (Of Image, Of Time, Of Water, Of Feeling, One Year's Work),* and pieces from his *Suppressed Imagery* series which, mark his first and rather rudimentary use of canvasboards. What is perhaps most significant about Taylor's commentary is that it situates Tillers in the general context of a new aesthetic—so new that the term 'postmodern' had not yet taken hold within the Australian art community. As has been noted, this new aesthetic consisted primarily of sophisticated Marxian and poststructuralist approaches to the interpretation of the strategy of photomediated appropriation. The role of Benjamin's landmark essay 'The Work of Art in the Age of Mechanical Reproduction' has also been noted.

In a significantly Benjaminian fashion, Taylor characterises the new genre he refers to as 'popism' as based primarily on 'photorhetoric' (Taylor 1982: 1). He observes that the visual arts has:

> failed to recognise and admit the influence that the rhetoric of photography bears on our history and culture. The art in POPISM, however, involves itself with this rhetoric and it is that to which we continually refer. (Taylor 1982: 1)

Taylor's focus on photography as the basis for the new 'rhetoric' of 'popism' can be compared with a similar focus on the importance of photography in Tillers' article 'Tom Roberts—Some Impressions' published in *Art and Australia* (Tillers 1981b). Significantly, Tillers' article was written in Autumn 1981, prior to Taylor's Popism essay. In this article Tillers quoted the science fiction author Isaac Asimov's suggestion that before photography nothing really existed:

> Before photography there was nothing. Before photography we lived in a world in which the passing moment died as it passed. Every bit of life was a flash that vanished as it appeared. (Tillers 1981b: 272)

Tillers also suggests that in taking us beyond the immediate present, photography produces a 'paper thin' 'parallel shadow world' (Tillers 1981b: 272). Taylor takes a similar approach in his Popism catalogue essay. He quotes the French poststructuralist philosopher Gilles Deleuze, unfortunately without any reference.

> Events, in their radical difference from things, are no longer sought in the depths but at the surface: a mirror that reflects them, a chessboard that 'flattens' them to a two-dimensional plane. By running along the surface, along the edge, one passes to the other side; from bodies to incorporeal events. The continuity of front and back replaces all levels of depth. (in Taylor 1982: 4)

The resonant phrase in this passage is: 'By running along the surface, along the edge, one passes to the other side; from bodies to incorporeal events.' The phrase becomes even more resonant when it is realised that Tillers' conception of photography as a 'paper-thin' 'parallel shadow world' relates to his interest in the possible existence of a fourth spatial dimension, and that he explains this dimension via analogy with a two-dimensional world intersected by three-dimensional objects.[29]

Taylor also notes, again without any reference, that Deleuze describes the situation outlined in the above passage using the term 'Carrollian language' after Lewis Carroll's *Through The Looking Glass* (Taylor 1982: 4). The detailed analysis of Tillers' theory and practice that forms the core of this study will show that Taylor's analysis of this new photorhetorical genre in terms of 'Carrollian language' can be related to the crucial and enduring role played by specular metaphor in Tillers' theory and practice.

Taylor's specific observations on Tillers' work are interesting due to the fact that as well as locating Tillers within the new discourse of appropriationism, he places considerably more reliance on Tillers' own ideas than is the case in previous commentaries. It appears, however, that this was not the result of a necessarily lengthy reading of Tillers' substantial body of writings, instead it would have been gleaned from conversations with Tillers.

For example, Taylor notes 'in Imants Tillers' *Suppressed Imagery,* non-referentiality between images and their original (didactic) contexts is totalised' (Taylor 1982: 4). In less jargon-laden terms Taylor appears to be suggesting that Tillers recontextualises his appropriated images and thereby interferes with their original signification in a manner akin to the methods outlined in Buchloh and Foster's interpretations of New York appropriationism examined in Chapter Three. A similar notion appears in Tillers' artist's book *Three Facts* published in the year prior to Taylor's Popism essay (Tillers 1981a). There Tillers argued that the replication of Heysen's *Summer* in a Chinese newspaper, with a vast distribution and a text by a Chinese art critic who had obviously not visited Australia, led to a totally different reading of the image than that offered by Australian art critics and historians (Tillers 1981a: 39).

Taylor also proposes that in Tillers' work: 'Mistakes, variations, misregistration and superimposition are staged as delays and collisions within photographic and illustrational continuums.' (Taylor 1982: 4, 12). In spite of the elaborate new ideas Taylor appears to have at his disposal, these observations accord with notions already evident in Tillers' writings. Thus the concept of 'misregistration' derives from the out-of-register Assisi postcard crucial to Tillers' *One Painting, Cleaving* (discussed in Chapter Nine). Also, Taylor's use of the term 'delay' stems from Tillers' observations on Duchamp's *The Green Box* in *A Companion to Conversations with the Bride* (Tillers 1978a: Table 4.3 § 4.1).

Three interrelated features emerge from an examination of Taylor's interpretation of Tillers. Firstly, Tillers is located within the canon of theorists and key ideas associated with appropriationism in the early 1980s; secondly, correspondences are made between Tillers' ideas and this canon; and thirdly, Tillers' involvement in the relationship between art and photomedia is brought to the fore. Thus by 1982 four major commentators—Myers, Gablik, Murphy and Taylor—had noted the relationship between Tillers' work and photomechanical reproduction. Myers is noteworthy for the perspicacity of his analysis in the absence of any knowledge of Benjamin's Work of Art essay. Gablik is important as she appears to have introduced Benjamin to the Australian avant-gardist art world. Murphy is distinguished by her ability to apply a close reading of Benjamin's Work of Art thesis to an interpretation of Tillers' photoconceptualism. Finally, Taylor is remarkable due to the fact that he combines his awareness of Tillers' ideas with his knowledge of poststructuralism in such a manner that he highlights the 'photo-rhetorical' and philosophical connotations of Tillers' work.

DONALD KUSPIT

By 1985 Tillers' Canvasboard System was well under way and he was building an international reputation as the major Australian practitioner of appropriationism. A salient indicator of this reputation is the fact that he was reviewed by the venerable American art critic Donald Kuspit. The review (Kuspit 1985) was of an exhibition of Tillers' canvasboard works at the Bess Cutler Gallery in New York. It was and still is a highly significant achievement for an Australian artist to be represented by a New York gallery. In addition, being reviewed by a major American art critic indicates the extent of international recognition Tillers had achieved via his canvasboard strategy only two years after he had fully developed it.

Unfortunately for Tillers, Kuspit is of an older generation of art critics who was, at that time, unsympathetic to the philosophies motivating deconstructive appropriation. Thus his review of Tillers' exhibition was somewhat negative. Yet, in view of Kuspit's antipathy it seems reasonable to claim that he was not criticising Tillers in particular but using Tillers' work as a prime example of the strategy of appropriationism. One of the distinctive features of Tillers' Canvasboard System lies in the fact that he does not 'deconstruct' mass media imagery as did most New York practitioners of appropriationism. In the first phase of his Canvasboard System, 1983-91, he appropriates exclusively from the field of fine art. It appears to have been this highly distinctive feature of Tillers' work that captured Kuspit's attention, but also his dissension. Kuspit's conservative position is evidenced by his claim that Tillers manipulates the images he appropriates:

> though he claims that he simply 're-articulates' images he admires but knows only from magazines, giving them the kind of 'body' they have in memory … by reversing the scale of the parodied works—a large Chia becomes small, a small de Chirico becomes large—Tillers turns each image into a caricature of itself. Also some of his paintings assemble bits and pieces from the oeuvre of one artist, creating a montage-like effect that undermines that artist's whole enterprise. (Kuspit 1985)

Kuspit's claim that Tillers' manipulative appropriation 'undermines' the original artist's 'whole enterprise' suggests that he subscribes to the traditional concept of the integrity of authorship and authenticity. But if Kuspit supports such notions then he would be equally opposed to a more faithful mode of appropriation. Accordingly, Kuspit's intellectual position seems to entail the rejection of *any* application of appropriationism to fine art.

Kuspit's rejection of appropriationism is less important than the fact that he focuses on Tillers despite the fact there were New York artists such as Sherrie Levine and Mike Bidlo who also appropriated from fine art.[30] Kuspit's focus on Tillers can be explained by the sheer scale of his appropriational system.

Even by 1985 the modularity of Tillers' Canvasboard System enabled him to assimilate any number of artists' works into his system. It is possible that Kuspit was aware that Tillers had created an appropriation 'machine', and it was this awareness that made him wary of such an enterprise.

THE PROVINCIALISM PROBLEM

By the mid-1980s appropriationism had become established as an international art movement focused primarily on New York artists and art theorists. The reception of Tillers in the second half of the 1980s acknowledged that he was a major Australian practitioner of this genre. In Australia two principal art writers dominate this period, Terry Smith and Terence Maloon. As with the other major critics examined in this chapter Maloon and Smith are intelligent and informed but, like the others, they were unable to identify any link between Tillers' theoretical writings and his work.

One of the outcomes of this feature of the reception of Tillers' Canvasboard System in the 1980s is that Australian critics such as Maloon and Smith imply that Tillers' entry into the international style of appropriationism can be understood in terms of Smith's analysis of provincialism in which he notes 'provincialism appears primarily as an attitude of subservience to an externally imposed hierarchy of cultural values' (Smith 1974: 54). It will be shown that both Maloon and Smith's analyses imply that Tillers' appropriationist Canvasboard System exhibits a significant degree of 'subservience to an externally imposed hierarchy of cultural values'.

It will be argued that this negative reception of Tillers can be explained by the lack of awareness of the substantive connections between his theoretical writings and his art practice that began with Brook and continued through Coombes, Myers and Murphy. Even Paul Taylor's knowledge of Tillers' ideas was gleaned from conversations with Tillers rather than via the time-consuming process of linking Tillers' writings to his work.

In the absence of any associations between Tillers' theory and practice in previous commentaries, Maloon and Smith became focused primarily on Tillers' Canvasboard System. It can be conjectured that if Smith and Maloon had some awareness of the intimate relationship between Tillers' theory and practice of the 1970s they would have realised that he had evolved from his photo-conceptualist works of the 1970s into his appropriationist works of the 1980s in a manner different from, yet parallel to, the evolution of artists such as Victor Burgin and Hans Haacke. But it is very easy to make such observations when one has the considerable benefit of hindsight.[31]

TERENCE MALOON

Terence Maloon published a substantial article on Tillers in the Winter 1986-87 issue of the then leading British contemporary art journal *Studio International*. By this time the discourse of deconstructive appropriation had become established in Australia, as is evidenced by the fact that Maloon refers to two powerful theorists associated with the discourse of deconstructive appropriationism and postmodern art: Walter Benjamin and Jean Baudrillard. Baudrillard's ideas were particularly influential upon Australian avant-gardist art and art theory, especially in Sydney, during the 1980s.[32]

One of the most interesting aspects of Maloon's analysis is that he identifies the relationship between Tillers' use of gridded arrays of canvasboards and Carl Andre's gridded, rug-like sculptures. Tillers was to underline this connection in a published interview with his partner in 1988 (Slatyer and Tillers 1988) and it seems most likely that Maloon discovered this link after speaking with Tillers. Maloon cites Andre's defence of minimalism:

> in which he declared that the environment already contained too many objects, and now 'requires significant blankness, ... some tabula rasa ... some space that suggests significant exhaustion. When signs occupy every surface, then there is no place for new signs'. (Maloon 1986-87: 34)

Ingeniously, Maloon then suggests that in his canvasboard paintings Tillers changed Andre's minimalist grid into its antithesis:

> Instead of being a locus of significant blankness, it began to support a profusion of overlaid, scrambled imagery. However, the image-overload (the return of the repressed) produced an oddly similar effect to the 'significant exhaustion' of classical minimalism. The excess of imagery cancelled itself out and caused the viewer to blank out in response. (Maloon 1986-87: 34)

In this passage Maloon provided one of the most concrete associations between Tillers' Canvasboard System and post-object art available in the literature on Tillers at that time.

Unfortunately, the correlation between Tillers' post-object period and his Canvasboard System is not pursued to the point where Maloon could have realised that Tillers had followed his own evolutionary path to deconstructive appropriation. Instead, Maloon begins to hint that Tillers is an implicitly 'provincialist' follower of a dominant international discourse. Reflecting on Tillers' account of his use of appropriation in his essay 'In Perpetual Mourning' (Tillers 1984) Maloon selects the following quotation:

> the dotscreen of mechanical reproduction has rendered all images equivalent, interchangeable, scaleless and surface-less: for the Australian artist it has made art in the reproduced form the perfect material for *bricolage.* (in Maloon 1986-87: 35)

Tillers' use of the term *bricolage* suggests that the medium of the photomechanical reproduction allows him to 'play' with the European and American 'authorities' rather than approach them with a provincialistic reverence. But Maloon appears somewhat unsympathetic to Tillers' position when he reports:

> Recently, [... Tillers] has tried to shift the focus away from his characterisation of the Australian artist as incorrigible copycat to emphasise his function as interpreter, entrepreneur and mixmaster of imagery. (Maloon 1986-87: 35)

Maloon's analysis is equivocal. On the one hand he interprets Tillers' strategy as going beyond mere, implicitly provincialist, mimicry. On the other hand, his use of the term 'mixmaster of imagery' suggests a disdainful attitude, as does the previous term 'copycat'.

The tone established by the terms 'copycat' and 'mixmaster' compound Maloon's earlier observation that Tillers 'trimming his sails to the winds of fashion has helped him maintain a high profile and retain his export value for the Australia Council [a governmental funding body for the arts]' (Maloon 1986-87: 34). It also relates to his remark that Tillers 'aspires for glory in the museums and Biennales in Europe and America' (Maloon 1986-87: 35).

The conclusion of Maloon's article is a culmination of the implicit criticisms listed above. It suggests that, in spite of a more informed position regarding appropriationism, like Kuspit, Maloon has fundamental reservations concerning this strategy. In a somewhat jaundiced description of Tillers' appropriation of leading contemporary European and American artists of the 1980s Maloon remarks:

> In a roomful of Baselitzes, Salles and Chias, Tillers' paintings would operate like those mirror-faced skyscrapers erected in the old quarters of cities, which harmonise with their surroundings by reflecting them. (Maloon 1986-87: 35)

Taken in the context of the other negative remarks in Maloon's text, the idea that Tillers' paintings 'harmonise with their surroundings by reflecting them' is quite a strong suggestion that Tillers is a provincialist follower of an international style. Ironically, the analysis of the relationship between Tillers' theory and practice, that is the core of the thesis presented here, will show that Tillers' work of the 1970s, which laid the foundation for his canvasboard strategy, is distinguished by his application of a specular rhetoric comparable with Rosalind Krauss' use of the notion of a 'hall of mirrors' to describe Cindy Sherman's appropriationism. Thus, Maloon's most adversely critical remarks paradoxically reflect one of the most poetic dimensions of Tillers' theory and practice.

TERRY SMITH

Terry Smith's analyses of Tillers' Canvasboard System parallel Maloon's, describing Tillers as an implicitly 'provincialist' follower of a hegemonic New York style. Smith's analyses also have an ironic twist because his landmark article 'The Provincialism Problem' (Smith 1974) was a major influence on Tillers' turn towards the appropriation of fine art imagery in *Conversations with the Bride,* 1974-75.

Smith's initial reception of Tillers was published in the *Times on Sunday* in November 1987 (Smith 1987: 33). The review is not entirely negative. In the course of his analysis Smith defines Tillers' use of appropriation in terms of 'alienation'. He proposes that 'alienation is an abiding concern' in Tillers' work, and adds that 'it appears quite directly, in the wandering figures, the no-place landscapes' (Smith 1987: 33). Smith's observation is precise and perceptive. Later in this analysis it will be argued that in his Canvasboard System Tillers uses Baselitz's distinctly unheroic depiction of human beings, in part, as a means of dislocating the hubris inherent in what Tillers referred to as the 'anthropocentric world view' (Tillers 1973a: Appendix A 9). Smith, however, could only have become aware of Tillers' anti-anthropic and eco-political position via familiarity with 'The Beginner's Guide to Oil Painting' and this does not appear to have been the case.[33]

As Smith's argument develops he shifts towards the position that the strategy of appropriationism is inherently 'alienated' as is evident when he asserts:

> Alienation is an abiding concern. But it is also there in the very process of obligatory appropriation … as if artists, nowadays, are condemned to endlessly spiralling self-reference. Until, that is, they are driven elsewhere, or surprise another content. The spiral, after all, can unravel too. (Smith 1987: 33)

Smith argues that the technique of appropriation is 'obligatory', thereby implying that it is imposed upon the provincial artist by the dominant international style. Thus, Tillers becomes implicated in this process and consequently in spite of his politically correct depiction of an alienated humanity he remains caught in what Smith referred to in his 1974 article as the 'provincialist bind' (Smith 1974: 56, 57, 58, 59).

Smith's implicit description of Tillers as a provincialist mimic becomes more explicit in his article 'Provincialism Refigured' published in the following year (Smith 1988). The latter was written after Smith had attended Tillers' one-person exhibition at London's prestigious avant-gardist artspace the Institute of Contemporary Arts (ICA) in 1988. For Tillers to have been given a one-person exhibition in such a prestigious London gallery accompanied by a substantial catalogue indicates an exceptional level of international recognition for an Australian artist working within an avant-gardist genre. Moreover, Tillers was only thirty-eight years old at the time. Yet, Smith's response indicates that he interpreted Tillers' success primarily in terms of provincialist mimicry. Smith recounts his responses to Tillers' exhibition as follows:

> as I stood in the main exhibition room of the Institute of Contemporary Arts, surrounded by the recent work of Imants Tillers … I realized that underlying his breathtaking appropriations and wry ridicule was a fantasy about avant-gardist purity: here was the ideal Museum of Modern Art, imaged from a vast cultural distance, as if by a dreamer who had never seen such an institution (certainly never seen behind it or through it) but who deeply desired its pure spaces. It was a brilliant reflection back of the mythology of Modernism which has been, for so many decades, exported abroad from past centres such as Paris, London and, especially, New York. (Smith 1988: 4)

One of the most clearly deprecating assertions in this passage is that Tillers had 'certainly never seen behind … or through' the art system. Smith suggests that Tillers is a 'dreamer' which connotes someone lost in fantasy, a hopeless romantic, out of contact with the world of art-political reality.

Both Smith and Maloon's negative evaluations of Tillers' use of authorial appropriation can be explained as arising out of the unavailability of any substantial analysis of the relationship between Tillers' pre-canvasboard theory and practice and his Canvasboard System. Although Maloon touched upon the existence of such a relationship a thorough understanding could only occur at a point in time that allows a sufficient degree of historical distance. Creating a coherent analysis of decades of an artist's theory and practice simply takes time.

With the benefit of historical hindsight it is possible to demonstrate that Tillers designed his canvasboard strategy in order to take advantage of the parallels between his own holistic systems aesthetic and deconstructive appropriation. And it is this demonstration that will controvert Maloon and Smith's interpretation of Tillers' canvasboard strategy as provincialist mimicry.

THE FIRST MONOGRAPH: WYSTAN CURNOW

The first monograph to be published on Tillers' work appeared in 1998, entitled *Imants Tillers and The Book of Power* (Curnow 1998). The text is by the New Zealand poet and writer Wystan Curnow and focuses on Tillers' Canvasboard System up to and including the Diaspora Trilogy 1992-94 and canvasboard works produced in 1996 prior to Tillers' move from Sydney to the country town of Cooma in New South Wales.

Curnow was kind enough to provide me with initial drafts of his text and I in turn provided him with drafts of this text. One observation I would make from this experience is that the first draft of Curnow's text had more emphasis on the theme of Roland Barthes' concept of the 'death of the author'. The published text takes a more biographical approach. Tillers' partner Slatyer notes that this was in large part due to the publisher Nevill Drury requesting the inclusion of a biographical introductory chapter after receiving Curnow's first draft. But the inclusion of a biographical introduction also tuned into a biographical turn in Tillers' Canvasboard System at the time Curnow was writing his text. The change began in 1992 with *Diaspora* which became a Trilogy when Tillers produced the companion pieces *Izkliede* and *Paradiso* in 1994.

Tillers' parents came to Australia as refugees from Latvia after harrowing experiences under the German and Russian occupation during the Second World War. Curnow portrays the Diaspora Trilogy as a biographical account of Tillers' family and other Baltic people who became 'displaced persons' dispersed across the world. In spite of the fact that there is an undeniably biographical aspect to the Diaspora Trilogy, the intensity of Curnow's focus on Tillers' family history leads to an uneasy relationship with his remaining references to the Barthesian concept of the 'death of the author'. On the other hand, this unease serves to emphasise the paradox inherent in Tillers' insertions of 'biographic' and 'autobiographic' material into his later work.

Another paradox revealed by Curnow's interpretation concerns the fact that although the Canvasboard System is largely based on imagery appropriated from photomechanical reproductions in books and periodicals Tillers is particularly proud of the fact that he uses the 'low tech' 'artisanal' means. Curnow pursues this aspect of Tillers' practice examining his use of materials such as oil sticks, stencils, canvasboard stacks and metallic paints. This is a very different approach from the analysis provided here, and provides a valuable insight into another facet of Tillers' practice.

Curnow's biographical approach is also evident in his discussion of the interactions between Tillers and the artists he appropriates. Thus he notes:

> Julian Schnabel, Philip Taaffe, Mike Bidlo, Sherrie Levine and Jiri Georg Dokoupil were among those who came by to check the second Bess Cutler show [New York 1985], either to see what Tillers had done with their work or in what way his work impinged on their own practice and career. A slightly peeved Ross Bleckner noted his own absence from Tillers' pantheon of the new. (Curnow 1998: 26)

Such anecdotal details, gleaned from conversations with Tillers, are interesting and provide an important complement to the attempt in this analysis to show how the Canvasboard System evolved out of Tillers' earlier theory and practice.

Another distinctive feature of Curnow's text lies in his personal responses to his encounter with the manifold of the Canvasboard System. They become particularly interesting when he evokes the manner in which the viewer becomes absorbed into the web of intra- and intertextuality that is the Canvasboard System. One example of this is evident in his contemplation of the theme of the door that recurs throughout the System (Curnow 1998: 104). Again Curnow's experience of the Canvasboard System is very different from the one provided here, indicating the multi-faceted nature of Tillers' project.

Perhaps one of the most substantive contributions provided by Curnow's text lies in the fact that he is a New Zealander and an authority on the New Zealand artist Colin McCahon. McCahon has become one of the most important appropriational sources for Tillers' Canvasboard System and accordingly Curnow's authority in this respect is extremely valuable.

Finally, Curnow, in common with most other commentators, does not demonstrate in any detail the ways in which Tillers' Canvasboard System arose out of his theory and practice of the 1970s. I cannot criticise Curnow for this omission, however, because our exchange of manuscripts was based on the agreement that he would not employ the analyses of Tillers' theory and practice of the 1970s that form the crux of this study.

THE RECEPTION OF TILLERS' APPROPRIATION OF ABORIGINAL ART

A final aspect of Tillers' reception needs to be dealt with—the reception of his appropriation of Aboriginal art. As this reception concerns a very specific facet of Tillers' work it will be prefaced with a brief account of the nature and extent of this feature of Tillers' theory and practice. In *Conversations with the Bride* and *Untitled*, 1978, Tillers' juxtaposition of Heysen's *Summer* with radical Euro-American avant-gardism possesses a parodic aspect that arises out of his use of *Summer* as an index of what he initially perceived to be the provincialism of the non-indigenous Australian landscape tradition. When he entered the burgeoning discourse of appropriationism in the early 1980s Tillers altered his strategy. He decided to continue to juxtapose antipodean art with Euro-American avant-gardism but sought powerful antipodean art that could confidently confront the best European and American art within the arena of his Canvasboard System.

Tillers' first choice was modern Aboriginal art, in particular a 'despiritualised' abstractionist style that originated in the early 1970s in the Papunya settlement in the Great Western Desert. By the 1980s this work was becoming better known not only to Australians, but also the international art world. Papunya painting can be considered 'modern' for three reasons: it is desacralised, it is 'abstractionist', and it utilises Western methods, acrylic paint on canvas. On these bases Tillers considered Papunya painting an important addition to Western art and accordingly wove imagery appropriated from

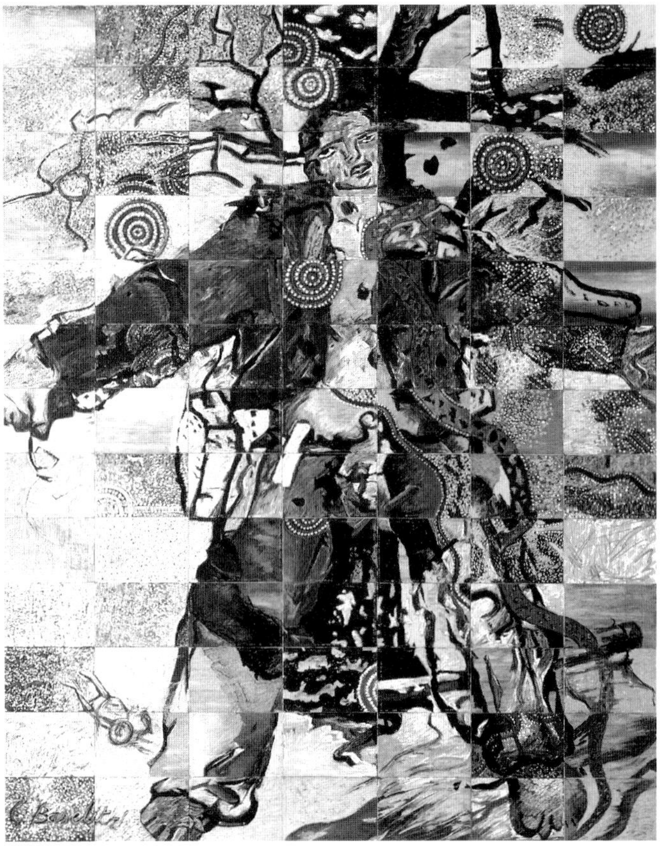

Imants Tillers, *The Nine Shots,* 1985. Synthetic polymer paint, oilstick on 91 canvasboards, Nos. 7215–7305, 330 x 266 cm. Collection: the artist. Photograph: D. James Dee.

Papunya artists into his appropriations from European and American art. One of the most outstanding examples of this strategy is apparent in *The Nine Shots*, 1985, illustrated left. The latter can be compared with another juxtaposition of Papunya art with European art, Tillers' *Fallen Man*, 1990 (opposite). In both cases Tillers appropriates figures from German neo-expressionist Georg Baselitz and montages them with imagery appropriated from a Papunya landscape painting by Michael Nelson Jagamarra in *The Nine Shots,* and Clifford Possum Tjapaltjarri in *Fallen Man*. Tillers' appropriations from Baselitz stem mainly from the latter's 1960s series *Der neue Typ* (the 'new man'). This series shows human figures standing unsteadily, tattered and dishevelled usually in a wasteland setting. The analysis of the first phase of Tillers' Canvasboard System in Chapter Ten will demonstrate that his conjunction of Papunya art with the work of Baselitz conveys an eco-political message based on Tillers' perception that there might be a correspondence between his anti-anthropic holistic aesthetics and the intrinsic role played by the land in traditional Aboriginal culture.

For the purposes of this analysis of the reception of Tillers' appropriation of Papunya imagery two of the most sophisticated examples of the contemporaneous reception of Tillers' early, and most contentious, appropriations of Aboriginal art will be examined. The first is by Colin Symes and Robert Lingard who published a section in an edited book for the Australian Bicentennial in 1988 (Symes and Lingard 1988). Their criticism of Tillers' appropriation of Papunya art presents a reasonably balanced analysis for the time it was written. The second text is Rex Butler's article on the urban Aboriginal painter Gordon Bennett who ingeniously appropriated one of Tillers' appropriations of Latvian imagery (symbolising his ethnic heritage) as a means of criticising Tillers' appropriation of Papunya art. Butler's analysis (Butler 1992) is outstanding in the context of the corpus of commentary assembled here because it approaches the issue of the appropriation from a poststructuralist standpoint. This genre of analysis was introduced in Chapter Three via an examination of what is referred to here as the Owens-Krauss interpretation of deconstructive appropriation.

A comparison of the Symes-Lingard and Butler commentaries reveals that one of the main reasons for criticising Tillers' appropriation of Aboriginal art stems either from a lack of familiarity, or sympathy, with three texts Tillers published in the early 1980s (Tillers 1982a, 1983, 1984) at the time he was formulating his Canvasboard System. In these texts Tillers makes it clear that he has considerable admiration for the modern Papunya style of painting, arguing that it could be understood as announcing the entry of Aboriginal art into the domain of international avant-gardist art.

The core of Tillers' position is evident in 'Fear of Texture' (Tillers 1983). In this essay Tillers argued that Aboriginal art had become congruent with Euro-American avant-gardism. He suggested that by using '[acrylic] paint on canvas' Papunya art became 'coextensive and in competition with other conventional forms of painting' (Tillers 1983: 15). Tillers' argument shifts into a more metaphorical exploration of the contemporariness of Papunya painting when he focuses on its distinctive use of an overall 'field' of painted dots. Using considerable poetic licence he compares this field with the 'dot-screen' of photomechanical reproduction observing: 'This "dot-screen" structure is most apparent in the works of the artists of Central Australia and the Western Desert who form the Papunya school of painters.' (Tillers 1983: 14). He expands his analogical conflation by subsuming it into his simplified metaphor for holism based on Germano Celant's notion that all paintings could exist as 'an enormous roll of diversified fabric woven in a single piece' (Tillers 1983: 15). He suggests that the 'truth of this proposition is clearly evident if we look at a room full of Papunya paintings. The initial impression is that each individual canvas is literally a fragment cut from the same cloth.' (Tillers 1983: 15). Tillers also suggested that the 'field' of dots that characterises Papunya art could be understood in terms of the concept of 'dematerialisation' used by theorists such as Lucy Lippard to interpret post-object art (Lippard 1973). Tillers proposed that whereas the dot screen of photomechanical reproduction serves to materialise images, the overall 'field' of Papunya dots 'dematerialise' images. He explained:

> because of the size of the dots and their continuity over the entire surface as a 'field' they tend to break down the image a the same instant as they define it: pictorial reality does not materialise out of the fusion of dots (as it does in mechanical and electronic reproduction techniques) but rather it dissipates into a cloud of dots. The 'dot-screen' becomes the image of dematerialisation. (Tillers 1983: 15)

Another facet of Tillers' analogical analysis concerns his perceptive observation that the dematerialising effect of the dot screen was used by Aboriginal artists as a means of hiding or removing sacred motifs. He reports that in changing over from sand painting to painting on canvas

Imants Tillers, *Fallen Man*, 1990. Oilstick, gouache, synthetic polymer paint on 91 canvasboards, Nos. 30003–30093, 350 x 267 cm. Collection: the artist.

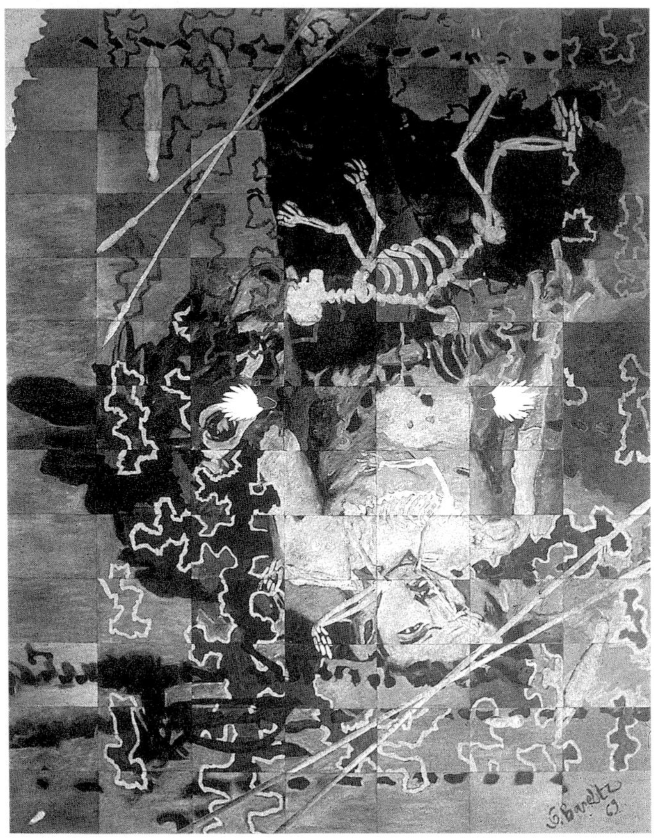

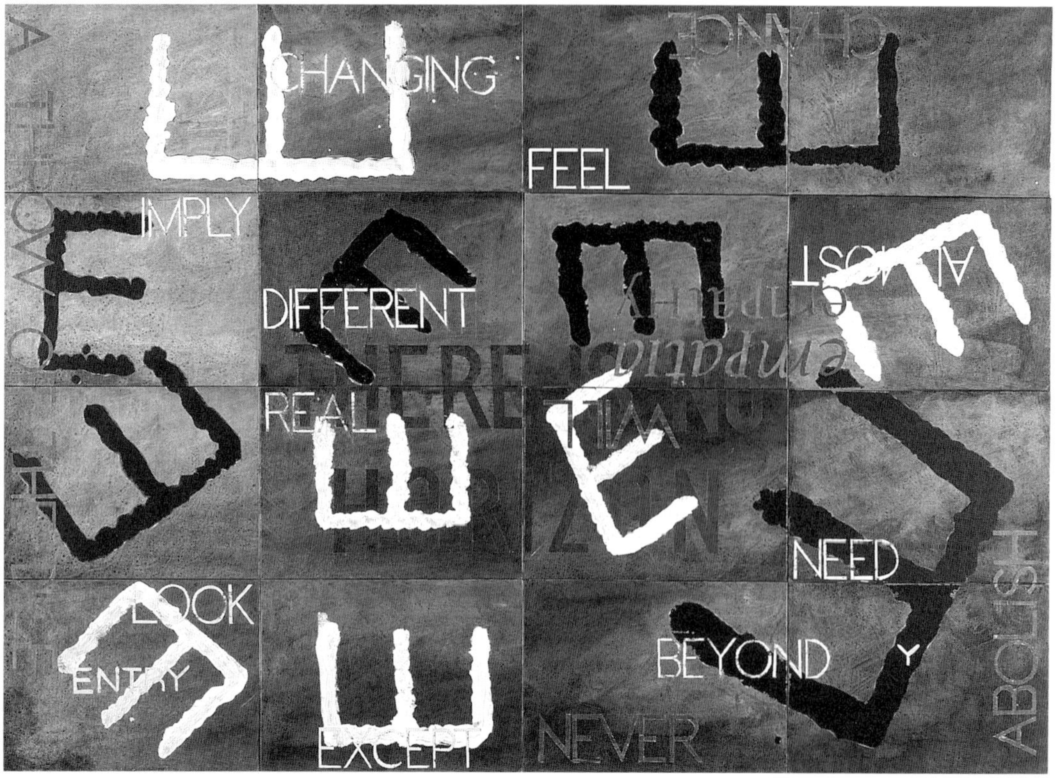

Imants Tillers and Michael Nelson Jagamarra, *Nature Speaks (Possum Dreaming): Y*, 2001. Synthetic polymer paint, gouache on 16 canvasboard panels, Nos. 69426–69440, 102 x 142 cm. Collaboration curated by Michael Eather, Fire-Works Gallery, Brisbane. Photograph: Schoo's Studio.

the 'Papunya artists were forced to eliminate much of their sacred imagery, in its place they substituted dots.' (Tillers 1983: 17). This is an important observation as it provides the most substantive basis for Tillers' argument that Papunya art can be treated in the same way as any other art, in the sense of being open to 'quotation'.

Although Tillers expressed his ideas in a poetic and sometimes somewhat surrealistic manner, his principal intuition accords with the subsequent evolution of contemporary Aboriginal art. A case in point is Tracey Moffatt who during the late 1980s and 1990s refused to be ghettoised as an 'Aboriginal artist' and subsequently attained an international profile as an artist and film-maker. In addition, whereas the sensitive art-political climate of the 1980s led to Tillers being castigated for his appropriation of Papunya imagery, the more relaxed climate of the 1990s and 2000s has allowed him to collaborate with Aboriginal artists. In 1993 he produced a collaborative work with Gordon Bennett as part of an exhibition of new Aboriginal art curated by Nicholas Tsoutas at the Institute of Modern Art in Brisbane. And in 2001 Tillers began a series of collaborative paintings with Michael Nelson Jagamarra, curated by Michael Eather of the Fire-Works Gallery, Brisbane. The first work arising out of this collaboration is reproduced above.

Of the two responses to Tillers' appropriation of Papunya art in the 1980s examined here Symes and Lingard seem to be unaware of, or unsympathetic to, the position evident in Tillers' texts of the early 1980s. Rex Butler's analysis of the appropriation of Aboriginal art on the other hand appears to be more sympathetic to Tillers' position. But it should also be noted that Butler's analysis was written at a later date, when the sensitivities of the 1980s were becoming ameliorated.

COLIN SYMES AND ROBERT LINGARD

Colin Symes and Robert Lingard's essay 'From the Ethnographic to the Aesthetic: An Examination of the Relationship between Aboriginal and European Culture in Australian Art 1788-1988' (in Foss 1988), approaches Tillers' appropriation of Aboriginal art by comparing it with the work of another avant-gardist non-indigenous Australian artist, Tim Johnson. In their essay Symes and Lingard assert:

> Tillers does not seem to operate with the same degree of political awareness as exists in Johnson: while the former appropriates Papunya and international art with equal facility, granting them a sort of parity of esteem, the latter is more circumspect. (Symes and Lingard 1988: 214)

It will be shown that a careful reading of Symes and Lingard's analysis reveals a contradiction which subverts the apparent confidence of their assessment. The crux of Symes and Lingard's claim is that Johnson demonstrates more 'political awareness' than Tillers, and this seems to rest upon their proposition that Johnson is aware of the problem of the co-option of Aboriginal art into Western art history and is more capable of preserving the essential 'difference' of Aboriginal culture. For Symes and Lingard:

> Tim Johnson is … a worthy example of the growing awareness amongst younger artists in Australia today of the need to oppose the seemingly inevitable passage from the ethnographic to the purely aesthetic in the reception of Aboriginal art. (Symes and Lingard 1988: 212)

The authors then point out that Johnson's strategy is based on combining Aboriginal appropriations with appropriations from Asian culture:

> In pursuit of a pictorial strategy for rendering the 'difference' of Aboriginal art, Johnson has sought examples from other non-European imagery. Thus he claims that 'Eastern art styles are similar to Central Australian art styles.' (Symes and Lingard 1988: 212)

After a lengthy discussion, Symes and Lingard conclude that Johnson's interrelationship of Aboriginal and Asian culture is problematical:

> Johnson particularly, by *equalising* Aboriginal and Eastern imagery, adopts a utopian perspective regarding the unique struggle of Aborigines for cultural independence … (Symes and Lingard 1988: 214)

This passage refers to a quotation from Johnson which suggests that Central Australian art styles seem 'to coincide with Buddhist theory and practice' (Symes and Lingard 1988: 212). Symes and Lingard's use of the term 'utopian' to describe Johnson's contentious comparison between two quite culturally distinct spiritual systems seems wholly justified. It seems reasonable to point out that characterising Johnson's strategy as 'utopian' effectively undermines the authors' assertion that 'Tillers does not seem to operate with the same degree of political awareness as exists in Johnson …' (Symes and Lingard 1988: 214). The ideological confusion inherent in Johnson's strategy is reinforced when the authors note: 'on the whole, even the present generation of artists have consistently failed to speak out against the real conditions of Australia's indigenous people' (Symes and Lingard 1988: 214). Symes and Lingard provide a much more convincing argument for the ideological superiority of Johnson's approach when they observe that Johnson actively collaborated with Aboriginal artists. In contrast, during the 1980s, Tillers worked mainly from photomechanical reproductions. As Symes and Lingard note:

> some of his [Johnson's] current work includes direct collaborations with Papunya painters or employs designs which they themselves have permitted him to use. … It needs to be said that Tim Johnson is very aware of the imperialist problems involved in the unacknowledged use of Papunya designs. (Symes and Lingard 1988: 212)

At this point it is possible to insert comments made by Tillers to the author in 1995,[34] when he remarked that it was Johnson who introduced him to Papunya art in the early 1980s. Tillers showed me an early example of Johnson's work which is a painting of a Papunya artist holding one of his paintings. According to Tillers these early works by Johnson were painted from photographs Johnson took in Papunya. Johnson obviously received permission to take the photographs, but Tillers points out that Johnson transformed these photographs into paintings that he went on to sell. Whether or not Johnson received, or needed to receive, permission to do this remains an unanswered question. Such considerations underline the complexities involved in the appropriation of a modern genre of Aboriginal art in a manner that inserts such art into the institutional processes of the Western art system.[35]

Tillers' observations do not affect the fact that Johnson pioneered a strategy of collaboration between Aboriginal and non-Aboriginal artists which is of great significance. However, they do point to the complexities inherent in the process of cross-cultural appropriation. And it is true that in the first phase of his Canvasboard System Tillers appropriated Papunya imagery from afar, but it seems somewhat unfair to condemn him for using a more rigorously appropriationist method that focused on photomechanical reproductions rather than original works of art. The logical extension of criticising Tillers for using this approach would be to suggest that the entire discourse of deconstructive appropriation that dominated avant-gardist art of the 1980s is 'politically incorrect'. This is extreme, especially as major Marxian-oriented critics such as Benjamin Buchloh and Hal Foster had constructed a more positive, although not entirely uncritical, analysis of deconstructive appropriation in the early 1980s.[36]

Indeed, at the conclusion of their analysis Symes and Lingard appear to acknowledge that there might be less difference in the 'degree of political awareness' between Johnson and Tillers, than seems to be the case earlier in their analysis, when they note:

> Clearly, though, there are positive aspects to both approaches; to their credit, Tillers and Johnson are aware of the problems inherent in a stance of 'cultural convergence'. (Symes and Lingard 1988: 214)

Symes and Lingard's analysis represents one of the most balanced critiques of Tillers' appropriation of Aboriginal modernism during the 1980s. But in common with less balanced criticisms it shows little appreciation of Tillers' published comments on Aboriginal art (Tillers 1982a, 1983, 1984).

REX BUTLER

Whereas Symes and Lingard take a broadly Marxian approach Rex Butler's analysis uses a poststructuralist framework. His analysis of Tillers' appropriation of Papunya art occurs in 'Two Readings of Gordon Bennett's *The Nine Ricochets'* (Butler 1992). There Butler's discusses the urban Aboriginal artist Gordon Bennett's reference to Tillers' appropriation of a Papunya landscape from Michael Nelson Jagamarra in *The Nine Shots*, 1985. The reference is evident in the title of Bennett's *The Nine Ricochets* and is reinforced in this work by his appropriation of Latvian imagery (the boy-bear) from Tillers' *Pataphysical Man,* 1984. Bennett's counter appropriation functions as a criticism of a white artist's appropriation of Aboriginal art in the context of the oppression of Aborigines. Butler's analysis is remarkable because he effectively challenges the validity of the censure of Tillers' appropriation of Papunya imagery without entering into the debate regarding political correctness that informed Symes and Lindgard's commentary.

What is interesting about Butler's approach is that it makes no distinction between white and Aboriginal art, both are taken as equal. He discusses the relationship between representation and appropriation using a model of an 'abyss' of self-referentiality akin to that examined in the writings of Owens and Krauss. For example, there is evidence of the influence of Derrida's notion of 'abyss' when Butler states:

> What Bennett's *The Nine Ricochets* manages to do is catch Tillers in an infinite and *abysmal* game of imitation, from which there is no escape … (Butler 1992: 21) [my emphasis]

The second stage of Butler's argument begins with the introduction of a Derridean-like notion that capacity of representation for self-reflection leads into an infinite regress, or 'abyss'. Butler's use of this notion is evident in the following passages:

> Aboriginality is not to be appropriated … because it is that prior appropriation that makes this appropriation possible.
> … Aboriginality is always being appropriated, but it never finally can be because it is that medium in which this appropriation takes place …
> … Aboriginality for Bennett is always that appropriation before any appropriation that makes that appropriation possible. (Butler 1992: 21)

Each of the phrases quoted above is marked by an almost poetic expression of self-referentiality that echoes Craig Owens' focus on Derrida's notion of an 'abyss' latent in all representation discussed in Chapter Three.

Butler's assertion that 'Aboriginality is not to be appropriated … because it is that prior appropriation that makes this appropriation possible.' (Butler 1992: 21) suggests that Aboriginal art is already appropriated even before an artist such as Tillers can appropriate it. This analysis finds support in Tillers' discussion of the nature of Papunya painting in 'Fear of Texture' (Tillers 1983). As noted previously, in this essay Tillers explains how, in changing over from sand painting to painting with acrylic on canvas, the Papunya artists of the Western Desert recoded their sacred imagery into abstractionistic fields of dots. If this process is understood as Aborigines effectively appropriating their own art then we are led to a situation wherein Tillers' appropriation of Papunya painting is actually the appropriation of an appropriation. In this particular case at least it appears possible to suggest, like Butler, that 'Aboriginality' is always already appropriated.

Similarly, when Bennett appropriates Tillers' appropriation of Latvian imagery he is also appropriating an already appropriated ethnicity. Both instances can be described in terms of the model of the *mise en abyme* or Derrida's notion of 'the representation of representation' falling into an 'abyss' of 'indefinite multiplication' (Owens 1978: 77; Derrida 1976: 163). Although primarily an analysis of Gordon Bennett's work, Butler's argument has relevance to Tillers' practice. In fact, in the following chapters it will become apparent that Butler's approach acquires even more substance when it is recognised that self-referentiality plays a crucial and enduring role in Tillers' theory and practice. As this text progresses it will become increasingly apparent that a poststructuralist concern with the deconstructive rhetoric of the *mise en abyme* possesses significant parallels with Tillers' holistic systems aesthetic.

Butler's analysis of Tillers is interesting because it tackles the complex interrelationship between the modernist abstraction of Papunya painting and the deconstructive appropriationism apparent in Bennett and other urban Aboriginal artists who emerged in the latter part of the 1980s. His analysis is also significant as it uses a frame of reference particularly applicable to Tillers' theory and practice.

SUMMARY

The analysis of key instances of the reception of Tillers' work in the period 1971-98 shows a distinct pattern consisting of two major threads. The first is that most writers were able to locate Tillers within an art historically appropriate context. The second is that most commentators were not in a position to be able to discern the degree of correspondence between Tillers' writings and his practice that is a prerequisite for defining the originality of his contribution.

The last point can be explained as a cumulative problem that began when Donald Brook was faced with the problem of relating the ideas in 'The Beginner's Guide to Oil Painting' with the visual rhetoric of *Moments of Inertia*. He was unable to do so, which is best explained by the extreme complexity and lack of coherence evident in *Moments of Inertia*. Unfortunately the fact that Brook was, understandably, unable to link Tillers' theory to his practice at the very beginning of the reception of Tillers' work meant that both 'The Beginner's Guide to Oil Painting' and *Moments of Inertia* fell into relative obscurity.

A lack of critical awareness of these two seminal works constitutes a major problem for three reasons: firstly, 'The Beginner's Guide to Oil Painting' is a highly sophisticated application of 'systems theory' to post-object art; and, secondly, the ideas contained in this seminal text, such as the equation of negentropy and creativity and Tillers' ecopolitical stance can be traced throughout his oeuvre; thirdly, *Moments of Inertia* is crucially important because it is in this work that Tillers developed the technique of isomorphic mapping that provides an important basis for the originality of his holistic systems aesthetics. It can, and will, be demonstrated that these two seminal works provide the keys for understanding the interplay between Tillers' theory and practice throughout the 1970s and 1980s.

In brief, the major commentators on Tillers in the period 1973-91 provided the most intelligent analyses possible in the absence of any substantive associations between Tillers' writings and his work. Moreover, it is the contention here that establishing such connections is confronted from the beginning with the extremely difficult task of making sense of a highly complex, experimental and incomplete work such as *Moments of Inertia.* It is only with sufficient historical distance and the time to pursue an analysis, such as will be presented here, that the correspondences between *Moments of Inertia* and 'The Beginner's Guide to Oil Painting' can be determined. When this is achieved the doors to understanding the rest of Tillers' work in the period 1971-2001 are relatively easy to unlock.

Part Two consists of two chapters which will examine the special relationship between 'The Beginner's Guide to Oil Painting' and *Moments of Inertia*. The latter was produced simultaneously and in parallel with 'The Beginner's Guide to Oil Painting' and represents Tillers' initial articulation of his holistic systems aesthetic in art practice. Articulating the links between Tillers' theory and practice in 'The Beginner's Guide to Oil Painting' and *Moments of Inertia* will provide a basis for understanding the relationship between Tillers' theory and practice throughout the period 1971-2001 and enable an evaluation of the originality of his contribution to the avant-gardist art discourses within which he worked.

5

'THE BEGINNER'S GUIDE TO OIL PAINTING' AND CREATION WITHOUT A CREATOR

The crux of this analysis of 'The Beginner's Guide to Oil Painting' will be the identification of an approach to art based upon a concept of 'creation without a creator'. This involves key notions such as Tillers' equation of creation and creativity with 'negentropy' and what will be referred to here as Tillers' 'anti-anthropic', ecopolitical position.[37] As this text develops it will become apparent that this position—originally outlined in 'The Beginner's Guide to Oil Painting' and initially articulated in artistic practice in *Moments of Inertia*—laid the foundation for Tillers' questioning of the primacy of authorship in *Untitled*, 1978, and his Canvasboard System. Accordingly, it is this aspect of Tillers' seminal theory and practice that provides the key for understanding the relationship between his theory and practice throughout the period 1971-2001. Moreover, an articulation of this correlation enables the evaluation of the originality of Tillers' contribution to the avant-gardist art discourses within which he worked during that period.

'The Beginner's Guide to Oil Painting' is a substantial, scholarly text written by Tillers as part of the Honours requirements for his BSc in Architecture at the University of Sydney (Tillers 1973a: Appendix A).[38] As it is an unpublished text, and will be referred to throughout this analysis, it has been included here as Appendix A.

Tillers honed his appreciation of post-object art by focusing on the writings of Jack Burnham, a leading American theorist of 1960s avant-gardism. Burnham's contribution was to provide a theoretical framework for understanding post-object art in terms of 'systems'. Tillers used this as the basis for the aesthetic he developed in 'The Beginner's Guide to Oil Painting' and *Moments of Inertia*. Although indebted to Burnham, it will be shown that Tillers formulated a sophisticated elaboration of Burnham's aesthetic especially evident in his addition of a 'holistic' dimension to the concept of systems—holism, here, being understood in the scientific, as opposed to 'new ageist' sense of the term. The sources for this important elaboration were the biologist and mathematician Ludwig von Bertalanffy's General Systems Theory, and Ian McHarg's ecological and ecopolitical theory of design. The result of Tillers' elaboration of Burnham's systems aesthetic will be referred to here as Tillers' 'holistic systems aesthetic'.

JACK BURNHAM'S 'SYSTEMS ESTHETICS'

As has been noted, Tillers' systems aesthetic was primarily influenced by Burnham's articles 'Systems Esthetics' and 'Real Time Systems' (Burnham 1968, 1969). In these works Burnham developed a concept of systems based on information theory and cybernetics. This is evident in his use of terms such as 'real-time', 'information', 'information processing', 'programming', and 'meta-programming'. The influence of Burnham is crucial because when recognised it requires that Tillers' photo-conceptual works *Conversations with the Bride*, 1974-75, and *Untitled*, 1978, be understood in terms of a strategy of 'processing' readymade 'art information', or as a species of information processing within the 'art system'. This Burnhamian aspect to Tillers' mode of appropriation also extends into his Canvasboard System in a manner that demands an expansion of our understanding of the strategy of appropriation.

It is also the case that when Tillers notes that 'the institutions which process art data are as important components of the system as the producers of data' (Tillers 1973a: Appendix A 18) he provides an unequivocal statement of a shift from the traditional concept of the transcendental role of the artist-creator towards one that conceives the artist as immanent within the systems in which he or she operates.[39] As this analysis develops it will become apparent that such ideas provide a foundation for Tillers' questioning of the primacy of authorship in *Untitled*, 1978, and the Canvasboard System.

LUDWIG VON BERTALANFFY'S HOLISTIC SYSTEMS THEORY

Tillers' Burnhamian systems aesthetic develops into a holistic systems aesthetic due to the addition of two critical influences: Ludwig von Bertalanffy and Ian McHarg. Tillers' interest in systems led him to F. E. Emery's compilation of essays entitled *Systems Thinking* (Emery 1969). It was here that he began to appreciate the revolutionary nature of von Bertalanffy's General Systems Theory, understanding it as marking a transition from a mechanistic to a holistic conception of systems. Tillers' involvement with holistic systems was enhanced by his contact with Ian McHarg's ecological theory of design (McHarg 1969) during the course of his BSc in architecture.

Ludwig von Bertalanffy (1901-1972) was a biologist and one of the principal sources cited by Tillers is 'The Theory of Open Systems in Physics and Biology' (von Bertalanffy 1950). In this work von Bertalanffy sought a mathematical description of the systems found in the biological domain. To this end he made a distinction between 'open' and 'closed' systems. The adjective 'open' referred to biological systems whereas 'closed' referred to the systems described by classical physics. Tillers' account of von Bertalanffy's theory describes the concentration of classical physics on closed systems as 'mechanistic', as is evident when he notes:

> [von] Bertalanffy … sees the significance of the systems view as a reorientation of our conceptual framework … from a mechanistic to an open systems view. The mechanistic view resolved happenings into linear causal chains … reduced all biological processes to laws known from inanimate nature. The open systems view is that the world is based on … a dynamic expansion of physical laws in light of biological laws. (Tillers 1973a: Appendix A 15)

Tillers' antitheses—physics vs. biology; mechanistic vs. open systems; and linear vs. non-linear causality—begin to evolve into an aesthetic dichotomy when he adds the crucial opposition between 'entropy' and 'negentropy'. Although these terms are scientific they carry with them distinctly poetic connotations, entropy being associated with 'death' and negentropy with 'life'. Tillers introduces the connection between closed systems and entropy when quoting from von Bertalanffy's 'The Theory of Open Systems in Physics and Biology' (von Bertalanffy 1950):

> A closed system must according to the second law of thermodynamics eventually attain a time-equilibrium state with maximum entropy and minimum free energy. (Tillers 1973a: Appendix A 13)

'The second law of thermodynamics' referred to by von Bertalanffy defines the phenomenon of entropy.[40] According to classical physics, in a closed system, energy, conceived thermodynamically in terms of 'heat', inevitably dissipates until it reaches the ultimate state of thermodynamic equilibrium, or stasis—sometimes referred to, somewhat poetically, as 'heat death'. Tillers notes, again after von Bertalanffy, that 'open systems' exhibit a characteristic antithetical to entropy referred to in science as 'negative entropy' or 'negentropy'. The latter is marked by an *increase* in the energy in a system leading to *greater* complexity and organisation. Tillers observes:

> the open system is characterised by negative entropy (negentropy) … Thus open systems tend to states of most improbable distribution i.e. states of increased order and organisation. (Tillers 1973a: Appendix A 13)

To summarise, Tillers' understanding of von Bertalanffy's theory suggests that entropy is a process associated with closed systems that leads to a condition akin to 'death'.[41] Negentropy on the other hand is a process associated with open systems and is intimately related to the phenomenon of life. It is obvious that this scientific dichotomy also possesses poetic connotations that could inform an aesthetic framework. Indeed, it will be shown that negentropy plays a crucial role in Tillers' development of his holistic systems aesthetic. He lays the foundation for such a poetic application of the concept of negentropy when he associates it with 'creation' observing that:

> the tendency of living organisms to raise matter to a higher order by entrapping energy from outside the organism and forcing it to do work is called negentropy or creation. (Tillers 1973a: Appendix A 11)

Later in his text he reinforces the aesthetic role of negentropy by linking it with creativity, noting: 'in the thermodynamic sense creativity is negentropy or ordering of an organism to a higher energy or information level' (Tillers 1973a: Appendix A 28).

NEGENTROPY AND INFORMATION PROCESSING

Tillers' description of negentropy in terms of information provides an elegant synthesis of Burnham's cybernetic, or informatic, model of art systems with von Bertalanffy's attempts to describe the complexity of biological systems. The applicability of Tillers' synthesis to post-object art is apparent in a section of 'The Beginner's Guide to Oil Painting' entitled 'Art as Information Processing'. Here Tillers applies a framework that encompasses both the Burnhamian and von Bertalanffian paradigms. He refers to the American conceptual artist Joseph Kosuth's definition of art's function as: 'being to increase the complexity of the concept of art … i.e. the function of art is to increase the creativity of art' (Tillers 1973a: Appendix A 28). Tillers uses Kosuth to support his contention that the task of the artist is to create more complexity. This not only relates directly to his analogy between negentropy and creativity but to the ecological and ecopolitical dimension of Tillers' holistic systems aesthetic that stems from his contact with the design theory of Ian McHarg.

IAN McHARG'S ECOPOLITICS

Tillers added another facet to his systems aesthetic after his contact with Ian McHarg's *Design with Nature* (McHarg 1969), which arose out of his architectural training at the University of Sydney. He read and was affected by McHarg's ecological and ecopolitical stance. It is also evident that Tillers was able to draw parallels between von Bertalanffy's holistic conception of systems and McHarg's ecopolitical approach to design, as is apparent when he explains McHarg's stance using his von Bertalanffian conception of negentropic creativity observing that McHarg:

> pointed out that man's creative role in nature should be considered thermodynamically as increasing the complexity, diversity, stability, quantity of species, number of symbioses and lowering entropy in the biosphere. (Tillers 1973a: Appendix A 25)

Tillers' contention that human creativity should be 'considered thermodynamically as increasing complexity' and 'lowering entropy' is a reference to his pivotal analogy between creativity and negentropy. Accordingly, in this passage Tillers makes a substantive connection between McHargian ecopolitics and von Bertalanffian holistic systems theory creating a unified notion of holistic systems that can be understood as a significant elaboration of Burnham's cybernetically oriented systems aesthetics.

Tillers' addition of von Bertalanffian and McHargian perspectives to his Burnhamian systems aesthetic had two important outcomes. Firstly, it added a powerful aesthetic metaphor based on Tillers' analogy between negentropy and creativity. Secondly, Tillers added an ecopolitical dimension to Burnham's concern for art systems interrelating with real-time or 'day-to-day' real world systems. Ecopolitics will be shown to be an enduring concern in Tillers' theory and practice apparent in works from the early *Conversations with the Bride,* 1974-75 to his most recent Nature Speaks series, 1998-2002. Additionally, it can be noted that ecopolitics has become an increasingly powerful political issue in late capitalist culture, a fact that indicates the socio-critical relevance of this facet of Tillers' oeuvre.

TILLERS' ANTI-ANTHROPIC, ECOPOLITICAL POSITION

Tillers' conception of creation without a creator also corresponds with his ecopolitical stance. In a subsection entitled 'The Anthropocentric View of the World' he investigates Western rational humanism and its influence upon the development of modern 'classical' science. He begins by quoting the ecologically oriented designer Ian McHarg from his book *Design with Nature* (McHarg 1969):

> Western society at large believes that the world, if not the universe, consists of a dialogue between men, or between men and an anthropocentric God: the result of this view is that man … is … given dominion over all life, enjoined among all creatures to subdue the earth. Nature is then an irrelevant backdrop to the human play called progress, or profit. If nature is to be brought to the foreground, it is only to be conquered—man versus nature. (in Tillers 1973a: Appendix A 9)

The passage Tillers selected from McHarg describes a concept of creation and creativity that informs what Tillers refers to as an 'anthropocentric view of the world'. It is this anthropocentric notion of creator and creativity that Tillers wishes to dispel by means of his synthesis of Burnham's systems aesthetic with von Bertalanffian holistic systems theory and McHarg's ecopolitics. The question arises as to what replaces the anthropocentric-theological conception of creator and creativity? Tillers puts forward a McHargian ecological and ecopolitical alternative to the anthropocentric creator-God asserting:

> the antithesis of the exploitative view of nature is the ecological view of man's dependence on nature not as a separate entity but as part of many interdependent systems. The complexity and holistic organisation of a system is in direct contrast to the simple relational man-nature dualism of the anthropocentric world view. (Tillers 1973a: Appendix A 11-12)

In this passage Tillers puts forward the notion that human beings are 'part of many interdependent systems' where the phrase 'many interdependent systems' can be related to his use of the phrase 'holistic organisation'. He then contrasts this idea with the 'anthropocentric world view'. For the purposes of brevity, Tillers' standpoint will be referred to here as his 'anti-anthropic' position.[42] As this analysis develops it will become evident that this position—initially outlined in 'The Beginner's Guide to Oil Painting' and originally articulated in artistic practice in *Moments of Inertia*—laid the foundation for Tillers' questioning of the primacy of authorship in *Untitled*, 1978, and his Canvasboard System. Accordingly, it is this aspect of Tillers' seminal theory and practice that provides the key for understanding the relationship between Tillers' theory and practice throughout the period 1971-2001 and enables an evaluation of the originality of his contribution to the avant-gardist art discourses within which he has worked.

The crux of the sophistication of Tillers' early theoretical position lies in the conjunction of his anti-anthropic stance with his poetics of negentropy. The outcome is a concept of creativity that does not require an anthropocentric 'creator'. Open, holistic, systems are capable of generating negentropic complex organisation without the need of any external agency and in Chapter One it was shown that this view informed Tillers' analysis of post-object art in 'The Beginner's Guide to Oil Painting'. It was shown that he forcefully foregrounded autonomous systems over the individual artist, celebrating the fact that Haacke, Oppenheim, Huebler, and Barry all selected readymade systems that were able to, more or less, 'organise themselves' (Tillers 1973a: Appendix A 23-25). It has also been noted that, under the heading 'Art as Information Processing', Tillers referred to the American conceptual artist Joseph Kosuth's definition of art's function as: 'being to increase the complexity of the concept of art ... i.e. the function of art is to increase the creativity of art' (Tillers 1973a: Appendix A 28).

The following chapter will show that in his first major work, *Moments of Inertia,* Tillers confronted the task of setting up a 'self-organising' system that would 'increase the complexity' and 'increase the creativity' of his own work. It will be shown that Tillers was most successful in his development of a complex self-reflexive image via the artistic application of a mathematical process known as 'isomorphic mapping'. Moreover, it will be established that this process is especially appropriate for 'information processing' because it entails making transformational 'copies' in the manner of a mirror reflection, a perspectival projection, or the projection of the earth's curved surface onto a flat plane. What is significant about this process is that it is both sophisticated and, within the context of art practice in the early 1970s, significantly original.

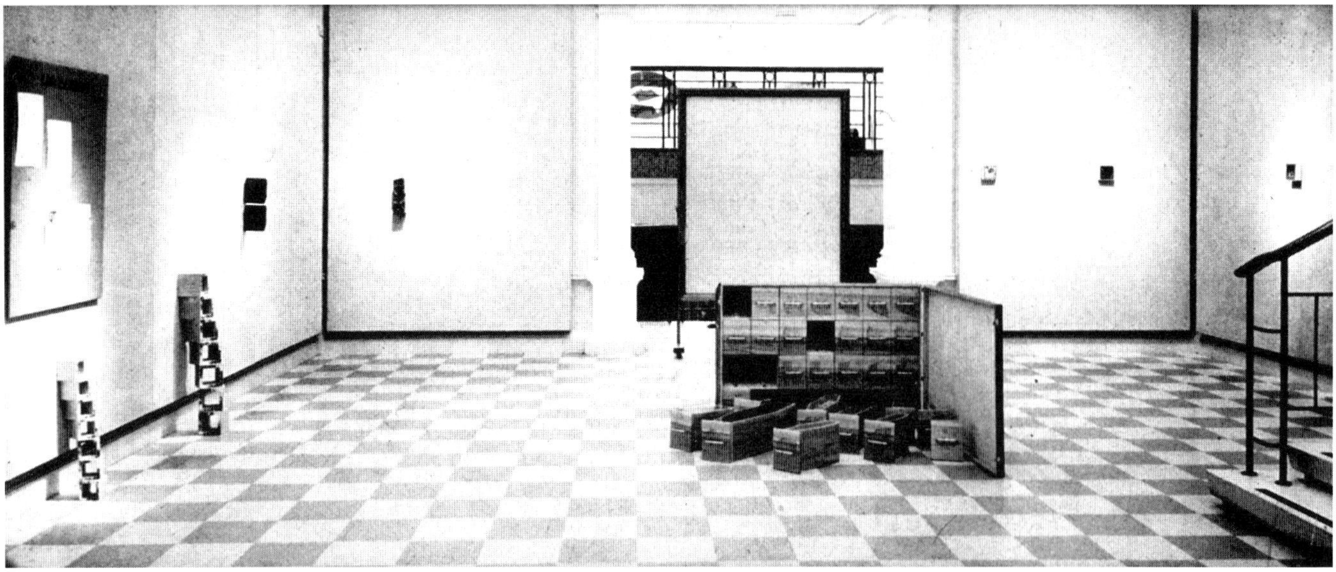

Moments of Inertia: Still Life 2, 1972–73.
Installation views of the Link Exhibition in the Art Gallery of South Australia, Adelaide,1974.

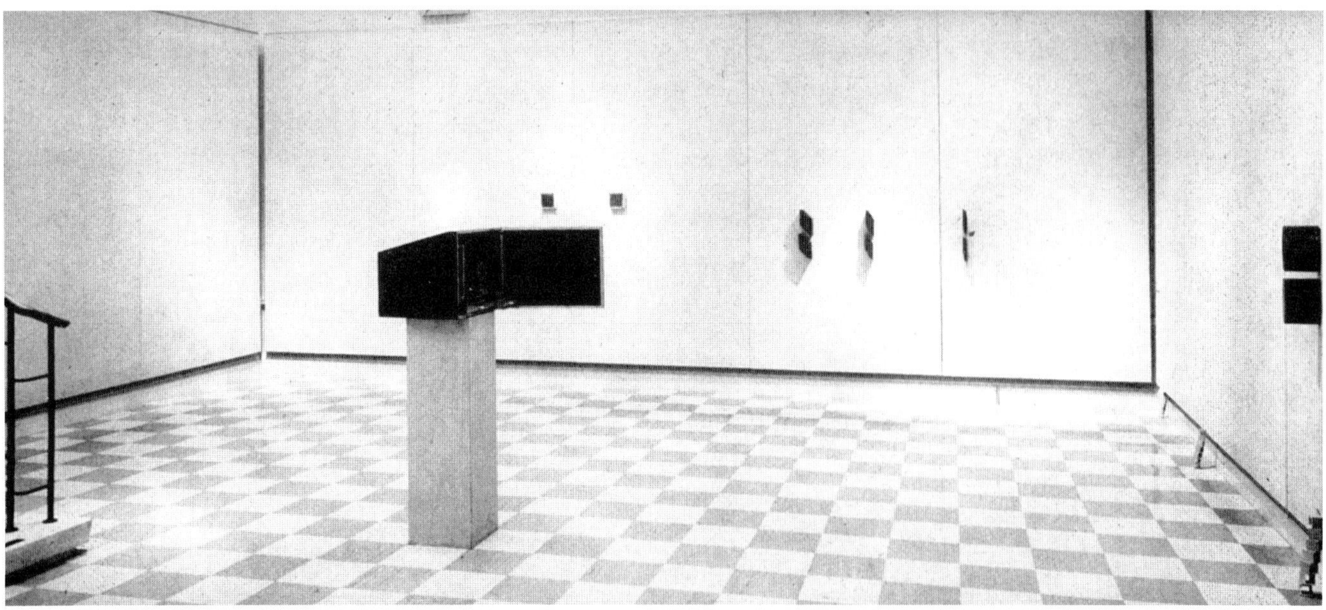

6

MINIMALISM *EN ABYME*: *MOMENTS OF INERTIA*, 1972–73

At the same time Tillers outlined his holistic systems theory in 'The Beginner's Guide to Oil Painting' he formulated and constructed his first major work *Moments of Inertia*, 1972-73.[43] In this work he developed a highly original approach to visual rhetoric that he continued to elaborate throughout the period dealt with in this analysis (1971-2001). At the simplest level this rhetoric involves a transgressive intersection of imagery with minimalist seriality. By adding images to minimalist formalism Tillers deliberately set out to deconstruct the linear geometric abstraction that is a defining feature of minimal art.

The methodology Tillers developed in *Moments of Inertia* will be referred to using key terms Tillers used in writings associated with *Moments of Inertia* and *Conversations with the Bride,* 1974-75. The terms are 'isomorphism' and 'mapping' respectively. Both terms are derived from mathematics where they are intimately interrelated to the extent that the phrase 'isomorphic mapping' will be used to designate the process Tillers developed.[44]

It will be shown that isomorphic mapping enabled Tillers to transpose a Burnhamian notion of 'information processing' into the realm of art practice. Essentially, Tillers appropriated formal characteristics from minimal art and used isomorphic mapping to 'process' these characteristics so that they took on a complexity that expressed his understanding of negentropy and holism.

The goal of formulating a negentropic mode of art-information processing was an ambitious one and it is not surprising to find that *Moments of Inertia* is not an entirely coherent work. It is composed of two interrelated parts, the first part, subtitled *Still Life 2,* is coherent and complete but the second part, subtitled *Still Life 1,* is incomplete and much less coherent. Originally, *Still Life 2* was designed as a prototype for the more ambitious *Still Life 1,* but in practice it is *Still Life 2* that is the more successful work. Accordingly, this analysis will focus primarily on *Moments of Inertia: Still Life 2;* but there will also be a summary examination of some of the more radical features of *Still Life 1.*

The background to Tillers' use of isomorphic mapping can be found in 'The Beginner's Guide to Oil Painting' where under the subheading 'Isomorphisms' Tillers discusses the body art of Dennis Oppenheim observing that:

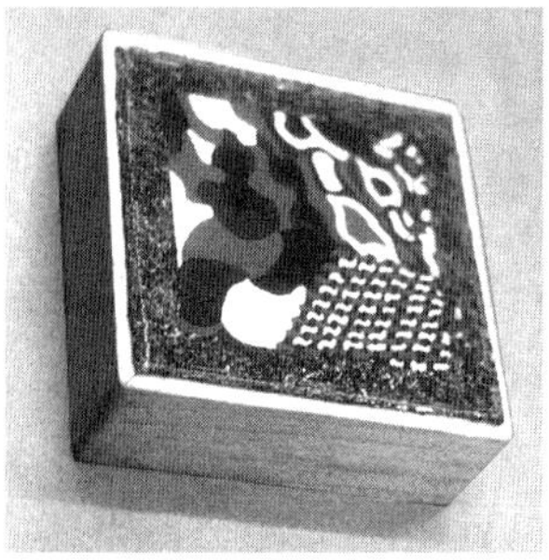

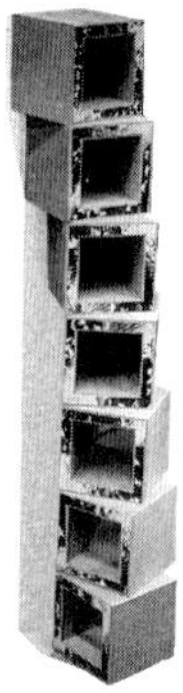

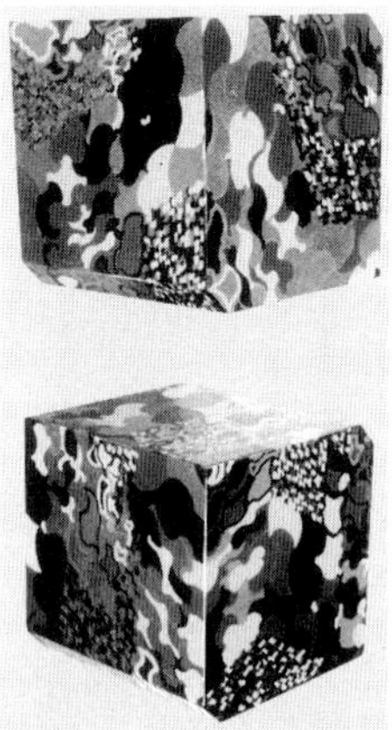

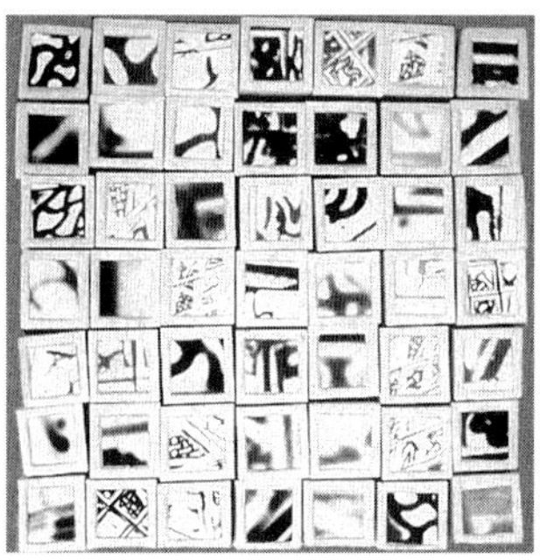

FROM TOP TO BOTTOM: Examples of Wallpiece, Frame, Box, and Floorpiece objects from *Moments of Inertia: Still Life 2*, 1972–73.

> Oppenheim's body art ... tries to set up morphological connections between his body processes and the land's processes. A film made in conjunction with Bob Fiore correlates an incision on Oppenheim's wrist and the subsequently slow healing process with a cut or a large ditch in natural terrain. (Tillers 1973a: Appendix A 24)

Tillers also refers to another work by Oppenheim in which the artist uses a similar technique: 'In a work called *Backtrack* he [Oppenheim] compares the evidence of past wounds or scars on his body to the characteristics of land also manifesting its past in tangible forms.' (Tillers 1973a: Appendix A 24).

The term 'isomorphism' recurs in an illustrated conceptual outline of *Moments of Inertia* by Tillers published in the Sydney based *Contemporary Art Society Broadsheet* (Contemporary Art Society 1974). The text was published on the occasion of an exhibition of *Moments of Inertia* at the Art Gallery of South Australia. In his description of the systems approach he employed in the work Tillers notes that there are: '2 discrete systems (which are isomorphic to each other) and are overlaid simultaneously to produce the final piece' (Contemporary Art Society 1974: n.p.).

ISOMORPHIC MAPPING AND INFORMATION PROCESSING

In mathematics there is a strong link between the notion of isomorphism and transformation that makes the process especially useful as a means of 'information processing'. The mathematician Douglas Hofstadter provides a precise definition of this relationship in his Pulitzer Prize winning book *Gödel, Escher, Bach*, when he defines isomorphism as 'an information-preserving transformation' (Hofstadter 1980: 8).

Hofstadter elaborates his description of the relationship between isomorphism and transformation by drawing an analogy with the construction of J. S. Bach's canons. Hofstadter notes that in Bach's canons 'copies' of a theme are played against each other. Crucially, isomorphic mapping does not lead to one-to-one copies but always involves an information-preserving transformation. Hofstadter observes that in Bach's canons such 'isomorphic copies' undergo a variety of systematic transformations. They are shifted out of synchronisation in time, altered in pitch, in speed, or the theme can be inverted (Hofstadter 1980: 8-9). In *Moments of Inertia* Tillers essentially took basic formal elements from minimal art and subjected them to processes analogous to Hofstadter's description of the canon in music. Hofstadter's phrase 'information preserving transformation' also indicates a parallelism between isomorphic mapping and the Burnhamian conception of art as 'information processing'. It seems probable that Tillers' choice of isomorphic mapping as a method was based on the recognition of that kind of parallelism.

TILLERS' 'TRANSFORMATION FUNCTION'

Chapter One demonstrated the influence of minimal art on the four basic object types (illustrated opposite) that make up the first and most coherent part of *Moments of Inertia, Still Life 2.* It was shown that what Tillers referred to as the Floorpiece was influenced by Carl Andre, the Box (pair) and Frame by Donald Judd, and the Wallpiece by Frank Stella. The following analysis will focus on two aspects of Tillers' use of isomorphic mapping to 'process' minimalist formalism. The first concerns his application of what he referred to as 'transformation functions' to his object-types and the second concerns his application of an image structure to every object making up *Moments of Inertia*: *Still Life 2*.[45] It will be argued that of the two strategies Tillers' image structure is by far the more successful method. A brief description of Tillers' application of his 'transformation functions' to his object types will be followed by a more detailed analysis of the image structure.

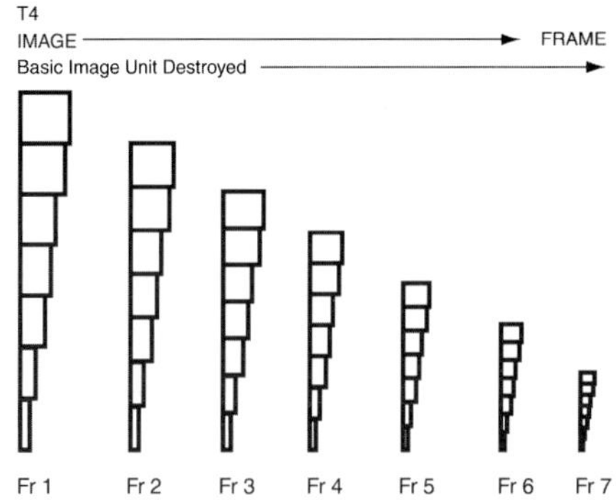

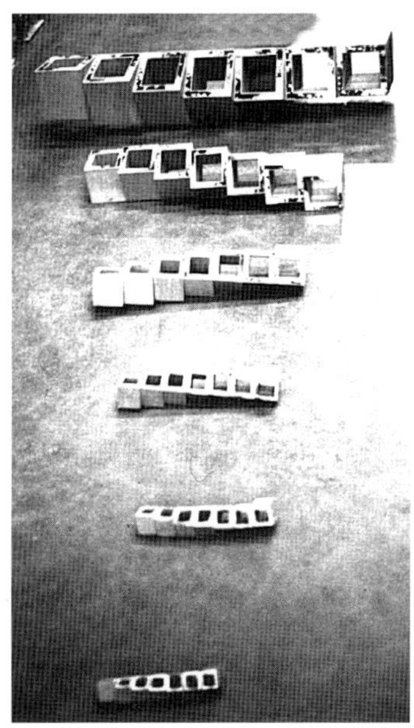

TOP: Reconstruction of Imants Tillers' diagram of the seven transformations of his Frame type, in *Moments of Inertia: Still Life 2.* BOTTOM: photograph of six of the seven Frame objects on the floor of the archive in the National Gallery of Australia, Canberra.

PROCESSING THE OBJECT TYPES IN *STILL LIFE 2*

Tillers provided an explanation of the 'transformation functions' he applied to the four object types in an illustrated conceptual outline for *Still Life 2* which accompanied 'The Beginner's Guide to Oil Painting' (Tillers 1973c). For example, the transformations pertaining to the Frame objects were defined by Tillers as follows:

> 1. Reduction in size of shape at a steady rate U1 = 4′, U7 = 4″ (Tillers 1972: n.p.)

Translated this means that the first unit is four feet high and the seventh unit is four inches high. Tillers also described these transformations with a diagram, a reconstruction of which is illustrated top right. He defines the second transformation as follows:

> 2. Reduction of contrast from black-white to white all over at a steady rate of change. (Tillers 1972: n.p.)

The second transformation concerns the image structure which in this case moves from a dark to a very light image. A photograph of six of the seven Frames unmounted on the floor of the archive in the National Gallery of Australia, Canberra is shown bottom right. When exhibited the Frame objects would be distributed around the space of the gallery and rest between the floor and wall as is evident in the installation views at the beginning of this chapter. Tillers applied similar transformations to the Box objects. These are apparent in the examples reproduced on the following page. When installed they would be placed on a wall in a manner that echoes Donald Judd's wall mounted boxes.

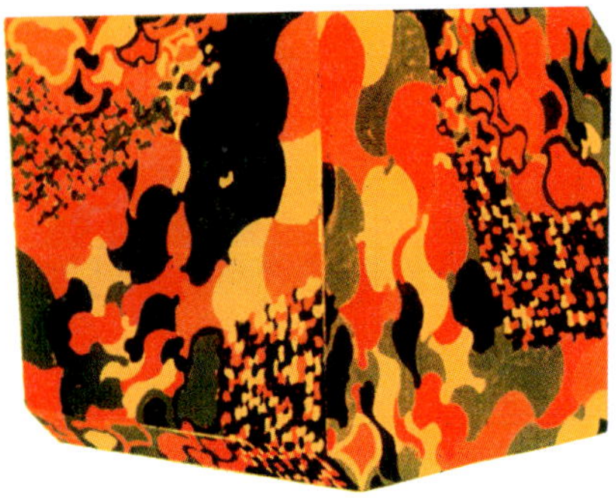

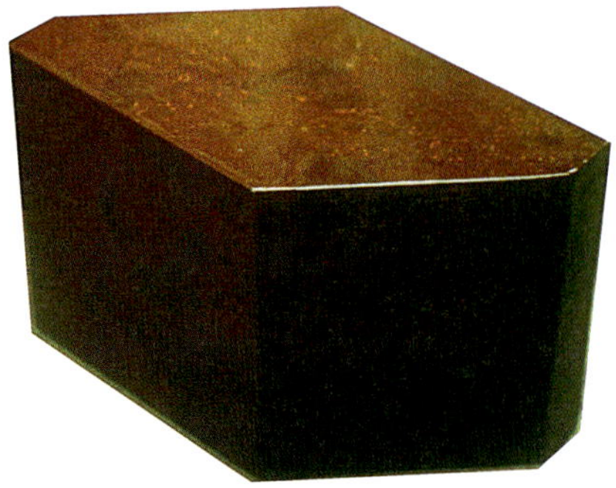

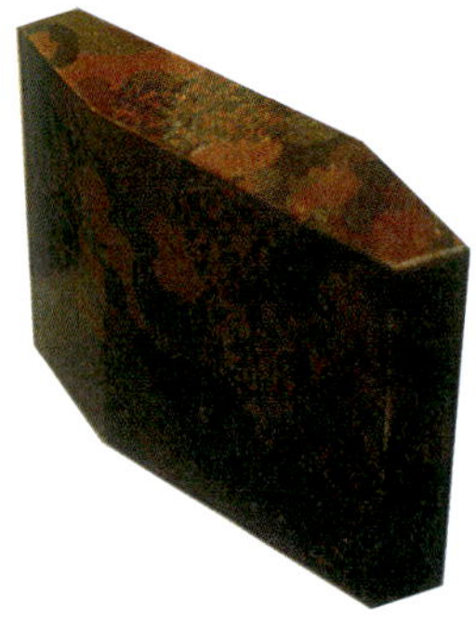

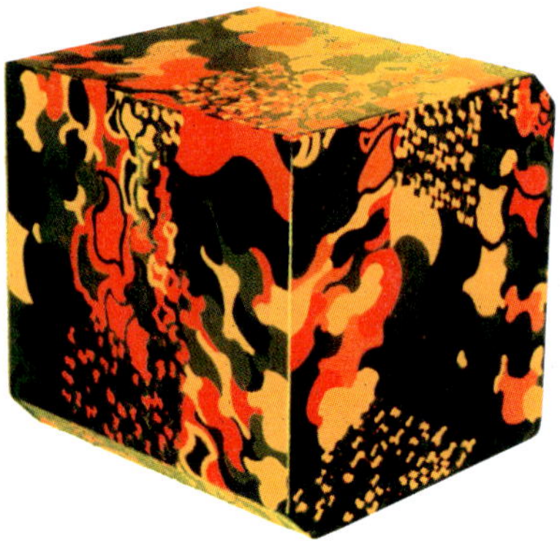

TOP LEFT: The first of the seven variants of paired Box objects making up *Moments of Inertia: Still Life 2*. TOP CENTRE: Top half of third Box object pair. TOP RIGHT: Top half of sixth Box object pair. Collection: National Gallery of Australia, Canberra. Paint on wood, largest unit 12 cm³. BOTTOM (FROM LEFT TO RIGHT): Wallpiece, Frame, and Floorpiece from, *Moments of Inertia: Still Life 2*.

The first of the seven truncated Box shapes is shown above left. The centre and right hand illustrations display two transformations imposed on the Box object-type: the first being a physical narrowing or squeezing of the original truncated cube shape; the second affects the visibility of the image structure. Tillers described the transformation function that led to the narrowing of the object as an 'oblique projection of box parallel to wall rotated by steps of 15°' (Tillers 1972: n.p.). It should be noted that the seven Box objects consist of paired boxes as shown above left. The examples of the Box objects illustrated above centre and left show only the top parts of each pair.

Tillers' implementation of isomorphism in the transformations of the object types in *Still Life 2* is not especially radical. If he had stopped at this point then his work could be seen as a small contribution to the, by then ageing, genre of minimal art. It is in Tillers' implementation of isomorphic transformations in his image structure that he breaks out of the linear formalism of minimal art and begins to achieve a negentropic-like complexity.

THE IMAGE *EN ABYME*

It is in his application of what he referred to as his image structure to the objects making up *Moments of Inertia* that Tillers comes closest to achieving a visual representation of his theoretical concepts of negentropy and holism using his technique of transformational isomorphism. The primary focus of the following analysis of Tillers' image structure will be on the completed and therefore more coherent part of *Moments of Inertia: Still Life 2*. The reproduc-

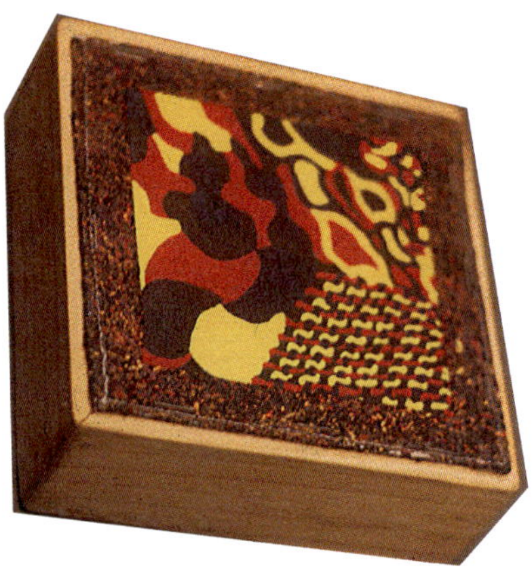

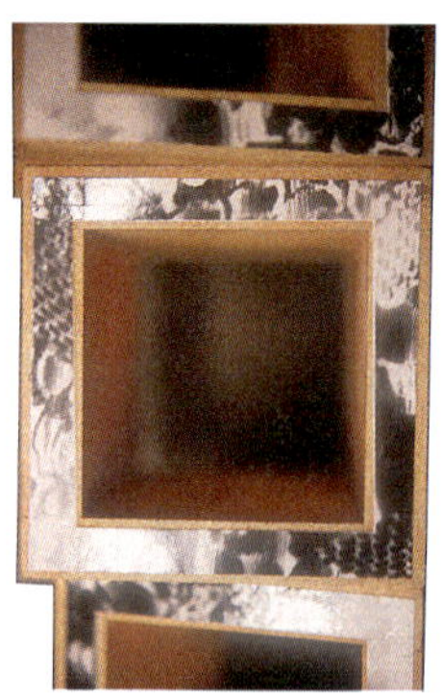

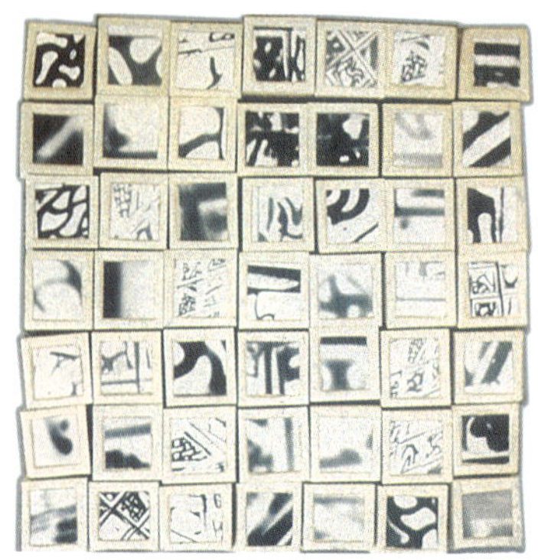

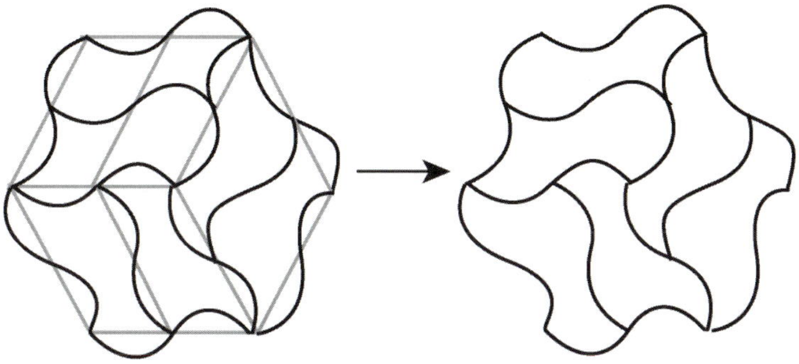

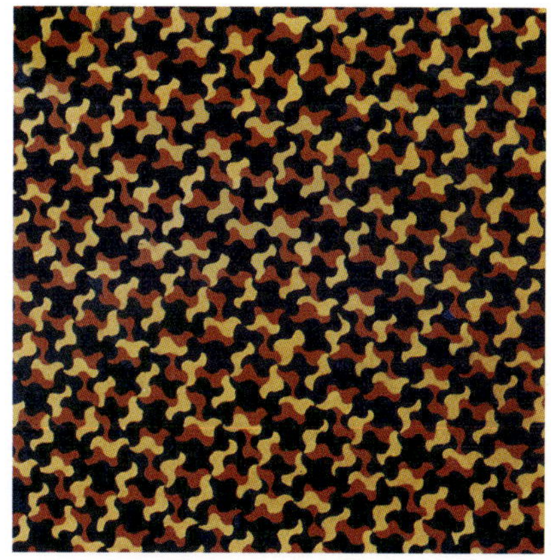

LEFT: Diagram based on a sketch by Tillers showing how he transformed a cuboid configuration of parallelograms into a curvilinear field pattern. RIGHT: Tillers' prototypical image structure illustrated in his conceptual plan for *Moments of Inertia* (Tillers 1973c).

tions below opposite show that each object type in *Still Life 2* had the image-type inscribed on it either with paint or photographic material. [46]

As the analysis of Tillers' image structure progresses it will become apparent that this interrelating of parts to whole is more complex than simply applying this motif to every element of the work. It will be established that not only does every object type refer to the image structure but that the image structure refers to every object type. The result is a more sophisticated and innovative translation of isomorphic mapping into visual rhetoric than is evident in Tillers' systematic transformation of his object types.

Tillers has explained (in Coulter-Smith 1991) that the basis for the image structure was a configuration of parallelograms locked together to form an isometric cube. Tillers recalls that he then modified the basic cube framework of the image structure by substituting 's' shaped curves for the straight lines of the parallelograms, as is diagrammed top left. The diagram is based on a sketch by Tillers that demonstrates how he transformed a cuboid configuration of parallelograms into a curvilinear design. Top right is a prototypical 'image structure' from Tillers' illustrated conceptual plan for *Moments of Inertia* (Tillers 1973c) showing how he turned his curvilinear design into a field pattern.

Another diagram illustrated below left demonstrates how Tillers' field pattern for his prototypical image-type would appear if it were not processed into curves. It is interesting to compare this diagram with Andre's grid pattern reproduced below right. The linearity of the diagram does not disturb the rhetoric of minimal art due to the fact that linearity is such a pivotal feature

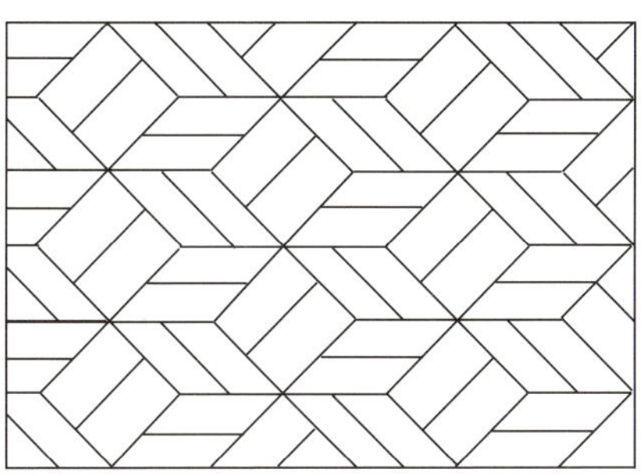

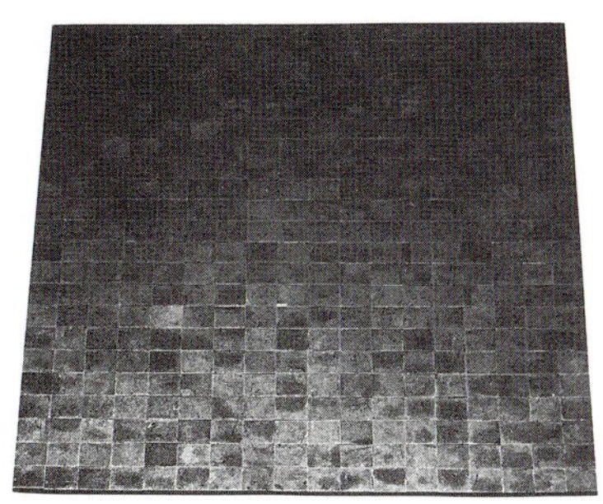

LEFT: Author's diagram of basic gridded nature of Tillers' prototypical image structure omitting the transformation from linear to curvilinear. RIGHT: Carl Andre, *Brooklyn Field,* 1966. Alnico magnets; 356 units each 2.5 x 3 cm; overall dimension 55.9 x 55.9 cm. Private collection, Elko, Belgium.

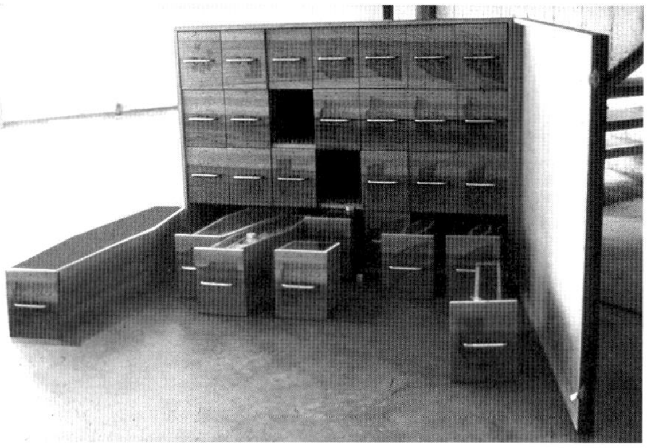

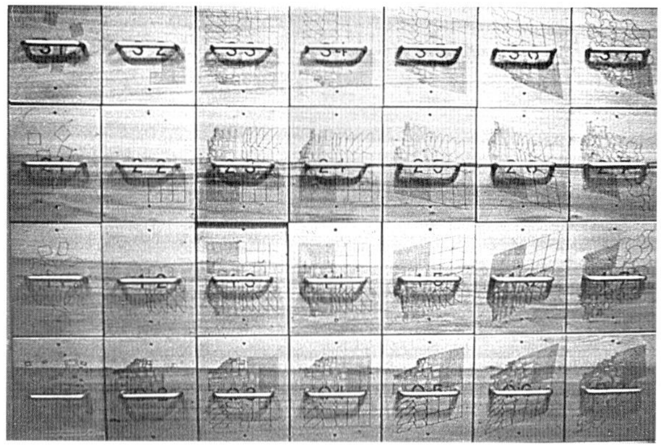

LEFT: Photograph of the cabinet in which the 28 objects making up *Moments of Inertia: Still Life 2* are stored. Wood, 85 x 120 x 100 cm. RIGHT: Frontal view of the 28 cabinet drawers.

of that discourse. In contrast, the curvilinearity of Tillers' prototypical image structure breaks this key generic feature of minimal art and accordingly can be described as a creative deconstruction of minimalist rhetoric. The extent of this deconstruction of minimalism is underscored by the fact that the curvilinearity is only one feature of Tillers' creative departure from the discourse of minimalism. The next stage of his application of a rhetorical mode of 'information processing' is inscribed on the cabinet which was built to house the 28 objects making up *Moments of Inertia: Still Life 2*, illustrated above left. The illustration above right shows the entire set of drawers. As can be seen there are four rows of drawers, one row for each of the four object types. The illustration below left is a close up of drawer '34' annotated to show that the image structure is a diagrammatic representation of the 28 objects making up *Moments of Inertia*: *Still Life 2*. Tillers explains:

> I drew all [28] objects from frontal view: Frames, Boxes, Wallpieces, Floorpieces. Then I used them as a grid to generate the image that would be on those objects. (in Coulter-Smith 1991: n.p.)

Detail of drawer 34 of the cabinet that holds the 28 objects making up *Moments of Inertia: Still Life 2.*

Boxes (in pairs) **Wallpieces**

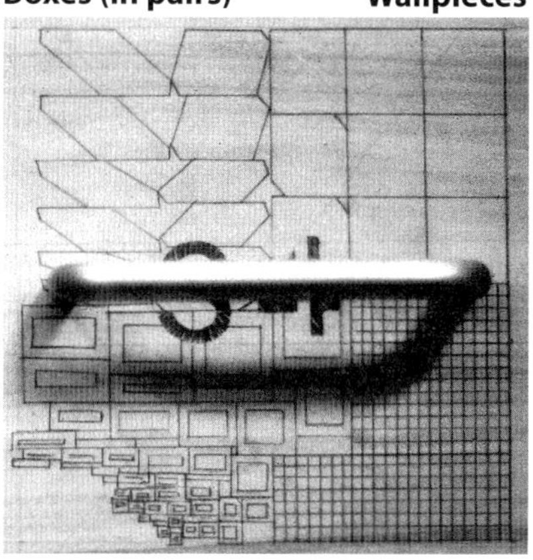

Frames **Floorpieces**

Drawers 35-37, illustrated at the top of the facing page, indicate how Tillers then subjected the diagram of the 28 objects to transformational processes so as to create the image-type that was applied to all the objects making up *Moments of Inertia*. Drawers 35 and 36 show Tillers rotating the diagram in an anticlockwise direction. The tilting effect appears to be a means of allowing it to assume a cuboid configuration as indicated in the appended diagram. The tilting process echoes the cuboid configuration that served as a matrix for Tillers' prototypical image structure, an interpretation reinforced by drawer 37 which shows Tillers applying a curvilinearity that stems from the method used in his prototypical image structure. A very clear example of Tillers' application of this more complex image structure to an object is the doubled Box object from *Still Life 2*, reproduced opposite, bottom right. At least five features show how far Tillers had moved from the discourse of minimalism.

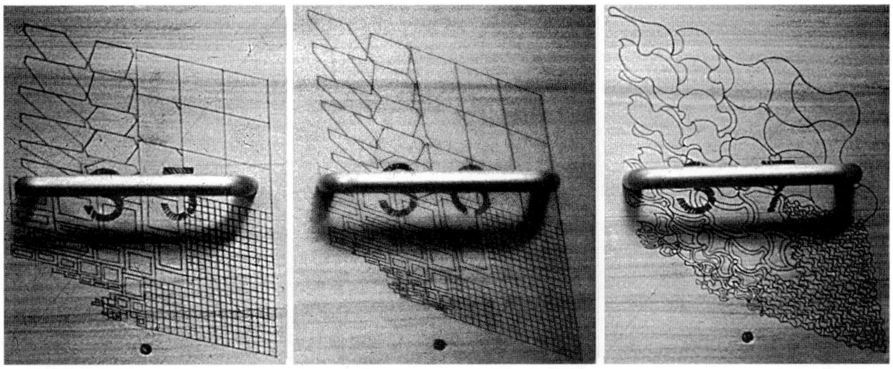

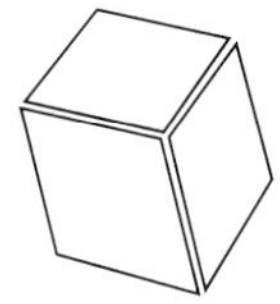

LEFT: Details of drawers 35–37 of the storage cabinet for the 28 objects making up *Moments of Inertia: Still Life 2*. ABOVE: Author's diagram showing how the rotation of the diagram on drawers 36 and 37 can form the basis for a cuboid configuration. BOTTOM: A pair of Box objects from *Moments of Inertia: Still Life 2*, displaying the image-type pattern. Each unit 12 cm³

Firstly, the pattern is non-linear, secondly it is multi-coloured (see page 108), thirdly it is very complex, fourthly it is an image, fifthly the image-type suggests a specular *mise en abyme*. The fifth difference concerns the fact that the image-type applied to all the objects making up *Moments of Inertia*: *Still Life 2* is a diagram of all the objects making up *Moments of Inertia*: *Still Life 2*. Each of the objects reflects the whole creating what is a metaphorical expression of the interconnectivity Tillers knew was an intrinsic feature of holistic systems such as biological organisms and ecosystems.

In *Moments of Inertia*: *Still Life 2* Tillers forged a sophisticated rhetorical device that allowed the expression of two pivotal features of the holistic systems aesthetic he formulated in 'The Beginner's Guide to Oil Painting': firstly, a system in which each element reflected the whole; and, secondly, a system that produced complexity. The last point is important as it represents Tillers' most successful visual expression of the concept of negentropy that is so crucial to his holistic systems theory in 'The Beginner's Guide to Oil Painting'.

There are two interrelated aspects to Tillers' visual expression of negentropic complexity. Firstly, there is the holistic-like inscription of a diagrammatic depiction of all twenty-eight objects onto all twenty-eight objects. Secondly, there is the quality of the isomorphism involved. It has been noted that in mathematics isomorphism entails an 'information-preserving transformation'. The examination of Tillers' application of transformation functions to his object types indicated quite simple transformations such as rotation, and diminution in size (in the Frame objects). The image structure introduces what is perhaps the most complex mode of isomorphic transformation, self-reflexivity.

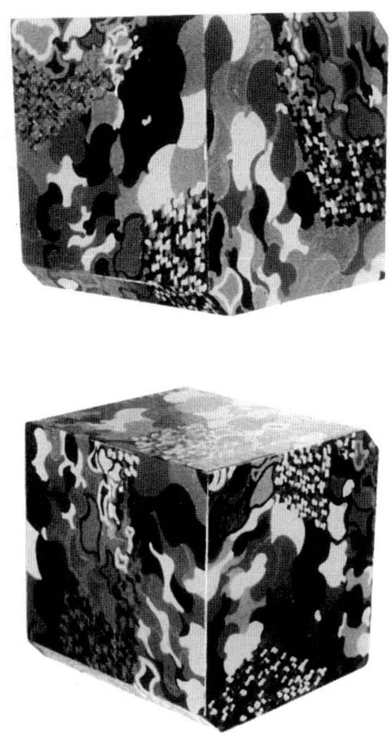

It can be shown that Tillers had a conceptual awareness of self-reflexivity. His reference to isomorphism in 'The Beginner's Guide to Oil Painting' was described above, and it is also the case that he referred to a phenomenon he describes as 'a dilemma known in philosophy as logical regression' (Tillers 1973a: Appendix A 25). Logical regression, or *mise en abyme,* is not only evident in Tillers' image structure it is also evident in the cabinet he had built

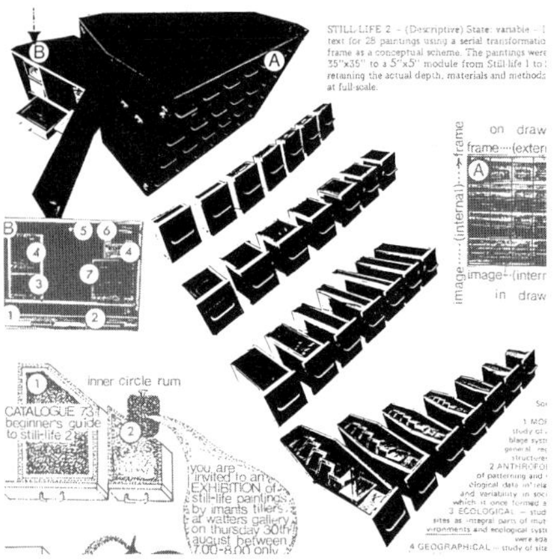

Detail from Tillers' explication of *Moments of Inertia: Still Life 2* in the *Contemporary Art Society Broadsheet,* 1974. Parts of the image have been greyed out for the purposes of emphasis.

to house the 28 objects making up *Moments of Inertia: Still Life 2*. In 1974 Tillers published an exploded view of this cabinet in the *Contemporary Art Society Broadsheet* (illustrated left). Tillers' numeric indexing of the objects stored in this cabinet suggests that it should be classified in the genre of cabinets designed for filing. Yet, the exploded view of the cabinet indicates that it reverses the usual logic of filing cabinets. Instead of the objects fitting into drawers the drawers are fitted for the objects. Cecil Pitman, who constructed the cabinet, was instructed by Tillers to design the drawers, in a glove-like manner, to fit the twenty-eight objects they were to house. And the cabinet that housed the drawers was designed to fit the shape of the resulting array of drawers. The result is isomorphic in a self-reflexive and holistic-like manner due to the fact that the shape of the cabinet echoes the overall shape of the 28 objects arranged in a gridded configuration.

It is also interesting to note that the visual representation of self-reflexivity and logical regression is also apparent in the work of Tillers' fellow avant-gardist Noel Sheridan who created the work *On Reflection*, illustrated below left. Sheridan's Magritte-like self-reflexive visual trope echoes Tillers' use of the rhetoric of *mise en abyme* in *Moments of Inertia*. More remarkably, Sheridan's image was on the cover of the same *Contemporary Art Society Broadsheet* that contained Tillers' exploded view of the cabinet housing *Moments of Inertia: Still Life 2*. Apparently there was no direct relationship between the two instances of visual self-reflexivity but the coincidence does suggest that, in the context of the Australian avant-garde, an awareness of the visual possibilities of self-reflexivity extended beyond Tillers. This interpretation is reinforced by the fact that another Australian, Michael Scullion, introduced Tillers to the self-reflexive paradox inherent in Gödel's Incompleteness Theorem that provided a sophisticated theoretical framework for Tillers' deconstructive approach to authorial appropriation in *Untitled*, 1978.

Tillers' use of self-reflexive isomorphism is arguably the single most significant feature of *Moments of Inertia* because it indicates that his artistic interpretation of isomorphic mapping has a distinctly specular dimension. Tillers' varied articulations of specularity and a concomitant rhetoric of the *mise en abyme* will be shown to be a vital thread running throughout his oeuvre.

Detail of front cover of the *Contemporary Art Society Broadsheet*, 1974, showing Noel Sheridan, *On Reflection*.

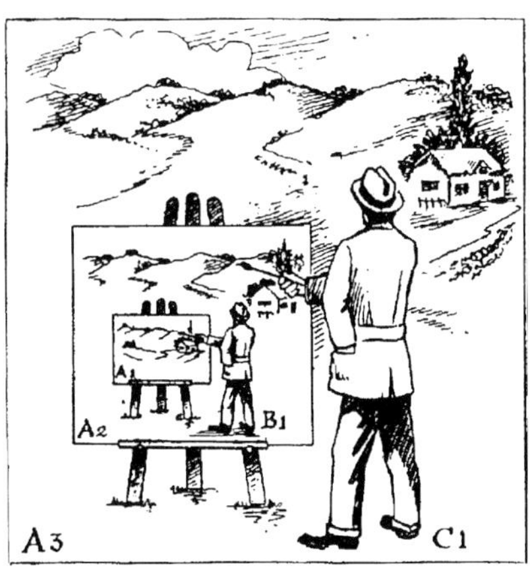

MOMENTS OF INERTIA: STILL LIFE 1 AND HYPER-COMPLEXITY

Tillers went on to apply his image structure to *Still Life 1* but here the impact of the metaphor is less powerful. *Still Life 1* was intended to be made up of 112 objects which would involve a more radical physical transformation of the four object types. Unfortunately, the designs for these objects were so complex that Tillers only constructed twenty-one objects and most of these are unfinished. Moreover, he applied the image structure developed in *Still Life 2* to the objects in *Still Life 1* rather than redesigning it to include the

112 new transformations. However, a careful observer would have noted that the diagrams of the objects on the drawers of the cabinet built to contain *Moments of Inertia*: *Still Life 2* appear to show more than seven objects for each type. This is due to the fact that the Boxes are in pairs, each of the Floorpieces is made up of forty-nine tiles, each of the Frames are made up of seven open-ended box sections, only the Wallpiece objects consist of a single element.[47] Accordingly, the image structure does not include diagrams of the objects making up *Moments of Inertia: Still Life 1*. Such considerations lead this analysis of *Moments of Inertia* to the conclusion that Tillers' attempts to increase the complexity of his formal transformations in *Still Life 1* are less significant than his much more coherent application of the image structure in *Still Life 2*.

In *Moments of Inertia: Still Life 1* Tillers intended to use isomorphic mapping to achieve an even greater degree of negentropic complexity. He set out to achieve this by the introduction of two isomorphic systems. In his illustrated text published in the *Contemporary Art Society Broadsheet* Tillers noted that there are: '2 discrete systems (which are isomorphic to each other) and are overlaid simultaneously to produce the final piece' (Contemporary Art Society 1974: n.p.). 'System 1' consists of a plan to generate 112 objects from the 28 objects making up *Still Life 2*. 'System 2' is an entirely new set of objects which correspond to the location of the installation. In order to create 'System 1' Tillers developed four 'classes' of isomorphic transformation to be applied to the object types. The first class is based on the 28 objects making up *Still Life 2* which together with three more 'classes' multiplies the number of objects in *Still Life 1* to 112. However, the degree of complexity was so extreme that he was able to produce only 21 out of the 28 objects making up 'class 1'. The remaining 91 were recorded in the form of a book, *Works* (Tillers 1973b), that can be considered as a work of conceptual art. Tillers did achieve a more radical negentropic effect in his *Still Life 1* objects, but the impact of this is lessened by the lack of completion.

As noted, the 'System 2' objects relate to the location of the installation, an approach informed, in part, by the minimalist premise that the work should interact with its location. Except that, instead of being based upon physical relationships to the environment such as the bolting of Judd's boxes to the wall or the intimate relationship of Andre's gridded floorpieces to the floor, Tillers uses objects that carry domestic connotations far removed from the emphasis of American minimalist art on industrial materials and processes. In her scholarly analysis of minimal art Frances Colpitt notes the minimal artist's preference for industrial materials when she notes 'Judd depends primarily on [industrial] fabrication for its neat and austere results, the same reason he employs industrial materials.' (Colpitt 1993: 19). It is also apparent that Tillers was well aware of this aspect of minimal art when he comments that Carl Andre 'uses convenient commercially available objects, like bricks,

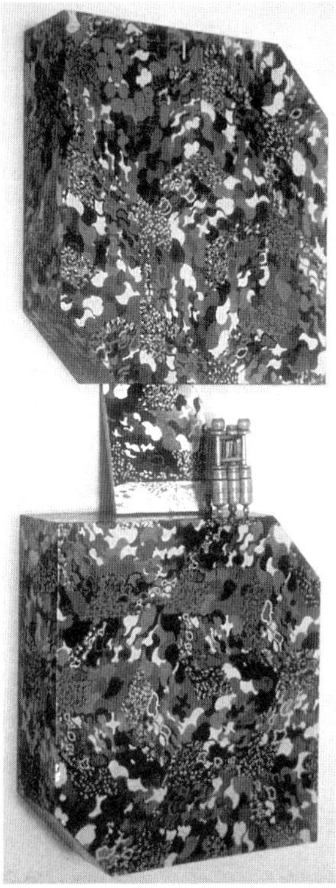

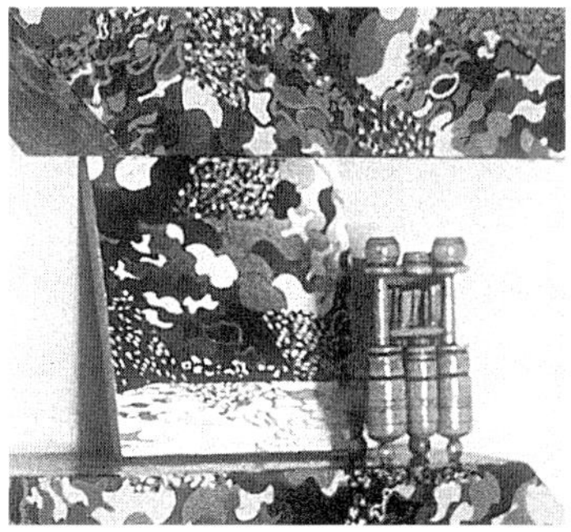

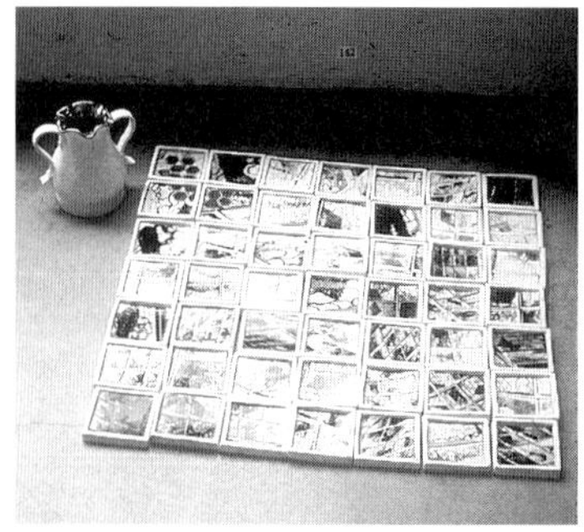

TOP LEFT: from *Moments of Inertia: Still Life 1*, showing *Still Life 1* Box 121 with 'System 2' attachments. TOP CENTRE: close-up of the 'System 2' component of Box 121. TOP RIGHT: a completed *Still Life 1* Floorpiece object with a 'System 2' object (the vase top right). BOTTOM: Tillers' diagram of the transformations occurring in *Moments of Inertia: Still Life 1*.

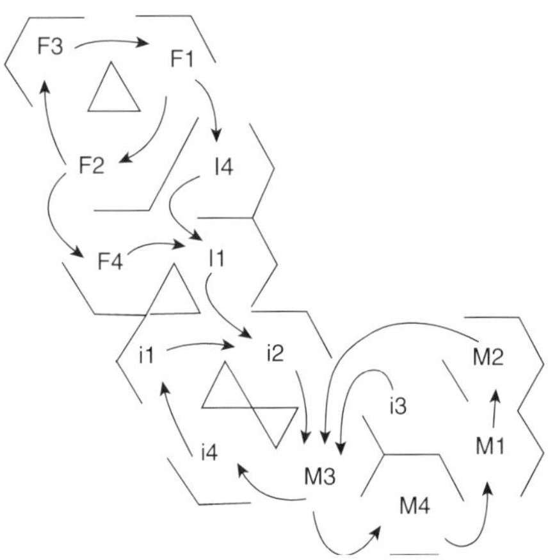

styrofoam planks, ceramic magnets, cement blocks and wooden beams' (Tillers 1973a: Appendix A 21). It appears that Tillers deliberately sought out a different, even antithetical, mode of expression.

Examples of Tillers' use of domestic motifs in 'System 2' are reproduced above. On the left is Box 121 from *Still Life 1*, and top centre is a detail of its System 2 appendage which is a candlestick-like object carved out of wood. On the far right is a completed *Still Life 1* Floorpiece which has a ceramic vase as its System 2 attachment.

Although Tillers was unable to fully realise the transformational strategy devised for the *Still Life 1* objects, there is enough evidence to indicate that he came close to achieving a highly negentropic effect. The level of negentropic complexity that Tillers wished to attain via isomorphic transformations between System 1 and 2 is explained in his *Contemporary Art Broadsheet* text (Contemporary Art Society 1974). There he used the diagram illustrated below left to show how 'the properties of one class are transformed into the properties of another class'. He also inscribed each of the *Still Life 1* objects with this diagram. For example, it is evident in the top left hand corners of the *Still Life 1* Wallpieces reproduced on the following page. It is also significant that Tillers has mirror-inverted the text on these images as it reinforces my argument that he translated the mathematical process of isomorphic mapping into visual rhetoric via specularity.

In his diagram Tillers uses alphanumeric designations for the 112 objects planned for *Still Life 1*. The system is explained by Tillers in his *Contemporary Art Broadsheet* text as follows: F = frame shape; i = image type [transformational stages applied to the image structure]; I = image structure; and M = medium. Tillers elaborates:

> the frame shape (i.e. the physical limits of the piece), image structure, (i.e. whether it is linear, tonal, coloured or combinations of these), image structure (i.e. the pattern by which the image structure is structured), and the material properties (i.e. whether the medium is hard or soft, opaque or transparent etc.). (Tillers 1974: n.p.)

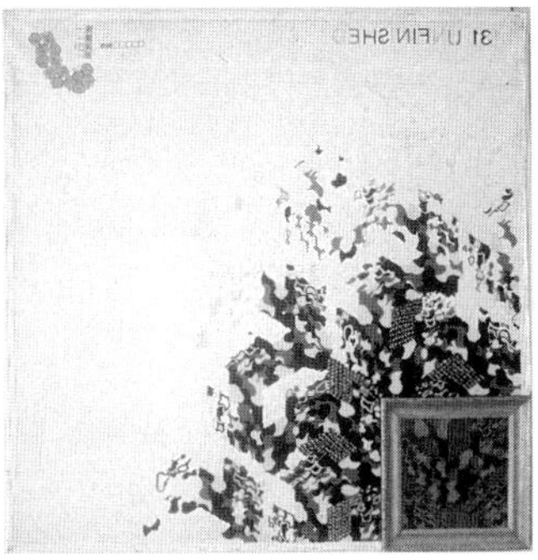
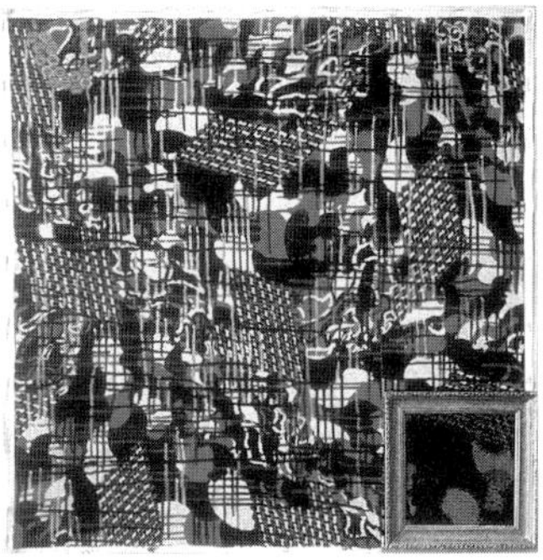
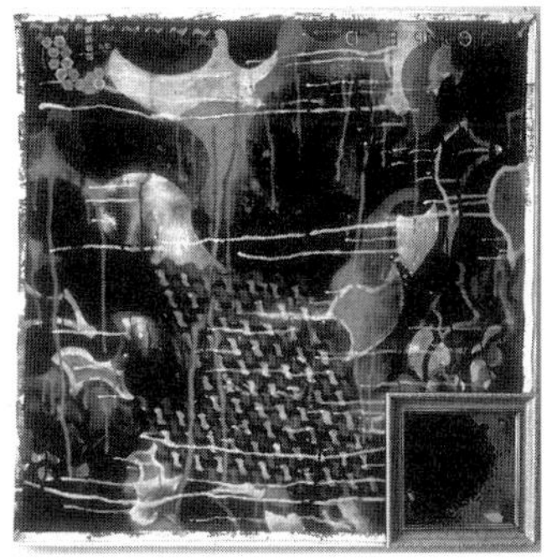
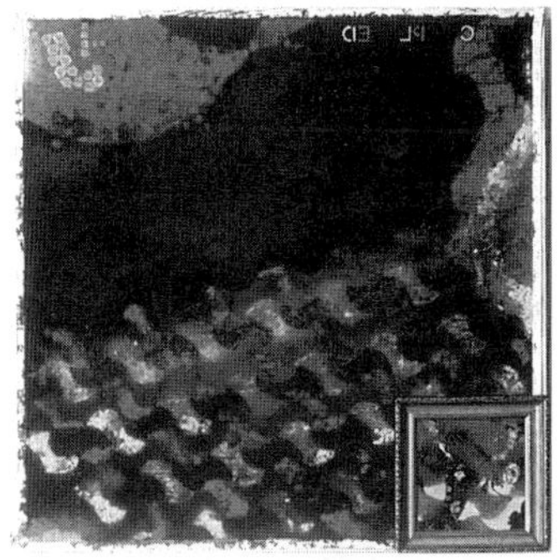

The numeric part of the labelling system refers to the four classes. Thus F3 means frame shape in class three.

The *Still Life 1* Wallpieces can be used to illustrate how Tillers' more complex transformation functions operated in practice. The illustrations at the top of this page show Wallpieces 131-134 and 137 (where '137' designates, class 1, object 3, transformation stage 7): 'System 2' can be seen in the form of a painting in a gilded frame appended to the bottom right hand corner of all the *Still Life 1* Wallpieces. Each of the stages shows both systems transforming according to 'transformation functions' similar to those used in *Still Life 2*. What is especially interesting is that in element 137 the System 2 appendage transforms into a flower painting within the gilded frame. Like the title of 'The Beginner's Guide to Oil Painting' Tillers' floral still life in a gilded frame is a parodic reference to traditional concepts of art, or more precisely to notions of art antithetical to post-object avant-gardism. In addition, because the floral still life is appropriated from the Australian painter Adrian Feint it can be read as a parody of what Tillers then understood as the 'provincialism' of historical, non-indigenous Australian art. In the context of *Moments of Inertia* this initial instance of Tillers' appropriation of 'readymade' 'art information' can also be understood as a culmination of his deconstruction of minimal formalism. His appropriation of Feint's painting is a seminal feature that later burgeoned into the transposition of imagery appropriated from fine art onto a minimalist-like grid array in *Conversations with the Bride*, 1974-75.

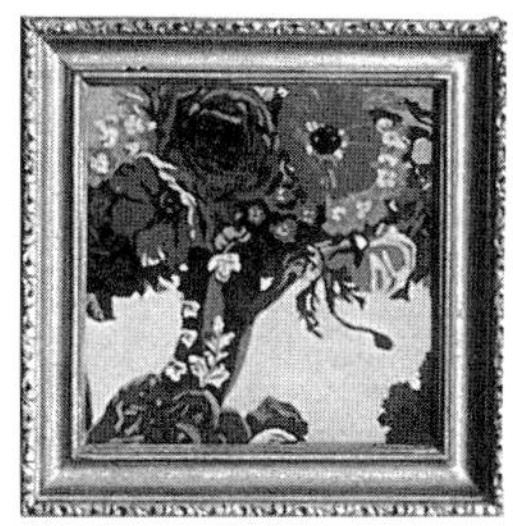

LEFT TO RIGHT: *Moments of Inertia: Still Life 1* Wallpieces 131, 132, 133, 134, 137, and a detail of the System 2 gilded framed still life (appropriated from Adrian Feint) attached to the bottom right-hand corner of each Wallpiece. Collection: Art Gallery of New South Wales, Sydney (gift of Patrick White). [Note: the text on the Wallpieces is mirror inverted.]

One of the best examples of Tillers' attempt to introduce a much more radical processing of his four object types than that evident in *Still Life 2* is demonstrated by his *Still Life 1* version of the Frame objects. These objects are reproduced on the following page as an installation view and in close-up. The reproductions show that the isomorphic transformation functions or 'mappings' described by Tillers' complex diagram have resulted in a radically different form from that in *Still Life 2*. Instead of the frames being objects that stand upright against wall and floor, they flop between wall and floor. One detects an element of humour here as in Tillers' appropriation of Adrian Feint's floral still life, and the whimsical title of his otherwise serious text 'The Beginner's Guide to Oil Painting'.

91 MISSING WORKS

Tillers' ambition to create a much more radical transformation of his four object types in *Still Life 1* proved too extreme to be fully realised. He managed to produce only the objects in class 1, and seven of these remained unfinished, which left 91 'missing objects'. Tillers tackled this problem by producing a work of conceptual art, in the form of a unique loose leafed book made with tracing paper pages onto which he drew annotated diagrams in Rotring pen, thereby describing how the unmade objects would be generated from his transformation of the properties of one class into those of another. He also produced several bound volumes of dyeline prints of *91 Missing Works* from the tracing paper master. The work shows the influence of the genre of conceptual art in which a text acts as a post-object work of art. The extreme complexity which would result from the feedback system described in the transformational diagrams is graphically demonstrated in the details from *91 Missing Works* reproduced above opposite.

The complexity and sense of dynamic process is very different from the static classical purity of much American minimal art, as was evident in an interview in July 1991 (Coulter-Smith 1991) when Tillers explained the diagrams. They concern a transformation Tillers designated 'F4 $\rightarrow$ I1' in which class 4 Frame objects are mapped onto the Image structure for class 1. He explained that the objects in class 4 were to be made of soft, clear PVC sheeting. He recalled:

> Each [component] would be a separate object put together in that form so the shapes of its internal parts are the same as the image structure to the actual object. It is the same as the image structure. There is no image … because it is just clear PVC, [the structure] is the image. So that's how the frame shape from Class 4 produces the image structure for Class 1. (in Coulter-Smith 1991: n.p.)

In this case, 'the transformation of the property of one class into the property of another class' means that the frame shape and the image structure combine, the image structure becomes the frame shape. One structure is embedded

RIGHT: Installation view of *Moments of Inertia: Still Life 1* Frame objects, Watters Gallery, Sydney. 1973. LEFT: Frame 111. Collection: National Gallery of Australia, Canberra.

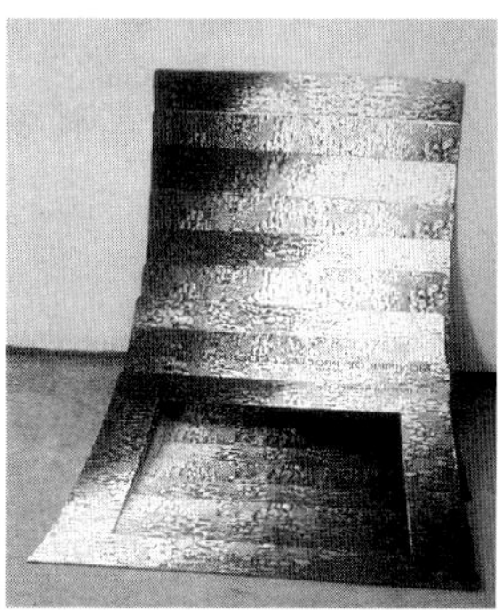

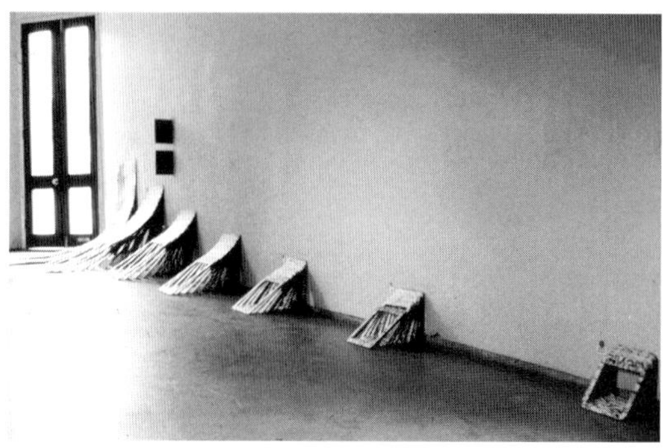

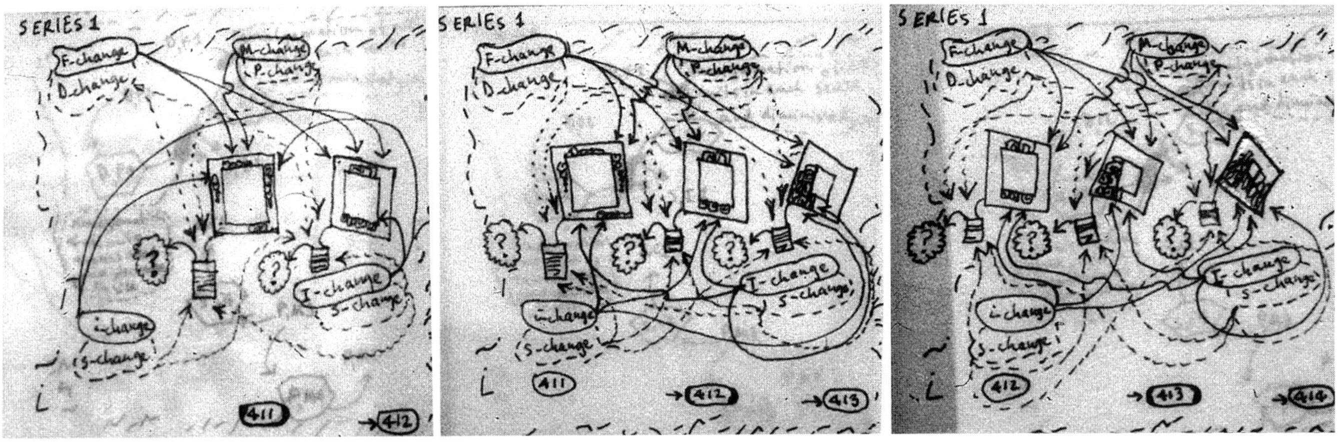

Details from unique master *91 Missing Works*, 1973. Rotring pen drawings on tracing paper. Collection: the artist.

in another in a frenzy of isomorphic transformations exhibiting a degree of self-reflexivity that, like Tillers' panel 24d from *Conversations with the Bride*, suggests a *mise en abyme*. It is also worth noting that the cartoon-like style of Tillers' drawing in *91 Missing Works* suggests that he was aware that his ambition to achieve a negentropic hypercomplexity had a ludicrous, pataphysical, aspect.

In spite of the hypercomplexity and abstruseness of *Still Life 1, Moments of Inertia* is an extraordinary work for three main reasons: firstly, in this work Tillers invented a method of 'isomorphic mapping' that provided a foundation for his approach in *Conversations with the Bride*, *Untitled*, 1978, and the Canvasboard System; secondly, it was in this work that we discover his first act of appropriating imagery from reproductions of works of art (the floral still life appropriated from Adrian Feint); and thirdly, *Moments of Inertia* shows Tillers using his understanding of isomorphic mapping to formulate a specular rhetoric which, even at this early stage in his career, has as its corollary a sophisticated visual rhetoric of *mise en abyme*.

7

A POETICS OF SPECULARITY: *CONVERSATIONS WITH THE BRIDE,* 1974–75

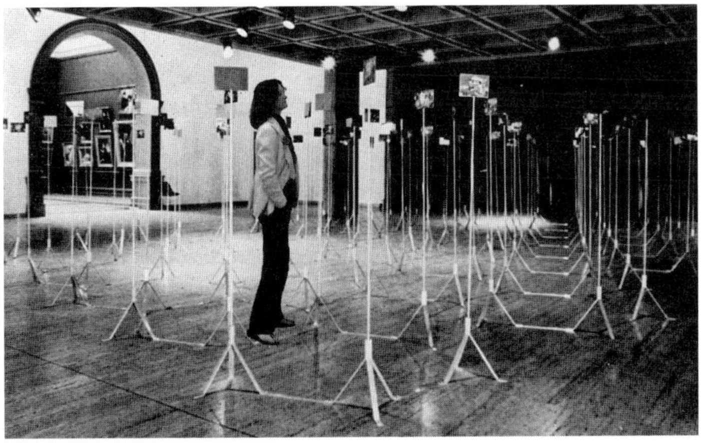

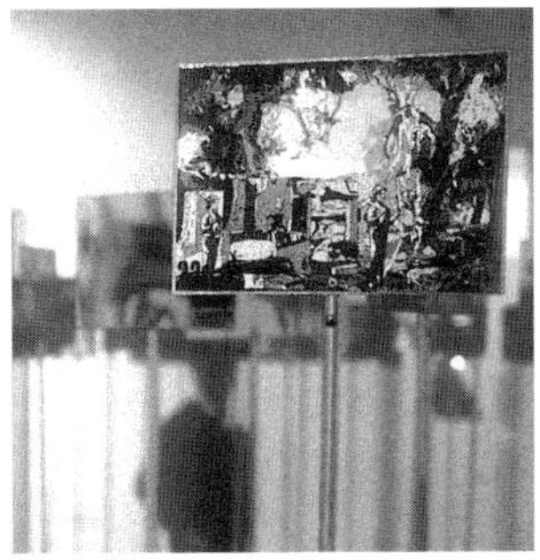

LEFT: *Conversations with the Bride,* 1974–75. 112 images, gouache and Resene Imperite acrylic-epoxy on chrome plated aluminium with mirrored backs mounted on aluminium stands. Each image 8.5 x 11.8 cm, stand height 163 cm, space between stands 75 cm. Collection: Art Gallery of New South Wales, Sydney. Spectator digitally inserted. RIGHT: detail.

Conversations with the Bride, as previously mentioned, is an installation (reproduced above left) consisting of a minimalist-like gridded array of 112 postcard-sized images perched on stands, as shown in the detail above right. The images consist predominantly of a montage of manipulated versions of the Australian landscape painter Hans Heysen's *Summer*, 1909, with fragments from Marcel Duchamp's *The Large Glass,* 1915-23. A reproduction of Hans Heysen's *Summer* is shown below left together with panel 05a from *Conversations with the Bride.* If the two images are compared it can be seen that Tillers used a mirror-inverted version of *Summer* as a background or *mise en scène* for panel 05a. In fact Tillers used *Summer* as the *mise en scène* for most of the 112 images that comprise *Conversations with the Bride.*[48]

LEFT: Hans Heysen, *Summer,* 1909. Watercolour, 56.5 x 78.4 cm. Collection: Art Gallery of New South Wales. RIGHT: Panel 05a from *Conversations with the Bride,* 1974–75. Gouache and Resene Imperite acrylic-epoxy on chrome plated aluminium, 8.5 x 11.8 cm.

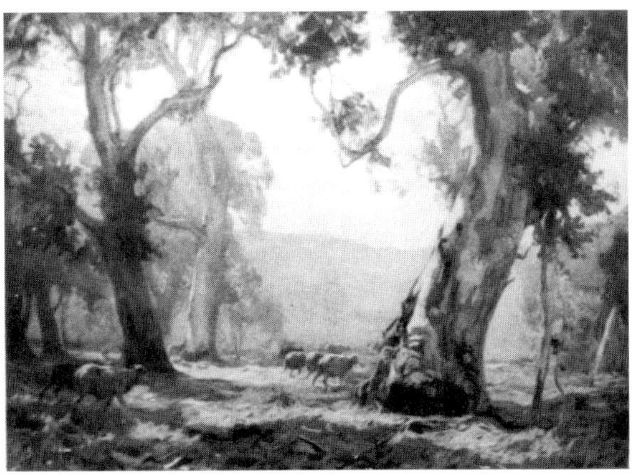

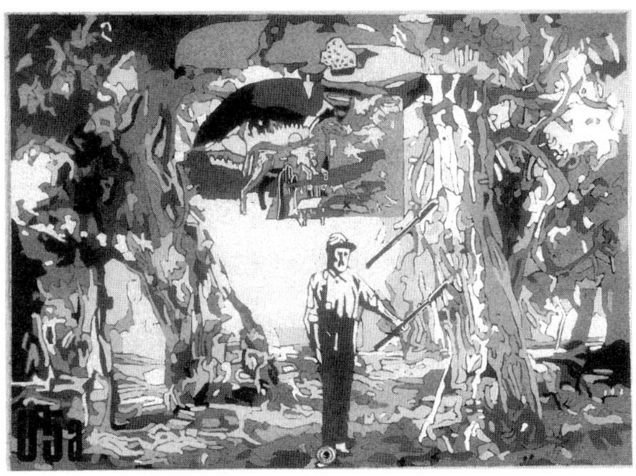

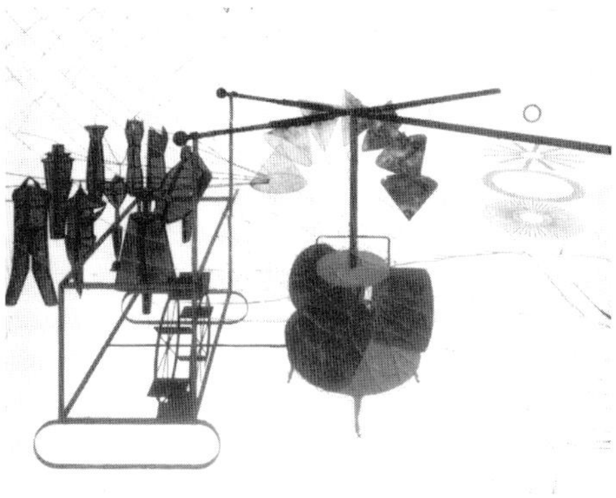

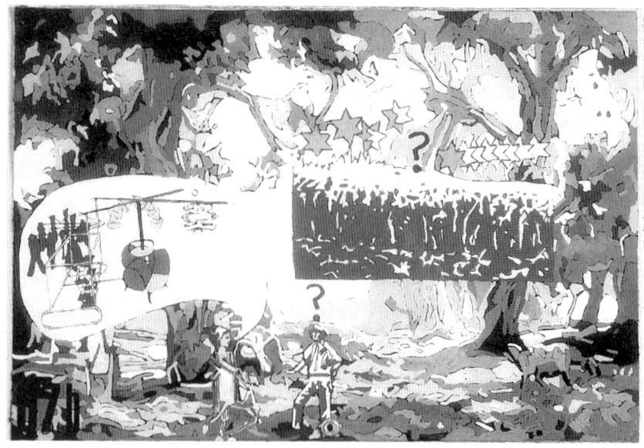

LEFT: Detail (of bottom half) Marcel Duchamp, *The Bride Stripped Bare by Her Bachelors, Even* (*The Large Glass*), 1915–23. Oil, varnish, lead foil and wire, and dust on glass mounted between two glass panels, 274.3 x 0.6 x 274.9 cm. Courtesy of The Philadelphia Museum of Art, Katherine S. Dreier Bequest. RIGHT: Panel 07b from *Conversations with the Bride*, gouache and Resene Imperite acrylic-epoxy on chrome plated aluminium, 8.5 x 11.8 cm.

The analysis of *Moments of Inertia* in Chapter Five noted that Tillers' innovative transposition of isomorphic mapping into the domain of art practice focused on mirror inversion and its more complex corollary, the *mise en abyme*. It will be shown that in *Conversations with the Bride* Tillers made specularity the poetic armature of the work. In addition to the mirror inversion of Heysen's *Summer* the backs of all 112 images making up *Conversations with the Bride* are mirrored, making the gridded array a maze of mirrors. The second major appropriational source of fine art imagery in *Conversations with the Bride* is Marcel Duchamp's *The Bride Stripped Bare by Her Bachelors, Even*, 1915-23, also known as *The Large Glass*. The image reproduced above left shows the bottom half of *The Large Glass* and to the right is panel 07b from *Conversations with the Bride*. If 07b is examined it can be seen that the bottom section of Duchamp's *The Large Glass* is visible in the middle part of the left hand side. Tillers' juxtaposition of segments of Duchamp's *The Large Glass* with Heysen's *Summer* is present in most of the 112 images making up *Conversations with the Bride*.

'SOLVING' THE PROVINCIALISM PROBLEM

At its simplest narrative level this juxtaposition can be read as a parody of what Tillers then considered to be the provincialism of non-indigenous Australian art. The parodic moment hinges on Tillers' juxtaposition of a work by one of the most radical avant-gardist artists of the twentieth century with an example of what he initially understood as a paradigmatic instance of the 'provincialism' of the landscape tradition that characterises historical, non-indigenous Australian art. It is also possible, however, to understand Tillers' appropriation of fine art imagery in *Conversations with the Bride* as an attempt to 'solve' the 'provincialism problem'. Tillers has acknowledged the fact that his juxtaposition of Heysen and Duchamp was influenced by Terry Smith's landmark essay 'The Provincialism Problem' published in *Artforum* in 1974. On the surface Smith's essay offers little hope to the antipodean artist. Smith hammers home the 'problem' via constant reference to an allegedly inescapable 'provincialist bind' (Smith 1974: 56, 57, 58, and 59). The relentless pessimism of Smith's analysis is also evident in categorical statements such as 'in Australia no avant-garde art … has emerged' (Smith 1974: 56). On the other hand, this pessimism affords Smith's essay its forcefulness and interest, and it can be read as a provocation, as an attempt to wake up Australian art. Tillers most certainly read it in such a way, as a call to 'solve' the provincialism problem; and the solution lies latent within Smith's essay.

To begin with, Smith's definition of provincialism as 'an attitude of subservience to an externally imposed hierarchy of cultural values' (Smith 1974: 54) is not entirely convincing, especially when he notes that the majority of artists throughout the world can be described as working within cultural discourses that can be said to be 'external'. This is apparent when Smith notes that New York is:

> the centre for the visual arts, to which artists living in the rest of America, in Holland, Germany, Brazil, England, France, Japan, Australia, etc. stand in a provincial relationship. (Smith 1974: 56)

Moreover, in an earlier passage he suggests that even artists in New York are provincial: 'most New York artists, collectors, dealers, and gallery-goers are provincialist in their work, attitudes, and positions within the system' (Smith 1974: 54-55). The notion that provincialism is the norm is augmented by Smith's observation that art is a 'rule-governed activity'. He suggests that 'whereas most artists are rule-following, there are both rule-following and *rule-generating* creators' (Smith 1974: 58). The concept of 'rule-following' and 'rule-generating' is less emotively loaded than his definition of provincialism as *subservience* to external cultural *values*. If the emotive words 'subservience' and 'external values' are replaced with the notion of 'following external rules' then Smith's definition of provincialism dissolves into a description of virtually any art making activity, without prejudice. Even New York artists such as Frank Stella, Donald Judd and Carl Andre who 'generated' the rules for minimal art that others 'followed' could not have generated such rules without themselves following other 'external' rules generated by the pioneers of European geometric abstraction in the first half of the twentieth-century. In turn these pioneers of abstraction were indebted to their symbolist predecessors, and so on.

So, if following 'external … cultural' 'rules' is not the crux of provincialism, then what is? The answer is apparent in Smith's essay, although he does not foreground it. Essentially the crux of provincialism seems to depend upon the degree of understanding of the 'rules'. Smith argues that Australian artists do not adopt external rules, or stylistic formations, 'whole'. Instead, he argues:

> Their character is distorted, acquaintance with them is late, usually with the mature forms of the style. The early innovative struggles are simply not

> available outside of the limited cultural situation in which they arise. If a visiting artist chances upon them, they are usually incomprehensible to him. Further distortions occur when works are seen only in reproduction, and are accompanied by inadequate criticism and gnomic artists' statements. (Smith 1974: 55)

It is at this point that Smith's analysis is contested by the case of Imants Tillers. It is true that Tillers' understanding of post-object art was dependent on 'works seen only in reproduction' in journals such as *Artforum* and *Studio International*. But instead of being 'accompanied by inadequate criticism and gnomic artist's statements', the articles in these journals were written by art theorists of the calibre of Jack Burnham. In addition, in 'The Beginner's Guide to Oil Painting' Tillers makes the important point that:

> the nature of the new work, because of its typical presentation in the form of documents or photographs, is readily accessible.
> … its media lends itself to distribution to any part of the globe (as books, photographs, films, tape recordings, television) (Tillers 1973a: Appendix A 2)

In this passage Tillers argues that the movement of conceptualist art away from the aesthetic object into a condition of information meant that it becomes more easily transmissible via photomechanical reproduction. And the more art becomes understood as 'information' the more available it is for 'processing'. The crucial concept informing Smith's definition of provincialism is 'subservience' and it is apparent that Smith argued that subservience arises out of ignorance. It is at this point that it is possible to understand how Tillers interpreted Smith's account of provincialism as provocative rather than as hopelessly pessimistic, because Tillers was far from ignorant. 'The Beginner's Guide to Oil Painting' provides ample evidence that he had a very substantial, comprehensive and sophisticated understanding of avant-gardist art of the 1960s. It was this depth of understanding that enabled him to respond to Smith's trenchant and provocative attack on non-indigenous Australian art in a manner that turned around the very crux of that attack—which is not about following rules, but about following rules in an uninformed manner. But Tillers went further because he was capable of not only understanding the 'rules' and 'following' them but also capable of intelligently bending them, as is evident in *Moments of Inertia*. It is at this point that Smith's discussion of 'following' and 'generating' 'rules' intersects with Tillers' Burnhamian discussion of art as 'information processing'.

In *Conversations with the Bride*, Tillers took works of art 'seen only in reproduction' and subjected this 'readymade' 'art information' to 'information processing'. Therein lies the core of Tillers' 'solution' to the 'provincialism problem' in *Conversations with the Bride* and it laid the basis for his strategy throughout the 1970s and into his Canvasboard System. The power of his new approach lies in the fact that the act of appropriation is not one of 'following rules' but one of 'processing information' in a manner that allows a significant degree of 'rule generation'. Tillers' mode of information processing had been developed in *Moments of Inertia* via his translation of the process of isomorphic mapping into a self-reflexive visual rhetoric capable of generating a formal complexity that deconstructs the linearity of minimal art.

In *Conversations with the Bride* Tillers' elaborated upon his strategy of self-reflexive isomorphism by developing a substantive specular poetics that was reinforced by his study of Duchamp's writings associated with *The Large Glass*. Tillers was fascinated to find that Duchamp was deeply involved in the mathematical hypothesis concerning the existence of a fourth spatial dimension. Metaphorically, Tillers' use of specularity 'inverts' the provincialism problem. Inside the mirror-maze that is *Conversations with the Bride* the juxtaposition of Heysen and Duchamp is transported beyond mere parody. Instead, Tillers' specular apparatus is designed to create a radical isomorphism between *The Large Glass* and *Summer*, essentially mapping *The Large Glass* onto *Summer* and vice versa. In the mirror world of *Conversations with the Bride* the subordination of *Summer* to *The Large Glass* is abolished. Metaphorically, *Summer* becomes as radically avant-garde as *The Large Glass* and the 'provincialism problem' is 'solved'.

There is also an authorially deconstructive aspect to Tillers' matrix of mirrors. He designed *Conversations with the Bride* in such a way that the viewer is given a crucial role in the mapping process. The reproduction of *Conversations with the Bride* below right shows that it is designed to allow the viewer to walk into the gridded array of image-mirrors. In his unique artist's book *A Companion to Conversations with the Bride* (Tillers 1978a) Tillers explained that he used mirrored backs to increase what he referred to as the 'coupling' of image to image. Tillers used a diagram (bottom left) to show how the mirrored backs of the images allowed a 'coupling' to occur when the viewer enters into

LEFT: Tillers' diagram for the effect of coupling via the mirrored backs of the images in *Conversations with the Bride*, published in his artist's book *A Companion to Conversations with the Bride* (Tillers 1978a: Table 9/1, § 9.1). RIGHT: *Conversations with the Bride*, 1974–75, installation consisting of 112 images on stands with mirrored backs. Spectator digitally inserted.

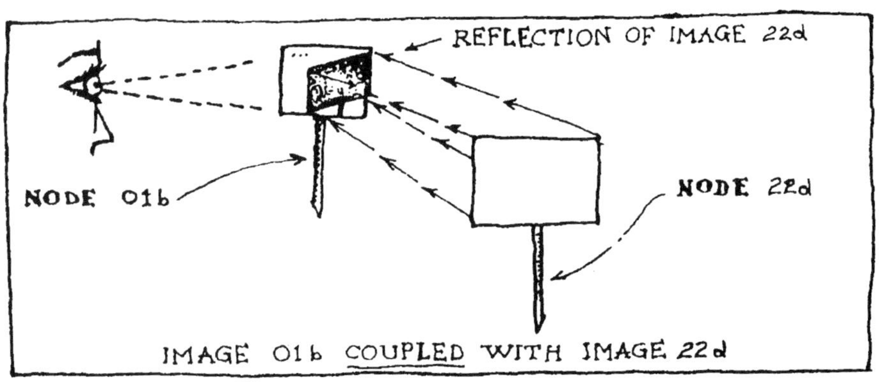

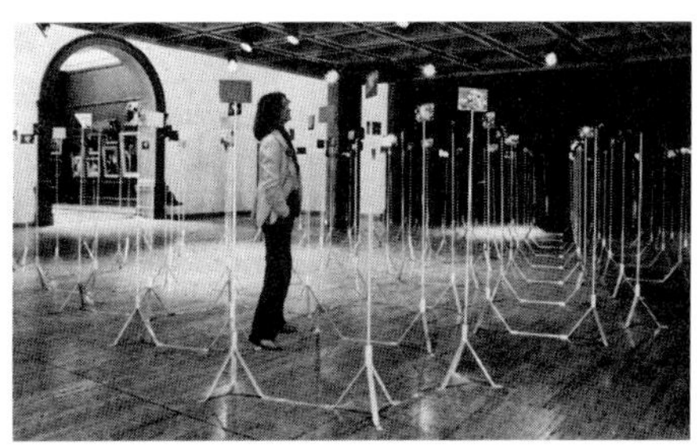

and walks around the 112 images. In the text accompanying the diagram Tillers describes *Conversations with the Bride* as:

> an installation on aluminium stands ... the relative position of adjoining images is determined by a disinterested arbitrariness. Furthermore, each image is part mirror to facilitate the 'coupling of moments' (Tillers 1978a: Table 9/1, §9.1)

By actively encouraging viewers to wander around the 'image matrix' in a condition of 'disinterested arbitrariness' Tillers creates a radical involvement of the spectator with the work to the extent that it is the *viewer's* coupling of images that gives rise to the maximalist, negentropic-like effect so crucial to this work. This reading is reinforced by the fact that Tillers notes that: 'coupling enables any of the 112 images to be linked to any other' (Tillers 1978a: 5/1 §5.1). The idea that 'coupling enables any of the 112 images to be linked to any other' suggests a holistic-like interrelationship between the images wherein they are considered as a single entity. One can compare this to the way in which Tillers interrelated all the objects making up *Moments of Inertia: Still Life 2* via his image structure which effectively meant that each object reflected the whole and vice versa. Tillers' use of mirrors in *Conversations with the Bride* seems to perform a similar role, an interpretation supported by panel 24d, reproduced below, which provides a correspondence between the substantive and sustained specular poetics evident in *Conversations with the Bride* and the seminal specular poetics apparent in *Moments of Inertia: Still Life 2*. In panel 24d the entire 'image matrix' of 112 images on their stands is shown embedded in one of the 112 images. In 1973 Tillers referred to this process in his theoretical text 'The Beginner's Guide to Oil Painting' as 'a dilemma known in philosophy as logical regression' (Tillers 1973a: Appendix A 25). Tillers' rhetoric of *mise*

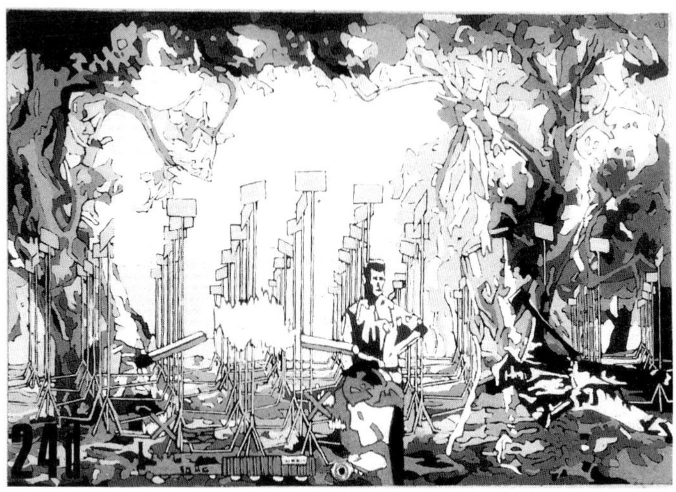

Image 24d from *Conversations with the Bride*, 1974–75. Gouache and Resene Imperite acrylic-epoxy on chrome plated aluminium with mirrored back, 8.5 x 11.8 cm. Collection: Art Gallery of New South Wales, Sydney.

en abyme in panel 24d is closely related to his statement that 'coupling enables any of the 112 images to be linked to any other' (Tillers 1978a, 5/1 §5.1). All the images in *Conversations with the Bride* are metaphorically reflected in 24d which in turn suggests that any of the 112 images reflects all the images.

There is an affinity between specularity and the *mise en abyme*, as is evident in the title of Lucien Dällenbach's *Le récit speculaire: essai sur la mise en abyme* (*The Specular Narrative: Essay on the Mise en Abyme*). In Chapter Three it was noted that Craig Owens used Dällenbach's analysis of the specular *mise en abyme* as a foundation for an innovative poststructuralist theory of visual culture. It is also noteworthy that Rosalind Krauss' pioneering poststructuralist interpretation of Cindy Sherman (Krauss 1984a) used the metaphor of a 'hall of mirrors', a metaphor that has obvious applicability to the mirrored images making up *Conversations with the Bride*. Owens' use of the term *mise en abyme,* however, came in the late 1970s and Krauss' analysis of Sherman first appeared in the early 1980s. Accordingly, one must be wary of anachronistic interpretations of *Conversations with the Bride*. On the other hand, it is not anachronistic to note that at the time he was creating this work Tillers' understanding of the ramifications of his specular metaphor had attained a high level of sophistication. The examination of 'The Beginner's Guide to Oil Painting' in Chapter Five showed that the primary basis of Tillers' theoretical sophistication stemmed from his understanding of science and the language of science, mathematics. This continues to be the case in *Conversations with the Bride* and *Untitled*, 1978.

One instance is indicated by the fact that Tillers' specular rhetoric is intimately related to the technique of isomorphic mapping which he originally articulated in *Moments of Inertia*. In his artist's book *A Companion to Conversations with the Bride* (Tillers 1978a) Tillers provided a table showing how he transposed the technique of isomorphic mapping developed in *Moments of Inertia* onto the imagery used in *Conversations with the Bride*:

(a) Woodsmen = (Priests of Nemi) = Bachelors
(b) Their Tree = (Diana) = Bride
and
(a) 'Summer' 1909 = (Diana's Mirror) = Bride's Domain
(Tillers 1978a: Table No. 6/1)

In these isomorphic chains Tillers designates the process of mapping with equals signs; but, in mathematics, the process of mapping is symbolised by an arrow sign '→'. Nonetheless, an association between Tillers' use of equals signs and the symbols for mathematical mapping is graphically por-

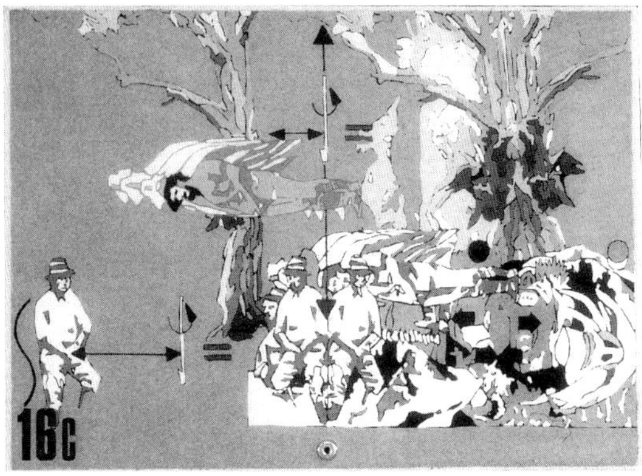

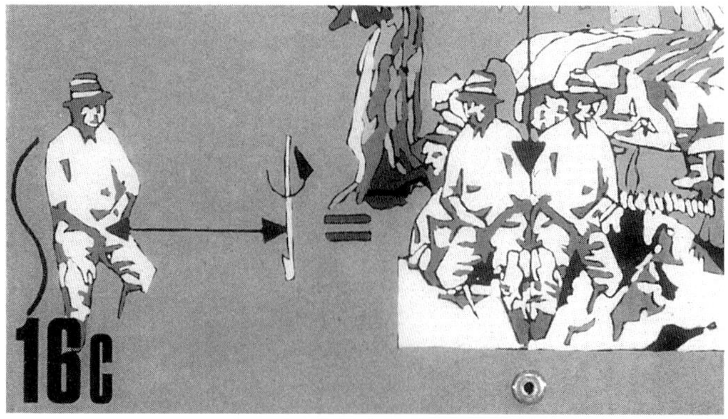

LEFT: Panel 16c from *Conversations with the Bride*, 1974–75. Gouache and Resene Imperite acrylic-epoxy on chrome plated aluminium with mirrored backs mounted on aluminium stands. Image size 8.5 x 11.8 cm. RIGHT: detail of 16c.

trayed in panel 16c from *Conversations with the Bride* which consists of parts of Heysen's *Summer* together with hatted male figures. The panel is reproduced top left. The image also contains a number of arrows and equals signs. The male figures are the 'woodsmen' referred to by Tillers in *A Companion to Conversations with the Bride* in his equation: '(a) Woodsmen = (Priests of Nemi) = Bachelors'. The detail of 16c, above right, focuses on Tillers' use of arrows and equals signs in conjunction with the woodsmen. In this context the arrows are used as symbols for 'mapping'. Tillers' use of the equals signs in conjunction with the arrows may be due to the realisation that an art audience might not be aware of the mathematical significance of the arrow symbols.[49] Strictly speaking mapping has nothing to do with the equals sign as mapping results in transformational, not identical, configurations. Yet, as Douglas Hofstadter notes, isomorphic mapping is an 'information-preserving transformation' (Hofstadter 1980: 8), and in this sense there is a degree of equivalence.

One of the simplest examples of such an information preserving transformation is that of mirror reflection. Significantly, as has been noted, this classic instance of isomorphic mapping plays a large role in *Conversations with the Bride*, and Tillers points to this graphically in the detail of panel 16c shown top right. The detail shows a mirror reflected version of the 'Woodsmen' bisected by an arrow. In conjoining the arrow symbol with the mirror inversion Tillers makes it apparent that, in the context of *Conversations with the Bride*, there is a direct correspondence between the technique of isomorphic mapping and the specular rhetoric that is so pervasive in *Conversations with the Bride*.

Tillers' translation of the mathematical process of isomorphic mapping into a specular visual rhetoric first emerged in *Moments of Inertia*, and is especially apparent in his self-reflexive image structure. In the analysis of *Moments of Inertia* in Chapter Six it was noted that Tillers focused on the mathematical process of isomorphic mapping because it provided a powerful means for 'information processing'. His interconnection of specularity and information processing is taken to a significantly more sophisticated level of articulation in *Conversations with the Bride.* In particular, his more intensive development of isomorphic mapping into a specular rhetoric is used to process 'readymade' 'art information'.

In retrospect this can be seen to be an extremely important development in Tillers' oeuvre as he became able to follow the path he delineated in 'The Beginner's Guide to Oil Painting' when he celebrates the fact that Haacke, Oppenheim, Huebler, and Barry all selected readymade systems that were able to, more or less, 'organise themselves' (Tillers 1973a: Appendix A 23-25).

In short, in *Conversations with the Bride* Tillers invented a method of processing already extant art information in a manner that is, paradoxically, highly original. Moreover, in spite of the fact that *Conversations with the Bride* is a tribute to Duchamp, Tillers' approach in this work is not simply a variation on the Duchampian 'readymade'. The readymade art information is not left as it was but is instead subjected to 'information processing' with the aim of generating negentropy. This aspect of *Conversations with the Bride* can be traced back to the subsection entitled 'Art as Information Processing' in 'The Beginner's Guide to Oil Painting'. There Tillers refers to the American conceptual artist Joseph Kosuth's definition of art's function as: 'being to increase the complexity of the concept of art … i.e. the function of art is to increase the creativity of art' (Tillers 1973a: Appendix A 28). As was noted in the analysis of 'The Beginner's Guide to Oil Painting' in Chapter Five this not only relates directly to Tillers' analogy between negentropy and creativity but also to the ecological and ecopolitical dimension of his holistic systems aesthetic that stems from his contact with the design theory of Ian McHarg. Interestingly, this correspondence is especially apparent in *Conversations with the Bride* in the 'woodsmen' Tillers inserted into Heysen's *Summer*, as will be examined later in this chapter.

If Tillers were simply copying the work of others then he could be accused of provincialist mimicry, but his extension of his technique of isomorphic mapping into a poetics of specularity indicates that his authorial appropriation is more accurately described as a transformational processing of readymade art information. In addition, when one connects *Conversations with the Bride* with the theory and practice informing 'The Beginner's Guide to Oil Painting' and *Moments of Inertia* it becomes evident that Tillers' transformational processing is informed by sophisticated concepts of anti-anthropic and negentropic creativity. Moreover, in *Conversations with the Bride* such notions are interwoven with Tillers' intensive study of Duchamp's writings. In particular, it will be shown that his understanding that Duchamp's concern with the possible existence of a fourth spatial dimension was connected with his involvement in chance can be related to Tillers' notion that negentropy entails an 'improbable' and inexplicable holistic connectivity.

CONVERSATIONS WITH THE FOURTH DIMENSION

In Chapter One it was noted that 'The Beginner's Guide to Oil Painting' indicates that Tillers had a reasonable understanding of the Duchampian readymade.[50] Tillers' understanding of Duchamp's theory and practice became significantly more complex and fluent in *Conversations with the Bride*. On the one hand this arises out of his increased knowledge of Duchampian theory and practice. On the other hand it is also due to the ingenious ways in which he articulates this knowledge in *Conversations with the Bride*.

In order to understand *The Large Glass* Tillers studied the notes Duchamp produced in the course of preparing for and making this work. He accessed these via Arturo Schwarz's *Notes and Projects for the Large Glass* (Duchamp and Schwarz 1969). The extent of Tillers' study is evident in the two artist's books that accompany *Conversations with the Bride*: *A Companion to Conversations with the Bride* (Tillers 1978a) and *Rendezvous with Configuration P* (Tillers 1978b). In addition, Tillers wrote a text for a catalogue that accompanied the exhibition of *Conversations with the Bride* at the Bienal São Paulo in 1975 (Tillers 1975). All three texts exhibit a sophisticated understanding of Duchamp. On reading Duchamp's working notes for *The Large Glass* it became apparent to Tillers that it was influenced by the hypothesis—arising out of non-Euclidean geometry—that there could be a fourth spatial dimension. The possible existence of a fourth spatial dimension became popularised as early as the 1890s and the art historian Linda Dalrymple Henderson, in particular, has shown that published accounts of the fourth spatial dimension directed at the lay reader had a significant impact on a broad range of European avant-gardist art movements in the early twentieth century (Henderson 1983).

A diagram from Claude Bragdon's *A Primer of Higher Space* reproduced in *A Companion to Conversations with the Bride*. (Tillers 1978a: Table 3/1, § 3.1).

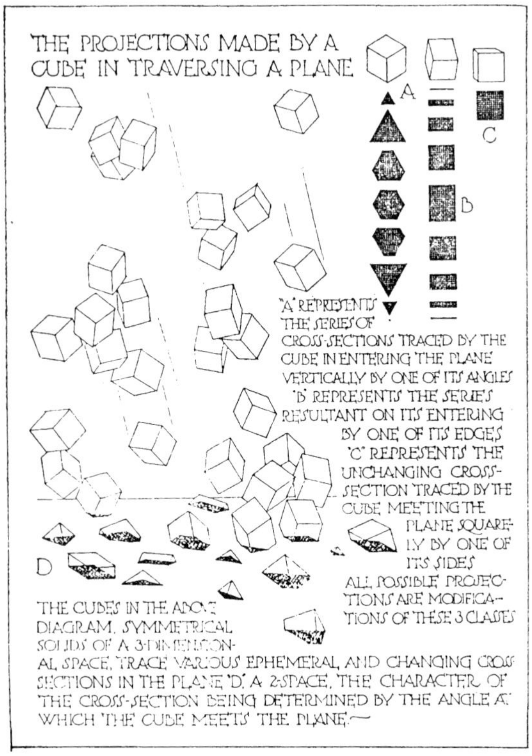

THE TWO-DIMENSIONAL ANALOGY

In her examination of the impact of the notion of a fourth spatial dimension on avant-gardist early twentieth century art, Henderson uses the term 'two-dimensional analogy' to label the standard model for describing how a four-dimensional object might appear to our three-dimensional minds (Henderson 1983: 18, 452). Although the two-dimensional analogy was originally developed in the mid nineteenth century it is still used in explanations of non-Euclidean geometry.[51] Duchamp uses the two-dimensional analogy in his notes for *The Large Glass*, but his notes are riddled with abbreviations and are consequently somewhat obscure. Fortunately, Tillers provides a more accessible exposition, taken from Claude Bragdon's book *A Primer of Higher Space* (Bragdon 1923). In *A Companion to Conversations with the Bride* (Tillers 1978a) Tillers reproduces the diagram from Bragdon's book (Tillers 1978a: Table No. 3/1, § 3.1) which is illustrated left. The basis of the two-dimensional analogy is that one imagines a two-dimensional world inhabited by two-dimensional sentient beings. Then one imagines that this flat world is intersected by three-dimensional objects. Bragdon's diagram shows how cubes might appear when they intersected such a two-dimensional world. In *A Companion to Conversations with the Bride* Tillers quotes Bragdon's explanation of the diagram:

> Consider a world which has only 2 dimensions; whose objects and inhabitants have area but not volume. This world is not entirely without thickness but exists as a thin membrane, like a film of oil on water. It exists concurrently with events in our everyday world and occasionally 3-dimensional objects penetrate and pass through the membrane. To an inhabitant of the membrane this is an unaccountable event.
>
> The object appears mysteriously as a point, line or plane on its orientation at the moment of entry and it appears to develop or grow as its successive cross-sections are traced by the film. Its subsequent and inevitable exit is equally mysterious. (in Tillers 1978a: §3.2)

In the context of an analysis of Tillers, the most important point in this passage is that the three-dimensional object appears as 'successive cross-sections' which, as Bragdon's diagram shows, are different in shape. The last point is significant as it suggests that the two-dimensional consciousness can never grasp the three-dimensional object as whole, but only as a series of apparently unconnected 'cross-sections'. Yet these cross-sections are interconnected as a coherent entity in an invisible 'higher dimension'.

Like Bragdon, Duchamp makes use of the two-dimensional analogy. In the first passage from Duchamp's notes[52] quoted by Tillers, Duchamp illustrates the intersection of the four-dimensional object with the third-dimension:

> by analogy with the method by which architects depict the plan of each story of a house, a 4-dim'l figure can be represented (in each one of its stories) by three-dimensional sections. These different stories will be bound to one another, by the 4th dim. (in Tillers 1978a: 1/3)

Duchamp's analogy with the layers of an architect's plan parallels Bragdon's observation that the 'successive cross-sections' of a four-dimensional object 'are traced by the film' which is the two-dimensional world. Accordingly, it is possible that Duchamp chose glass as a support, which is rare in the history of European art, due to his awareness of the two-dimensional analogy. The transparency of glass certainly provides one of the closest material analogies to absolute two-dimensionality available in our ineluctably three-dimensional universe.

At least this aspect of *The Large Glass* appears to have encouraged Tillers in his use of mirror devices in *Conversations with the Bride*. The link between the transparency of Duchamp's glass support and use of mirror inversion by Tillers in *Conversations with the Bride* is quite direct because *The Large Glass* is not hung on a wall but is exhibited free-standing, like a sculpture, thereby allowing the viewer to see it from both sides in a manner similar to the way one can view a photographic transparency. This unusual viewing method can be compared with Tillers' equally unusual 'image matrix' which invites the viewer to enter a maze of image-mirrors. The parallel is reinforced in one of the quotations from Duchamp's notes cited by Tillers in *A Companion to Conversations with the Bride.* In the passage Tillers quotes Duchamp noting that as the four-dimensional object intersects our three-dimensional world via 'an ∞ of 3-dim'l sides … one can move around the 4 dim'l figure' (Tillers 1978a: Table No. 1/3).

The Large Glass can also be compared with the transparency of photographic film, be it negative or positive (as in cinematographic film). Importantly, in the context of photo-conceptual art, this observation has direct parallels with comments in Duchamp's notes on *The Large Glass* quoted by Tillers in a catalogue essay that accompanied the exhibition of *Conversations with the Bride* at the Bienal São Paulo (Tillers 1975). In the essay Tillers refers to Duchamp's references to 'waiting for "the moment to come" at which "to inscribe a readymade"' (Tillers 1975: col. 4), 'film phenomena' (Tillers 1975: col. 1) and the 'snap-shot' (Tillers 1975: col. 3).[53] Tillers also provided similar references to Duchamp in *A Companion to Conversations with the Bride* (Tillers 1978a).

CONVERSATIONS WITH THE BRIDE AND *THE LARGE GLASS*

Apart from his juxtaposition of appropriations from *Summer* and *The Large Glass*, and his use of the 'coupling' effect of mirrors it is possible that the transparent ground for *The Large Glass* also contributed to Tillers' conflation of *Summer* and *The Large Glass*. The evidence for this is not contemporary with *Conversations with the Bride* but appears six years later in Tillers' most substantial artist's book to date *Three Facts*, published in 1981 (Tillers 1981a). In *Three Facts* Tillers provides two reproductions of *Summer* the first of which is oriented as in the original Heysen, and a second which is mirror-inverted. Tillers' use of these two photomechanical reproductions of *Summer* is executed in a manner that suggests a correspondence between Tillers' mirror inversion of Heysen's *Summer* in *Conversations with the Bride* and Duchamp's use of a transparent ground for *The Large Glass.* The two images of Heysen's *Summer* are reproduced below opposite as they appeared on the recto and verso of page 43 in Tillers' *Three Facts.* On page 43 Tillers reproduced Heysen's *Summer* in its correct orientation, but on the other side of the page he reproduced a mirror-inverted version of the same image perfectly aligned with that on page 43. The effect is as if the page were transparent. In fact, to fully appreciate this effect one has to hold the page up to a strong light thereby making the page translucent. Tillers also mirror inverts the text on page 43, including the page number and the caption which reads 'The Two Paintings'. The image, the page number and the caption are perfectly aligned on the other side of page 43. Thus instead of this page being designated '44' the other side of page 43 is designated Ɛ4 which is, interestingly, unpronounceable. Tillers treated the caption in the same way. Although this connection appears in a text published six years after the completion of *Conversations with the Bride* there is a direct parallel between the two texts apparent in panel 16c from *Conversations with the Bride* a detail of which is reproduced to the right of the illustration of pages 43 and Ɛ4 below. The figures of the woodsmen in the centre of 16c are mirror doubled in a similar manner to Tillers' doubled depiction of *Summer* in *Three Facts*.

THE ANTIPODES AS A COUNTER-RATIONAL PARALLEL WORLD

Tillers' notion of Heysen's *Summer* becoming 'The Two Paintings' in *Three Facts* can be discussed in the context of an idea that began to preoccupy Tillers' work from *Conversations with the Bride* onwards—the notion that the antipodes can be conceived mythopoetically as a counter-rational parallel world. Tillers alluded to this aspect of *Conversations with the Bride* in an interview with his partner in 1988, where he revealed that his use of mirrors in *Conversations with the Bride* was inspired by reading Jorge Luis Borges' short story 'Tlön, Uqbar, Orbis Tertius'. Tillers recounts:

> 'Tlön, Uqbar, Orbis Tertius' was of great importance to me then, as it expanded on the idea of a novel in the first person in which the narrator would omit or disfigure the facts and indulge in various contradictions which would permit a few readers to perceive, as Borges describes it, 'an atrocious or banal reality'. But *even more fascinating was the idea of a fantastic world (that of Tlön) intruding secretly into the world of reality and then subtly and irrevocably displacing the real.* [emphasis added] (Slatyer and Tillers 1988: 2)

LEFT: Hans Heysen's *Summer*, 1909, as reproduced on the recto and verso of page 43 in *Three Facts*, 1981. RIGHT: Detail of the centre of panel 16c from *Conversations with the Bride*, 1974–75.

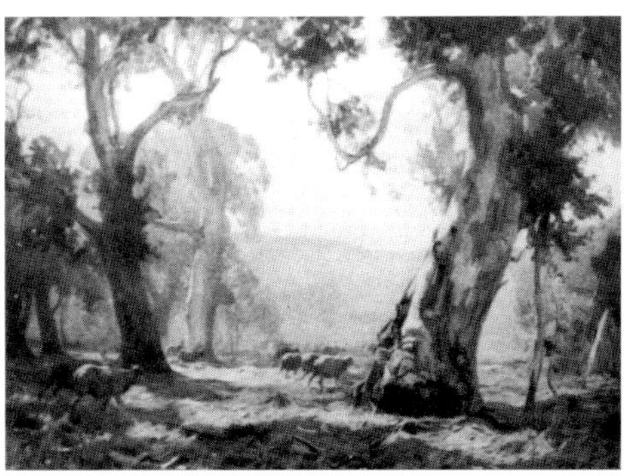

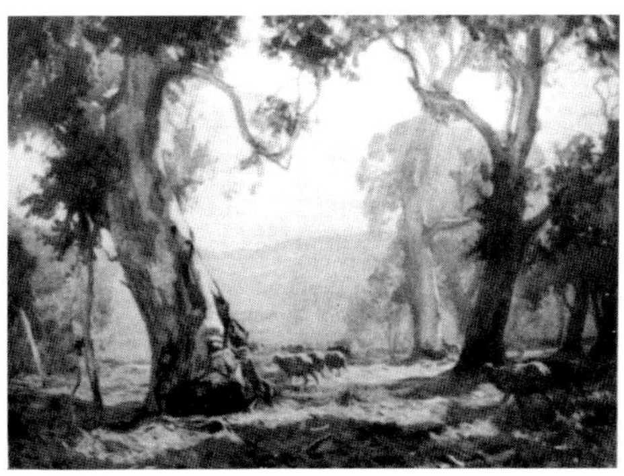

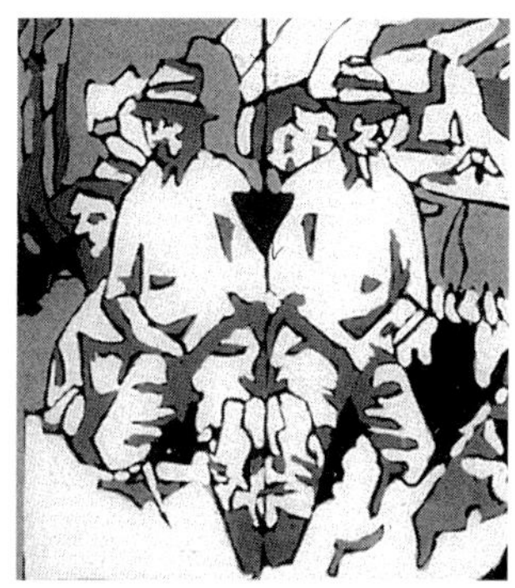

Tillers' revelation of his knowledge of 'Tlön' and his fascination with 'the idea of a fantastic world … intruding secretly into the world of reality and then subtly and irrevocably displacing the real', relates very closely to his Duchampian-inspired conception of the interpenetration of our third dimension by four-dimensional objects. If it exists, the fourth spatial dimension is a domain that lies beyond the grasp of what Tillers referred to in 'The Beginner's Guide to Oil Painting' as an 'anthropocentric world view' (Tillers 1973a: Appendix A 9). Tillers metaphorically projected *Summer* into this subversive parallel world in two stages. Firstly, his mirror inversion of *Summer* can be interpreted as metaphorically emphasising its 'antipodeanness'. Secondly, he creates an analogy between this antipodean mirror-world and the fourth spatial dimension using specularity to isomorphically conflate *Summer* with *The Large Glass*. Indeed, it can be argued that the projection of one dimension into another can itself be understood as an analogue of isomorphic mapping. Certainly, such a metaphorical expansion of scientific and mathematical principles typifies the approach evident in Tillers' theory and practice following 'The Beginner's Guide to Oil Painting'.

The 'transparent' version of *Summer* on pages 43-Ɛ4 in *Three Facts* is an instance where *Conversations with the Bride* can be seen as a precursor to *Untitled*, 1978, as *Three Facts* is primarily an account of, and elaboration on, the ideas and methods associated with *Untitled*. Tillers' fascination with Duchamp's involvement in the fourth dimension of space can also be traced back to 'The Beginner's Guide to Oil Painting'. The idea that the interconnectivity of four-dimensional objects remains beyond the conception and perception of three-dimensional human beings relates to the mystery inherent in Tillers' poetic equation of negentropy with creation and creativity in the absence of a creator. In 'The Beginner's Guide to Oil Painting' Tillers defines negentropy in terms of an 'improbable' interconnectivity that resonates with his description of the metaphysical interconnectivity of a four-dimensional object when he observes:

> entropy can be expressed as a measure of probability and so a closed system tends to a state of most probable distribution. For example in a box of green and yellow marbles, it is highly improbable that all green marbles and all yellow ones align themselves on the left and right sides respectively. In open systems, since there is a steady import of energy from the environment the operation of entropy is counteracted and the open system is characterised by negative entropy (negentropy) rather than positive entropy. Thus open systems tend to states of most improbable distribution i.e. states of increased order and organisation. (Tillers 1973a: Appendix A 13)

Tillers' definition of negentropy in terms of 'improbability' resonates strongly with the fact that his fascination with Duchamp's involvement in the theory of the fourth dimension was accompanied by his increasing attraction to Duchamp's concern with chance. Tillers makes direct reference to chance in *A Companion to Conversations with the Bride* when discussing the 'coupling' of images by the spectator walking inside *Conversations with the Bride*:

> The notion of 'coupled moments' results in a structure susceptible to chance or at least it allows acausal connections and unpredictable configurations to occur within a set of structured images tied to the unknown trajectories and observations of spectators. (Tillers 1978a: 9/1L, 9.1)

It is interesting to note that Tillers' use of the term 'acausal connections' in this passage from an artist's book produced in 1978 provides evidence of his awareness of quantum theory and what I will refer to in Chapter Nine as the 'Jung-Paulian' notion of an 'acausal connecting principle' that suggests that the incomprehensible interconnectivity between quantum phenomena might influence, interpenetrate, or map onto our material world. In the context of the present discussion the notion of acausal connectivity suggests that instead of understanding chance and coincidence as merely random it can be understood as evidence of a 'hidden order'. Tillers became very concerned with coincidence in the course of producing *Conversations with the Bride* and this concern has endured. Indeed, this facet of Tillers' theory and practice is substantial enough to provide another perspective onto Tillers' oeuvre that would complement the present analysis.

AN ECOPOLITICAL ALLEGORY

Tillers' use of specular rhetoric in *Conversations with the Bride* represents a successful expansion of the technique of isomorphic mapping in *Moments of Inertia: Still Life 2* in a manner that is complex yet elegant. It is also apparent that Tillers attempted to introduce a negentropic interaction between the repertoire of motifs that appears in his outline of isomorphic relationships between specific motifs apparent in Table No. 6/1 in *A Companion to Conversations with the Bride* reproduced below:

> (a) Woodsmen = (Priests of Nemi) = Bachelors
> (b) Their Tree = (Diana) = Bride
> and
> (a) 'Summer' 1909 = (Diana's Mirror) = Bride's Domain
> (Tillers 1978a: Table No. 6/1)

When one attempts to trace the references in Table No. 6/1, however, one is confronted with a labyrinthine complexity reminiscent of that evident in the second part of *Moments of Inertia: Still Life 1*. On the basis of this I would suggest that Tillers' attempt to create complex narrative layering via isomor-

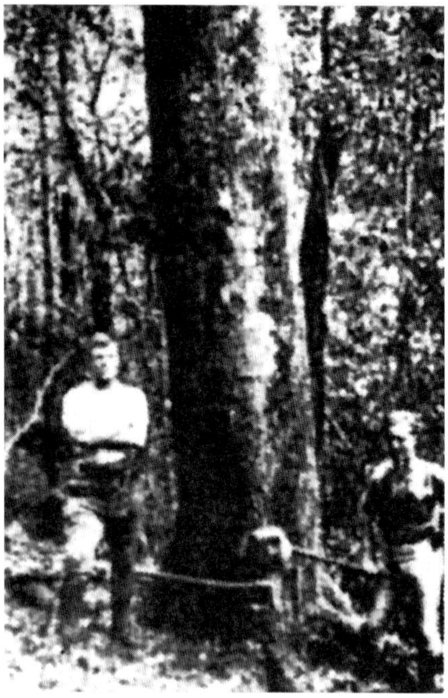

phic mapping is less successful than his specular poetics. Nevertheless, his seminal attempts to create negentropic interactions between elements of figurative imagery can be understood as laying a valuable foundation for his successful generation of a web of resonances between appropriated motifs in his Canvasboard System.

Table No. 6/1 in *A Companion to Conversations with the Bride* shows nine motifs or actants that stem from four sources. The actants and their sources are tabulated below:

'Summer', 1909	Hans Heysen's *Summer*, 1909
Priests of Nemi	James G. Frazer's *The Golden Bough*
Their Tree	James G. Frazer's *The Golden Bough*
Diana's Mirror	James G. Frazer's *The Golden Bough*
Bachelors	Marcel Duchamp's *The Large Glass*
Bride	Marcel Duchamp's *The Large Glass*
Bride's Domain	Marcel Duchamp's *The Large Glass*
Woodsmen	W.D. Francis' *Australian Rainforest Trees*

It is Tillers' introduction of motifs from James G. Frazer's *The Golden Bough* (Frazer 1994 [orig. 1890]) which lead to a degree of hypercomplexity that could be termed abstruse. Accordingly, the analysis here will not delve into this aspect of Table No. 6/1. However, it can be noted that the complex narrative that arises from tracing the meaning of Tillers' mapping of these sources onto each other is essentially an ecopolitical allegory. And this is epitomised in the motif of the 'woodsmen'.

TOP: Photograph from W. D. Francis' *Australian Rainforest Trees* (Francis 1970) reproduced from *Rendezvous with Configuration P* (Tillers 1978b). BOTTOM: Panel 05a from *Conversations with the Bride*, 1974-75. Gouache and Resene Imperite acrylic-epoxy on chrome plated aluminium with mirrored back, 8.5 x 11.8 cm

The first term in Table No. 6/1 '(a) Woodsmen …' symbolises the destruction of nature by Western culture. The image reproduced bottom left is 05a from *Conversations with the Bride*. It shows a woodsman standing in a mirror-inverted Heysen landscape holding an axe which is buried in a tree. The 'Woodsmen' motif occurs throughout *Conversations with the Bride* and in *A Companion to Conversations with the Bride* Tillers cites the source as W.D. Francis' *Australian Rainforest Trees* (Francis 1970.). But it is only in another artist's book, *Rendezvous with Configuration P* (Tillers 1978b) that Tillers reproduces a photograph from W. D. Francis' text which establishes the latter as the source for the 'woodsmen'. This photograph is reproduced top left and shows two woodsmen standing proudly by a large tree. Significantly their axes are visible, jutting out between them from a tree stump or root. It appears that this image was the source for the woodsmen-tree-axe(s) motif which Tillers inserted into many of the images in *Conversations with the Bride*. The Woodsmen have the effect of introducing the ecological core of Tillers' hidden allegory in *Conversations with the Bride*. This becomes apparent when the woodsmen-rainforest tree-axe(s)

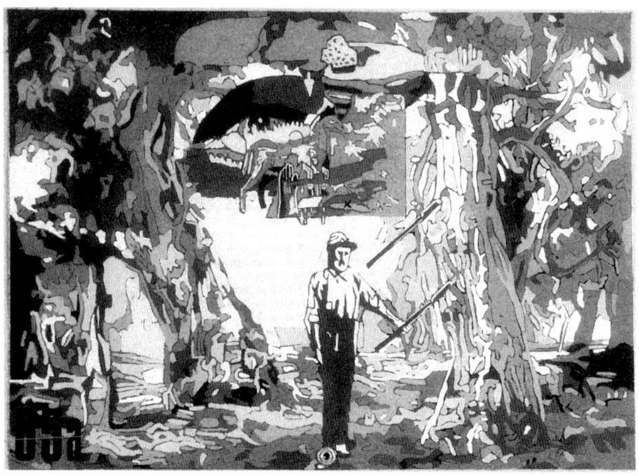

motif is considered in the context of Tillers' ecological stance promulgated in 'The Beginner's Guide to Oil Painting'. The following passages from that text make his position very clear:

> As a society our model of reality is one based on economics—the world is seen as a commodity, not as a series of interrelationships which incorporate physical and biological processes. We know how to exploit the seashore for profit, sterilise the landscape for profit, fell the great forests for profit, fill protective marshes for profit. (Tillers 1973a: Appendix A 9)

Tillers pursues this theme further mapping the Woodsmen onto the Priests of Nemi, Duchamp's Bride onto Frazer's version of Diana, and the tree in Heysen's *Summer* onto the tree associated with the Priests of Nemi. These analogies will not be examined here because the outcome of an analysis of these labyrinthine associations largely underscores the ecopolitical message outlined above. As was noted earlier Tillers' attempt to subject narrative elements to information processing in order to produce negentropic ('self-organising') complexity becomes much more adept in his Canvasboard System. Indeed it is worth speculating on whether he would have been so successful if he had not made an initial attempt in *Conversations with the Bride*. In the final analysis *Conversations with the Bride* is a remarkable work and a valuable contribution to the genre of photo-conceptual art due to Tillers' complex yet elegant and coherent articulation of specular devices, not least that of the *mise en abyme*. The following chapter will show that the specular rhetoric Tillers developed in *Conversations with the Bride* is an important feature informing an even more remarkable work, *Untitled*, 1978.

8

FROM PHOTO-CONCEPTUALISM TO APPROPRIATIONISM: *UNTITLED*, 1978

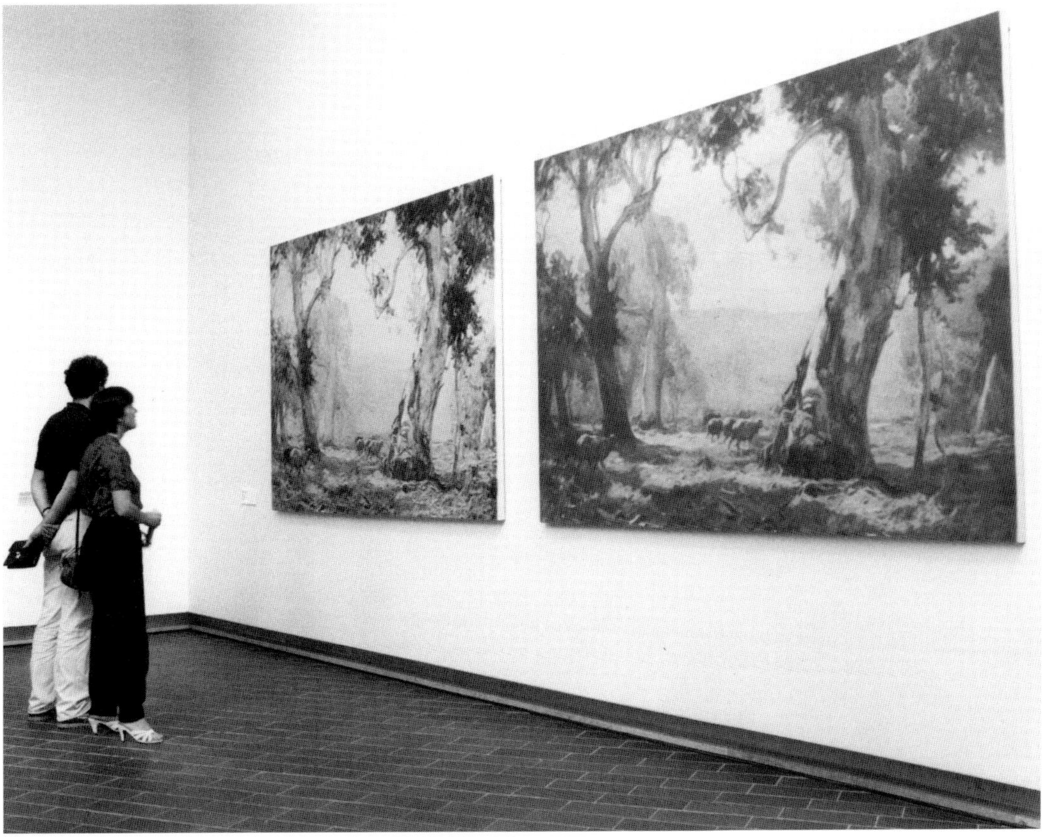

***Untitled*, 1978. Neco digital paint-jet print on canvas. Two parts each 163.9 x 185.5 cm. Collection: in National Gallery of Australia, Canberra, until lost or accidently destroyed.**

It is possible that *Untitled*, 1978, is the single most sophisticated work that Tillers has produced. It is elegant and all the more powerful due to its aesthetic economy. Essentially, it will be shown that in *Untitled*, 1978, Tillers successfully transposed his specular poetics onto the medium of photomechanical reproduction and the act of photomechanically mediated authorial appropriation. The result is an instance of proto-appropriationism comparable in its sophistication with the seminal appropriationist works produced in the late 1970s by major international figures such as Haacke, Burgin, Sherman, or Levine. Moreover, *Untitled*, 1978, increases in importance when it is acknowledged that it provided a substantial foundation for Tillers' Canvasboard System. The fact that Tillers was able to extend the elegance and sophistication of *Untitled*, 1978, into such a monumental project of deconstructive authorial appropriation, affords *Untitled*, 1978, a special place not only in Tillers' oeuvre but also in the history of late twentieth century avant-gardist art.

Two principal features of *Untitled*, 1978, make such an evaluation possible: firstly, it was produced by the Neco process; and, secondly, Tillers' use of authorial appropriation in this work was informed by an understanding of Kurt Gödel's Theorem, or Proof. As far as I am aware no other artists used the Neco process as early as 1978 or Gödel's Proof, let alone both. The closest parallels would be with Sherman's direct use of photography to reproduce photography in her Untitled Film Stills series which began around the time Tillers was working on *Untitled*, 1978, (neither was aware of the other), or Levine's use of photography to reproduce photography in her appropriations of 'master photographers' in 1981. The relationship of Tillers' work to Levine's is treated in Chapter Three.

In the same chapter it was noted that in her pioneering application of poststructuralist art theory to Sherman's Untitled Film Stills series Krauss observed that 'the images reproduce what is already a reproduction' (Krauss 1984a: 59); an observation that echoes Owens' essay on the *mise en abyme* where he cites a passage from Derrida that uses the phrase 'the representation of representation' (Owens 1978: 77). It was also pointed out that Krauss argued that this strategy led Sherman into the realm of authorial self-deconstruction. In this chapter it will be demonstrated that Tillers' understanding of Gödelian 'undecidability' played a crucial role in enabling him to realise that his photomechanical reproduction of a photomechanical reproduction led to an authorial 'undecidability'. It is especially interesting that Tillers arrived at this point along a very different path to that taken by the New York school of deconstructive appropriationism.

PAINTING AS PHOTOGRAPHY—THE NECO PROCESS

To produce *Untitled, 1978,* Tillers used the Japanese Neco process which in 1978 was at the forefront of industrial photomechanical technology. Tillers explains that Neco is:

> An advanced computerised process that can accurately transform any photographic image into pigment on canvas. Until recently the process has been used exclusively for fabricating large advertising photo-murals. (Tillers 1981a: 41)

Tillers contacted a company in Perth, Western Australia, which used this new technology and sent two colour photographic transparencies taken from two different reproductions of Heysen's *Summer*. There was a noticeable, distinction between the two reproductions owing to variations in their colour casts (see page 4). In the Neco process the photographic transparencies were scanned by a device which converted the images into digital information that was fed into a computer controlling a precision, industrial paint-jet device that produced a large scale, full colour photomechanical reproduction. As Tillers observes in the passage quoted above: 'the process has been used exclusively for fabricating large advertising photo-murals', however, on this occasion it was used to make a conventional painting consisting of paint on a stretched canvas. Tillers' use of canvas makes the work redolent with 'fine art' connotations which are reinforced by the fact that the apparatus uses 'paint'. The only thing missing is the quality of brushwork—the 'signature' of the artist's individual style of handling paint.

It is apparent that Tillers was very aware of the paradoxical ramifications involved in the process of making a photomechanical reproduction of a photomechanical reproduction that consisted of paint on canvas, as is evident in the following statement in *Three Facts*:

> With this ingenious *Japanese* process, it was possible for Tillers to produce his own version of *'Summer'* which, when reproduced, was *indistinguishable* from the reproduction of Heysen's original. Thus *any* reproduction of '*Summer*' could be a reproduction of both Heysen's original and Tillers' version of it. (Tillers 1981a: 38, §2.5)

Tillers is making an important point in this passage. He is not suggesting that the two large canvases that constituted *Untitled*, 1978, are identical to Heysen's original. He is pointing out that *when reproduced, Untitled*, 1978, is indistinguishable from a *reproduction* of Heysen's original. It has been noted that *Untitled*, 1978, is a photomechanical reproduction of a photomechanical reproduction. Tillers' acute observation in the above passage points to the fact that when reproduced *Untitled*, 1978, falls even further into the *mise en abyme* becoming a photomechanical reproduction of a photomechanical reproduction of a photomechanical reproduction.

It will be argued that Tillers' awareness of the paradox inherent in the *mise en abyme*-like process of making a photomechanical reproduction of a photomechanical reproduction and the ramifications of this for traditional concepts of authorship was based on a theoretical framework that possesses a degree of sophistication comparable with the application of poststructuralist theory in the texts by Owens and Krauss mentioned earlier.

GÖDEL'S THEOREM AND AUTHORIAL DECONSTRUCTION

Untitled, 1978, is informed by Tillers' understanding and artistic interpretation of Kurt Gödel's Incompleteness Theorem. In the context of mathematics a 'theorem' is not a theory but a proof. The importance of Gödel's Theorem, or Proof, is apparent in histories of mathematics, thus in *A History of Mathematics* Carl Boyer notes that 'Gödel's Theorem, is 'sometimes regarded as the most decisive result in mathematical logic' (Boyer 1968: 656). In a more recent history of mathematics Roger Cooke is even more emphatic asserting: 'The most influential figure in mathematical logic during the twentieth century was Kurt Gödel (1906-1978).' (Cooke 1997: 444).

Gödel is also interesting because his Incompleteness Theorem had an impact upon the New French Theory that underpins the poststructuralist theory of art which emerged in the late 1970s and 1980s. The status of Gödel is evident in the fact that in their critique of the use of scientific and mathematical theory by French philosophers Alan Sokal and Jean Bricmont dedicate an entire chapter to the alleged abuses of Gödel's Theorem by contemporary French intellectuals (Sokal and Bricmont 1998). They argue that the French philosophers who referred to Gödel's Theorem lacked sufficient training in mathematics to fully appreciate its intricacies. But Sokal and Bricmont are theoretical physicists, and it could be argued that they may be equally unable to fully understand the intricacies and ramifications of the discourses of philosophy, Lacanian psychoanalysis, and cultural theory which they so confidently critique. The French intellectuals Sokal and Bricmont attack were most probably attracted to Gödel's Theorem due to perceived resonances with their philosophical and metaphorical frames of reference rather than by a desire to embark upon rigorous mathematical practice.

Tillers was trained in mathematics and was able to grasp the essentials of Gödel's Theorem. Nevertheless, his *application* of Gödel's Theorem undergoes necessary processes of poetic and artistic interpretation. In consequence, the focus of critical attention in this analysis is on the elegance of Tillers' poetic transposition of a scientific theory into artistic practice. Indeed, it could be argued that Tillers interprets Gödel in a manner comparable to Duchamp's interpretation of the non-Euclidean hypothesis concerning the existence of a fourth spatial dimension.

It is also the case that Sokal and Bricmont's chapter on the 'misuse' of Gödel's Theorem by Julia Kristeva, Paul Virilio, Régis Debray, Michel Serres, and Alain Badiou serves to indicate that Tillers' involvement in Gödel's Theorem is not simply an isolated idiosyncratic instance but can be compared instead with the impact of Gödel's Theorem on a substantial contemporary intellectual discourse. Moreover, this discourse has had a major impact on contemporary art theory. Indeed, this analysis of Tillers' poetic translation of Gödel's Theorem into artistic practice elicits interesting parallels with Owens and Krauss' pioneering applications of contemporary French theory in the field of art theory, examined in detail in Chapter Three.

TILLERS' INTRODUCTION TO GÖDEL'S THEOREM

Tillers encountered Gödel's Theorem while he was on a three month exchange as art lecturer at the South Australian School of Art, Adelaide.[54]

It was during this time that he was fortunate enough to meet Michael Scullion who at that time was a postgraduate candidate working on an innovative interdisciplinary thesis which involved understanding artistic representation using a framework based on Gödel's Theorem, which Scullion referred to, quite legitimately, as 'Gödel's Proof'. Tillers would have been drawn to Scullion due to the fact that a central feature of Gödel's Proof is his use of isomorphic mapping, the mathematical procedure that Tillers used as a foundation for his artistic methodology in *Moments of Inertia* and *Conversations with the Bride*.

At the end of April 1978 Tillers and Scullion were part of a South Australian School of Art excursion to a campsite near Brachina Gorge in the Flinders Ranges National Park in South Australia. In *Three Facts* Tillers notes: 'In the bus, *Gödel's Proof* was the somewhat unlikely subject of the conversation between Michael Scullion and Imants Tillers.' (Tillers 1981a: 11, §1.2). Tillers' account of his encounter with Scullion in *Three Facts* was not published until 1981 by which time appropriationism was beginning to burgeon into an international style. Accordingly it does not provide an entirely accurate record of Tillers' understanding and interpretation of Gödel's Proof at the time he formulated *Untitled*, 1978. Fortunately, Tillers' account of his introduction to Gödel's Theorem in *Three Facts* is based on an earlier version published shortly after Tillers and Scullion's trip in 1978 in the form of an article entitled 'Dialogue on False Mt. Hayward' published in *ZX* magazine (Scullion and Tillers 1978). This earlier text will be used in preference to the more elaborate account in *Three Facts*.

In 1978 Tillers was in a perfect position to assimilate Gödel's ideas into his increasingly sophisticated adaptation of isomorphic mapping to artistic practice. There are two reason for this: firstly, Gödel's Theorem is based on the application of isomorphic mapping; secondly, Tillers' poetic interpretation of isomorphic mapping apparent in his rhetoric of specularity and *mise en abyme* also possesses strong resonances with the role played by 'self-referentiality' in Gödel's Theorem. Writing on Gödel's Theorem the theoretical physicist and science writer Paul Davies notes that:

> Gödel's Theorem springs from a constellation of paradoxes that surround the subject of self-reference. Consider as a simple introduction to this tangled topic the disconcerting sentence: 'This statement is a lie. If the statement is true, then it is false; and if it is false, then it is true'. (Davies 1992: 101)

The mathematician and theoretical physicist Douglas Hofstadter's Pulitzer Prize winning book *Gödel, Escher, Bach* (Hofstadter 1980) explains the revolutionary nature of Gödel's Proof in lay terms, highlighting the self-referentiality that Davies was to cite thirteen years later. Hofstadter recounts how

Bertrand Russell set out with Alfred North Whitehead to banish paradox from mathematical logic making the important point that 'There seems to be one common culprit in these paradoxes, namely self-reference … So if the goal is to ban all paradoxes, why not try banning self-reference and anything that allows it to arise?' (Hofstadter 1980: 21). Hofstadter describes *Principia Mathematica* as 'a mammoth exercise in exorcising [self-reference] from logic, set theory, and number theory' (Hofstadter 1980: 21).

This chapter will demonstrate that Tillers' understanding of Gödel's focus on self-referentiality, crystallised in the concept of 'undecidability', was a critical influence on *Untitled*, 1978, enabling Tillers to bring together notions of paradox, specularity, *mise en abyme*, photomechanical reproduction and authorial deconstruction. It is the fact that what appears to be at first sight a rather simple work actually maps onto such a sophisticated conceptual framework that makes *Untitled*, 1978, a remarkable work not only in the context of photo-conceptual art and appropriationism but in the context of avant-gardist art of the late twentieth century.

In 'Dialogue on False Mt. Hayward' Scullion provides Tillers with an accurate account of the essential components of Gödel's Theorem together with some speculative elaborations which were also beneficial to Tillers' theory and practice. He begins by telling Tillers that Gödel formulated the Theorem in the 1930s (in 1930 to be precise)[55] 'when people were trying to axiomatise mathematics, make it more machine-like' (Scullion and Tillers 1978: 7).[56] The 'people' Scullion is referring to are Russell and Whitehead and his reference to their making mathematics 'more machine-like' is echoed in Hofstadter's account that Russell and Whitehead used a 'rigid' hierarchy of 'types' of sets in set theory to banish the effect of self-reference. Hofstadter adds that *Principia Mathematica* eliminated paradox 'but only at the cost of introducing an artificial seeming hierarchy' (Hofstadter 1980: 21). Hofstadter's description is reinforced by Boyer's history of mathematics in which he refers to Russell and Whitehead's *Principia Mathematica* as 'a rigidly logical system' (Boyer 1968: 655).

Scullion goes on to introduce Tillers to the crucial notion of Gödelian 'undecidability', explaining that Gödel 'found some arithmetical propositions which were undecidable, they were both true and false … (undecidable)' (Scullion and Tillers 1978: 7). As Scullion notes Gödelian 'undecidability' refers to a genre of propositions which are highly paradoxical as they are 'both true and false'. Such paradox is anathema to classical logic, as is made clear when in the course of a discussion of Gödel's Theorem the theoretical physicist Paul Davies' makes the observation that Bertrand Russell asserted:

> the existence of … paradoxes strikes at the very heart of logic, and undermines any straightforward attempt to construct mathematics rigorously on a logical foundation. (in Davies 1992: 101)

Having noted the paradox inherent in Gödelian undecidability, Tillers asks Scullion the leading question '... how does MAPPING come into it?' (Scullion and Tillers 1978: 7). The question obviously stems from Tillers' own use of isomorphic mapping in *Moments of Inertia* and *Conversations with the Bride*. Scullion responds by informing Tillers 'that was how Gödel got his results'. Scullion elaborates:

> [Gödel] made a series of pictures, as it were, isomorphic resemblances between two categories, like these two hands—whatever one did was matched by the other, until he got this double reflection, as it were, in his results. (Scullion and Tillers 1978: 7).

Scullion's two hands analogy has the advantage of reinforcing the relationship between Gödel's use of isomorphic mapping and Tillers' extensive use of a classic instance of isomorphic mapping, the mirror reflection. Indeed Scullions' two hands metaphor bears more than a passing resemblance to Tillers' specular rhetoric in the centre of panel 16c from *Conversations with the Bride* illustrated as a detail below left. In Chapter Seven this detail was compared with the perfectly aligned reproductions of Heysen's *Summer* on the recto and verso of page 43 in *Three Facts* (Tillers 1981a). This led to a doubling of *Summer* in which one version was mirror inverted, see below right. Tillers gave this doubled version the caption 'The Two Paintings' thereby underlining the reference to the doubling of *Summer* in *Untitled*, 1978. Indeed it is possible that in making *Untitled*, 1978, Tillers could have asked the Neco technicians to print one of the canvases with a mirror inversion. He did not, and in retrospect it is possible to appreciate that such an approach would have been too programmatic. Instead Tillers took a quantum leap, transposing his specular rhetoric into the domain of deconstructive authorial appropriation creating a work that was not only an 'undecidable' painting, but also one created by an 'undecidable' artist. This becomes evident when immediately after Scullion introduces the two hands analogy he adds that Gödel's 'results were suggestive of all sorts of things—Creation, the idea of self-as-founded-on-contradiction' Scullion is suddenly cut off and the following passage is inserted:

LEFT: Detail of panel 16c from *Conversations with the Bride*, 1974-75. CENTRE: Photograph of two hands to illustrate Michael Scullion's two hands analogy (Scullion and Tillers 1978: 7). RIGHT: Hans Heysen's *Summer*, 1909, as reproduced in *Three Facts* on the recto and verso of page 43 (Tillers 1981a: 43).

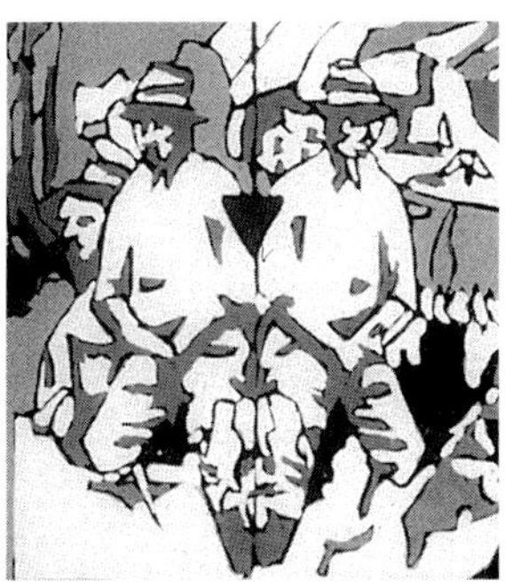

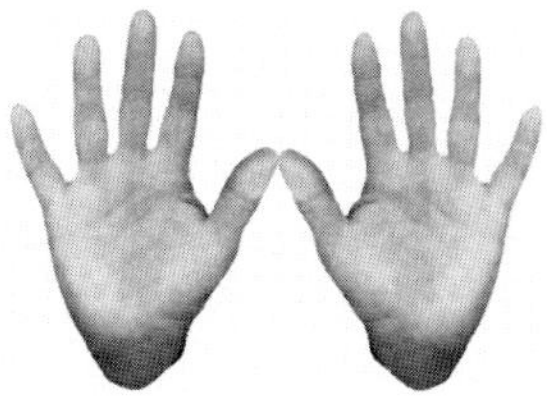

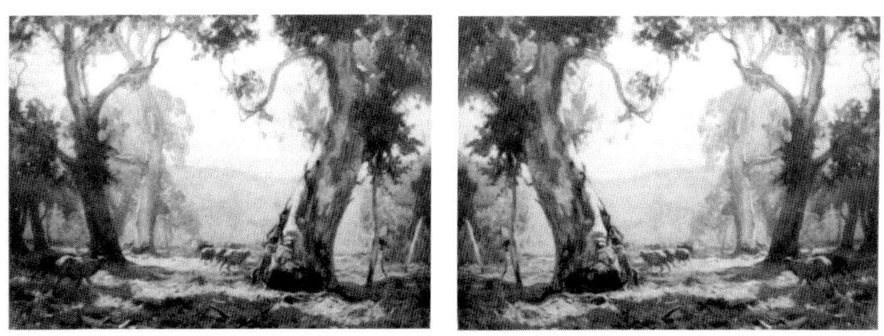

> At this point contingent circumstances intervene and IT and MS are spontaneously exchanged—IT is mapped onto MS and conversely MS is mapped onto IT. (Scullion and Tillers 1978: 7).

Obviously, 'IT' represents Imants Tillers and 'MS' Michael Scullion. Accordingly, Tillers is mapped onto Scullion and Scullion onto Tillers. This passage is crucial because it follows on immediately from Scullion's observation that Gödelian 'undecidability' implies notions such as 'self-as-founded-on-contradiction'.[57] But the correspondence between Gödelian 'undecidability' and the issue of identity does not end there. As the dialogue continues, Tillers tells the story of his walk along the mountainside, recounting that he came across a road with a sign stating, paradoxically, 'NO ROAD' (Scullion and Tillers 1978: 8). Tillers reports that he 'followed it instinctively, thinking that such a false sign must surely lead to a false place' (Scullion and Tillers 1978: 9). To which Scullion responds: 'Aha … the way to False Mount Hayward—you were Heysen bound' and Tillers replies 'Wholly Encompassed' (Scullion and Tillers 1978: 9).

What is remarkable about this passage is that it indicates that Scullion and Tillers were able to link ideas related to Gödelian undecidability with issues of authorial identity. When Scullion tells Tillers that he was 'Heysen bound' the inference is that not only was Tillers moving towards a mountain range that Heysen used to paint, but also that Tillers was bound up in Heysen, a connotation reinforced by Tillers' reply that he is 'Wholly Encompassed'. By suggesting that he has become wholly encompassed by Heysen, taken over by Heysen, Tillers underscores Scullions' suggestion that Gödelian 'undecidability' leads to 'the idea of self-as-founded-on-contradiction'. The appropriator becomes appropriated by his appropriation, an effect that will be shown to be increasingly apparent in Tillers' Canvasboard System.

But most importantly, Tillers was able to translate his and Scullion's 'dialogue' into artistic practice in *Untitled*, 1978. As was noted earlier, *Untitled*, 1978, is an extremely radical appropriation of another artist's work at a time when it was not generally recognised as an avant-gardist strategy. It can be compared with Sherrie Levine's photographic appropriations of 'master' photographers produced three years after *Untitled*, 1978, in 1981. The parallel with Levine is examined in more detail in Chapter Three where it is noted that apart from Levine there are few contemporaneous instances of the appropriation of fine art imagery that can challenge the deconstructive credentials of *Untitled*, 1978. This analysis would also suggest that *Untitled*, 1978, is such a substantial work that it provides, together with *Conversations with the Bride*, an extremely firm foundation for Tillers' massive project of authorially deconstructive appropriation that is his Canvasboard System.

It can also be noted that Tillers' articulation of Gödelian 'undecidability' in terms of authorial deconstruction in *Untitled*, 1978, can be traced back to his analysis of avant-gardist artists of the 1960s and early 1970s in 'The Beginner's Guide to Oil Painting'. As was noted in Chapter One, Tillers consistently focused on art that foregrounded systems over and above the artist-creator. He celebrated the fact that Haacke, Oppenheim, Huebler, and Barry all selected readymade systems that were able to, more or less, 'organise themselves' (Tillers 1973a: Appendix A 23-25).

In conclusion, *Untitled*, 1978, is a remarkably successful work because it is such an elegant translation of Gödelian 'undecidability' into artistic practice. As well as being 'an undecidable painting' it is also a work that can be metaphorically designated as having been produced by 'an undecidable artist'—a feature that becomes a valuable contribution to the poetics of authorial invisibility that begin to emerge in Tillers' work after *Untitled*, 1978.

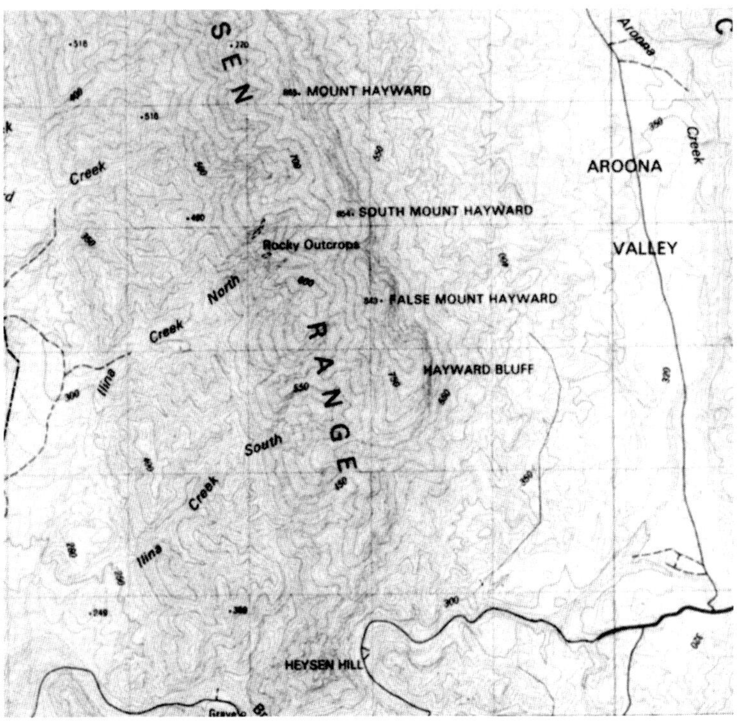

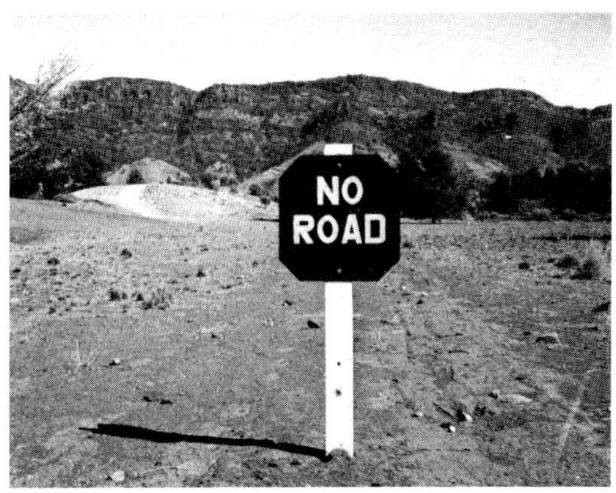

LEFT and RIGHT: Illustrations from *Three Facts* (Tillers 1981a: 27, 33).

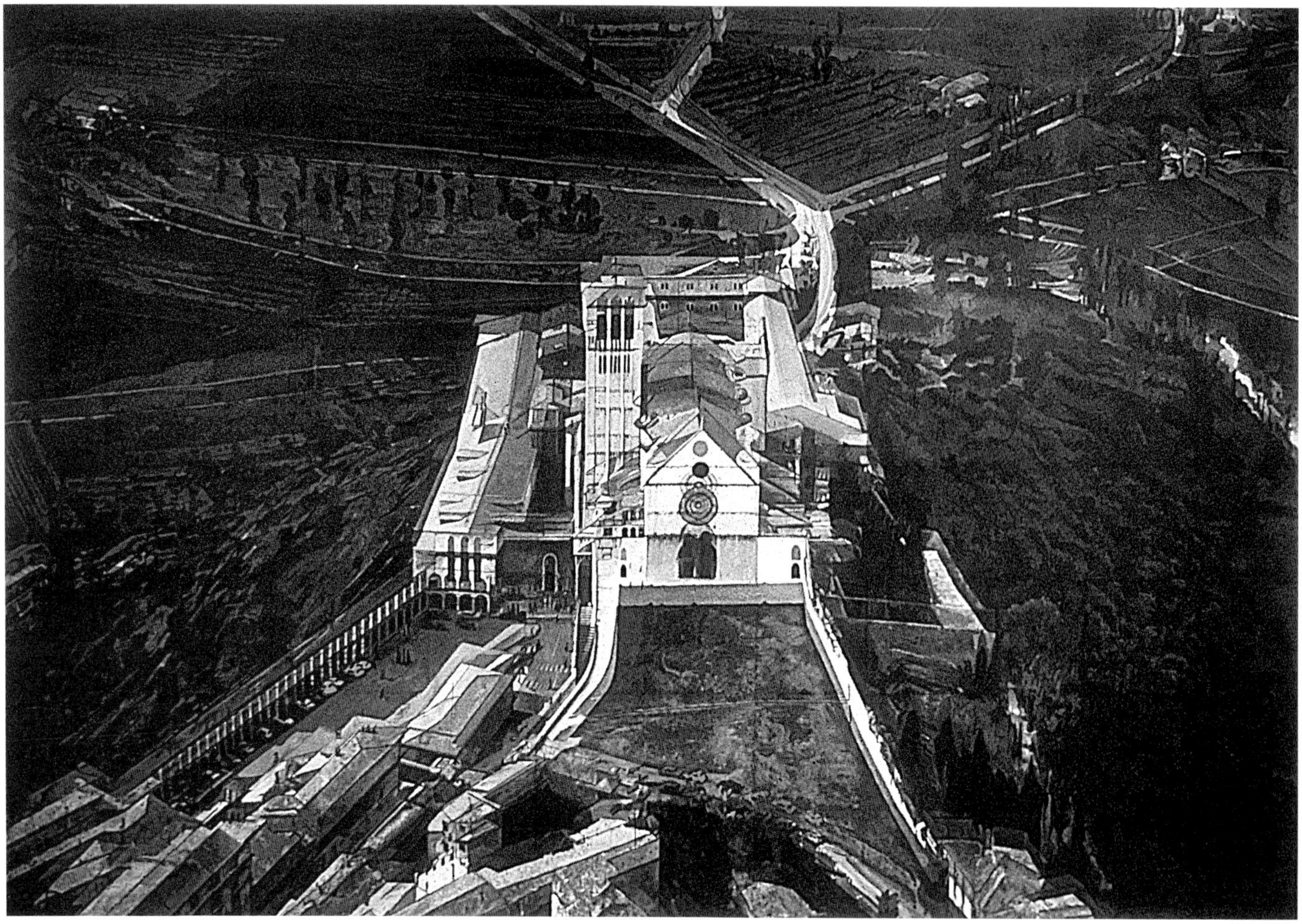

From *One Painting, Cleaving,* 1980–81. Synthetic polymer paint on canvas, 185.5 x 263.9 cm. Collection: National Gallery of Victoria, Melbourne.

9

TRANSITION: *ONE PAINTING, CLEAVING* AND TILLERS' POETICS OF INVISIBILITY

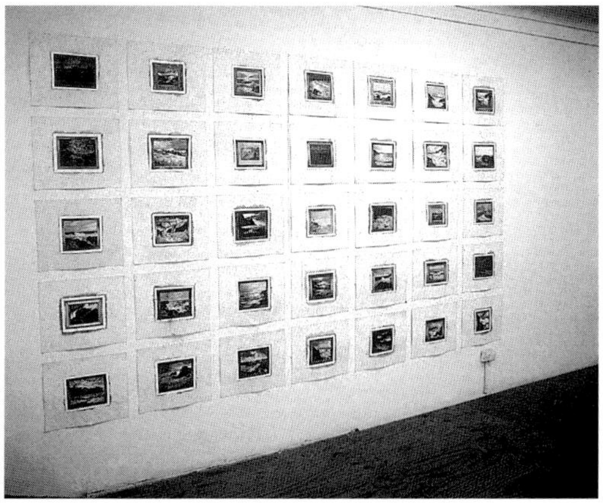

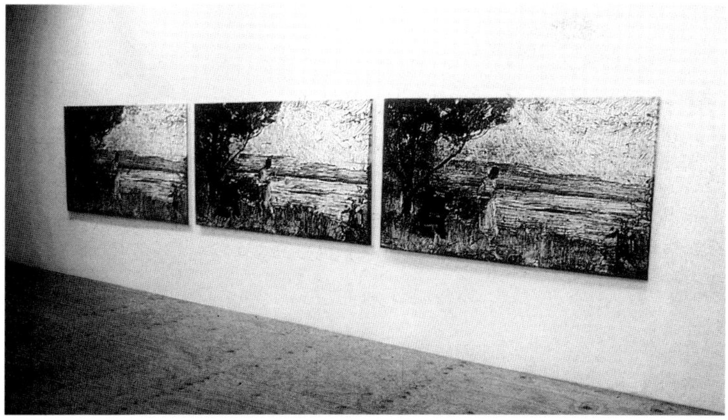

TOP LEFT: Detail of the painted component of *52 Displacements (Of Image, Of Time, Of Water, Of Feeling, One Year's Work)*, 1979–80. 52 parts gouache on canvas and 52 parts framed texts. Each canvas 34.4 x 42.5 cm; each framed text of varying dimensions. Various private and public collections. TOP RIGHT: *Four Impressions*, 1980. Each part synthetic polymer paint on canvas, 185.5 x 263.9 cm. Private Collection.

Untitled, 1978, was followed by several notable works: *52 Displacements (Of Image, Of Time, Of Water, Of Feeling, One Year's Work)*, 1979-80; *Four Impressions*, 1980, and *One Painting, Cleaving*, 1980-81. Of these three works *One Painting, Cleaving* appears to be the most significant in the sense of augmenting the poetics Tillers formulated in works such as *Conversations with the Bride* and *Untitled*, 1978. Accordingly, this chapter will focus on *One Painting, Cleaving* and refer to the other two works in the course of analysing that work. In addition, as in the case of *Moments of Inertia*, *Conversations with the Bride*, and *Untitled*, 1978, *One Painting, Cleaving* is accompanied by writings: 'Tom Roberts—Some Impressions' (Tillers 1981b) and '*One Painting, Cleaving:* Triangle of Doubt' (Tillers 1982b). These pertinent writings will also be examined in this chapter.

Tillers' original concept for *One Painting, Cleaving* was to produce one painting which would be simultaneously a number of paintings. He planned to achieve this by painting one painting over another leaving only the last painting visible. What distinguishes the strategy in *One Painting, Cleaving* is the fact that it entails a visual rhetoric based on invisibility. In this sense *One Painting, Cleaving* can be understood as a paradoxical painting in a manner that possesses poetic similarities with *Untitled*, 1978. The dada-like absurdity of this palimpsestic project is augmented by fact that the artist has to spend considerable time and effort creating works no-one will ever see—at least not without the aid of an x-ray device. What results is a perplexing metaphor that is difficult to decode unless placed in the context of works such as *Conversations with the Bride* and *Untitled*, 1978.

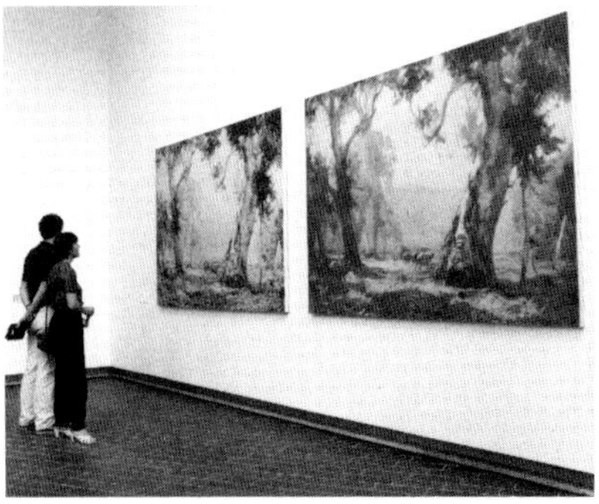

***Untitled*, 1978. Neco digital paint-jet print on canvas. Two parts each 163.9 x 185.5 cm. Collection: National Gallery of Australia until lost or accidentally destroyed.**

THE CLOVEN PAINTINGS

When it came to actually producing *One Painting, Cleaving* Tillers decided to modify the original concept. Instead of making one work with a number of invisible underlayers he decided to produce a series of paintings each of which consisted of one hidden underpainting covered by a surface image which would remain the same in a manner that echoes the seriality of *Untitled*, 1978. The relationship between the design of *One Painting, Cleaving* and *Untitled*, 1978, is very evident in an intervening work *Four Impressions*, 1980, reproduced top right on page 147.

In *Four Impressions* Tillers continued the approach taken in *Untitled*, 1978. On this occasion he used a reproduction of a work by the distinguished Australian landscape painter Tom Roberts and subjected it to the same Neco process used to produce *Untitled*, 1978. The fact that Tillers produced three versions instead of two, as in *Untitled*, is evidence of the continuing influence of minimalist seriality on Tillers' work. But due to its similarity with *Untitled*, 1978, *Four Impressions*, is less impressive, and it is Tillers' turn towards a poetics of invisibility in *One Painting, Cleaving* that produces a more substantial successor to *Untitled*, 1978. In addition, although *Four Impressions* has the distinction of relating to Tillers' essay 'Tom Roberts—Some Impressions' (Tillers 1981b) the analysis of this text will show that it is more valuable as a means of understanding the poetics of invisibility inherent in *One Painting, Cleaving*.

As far as I am aware *Four Impressions,* 1980, has never been hung in conjunction with *One Painting, Cleaving* in the manner shown below. Bottom left is *Four Impressions*, 1980; bottom centre, a digitally fabricated, but entirely possible, hanging of three panels from *One Painting, Cleaving*. What this 'digital hanging' shows is that the two works possess common features that point to the influence of *Untitled,* 1978. As in *Untitled*, an image expresses the process of photomechanical reproduction via its medium or via its source and is repeated in a manner akin to minimalist serialism.

The diagram shown to the right of the reproductions below shows that one of the crucial ways in which *One Painting, Cleaving* augmented the poetics of Gödelian 'undecidability' apparent in *Untitled*, 1978, and reiterated in *Four Impressions*, 1980 is that it quite simply added an additional dimension. Less

LEFT: *Four Impressions*, 1980. Each part synthetic polymer paint on canvas, 185.5 x 263.9 cm. Private collection. CENTRE: Three parts from *One Painting, Cleaving*, 1980–81. All parts synthetic polymer paint on canvas. Smaller parts, 132 x 193 cm. Larger part, 185.5 x 263.9 cm. Combination of parts digitally constructed. Various collections. RIGHT: Diagram of *One Painting, Cleaving* indicating the hidden image layer behind the surface image.

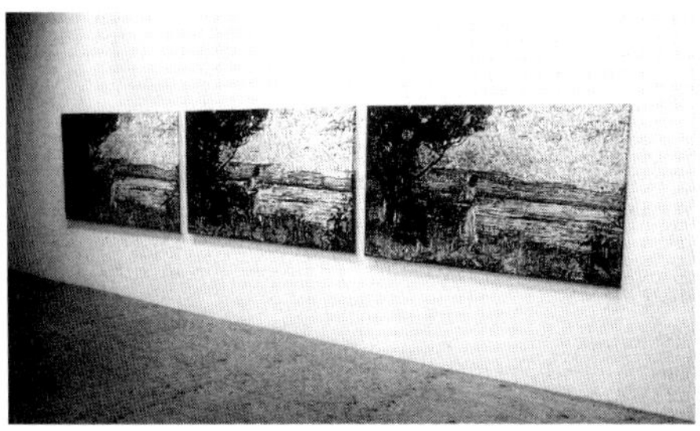

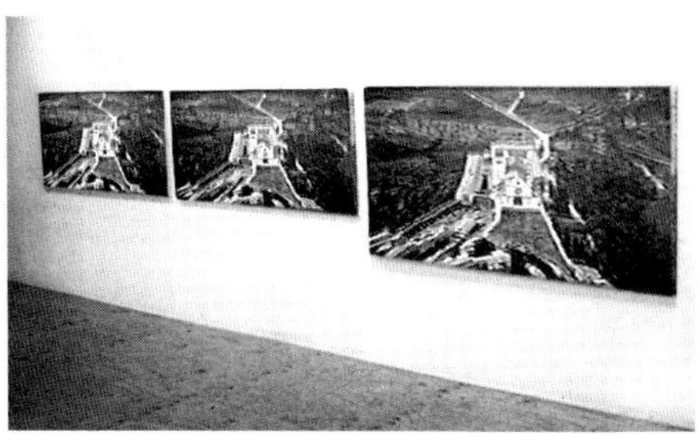

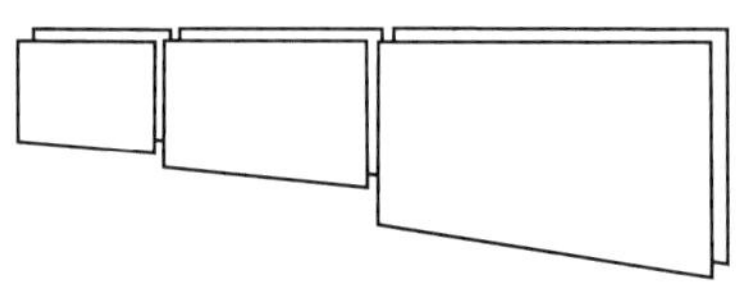

simply this dimension is invisible. An explanation for Tillers' strategy of invisibility is available in his essay 'Tom Roberts—Some Impressions' (Tillers 1981b) in which he reveals the continuing influence of Duchamp's concern with the invisible fourth spatial dimension that constitutes an important poetic theme in *Conversations with the Bride*. But it will also be shown that in his Tom Roberts essay Tillers elaborates his poetics of invisibility by conflating the metaphor of the fourth dimension with what he refers to as the 'paper-thin' quasi-immateriality of a photographic 'shadow-world'.

Photography and photomechanical reproduction are crucial features in the image Tillers chose to be the surface image for all the paintings making up *One Painting, Cleaving*. The single image that one sees when viewing the versions of *One Painting, Cleaving* is derived from a postcard image of the Basilica of St. Francis in Assisi in which the four process colours (cyan, yellow, magenta and black) used to photomechanically reproduce a photographic image are misregistered, creating a shaken or 'cloven' effect. It can also be noted that the fact Tillers decided to create a serial 'one painting' instead of a single work actually reinforces the cloven effect. Moreover this aspect of the work also anticipates the extreme seriality and deconstructionism of the Canvasboard System.

In 1990 Tillers recalled that he acquired the image when he purchased 'a postcard of the Basilica of St. Francis, bought at Assisi in April 1979' (Tillers 1990: 2). In 1982 he noted that the image was 'found to be "out of register."' and adds, 'This is not a local mirage. Nor is it bad luck.' (Tillers 1982b: n.p.). Tillers' use of the phrase 'local mirage' suggests a species of optical

From *One Painting, Cleaving*, 1980–81. Synthetic polymer paint on canvas, 185.5 x 263.9 cm. Collection: National Gallery of Victoria, Melbourne. Surface image derived from a misregistered colour postcard of the Basilica of St. Francis in Assisi.

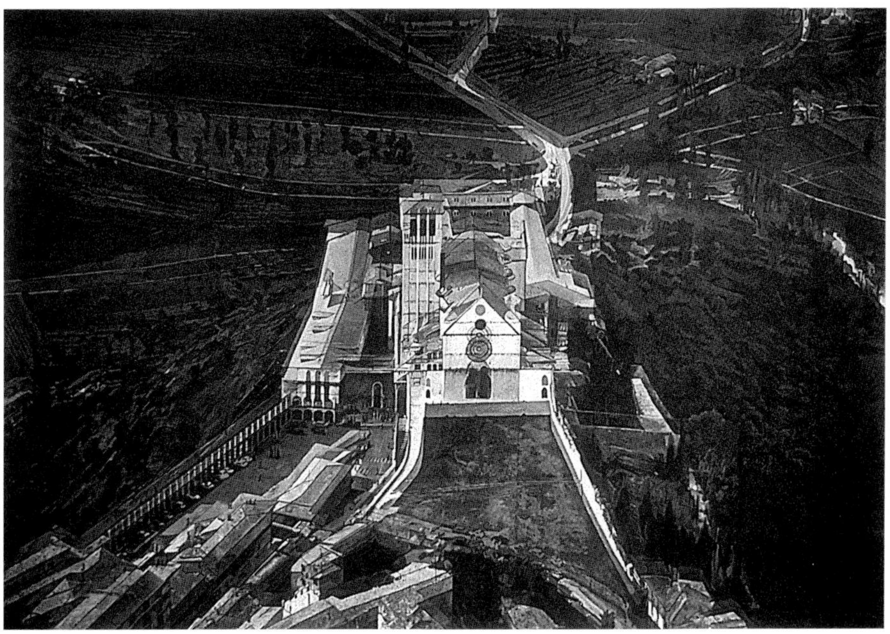

transformation in accord with his experiments with specular isomorphic mapping in *Conversations with the Bride* and *Untitled*, 1978. There is the implication that an image from one side of the globe appears distorted when seen on the other side—a notion that relates to Terry Smith's observation on the antipodean isolation in 'The Provincialism Problem' when he notes that 'distortions occur when works are seen only in reproduction' (Smith 1974: 55). This interpretation is reinforced by Tillers' discussion of the relationship between art and photomechanical reproduction in 'Tom Roberts—Some Impressions'. Tom Roberts is a major figure in the history of Australian landscape painting and Tillers begins his article with the following observation:

> Apart from several well-known paintings (such as *Bailed Up*), which are on permanent display in the Art Gallery of New South Wales, my experience of Tom Roberts's oeuvre has been entirely through reproductions in books and magazines. However, I do not consider this to be a deficiency. (Tillers 1981b: 272)

Tillers' phrase 'I do not consider this to be a deficiency' indicates that, as an artist, he sees no need for a direct contact with the original work of art. Such an attitude is not surprising when the early, yet enduring, influence of post-object art on Tillers is taken into account. It should also be noted that by this time Tillers would have read Suzi Gablik's article on Australian art in which she interprets *One Painting, Cleaving* making creative use of ideas taken from Benjamin's 'The Work of Art in the Age of Mechanical Reproduction' (Gablik 1981b, 1981a).[58] Gablik observed:

> If, as Walter Benjamin says, that which decays in the age of mechanical reproduction is the 'aura' of the work of art, then Tillers' effort must be seen as reclaiming for the mechanical reproduction a unique existence and endowing it with the 'aura' of the original. (Gablik 1981b: 37)

Tillers' contact with Gablik's essay would have provided him with greater confidence in the sophisticated poetic articulation of photomechanical reproduction he developed in *Untitled*, 1978. This is borne out by his speculations on art in the age of photomechanical reproduction in his Tom Roberts essay. There Tillers uses the ideas of the science fiction writer Isaac Asimov to suggest that photographic images can be understood as a species of parallel world. Tillers quotes Asimov: 'Before photography there was nothing. Before photography we lived in a world in which the passing moment died as it passed. Every bit of life was a flash that vanished as it appeared.' (in Tillers 1981b: 272). Tillers observes that 'according to Asimov, through photography the passing moment can be captured, the world stopped and thus corroborated' (Tillers 1981b: 272). This concept can be linked to Tillers' poetic exegesis of Duchamp's notes for *The Large Glass* in *A Companion to Conversations with the Bride* where he cites Duchamp describing Readymades as 'delays' and in terms of a 'snapshot effect' (in Tillers 1978a: § 4.4).[59] In the same text Tillers also notes the relationship between Duchamp's concept of the 'delayed' or 'snapshot' Readymade and his notion of it as a four-dimensional 'shadow'.[60] This is echoed in 'Tom Roberts—Some Impressions' when Tillers observes that the Asimovian process of capturing the 'passing moment' and 'corroborating' it 'yields a parallel "shadow-world" populated by melancholy residues—paper-thin displacements of the 3-D objects to which they refer' (Tillers 1981b: 272).

Read in association with the implicit evocation of the fourth spatial dimension in 'Tom Roberts—Some Impressions', Tillers' rhetoric of misregistration in the appropriated Assisi image can be read as a photographic earthquake that fissures the surface of representation revealing, metaphorically, a world that lies beyond representation. Substantiation for this reading is provided by the fact that Tillers adds another correspondence with the poetics he formulated in *Conversations with the Bride* when he associates Asimov's speculations on photography with Jorge Luis Borges' counter-rational parallel world of Tlön:

> In the global task of ensuring the continuity of the world, Asimov recommends the use of the SX-70 system (sonar guided, autofocused, colour Polaroid). Thus he is no slave to photographic 'realism', but envisages a world, like Tlön, whose objects can be convoked and dissolved according to the purely poetic needs of each man, woman and child. For the SX-70 renders the entire world 'photogenic' and every user an artist. (Tillers 1981b: 272)

Tillers' reference to Borges' Tlön in this passage corresponds with the previously mentioned interview in 1988 (Slatyer and Tillers 1988) in which he revealed that his use of mirrors in *Conversations with the Bride* was inspired by reading Borges' short story 'Tlön, Uqbar, Orbis Tertius'. In *One Painting, Cleaving* Tillers shifts from specular to photomechanical and photographic metaphors, an observation reinforced by the fact that he took Polaroid photographs of the underlayer paintings in his *One Painting, Cleaving* works before covering them with the Assisi image. At this point the perplexing poetics of *One Painting, Cleaving* seems clearer. Tillers' rhetoric of invisibility and 'cleaving' relates to his notion of photography as a Tlön-like 'shadow-world' of 'displacements'. What appears, at first, to be a very strange strategy actually maps back onto the poetics of *Conversations with the Bride*.

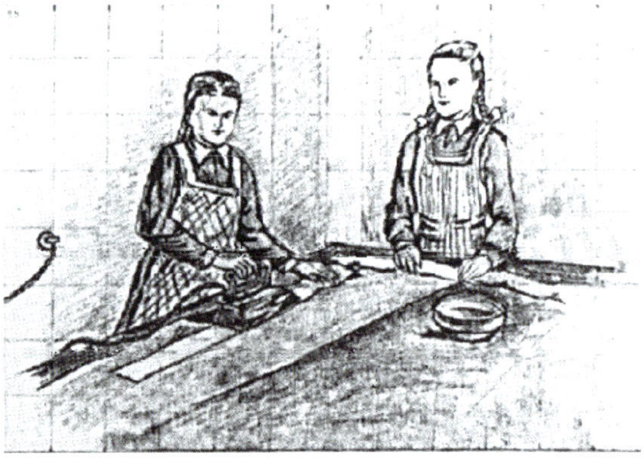

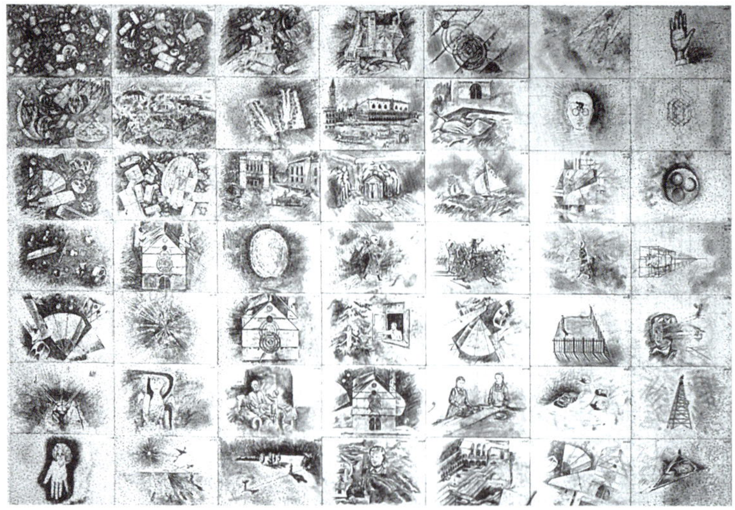

TOP RIGHT: ***Suppressed Imagery*****, 1981. Pencil on 49 canvasboards Nos. 1-49, 178 x 267 cm. Private collection, Melbourne.**
TOP LEFT: from ***Suppressed Imagery*****, 1981.**
BOTTOM LEFT: Assisi surface image from ***One Painting, Cleaving*****.**
BOTTOM RIGHT: From a 35 mm photograph taken by Tillers when painting over a ***Suppressed Imagery*** **image with the Assisi image while producing part of** ***One Painting, Cleaving*****.**

ONE PAINTING, CLEAVING **AND THE CANVASBOARD SYSTEM**

As well as referring back to Tillers' earlier work, *One Painting, Cleaving* overlaps with the seminal stages of Tillers' Canvasboard System. Tillers' initial experiments with canvasboards took place in 1981 when he produced a suite of works entitled *Suppressed Imagery*, 1981. A collection of these works is illustrated above right. Some of the imagery Tillers used in the *Suppressed Imagery* suite were also used for the invisible under-images in *One Painting, Cleaving*. One such image, appropriated from a Latvian childrens' story book, is reproduced above left. Below left is the Assisi surface image and below right is a photograph Tillers took of the intermediate stage when the surface image was beginning to cover the *Suppressed Imagery* image. Tillers' photograph of the process of 'suppressing' the under-image is interesting as it shows an interweaving of the under-image with the Assisi surface image. This effect echoes the misregistration in the Assisi image, if the latter is read as a photographic earthquake that fissures the surface

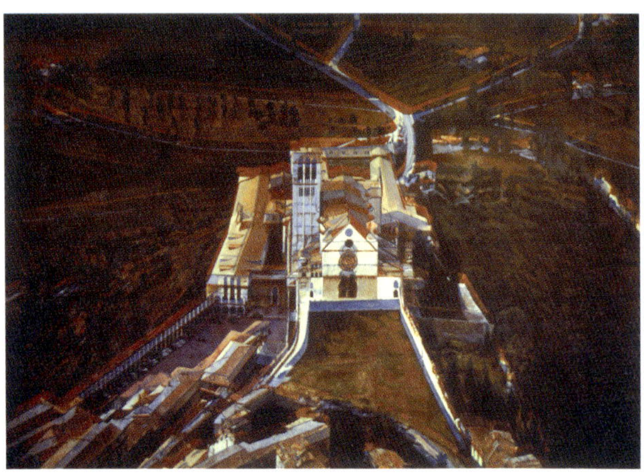

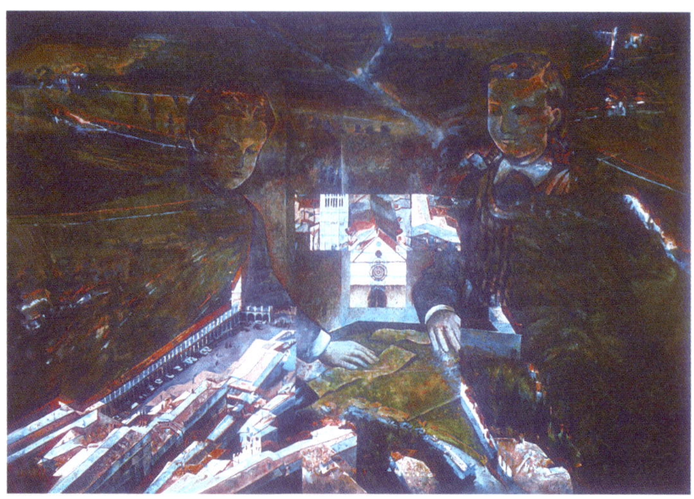

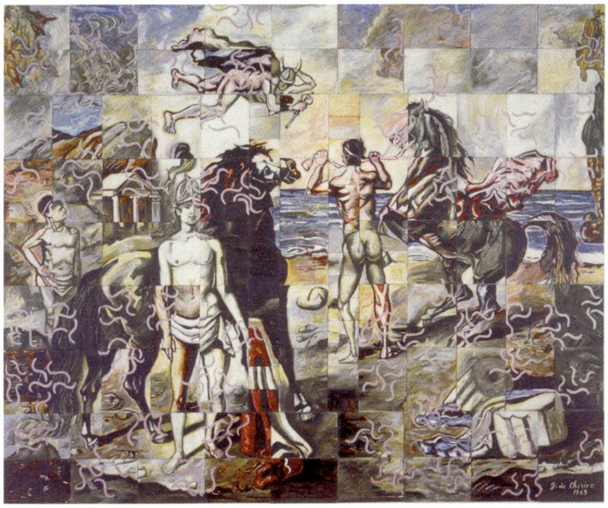

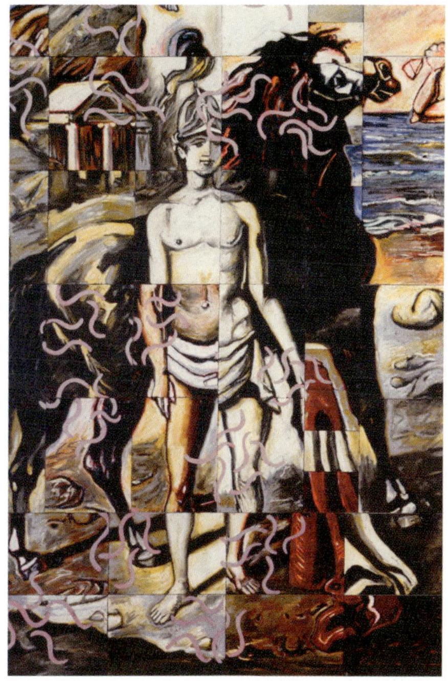

of representation revealing, metaphorically, a world that lies beyond our common sense reality.

The visual effects of misregistration and the interweaving of image layers in the Assisi image and Tillers' photograph are echoed in Tillers' Canvasboard System. In the latter the modular canvasboard 'pictemes' often misregister and disintegrate the imagery, allowing the recombination and intersection of different image particles, as is apparent in the detail from *La Citta di Riga*, 1988, reproduced above right. The detail shows the effect of misregistration between the individual canvasboards. It is evident that Tillers is emphasising this effect and it has obvious links with his obsession with the 'out-of-register' Assisi image. But it also relates to Tillers' curious palimpsestic photograph in which two very different image sources are interwoven. The effect of interweaving imagery from distant sources is also apparent in *The Nine Shots*, 1985, a detail of which is reproduced below left. As in *La Citta di Riga*, there is considerable misregistration between the canvasboards. It is also evident that the mis-

TOP LEFT: *La Citta di Riga,* 1988. Oilstick, gouache, synthetic polymer paint on 119 canvasboards, Nos. 16593–16711, 279.4 x 342.9 cm. Private collection, Sydney. Photograph: Fenn Hinchcliffe.
TOP RIGHT: detail.
BOTTOM RIGHT: *The Nine Shots,* 1985. Synthetic polymer paint, oilstick on 91 canvasboards, Nos. 7215–7305, 330 x 266 cm. Collection: the artist. Photograph: D. James Dee.
BOTTOM LEFT: Detail.

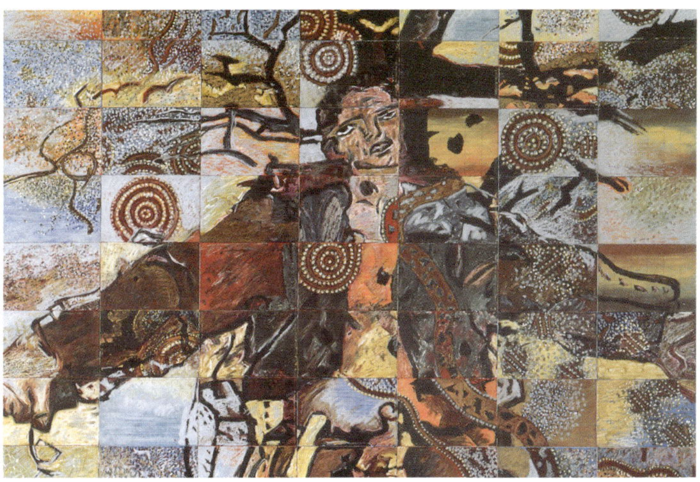

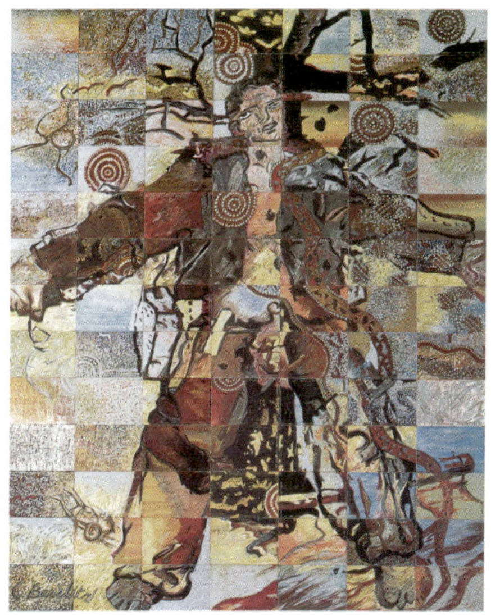

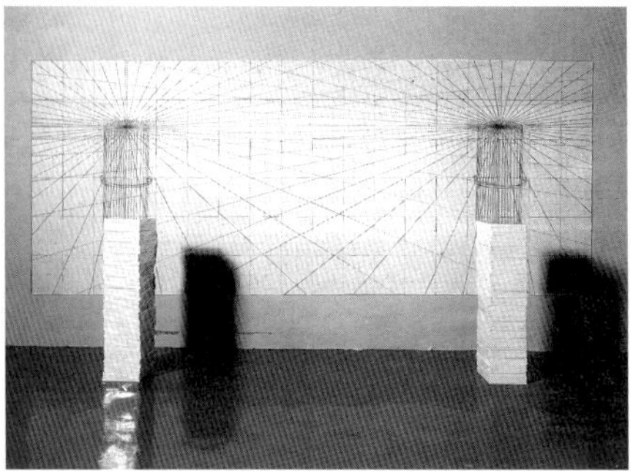

registration plays a part in the extremely fluid interaction of imagery appropriated from the modern Aboriginal art of Michael Nelson Jagamarra and the German neo-expressionist Georg Baselitz. In spite of the fact that the work is a painting, and perforce static, the canvasboard modules impart a narrative-like movement akin to the frames of a film. The analogy with film is reinforced when it is acknowledged that Tillers conceives his Canvasboard System as a single work and that this system is made up of tens of thousands of 'frames', as is a film.

ONE PAINTING, CLEAVING AND TILLERS' CANVASBOARD STACKS

Another important visual rhetorical relationship between *One Painting, Cleaving* and the Canvasboard System concerns Tillers' use of stacks. It has been noted that one of the advantages of Tillers' Canvasboard System is that even very large paintings (presently up to 8 x 3 metres) demount into easily transportable stacks. Apart from the practical advantages of this feature of the Canvasboard System, Tillers also became aware that the demounted canvasboard works had a sculptural quality which meant they could be exhibited as sculptures as well as paintings hung on a wall. His sculptural use of canvasboard stacks is apparent in *The Forming of Place*, 1987, and *The Bridge of Reversible Destiny*, 1990, both of which are illustrated left. In each case a mounted canvasboard painting is exhibited in conjunction with canvasboard stacks. In *The Forming of Place* a mounted canvasboard work of two 'I'-like motifs is confronted by two tall canvasboard stacks. In *The Bridge of Reversible Destiny*, 1990, Tillers exhibited a large number of canvasboard works in stack form. The artistic value of these stacks is not limited to their sculptural qualities. They also have a strong resonance with *One Painting, Cleaving* in the sense that only the top canvasboard is visible and all the other image material is hidden. But the connection between Tillers' exhibition of stacks in his Canvasboard System and the poetics of invisibility informing *One Painting, Cleaving* is more pronounced in *The Forming of Place*. In this work the two stacks are made up of blank canvasboards that have not been taken out of their plastic wrapping. Moreover, Tillers has never exhibited this work—it exists only in the 'shadow world' of photographic 'displacements'.

TOP: Imants Tillers, *The Forming of Place,* 1987. Exists only in the condition of a photograph. Photograph: Fenn Hinchcliffe. Collection: the artist. BOTTOM: *The Bridge of Reversible Destiny,* 1990. 7445 panels. Vitreous enamel on steel; gouache, synthetic polymer paint, oilstick on plywood; oilstick, gouache, oil, synthetic polymer paint on canvasboards; blank canvasboards. Panels executed between December 1981 and March 1990, Nos. 21892–29336, 1180 x 279 x 140 cm. Installation at Yuill/Crowley Gallery, Sydney. Photograph: Paul Green.

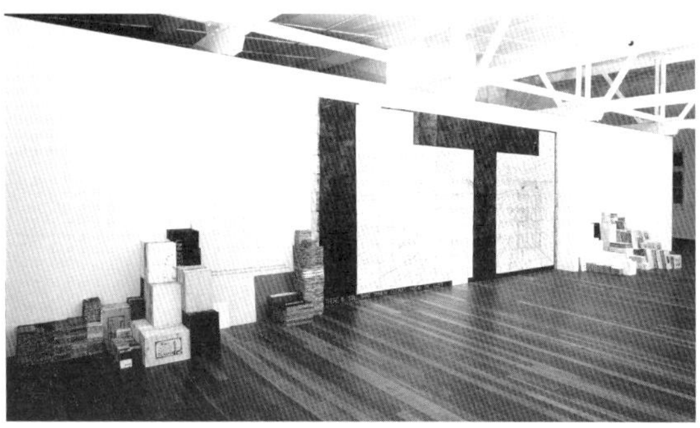

SHUSAKU ARAKAWA AND MADELINE GINS: CLEAVING AND *CLEOFUNG*

In *The Forming of Place* the blank stacks face a wall-mounted canvasboard painting with an 'I' shaped motif Tillers appropriated from the Japanese-American artist Shusaku Arakawa. It will be shown that it is a particularly important motif in Tillers' Canvasboard System due to its self-deconstructive assertion of identity via an 'I'-like motif appropriated from another artist. Significantly, the first direct sign of Arakawa's influence is in *One Painting, Cleaving*. Tillers acknowledges that his use of the term 'cleaving' is derived from Arakawa and Madeline Gins' artist's book *The Mechanism of Meaning* (Arakawa and Gins 1971, 1979).[61]

The term 'cleaving' occurs in the context of Arakawa and Gins' description of a proposed installation work consisting of 'a brick wall made of mesh' (Arakawa and Gins 1988: 96). The notion of 'cleaving' relates to their explanation that 'this is a wall that is made to be walked into' (Arakawa and Gins 1988: 96). Following this description the authors introduce the notion of 'cleaving' stating: 'The name [of the work] "cleofung" is taken from the thirteenth-century Anglo-Saxon word for "cleaving"' (Arakawa and Gins 1988: 101). Arakawa and Gins' concept of 'cleaving' in the context of their notion of 'a wall that is made to be walked into' is reminiscent of Tillers' revolutionary 'walk-in' painting *Conversations with the Bride*, 1974-75. Following *One Painting, Cleaving* Arakawa was to become a major appropriational source within Tillers' Canvasboard System. Indeed, Tillers' involvement and dialogue with Arakawa continued up to 2001.[62] The reason for Tillers' admiration for Arakawa is clear—Arakawa, like Tillers, works in a conceptual manner that is also guided by a poetic interpretation of science.

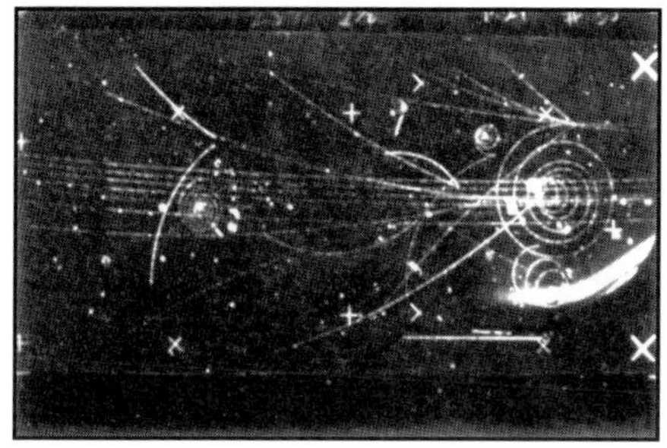

A photograph reproduced in Arakawa and Gins' *The Mechanism of Meaning* of the 'vapour trails' that represent subatomic events in the cloud or bubble chamber of a subatomic particle accelerator.

Arakawa and Gins' concern with science is focused on quantum theory, as is apparent in *The Mechanism of Meaning* when the authors reproduce a photograph representing subatomic events occurring in the 'cloud' or 'bubble' chamber of a particle accelerator (Arakawa and Gins 1988: 25).[63] The photograph Arakawa and Gins use is reproduced above right.

Significantly, Arakawa and Gins gave their cloud chamber image the caption 'Quantum as particle or wave' (Arakawa and Gins 1988: 25). Quantum theory—originally formulated in 1927 by Niels Bohr and Werner Heisenberg—began with the discovery that one method of investigating subatomic phenomena (for example, electrons) indicated that the phenomena is made up of particles whereas another, equally valid, experiment showed subatomic phenomena to be wave-like. Such contradictory, yet equally valid, experimental results had never been encountered before in the realm of physics. The science writer Nick Herbert observes: 'The electron is in reality neither particle nor wave, but an entity entirely new to human experience which exhibits the properties of both.' (Herbert 1985: 63-64).

Quantum theory was formulated to describe this paradoxical phenomenon. Heisenberg characterised it via his principle of 'uncertainty' or 'indeterminacy', and Bohr in terms of the principle of 'complementarity'. Applied to the particle-wave paradox Bohr's principle of complementarity suggests that whether the observer perceives subatomic phenomena as particle or wave depends upon how the experiment is conducted. The theoretical physicist Heinz Pagels explains:

> Bohr emphasized that when we are asking a question of nature we must also specify the experimental apparatus that we will use to determine the answer.

> … In classical physics we do not have to take into account the fact that in answering the question—doing an experiment—we alter the state of the object. We can ignore the interaction of the apparatus and the object under investigation. For quantum objects like electrons this is no longer the case. The very act of observation changes the state of the electron. (Pagels 1983: 92)

In *The Mechanism of Meaning* Arakawa and Gins take a position that appears to be informed by an understanding of Bohr's principle of complementarity when they state:

> There is no space except that which the perceiver forms. Space does not exist as anything on its own apart from the 'fiction of place', which sends it forth. (Arakawa and Gins 1988: 102)

The phrase 'there is no space except that which the perceiver forms' expresses a conception very similar to Pagel's explanation that Bohrian complementarity asserts that the observer affects, and even creates, what is observed: 'The very act of observation changes the state of the electron.' (Pagels 1983: 92).[64]

In the context of *One Painting, Cleaving,* it would appear that Arakawa and Gins' poetic interpretations of quantum theoretical notions of 'complementarity', 'uncertainty' and 'indeterminacy' were assimilated by Tillers into his poetics of 'mapping'. This is apparent in a text written by Tillers on the occasion of an exhibition of *One Painting, Cleaving* at John Nixon's Art Projects art space in Melbourne in 1982. A modest catalogue accompanied this exhibition including Tillers' text '*One Painting, Cleaving:* Triangle of Doubt' (Tillers 1982b). In this text Tillers uses the metaphors of a 'triangle of doubt' and 'cleaving' to explain *One Painting, Cleaving* together with the two diagrams reproduced below. Tillers recalls that his diagrams were based on the use of triangulation by cartographers to determine distance and location.[65] It will be argued that combined with his interest in Arakawa and Gins' quantum poetics, this cartographical allusion can be understood as a metaphorical extension of Tillers' ongoing concern with 'mapping'. In cartographical terms the

Diagrams used by Tillers in 'One painting, Cleaving: Triangle of Doubt' (Tillers 1982b).

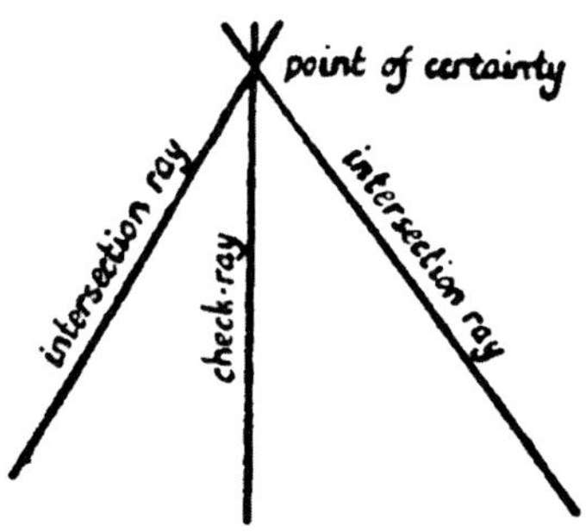

fig. 1

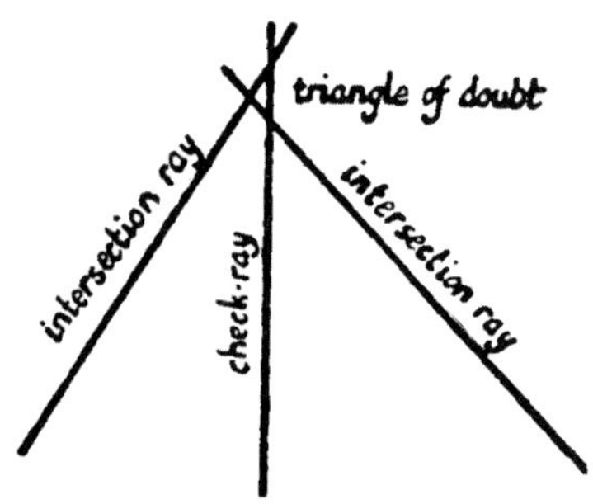

fig. 2

intersection of the three 'rays' at the apex of 'fig. 1' suggests that distance and location are determined with certainty. In 'fig. 2' Tillers appears to employ Arakawa and Gins' ideas to create a poetic conceit based on quantum theoretical 'uncertainty'. What results is a metaphor Tillers refers to as the 'triangle of doubt' which depicts a situation in which the process of 'mapping' is permeated with quantum uncertainty, indeterminacy and complementarity, an association that underscores and augments his understanding, and poetic interpretation, of Gödelian 'undecidability' in *Untitled*, 1978.

In Tillers' 'triangle of doubt', 'Fig. 2', 'doubt' is conveyed via the misaligned 'intersection rays'. The misalignment adds another metaphorical layer to the 'out-of-register' or 'displaced' character of the Assisi postcard. It also adds another layer to the influence of Arakawa on Tillers as it combines the metaphor of cleaving with Arakawa and Gins' quantum theoretically inspired notion of 'meaning' as inherently ambiguous.

In the context of '*One Painting, Cleaving*: Triangle of Doubt' it is evident that 'doubt' is represented by the 'cloven' apex of 'fig. 2' which represents the 'triangle of doubt'. Logically, the perfectly aligned apex of 'fig. 1' must represent 'certainty', and this is borne out when Tillers notes that 'the point of certainty' [the uncloven apex of 'fig. 1'] is 'inexplicably bound to fail' (Tillers 1982b: n.p.). Tillers elaborates:

> The desired unambiguous 'point' expands into an 'area' of concern—the <u>triangle of doubt</u> (figure 2). Thus for example, the work in this exhibition while attempting to be <u>one painting</u> becomes instead <u>one painting, cleaving</u>. The <u>triangle of doubt</u> expresses the failure of desire (or overt intent) but at the same time represents an expansion of possibility and knowledge. (Tillers 1982b: n.p.)

Tillers' statement can be compared to a passage in *The Mechanism of Meaning* where Arakawa and Gins formulate a quantum theoretical inspired notion of meaning:

> Everything is ambiguous as well as the judgement that something is ambiguous. As soon as any fact is presented, ambiguity appears as the zone of alternate possibilities. (Arakawa and Gins 1988: 19)

The assertion that 'ambiguity appears as a zone of alternate possibilities' resonates strongly with Tillers' declaration that 'the triangle of doubt … represents an expansion of possibility and knowledge' (Tillers 1982b: n.p.). Accordingly, it seems reasonable to suggest that the cloven apex of Tillers' 'triangle of doubt' has reference to Arakawa and Gins' poetic conception of 'meaning' informed by quantum theoretical notions of 'uncertainty', 'indeterminacy' and 'complementarity'.

There is considerable evidence to substantiate the claim that Tillers was inspired by Arakawa and Gins' quantum aesthetics and their redefinition of 'meaning'. Firstly, Tillers possesses a first edition of *The Mechanism of Meaning*, published in German as *Mechanismus der Bedeutung: (Werk im Entstehen: 1963-1971)* [*Mechanism of Meaning: Work in Progress: 1963-71*] (Arakawa and Gins 1971). Secondly, he acquired this edition around the time he was engaged in preparatory work for *Conversations with the Bride* in 1974. Thirdly, when preparing for *Conversations with the Bride* Tillers' research led him to two texts on the subject of chance that also contained substantial references to quantum theory. Lastly, after completing *One Painting, Cleaving* and developing his canvasboard strategy Tillers wrote an essay, 'Locality Fails' (Tillers 1982a) which uses quantum theory as its primary focus.

When reading Duchamp's Notes for *The Large Glass*, during his preparation for *Conversations with the Bride* Tillers became fascinated by the relationship between the fourth spatial dimension and the phenomenon of chance in Duchamp's writings. Tillers researched the literature on chance and chose two main sources both of which related chance to quantum theory. He reports that the first book he read on the subject was Arthur Koestler's *The Roots of Coincidence: An Excursion into Parapsychology*, (Koestler 1973) orginally published in 1972 and purchased by Tillers in its 1973 paperback edition. Koestler's book has an entire chapter on quantum theory. The second book was Carl Jung's famous study of chance, *Synchronicity: An Acausal Connecting Principle* (Jung 1985) first published in English in 1955. Jung's study also makes significant reference to quantum theory. As Allan Combs and Mark Holland point out: 'Jung developed his ideas of the acausal nature of synchronicity in close collaboration with the quantum physicist Wolfgang Pauli.' (Combs 1994: 75).

The Jung-Paulian notion of an 'acausal connecting principle' suggests that the surreal behaviour of the quantum phenomena might influence, interpenetrate, or map onto our material world.[66] In the context of Tillers' theoretical writings, this notion that can be compared with the idea that our three-dimensional world might be interpenetrated by four-dimensional objects which would appear disconnected because their internal connectivity would be invisible to us. As was shown in Chapter Seven this notion had a significant influence on *Conversations with the Bride* via Tillers' reading of Duchamp's notes for *The Large Glass.* The notion of an 'acausal connecting principle' also relates to Tillers' reference to Borges' surrealistic parallel world of Tlön in 'Tom Roberts—Some Impressions' (Tillers 1981b).

THE SURREALITY OF SCIENCE: 'LOCALITY FAILS'

The Jung-Paulian notion of an 'acausal connecting principle' is also important to this examination of Tillers because, together with his reading of Arakawa and Gins, its influence is apparent in the first published writing by Tillers in his canvasboard period, 'Locality Fails' (Tillers 1982a). This essay focuses on one of the most 'surreal' aspects of quantum theory which was most probably the inspiration for Pauli's contribution to the Jungian notion of an 'acausal connecting principle'. Quantum theory entails the proposition that a subatomic particle at one end of the universe can have an effect on another at the other end—billions of light years away. This corollary of quantum theory not only confounds common sense but also contradicts a fundamental principle in classical physics known as 'local-causality'. According to this principle only local events need to be taken into account when examining cause and effect relationships. Tiny events taking place billions of trillions of miles away can be safely discounted, according to local causality. The contradiction of the apparently self-evident truth of local causality by quantum theory led even the revolutionary physicist Albert Einstein to the conclusion that the quantum theory must be seriously flawed. In 1935 Einstein and his colleagues, Nathan Rosen and Theodor Podolsky, constructed a critique of quantum theory based on the argument that as the possibility of non-local causality was an intrinsic feature of quantum theory, the theory must be incomplete. The 'EPR' argument, as it is known, concludes that an as yet indetectable local causality will be discovered in the subatomic domain.

Tillers' essay 'Locality Fails' was written in 1982, the same year he produced his prototypical canvasboard work *The Field*. In it he applauds John Bell who, in 1965, disproved the EPR argument by proving that non-local causality *could* occur at the quantum level. Moreover, Bell's Theorem, or Proof, laid the foundation for the later experimental validation of quantum theory. Tillers' text indicates that Bell's Theorem was attractive to him because it represents a 'hard' scientific validation of what is probably the most surreal discovery of twentieth century science, as is evidenced when Tillers explains that according to Bell's Theorem:

> the failure of the principle of local causes implies that there can be unexplained connectedness between events in different 'space-like separated' places and that this connectedness allows for example, an experimenter (e.g. an artist) in one place to affect the state of a system in another remote (apparently unconnected) place. (Tillers 1982a: 56-57)

Tillers' repeated use of the term 'connectedness' in this passage seems to echo his earlier encounter with quantum theory and the Jung-Paulian notion of an 'acausal connecting principle'.

In the context of the Canvasboard System Tillers' poetic interpretation of non-local causality reinforces his visual rhetoric of specularity and *mise en abyme*. It provides a metaphorical extension of the methodology Tillers devised in *Conversations with the Bride* where 'coupling enables <u>any</u> of the 112 images to be linked to <u>any</u> other' (Tillers 1978a: 5/1 §5.1). In the following chapter it will be argued that Tillers' Canvasboard System can be conceived as an epic version of *Conversations with the Bride* in which thousands of images interpenetrate and intermingle, creating countless 'couplings' that transcend the intentionality of the artist who compiled them. This is one sense in which Tillers' concept of his Canvasboard System as 'self-organising' can be understood. Indeed one is reminded at this point of the passage in Roland Barthes' 'Death of the Author' where he refers to the post-authorial text as 'a multi-dimensional space':

> We know now that a text is not a line of words releasing a single 'theological' meaning (the 'message' of the Author-God) but a multi-dimensional space in which a variety of writings none of them original, blend and clash. The text is a tissue of quotation drawn from the innumerable centres of culture. (Barthes 1977: 146)

Tillers was unaware of Barthes at the time he devised *One Painting, Cleaving* and wrote '*One Painting, Cleaving*, the Triangle of Doubt', but he—along with other avant-gardist artists in the late 1970s and early 1980s—was certainly moving in a Barthesian direction as his next project was to be one of the most monumental instances of deconstructive authorial appropriation in the history of avant-gardist art: the Canvasboard System.

10

'INVISIBLE' AUTHORS: PHASE ONE OF THE CANVASBOARD SYSTEM, 1983–91

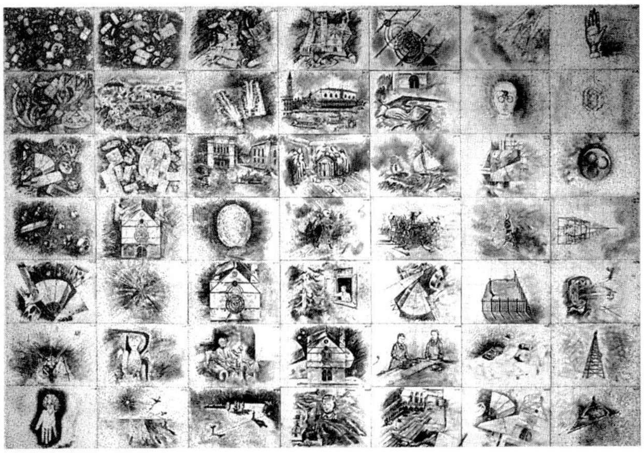

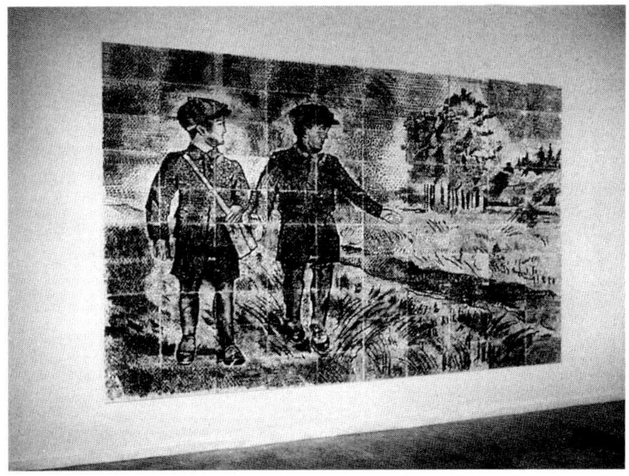

LEFT: *Suppressed Imagery*, 1981. Pencil on 49 canvasboards Nos. 1–49. 178 x 267 cm. Private collection, Melbourne. RIGHT: *The Field*, 1982. Charcoal on 100 canvasboards, Nos. 196–295, 254 x 380 cm. Collection: National Gallery of Victoria, Melbourne. Photograph: John Nixon.

Tillers began to experiment with canvasboards in 1981 producing numerous pencil drawings of imagery appropriated from sources such as reproductions of Giorgio de Chirico's paintings and illustrations in Latvian childrens' books. In his early *Suppressed Imagery* works (above left) each canvasboard bears a single image and is systematically indexed with a rubber-stamped number, a procedure that can be traced back to his minimalist-conceptualist inspired numbering systems in *Moments of Inertia* and *Conversations with the Bride*. Indeed, Tillers' numbering of each canvasboard has become an integral feature of his Canvasboard System. In 1982 he made the leap from images inscribed onto individual canvasboards to creating a large-scale image on a gridded array of canvasboards. The first such work is *The Field*, illustrated above right. Tillers' use of charcoal as the medium for *The Field* indicates its prototypical status.

In 1983 Tillers' Canvasboard System crystallised into a powerful artistic strategy when he acquired sufficient confidence in his new method to begin the production of large scale paintings. The modularity of Tillers' canvasboard grids is a powerful and original approach to painting because it enabled him to produce very large works with a minimum of means. Indeed the technique is so successful that it has become a hallmark of his style. Typical works from 1983 such as *Spirit of Place* and *The Great Metaphysical Interior* are reproduced on pages 46-47. Both works measure 254 x 648 cm (8.3 x 21.25 feet) exhibiting the capacity of small-scale canvasboard modules to create impressive large-scale paintings. As

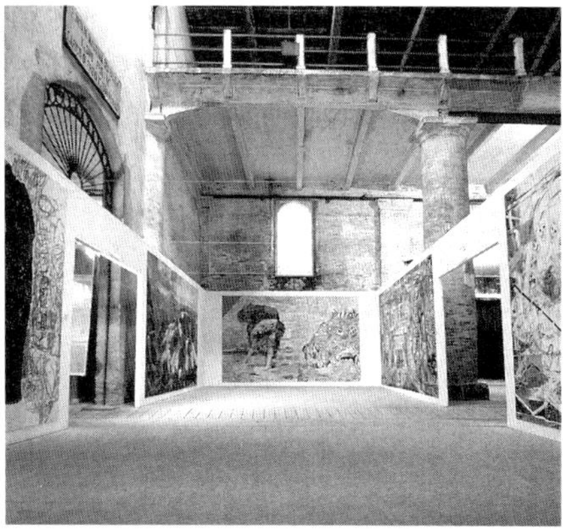

Tillers representing Australia at the Venice Biennale, 1986.

was noted in the Introduction, by 1986 Tillers was able to use the impressive scale of his modular paintings to make a major statement at the 1986 Venice Biennale (see left).

Tillers' Canvasboard System is also marked by a radical expansion of his strategy of appropriating the work of other artists from reproductions in books and magazines. It has been shown that he initiated this strategy in *Conversations with the Bride* and quickly elaborated it into a highly sophisticated mode of deconstructive authorial appropriation in *Untitled*, 1978. Both works are marked by Tillers' obsession with the non-indigenous Australian landscape tradition, in particular Hans Heysen's *Summer*, 1909. Tillers selected Heysen's *Summer* on the basis that during the 1970s it was one of the most reproduced examples of Australian landscape painting, adorning the walls of suburban living rooms and motels. There is a parodic register to Tillers' use of this image, as has been noted. But what is more important is the fact that Tillers wanted to break out of what Terry Smith referred to as the 'provincialist bind' (Smith 1974: 56, 57, 58, 59). This is apparent in his construction of what can be described, in retrospect, as a pataphysical mirror machine—*Conversations with the Bride*—to generate 'acausal connections' between *Summer* and *The Large Glass* thereby transmogrifying a somewhat conservative landscape painting into radical avant-gardist art. Tillers' strategy of appropriation was amplified by his extremely direct quotation of Heysen's *Summer* in *Untitled*, 1978, which was a very radical gesture for that time. But even such an apparently plagiaristic appropriation involved considerable 'information processing' in terms of scale, medium, and most importantly a Gödelian concept of undecidability applied to the question of authorship.

TILLERS' ANTIPODEAN CHALLENGE

By 1983 appropriationism had become an international style. Tillers' obsession with Heysen had been assuaged and he was ready to embark upon a much broader and ambitious appropriationist project that would penetrate into the heart of Euro-American avant-gardist art while simultaneously confronting such art with an antipodean challenge. On this occasion Tillers' antipodean source material was not 'provincialist'. On the contrary it consisted of the most powerful forms of antipodean art he could find. The first such source was the desacralised, modern acrylic paintings of the Aboriginal Papunya settlement situated in the Great Western Desert in Central Australia. Papunya art, characterised by regular patterns of sharp-edged dots, originated in the 1970s and by the early 1980s was beginning to come to the attention of the non-indigenous Australian art world. By the mid-1980s Papunya art was acquiring an international profile in its own right and Tillers came under intense criticism for his appropriation of this work. This aspect of Tillers' work was dealt with in Chapter Four. Tillers suspended his use of this imagery and turned to another powerful antipodean source in the form of the dark, text-based religious paintings of the New Zealander Colin McCahon, a remarkable artist still relatively unknown in the Northern Hemisphere.

The European and American sources Tillers has employed are various. A list of Tillers' sources is compiled in Curnow's monograph *Imants Tillers and 'The Book of Power'* (Curnow 1998: 136-139). Using Curnow's list it is apparent that in the period 1981 to 1985, the year before he exhibited at the Venice Biennale, Tillers' sources included: Giorgio de Chirico, Georg Baselitz, Arnold Böcklin, Anselm Kiefer, Kasimir Malevich, Frida Kahlo, Marcel Duchamp, Fernand Léger, Shusaku Arakawa, Julian Schnabel, Enzo Cucchi, David Salle, Gerhard Richter, Frederic Lord Leighton, Marina Abramovic and Ulay, Brice Marden, Jackson Pollock, Jonathan Borofsky, Kurt Schwitters, Ken Unsworth, Jasper Johns, Jiri Dokoupil, and On Kawara.

The very fact that Tillers' Canvasboard System is made up of serial permutations of fine art imagery appropriated from photomechanical reproductions in books and art journals indicates that his System cannot be addressed from the traditional standpoint of individual works created by an individual artist. Unlike traditional painting the Canvasboard System is a complex whole 'cloven' into discrete 'paintings' that are in turn split into scores of canvasboard panels. The individual canvasboard paintings are part of a modular system which entails that each painting remains open to recombination and recycling, while it remains in Tillers' hands, and reappropriation when it leaves his possession.

As noted earlier, Tillers' Canvasboard System is an almost paradigmatic realisation of Roland Barthes' 'multi-dimensional space in which a variety of writings none of them original, blend and clash' and as 'a tissue of quotation drawn from the innumerable centres of culture' (Barthes 1977: 146). One only needs to change Barthes' use of the term 'writings' to 'images' to make the description complete. Although Tillers probably would have been familiar with Barthes' statement by 1982, the whole thrust of this analysis has been to demonstrate that he arrived at this point via his own unique route and that it is this fact that endows his radically appropriationist project with a paradoxical 'originality'.

KEY APPROPRIATIONAL SOURCES IN PHASE ONE OF THE CANVASBOARD SYSTEM

Although the appropriational sources are manifold it will be suggested that in the period 1983-91 the outstanding sources are represented by selective imagery appropriated from Papunya art; Colin McCahon; Giorgio de Chirico; Shusaku Arakawa; and Georg Baselitz. It will be argued that these sources appear to resonate most powerfully with the sophisticated poetics that Tillers formulated in *Conversations with the Bride*,

Untitled, 1978, *One Painting, Cleaving* and the writings associated with these works.

This chapter will focus on the period, 1983-91, which will be referred to as the first phase of Tillers' Canvasboard System. Chapter Eleven will examine what will be referred to as the second and third phases, the former spanning 1991-96; and the latter 1997-2001. In the following analysis of the first phase of the Canvasboard System it will be established that within the expansive dimensions of this system Tillers is able to create an interplay between his poetics of specularity, *mise en abyme*, and authorial invisibility. The first important point to recognise is that although the canvasboard works appear to be discrete paintings they function as components of a holistic-like system. A helpful paradigm is available in the form of *Conversations with the Bride*. The latter is composed of 112 discrete images, however, these images are interrelated in such a way that 'coupling enables <u>any</u> of the 112 images to be linked to <u>any</u> other' (Tillers 1978a: 5/1 §5.1). In certain respects Tillers' Canvasboard System can be understood as a much more ambitious variation on the artistic methodology delineated in *Conversations with the Bride*.

The fact that Tillers conceives his canvasboard works as an integral holistic-like system is evident in the published conversation with his partner referred to previously (Slatyer and Tillers 1988). Tillers discussed his Canvasboard System in the context of his understanding of holistic, as opposed to mechanistic, systems. He described his canvasboard paintings, after Stéphane Mallarmé, as a 'Book of Power', where each consecutively numbered canvasboard could be conceived as a page in the book. He explained:

> The idea comes from the French poet Mallarmé who wrote in 1895: 'Everything, in the world, exists to end up in a book'. The panels have been numbered right from the start and the panel count is continuous from 1 to ∞. I've almost reached 15,000 … All modes of art can be accommodated within this book, and all modes of expression: from the trivial to the serious, the banal to the profound, the pious to the blasphemous, etc. My intention is the exhaustion of all possible categories and I'll spend the rest of my life working towards achieving this goal. (Slatyer and Tillers 1987: 111)

Tillers' metaphor leads one to imagine the numbered canvasboards are analogous to pages and individual canvasboard paintings as comparable to chapters or subsections. The problem with this metaphor is that it suggests a linear model that contradicts the paradigmatic instance of *Conversations with the Bride*. The latter is a valuable model as it provides a graphic illustration of the inherent 'undecidability' and 'acausality' of the image 'couplings' generated by the viewer passing through what Tillers termed the 'image matrix'.

Tillers provided a more complex metaphor for the holistic-like nature of his Canvasboard System in an article entitled 'Fear of Texture' published in 1983—the year he developed a successful formulation of his canvasboard strategy (Tillers 1983). There he makes reference to an idea conceived by the distinguished Italian avant-gardist art critic Germano Celant.[67] Tillers introduces Celant's ideas explaining that according to Celant: 'a painting might be thought of not in terms of a finite object but as a property of a continuous surface existing in time ad infinitum' (Tillers 1983: 15). Tillers continues quoting a passage from Celant in which he states: 'I propose that painting be thought of as an enormous roll of diversified fabric woven in a single piece ...' (Tillers 1983: 15). The metaphor becomes more sophisticated when it is proposed that as the 'enormous roll' is 'unrolled in time and space' it 'extends for miles and miles but never appears on display' (Tillers 1983: 15).

The notion that Celant's holistic-like 'enormous roll' 'never appears on display' is important because it relates to the poetics of invisibility informing *One Painting, Cleaving* which in turn developed out of Tillers' specular poetics in *Conversations with the Bride* and *Untitled*, 1978. Such associations are reinforced when Tillers adds that the continuity of the 'enormous roll' is:

> interrupted and broken up—cut into—to form innumerable fragments and portions of canvas (paintings), creating intervals and separations the understanding of which could greatly influence our way of thinking about and seeing painting, or for that matter continuity in the history of painting. (Tillers 1983: 15)

The idea of the continuous painting being 'cut into' has obvious reference to the notion of 'cleaving' in *One Painting, Cleaving* and avoids the linearity of the book metaphor. It is possible to understand the modular paintings that make up the Canvasboard System as cut out of, or cloven from, a continuous and invisible whole. There is also a resonance here with Tillers' detailed discussion of Duchamp's fascination with the non-Euclidean concept of the fourth spatial dimension and its description via the two-dimensional analogy.[68] As noted earlier, in *A Companion to Conversations with the Bride* Tillers quoted a passage from Duchamp's notes on *The Large Glass* where he likens the intersection of a four-dimensional object with our three-dimensional world using the analogy of an architect's plan that depicts each story of a house. Duchamp observes that: 'a 4-dim'l figure can be represented (in each one of its stories) by three-dimensional sections. These different stories will be bound to one

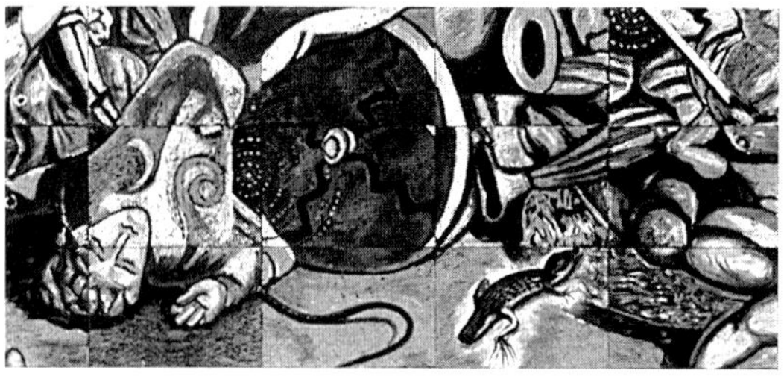

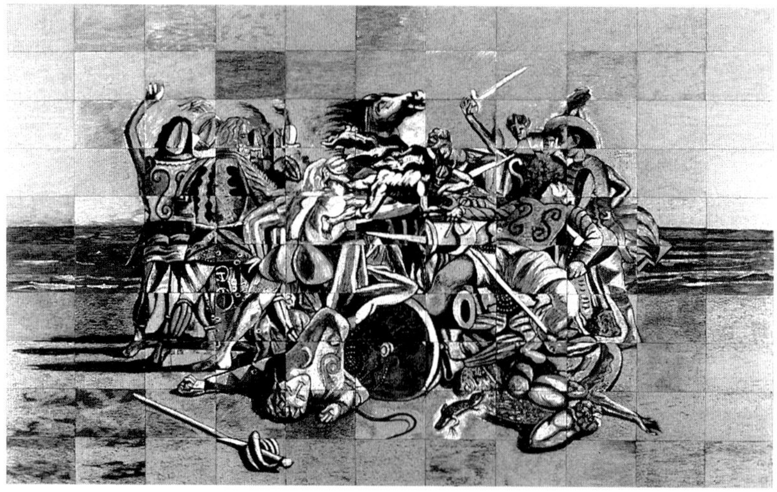

RIGHT: ***When False is True,*** **1985. Oilstick, synthetic polymer paint on 110 canvasboards, Nos. 7306–7415, 254 x 419 cm. Collection: Tasmanian Museum and Art Gallery, Hobart. Photograph: D. James Dee. LEFT: Detail**

another, by the 4th dim.' (in Tillers 1978a: 1/3). Duchamp's account suggests that what appears to be disconnected in one dimension is actually connected in another. Tillers provides a radical imaging of this concept in *One Painting, Cleaving* where only the surface image is visible hiding layers that exist, metaphorically, in another dimension. In the case of *One Painting, Cleaving* this dimension is the medium photography, i.e. the Polaroids and 35 mm photographs Tillers took of the underlayer paintings before covering them with the 'cloven' Assisi image.

Tillers wrote about Celant's 'enormous roll' in 1983 when in the thick of the first fully fledged components of his Canvasboard System. By then he would have been aware that his modular canvasboard paintings possess a capacity for 'infinite' expandability that articulates the notions of specular interconnectivity, 'acausal connectivity' and invisibility he had developed in his photo-conceptualist period.

Crucially, it becomes apparent that the poetics of invisibility that appears at first sight to be somewhat absurd in *One Painting, Cleaving* is articulated in the Canvasboard System in a manner that indicates Tillers is referring to the poetic possibility of 'invisible', or acausal, connections between apparently discrete images. It will be shown that in the Canvasboard System authors, including Tillers, are subordinated to the possibility of interconnections that are 'invisible' in the sense that they transcend the intentionality of either Tillers or his sources. Tillers' poetics of authorial invisibility has its roots in his understanding of the negentropic self-organising character of holistic systems in 'The Beginner's Guide to Oil Painting', his valorisation of system over authorship in the same text,[69] and his radical deconstruction of authorship in *Untitled*, 1978. The more one becomes absorbed in the specular dimensions of the Canvasboard System the more one begins to realise that it is replete with resonances and Baudelairean correspondences. It is in this sense that Tillers' canvasboard works function as a 'system'—not a mechanistic system, but a poetic system.

Support for this interpretation is afforded by an interesting passage from an interview between Tillers and his partner published in the catalogue of the Australian Bicentennial Perspecta exhibition (Slatyer and Tillers 1987). The relevant portion of the interview regards Tillers' synthesis of elements from de Chirico and Arakawa in *When False is True,* 1985, reproduced opposite right with a relevant detail to the left. Tillers begins by reporting that in 1985 he exhibited a painting in New York called *When False is True*. He notes that:

> it was based on an image by Giorgio de Chirico—gladiators fighting on a deserted beach—painted over fragments from several earlier paintings I'd abandoned. On one of these earlier fragments was the image of a lizard escaping by shedding its tail, [see the detail reproduced opposite left] the squirming tail held firmly by a cat's paw. In my New York painting this lizard ran free of the wild mêlée on the beach, its tail trapped instead by a fallen shield. The original image of the lizard came from a small detail entitled *Escapism* in Arakawa and Gins' book *The Mechanism of Meaning.* When Arakawa and Madeleine Gins saw my painting they were very impressed by this juxtaposition of motifs. They then told me that when they'd met de Chirico in New York in 1978 and had shown him *The Mechanism of Meaning,* de Chirico had been totally disinterested until he, too, came across this escaping lizard. This page struck a chord in him and triggered off an enthusiasm for the rest of this volume. After that incident, I realised that at the core of my work lies intuition and resonance. (Slatyer and Tillers 1987: 114-115)

Tillers' anecdote underscores the poetic dimension of his appropriationist project and the fact that key appropriational sources such as Arakawa and de Chirico assume a meta-authorial presence within the space of the Canvasboard System. But the Canvasboard System not only 'resonates' within itself but also with Tillers' previous theory and practice.

COLIN McCAHON, SHUSAKU ARAKAWA AND *THE BRIDGE OF REVERSIBLE DESTINY*

This examination of the relationship between Tillers' pre-canvasboard works and his Canvasboard System hinges on what will be argued is a pivotal canvasboard work, *The Bridge of Reversible Destiny*, 1990, reproduced on the following page. *The Bridge of Reversible Destiny* appeared towards the end of the first phase of the Canvasboard System and, in retrospect, appears to be a culminating statement of that phase. It provides an outstanding instance of how the sophisticated mode of deconstructive authorial appropriation apparent in *Untitled*, 1978, became articulated within Tillers' Canvasboard System.

The Bridge of Reversible Destiny consists of an installation made up of a large canvasboard painting accompanied by numerous stacks of unmounted canvasboard paintings. It is obvious that the gigantic 'IT' dominating *The Bridge of Reversible Destiny* can be read as a somewhat ostentatious statement of authorship on Tillers' part. But this assumption is deconstructed by the fact that Tillers appropriated these letters from works by the New Zealand painter Colin McCahon (1940-1987). In particular, Tillers focused on McCahon's use of the letters 'I' and 'T' which not only form Tillers' initials but also imply an inanimate or abstract thing. The sources for the 'IT' dominating *The Bridge of Reversible Destiny,* 1990, are evident in Tillers' more direct appropriations of McCahon's use of 'I' and 'T' in *The Letter I* and *The Letter T*, both made in 1988 and reproduced opposite. As will be noted in Chapter Eleven which deals with phases two and three of Tillers' Canvasboard System McCahon has become an increasingly important appropriational source to the point where McCahon seems to appropriate Tillers; an effect that echoes the exchange of identities in 'Dialogue on False Mt. Hayward' which led to Tillers declaring himself 'Wholly Encompassed' by Hans Heysen (Scullion and Tillers 1978: 9). Certainly, in the first phase of the Canvasboard System Tillers was so impressed with McCahon's extensive use of text that he assimilated McCahon into his use of the Mallarméan metaphor of the 'Book of Power'. Tillers notes:

> As the New Zealand critic Wystan Curnow observed, McCahon was mindful of 'the book of his own work', as year by year his collections of quotations grew. ... he was concerned with how the addition of this or that text reinforced or complicated the story so far. But all-encompassing books are destined to remain unfinished. So in 1987 McCahon died 'mid-sentence'... (in Slatyer and Tillers 1988: 4)

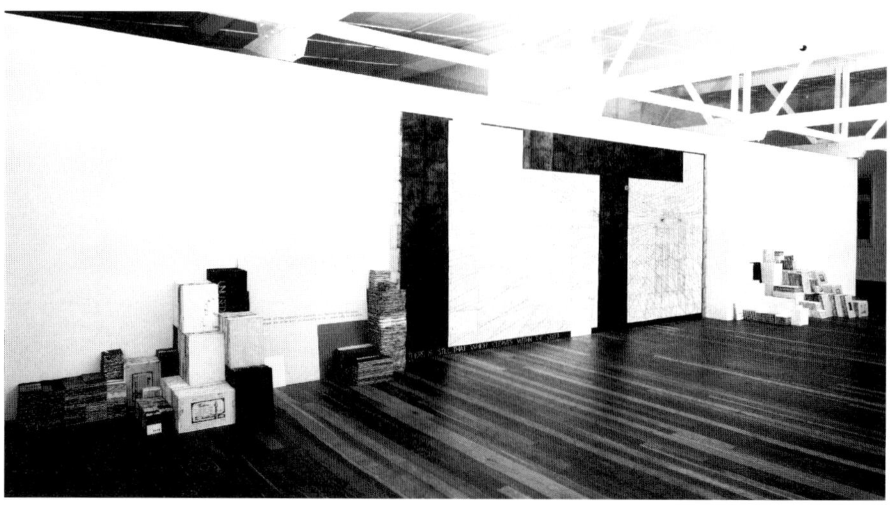

***The Bridge of Reversible Destiny,* 1990. 7445 panels (mounted and unmounted). Vitreous enamel on steel; gouache, synthetic polymer paint, oilstick on plywood; oilstick, gouache, oil, synthetic polymer paint on canvasboards; blank canvasboards. Panels executed between December 1981 and March 1990, Nos. 21892–29336, 1180 x 279 x 140 cm. Installation at Yuill/Crowley Gallery, Sydney. Photograph: Paul Green.**

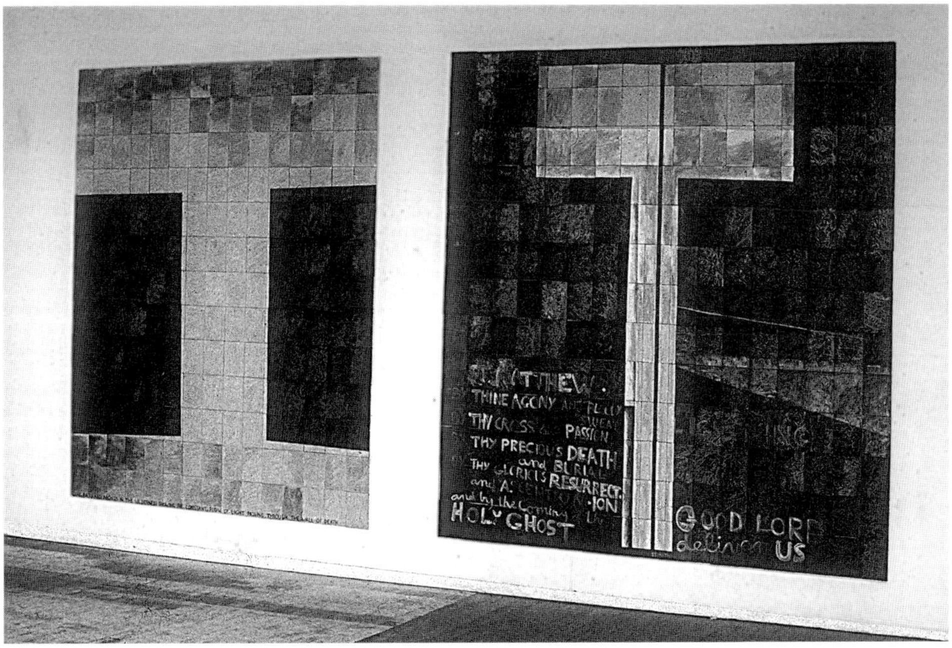

LEFT: Imants Tillers, *The Letter I*, 1988. Oilstick, gouache and synthetic polymer paint on 195 canvasboards, Nos. 17438–17632, 231 x 190.5 cm. Private collection. RIGHT: Imants Tillers, *The Letter T*, 1988. Oilstick, gouache, and synthetic polymer paint on 221 canvas-boards, Nos. 18579–18799, 231 x 215.9 cm.

In his monograph *Imants Tillers and the 'Book of Power'* Wystan Curnow has provided an impressive account of the influence of McCahon on Tillers (Curnow 1998: 145-46). Curnow suggests that Tillers would have been attracted to the complexity and contradictions apparent in McCahon's work. He notes that McCahon's contact with 'New American Painting' in the form of Alan Kaprow's installation art and Jackson Pollock's field paintings enters into a fascinating confrontation with the radically 'marginal' influence of religious painting, evident in McCahon's obsession with quoting biblical texts painted in a child-like script onto tar-black backgrounds. Curnow points to the fact that it is intertextual tensions such as these that explain Tillers' fascination with McCahon and quotes a revealing passage from an interview with the curator and art historian Jenny Harper in which Tillers states:

> McCahon's use of a contemporary scale (a la Rothko and Newman), the 'arte-povera' painting surfaces he sometimes employs (coarse hessian, readymade blinds, old doors, tarpaulins, etc.); the 'conceptual' flavour in his use of numbers and words; the, at times, ephemerality of his gesture and his radical disregard for the traditional niceties of finish and, in the late works, a severely monochrome palette. Also, in certain works, his radical hybridization of received styles and ideas (Barnett Newman, Mark Rothko, Mondrian, etc.) and his use of textual quotation (albeit biblical) gives his work a simultaneously archaic and contemporary presence. There is a constant tension between the search for meaning, the desire for transcendence and a pervasive, immovable skepticism. It is this aspect of

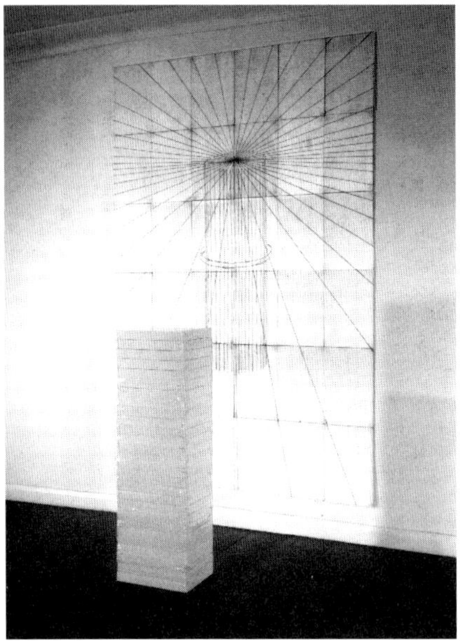

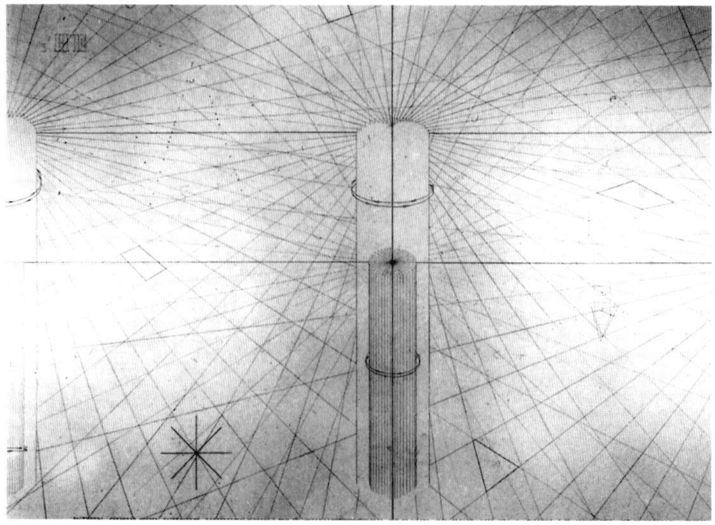

McCahon that I find most interesting and most relevant to our condition today. (in Curnow 1998: 146)

TOP LEFT: Imants Tillers, *The Fountainhead,* 1986. Pencil, synthetic polymer paint on 36 canvasboards and stack of 324 canvasboards, Nos. 10759–11118. Collection: the artist. Photograph: Fenn Hinchcliffe. TOP RIGHT: Shusaku Arakawa, *Degrees of Return,* 1975. BOTTOM LEFT: Imants Tillers, *The Forming of Place,* 1987. Exists only in the condition of a photograph. Collection: the artist. BOTTOM RIGHT: Reproduction of photograph of *The Forming of Place* with a centre line drawn to emphasise the compositional symmetry.

Tillers' appropriation of his own initials from the work of McCahon is echoed by his appropriation of an 'I'-shaped motif from the Japanese-American artist Shusaku Arakawa. Tillers' first use of this motif is evident in *The Fountainhead*, 1986, which is reproduced above left together with an example of Arakawa's use of the 'I' motif above right. The relationship between Tillers' use of the Arakawian motif and the concept of 'I' becomes very clear in *The Beacon,* 1989, reproduced above opposite. In *The Beacon* Tillers superimposes the Arakawian motif over an appropriation from a painting by McCahon. What would have been an 'I' in McCahon's biblical reference 'I AM' indicates quite clearly that Tillers uses the Arakawian motif as a means of

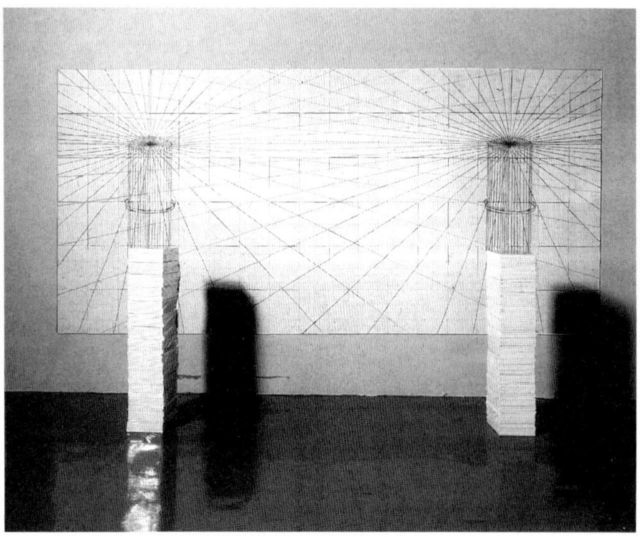

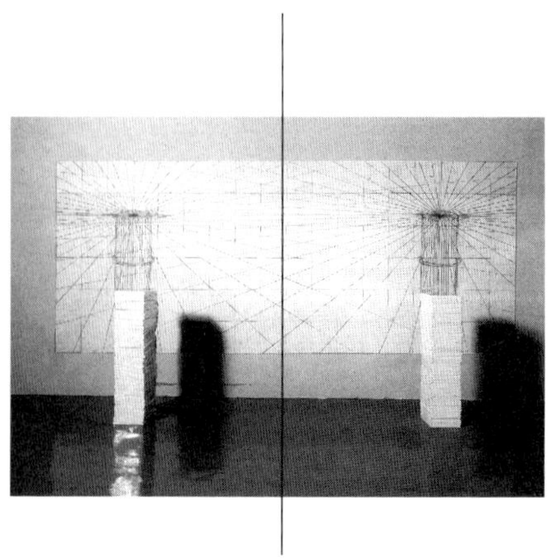

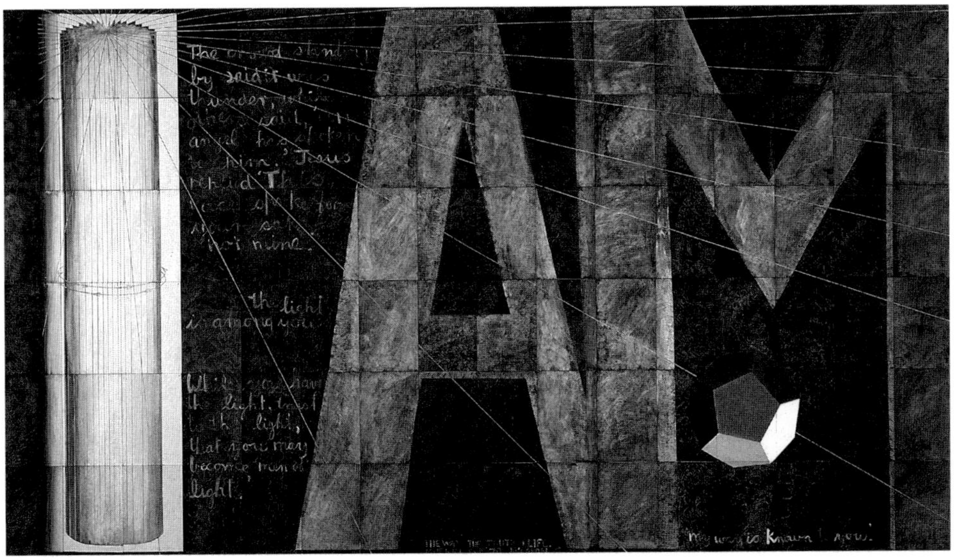

conveying the concept of 'I'ness. In addition, his use of the term 'beacon' to refer to the rays emanating from the 'I' is very descriptive of Arakawa's motif. It can also be noted that the superimposition of the Arakawian motif over McCahon's 'I' in *The Beacon* relates the beacon-'I' motif with Tillers' appropriations of 'I' and 'IT' from McCahon. This relationship is amplified by the fact that Tillers' use of a massive McCahonian 'IT' in *The Bridge of Reversible Destiny*, 1990, is accompanied by a doubled beacon-'I' motif under the left arm of the 'T' as shown in the detail below right. As in *The Beacon*, 1989, Tillers establishes a direct relationship between his McCahonian 'IT' motif and his beacon-'I' motif. Moreover, it can be noted that the doubled beacon-'I' motif in *The Bridge of Reversible Destiny* is echoed in *The Forming of Place*, 1987, reproduced opposite below left. To the right is another illustration of *The Forming of Place* with a centre line added to the photograph to show that it displays an almost an symmetrical, mirror-like doubling. This doubling can be compared with Tillers' specular rhetoric in panel 16c, *Conversations with the Bride*, and on the recto and verso of page 43 in *Three Facts* (Tillers 1981a). The reproductions on page 143 indicate how this rhetoric became enhanced by Gödelian 'undecidability' in *Untitled*, 1978. Accordingly it seems reasonable to suggest that the doubling of the beacon-'I' motif and the stacks in *The Forming of Place*, 1987, can be understood as possessing formal and poetic resonances with *Untitled*, 1978.

The association is reinforced by the fact that *The Forming of Place* has a very special position within Tillers' Canvasboard System because he only assembled it for the purposes of photo-documentation. It has never been and, according to Tillers, never will be exhibited in public. The reason for this is that Tillers wanted a part of his Canvasboard System to exist solely in what he referred to in 'Tom Roberts—Some Impressions' as 'a parallel "shadow-

TOP: *The Beacon,* 1989. Synthetic polymer paint, gouache on 96 canvasboards, Nos. 19984-20079, 229 x 406 cm. Photograph: Fenn Hinchcliffe. BOTTOM: Detail of *The Bridge of Reversible Destiny,* 1990.

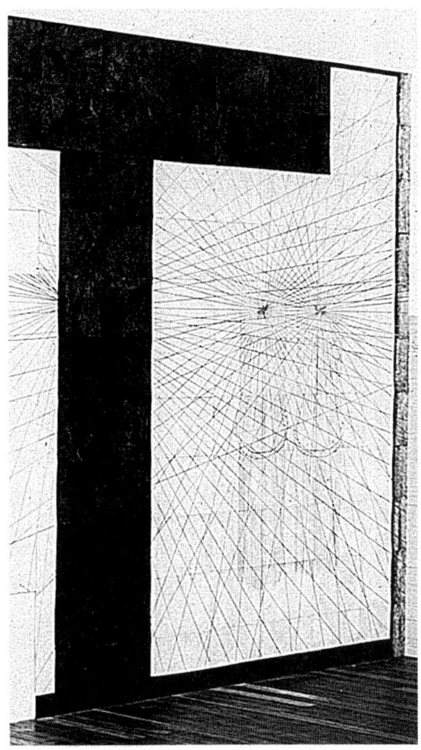

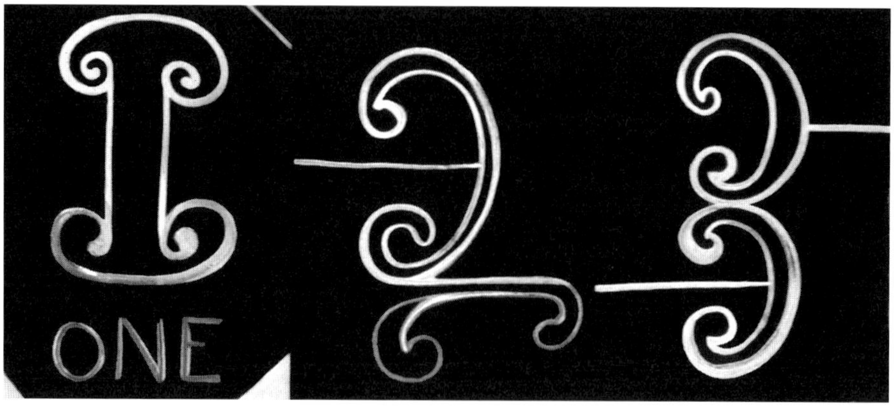

world"' of photographic 'displacements' (Tillers 1981b: 272). In the 1980s the National Gallery of Australia, Canberra, which owned *Untitled*, 1978, discovered that they had lost or accidently destroyed the work. Accordingly, like *The Forming of Place*, *Untitled*, 1978, now exists only in the 'parallel "shadow-world"' of photographic 'displacements'.

The Forming of Place, 1987, not only provides an important link between Tillers' Canvasboard System and *Untitled*, 1978, but also to the poetics of invisibility informing *One Painting, Cleaving*, and to Tillers' broader mythopoetic conception of the antipodes as a parallel world which he initiated in the specular aesthetics informing *Conversations with the Bride*. It is true that *The Forming of Place*, 1987, is the only element in Tillers' Canvasboard System that was relegated to this 'parallel shadow world' in a premeditated fashion, but the fact that the Canvasboard System should be considered as a whole suggests that *The Forming of Place*, 1987, functions—like images 24d and 16c in *Conversations with the Bride*—to alert the viewer to important features of the whole. This is borne out by the fact that the reprocessing, recycling and reappropriation of imagery is an important aspect of the Canvasboard System that effectively relegates what were once individual canvasboard works to a purely photographic existence. Indeed, this was the fate of *The Bridge of Reversible Destiny*.

There are other important features of *The Forming of Place*, 1987, that relate it to Tillers' photo-conceptualist poetics. If the reproduction of *The Forming of Place* (bottom left page 170) is examined it can be seen that the two beacon-'I' motifs are confronted by two stacks of canvasboards. In the analysis of *One Painting, Cleaving* it was noted that Tillers' canvasboard stacks indicate the relationship between the ideas informing *One Painting, Cleaving* and Tillers' Canvasboard System. It was also observed that Tillers has often exhibited his canvasboard works as demounted stacks, as is evident in *The Bridge of Reversible Destiny* installation, 1990. Stacks from that installation are reproduced as a detail below left. The difference in *The Forming of Place*, 1987, is that the stacks are blank canvasboards still in

TOP: Colin McCahon, *Untitled: (One, Two, Three)*, 1965.
BOTTOM: Detail of some of the stacked canvasboard works that form part of *The Bridge of Reversible Destiny*, 1990.

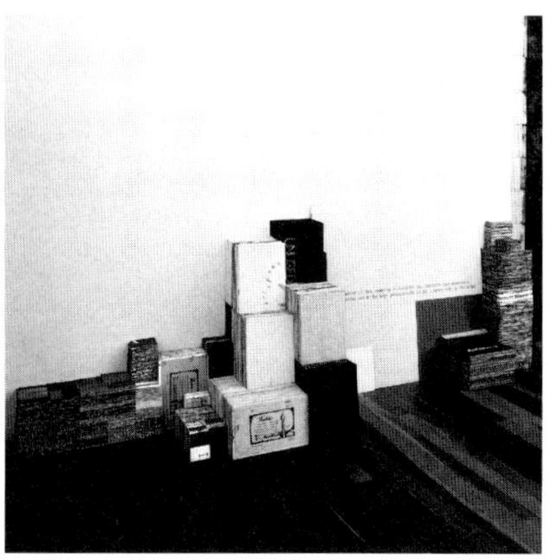

their plastic wrapping. Thus not only do they reflect the 'I' shape of Arakawa's beacon but they also map the 'I-ness' of authoriality onto a metaphorical blankness and invisibility.

Tillers' subversion of the 'IT' functioning as the artist's 'signature' relates to his tactic of sometimes signing his appropriated images with the name of another artist. Thus he will sign an appropriation of McCahon with de Chirico's signature. In this sense Tillers adds another dimension to his apparent status as artist *in absentia* amongst the panoply of appropriations that accumulate intratextually in the Canvasboard System. An example of the above tactic occurs in Tillers' appropriation of McCahon's *Untitled (One, Two, Three)*, 1965, in *Counting: One, Two, Three*, 1988. McCahon's original and Tillers' appropriation are reproduced opposite and below. The primary feature of interest is the '1' shape on the far left of McCahon's painting and Tillers' appropriation. It can be read as a '1' as it has the word 'one' painted under it. It does look, however, more like an 'I'. Certainly it seems obvious that, for Tillers this signifier would connote both identity and the initial for his own given name. Tillers preserves McCahon's original title and the crucial signifier which might mean 'one' but which looks much more like an 'I'. Tillers also manipulates McCahon's original work by superimposing it onto an appropriation of Eugène von Guérard's painting of New Zealand's Lake Wakatipu, *Lake Wakatipu with Mount Earnslaw*, 1877-79.[70]

The layering of appropriations in Tillers' *Counting: One, Two, Three* seem to echo the title. McCahon's '1' and 'I'—if read as signs of McCahon's identity—become 'cloven' in 'two' by the 'invasion' of McCahon's space by imagery from von Guérard. An invasion that also connotes the colonial invasion of New Zealand evoked by Tillers' insertion of a colonial artist's depiction of New Zealand. The 'three' could refer to a third appropriational source apparent in the bottom right hand corner of the work shown in the detail below right. Tillers' layering of authorial identities is amplified by 'signing' a work he constructed from the paintings of two other artists with the signature of a third, 'G. de Chirico'. It has been noted that Tillers was

LEFT: Imants Tillers, *Counting: One, Two, Three,* 1988. Synthetic polymer paint, gouache, oilstick on 162 canvasboards, Nos. 17188–17349, 251 x 639 cm. RIGHT: Detail of bottom right hand corner.

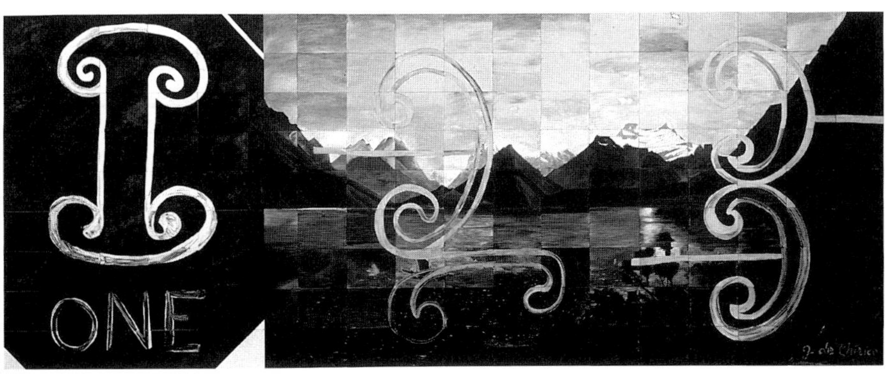

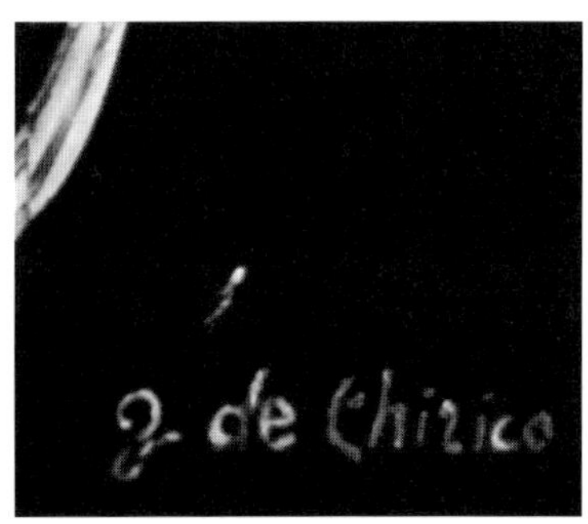

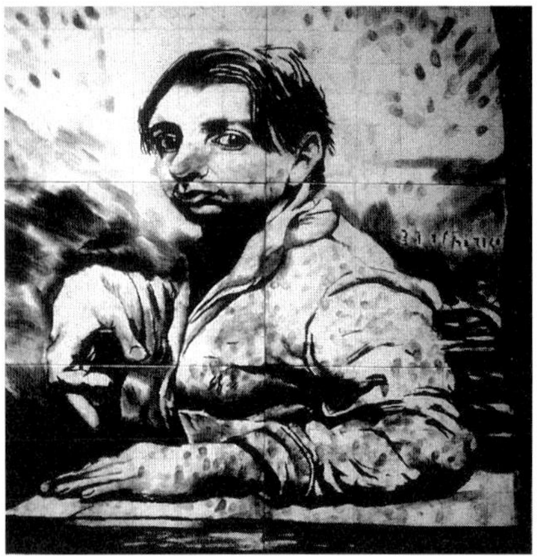

***A Life of Blank VI*, 1984. Charcoal on 6 canvasboards, Nos. 4006–4011, 76.2 x 76.2 cm. Private collection. Photograph: Fenn Hinchcliffe.**

attracted to McCahon, in part, due to 'the "conceptual" flavour in his use of numbers and words' (in Curnow 1998: 146). In metaphorical terms Tillers' version of *Counting, One, Two Three* seems to echo the seriality intrinsic to minimal and conceptual art. But when applied to authorship (as in *Counting: One, Two, Three*) seriality leads to a radical erasure of the '1' or 'I' by replacing 'it' with a system—a state of affairs applauded by Tillers as far back as 1973 in 'The Beginner's Guide to Oil Painting'.

GIORGIO DE CHIRICO AND 'A LIFE OF BLANK'

The interpretation of Tillers' use of the McCahonist 'IT' motif as a poetics of authorial 'invisibility' is also relevant to Tillers' appropriation of works by Giorgio de Chirico—another key source that recurs throughout the first phase of the Canvasboard System. In particular, it relates to the concept of authorial 'blankness' evident in Tillers' appropriation of a self-portrait by de Chirico given the title *A Life of Blank* by Tillers (see left).

Tillers' use of the concept of blankness appears to refer to the process of authorial appropriation in the Canvasboard System wherein authoriality, including that of the appropriator, is emptied out of the sources. It is also interesting to note that in 'The Provincialism Problem' Terry Smith referred to the antipodean artist as 'invisible': 'to the international audience he is mostly invisible, sometimes amusingly exotic' (Smith 1974: 56). From one perspective the assimilation and dissolution of authorship in the Canvasboard System can be read as a form of postcolonial vengeance wrought upon the hegemony of Euro-American 'masters'. From another it can be read as utilising the 'privileged' position of the antipodean artist—privileged in the sense that antipodean 'invisibility' makes it possible for Tillers to be intentionally non-intentional.

There appear to be two reasons why Tillers attributes 'blankness' to de Chirico. One relates to the fact that a typical motif used by de Chirico is a mannequin-like figure with a 'blank' face; another, more complex reason, concerns Tillers' identification of an element of minimal-conceptualist-like 'seriality' in de Chirico's oeuvre.

De Chirico's typical depiction of the human figure as a mannequin with a face-less, egg-shaped head is apparent in a variety of Tillers' appropriations from de Chirico such *Pataphysical Man*, and *The Vortex,* both of 1984, and *Voice,* 1988, (see opposite). All three show the blank-faced mannequin-like figures that are one of the characteristic attributes of de Chirico's work. Another feature contributing to Tillers' attribution of 'blankness' to de Chirico relates to an element of minimal-conceptualist-like 'seriality' and self-deconstructive auto-appropriation evident in de Chirico's oeuvre. Tillers has explained that his fascination with de Chirico's work derives from his perception of it as a 'field' of images in a condition he describes as 'a steady state'. Tillers owns, and has carefully studied, the three volume catalogue raisonné of de Chirico's

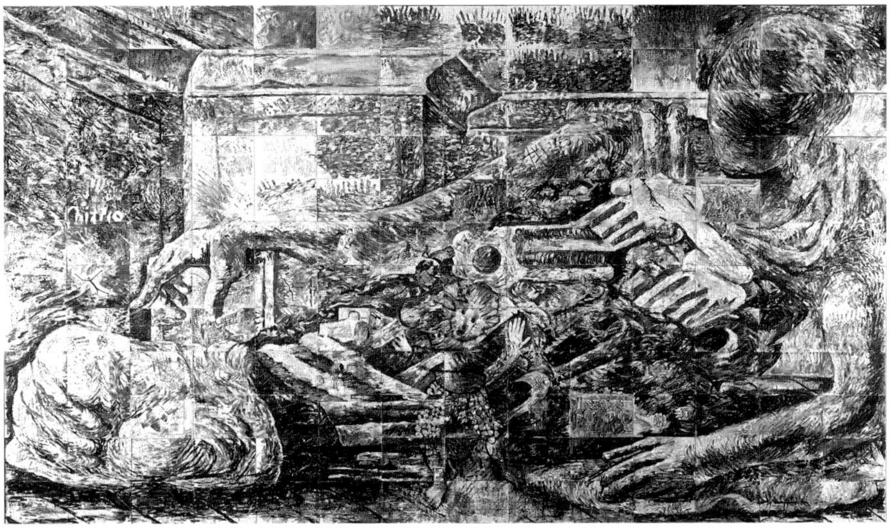

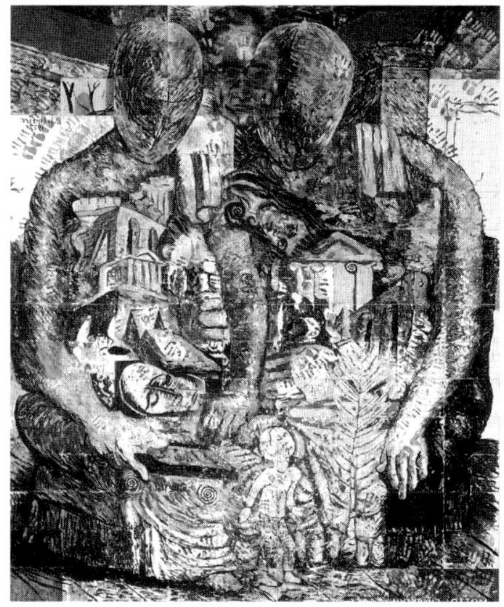

works (Bruni Sakraischik et al. 1971) and reveals his conception of de Chirico's oeuvre in the following statement:

> The volumes [of the catalogue raisonné] cover three periods from 1908-1930, from 1931-1950 and from 1951 to 1971. But the contents of each volume are virtually the same. So it's like there is this homogeneous grouping of images in each period [but with] hundreds of variations. (in Coulter-Smith 1991: n.p.)

If one examines de Chirico's catalogue raisonné it appears he had a repertoire of images that he randomly recycled over his entire career creating the homogeneity Tillers refers to above. Works originally painted in the teens of the twentieth century recur in the 1930s and 1950s and 1970s. In effect de Chirico is quoting or appropriating from himself, and in so doing deconstructs the notion of an original work of art. In this sense de Chirico's oeuvre can be understood as a precursor of Tillers' Canvasboard System which is also based on a process of 'recycling'. The difference is, whereas de Chirico appropriated his own work, Tillers appropriates not only the work of others but also his previous appropriations—a development especially evident in the second and third phases of the Canvasboard System. In this sense Tillers introduces de Chirico's strategy to the deconstructive rhetoric of the *mise en abyme*. Such observations are reinforced by Tillers' 1994 statement that when he saw one of his sources reproduced in a magazine or book 'it would be like a virtual version of my own work. It would have that same effect on me personally' (in Coulter-Smith 1994).

By extension, all of Tillers' appropriations of other artists could be perceived by him afterwards as 'virtual' works of his own. Translated into the terms used by Tillers and Scullion in 'Dialogue on False Mt. Hayward' (Scul-

TOP LEFT: *Pataphysical Man*, 1984. Acrylic paint, charcoal, pencil on 168 canvasboards, Nos. 2466–2633, 304.8 x 530.9 cm. Collection: Art Gallery of New South Wales, Sydney. Photograph: Fenn Hinchcliffe. TOP RIGHT: *The Vortex*, 1984. Synthetic polymer paint, watercolour, charcoal on 144 canvasboards, Nos. 3590–3733, 406 x 342 cm. Collection: the artist. Photograph: MARCO, Museum of Contemporary Art, Monterrey. BOTTOM: *Voice*, 1988. Gouache, synthetic polymer paint on 90 canvasboards, Nos. 18470–18559 160 x 127 cm. Private collection. Photograph: Fenn Hinchcliffe.

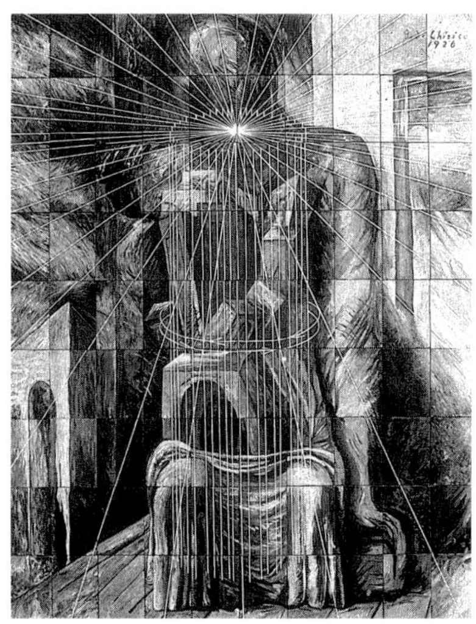

lion and Tillers 1978), Tillers 'maps' himself onto the authors he appropriates and vice versa. The appropriator becomes appropriated by the appropriation. Moreover, when the visual fabric is composed of hundreds of large scale paintings and tens of thousands of canvasboard modules or 'pictemes', the extent of the authorial mapping really does appear to be a concrete manifestation of the abyme-like condition described by Krauss in her pioneering analysis of Cindy Sherman (Krauss 1984a). There Krauss employs specular metaphors to elaborate her suggestion that Sherman's Untitled Film Stills series evokes a 'total collapse of difference':

> With this total collapse of difference, this radical implosion, one finds oneself entering the world of the simulacrum—a world where, as in Plato's cave, the possibility of distinguishing between reality and phantasm, between the actual and the simulated, is denied. (Krauss 1984a: 59-62)

Krauss elaborates on the image of Plato's cave in a discussion of the 'simulacrum' as a 'false copy' which introduces the specular metaphor that Krauss' colleague, Craig Owens identified in Derrida's theory of deconstruction in his essay 'Photography *en abyme'* (Owens 1978). Krauss states:

> the false copy is a paradox that opens a terrible rift within the very possibility of being able to tell true from not-true. The false copy takes the idea of difference or nonresemblance and internalises it, setting it up within the given object as its very condition of being. If the simulacrum resembles anything, it is the [Platonic] Idea of nonresemblance. Thus a labyrinth is erected, a hall of mirrors, within which no independent perspective can be established from which to make distinctions—because all of reality has now internalised those distinctions. The labyrinth, the hall of mirrors, is, in short, a cave. (Krauss 1984a: 62)

It was suggested in Chapter Three that Krauss' analysis succeeds in bringing together two crucial components of Derridean deconstruction: the specular metaphor of an abyss of self-reflection and the connotations that make Derridean deconstruction a deconstruction of traditional conceptions of authorship. It is this conjunction that makes her analysis of Sherman an especially elegant example of the post-structuralist interpretation of a mode of appropriation defined as authorially deconstructive. Moreover, it is this conjunction that makes her analysis so appropriate to an understanding of the poetics of authorial invisibility informing Tillers' Canvasboard System.

PAPUNYA PAINTING AND GEORG BASELITZ'S *'DER NEUE TYP'*

Of the key appropriational sources mentioned at the beginning of the chapter, two remain unexamined: Tillers' appropriation of modern Aboriginal Papunya art and the work of Georg Baselitz. Both sources will be examined together in instances where Tillers combines them. It will be shown that Tillers' juxtaposition of Papunya painting and Baselitz introduces a new register into his concern with identity that seems to create a correspondence between the authorial self-deconstruction apparent in the McCahon-Tillers 'IT' motif and Sigmund Freud's suggestion that even apparently 'civilised', white Europeans are prone to being taken over by what he referred to as *'das Es'*, the 'It' or Id. This is demonstrated by Tillers' implicit interconnection of references to the barbarism committed by Western civilisation in the colonisation of Australia and during the Nazi-period.

Tillers predominantly appropriates figures from Baselitz's ironically entitled *Der neue Typ* series produced in the 1960s. The series depicts human figures standing unsteadily, tattered and dishevelled usually in a wasteland setting. The scenes can be described as 'post-Holocaust' in the light of the fact that Baselitz was born in Germany in 1938, one year before the beginning of the war.

In art historical terms Baselitz is classed with artists such as Markus Lüpertz, Jorg Immendorf, and A. R. Penk as part of the German 'neo-expressionist' movement that picked up the pieces of the German expressionist movement of the first half of the twentieth century, shattered by the Nazis, who condemned such art as 'degenerate' (see Zuschlag 1995; Barron et al. 1991). Baselitz's return to this earlier discourse—as opposed to the minimal conceptualism that had such an impact on younger artists such as Tillers—is evident in a quotation recorded in 1966 where Baselitz states: 'The picture is an ideal image, a gift from God, unavoidable—a revelation.' (in Dahlem 1990: 24). It is also worth noting that the tone of Baselitz's statement resonates strongly with McCahon's contemporary religious art.

In her study of Baselitz, the art historian Diane Waldman defines his mode of expressionism by comparing his figurative paintings of the 1960s with the American expressionist painter Willem de Kooning's Women series of the 1950s which depict women via a savage gestural expressionist style. She notes:

> For both artists, the figure is the focal point of their paintings, though Baselitz's antiheroes and working men are vastly different from de Kooning's subjects. … Baselitz's palette is that of the forest—muted earthtones, deep greens, and blues; de Kooning employed … luscious colours … (Waldman 1995: 60)

Waldman associates Baselitz's figures with the wildness and savagery of de Kooning's Women series, but notes that Baselitz's treatment is more 'muted' his figures are 'antiheroes' set in a dark 'forest'-like landscape. Following her description it could be said that whereas de Kooning depicts the wildness and savagery of human nature Baselitz depicts its aftermath.

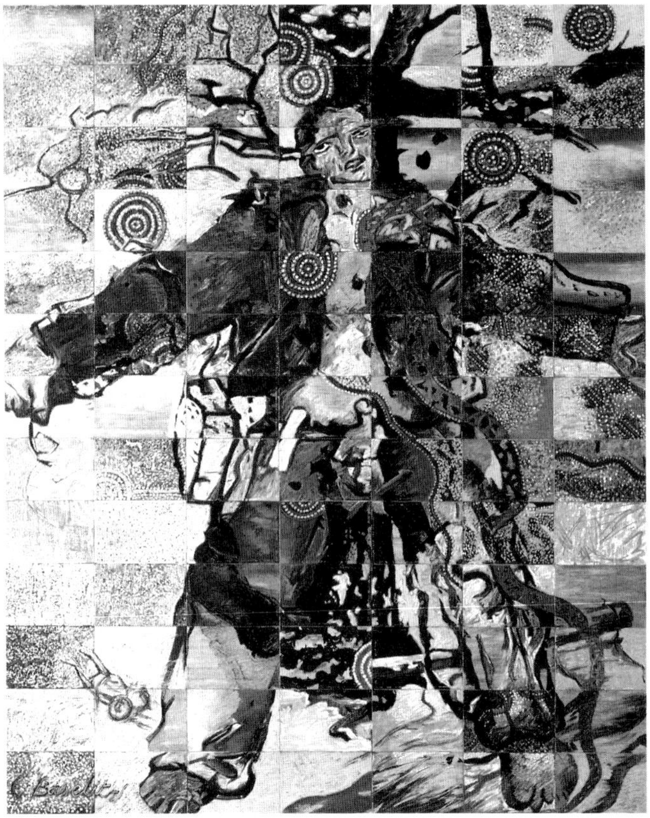

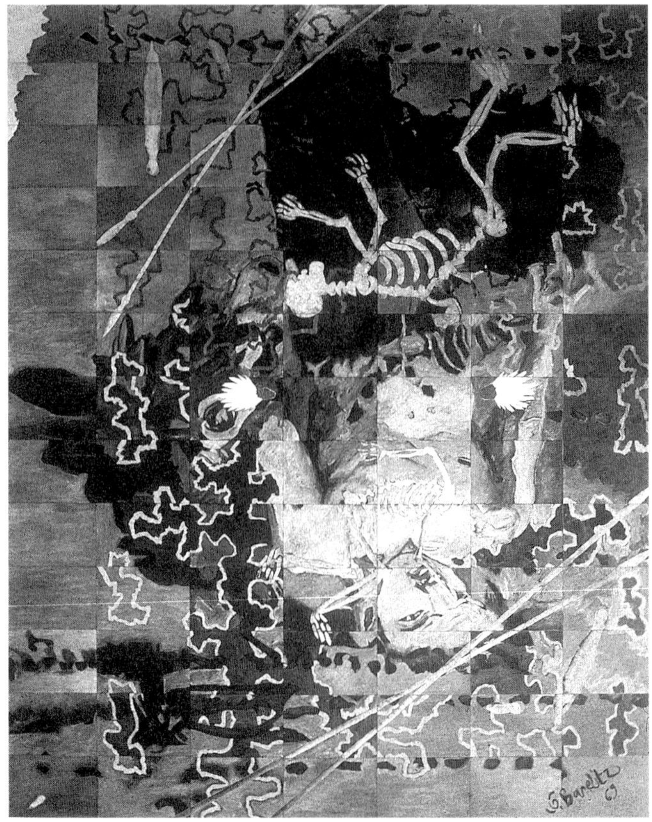

LEFT: ***The Nine Shots,*** **1985. Synthetic polymer paint, oilstick on 91 canvasboards, Nos. 7215–7305, 330 x 266 cm. Collection: the artist. Photograph: D. James Dee.**
RIGHT: ***Fallen Man,*** **1990. Oilstick, gouache, synthetic polymer paint on 91 canvasboards, Nos. 30003–30093, 350 x 267 cm. Collection: the artist.**

A typically bedraggled looking Baselitzian *neue Typ* is portrayed in Tillers' *The Nine Shots,* 1985, reproduced above left. In this work the figure is entangled in a Papunya landscape appropriated from Michael Nelson Jagamarra. Another juxtaposition of a Papunya painting, in this case by Clifford Possum Tjapaltjarri, with a Baselitzian figure is apparent in Tillers' *Fallen Man*, 1990, above right. In the context of *The Nine Shots* and *Fallen Man* Baselitz's post-Holocaust 'fallen men' implicitly refer to the descent of Western civilisation into barbarism in the Nazi period. Tillers' conflation of this connotation with Aboriginal imagery creates a parallel with the attempts at genocide by European settlers in Australia. *Fallen Man* shows a fragmented, dismal naked and very white man suspended upside down within an Aboriginal landscape scene. Significantly, Tjapaltjarri's imagery includes implicitly Aboriginal skeletons. It is via this juxtaposition of a post-Holocaust 'fallen man' with Aboriginal skeletons that Tillers suggests a parallel between the Holocaust and European settlers' attempts at genocide during the colonisation of Australia.

Texts written by Tillers in the early years of the Canvasboard System support this reading. In 'Locality Fails' Tillers refers to 'the successful extermination of the Tasmanian Aborigines by the white settlers' (Tillers 1982a: 57) and 'In Perpetual Mourning' he observes:

> The recent and brutal history of Australia is strewn with many corpses. For example the term 'isles of the dead' referred to those islands off the Western coast of Australia where Aboriginal tribes, often sick and dying from their lack of resistance to the most harmless of white man's diseases, were herded together with no regard for their totemic differences and left to die. (Tillers 1984: 23)[71]

Tillers' depiction of Europeans as 'fallen men' resonates with his appropriation of McCahon's child-like daubing of Biblical quotations on a tar-black ground that echoes Baselitz's wastelands. The 'fallen man' theme is also relevant to the second phase of Tillers' Canvasboard System which deals with his Latvian heritage and the barbarism imposed on the Baltic States by Hitler and Stalin's armies. This 'biographical' turn in Tillers' Canvasboard System will be dealt with in the following chapter.

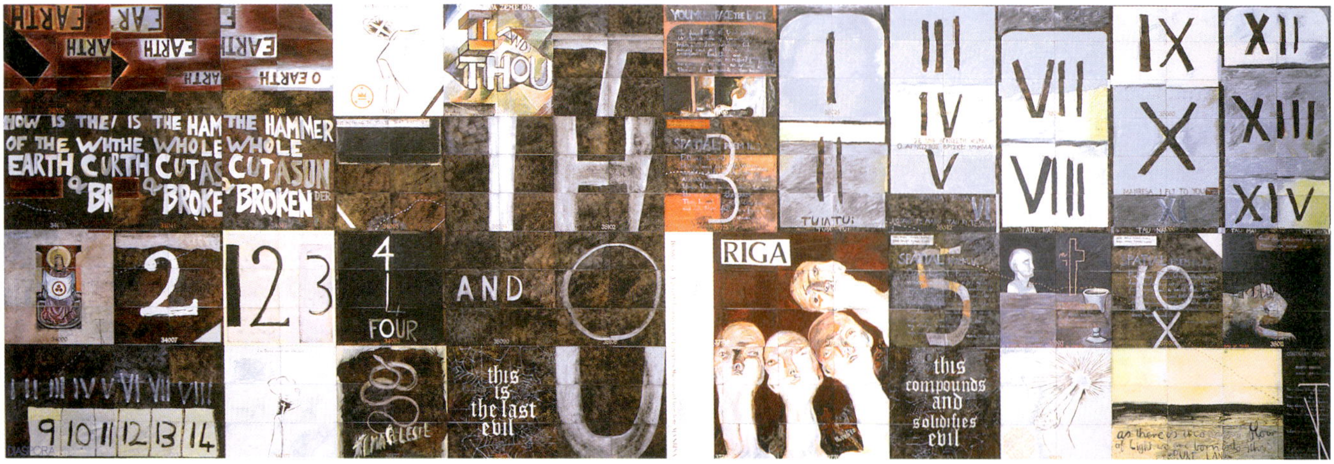
RIGA
AND
FOUR
this is the last evil
this compounds and solidifies evil
DIASPORA

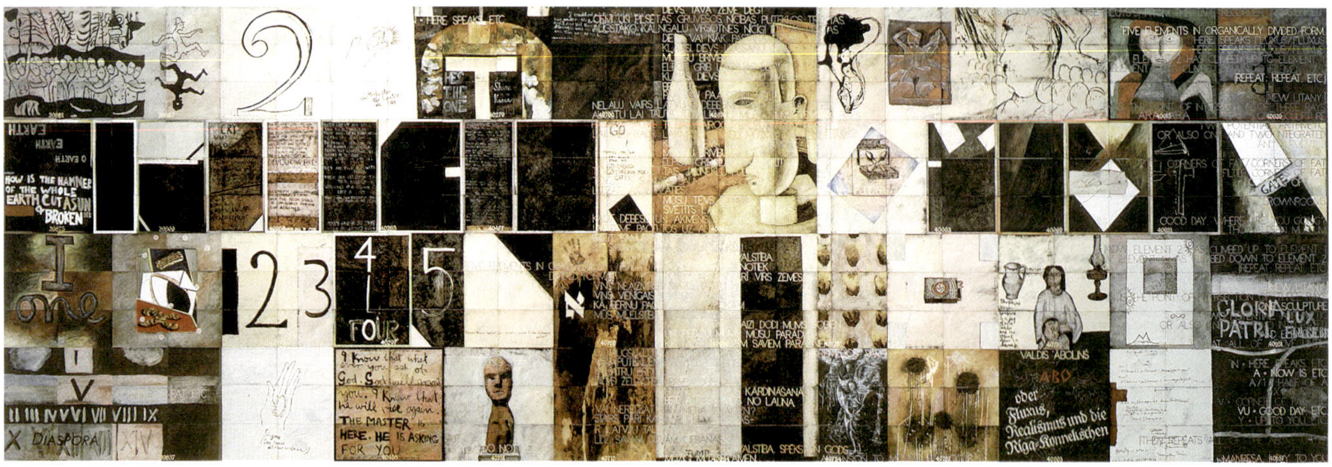
FIVE ELEMENTS IN ORGANICALLY DIVIDED FORM
HOW IS THE HAMMER OF THE WHOLE EARTH CUT ASUN BROKEN
FOUR
VALDIS ABOLINS
DIASPORA

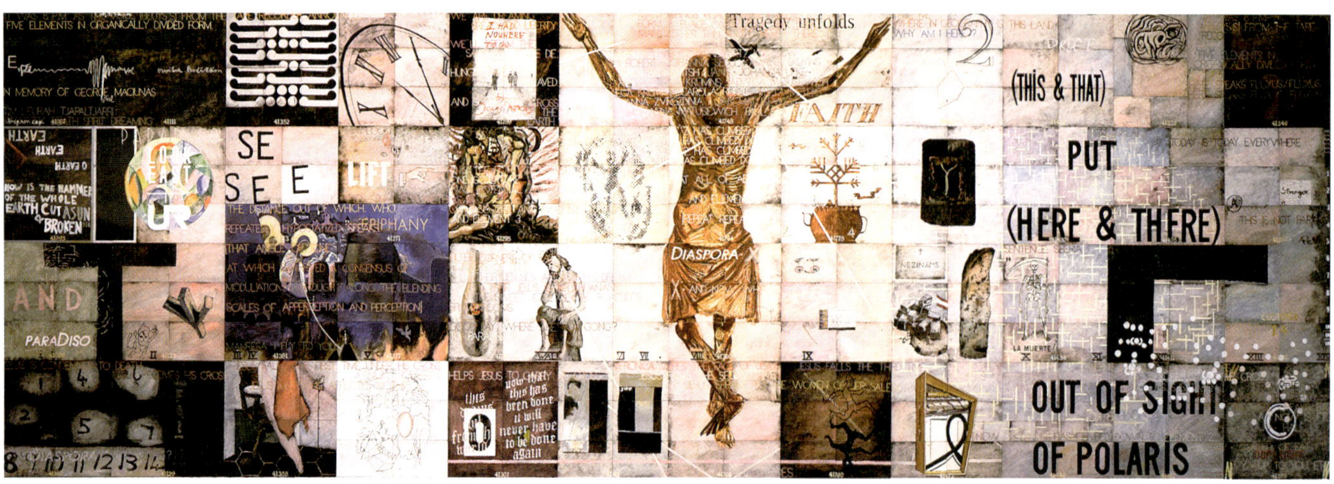
FIVE ELEMENTS IN ORGANICALLY DIVIDED FORM
IN MEMORY OF GEORGE MACIUNAS
Tragedy unfolds
FAITH
(THIS & THAT)
PUT
(HERE & THERE)
DIASPORA
AND
PARADISO
OUT OF SIGHT
OF POLARIS

11

PHASES TWO AND THREE: THE DIASPORA TRILOGY AND THE COOMA WORKS

PHASE TWO: THE DIASPORA TRILOGY

After creating a monumental deconstruction of authorial identity *in The Bridge of Reversible Destiny*, 1990, Tillers began a project that resulted in three very large and interconnected works, his Diaspora Trilogy. These works have such internal coherence both in terms of form and content that they can be understood as marking a new phase of his Canvasboard System. The Diaspora Trilogy is characterised by four salient features: firstly it refers to Tillers' Latvian heritage; secondly, it is made up of modules of six canvasboards creating a strong sense of dislocation that serves to reinforce the theme of diaspora; thirdly, the Trilogy consists of three very large and long works that have an identical format; fourthly, the Trilogy utilises a great deal more text than is the case in Tillers' previous canvasboard works and in this sense echoes the influence of conceptual art on his earlier work, and also the increasing role of McCahon.

The first work in the Trilogy, *Diaspora*, was completed in 1992. The second and third works were produced in 1994 and entitled *Izkliede* and *Paradiso*. 'Izkliede' is Latvian for diaspora and 'paradiso' is an anagram of diaspora. The Latvian theme is particularly salient in the Diaspora Trilogy. Tillers' Latvian parentage has been noted previously, specifically with regard to his appropriation of imagery from Latvian childrens' books initially in *One Painting, Cleaving* and then throughout the first phase of his Canvasboard System. In October 1991 Latvia declared its independence from the crumbling Soviet Union and in November Tillers visited Riga to discuss an exhibition in Latvia's National Art Museum, which led to the creation of the first part of the trilogy, *Diaspora,* in 1992.

Diaspora, *Izkliede* and *Paradiso* are all very large works each measuring 304.8 x 914.4 cm (10 x 30 feet). As the National Art Museum did not have the capacity to show very large works Tillers used modules made up of six canvasboards which could be exhibited as separate works. When assembled into a single large work these modules create the *mise en abyme*-like effect of a very large canvasboard painting made up of smaller canvasboard paintings. The self-reflexivity of this nested structure is intensified if it is accepted that the internal coherence of the Diaspora Trilogy can lead to understanding it as a small-scale canvasboard system nested, or enfolded, within the larger Canvasboard System.

OPPOSITE TOP: *Diaspora,* 1992. Oilstick, gouache, synthetic polymer paint on 228 canvasboards, Nos. 34000–38183, 304.8 x 914.4 cm. OPPOSITE CENTRE: *Izkliede,* 1994. Oilstick, gouache, synthetic polymer paint on 292 canvasboards, Nos. 39840–40805, 304.8 x 914.4 cm; OPPOSITE BOTTOM: *Paradiso,* 1994. Oilstick, gouache, synthetic polymer paint on 299 canvasboards, Nos. 41087–41820, 304.8 x 914.4 cm.

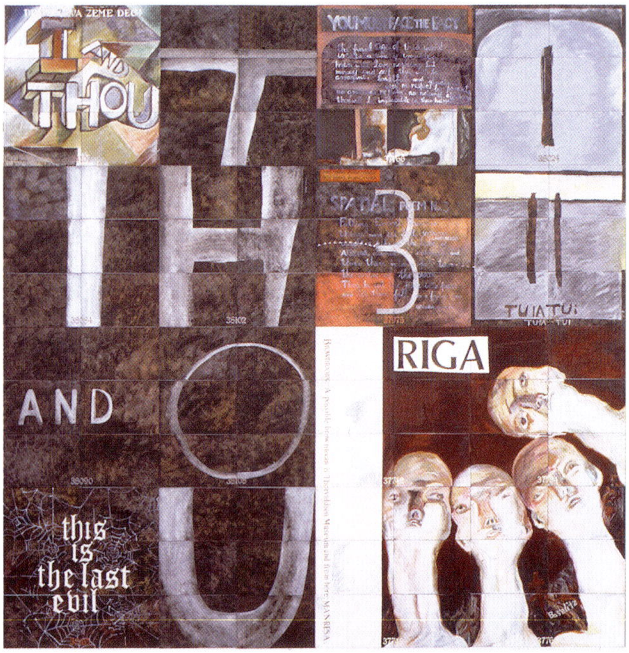

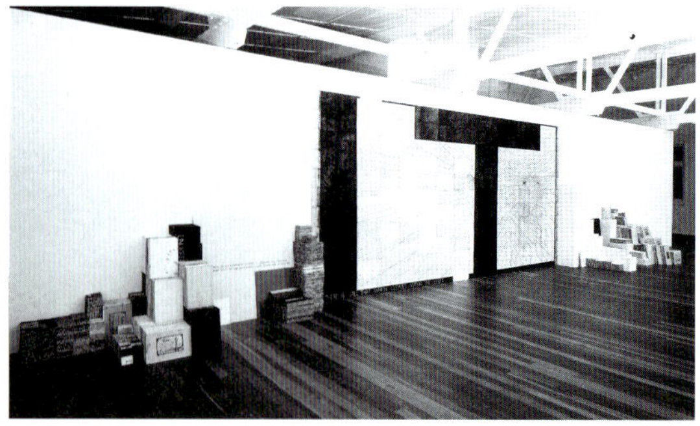

LEFT: Detail, *Diaspora*, 1992. RIGHT: *The Bridge of Reversible Destiny*, 1990. Installation at Yuill/Crowley Gallery, Sydney.

The fact that each of the paintings in the Trilogy is identical in format also relates to Germano Celant's concept that all the paintings in the world might form an 'enormous roll', a metaphor Tillers employed to describe his conception of the Canvasboard System as 'one painting'. It would be possible, given a suitably large gallery, to hang the three works as a single work 27.4 metres (90 feet) long. An impression of the result is evident in the reproduction of the three works on page 180. Conceived of as a Celantian 'enormous roll' the Diaspora Trilogy can be understood as a symbolic mirror of the entire Canvasboard System metaphorically reflecting both its past and future configurations. And somewhere within this mirror is the reflection of Tillers.

There is also a self-reflexive interrelationship between the Diaspora Trilogy and *The Bridge of Reversible Destiny* which is based on the fact that in both cases Tillers uses McCahon's 'voice' in a paradoxical mode of self-expression. McCahon's 'voice' resounds across the entire surface of *Diaspora* in the form of appropriations of McCahon's biblical quotations and Roman numerals containing a high percentage of 'I's. The problem of authorial identity posed by *Diaspora* is particularly apparent in the central section, reproduced above left.

This section of *Diaspora* possesses significant parallels with *The Bridge of Reversible Destiny*. In *Diaspora* Tillers creates large scale graphic statements of identity apparent in the repetition of 'I and Thou' in the top left hand corner of the detail; in the use of roman numerals in the top left which conflate '1' with 'I' and a doubled 'I' which in the context of Tillers' Canvasboard System can be read as a metaphor for appropriation. There is also a modernistic white, sans serif 'I'-shape in the bottom centre adjacent to four long-necked 'I'-shaped faces, bottom right. The faces are reappropriations of Tillers' appropriation of a motif from Baselitz in *A Painting Which Does Not Speak*, 1989. Indeed there are a number of such reappropriations within the Diaspora Trilogy that intensify the specular enfolding and consequent sense of *mise en abyme* produced in this second phase of the Canvasboard System.

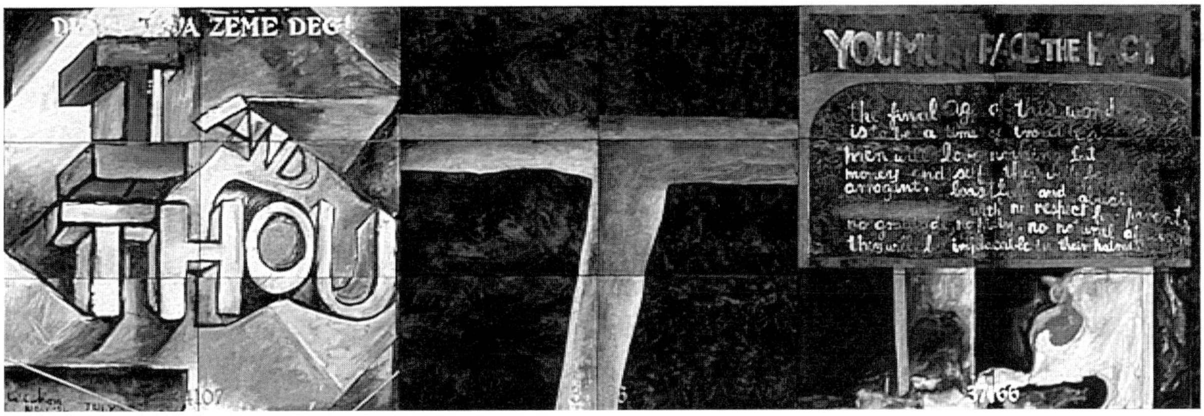

Detail of top middle section of *Diaspora*, 1992.

In the context of *Diaspora* Tillers seems to be announcing the fact that 'I' is not 'I' or '1', and that what appears at first sight to be an 'autobiography'—or more accurately, his family history—is rendered even more diasporatic by his need to articulate it via the voices of others. The dominant voice of McCahon is augmented by the fact that the latter's religious obsession is carried across the entire trilogy in the form of biblical quotations appropriated from McCahon and religious motifs appropriated from other sources as if by a sensibility akin to that of McCahon. Indeed it is as if Tillers is taken over by McCahon in a manner reminiscent of Tillers' description of himself becoming 'Wholly Encompassed' by Heysen (in Scullion and Tillers 1978: 9).[72] With respect to Tillers' use of McCahon's 'voice' in the *Diaspora* Trilogy, the crucial point is that the appropriator can become appropriated by the act of appropriation, which is especially evident when the author is unable to tell his own story in his own voice.

The top centre section of *Diaspora* reproduced above shows Tillers using his six panel modules in a cinematic-like fashion. A six panel McCahonian 'I and Thou' leads on to a six panel McCahon-Tillers 'T' and then to a biblical text from McCahon that reads:

> You Must Face the Fact / The final Age of this world / Is to be a time of troubles / Men will love nothing but / Money and self, they will be / Arrogant, boastful and abusive / With no respect for parents, / No gratitude, no piety, no natural affections / They will be implacable in their hatreds.

The biblical reference is taken from McCahon but in the context of *Diaspora* the text seems to refer more to the Second World War. Tillers' parents underwent harrowing experiences during the war. In July 1940 the Soviets invaded Latvia, Lithuania and Estonia. The following year the Russians were driven out by the Nazis. In October 1944 the Soviets occupied Latvia again. When the war ended Tillers' parents escaped to the British occupied sector of Ger-

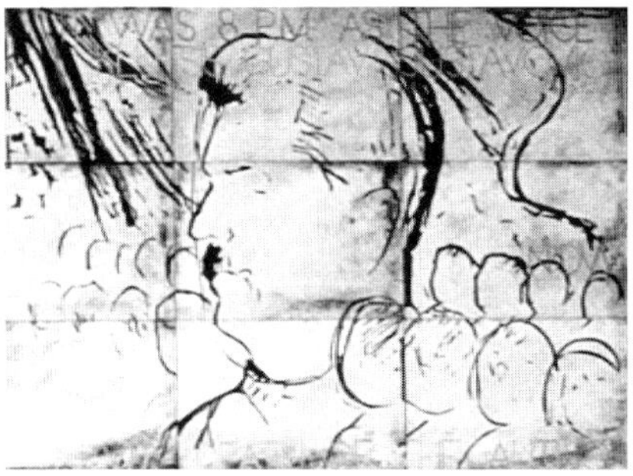

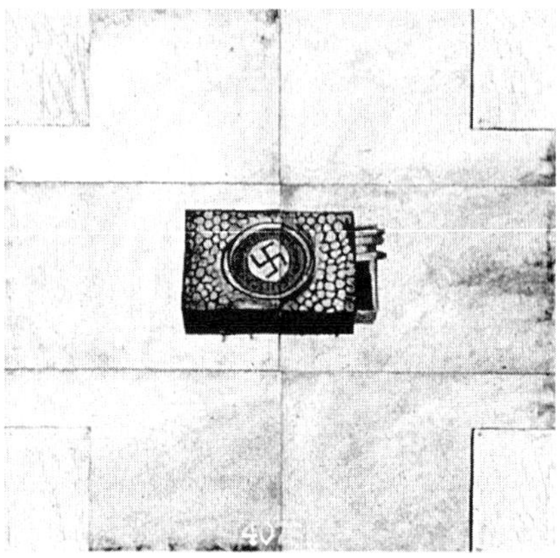

TOP: Details from *Izkliede.*

many where they were interned in a displaced persons camp until they were eventually offered passage to Australia. Tillers reports that both his parents were emotionally scarred for life by their experiences and that their trauma has made a deep impression on his psyche. References to the events in Europe in, and after, the war run through the whole Trilogy, two significant details from *Izkliede,* 1994, reproduced left, provide self-evident references to Stalin and Nazism. A detail from *Paradiso,* 1994, reproduced top right opposite, includes a depiction of the cover of a book *I Had Nowhere to Go* by Jonas Mekas, abutted from beneath by an appropriation of Baselitzian 'fallen' people. Like Tillers' parents Mekas, a Lithuanian, became a 'displaced person' who was able to escape, in his case to New York where he became a filmmaker. This sign of displacement becomes linked to the Baselitzian figures below when Tillers reports that the impact of his parents' trauma on his own sensibility has made him more sensitive to the imagery of artists such as Baselitz and Anselm Kiefer.[73] On the other hand, the personal aspect of the Diaspora trilogy is ineluctably interwoven into the web of intra- and intertextuality that Tillers weaves. What results is another paradoxical twist of the fabric of the Canvasboard System, another self-reflexive enfolding.

A variety of features underscore this interpretation: firstly, Tillers' use of others' voices to tell his family history; secondly, the highly conceptualist nature of the Trilogy apparent in Tillers' extensive use of text; and, thirdly, the permutational modularity of the six panel modules. These three features indicate the fact that in spite of its more 'personal' subject matter the Diaspora Trilogy is firmly located within the Canvasboard System informed by Tillers' involvement in art as information and information processing, and his attempts to allow the System to become 'self-organising'. Such observations are supported by a published conversation on the topic of the Diaspora Trilogy between Tillers and his partner Slatyer. There Slatyer notes that:

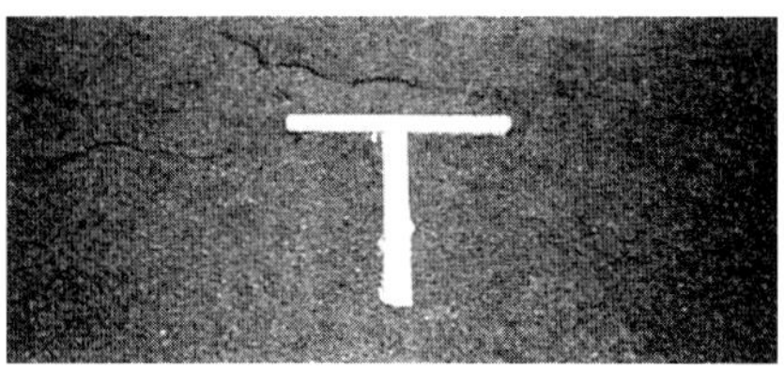

> in *Izkliede*, and even more so in *Paradiso*, there is a notable intensification in the complexity of the rich network of visual and textual references that we find first in *Diaspora*. The viewer can also detect a changing relationship amongst the sources, moving away from the strictly art-world, or primary, sources to encompass a secondary layer of more esoteric, autobiographical or anecdotal references from the real world. (Slatyer and Tillers 1995: 95)

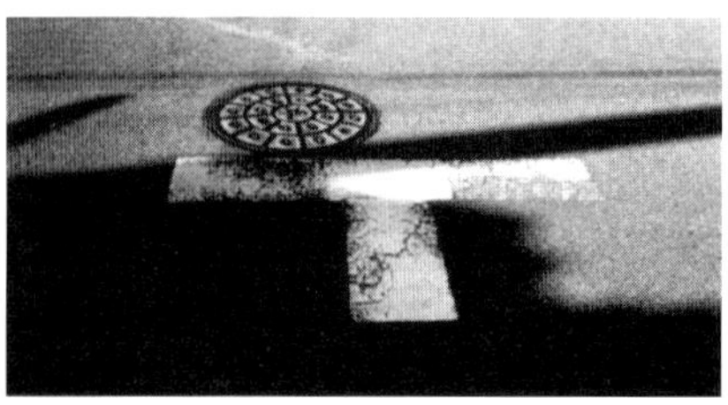

It is significant that Slatyer should discuss the 'autobiographical' character of the Diaspora Trilogy in terms of Tillers' insertion of images taken from his everyday life in Sydney rather than with reference to his use of images referring to the invasion of the Baltic States by Hitler and Stalin. Equally significant is Tillers' response, in which he discusses his appropriations in an impeccably conceptualist manner as 'encoding' noting that his Diaspora Trilogy:

> encodes information from everyday (quotidian) sources, like the postcard sent to me by Eugenio Dittborn, local graffiti ('Abo Boys'), a wine label ('Faith Shiraz'), a newspaper caption ('Tragedy unfolds') and images or text from photographs I have been taking since 1991. These record the kinds of commonplace signs, minor objects and subtle phenomena that are all around me in my local precinct but that normally pass unnoticed. (Slatyer and Tillers 1995: 95-96)

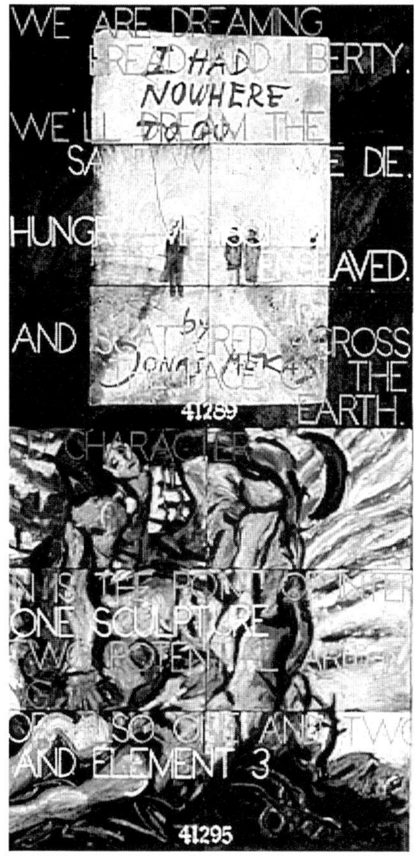

TOP: Detail from *Paradiso,* 1994. BOTTOM and OPPOSITE PAGE: Snapshots taken by Tillers in the vicinity of his old Sydney studio.

The notion that the Diaspora Trilogy should be received in the manner of the works of the tormented religious alcoholic McCahon or post-Holocaust Baselitz is deconstructed by Slatyer and Tillers' observations. We are reminded that what appear to be the most profound statements in the Trilogy are uttered through McCahon and Baselitz as if they were mediums for the deepest sentiments of an invisible author. Tillers' 'voice', in contrast, is evident in the details of his everyday life in Sydney, ten thousand miles and fifty years away from the turmoils of a war-torn Europe. Thus in spite of appearances to the contrary the Trilogy is like the entire Canvasboard System, a project of information processing, encoding and authorial deconstruction.

Yet, at the same time perhaps the Diaspora Trilogy is profoundly personal due to the pathos inherent in the possibility that it is because Tillers is so geographically *displaced* that he cannot tell his family's story in his own voice. Such an interpretation is reinforced by the fact that Tillers' attempts to insert his own voice are profound in their banality, in their Duchampian attraction to mundane found objects. The images reproduced below, on this and the facing page, are examples of photographs taken by Tillers in the neighbourhood of his Sydney studio reproduced in Curnow's book on Tillers (Curnow 1998: 54-55). These are literally snapshots taken by Tillers on his way to the bus stop after a day's work at his studio.

The images reproduced below opposite show two T's painted on the street one delimiting parking zones the other possibly marking a spot for roadworks. These have obvious reference to Tillers' appropriation of his initial 'T' from McCahon. Other images include 'I AM' and 'Truth Works' both in the form of religious advertising. Again these refer to McCahon, in particular to his use of biblical quotation. Another image displays Aboriginal graffiti which relates both to Tillers' appropriation of modern Aboriginal art

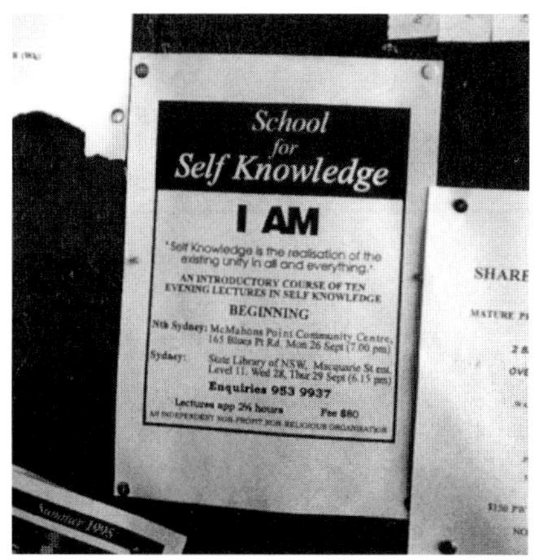

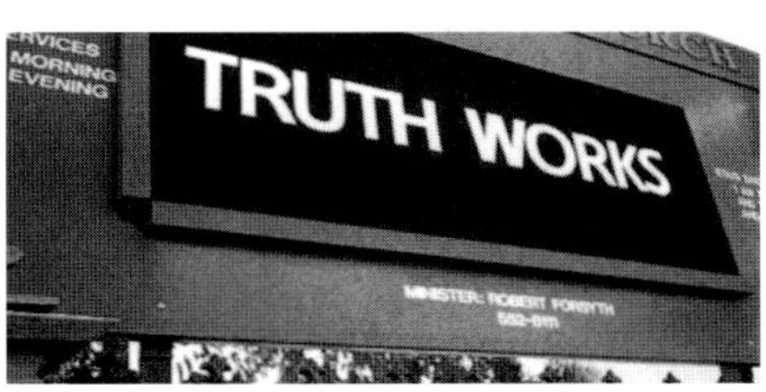

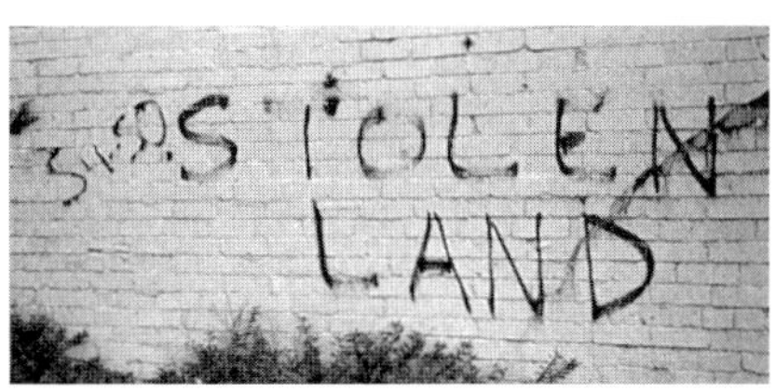

and his ecopolitical stance apparent in 'The Beginner's Guide to Oil Painting' and *Conversations with the Bride*.[74] What these images show is that even Tillers' putatively 'autobiographical' snapshots echo the voices of his appropriational sources. They emphasise the fact that he lives in a world of resonances generated by the Canvasboard System. And these resonances proliferate: the 'I AM' alludes to a McCahonian reference to God, but possibly also to Barthes' references to the 'death' of the 'author-God', which resonates in turn with Nietzsche's concept of 'the death of God'. One is reminded here of the 'couplings' Tillers wanted to facilitate by making the viewer enter into the maze of image-mirrors that constitute *Conversations with the Bride*.

Tillers' snapshots also evoke *A Companion to Conversations with the Bride* in which Tillers refers to Duchamp's discussion of the process of waiting and looking for a readymade to appear, and his use of the analogy of the 'snapshot' to describe how one might 'wait' to 'inscribe a readymade' (Tillers 1978a: Table No. 4/3 § 4.4).[75] Tillers 'snapshots' can also be linked to his discussion of photography in terms of a 'parallel shadow world' in 'Tom Roberts—Some Impressions' (Tillers 1981b: 272); his photographs of the hidden layers of *One Painting, Cleaving*; and the fact that the canvasboard work *The Forming of Place* exists only in the form of a photograph—as does Tillers' masterwork *Untitled*, 1978. As previously mentioned, the latter was lost or accidentally destroyed by the National Gallery of Australia, Canberra in the late 1980s. Accordingly, rather than being 'autobiographical' Tillers' snapshots appear to function in a more complex manner as yet another layer of resonance within the multiplicity of 'voices' constituting his multi-dimensional, appropriational matrix.

PHASE THREE: TILLERS' FIRST COOMA WORKS

In 1997 Tillers moved from Sydney to Cooma, a small town in south-eastern New South Wales in the shire of Cooma-Monaro. He reports that:

> The move was an impulsive response to an untenable situation in Sydney that coincided with an opportunity to purchase a property 'Blairgowrie' in Cooma. It was not a completely conscious and considered choice. (Tillers 2001a)

The move from Sydney, with his partner and two daughters, to a country town was obviously a radical shift in Tillers' life. In a manner that follows on from the Diaspora Trilogy the move to Cooma has facilitated another dynamic interaction of the 'personal', 'appropriational' and 'systematic' aspects of the Canvasboard System. The personal dimension is evident in Tillers' references to his new environment. Yet, Tillers' Cooma works also serve to reinforce the argument pursued here that, in the context of his Canvasboard System, what appears to be 'personal' is better interpreted as 'self-reflexive'—informed as much by the deconstructive logic of the *mise en abyme* as by any attempt at 'self-expression'. Tillers supported this approach to his work in a conversation with the author in September 2001:

> The selection of images is not neutral, it is directed by an underlying psyche that might gravitate towards Baselitz, McCahon or de Chirico. It hasn't been an entirely random process so in a sense the 'personal' has been there from the start. But 'personal' is not quite the right way of putting it. It's more to do with one's focus. I have focused on art for a long time but in the past few years that focus has increasingly expanded into a panorama that allows many other things to be included. The system is flexible enough to allow a range of inputs, and moving to Cooma has given me a new point of view. The imagery I use is filtered through this locale, not just the town but the landscape and many other aspects of this new location. (Tillers 2001a: n.p.)

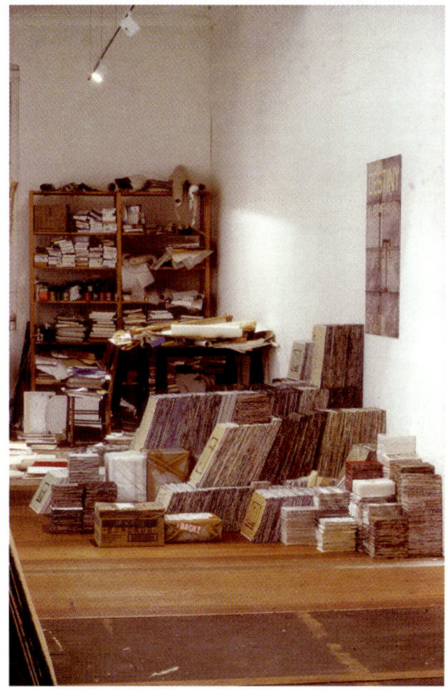

Tillers' photograph of the process of packing up the Sydney studio for the move to Cooma.

There are at least three features of Tillers' Cooma works that indicate that they constitute a body of works that can be understood as yet another self-reflexive enfolding of the continuous, yet 'cloven', fabric that is the Canvasboard System: firstly, some of the Cooma works employ a scale and format that bears a direct relationship with the Diaspora Trilogy; secondly, the Cooma works are significantly informed by the culminating feature of the first phase of the Canvasboard System, *The Bridge of Reversible Destiny*, 1990; thirdly, the Cooma works have generated a repertoire of motifs that makes them highly interrelated in a manner that suggests—as in the case of the Diaspora Trilogy—a canvasboard system within the Canvasboard System.

THE RETURN OF REVERSIBLE DESTINY

One of the most interesting aspects of the Cooma works is the fact that they exhibit an important interconnection with the first phase of Tillers' Canvasboard System. The analysis of the first phase provided in Chapter Ten suggested that *The Bridge of Reversible Destiny,* 1990, was a culminating statement of authorial self-deconstruction. It is therefore significant that this work should resurface ten years later in the most recent canvasboard works. The reconnection began in 1998 when Tillers was invited to be part of a large multi-national group exhibition, Five Continents and a City, to be held in Mexico City. The curator for Asia/Oceania, Yu Yeon Kim asked specifically for *The Bridge of Reversible Destiny*, 1990. However, the mounted canvasboard aspect of the original installation had already been recycled into a new work, *There is Still that which Cleaves within the Cleft,* 1992. In addition, Tillers was unable to locate and retrieve the exact canvasboard

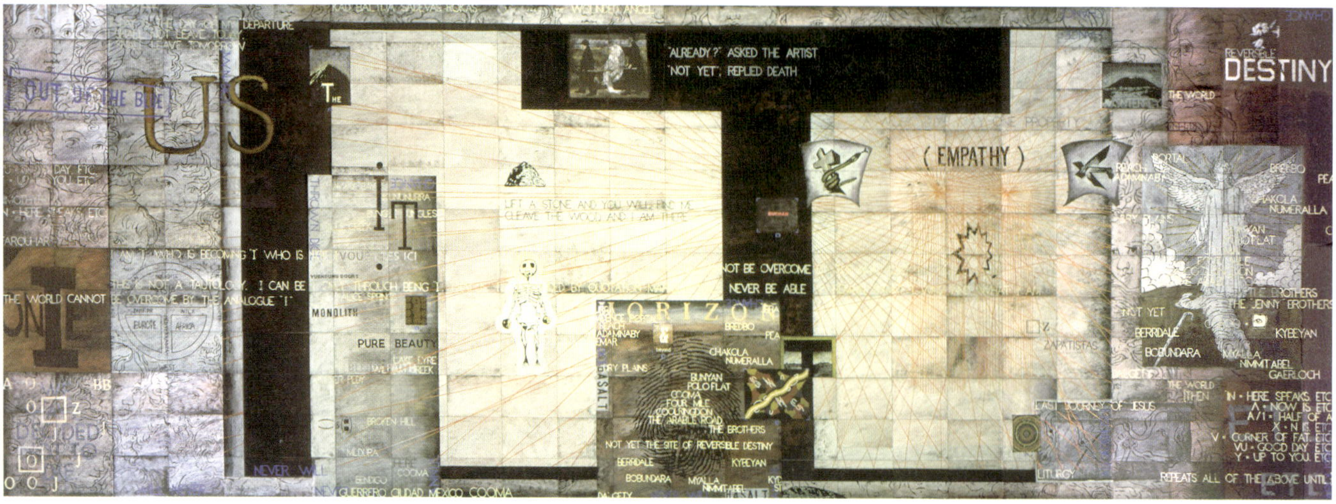

TOP: ***Mexico, etcetera*****, 2001. Synthetic polymer paint and gouache on 294 canvasboards, Nos. 69047–69340, 305 x 853 cm. Installation view at Pori Art Museum, Pori, Finland. Collection: the artist. Photograph: Erkki Valli-Jaakola.**
BOTTOM: ***Landing Sites: A, B, C*****, 2000. Synthetic polymer paint, gouache and oil stick on 184 canvasboards, Nos. 65962–66145, 279 x 569 cm. Collection: National Gallery of Australia, Canberra. Photograph: Mick Bradley.**

works that formed the stacked component of *The Bridge of Reversible Destiny*, 1990. A completely new version of *The Bridge of Reversible Destiny* installation had to be created for the Five Continents and a City exhibition, but one that resembled the original version as much as possible. In effect Tillers had to create a copy or simulacrum of the 'original', which being appropriational was never entirely original.

The case of *The Bridge of Reversible Destiny* is significant because it points to an important feature of the Canvasboard System—while the modular canvasboard works remain in Tillers' possession they are unmounted in stacks, literally deconstructed and in a state of potential flux. Tillers reports

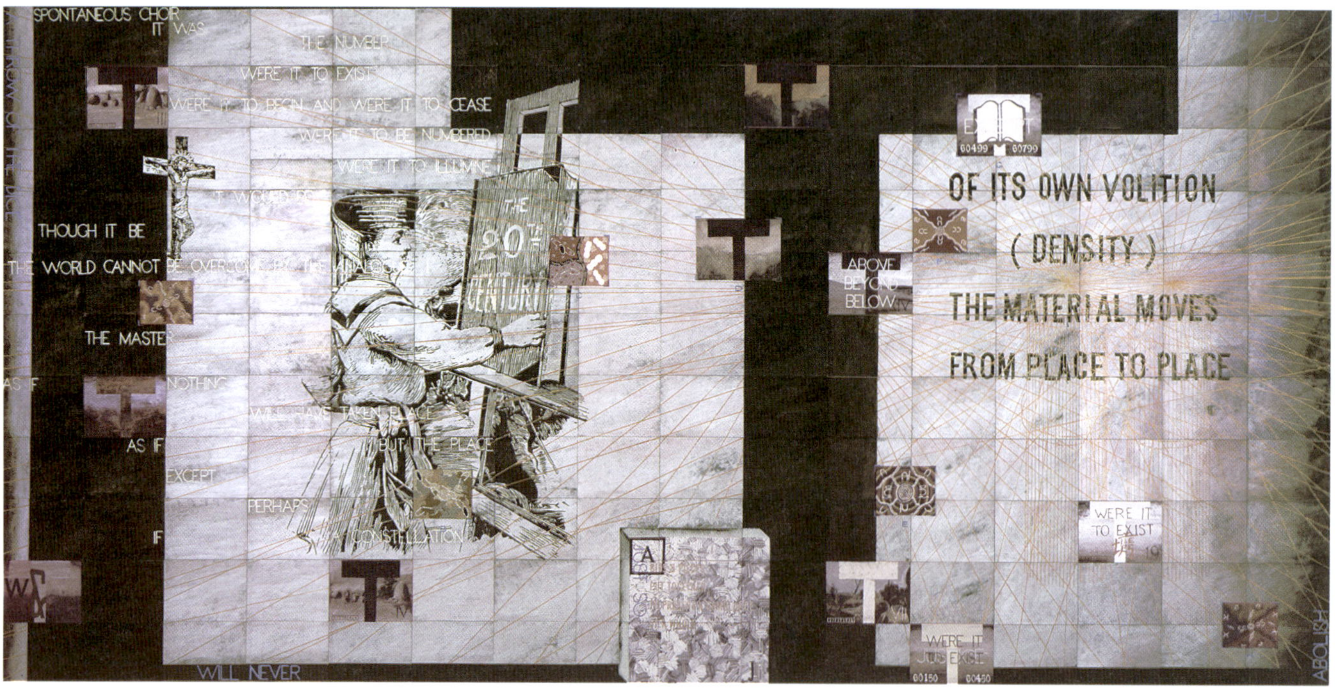

that he relies on his partner as a 'resident tracker and archivist' who can follow and document:

> the, at times, elusive trajectory of what are essentially unstable works—as they coalesce, dissolve, recombine or, alternatively, are discarded, recycled or remade according to the demands of the system or the possibilities of the moment. (Tillers 2001a: n.p.)

The most obvious impact of Tillers' reconstruction of *The Bridge of Reversible Destiny* on his Cooma works became evident in Diaspora-scale works produced in 2000 and 2001: *Landing Sites: A, B, C*, 2000; and *Landing Sites: D, E, F*, 2000; and *Mexico, etcetera*, 2001 which are dominated by a large 'IT' as is apparent in the two examples illustrated opposite. The fact that ten years separates the Landing Sites works and *Mexico, etcetera* from the original *The Bridge of Reversible Destiny* is testimony to the fact that Tillers continues to conceive of his canvasboard works as a holistic system that creates complexity via both intertextual and intratextual 'information feedback' and 'information processing'.

The act of reconstructing *The Bridge of Reversible Destiny* also influenced Tillers' earlier Cooma works, adding a paradoxical dimension to his inclusion of apparently 'personal' references to the landscape surrounding his new home. To facilitate the process of integrating into his new environment and what he describes as 'a kind of reconnaissance of the terrain' (Tillers 2001a) he joined a group of amateur painters on *plein-air* landscape painting expeditions. Unsurprisingly he painted on his standard canvasboard modules and thereby introduced the first original painted images into his work since the image structure in *Moments of Inertia,* 1972-73.[76] But, as with his introduction of photographs of his locale into the Diaspora Trilogy, Tillers' *plein-air* landscapes resonate with, and are directed by, the constellation of appropriations that make up his Canvasboard System. Two of Tillers' *plein-air* canvasboard paintings are reproduced top and centre right. The third illustration, bottom right, is one of a series of canvasboards produced simultaneously with the *plein-air* painting but in the studio. Together the two types formed a pool of single panel modules all of which have large 'T's superimposed over them as if Tillers were trying to map himself onto the land. A self-deconstructive register appears, however, when it is acknowledged that the 'T' is a reawakened reference to the 'IT' in *The Bridge of Reversible Destiny* where Tillers' apparent assertion of identity is deconstructed by the fact that he appropriated his initials from another artist, McCahon. The self-deconstructive nature of Tillers' reference to himself is amplified by the fact that before beginning his *plein-air* paintings he had discovered that McCahon had produced a series of 'T's on canvasboard panels. The phrase 'WERE *IT* TO EXIST' [emphasis added] in the third reproduction reinforces this

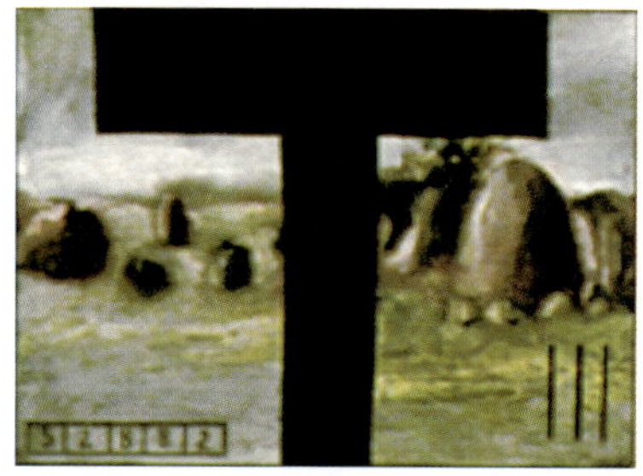

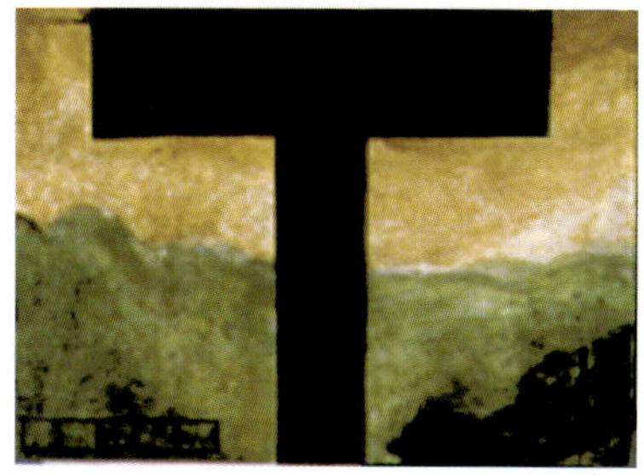

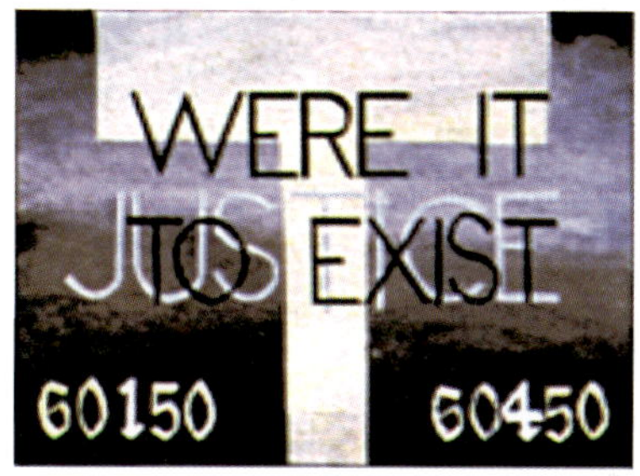

TOP and CENTRE: Two canvasboards with landscapes painted by Tillers on his plein-air landscape painting expeditions with an amateur painters' group in Cooma, 1998. Synthetic polymer paint on canvasboards, each measuring 25.4 x 35.6 cm. BOTTOM: One of a series of single panel canvasboard modular works produced at the same time as the plein-air paintings but in the studio. Synthetic polymer paint on canvasboards, each measuring 25.4 x 35.6 cm.

interpretation. After his initial reconnaissance Tillers produced the first of his Diaspora-sized Cooma works: *Monaro,* 1998 (see below).

Although there is no large 'IT' dominating *Monaro* a reference to *The Bridge of Reversible Destiny* is evident in the fact that Tillers has incorporated a number of his single panel landscape 'T' paintings into the work. A similar strategy is evident in the other Diaspora-scale Cooma works to date, with the difference that instead of incorporating the landscape 'T' panels into *Monaro* Tillers superimposed them on the surface, together with single canvasboard panel Aboriginal paintings which he purchased.

Another significant feature of *Monaro* and the other Diaspora-scale Cooma works is that they can be understood as continuing Tillers' reference to Germano Celant's metaphor of painting as an 'endless roll' that appears so appropriate for the large, elongated format of the Diaspora works.[77] *Monaro,* 1998, and *Mexico, etcetera,* 2001, are both the same height as the Diaspora Trilogy but slightly shorter (by 61.4 cm, approximately two feet) due to the fact that Tillers used slightly shorter canvasboard panels. *Landing Sites: A, B, C,* 2000 and *Landing Sites: D, E, F,* 2000 are significantly shorter (by 345.4 cm, 11 ft. 4 in.) and lower (by 26 cm, 10 in.) than the Diaspora works. Nevertheless these two works remain monumental enough to remain associated with the Diaspora Trilogy.

Monaro, 1998, is distinguished by the fact that it is the first Diaspora-scale Cooma work and its seminal status is evident in its title which refers to the

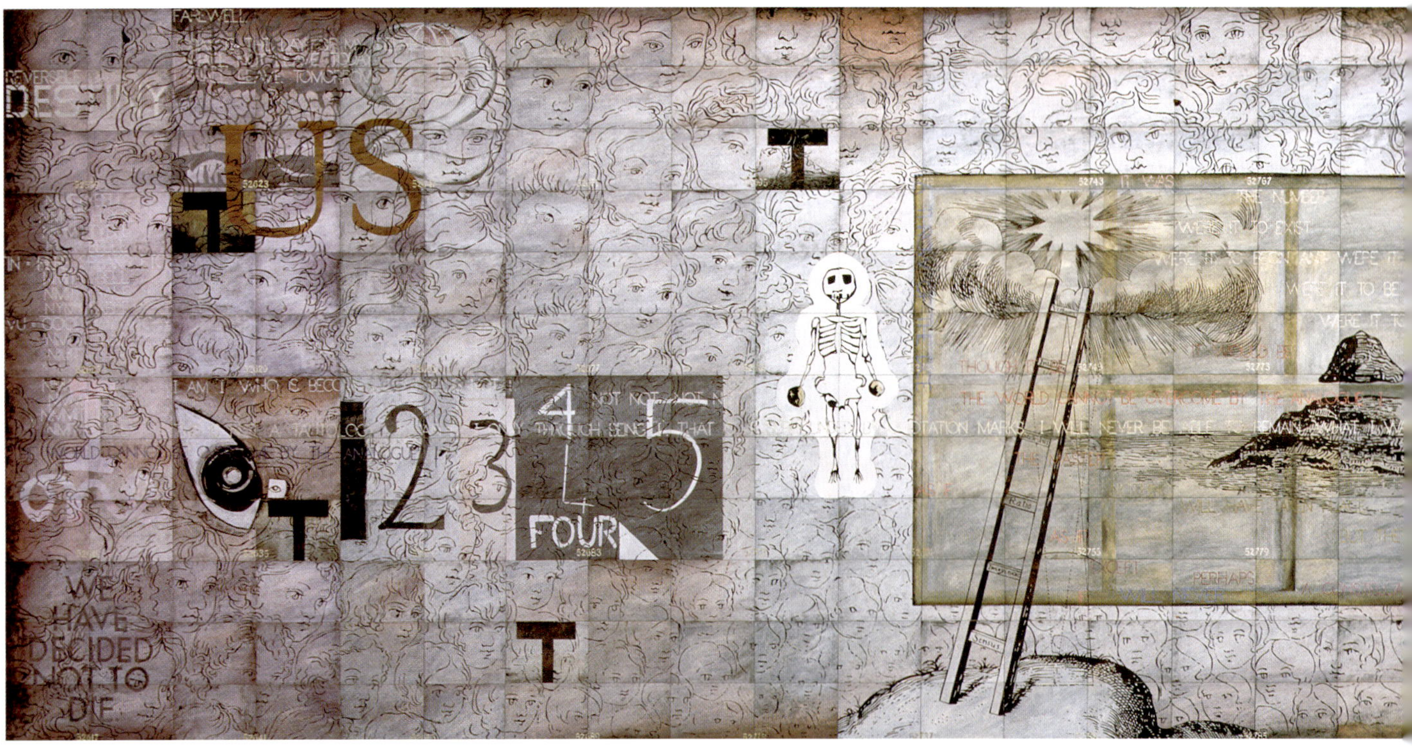

***Monaro,* 1998. Synthetic polymer paint, gouache on 288 canvasboards, Nos. 52,594–52881, 305 x 853 cm. Collection: the artist. Photograph: Paul Green.**

broader region in which the Cooma-Monaro shire is located. The landscape in this region is an austere tableland with a granite and basalt geology and a climate that encompasses extremes of cold and heat. In *Monaro* and Tillers' Cooma works in general he has moved towards an overall field-like quality that reflects the landscape of the Monaro region. This reference to the landscape is reinforced by the single panel landscape-'T' paintings which he incorporated into *Monaro*. Some of the single panels derive from his *plein air* painting expeditions, but most are in fact auto-appropriations suggesting that in spite of his *plein air* experience he remains dedicated to the simulacral as opposed to the unique original. Perhaps the most distinctive feature of *Monaro* is the field of cherubic faces that cascades across the enormous canvasboard expanse replacing Tillers' field of McCahonian inspired text in the Diaspora Trilogy with a multitude of angels derived from a drawing by Philipp Otto Runge. Tillers reports that Runge's drawing of cherubim:

> dates from around 1806. Runge was older than Caspar David Friedrich, and is understood as a precursor of the romanticism that leads onto contemporary German artists such as Polke, Beuys and Baselitz. (in Coulter-Smith 2001: n.p.)

Tillers no doubt mentions the associations with Polke, Beuys and Baselitz because they are important appropriational sources in the Canvasboard System. Yet, he also reports that he was unaware of this connection when he first used the Runge motif.[78] Tillers continues: 'Runge wanted to produce four masterworks: *Morning*, *Day*, *Afternoon*, *Evening*. They would be an allegory of life and would take his entire life to produce.' (in Coulter-Smith 2001: n.p.). Tillers' comments are interesting as they suggest that he understands Runge's romantic imagery in terms of a systematic conceptualist approach similar to the one he adopted in the Canvasboard System and articulated in a published conversation with his partner when he explained:

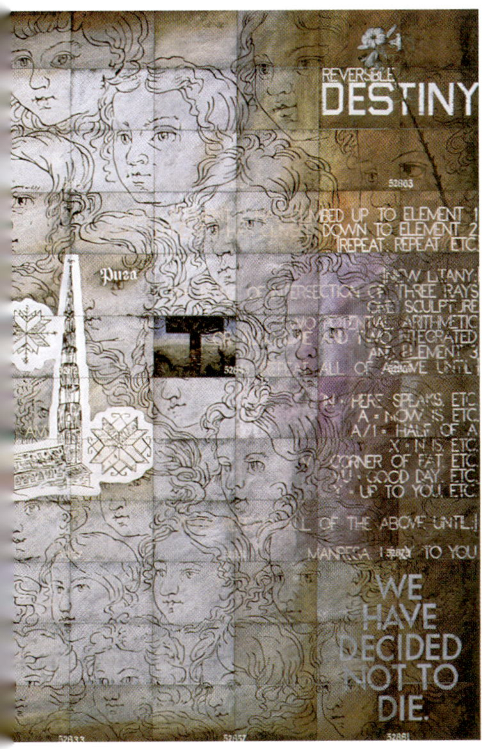

> The panels have been numbered right from the start and the panel count is continuous from 1 to ∞. … All modes of art can be accommodated within this book, and all modes of expression … My inten-

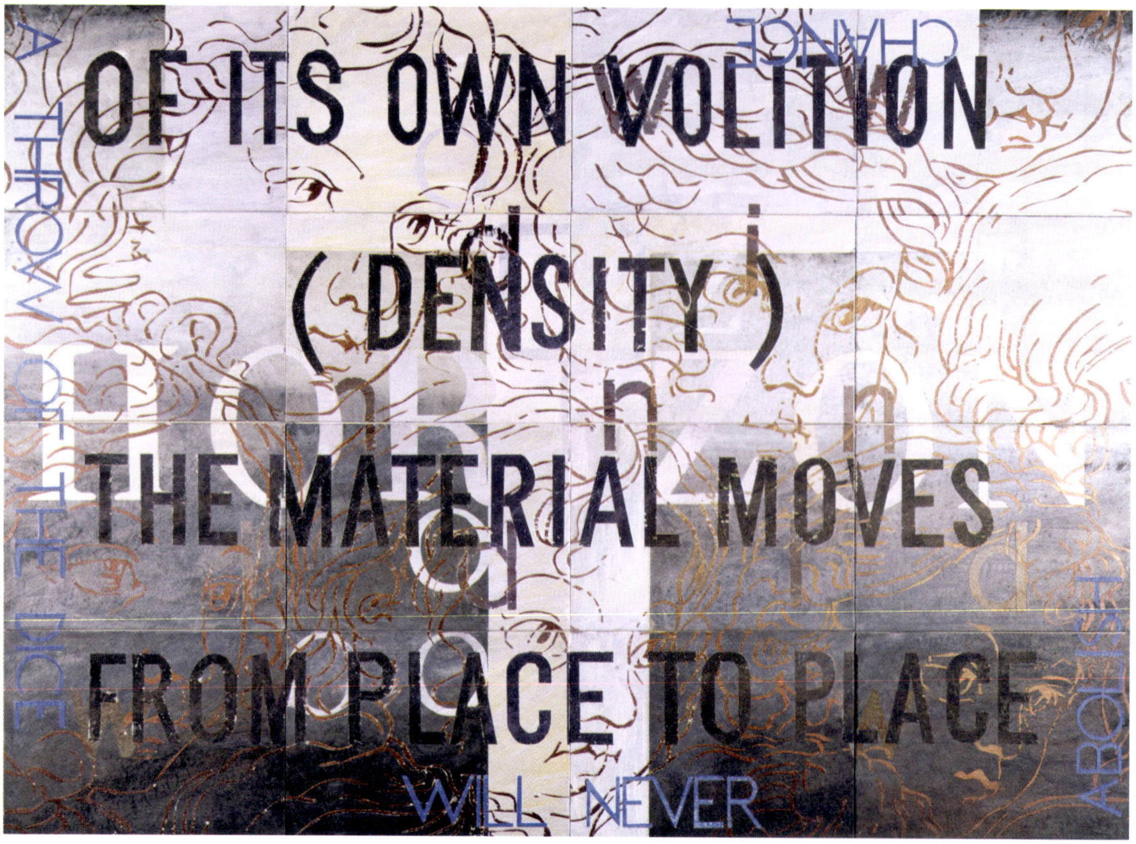

***Nature Speaks (Volition)*, 1999. Synthetic polymer paint, gouache on 16 canvasboards, Nos. 61412–61427, 102 x 142 cm. Collection: the artist. Photograph: Schoo's Studio.**

> tion is the exhaustion of all possible categories and I'll spend the rest of my life working towards achieving this goal. (Slatyer and Tillers 1987: 111)

Tillers also notes that Runge died in his early thirties and little survives of his project for *Morning*. Tillers was particularly struck by one of the preparatory studies which consists of a large pen drawing of a field of cherubim dated 1809, and comments:

> The work seemed remarkably modern when seen as a drawing and appealed to me for some reason. I could see possibilities in using something so linear; a pattern that could function as a detail or as a whole. (in Coulter-Smith 2001: n.p.)

Tillers' description of the Runge motif as a 'pattern' that 'could function as a detail or as whole' is reminiscent of the holistic systems theory informing his image structure in *Moments of Inertia*. This was also a field-like image that functioned as part and as whole. In addition, as the analysis in Chapter Six showed, it also marks Tillers' first use of specular poetics to express the complexity of organic systems. When located in this context the Runge motif can be understood as a self-reflexive reference to the way in which the Canvasboard System is made up of parts that function as a whole.

SYSTEMS WITHIN SYSTEMS

Taken as a whole the Cooma works exhibit a Russian doll-like structure of systems within systems. The most encompassing works are the Diaspora-scale paintings that connect the Cooma works with both the Diaspora Trilogy and the first phase of the Canvasboard System via their reference to *The Bridge of Reversible Destiny*, 1990. The Diaspora-scale works are followed by medium scale works which at present consist of a series of works with the title 'The Enigma of Arrival' followed by a Roman numeral, and another series with the generic title 'Nature Speaks' followed by a Roman numeral, a word in brackets, or an alphabetic letter. The medium scale works in turn encompass a system of smaller sixteen panel works that Tillers intends will be a set of exactly one hundred works. Finally, there are the single panel landscape 'T' works. These nested systems create a complex whole in which the repertoire of motifs emerging from the Cooma works is subjected to dynamically interrelated 'information processing'. Moreover, this systematic processing and 'reprocessing' also includes the reappropriation of appropriated imagery from the first phase of the Canvasboard System. Indeed Tillers notes that in the Cooma works as a whole the process of 'recycling from earlier works is increasing' (Tillers 2001b).

THE SIXTEEN PANEL SYSTEM

The sixteen panel system, in particular, appears to crystallise key motifs that occur in the current body of Cooma works and accordingly provides a valuable means of understanding important features of the Cooma works as a whole. However, it is difficult to extricate this system from the Nature Speaks series in which it is nested. Accordingly the following analysis will take a 'nonlinear' path through the Cooma works focusing on the repertoire of motifs that Tillers has fed into the permutational sixteen panel system. It will be shown that the sixteen panel system is not only a self-reflexive nested system, but also that the individual motifs that recur in this set of works exhibit distinctly self-reflexive properties. The sixteen panel system is nonlinear and can be entered at any point; for example *Nature Speaks (Volition)*, 1999, (see opposite) appropriates a text from the American conceptual artist Lawrence Weiner, who has become a regular contributor to the third phase of Tillers' Canvasboard System. Weiner's text 'of its own volition (density) the material moves from place to place' seems to be deployed as an embedded reference to the entire Canvasboard System. The phrase 'of its own volition' reflects Tillers' desire for the System to become

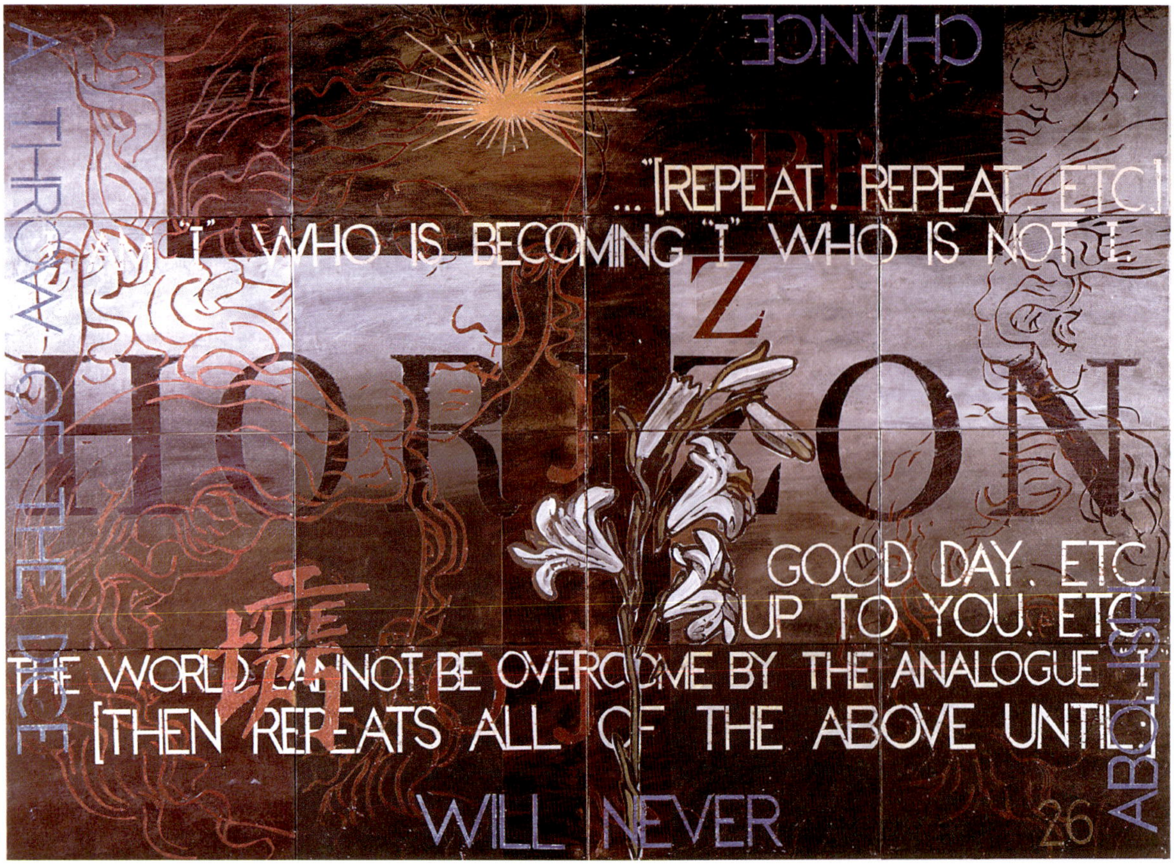

***Nature Speaks IV*, 1998. Synthetic polymer paint and gouache on 16 canvasboard panels, Nos. 60800–60815, 102 x 142 cm. Private collection. Photograph: Schoo's Studio.**

'self-organising', and the notion of material moving 'from place to place' can be read as an allusion to Tillers' recombination of canvasboard modules into new works, a process that adds to the intertextual, interconnectivity of the System.

It is also important to note that the paradoxical nature of Tillers' authorial identity is also woven into and out of this intertextual interconnectivity, as is particularly apparent in *Nature Speaks IV,* 1998, shown above. In the top section of the work there is a phrase which reads 'I am "I" who is becoming "I" who is not I' and is a quotation from the postmodern writer Haniya Yutaka.[79] In the bottom part of the work is another phrase 'The world cannot be overcome by the analogue "I"'. Tillers notes that he has 'used this over and over again because it is such a resonant text'. It is a quotation from the late John Anderson, a Melbourne poet who suffered from narcolepsy. Tillers reports that Anderson: 'would write down phrases and words as he moved involuntarily from the waking to the sleeping state almost like a medium' (Tillers 2001a). Tillers also notes that 'analogue is a powerful word for me because it has to do with maps, mapping and Mount Analogue' (in Coulter-Smith 2001: n.p.).

Tillers' reference to Mount Analogue relates to *Mount Analogue,* 1985, a work from the first phase of the Canvasboard System in which he appropri-

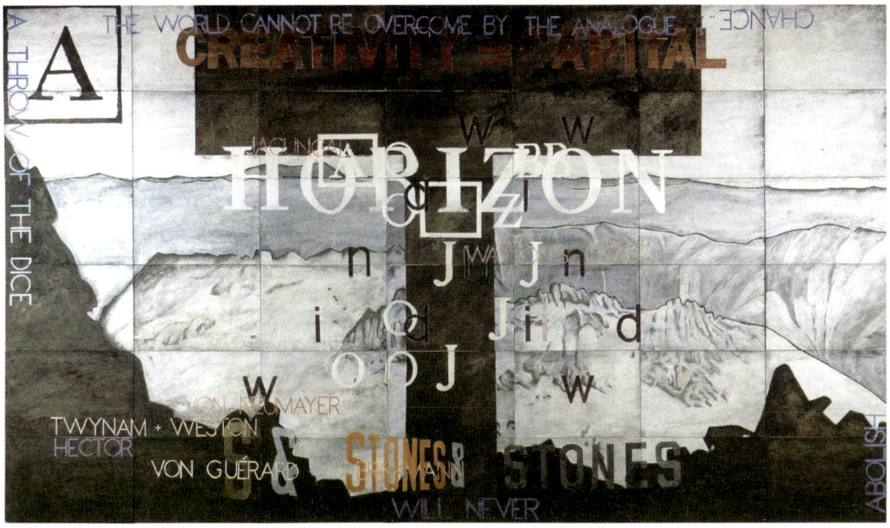

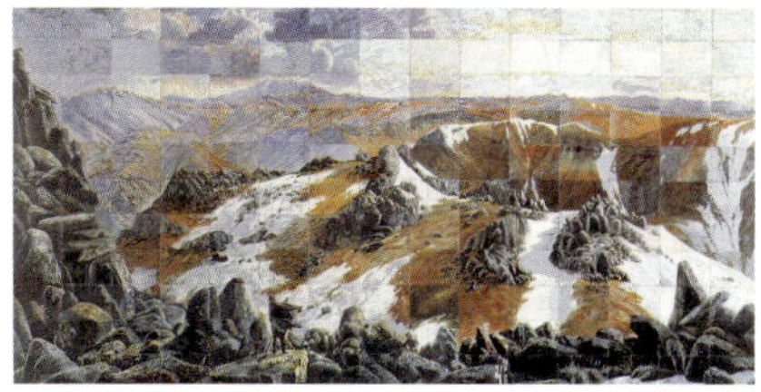

LEFT: *The View from K*, 1997–98 Synthetic polymer paint and gouache on 24 canvasboards, Nos. 60451–60492, 152 x 267 cm. Private collection. Photograph: Schoo's Studio. RIGHT: *Mount Analogue*, 1985. Oilstick, synthetic polymer paint on 165 canvasboards, Nos. 7416–7580, 279 x 571 cm. Collection: National Gallery of Australia, Canberra. Photograph: Fenn Hinchcliffe.

ated a painting of Mount Kosciuszko (the highest mountain in Australia) by Eugène von Guérard (see top right). The title *Mount Analogue* stemmed from Tillers reading René Daumal's pataphysical novel *Mount Analogue: A Novel of Symbolically Authentic Non-Euclidean Adventures in Mountain Climbing* (Daumal 1960). Daumal's story is of an expedition to an invisible mountain. Tillers' parallel between Daumal's *Mount Analogue* and Anderson's 'analogue I' in the Nature Speaks series suggests that his layering of self-reflexive motifs leads authorial identity into a *mise en abyme* that renders it 'invisible' by becoming 'meta-' or 'inter'-authorial.

This reading is supported by another motif in the Nature Speaks series which underscores the relationship between Mount Analogue, and the 'analogue I'. By sheer coincidence Tillers' move to Cooma brought him close to Mount Kosciuszko and led him to include it as a motif in the Nature Speaks series as is evident in *The View from K*, 1997, reproduced above left. *The View from K* is based on a lithograph by von Guérard which bears the same title as the source for Tillers' *Mount Analogue.* Tillers was attracted to the reproduction of this lithograph in a book by Alan E. J. Andrews (Andrews 1991) because it is a more graphic depiction than the *Mount Analogue* source. The title of the lithograph is *North-East View from the Northern Top of Mount Kosciuszko*, but Andrews notes that the view is probably from the adjoining Mount Townsend. In the bottom left corner of *The View from Mount K* Tillers has superimposed von Guérard's name onto the landscape as well as the names of the people who accompanied him: von Neumayer, Twynam, Weston and Hector (a dog), plus the names of mountains that form part of the vista: Jagungal, and Watson's Crags.

The mountain these Europeans climbed has an English name (Townsend), the mountain they thought they were climbing has a Polish name and was first painted by an artist with a Swiss name, and the vista they looked out on

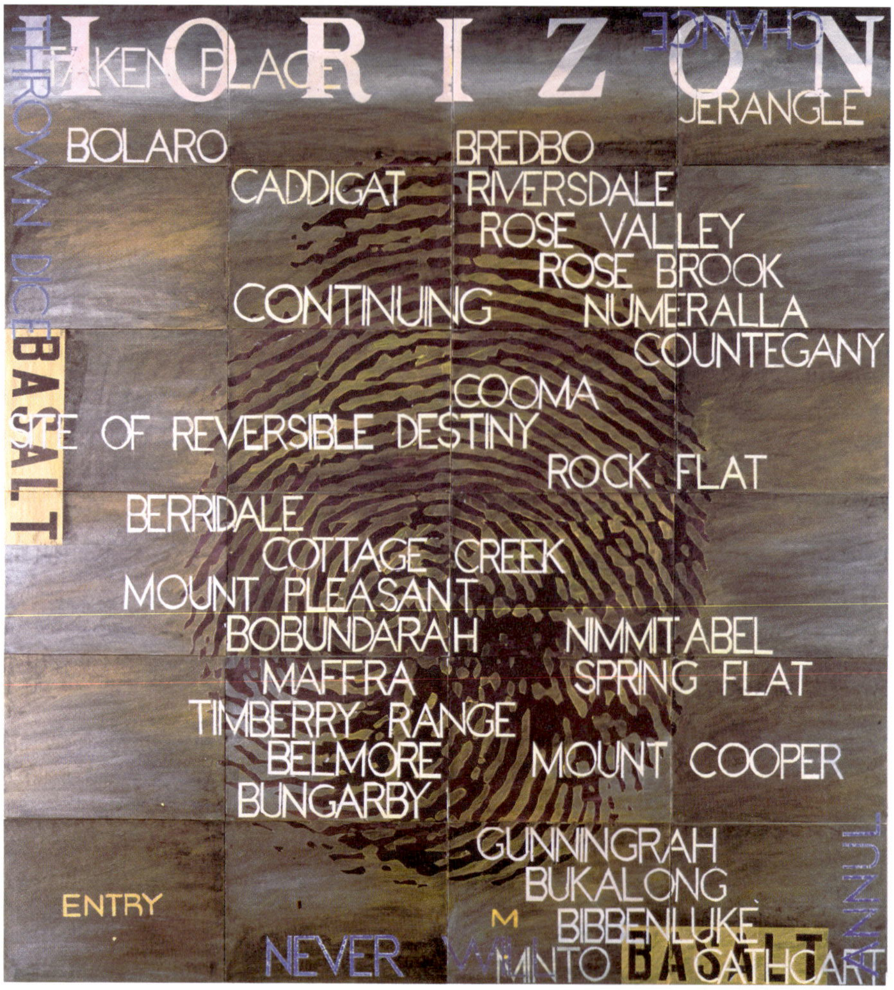

***Nature Speaks: M*, 2000. Synthetic polymer paint on 24 canvasboards, Nos. 66749–66772 cm. Private collection. Photograph: Schoo's Studio.**

includes Jagungal and Watson's Crags. The fact that the European names outnumber the Aboriginal name listed by Tillers in *The View from Mount K* is significant, suggesting that by superimposing names onto the landscape Tillers is referring to issues of colonisation and ownership of the land. The question can be posed as to whether Tillers' imposition of a giant 'T' on the landscape can be read as a species of colonisation. In the light of *The Bridge of Reversible Destiny*, Tillers' discovery of McCahon's canvasboard 'T's, and the 'analogue I' the answer appears to be no. Instead the 'T' in *The View from K* can be read as reflecting upon issues of colonisation in a manner that parallels the self-reflexivity generated by the process of appropriation, in particular the phenomenon wherein parallels, resonances and interrelationships evolve between the appropriator and the appropriated. Another work *Nature Speaks: M, 2000*, reproduced above, supports this interpretation: *Nature Speaks: M* makes use of place names around Cooma against a background that evokes the colours of the landscape of the Monaro region. It also evokes the aerial viewpoint of

Aboriginal landscape, a reference reinforced by the fact that the names on the map combine white settler and Aboriginal place names. Tillers explains that the names were derived from a genealogical book based on the study of headstones in graveyards. It interested him that although they are all Anglo-Saxon graveyards, a significant number have Aboriginal names. This led him to observe that: 'The graveyards are like Christian sacred sites, that now exist in the land as do Aboriginal sacred sites.' (in Coulter-Smith 2001). Tillers' interpretation of the mix of names suggests a complex intercultural relationship between inhabitants and the land. It is also noteworthy that *Nature Speaks: M* does not contain a 'T'—instead a giant thumbprint leaves its mark on the landscape. The thumbprint is appropriated from Piero Manzoni (famous for deconstructive gestures including signing peoples' bodies and exhibiting his excrement in small tin cans) and functions very much like the 'T'. Indeed the Manzoni thumbprint is just as much a sign of 'Tillers'—the 'author' of the system—as is the 'T'. Both signs are appropriated from other artists, the one Manzoni the other McCahon. Accordingly the 'T' is less a personal imprint on the land than a sign that reflects upon the question 'to whom does the land belong?', and the answer can be traced back to Tillers' anti-anthropic position in 'The Beginner's Guide to Oil Painting' where he stated:

> the world is seen as a commodity … We know how to exploit the seashore for profit, sterilise the landscape for profit, fell the great forests for profit, fill protective marshes for profit. (Tillers 1973a: Appendix A 9)

and suggested as an alternative that:

> the antithesis of the exploitative view of nature is the ecological view of man's dependence on nature not as a separate entity but as part of many interdependent systems. The complexity and holistic organisation of a system is in direct contrast to the simple relational man-nature dualism of the anthropocentric world view. (Tillers 1973a: Appendix A 11-12)

Tillers' anti-anthropic assertion that 'the ecological view of man's dependence on nature not as a separate entity but as part of many interdependent systems' remains relevant today, as can be seen in a statement made by Tillers in 1998 when he observed:

> Atoms are wholes consisting of sub-atomic parts … likewise cells within tissues within organs within organisms, organisms within societies, societies within ecosystems, ecosystems within Gaia, Gaia in the Solar System, the Solar System in the Galaxy and so on (Tillers 1998: 34)

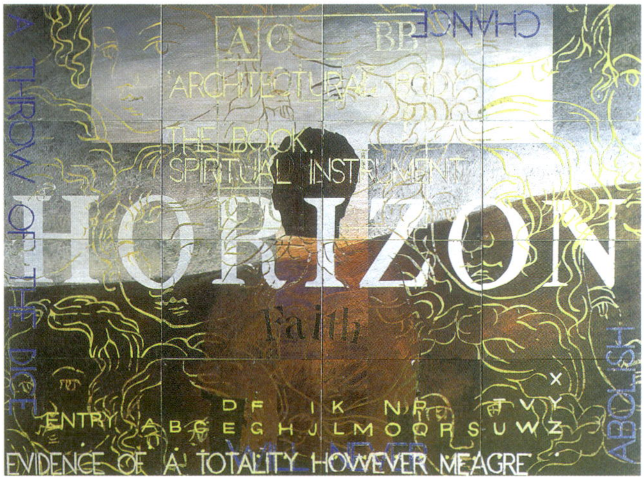

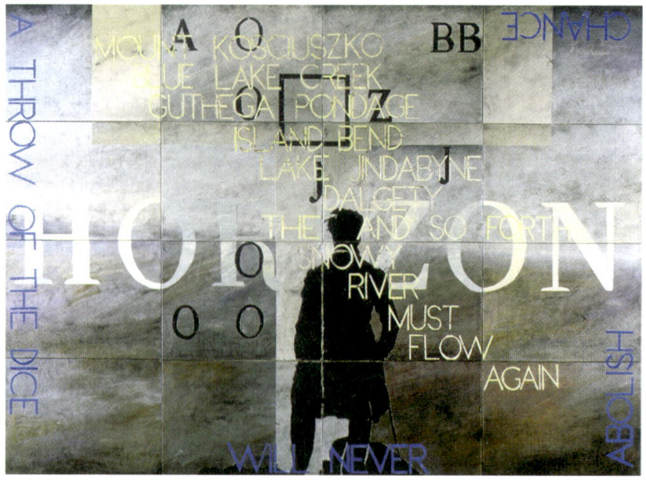

TOP LEFT: ***Monaro Index II*, 2000. Synthetic polymer paint and gouache on 16 canvasboards, Nos. 65734–65749, 102 x 142 cm. Private collection. Photograph: Schoo's Studio. TOP RIGHT:** ***Nature Speaks (Kosciuszko)*, 1999. Synthetic polymer paint and gouache on 16 canvasboards, Nos. 65734–65749, 102 x 142 cm. Private collection. Photograph: Schoo's Studio. BOTTOM:** ***Monaro Millennium I*, 2000. Synthetic polymer paint and gouache on 16 canvasboards, Nos. 65734–65749, 102 x 142 cm. Private collection. Photograph: Schoo's Studio.**

Accordingly, it is reasonable to assume that Tillers' inscription of the Nature Speaks landscapes with large 'T's is not only a self-deconstructive assertion of self in the manner of the 'IT' in *The Bridge of Reversible Destiny* but also an expression of his enduring anti-anthropic ecopolitics informed by his understanding of the nested set structure of holistic systems in nature. One is also reminded here of the photographs Tillers took of his local environment around his old Sydney studio: His snapshots (see pages 184-185) combine self-deconstructive evocations of decentred selfhood with the issue of Aboriginal land rights that remains such a pressing concern in Australia. Tillers' inscription of the names onto the landscape in *The View from K*, 1997-98, seems to be similarly deconstructive. In the geographical context Mount Kosciuszko faces Mount Townsend; in the poetic context of the Canvasboard System they face Mount Analogue; and within the nested subsystems constituted by the Nature Speaks series and the sixteen panel Nature Speaks system, the giant 'T' seems to echo the phrase 'the world cannot be overcome by the analogue I', where the 'analogue I' is associated with the '"I" who is becoming "I" who is not I'.

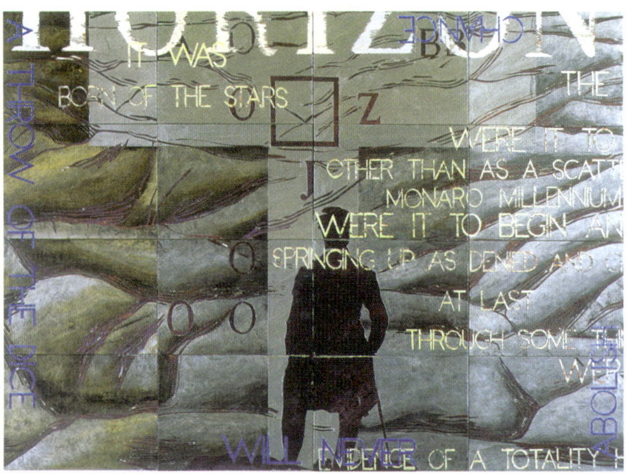

Such a reading is supported by three works from the sixteen panel system—*Monaro Index II*, 2000; *Monaro Millennium I*, 2000; and *Nature Speaks (Kosciuszko)*, 1999, reproduced above and below. Each work shows a figure standing in front of Tillers' renditions of the Cooma-Monaro landscape. In each instance the giant 'T' is conflated with a figure, two of which are appropriated from Caspar David Friedrich. The fact that we see the only the back of the person suggests absence. One is reminded of Magritte's image of a man standing in front of a mirror that reflects the back view we see standing in front of the mirror—an inter-

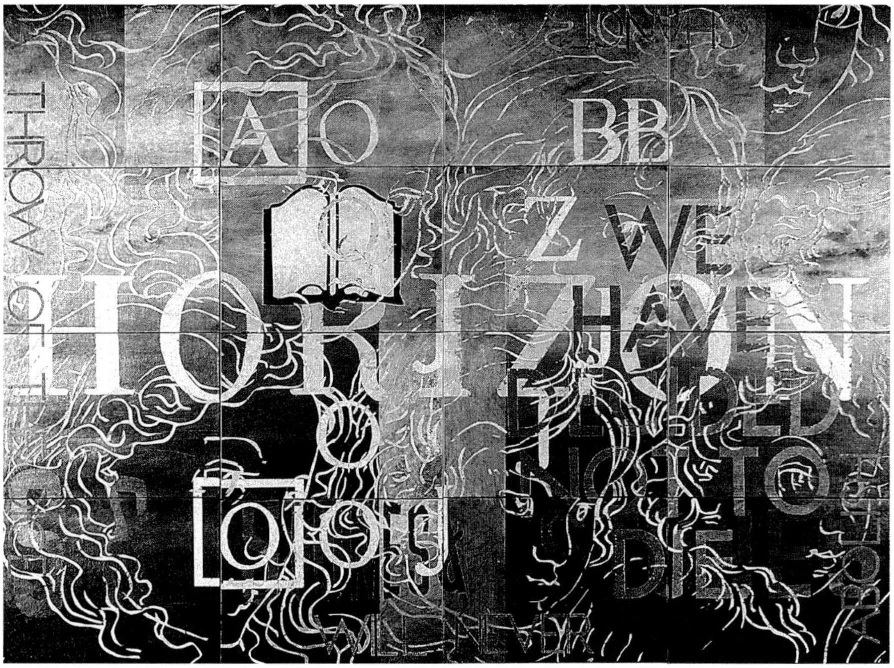

***Nature Speaks: III*, 1998. Synthetic polymer paint, gouache on 16 canvasboards, Nos. 60128–60143, 102 x 14.2 cm. Private collection. Photograph: Schoo's Studio.**

esting instance of *mise en abyme*. The image of the silhouetted man juxtaposed with the 'T' connotes an infinite regress of presence and absence that is intensified by the systematic, layered nature of these works.

Apart from the 'T', another leitmotif in the Nature Speaks series is the phrase: 'A Throw of the Dice Will Never Abolish Chance' which runs around the periphery of most of the works in the series. The phrase is the title of a poem by Stéphane Mallarmé (transposed into a typeface appropriated from the conceptual art of Robert Barry). The motif is self-reflexive due to its relationship with Tillers' use of Mallarmé's metaphor of the 'Book of Power' to describe his Canvasboard System. As mentioned previously, Tillers' use of this metaphor stems from Mallarmé who wrote in 1895: 'Everything, in the world, exists to end up in a book.' (in Slatyer and Tillers 1987: 111). This metaphor became the title of the first monograph on Tillers, *Imants Tillers and the 'Book of Power'* (Curnow 1998) in which Wystan Curnow focused on Tillers' use of the Mallarméan metaphor to refer to the Canvasboard System. A very direct reference to the 'Book of Power' is apparent in *Nature Speaks: III*, 1998, reproduced above. In this work a centrally located open book motif, with a pictographic appearance, reflects Tillers' metaphor of the 'Book of Power'. The connotations of the book motif also resonate with the title of Mallarmé's poem 'A Throw of the Dice Will Never Abolish Chance' which surrounds the periphery of *Nature Speaks: III*. This leitmotif also runs round the periphery of *Nature Speaks: V*, reproduced overleaf. In this work the peripheral text is reinforced by a quote from 'A Throw of the Dice Will Never Abolish Chance' imposed as yellow text

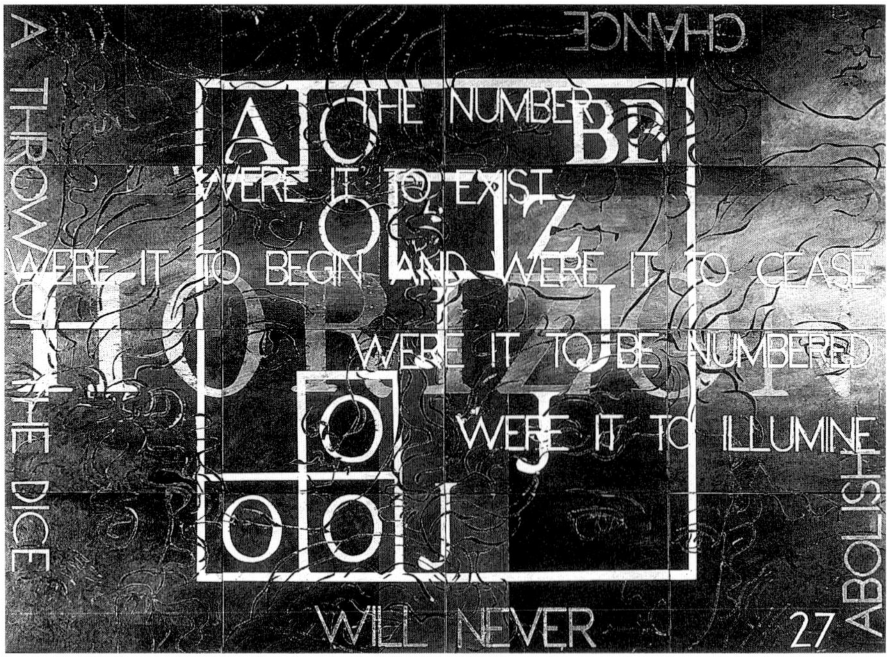

***Nature Speaks: V*, 1999. Synthetic polymer paint, gouache on 16 canvasboards, Nos. 60824–60839, 102 x 142 cm. Private collection. Photograph: Schoo's Studio.**

across the picture plane, reading: 'The Number / Were it to Exist / Were it to Begin and Were it to Cease / Were it to be Numbered / Were it to Illumine'. In January 2001 Tillers suggested that this text 'almost describes The Book of Power' adding that it is 'a verbal aspect that refers to the whole [canvasboard] project' (in Coulter-Smith 2001: n.p.).

Tillers' observation indicates that his references to Mallarmé are another addition to the battery of interrelated self-reflexive motifs that constitute his Cooma works. In *Nature Speaks: V* such self-referential interconnectivity is intensified by the fact that the quotation from Mallarmé is superimposed over an appropriation of Kurt Schwitters' 'Typeset Picture-Poem', 1922,[80] consisting of letters locked into a grid-like construction. There is a minimalist-like systemicity to Schwitters' poem that reflects the systematic nature of Tillers' Canvasboard System and the Nature Speaks series; an interpretation reinforced by the fact that Tillers refers to Schwitters' poem as 'a kind of encoding' (in Coulter-Smith 2001: n.p.).

Tillers' reference to 'encoding' highlights the argument presented here that he continues to understand his work in terms of a 'holistic system aesthetic' that can be traced back to the concern with systems in conceptual art. But over the years Tillers' conceptual framework has evolved from the scholarly seriousness of his seminal scientific aesthetic, outlined in 'The Beginner's Guide to Oil Painting' (Tillers 1973a: Appendix A) into a scientific poetics that incorporates paradoxical, intuitive and playful facets. The latter is evident in another motif apparent in *Monaro Index I*, 2000, shown opposite. Along the bottom of this work there is a systematic, code-like

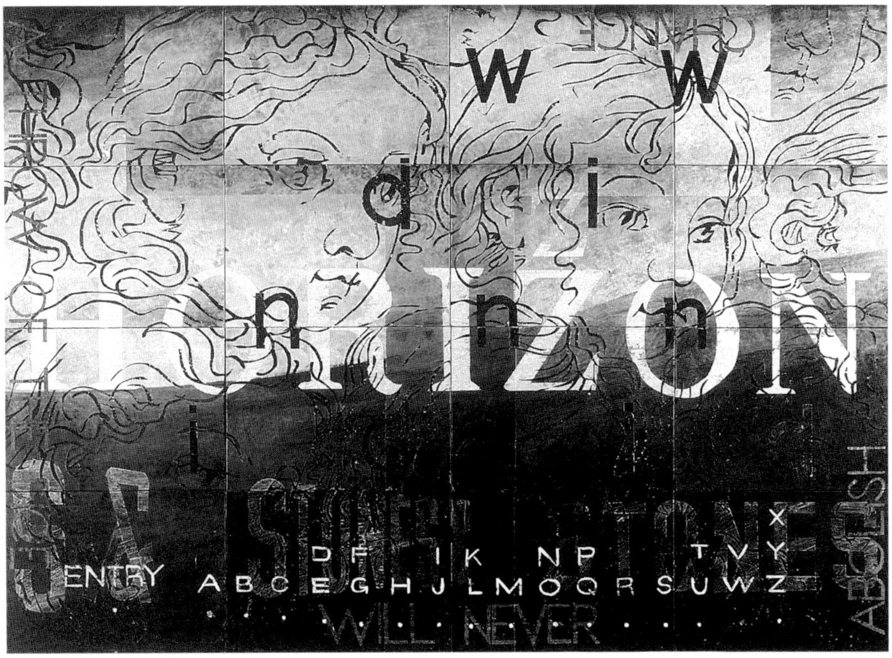

***Monaro Index I*, 2000. Synthetic polymer paint, gouache on 16 canvasboards, Nos. 65670–65685, 102 x 142 cm. Private collection. Photograph: Schoo's Studio.**

alphabetic series. It is not simply an alphabet, the 'D' is placed above the 'E', the 'F' over the 'G' and the 'X' and 'Y' over the 'Z'. In fact the source is quite mundane, it was inspired by Tillers' telephone index. Tillers wove this reference into the Cooma works, firstly, due to his long standing fascination with systems;[81] and, secondly, because the cover of Tillers' telephone index has a graphic curve inscribed on it that reminded him of the hilly terrain of Cooma-Monaro, an association articulated in *Monaro Index I* in the curve of the horizon.

Here is another instance of an 'autobiographical' insertion that deconstructs the concept of autobiography due to the fact that it is only given meaning by the system into which it is inserted. It underscores the notion that Tillers has become 'wholly encompassed' by the web of intertextuality that is the Canvasboard System. The logical extension of this idea is that the authority of the author of this system is, in the final analysis, dependent on his position *within* the system, as opposed to a 'God-like' authorial transcendence over his creation. Support for this reading can be found in 'The Beginner's Guide to Oil Painting' (Tillers 1973a: Appendix A) where in a section entitled 'The Art System' Tillers observed that Jack Burnham noted:

> that artists are the equivalent *in their position in the system* to that of programs and subroutines in a computer—i.e. they prepare new codes and analyse data in making works of art. (Tillers 1973a: Appendix A 18) [emphasis added]

In another section of 'The Beginner's Guide to Oil Painting' Tillers reinforces this Burnhamian notion when considering radical instances of post-object art:

> it becomes difficult to assign economic value to a pile of dirt, some photographs, holes in the desert, a work consisting of a two mile walk or a person cutting himself. It also becomes difficult to consider the presentation of these items as objects or things in themselves, it becomes necessary to consider them within some system—the meaning of these items is not in their intrinsic worth …but in *their positional value in some system*. (Tillers 1973a: Appendix A 17) [emphasis added]

Such ideas inform the central premise of this analysis of Tillers' oeuvre which is based on the argument that when Tillers came to produce *Untitled*, 1978, he was able to translate the concept of 'positional value' into a unique mode of *systems theoretical* deconstructive authorial appropriation. What is significant here is that this unique mode continues to inform his Canvasboard System into the 2000s and gains its strength from Tillers' enduring and constantly evolving scientific poetics. It is the elegant complexity of this poetics that makes his mode of deconstructive authorial appropriation original, and capable of further evolution when other modes of appropriationism have waned.

APPROPRIATION IN AN EXPANDED FIELD

There is an enormous difference between an artist who follows a readymade style and one who takes part in the development of a new genre. Moreover, there are also major and minor artistic genres and an artist, such as Tillers, who takes part in the development of a major genre is of considerable significance. I would argue that appropriationism is a major genre because it is an integral component of a much broader discursive formation. Deconstructive appropriation is not a simple strategy, it has art historical roots that reach back into photo-conceptualism, post-object art and the Duchampian readymade.

My analysis of the evolution of Tillers' appropriational strategy has established that his approach to appropriation is composed of at least three components that have extensive historical roots: a movement away from the sovereignty of authorship and towards a foregrounding of the viewer; alternatives to linear (classically rational) modes of order, such as those offered by chance; and the juxtaposition and layering of imagery (montage).[82] None of these components are necessarily tied to the strategy of appropriation. Moreover, each one not only reaches back into the history of twentieth century art but is also sufficiently vital to continue to inform artistic practice.

To these points can be added Tillers' Burnhamian concern with art as information and information processing. I have traced this more recent development through the 1960s to the 1980s, and in the light of the emerging digital forms of art in the 1990s and 2000s it is obvious that this tendency will continue to evolve.

The breadth and depth of even a provisional sketch of the historical roots and contemporary ramifications of appropriationism indicates that it is part of a complex of interrelated ideas, desires, and methods that constitutes something much more substantial than a single art movement. I would argue that the term 'appropriationism' is best used as a label for a specific style or genre such as ideological and parodic appropriation of the late 1970s and 1980s, and the Australian school of authorially deconstructive appropriation pioneered by Tillers. But the wider discursive formation that appropriationism maps onto requires the breadth offered by the term 'postmodern art'. Whereas geometric abstraction evident in art, design and architecture from the early twentieth century onward is usually described historically as 'modernist', I would suggest that postmodern art is as yet less defined and still evolving. Appropriation gains its power, significance, and perhaps its perplexity, from the fact that it is part of a discursive formation that remains open-ended.

FROM APPROPRIATION TO INTERTEXTUALITY

However, my restriction of the term appropriationism to the genres of avant-gardist art that arose in the late 1970s and 1980s poses a problem when approaching Tillers' work in the 1990s and 2000s. If appropriationism is now an *historical* movement the question can be posed, is Tillers passé? Or has the fact that his strategy is made up of the fertile components outlined above allowed him to continue to create work that can parallel the vitality of the post-appropriationist modes of art of the 1990s and 2000s?

When I came to analyse the development of Tillers' Canvasboard System in the 1990s and 2000s I began, almost unconsciously, to use the term 'intertextuality' in a manner which suggested that Tillers' continued practice of appropriation was simultaneously an expansion of that strategy. The term intertextuality is strongly related to the Barthesian notion of the 'death of the author' and is therefore particularly pertinent for an analysis of the genre of authorial appropriation. And Tillers' mammoth Canvasboard System and its substantial precursors—*Conversations with the Bride*, *Untitled*, and *One Painting, Cleaving*—must make him a major figure within this genre.

Julia Kristeva pioneered the semiotic use of the term 'intertextuality' (Allen 2000: 15) and her definition of the concept assists in expanding our understanding of Tillers' Canvasboard System. Kristeva observes:

> The term *inter-textuality* denotes … [the] transposition of one (or several) sign systems into another; but since this term has often been understood in the banal sense of "study of sources," we prefer the term *transposition* because it specifies … the passage from one signifying system to another … If one grants that every signifying practice is a field of transpositions of various signifying systems (an intertextuality), one then understands that its "place" of enunciation and it denoted "object" are never single, complete, and identical to themselves, but always plural, shattered … (Kristeva 1984: 59-60)

It is significant that in tracing the origin of the postmodern use of the term intertextuality one finds oneself back in the realm of systems of information that formed the matrix for Tillers' major works of the 1970s and his Canvasboard System.

It is also interesting that Kristeva shuns the term intertextuality because of its banal connotations with the 'study of sources' (which can also inform a banal interpretation of appropriation) and puts forward the supplementary concept of 'transposition'. Kristeva's use of this term becomes especially significant when we address the fact that in the late 1980s Tillers was becoming tired of being branded as a provincialist follower of the international style of appropriationism and attempted to reposition himself. This took the form of the interview published in the catalogue for his survey exhibition at the

Institute of Contemporary Arts (ICA), London, in 1988. Here he framed his Canvasboard System in terms of Mallarmé's statement that 'everything in the world exists to end up in a book' and continued:

> As Curnow points out, the process of 'quotation' in McCahon is simply the extraction of signs from one context and their transference into another. … I like the poetry of 'translation'. 'To translate' can mean a lot of things: 1. bear away, convey or remove from one person, place or condition to another, to transfer, transport; 2. to turn from one language into another; 3. to interpret, explain, to express one thing in terms of another; 4. to change in form, appearance or substance, to transmute, to transform. I much prefer these meanings to those of that other word, recently devalued by overuse, 'appropriation'. (Slatyer 1988: 4-5)

Thus in 1988 we find Tillers trying to extricate himself from the sticky label of appropriation. Unlike many appropriationist artists in the English speaking world he was not especially interested in postmodern theory. He had his own holistic systems aesthetic. But his use of the term 'translation' possesses an intriguing resonance with Kristeva's notion of 'transposition' as 'the passage from one signifying system to another'. It is also evident that Tillers' technique of isomorphic mapping can quite readily be described both as a mode of translation and transposition. No doubt Tillers avoided referring to his concept of isomorphic mapping in his 1988 interview because he realised that even sixteen years after he first developed the technique and described it in his writings it had provoked no interest in the art community. But his use of the term 'translation' met a similar fate, as did Kristeva's notion of 'transposition'. Intertextuality on the other hand now has the advantage of being part of the currency of postmodern theory.

Despite Kristeva's reservations it is also the case that the term intertextuality is less prone to a vulgar reading than is appropriation. Moreover, intertextuality is a literary term that expands the concept of appropriation by mapping postmodern art onto a parallel universe of ideas and methodologies: postmodern literature and literary theory. Indeed, this mapping between the literary and the artistic domains functions in itself as a mode of Kristevian 'transposition'.

Certainly, my use of the term intertextuality to analyse Tillers' Canvasboard System is informed by an awareness that Tillers' authorial appropriation exhibits multiple and nonlinear narrative dimensions. This was apparent when I mentioned that although Tillers was not influenced by Roland Barthes' writings, his Canvasboard System appears to be a concrete realization of Barthes' statement that a text is 'a multi-dimensional space in which a variety of writings, none of them original, blend and clash … a tissue of quotations drawn from the innumerable centers of culture' (Barthes 1977: 146). As

I observed in Chapter Ten all one needs to do is replace the word 'writings' with 'images' in order to achieve a perfect fit.

The narrative dimensions of Tillers' Canvasboard System are intensified in his later works—the Diaspora Trilogy and the Cooma works—due to the considerable role played by written text. Text becomes another layer or parallel dimension resonating with the imagery. What results is an increasingly complex intertextuality that intersects the literary with the visual. This is evident in Tillers' Cooma works in his quotations from Mallarmé, Kurt Schwitters, Haniya Yutaka, and the Melburnian poet John Anderson. This is a crucial development for a variety of reasons, one being that Tillers' increased introduction of text that began in the Diaspora Trilogy was primarily influenced by the antipodean artist Colin McCahon rather than an artist working in the cultural centres. McCahon's use of biblical and Maori texts makes his art an especially distinctive instance of a visual art form that operates intertextually, or transpositionally.

THE BIRTH OF THE READER

In this analysis I have stressed Tillers' deconstruction of authorship tracing it back to his admiration for post-object artists who dealt with readymade systems, and further back to the Duchampian readymade. But it is a self-evident fact that despite Barthes' brilliant essay the author is not dead: in the final analysis the Canvasboard System belongs to Tillers. But, crucially, he does not own how it is read. Barthes explored what he referred to as the 'birth of the reader' (Barthes 1977: 148) when he made the distinction between the readerly (*lisible*) and the writerly (*scriptable*) text in *S/Z* (Barthes 1990 [orig. 1973]). Barthes explained that the writerly text invites the reader to be an active participant in the construction of meanings: 'the goal … is to make the reader no longer a consumer, but a producer of the text' (Barthes 1990: 4).

Tillers' Canvasboard System can be described as 'writerly' because it does not impose the author's point of view onto the reader. Instead it provides an array of data that encourages the viewer to become an active participant in the construction of meaning. In this sense the Canvasboard System follows on from *Conversations with the Bride*, 1974-75, in which Tillers invites the viewer to enter into an 'image matrix' in order to produce 'couplings'.

A key feature of writerly intertextuality is that it does not possess a conventional narrative structure. In the case of Tillers' Canvasboard System the structure can be described as 'nonlinear'. Nonlinearity is an absolutely essential aspect of Tillers' scientific appreciation of holistic systems that can be traced back to his understanding of Ludwig von Bertalanffy's descriptions of biological systems and his artistic expression of negentropy in *Moments of Inertia*, 1972-73. This legacy should alert us to the fact that in the case of the Canvasboard System nonlinear narrativity does not mean randomness. A holistic system is not random, instead it displays a complexity that accommodates unpredictability. It is a living machine that works and, crucially, evolves.

ONE PERSPECTIVE

What makes the Canvasboard System fascinating is that its multi-dimensional nonlinearity allows many narratives to be woven from it. And the more the Canvasboard System grows the more narrative perspectives can emerge out of this enormous, holistic image matrix. An exhibition of all the canvasboard works would take over the entire surface of a major art gallery, and the viewer would need to examine the works carefully in order to create an informed reading.

One such narrative is demonstrated by the reading I have offered here. But I have only scratched the surface of the Canvasboard System, my main aim having been to show the way in which it arose out of Tillers' earlier work. My perspective on the Canvasboard System is simply that, *a* perspective. And my reading is not Tillers' reading, although he says my perspective adds to his own, which is constantly evolving. My conversations with him indicate that what is most important to him is the empathy he feels with his key appropriational sources, the resonances between sources and the many instances of synchronicity he has experienced since creating his first appropriational work *Conversations with the Bride*, 1974-75.

Tillers' Canvasboard System is an important monumental and paradigmatic intertextual project that helps us understand that intertextuality does not lead to the 'death' of the author so much as it places the author in the space of the viewer. The author's point of view becomes one more perspective, no more valid than that of an informed interpreter such as myself.

FURTHER PERSPECTIVES

My perspective on Tillers' Canvasboard System and indeed his entire oeuvre is by no means definitive. There are aspects of which I am aware but which I have not pursued. One instance of this is Tillers' deep interest in chance, coincidence and its relationship to intertextual 'resonances' that defy rational explanation.[83] This concern with coincidence began with his preparations for *Conversations with the Bride*. Even at that early point in Tillers' career it was not simply a case of being interested in Duchamp's comments on chance, it became part of his personal experience pointing to a metaphysical dimension of his oeuvre that has only been touched upon here in passing and certainly merits further enquiry.

Another avenue for further exploration concerns the fact that the success of Tillers' distinctive approach to appropriation deconstructs Terry Smith's assertion in 'The Provincialism Problem' that 'in Australia no avant-garde art … has emerged' (Smith 1974: 56). According to the analysis provided here

Tillers pioneered a powerful Australian alternative to the New York school of appropriationism. Although a collection of essays has been published on appropriation and Australian art (Butler 1996), none make the simple yet extremely crucial point that the appropriation of fine art imagery by Tillers and his Australian colleagues—including, Gordon Bennett, Janet Burchill and Jennifer McCamley, Juan Davila, John Nixon, Lindy Lee, Julie Rrap, Dick Watkins, John Young and others—constitutes a distinctive, Australian avant-gardist movement. Accordingly, one hopes that a study of the various artists making up this movement will follow this account of the artist who is both its pioneer and its most profound practitioner.

1. For example the Imants Tillers-Michael Nelson Jagamarra campfire group collaboration curated by Michael Eather of the Fire-Works Gallery, Brisbane in 2001.
2. An anthology of critical writings on appropriation in Australian art in the 1980s and 1990s has been published entitled *What is Appropriation?* (Butler 1996). However, although it is an informative work, it does not make the simple observation that the appropriation of fine art by a significant number of Australian artists in the 1980s constitutes an original genre. Perhaps the next question should be 'what is Australian appropriation?'. Certainly, there is scope for a detailed study of the Australian appropriationists who followed Tillers' response to the challenge inherent in Smith's 'The Provincialism Problem'.
3. 'The Beginner's Guide to Oil Painting' is a thirty thousand word dissertation that was part of Tillers BSc Honours in Architecture at the University of Sydney. He received a first class Honours degree in 1973 and the distinction of being awarded a university medal.
4. The theoretical underpinning for this term is evident in Brook's University of Sydney Power Lecture, 'Flight from the Object' (Brook 1970).
5. The artists in the exhibition included: Ian Burn, Mel Ramsden, Aleksander Danko, Bill Gregory, Tim Johnson, Nigel Lendon, Clive Murray-White, Optronic Kinetics, Ti Parks, Robert Rooney, David Aspden, Simon Close, Tony Coleing, Neil Evans, Dale Hickey, Robert Hunter, Michael Johnson, Guy Stuart and Trevor Vickers.
6. The meaning of 'real-time' in its usage in computer terminology is defined by the *New Oxford Dictionary of English* as 'of or relating to a system in which input data is processed within milliseconds so that it is available virtually immediately as feedback to the process from which it is coming. e.g. in a missile guidance or airline booking system.' (Pearsall 1998).
7. This information was conveyed to me by the Australian conceptual artist Ian Burn who worked for ten years in the avant-gardist art circles of New York during the late 1960s and 1970s.
8. An exhibition of conceptual art entitled 'Information' at the Museum of Modern Art in New York 2 July – 20 September, 1970.
9. A form of symbolic logic, devised by George Boole (1815–64) in the middle of the 19th century, which provides a mathematical procedure for manipulating logical relationships in symbolic form. For example in Boolean algebra a + b means 'a or b', while ab means a and b. It makes use of set theory and is extensively used by the designers of computers to enable the bits 0 and 1, as used in the binary notation, to relate to the logical functions the computer needs in carrying out its calculations.
10. This imagery first appeared in *One Painting, Cleaving*, 1980-81, an important work that bridges Tillers' major works of the 1970s with his Canvasboard System. *One Painting, Cleaving* is examined in detail in Chapter Nine.
11. One can also cite another work *Island of the Dead*, 1982, in the National Gallery of Australia collection.
12. A discussion of postmodern art in the 1990s and 2000s is adumbrated in the Conclusion.
13. The concept of 'presence' in Derridean usage refers to self-presence. In the following passage from his essay *'Différance'* Derrida makes it clear that he believes that a direct contact between consciousness and the phenomenal world is probably impossible due to the constant mediation of symbolic activity—the activity of processes of representation (where the very term *re*-presentation effectively deconstructs the possibility of direct presence). Derrida comments:

> certainly the subject becomes a *speaking* subject only in its commerce with the system of linguistic differences; or yet, the subject becomes a *signifying* (signifying in general, by means of speech or any other sign) subject only by inscribing itself in the system of [semiotic] differences. Certainly in this sense the speaking or signifying subject could not be present to itself, as speaking or signifying, without the play of linguistic or semiological *différance.* (Derrida 1982: 16)

The notion that a direct presencing or contact between consciousness and phenomena or consciousness and the sense of self is mediated by virtually incessant symbolic processes of representation is amplified when the passage from Derrida quoted by Owens is taken into account.
14. The background to Krauss' comment concerning the 'notion of the artist as a consciousness which is both anterior to and distinct from it, a consciousness that knows the world by judging it' can be found in her previous essays. For example, in 1978 she published 'LeWitt in Progress' in which she attacked art critics for interpreting the work of the New York minimal artist Sol LeWitt from the standpoint of classical rationalism. She argued that the more 'discriminating reader might find it strange that':

> in the last quarter of the twentieth century there should have arisen an art dedicated to a triumphant Cartesianism, that when almost everything else in our cultural experience has instructed us about the necessity of abandoning the fantasy of the transcendental subject. (Krauss 1978: 48)

Here Krauss explicitly rejects the anthropocentrism of Western rationalism epitomised by Descartes' famous aphorism *'cogito ergo sum'*—which effectively defines human consciousness in terms of reason—and Kant's 'transcendental subject' which also linked consciousness with reason defining it as the 'subject of the thoughts …' (Kant 1929: 331).

15. In 1973 Tillers referred to this process in his theoretical text 'The Beginner's Guide to Oil Painting' as 'a dilemma known in philosophy as logical regression ….' (Tillers 1973a: Appendix A25).

16. This is evident when in 'The Beginner's Guide to Oil Painting' Tillers comments:

> The recognition that art is really concerned with information processing and not necessarily working from data in the form of objects was confirmed by the emergence of conceptual art. Sol LeWitt has stated 'since no form is intrinsically superior to another, the artist may use any form, from an expression of words (written or spoken) to physical reality, equally. (Tillers 1973a: Appendix A25)

17. The main theoretical text of Tillers' post-object period is 'The Beginner's Guide to Oil Painting' which constituted the main part of his Honours dissertation for his BSc in Architecture awarded at Sydney University in 1973. Tillers points out that Brook along with Terry Smith helped him with his research for 'The Beginner's Guide to Oil Painting' (reproduced here as Appendix A). However, Tillers also points out that although Brook and Smith helped him with his research they were not obliged to read the text, that was the duty of his supervisor in the Architecture Department, Jennifer Taylor. Brook's commentary on Tillers' art practice suggests that he was familiar with at least part of 'The Beginner's Guide to Oil Painting' but there is no evidence that Smith was familiar with this text.

18. *Conversations with the Bride,* 1974-75, has three related texts (Tillers 1975; 1978a; 1978b). *Untitled*, 1978 has two (Scullion and Tillers 1978; Tillers 1981a). Tillers' canvasboard works of the 1980s are accompanied by four: (Tillers 1982a; 1983; 1984; Slatyer and Tillers 1988).

19. Tillers notes that this was the first 'Link' exhibition, curated by Ian North.

20. The Roerich Museum's motto 'pax cultura' ('peace through culture') fits in well with the integration of Tillers' systems aesthetics with ecopolitics evident in 'The Beginner's Guide to Oil Painting'. Tillers has had a long standing admiration for Nicholas Roerich and has used Roerich's 'banner of peace' symbol in *One Painting, Cleaving*, 1980-81, and in the first and second phases of the Canvasboard System. The symbol is reproduced

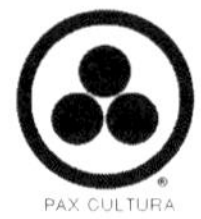

left. The museum's website offers the following explanation of the symbol: 'This sign of the triad which is to be found all over the world may have several meanings. Some interpret it as a symbol of past, present and future, enclosed in the ring of Eternity; others consider that it refers to religion, science and art, held together in the circle of Culture.' (www.roerich.org). The reference to science and art has particular relevance to Tillers.

21. His writings included: 'The Beginner's Guide to Oil Painting' (Tillers 1973a: Appendix A), his Bienal São Paulo catalogue essay (Tillers 1975), *A Companion to Conversations with the Bride* (Tillers 1978a), and *Rendezvous with Configuration P* (Tillers 1978b).

22. Tillers notes that Myers lectured with him at Sydney College of the Arts from 1977-79 in the Department of Sculpture.

23. Tillers reported Gablik's visit to me in an unrecorded conversation.

24. Her article was also published in June in *Art and Australia* (Gablik 1981b).

25. However, Gablik's comments regarding Tillers 'reclaiming for the mechanical reproduction a unique existence and endowing it with the "aura" of the original' indicates a creative interpretation of Benjamin's position in 'The Work of Art in the Age of Mechanical Reproduction' where he uses the term 'aura' in a pejorative sense together with the phrase 'cult value' to indicate the elitist fetishisation of the pre-industrial, pre-photomedia art of painting. For Benjamin photography and film were products of the industrial revolution and as such needed to be used by progressive artists. In addition, he makes the point that whereas fine art gains its value or 'aura' via its uniqueness and the concomitant *provenance,* photography and film are antithetical owing to their capacity for mass production which possesses the crucial advantage of being able to disseminate art to the masses.

26. Perspecta is a biennial exhibition held at the Art Gallery of New South Wales. It was instigated in 1981 to alternate with the predominantly international Biennale of Sydney and is generally oriented towards revealing new tendencies in Australian art.

27. This work is one of the Polaroids taken by Tillers of the hidden underlayer paintings in *One Painting, Cleaving*. For an analysis of this work see Chapter Nine.

28. Compare Murphy's statement with this passage from Ben-

jamin's 'The Work of Art in the Age of Mechanical Reproduction' 'One might generalize by saying: the technique of reproduction detaches the reproduced object from the domain of tradition. By making many reproductions it substitutes a plurality of copies for a unique existence.' (Benjamin 1973: 215).

29. This aspect of Tillers' theory is examined in detail in Chapter Seven and its relation to his references to a photographic 'shadow world' is explained in Chapter Nine.

30. Significantly, Tillers mentions Bidlo in one of his key writings of the 1980s 'In Perpetual Mourning', where he notes that 'on 15th August 1983, the *Sydney Morning Herald* carried the following report: Jackson Pollock's *Blue Poles* was reproduced in New York recently to mark the 27th anniversary of Pollock's death. Artist Mike Bidlo recreated the work on 132 masonite tiles and then gave them away to onlookers. Asked why he chose *Blue Poles,* Bidlo claimed that the canvas had 'helped change the government of Australia. When the Australian people found out what the government paid for it, they were outraged. They threw the government out.' Pollock's painting was bought for $1.3m by the Whitlam government in 1973 (Tillers 1984: 22).

31. When Tillers' partner Slatyer proofed this passage she added the comment 'he's too polite!'.

32. The impact of Baudrillard on the Sydney art scene in the 1980s is especially evident in a large conference organised by Alan Cholodenko of the Power Institute (now the Department of Art History and Theory), University of Sydney. The conference was organised around a paper given by Baudrillard who was flown to Australia for the first time for this event. I attended Baudrillard's presentation and it was held in a large lecture theatre packed with hundreds of people. The conference papers were consequently published (Grosz 1986). Somewhat unfairly, given the fact that he was a key figure in conceiving of and organising the conference, the Power Institute would not permit Cholodenko co-authorship of the publication. In an annotation to a final draft of this text Tillers noted that he 'chose not to attend' the conference as he 'was not particularly interested in absorbing Baudrillard's ideas'.

33. 'The Beginner's Guide to Oil Painting' was an Honours dissertation which is published here in Appendix A. If Appendix A is examined it can be seen that Smith is listed in the acknowledgements. In a telephone conversation, 24 October 2001, Tillers reported that his main supervisor was Jennifer Taylor in the University of Sydney Architecture Department in which he was a BSc Honours candidate. The department kindly allowed Tillers to seek assistance from Smith who was then working in the Power Institute in the same university. Tillers reports that Smith was very helpful in enabling Tillers to make contact with post-object artists including Ian Burn who was then living and working as a conceptual artist in New York. However, Tillers also reports that after assembling his research he wrote the text for 'The Beginner's Guide to Oil Painting' in ten days in order to meet the deadline for the completion of the dissertation. He claims that this meant that few of the people who assisted him in his research actually read what he had written. Certainly his main supervisor Jennifer Taylor would have read it and there is evidence, noted in Chapter Four, that Donald Brook, who also assisted Tillers' research had a degree of familiarity with the text. On the other hand, Tillers' partner Slatyer believes that as Smith helped Tillers with his research for 'The Beginner's Guide to Oil Painting' he may have looked at it. But even if this were the case it would probably have been as difficult for Smith as it was for Brook to make a substantive connection between Tillers' theory and his practice.

34. These remarks were reported to me in an unrecorded conversation in Tillers' studio in March 1995.

35. In addition, Tillers curated an exhibition of a series of these early works by Johnson together with the Aboriginal paintings he drew from. The exhibition was at the Yuill/Crowley Gallery, Sydney in 1984. The exhibition, Waiting for Technology, included work by Limpi Tjapangati, Emily Possum, Anatjari No. 1 and Don Tjungarrayi as well as Johnson.

36. These theorists are dealt with in Chapter Three.

37. The abbreviation of 'anthropomorphic' to 'anthropic' is derived from the existing term 'anthropic principle' defined by *The New Oxford Dictionary of English* as 'The cosmological principle that theories of the universe are constrained by the necessity to allow human existence.' (Pearsall 1998). As the analysis proceeds it will be shown that Tillers' anti-anthropic position is opposed to the Judeo-Christian concept of God. The appropriateness of the term anti-anthropic to Tillers' stance is supported by discussions of the anthropic principle which focus on the notion of God such as: *God and the New Cosmology: the Anthropic Design Argument* (Corey Michael 1993); and *Cosmos and Theos: Ethical and Theological Implications of the Anthropic Cosmological Principle* (Harris Errol 1992).

38. The quality of his dissertation is evident in the fact that Tillers' not only received first class Honours but also a University Medal.

39. In 'The Beginner's Guide to Oil Painting' Tillers' praises Robert Barry for merely selecting objects for 'art processing' (Tillers 1973a: Appendix A 25); lauds Haacke for allowing 'natural entities to organise themselves' (Tillers 1973a: Appendix A 23); commends Huebler for not producing 'any art data' and selecting 'a system already in the world' (Tillers 1973a: Appendix A 25); and compliments Oppenheim for using a 'day-to-day environment' with a 'minimum of reorganisation' (Tillers 1973: Appendix A 24).

40. R. Clausius (1822–88) stated the law in two ways: 'heat cannot be transferred from one body to a second body at a higher temperature without producing some other effect' and 'the entropy of a closed system increases with time'. These statements introduce the thermodynamic concepts of temperature (T) and entropy (S), both of which are parameters determining the direction in which an irreversible process can go. The temperature of a body or system determines whether heat will flow into it or out of it; its entropy is a measure of the unavailability of its energy to do work. (Oxford 1999).
41. Concerning the eventual fate of the Universe the Second Law of Thermodynamics predicts a condition known in physics as 'heat death'.
42. See note 37.
43. This work was initiated in response to an invitation to participate in Object and Idea curated by Brian Finemore at the National Gallery of Victoria in 1973.
44. Although he used the term 'isomorphism' in the context of discussing *Moments of Inertia,* 1972-73, Tillers did not use the term 'mapping' until his writings on *Conversations with the Bride,* 1974-75. However, he did use the term 'transformation function' with respect to *Moments of Inertia* and, in the context of mathematics, this term is synonymous with 'mapping'. Tillers was academically very able in the spheres of mathematics and science and would have been introduced to the concept of 'mapping' in the course of his tuition in mathematics in High School. For example, in a British secondary school textbook G. D. Buckwell notes the mathematical 'rule' that changes a value of 'x' into a value of 'y' is called a '*function* or *mapping*' (Buckwell 1988: 97). A high level of attainment in mathematics was also a prerequisite for his entry into the BSc in Architecture at the University of Sydney.
45. In his illustrated and annotated conceptual plan for *Moments of Inertia* Tillers used the term 'image structure type' (Tillers 1973c: n.p.), this has been abbreviated here to image structure.
46. Tillers used photographic material to apply the image structure to his Floorpiece and his Frame objects.
47. Until Tillers corrected me I had originally believed that there were more than seven variants for each object in the image structure diagrams and thought that this meant that Tillers was making an attempt to include references to the objects in *Moments of Inertia: Still Life 1.* The most significant feature contributing to such confusion is the fact that the Box objects are in pairs.
48. *Conversations with the Bride* was exhibited at the São Paulo Biennale 1975 and in a catalogue essay Tillers explained that in *Conversations with the Bride* 'The landscape, … is a mirror-image of Hans Heysen's 'Summer' (1909) …' (Tillers 1975: col. 6).
49. On the other hand the use of equals signs in *A Companion to Conversations with the Bride* might have been due to typographical limitations as the book was a low budget production. Significantly, Tillers' much more sophisticated artist's book *Three Facts* (Tillers 1981a) does use arrows to signify mapping in the course of providing the background to the theory informing *Untitled*, 1978.
50. It was noted in relation to his suggestion that a work by Dennis Oppenheim made use of 'readymade systems'. Tillers also makes reference to 'the Duchamp ready-made spade' (Tillers 1973a: Appendix A 17).
51. For example, the theoretical physicist Michio Kaku uses it in his explanation of the role played by the non-Euclidean geometric notion of higher spatial dimensions in the most sophisticated contemporary theory concerning the unification of physical forces. This theory, originally developed in the 1970s and 1980s, is known as 'superstring theory', 'string theory', or more aphoristically 'the theory of everything' (Kaku 1994: 46-48, 151-172).
52. From *The Green Box,* an assortment of notes accompanying *The Large Glass*.
53. The full passage quoted by Tillers is as follows:

> Specifications for 'Readymades' by planning for a moment to come (on such a day, such a date such a minute), '<u>to inscribe</u> a readymade.'—The readymade can later be looked for—(with all kinds of delays). <u>The important thing then is just</u> this matter of timing, this snapshot effect, like a speech delivered on no matter what occasion but at <u>such and such an hour.</u> It is a kind of rendezvous.—Naturally inscribe that date, <u>hour, minute, on the readymade as information</u>, also the serial characteristic of the readymade. (in Tillers 1978a: Table N<u>o</u> 4/3, § 4.4).

54. At that time Tillers was lecturing at Sydney College of the Arts.
55. Roger Penrose notes that Gödel formulated his Theorem in 1930 and it was published in 1931 (Penrose 1995: 90).
56. The term 'axiom' in its mathematical usage can be defined as 'a statement that is stipulated to be true for the purpose of constructing a theory …' (Borowski and Borwein 1989: 40). To be 'stipulated as true' requires that the axiom appears to be self-evident. In mathematics a 'postulate' is defined as 'an axiom of a specific theory …' (Borowski and Borwein 1989: 461). The self-evident character of axioms is evident in the first axiom, or proposition, in Euclidean geometry which states: 'a straight line segment can be drawn joining any two points' (Hofstadter 1980: 90).
57. The direct link with 'undecidability' is evident when Scullion's account is quoted in full:

> Well that was how Gödel got his results. He made a series of pictures, as it were, isomorphic resemblances between two categories, like these two hands—whatever one did was matched by the other, until he got this double reflection, as it were, in his results. There was the arithmetical proposition which implied the existence of its contrary. Then there was the proposition which was isomorphic with the statement "Arithmetic is consistent"—the isomorphic picture of this was also *undecidable*. Anyway the results were suggestive of all sorts of things—Creation, the idea of self-as-founded-on-contradiction … (Scullion and Tillers 1978: 7). [emphasis added]

58. Gablik's commentary on Tillers is examined in more detail in Chapter Four.
59. See note 53.
60. Tillers quotes Duchamp's description, after Jouffret, of shadows of four-dimensional objects: 'The shadow cast by a 4-dimensional figure on our space is a 3-dimensional shadow (see Jouffret Geom. à 4 dim. page 186. last 3 lines.).' (in Tillers 1978a: § 1.3).
61. Tillers was aware of this book in its earliest German edition, 1971, but it is noteworthy that a direct relationship between this text and Tillers' work is only evident after its first English translation 1979, which Tillers has acknowledged did influence *One Painting, Cleaving*.
62. In the late 1990s and the new millennium Tillers and Arakawa were planning a 'site of reversible destiny' (see Arakawa 1995) on the treeless plains of the Cooma-Monaro shire (New South Wales) where Tillers has been living since 1997. This plan was shelved in 2001.
63. The image reproduced by Arakawa and Gins is typical of photographs taken in the 'cloud' or 'bubble' chambers of particle accelerators. Exploring the subatomic domain requires massive energies and particle accelerators are very large and expensive. They are usually several miles long and accelerate a subatomic particle with an extremely powerful forward moving magnetic field. By the time the particle reaches the end of the accelerator it is travelling close to the speed of light (186,000 miles per second). Then it hits a target, an atom, which is 'smashed' into fundamental subatomic components (the list grew as more powerful machines were constructed: protons, neutrons, neutrinos, photons, bosons, positrons, anti-positrons, anti-neutrinos, and many more). The subatomic events cannot be directly perceived because the phenomena are so small they are invisible. However, the events can be represented if they occur in a chamber filled with a suitable fluid such as liquid hydrogen. Then a representation of the events is available in the form of vapour trail-like tracks of tiny droplets of the fluid in the chamber.
64. The notion that the observer can create what is observed is implicit in the 'Schrödinger's cat' problem posed by quantum theory (see Marshall, Zohar, and Peat 1997; Gribbin 1984).
65. In conversation with Tillers January 2001.
66. The surrealistic nature of quantum theory is evident when a Nobel prize-winning quantum theorist such as Richard Feynman can state:

> I think it safe to say that no one understands quantum mechanics. Do not keep saying to yourself, if you can possibly avoid it, 'But how can it be like that?' because you will go 'down the drain' into a blind alley from which nobody has yet escaped. Nobody knows how it can be like that. (in Pagels 1983: 135)

67. Tillers notes that Celant selected him and John Nixon to represent Australia at Documenta 7, Kassel, 1982. This was the first time Australia had been represented in this important international exhibition. Tillers exhibited components from *One Painting, Cleaving*, 1980-81.
68. This is examined in Chapter Seven.
69. See note 39.
70. McCahon is a New Zealand artist and Tillers' inclusion of a much earlier colonialist depiction of McCahon's country can be interpreted as underlining the fact that McCahon was a white New Zealander. Perhaps some of the darkness and lack of faith and identity is linked to the fact that New Zealand was taken by white Anglo colonialists from the native Maori.
71. Tillers gives a reference for this passage, (Bates 1938: 93).
72. See Chapter Eight. Interestingly, Tillers began his appropriation of Heysen in a mildly mocking manner that stemmed from Terry Smith's analysis of non-indigenous Australian art as 'provincial' (Smith 1974). In retrospect Tillers' parody of non-indigenous Australian artists' dependence on their landscape tradition is thoroughly deconstructed by the fact that his latest major work, the Nature Speaks series, begun in 1998, can be described as 'conceptual landscape painting', due to its juxtaposition of text with renditions of the Cooma-Monaro landscape.
73. In a telephone conversation 6th August 2001.
74. See Chapters Five and Seven.
75. The full passage quoted by Tillers is as follows:

> Specifications for 'Readymades' by planning for a moment to come (on such a day, such a date such a minute), 'to inscribe a readymade.'—The readymade can later be looked for—(with all kinds of delays). The important thing then is just this matter of timing, this snapshot effect, like a speech delivered on no matter what occasion but at such and such

an hour. It is a kind of rendezvous.—Naturally inscribe that date, hour, minute, on the readymade as information. also the serial characteristic of the readymade. (in Tillers 1978a: Table No 4/3, § 4.4)

Tillers' reference to waiting here is implicit in his concept of 'rendezvous' and is more explicit in another part of *A Companion to Conversations with the Bride* when he states:

> 4/1;4.2 The higher space forms are autonomous, relative to the lower space and the trajectory of their changing cross-sections is determined by a causality hidden from the inhabitant of the lower space. This means that the inhabitant of the lower space cannot influence, but must merely *wait* for these manifestations to occur. Duchamp's note [54] expresses this attitude: the readymade behaves like a free agent. It is not the product of conscious choice, instead one waits and meets it at the particular moment at which it occurs. (Tillers 1978a: 4/1, 4.2) [emphasis added]

76. Interestingly, Tillers has subsequently discovered that even this image structure is not entirely original because a similar, but much less systematic, pattern is evident in several paintings created around 1960 by a Spanish group of 'constructivist' artists calling itself Equipo 57 (see *De Este a Oeste* illustrated right). The artists in this group include: Juan Cuenca, Angel Duarte, José Duarte, Agustin Ibarrola and Juan Serrano.
77. It is also the case that Tillers produced a fourth work after the Diaspora Trilogy entitled *Farewell to Reason*, 1996, which has an identical format to the Diaspora works, but differs in content.
78. He reports that he read this interpretation in the catalogue for an exhibition of German Romanticism at the Royal Academy in London (Coulter-Smith 2001: n.p.).
79. His metaphysical novel *Death Spirits* has been described as 'affected by Kant and slapstick movies' (www.horagai.com/www/xwho/haniya.htm).
80. Thanks to James A. Walker for providing me with the title and date of the poem.
81. This fascination is evident in the indexing systems Tillers used in *Moments of Inertia*; *Conversations with the Bride*; and his Canvasboard System.
82. The strategies of montage and chance are particularly evident in dada and surrealism. In the context of contemporary Australian art Urszula Szulakowska commented on the relationship between postmodern art and dada quite some time ago (Szulakowska 1987). And Nicholas Zurbrugg also pointed to the relationship between dada and postmodern art around the same time. An especially systematic treatment of key dada and surrealist strategies of allegorical montage, automatism, chance, and the desire to overcome barrier between the traditional aesthetic object and the everyday world is available in Peter Bürger's *Theory of the Avant Garde* (1984 [orig. 1974]). Bürger's analysis also points to the relationship between such strategies and those informing postmodern art (which he refers to as the 'post avant-garde').
83. See his account of the coincidence associated with *When False is True* on page 167.

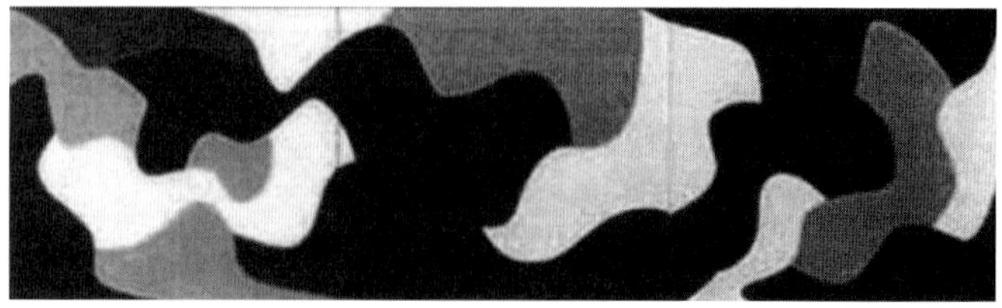

Equipo 57, *De Este a Oeste.*

Allen, Christopher. 1997. *Art in Australia: From Colonisation to Postmodernism*. London: Thames and Hudson.

Allen, Graham. 2000. *Intertextuality*. London: Routledge.

Andrews, Alan E. J. 1991. *Kosciusko: The Mountain in History*. Palmerston, A.C.T [Australia]: Tabletop Press.

Arakawa, Shusaku, and Madeline Gins. 1971. *Mechanismus der Bedeutung: (Werk im Entstehen: 1963-1971)*. Munich: Bruckmann.

———. 1979. *The Mechanism of Meaning: Work in Progress (1963-1971, 1978), Based on the Method of Arakawa*. New York: H. N. Abrams.

———. 1995. *Sites of Reversible Destiny*. London: Academy Editions.

———. 1988. *The Mechanism of Meaning (No.3)* 3rd ed. New York: Abbeville Press.

Archer, Michael. 1997. *Art Since 1960*. London: Thames and Hudson.

Archer, Michael, Nicolas de Oliveira, Nicola Oxley, and Michael Petry. 1994. *Installation Art*. London: Thames and Hudson.

Barron, Stephanie, Peter W. Guenther. 1991. *Degenerate Art: The Fate of the Avant-Garde in Nazi Germany*. Los Angeles, Calif., and New York: Los Angeles County Museum of Art and H.N. Abrams.

Barthes, Roland. 1973. *Mythologies*. London: Paladin.

———. 1990. *S/Z*. Oxford: Blackwell Publishers.

———. 1977. 'The Death of the Author'. In *Image-Music-Text*, pp. 142-148. London: Fontana.

Batcock, Gregory, ed. 1968. *Minimal Art: A Critical Anthology*. New York: E.P. Dutton.

Bates, Daisy. 1938. *The Passing of the Aborigines: A Lifetime Spent Among the Natives of Australia*. London: Murray.

Benjamin, Andrew, ed. 1993. *Art & Design: Installation Art*. Edited by N. Hodges. London: Academy Group.

Benjamin, Walter. 1973. 'The Work of Art in the Age of Mechanical Reproduction'. In *Illuminations*, pp. 211-244. London: Fontana. Originally published as an article, in 1936, through the University of Frankfurt Centre for Social Research. The *Illuminations* collection was originally published in Germany in 1955, and first published in Britain 1970 by Jonathan Cape Ltd. The English translation was sponsored by Harcourt, Brace & World, Inc., New York, in 1968.

Borowski, E. J. and J.M. Borwein. 1989. *Collins Dictionary of Mathematics*. London: Harper Collins.

Boyer, Carl B. 1968. *A History of Mathematics*. New York: John Wiley & Sons Inc.

Bragdon, Claude. 1923. *A Primer of Higher Space, the Fourth Dimension, to which is Added, Man the Square, a Higher Space Parable*. New York: A. A. Knopf.

Brook, Donald. 1970. *Flight from the Object*. Sydney: Power Institute of Fine Arts, University of Sydney.

———. 1973. 'Peeling the Onion in Post-Object Art'. *Nation Review* [Australia] no. 14 (September).

———. 1975. 'Imants Tillers and the Redefinition of Art'. *Art and Australia* no. 1, vol. 13: pp. 54-59.

Bruni Sakraischik, Claudio, Isabella Far, Giorgio de Chirico, Giuliano Briganti. 1971. *Catalogo generale: Giorgio de Chirico,* Milano: Electa.

Buchloh, Benjamin. 1982. 'Allegorical Procedures: Appropriation and Montage in Contemporary Art'. *Artforum* (September): pp. 43 -56 .

———. 1989. 'From the Aesthetic of Administration to Institutional Critique (Some Aspects of Conceptual Art)'. In *L'art conceptuel: une perspective. 1962-1969*, exhib. cat., curator Claude Gintz. Paris: Musée d'art moderne de la Ville de Paris.

Buckwell, G.D. 1988. *Work Out Mathematics GCSE*. London: Macmillan Education Ltd.

Bürger, Peter. 1984. *Theory of the Avant-Garde*. Translated by M. Shaw. Minneapolis: University of Minnesota Press.

Burn, Ian, Nigel Lendon, Charles Merewether, and Ann Stephen. 1988. *The Necessity of Australian Art*. Sydney: University of Sydney.

Burnham, Jack. 1968. 'Systems Esthetics'. *Artforum* (September): pp. 30-32.

———. 1969. 'Real-Time Systems'. *Artforum* (September): pp. 49-55.

Butler, Rex. 1992. 'Two Readings of Gordon Bennett's The Nine Ricochets'. *Eyeline* no. 19: pp. 18-23.

———, ed. 1996. *What is Appropriation? An Anthology of Critical Writings on Australian Art in the '80s and '90s*. Brisbane and Sydney: Institute of Modern Art and Power Publications.

Chambers, Ross. 1984. *Story and Situation: Narrative Seduction and the Power of Fiction*. Manchester & Minneapolis: Manchester University Press and University of Minnesota Press.

Colpitt, Frances. 1993. *Minimal Art: The Critical Perspective.* Seattle: University of Washington Press.

Combs, Allan. 1994. *Synchronicity: Science, Myth and the Trickster*. Edited by M. Holland. Edinburgh: Floris Books.

Contemporary Art Society. 1974. 'Imants Tillers: Moments of Inertia'. *Contemporary Art Society of Australia Broadsheet* (January).

Cooke, Roger. 1997. *The History of Mathematics: A Brief Course*. New York: John Wiley & Sons, Inc.

Coombes, Robin. 1979. 'Imants Tillers'. In *Biennale of Sydney: European Dialogue* n.p. Sydney: Art Gallery of New South Wales.

Corey Michael, Anthony. 1993. *God and the New Cosmology: The Anthropic Design Argument*. Lanham, Md: Rowman & Littlefield.

Coulter-Smith, Graham. 1991. Interview with Imants Tillers in his Sydney studio. Audio tape recording (January). Archive: Graham Coulter-Smith.

———. 1994. Interview with Imants Tillers in his Sydney studio. Audio tape recording (September). Archive: Graham Coulter-Smith.

———. 2001. Interview with Imants Tillers at the Fine Art Research Centre, Southampton Institute, England (January). Archive: Graham Coulter-Smith.

Crimp, Donald. 1984. 'Pictures'. In *Art After Modernism: Rethinking Representation*, edited by B. Wallis. New York: The New Museum of Contemporary Art in association with David R. Godine, Publisher, Inc., Boston.

Curnow, Wystan. 1998. *Imants Tillers and the 'The Book of Power'*. Sydney: Craftsman House.

Dahlem, Franz, ed. 1990. *Georg Baselitz*. Cologne: Benedikt Taschen Verlag.

Daumal, René. 1960. *Mount Analogue: A Novel of Symbolically Authentic Non-Euclidean Adventures in Mountain Climbing*. [1st American] ed. New York: Pantheon.

Davies, Paul. 1992. *The Mind of God: Science and the Search for Ultimate Meaning*. London: Penguin Books.

Derrida, Jacques. 1976. *Of Grammatology*. Translated by G. C. Spivak. Baltimore, Maryland: Johns Hopkins University Press.

Duchamp, Marcel, and Arturo Schwarz. 1969. *Notes and Projects for the Large Glass*. London: Thames & Hudson.

Emery, F.E., ed. 1969. *Systems Thinking*. Harmondsworth, Middlesex: Penguin Books.

Foss, Paul, ed. 1988. *Island in the Stream: Myths of Place in Australian Culture*. Sydney: Pluto Press.

Foster, Hal, ed. 1983. *The Anti-Aesthetic: Essays on Postmodern Culture*. Port Townsend, Washington: Bay Press.

———. 1985. *Recodings: Art, Spectacle, Cultural Politics*. Port Townsend, Washington: Bay Press.

Foucault, Michel. 1977. *Discipline and Punish: The Birth of the Prison*. 1st American ed. New York: Pantheon Books.

Francis, W. D. 1970. *Australian Rain-Forest Trees*. Canberra: Australian Government Printing Service.

Frazer, James G. 1994. *The Golden Bough*. London: Penguin Books. Originally published in 1890.

Gablik, Suzi. 1981a. 'Report from Australia'. *Art in America* vol. 69, no. 1: pp. 29-37.

———. 1981b. 'Report from Australia'. *Art and Australia* vol. 18, no. 4: pp. 352-355.

Godfrey, Tony. 1998. *Conceptual Art, Art & Ideas*. London: Phaidon.

Goldstein, Ann, and Anne Rorimer. 1995. *Reconsidering the Object of Art: 1965-1975*. Cambridge, Massachusetts: MIT Press.

Gribbin, John R. 1984. *In Search of Schrödinger's Cat: Quantum Physics and Reality*. Toronto and New York: Bantam Books.

Grosz, E. A., ed. 1986. *Futur*fall: Excursions into Post-Modernity, Power Institute Publications 4*. Sydney: Power Institute of Fine Arts, University of Sydney.

Harris Errol, E. 1992. *Cosmos and Theos: Ethical and Theological Implications of the Anthropic Cosmological Principle*. New Jersey and London: Humanities Press.

Henderson, Linda Dalrymple. 1983. *The Fourth Dimension and Non-Euclidean Geometry*. Princeton, New Jersey: Princeton University Press.

Herbert, Nick. 1985. *Quantum Reality: Beyond the New Physics*. New York: Anchor (a division of Doubleday Dell Publishing).

Hofstadter, Douglas, R. 1980. *Gödel, Escher, Bach: An Eternal Golden Braid—A Metaphorical Fugue on Minds and Machines in the Spirit of Lewis Carroll*. London: Penguin Books.

ICA, and Philip Morris, Europe. 1969. *When Attitudes become Form: Works-Concepts-Process-Situations-Information*, exhib. cat., London: Institute of Contemporary Arts.

Jung, Carl, Gustav. 1985. *Synchronicity: An Acausal Connecting Principle*. Translated by R. F. C. Hull. London: ARK Paperbacks, an imprint of Routledge.

Kaku, Michio. 1994. *Hyperspace: A Scientific Odyssey through Parallel Universes, Time Warps, and the 10th Dimension*. New York: Oxford University Press.

Kant, Immanuel. 1929. *Critique of Pure Reason*. London: The Macmillan Press Ltd.

Kastner, Jeffrey, and Brian Wallis. 1998. *Land Art and Environmental Art*. London: Phaidon.

Koestler, Arthur. 1973. *The Roots of Coincidence: An Excursion into Parapsychology*. New York: Vintage Books, a division of Random House.

Krauss, Rosalind. 1978. 'LeWitt in Progress'. *October* no. 6 (Fall): pp. 46-60.

———. 1984a. 'A Note on Photography and the Simulacral'. *October* no. 31 (Winter): pp. 49-68.

———. 1984b. 'The Originality of the Avant-Garde: A Postmodern Repetition'. In *Art After Modernism: Rethinking Representation*, edited by B. Wallis, pp. 12-29. New York: The New Museum of Contemporary Art.

Kristeva, Julia. 1984. *Revolution in Poetic Language*. New York: Columbia University Press.

Kuspit, Donald. 1985. 'Imants Tillers at Bess Cutler'. *Art in America* (March): p.158.

Lippard, Lucy. 1973. *Six Years: The Dematerialisation of the Art Object from 1966 to 1972*. New York, Washington: Praeger Publishers.

———. 1984. 'Trojan Horses: Activist Art and Power'. In *Art After Modernism: Rethinking Representation*, edited by B. Wallis, pp. 340-358. New York: The New Museum of Contemporary Art.

Lynn, Victoria. 1991. *Australian Perspecta 1991*. Sydney: Art Gallery of New South Wales.

Maloon, Terence. 1986-87. 'Imants Tillers and the Museum without Walls'. *Studio International* no. 1015: pp.32-35.

Marsh, Anne. 1993. *Body and Self: Performance Art in Australia 1969-92*. Melbourne: Oxford University Press.

Marshall, I. N., Danah Zohar, and F. David Peat. 1997. *Who's afraid of Schrödinger's Cat?: All the New Science Ideas You Need to Keep Up with the New Thinking*. 1st ed. New York: Morrow.

McHarg, Ian L. 1969. *Design with Nature*. New York: The Natural History Press.

Murphy, Bernice. 1981. 'Imants Tillers'. In *Australian Perspecta 1981: A Biennial Survey of Contemporary Australian Art*. Sydney: Art Gallery of New South Wales.

Myers, Peter. 1980. 'Imants Tillers'. In *Survey 13: Imants Tillers* n.p. Melbourne: National Gallery of Victoria.

Owens, Craig. 1978. 'Photography en abyme'. *October* no. 5, (Summer), pp. 73-88.

———. 1984. 'The Allegorical Impulse: Towards a Theory of Postmodernism'. In *Art After Modernism: Rethinking Representation*, edited by B. Wallis, pp. 12-29. New York: The New Museum of Contemporary Art.

Oxford, University of. 1999. *Oxford Reference Shelf* [CD-ROM]. Oxford: Oxford University Publications.

Pagels, Heinz. 1983. *The Cosmic Code: Quantum Physics as the Language of Nature*. London: Michael Joseph Ltd.

Pearsall, Judy. 1998. *The New Oxford Dictionary of English*, chief editor, Patrick Hanks. Oxford: Clarendon Press.

Penrose, Roger. 1995. *Shadows of the Mind: A Search for the Missing Science of Consciousness*. London: Vintage, an imprint of Random House.

Rush, Michael. 1999. *New Media in Late 20th-Century Art*. London: Thames & Hudson.

Sandler, Irving. 1996. *Art of the Postmodern Era: From the Late 1960s to the Early 1990s*. New York: HarperCollins.

Scullion, Michael, and Imants Tillers. 1978. 'Dialogue on False Mt. Hayward'. *ZX* no. 2: pp. 6-10. Sydney: Sydney College of the Arts.

Slatyer, Jennifer and Imants Tillers. 1987. 'An Interview with Imants Tillers'. In *The Australian Bicentennial Perspecta*. Sydney: Art Gallery of New South Wales.

———. 1988. 'The Life-Motif: Interview with Imants Tillers'. In *Imants Tillers: Works 1978-88*, exhib. cat., pp. 2-6. London: ICA.

———. 1995. 'Via Paradiso: An Interview with Imants Tillers'. In *Diaspora in Context, Connections in a Fragmented World: Imants Tillers*, edited by M. Seppala. Pori: Pori Art Museum [Finland].

Smith, Terry. 1974. 'The Provincialism Problem'. *Artforum* (September): pp. 54-59.

———. 1987. 'Imants Tillers: Appropriation No Crime'. *Times on Sunday* [Sydney].

———. 1988. 'Provincialism Refigured'. *Art Monthly: Australia and International* no.13: pp. 4-6.

Sokal, Alan, and Jean Bricmont. 1998. *Intellectual Impostures*. London: Profile Books.

Symes, Colin, and & Robert Lingard. 1988. 'From the Ethnographic to the Aesthetic: An Examination of the Relationship between Aboriginal and European Culture in Australian Art 1788-1988'. In *Island in the Stream: Myths of Place in Australian Culture*, edited by P. Foss, pp. 188-215, 228-232. Pluto Press: Sydney.

Szulakowska, Urszula. 1987. 'Brisbane Dada'. *Eyeline* no. 1, May: pp. 14-16.

Taylor, Paul. 1982. 'Popism'. In *Popism*, exhib. cat., 16th June-25 July, pp. 1-4, 8. Melbourne: National Gallery of Victoria.

———. ed. 1984. *Anything Goes*. Melbourne: Art & Text.

Tillers, Imants. 1973a. 'The Beginner's Guide to Oil Painting'. Honours dissertation, Faculty of Architecture, University of Sydney, Sydney. Appended here as Appendix A.

———. 1973b. *From 91 Missing Works*. Unique unbound master copy of bound limited edition artist's book: Collection: Imants Tillers.

———. 1973c. Illustrated conceptual plan for *Moments of Inertia*. Unique document. Collection: Imants Tillers.

———. 1974. 'Moments of Inertia'. *Contemporary Art Society Broadsheet* (January): n.p. [Sydney].

———. 1975. 'Conversations with the Bride'. In *Bienal São Paulo: Australia: XIII,* exhib. cat. São Paulo: Bienal São Paulo.
———. 1978a. *A Companion to Conversations with the Bride*. Collection: Imants Tillers, on loan to the Museum of Contemporary Art, Sydney.
———. 1978b. *Rendezvous with Configuration P*. Adelaide: Experimental Art Foundation.
———. 1981a. *Three Facts*. Melbourne: Double Vision.
———. 1981b. 'Tom Roberts—Some Impressions'. *Art and Australia* vol. 18, no. 3: pp. 272-273.
———. 1982a. 'Locality Fails'. *Art & Text* no. 6: pp. 51-60.
———. 1982b.. 'One Painting Cleaving: Triangle of Doubt'. In *Notes on Art Practice*, n.p. Melbourne: Art Projects.
———. 1983. 'Fear of Texture'. *Art & Text* no. 10: pp. 8-18.
———. 1984. 'In Perpetual Mourning'. *Art & Text/ZG* (Summer): pp. 22-23.
———. 1990. 'One Painting, Cleaving'. In *Imants Tillers: One Painting, Cleaving*, exhib. cat., pp. 1-8. Woolongong, Woolongong City Gallery.
———. 1998. 'Remanence'. In *Justice is God's Mountain*, edited by M. Palmer. Melbourne: Melbourne International Festival of the Arts.
———. 2001a. Facsimile from Imants Tillers to Graham Coulter-Smith (September).
———. 2001b. Telephone conversation with Graham Coulter-Smith, 19 September.
von Bertalanffy, Ludwig. 1950. 'The Theory of Open Systems in Physics and Biology'. *Science* no. 111: pp. 23-29.
Waldman, Diane. 1995. *Georg Baselitz*. New York: Guggenheim Museum.
Wallis, Brian, ed. 1984. *Art After Modernism: Rethinking Representation*. New York: The New Museum of Contemporary Art.
Zuschlag, Christoph. 1995. *'Entartete Kunst': Ausstellungsstrategien im Nazi-Deutschland, Heidelberger kunstgeschichtliche Abhandlungen. Neue Folge; 21*. Worms: Wernersche Verlagsgesellschaft.

illustrations are indicated by italics, in some instances main entries are shown in bold

APPENDIX A

This previously unpublished text is presented here in its entirety.
The original pagination has been altered.

THE BEGINNER'S GUIDE TO OIL PAINTING
by
IMANTS ALFRED TILLERS

A thesis submitted in partial fulfilment of the requirements for the degree of Bachelor Science, (Architecture) (Honours)
University of Sydney, 1973.

"To put the final touch to your painting a frame is necessary"

CHAPTER 1: INTRODUCTION

1. PURPOSE OF STUDY

This thesis represents the findings of a study intended to relate recent art (manifested in scatter pieces, buried sculpture, earth art, ecological art, systems art, process art, body sculpture, mail art, auto-destructive art, art of nominating part of the world as art, conceptual art, language art) to a context beyond the art historical context.

With the gravity of environmental and social problems affecting the quality of man's life in an affluent industrial society, it seemed logical that artists and their work should be affected by these concerns as well. "Perceptiveness" is after all a quality often attributed to artists.

The apparent 'dematerialization' of this recent art and the consequences of this on the artwork as a commodity seemed to present a valuable point of departure. It seemed to show a desire for artists to make their art socially relevant to these recent issues of "quality of life" rather than continue its designated relevance to the socio-economic-political order. To verify this intuition is a further aim of this study. More specifically, the approach was to:

1) Examine the common features of this art and find a meaningful yet generalised framework which would specify the common intentions of the artists, beyond their specific individual concerns.
2) To identify the constraints on the artists' capacity to pursue a new social relevance and to examine ways in which the type of art under consideration reacts to these constraints.

2.LIMITATIONS OF UNDERTAKING.

While most of the art referred to has been done outside the local art context (except for Christo and Eventstructures Research Group projects) this is not to be considered as a major disadvantage.

Information is available through magazine appraisals and interviews as well as in some books, and the nature of the new work because of its typical presentation in the form of documents or photographs is readily accessible.

Part of the trend of this type of art is the breakdown of localised development in specific cultural centres, primarily because its media lends itself to distribution to any part of the globe (as books, photographs, films, tape recordings, television), as Seth Siegelaub (the curator who has organized several 'conceptual art' shows) has said, "I am interested in conveying the idea that the artist can live where he wants to—not necessarily in New York or London or Paris as he has had to in the past—but anywhere and can still make important art".

Nevertheless it is recognised that without direct contact with the artists and works described;[1] it is obvious that distortion of original intention has occurred through the bias of critics and misconceptions due to partial information will arise—however the critics themselves are considered as part of the art information generating system and thus it seems quite valid to accept their information-biases. As a consequence of this fact and the wide context considered, this study should be considered as a suggestion of a general trend rather than as an 'in-depth' study. It suggests a framework or an approach perhaps for a more intensive study in the future, applied perhaps specifically to the local context.

3. SUMMARY OF CONTENTS

What to Paint On

Chapter 2 tries to establish that there are in fact serious problems in our environment which affect the quality of life at the present time (Corporate State) and problems of a global scale which, though they seem distant are of an impending significance.The artist is part of this global-societal context and thus also subject to its problems.

Getting Ready

Chapter 3 examines specific views about society and the approaches which could be taken to solve what were identified in Chapter 2 as problems of the socio-economic-political matrix.

These approaches ascribe an important role to a "new aesthetic" or a "new sensibility" although none of them actually identify its characteristics.The implication on recent art is that the artist potentially could have social relevance in terms of changing this matrix by perhaps defining this 'aesthetic' in the nature of his works.

Setting the Palette

Chapter 4 examines ecological approaches to solving environmental problems which are threatening the survival of the human species. Underlying the solution is the need for a changed relationship between man and nature: from an anthropocentric view to a view which recognises that man is a part of the natural cycles and natural systems and dependent on them for his survival. Heizer's and Long's works are examined in relation to previous anthropocentric landscape traditions, to suggest a changing sensitivity to nature in recent art. The nature of the ecological sensibility is equated to an "aesthetic sensibility".

Useful Colour Charts

Chapter 5 places the ecological view into its wider context (i.e. as an open system). Since the open system view suggests a radical (possibly) reorientation of science from a mechanistic, reductionist viewpoint to a systems oriented, perspectivist viewpoint—it indicates a change from present major paradigm in science.

The ecological viewpoint can be seen as a subset of an open-systems viewpoint. Thus a solution to environmental problems involves an open-systems approach or a perspectivist method of analysis.

While the systems approach has not as yet been applied in the social sciences there are already signs that the 'Image of Man' in psychology, perception etc. is changing from a mechanistic robot-model to a more holistic systems model.

Painting a Picture

Chapter 6 demonstrates that there is a trend in some recent art towards an open-systems orientation.

The Chapter defines art in terms of criteria relating to an existing art context. It then examines the art world as a system which typically produces an output of art information. The input in this system is typically the raw data which the artist produces. This is then processed and transformed into information.

An examination of some recent art in relation to the systems model reveals a transition from object-orientation to a systems-orientation in both the works themselves and also in the development of a perspective outlook in the artists' attitudes.

The perspectivist viewpoint results in a recognition of the art world as a system and in a re-assessment of the artist's role from a producer of data to a processor of data, manifested in the increasing dematerialisation of the art-object and the interpretation of data not specifically created for interpretation but already present in the world.

This Chapter suggests the 'systems-oriented aesthetic' as the general framework in which to place some of the recent art and implies a shift from an object-oriented aesthetic to a systems-oriented aesthetic parallel to the shift in science.

CLEANING UP

Chapter 7 indicates the difficulty of ascribing a direct political role to a systems-oriented art because it is part of an art-system which is intrinsically tied to the existing socio-economic-political structure. The dilemma is that the art-system defines what art is and thus for the artist to move outside its boundaries totally, is to exclude himself from being an artist although in this new context his continued activity may be worthwhile.

While the systems aesthetic seems to be a valuable one in relation to the problem of improving the `quality of life', only broader changes in the nature of the entire art-system will allow the artist to be an effective agent for social change.

CHAPTER 2: WHAT TO PAINT ON

1. INTRODUCTION

The aim of this chapter is to briefly demonstrate that there are problems in the world and that they relate to affluent industrial man at a number of different levels. While it is easier to grasp those problems which are on a localized scale and thus are of direct relevance (issues such as local pollution, destruction of environment by highways and automobiles, decrease in quality of life) the macro-scale problems (such as over-population, diminishing resources and the threat of lethal warfare) are certainly more important concerns, however at this level solutions are usually more difficult.

One of the outcomes of a McLuhanesque age is that we are supposedly more aware of those global problems. According to McLuhan[2] the nature of our media has made large quantities of information available to a mass audience at a high speed from all parts of the globe. "In an electric information environment, minority groups can no longer be contained or ignored. Too many people know too much about each other. Our new environment compels commitment and participation."[3] Television for instance forces participation in the war in Vietnam, famines in Biafra and India, black riots in America, on the other hand it may be argued also that because of the overwhelming scale of problems to the average person, it instead breeds acceptance of these phenomena and in fact indifference and even callousness. Other factors associated with the goals of the particular society may also obscure the importance of these as relevant issues.

The aim then, is to present a context of some specific issues which the author considers of relevance to contemporary man and thus relevant to contemporary artists. Whether the artists respond to these or consider them relevant, whether they in fact react to them and thus modify their attitudes, sensibilities, content and methods of their activity is the question which this thesis is examining.

There is no intention to show the connectivity of causes and effects but rather to sketch in some aspects of the global and more local environments which seem relevant.

2. A GLOBAL PERSPECTIVE

Population Growth

Paul Ehrlich[4] attributes many of the world's problems (including environmental deterioration) to population growth. He argues that considering the present technology and patterns of behaviour, our planet is grossly overpopulated now and that a large absolute number of people and a high rate of population growth are major hindrances to solving human problems.

In this context then, the limits of human capability to produce food by conventional means have very nearly been reached. Problems of supply and distribution already have resulted in roughly half of humanity being undernourished. Some 10-20 million people are starving to death annually now.

But despite this inadequacy of supply other non-renewable resources—minerals and natural water—are being consumed quicker than natural processes can replenish them.

Much of the diminishing resources are due, moreover to the exploitative economic systems of the overdeveloped nations which persist in pursuing an affluence based on wastage.

Environmental Deterioration

Further, Ehrlich sees that the attempts to increase food production will tend to accelerate the deterioration of our environment which will in turn eventually reduce the capacity of the Earth to produce food.

Such technological "successes" as automobiles, pesticides and inorganic nitrogen fertilizers are major causes of environmental deterioration.

Most laymen tend to see the environmental deterioration as a problem which merely combines aesthetic decay with direct health hazards. These however are only minor consequences when we consider the effects of upsetting the ecosystem of the earth on which we are so dependent.

Ecological systems depend on complexity, so that everytime a forest is cleared or animal species exterminated, the complexity of the ecosystem is reduced.

Already other types of environmental deterioration are present—air pollution for example is changing the climate of the Earth—dust blankets over Southern Asia and murkiness of the atmosphere over the Pacific are manifestations of this. Already the atmosphere is cooling as less sunlight can penetrate the solid particles in the atmosphere and such weather changes could produce serious damage to world agriculture.

PLAGUE AND WARFARE

Another effect of population growth is that it increases the probability of a lethal world-wide plague and a thermonuclear war. A large weak population is ideal for disease-causing organisms, especially lethal viruses. In addition in a large population there is more chance of a lethal mutation of a common virus such as flu occurring. Also organisms could conceivably escape from biological warfare laboratories.

Thermonuclear war also becomes more likely as countries struggle for their share of diminishing resources. A struggle for the rich oil resources of the Middle-East is one of the factors behind political conflict in the area at present.

More frightening perhaps is the attitude of many corporations in the United States which are planning for the advantages they can reap through nuclear war. "... that our way of life including free enterprise, the oil industry and Socony Mobil Oil Company, can survive, recover and will win with it.[5]

* * *

The reality of considering these problems is however less than those closer to hand. After all, the affluent people in the affluent society can hardly see the immediacy or relevance of plague, famine or overpopulation in a society where steady consumption of commodities is the rule—the affluent consciousness does not feel dependent on natural processes—food is something that comes from the supermarket.

3.THE CORPORATE STATE

While the industrial societies are among the main offenders of global problems there are also important problems posed to the welfare of the individual by the structure of these societies. Both Charles Reich[6] and Kenneth Galbraith[7] have characterised the industrial state by the emergence of the structure known as the corporation. Galbraith notes that corporations are by no means the only structures which exist in the industrial state, however the influence of corporations is increasing and constituting a dominant element not only in the American economy but at social and political levels as well. There are moreover certain characteristics of corporations particularly in the pervasiveness of their power and the need to satisfy organisational rather than human needs that seem undesirable.

Charles Reich[8] has furthermore analysed the corporations and noted their close enmeshing with non-profit institutions, the education system and the government. Moreover the inter-relationship of these elements forms a greater whole than the parts.

Characteristics of the Corporate State

(i) Amalgamation and Integration.

Amalgamation and integration of many companies into one can occur in two ways. Firstly separate companies can follow parallel policies, making identical pricing decisions, identical products with identical methods of distribution and secondly by takeover of many diverse companies by a single management.

Amalgamation of the government and private sector occurs when the government provides services (such as educating people for industry) for the private sector and the private sector performs public function (such as Boeing building bombers for the government). Thus in the corporate state, diverse and pluralistic systems (i.e. the limitation of one kind of power by another) are dwindling at an increasing rate.

(ii) Hierarchical Administration.

Another feature of the Corporate State is that it is basically an administrative state and since the theory of administration emphasises rational control of activity by lines of authority, responsibility and supervision, this results in everyone being arranged hierarchically. There are no rules for every contingency and individual choice is minimised. The structure of bureaucracy then produces a small ruling elite who make all the decisions about what is produced, consumed, how resources are allocated, the conditions of work, etc. Further while the administration is valueless it functions most effectively when the status quo is maintained.

(iii) Autonomy.

The Corporate State is autonomous in that it is not subject to control by the people through the democratic process[9]; by the market in the private sector[10]; or by pluralism in the case of the government[11].

Further, those people in positions to exercise power are not in control either since the existence of bondholders, stockholders, banks and bankers, potential raiders seeking control, financial control by conglomerate ownership all result in impersonal demands of profits, growth and stability of income. The executive holding power is also dependent on the information he gets and thus he doesn't challenge the autonomy of the corporate state either.

(iv) Status—the New Property

According to Reich "the concept of status in the corporate state has replaced the role of private property in the market economy. Status, which defines an individual's relationship to organisations has become the chief goal in life—happiness is defined in terms of position in a complex hierarchy of status.

Galbraith's principle of consistency[12] is relevant here too. The principle states that there must be a symmetry in the motivation and goals of organisations and the individuals comprising them. Thus the corporation must somehow attribute social purpose to the goals of those who comprise it.

The technocracy is principally concerned with the manufacture of goods and with accompanying management and development of demand for these goods and thus it attributes social purpose to these in "a high standard of living" which is defined in terms of more goods (usually of those type that conserve muscular energy or raise calorie intake).

Thus the individual identifies his goals with those of the organisation and he does not want to exercise his freedom against authorities (i.e. he wants his homelife investigated, his psychological make-up, his friends and associations, political and cultural activities and past investigated, he wants his privacy invaded, to fulfil special conditions), since the organisations and society's well-being is identical to his own.

Since everyone is arranged in a hierarchy, inequality is clearly defined—everyone can feel the differences between himself and other statuses. As one man's special status benefits and privileges depend on the proper functioning of the rest of the organisation and the need for everyone else to be kept in their proper place, the individual becomes more and more the ROLE as less and less of his private life remains.

(v) Role of Law.

Reich's most startling analysis is in the role of law[13] in the corporate state. Law perpetuates and legalises the controls already executed by the corporate state to keep it running effectively. Reich notes that law in America changed from a medium which carried traditional values of its own to a value-free medium adapted to serve public policy—the public interest of the corporate state. We have already seen that the public interest is really an expression of the needs of the corporations (i.e. the principle of consistency).

Corporations are not subject to the Bill of Rights while they do exercise government powers (due to the emergence of the public-private state). They can decide on what is to be produced and what is not, how resources are allocated; also they can fire employees for using free speech or discriminate against those who do—newspapers, T.V. and magazines can refuse to carry public opinion.

Federal regulation of economic activity by law rationalizes and stabilizes industry—it does not protect the consumer, the individual, rather it polices outlaws, prevents unruly competition and limits entry into a field, creates monopolies and excludes particular groups in the allocation of valuable resources (e.g. T.V.)

In addition technology is not subject to law, this is best exemplified by the development of Mace as a police weapon. It was developed for profit by a private company; no tests or studies were made by scientific or government agencies; no approval made by any legislative body; no vote made by the public; no disclosure of information on its long-term effects made; no standards set as to when it would be appropriate to use it and in fact the law bars any redress to the victims.

The Law in fact functions in advancing private interests. The courts become the field for private manoeuvre for power, status and financial goals using the legal powers of the government to provide benefits, subsidies, allocate resources, franchise and to grant special favours and exceptions. For each status, class and position in society there are different sets of laws. Finally there are a great number of laws in the corporate state and consequently there is a large amount of discretionary power generated so that the law can be enforced selectively or arbitrarily.

* * *

In the context of this integrated and formidable structure it seems possible also to attribute many of the manifestations of environmental deterioration, deterioration of the quality of life to the corporations. When we examine their objectives the link becomes more obvious.

Goals of Corporations

The main objectives of corporations are "a secure level of earnings and a maximum rate of growth consistent with the provision of revenues for the requisite investment. Technological virtuosity and a rising dividend rate are secondary in the sense that they must not interfere with the first objectives".[14]

The corporation can only maintain its decision making autonomy if it has a steady level of earnings so that it is not vulnerable to outside influence. It maintains profit maximisation and expansion of output to expand the corporation itself and thus maintain its stability. (This behaviour is similar in organisms).[15]

Growth, moreover, while it is the goal of the organisation is also a social goal by the principle of consistency and thus we find that the almost universal acceptance of the annual increase in Gross National Product as a measure of a country's social success. Similarly technological advance as a goal of the corporation is consistent with technological advance as a social goal.

James Weaver goes on to make the link of environmental deterioration with the imperatives of economic growth[16]—nature is treated as a commodity (things like air, water, quiet and natural beauty are treated as 'free goods' and their use not as social costs). He demonstrates that economic growth results in overdeveloped countries which destroy natural resources for more commodities (increasingly supplying an artificially created demand for useless goods) and produce dangerous pollutants and waste. The link then between corporations and environmental deterioration is fairly obvious.

4. FURTHER CONSEQUENCES FOR THE INDIVIDUAL

So far we have shown some of global problems as they potentially affect the individual, some of the problems of the corporate state and how they directly affect the individual, we also have shown that there is a relationship between the global problems and the structure and goals of the corporate state. The next section then examines some further consequences on the individual of economic growth and of industrialisation even prior to the emergence of the corporate state.

The Consequences on Man of Economic Growth.

Under the directives of economic growth "labour becomes a commodity to be bought and sold on the market like sacks of flour or bales of hay"[17] and the point about labour markets is that they require differentiated incomes to operate, thus they generate income inequality. In addition as labour becomes more specialized—tasks are divided into minute tasks. Alienated labour is then required to do alienated tasks—and education is enlisted as was shown before to provide this labour—as much as anything else schools teach compliance and obedience to the system.

Other consequences discussed are the geographic mobility which results in despoliation of otherwise inaccessible areas; the destruction of cities and the loss of community.

Biological and Psychological Needs

Ian McHarg[18] provides in a case study a striking correspondence between the destruction of quality in the city environment (i.e. noise, pollution, sensory deprivation) and pathology. While it is difficult to predict correlations it seems that not only poverty but population density correspond to patterns of pathology (Psychological as well as physiological).

However this correlation could be due to the nature of employment of the people living there. Stephen Boyden[19] points out that the industrial system has replaced man's biological needs by false externally imposed needs (i.e. that one's status, one's self respect, self worth depends on the quantity and quality of goods consumed—the problem is that one's expectations always rise so one is never satisfied) which now have become part of the biology of man[20].

The falseness of these needs is emphasised if we compare the conditions of life of urban man today and the non-psychological needs of palaeolithic man.

"The industrial man is no longer subject to natural regulatory mechanisms that ensured his calorie consumption was not in excess or less than that required for growth, physical activity; the social environment now imposes a monophasic sleeping pattern whereas palaeolithic man slept when he became tired during the day; the emotional involvement of the average individual in the main activities of the day is now minimal; the average individual is not engaged daily in personal creative activities; the average individual is prevented from responding to personal tensions in a spontaneous way; the average individual is not surrounded by a visual environment full of interest; the average individual is separated from close relatives so that there is no opportunity for spontaneous conversation to share problems and anxieties; the average individual is seldom involved in meaningful co-operative group activities; most of his daily activities are not directly goal-directed."[21]

While this is a great generalisation it is not to deny its significance, for certainly the symptoms of biological maladjustment are growing, in the form of increased mental illness, growing suicide rates, and in anti-social behaviour such as crime and delinquency.

The interrelationship of these maladjustments as consequences of the corporate state and its objectives is also stressed, although these deprivations would have been relevant prior to the corporate state, however as the corporate state extends its influence as it has been described to do, we all will come to share the same deprivation of biological needs.

* * *

We have examined then problems of a global scale, those implicit in the structure of the corporate state, to those that affect the individual at a person level and shown the interrelationships which occur between the different levels. The aim was not to be comprehensive but rather to indicate areas of concern that seemed relevant.

The next chapter emphasises the need for changed attitudes and sensibilities to deal with these problems on a societal level and in chapter 4 on an environmental level.

CHAPTER 3: GETTING READY

1. INTRODUCTION

It is far beyond the scope of this thesis to examine theories as to how some of the man-man, man-society, man-technology problems outlined briefly in Chapter 1 are to be solved or what approach should be used in analysing them. There are many social and political and economic theories (which are often contradictory as to the extent to which social change must take place, in what form and with what basis liberation from the repression of the present corporate state must proceed—it is even more difficult to propose how these theories could be applied and whether the processes of social change actually taking place seem to correspond to their theoretical models.[22]

However, what is relevant to this is the proposal of several of these writers, who are influential in forming the views of certain artists referred to in Chapter 6, that "there is a need for the formation of a 'new aesthetic sensibility' as a prerequisite or necessary accompaniment to social change".

2. THE FURTHER DIMENSIONS OF THE CORPORATE STATE

Irrelevance of Ideology

The economist Galbraith[23] has insisted that the aims of the industrial state have been power and expansion. The needs of this state moreover have not been served by the complete expression of the aesthetic impulse at all, however he sees the future as a technocracy "guided by aesthetic decision-making".

He questions both Communism and American laissez-faire capitalism stressing that both societies have developed the same corporate structures despite their different ideologies. This is because the corporation itself has its own goals and develops its own autonomy (as has been already shown in Chapter 2) irrespective of its subjects' beliefs who tend to identify their own goals with those of the corporation. This fact also demonstrates that Marxism is a production orientated system and that its fundamental economic premises (i.e. of growth) are the same as those of capitalism.

"Marxism is the mirror image of bourgeois industrialism: an image reversed and yet unmistakably identical. For both traditions, the technocratic imperative with its attendant conception of life stands unchallenged. Ironically, it is the greatest single victory bourgeois society has won over even its most irreconcilable opponents: that it has inculcated upon them: its own shallow, reductionist image of man. Like classical economics, scientific socialism approached society as Newton approached the behaviour of heavenly bodies, seeking their immutable "laws of motion". Marx's view still aspired to the "myth of a social-scientific objectivity" in which society would be understood as "a process of natural history".[24]

The Technocratic Deception

Even so Galbraith does not think that the industrial system is a terminal phenomena as does Roszak—it is the product of a vast and autonomous transformation and still in the process of evolving. However as Galbraith points out "it has succeeded tacitly in excluding the notion that it is transitory and thus somehow an imperfect phenomena. Among the least enchanting words in business lexicon are planning, governmental control, state support and socialism. To consider the likelihood of these in the future would be to bring home the appalling extent to which they are already a fact."

In the economy the flow of instruction from the consumer to the market (i.e. the consumer buys goods and services in the market and opportunities that result for making more or less money, are the message of the market to the producing firms) what he calls the "Accepted Sequence"[25] has been reversed so that the mature corporation has readily at hand the means for controlling the prices at which it sells as well as those at which it buys and what the consumer buys at the prices which it controls. The problem is that the reversal of the sequence (The Revised Sequence) is not recognised and it is still believed that the individual is the ultimate source of power in the economy and this belief raises barriers against a wide range of social action, including government interference on questions of industrial squalor, air and stream pollution, sacrifice of aesthetic values—rhymed commercials and billboards. Also the individual subordinates his personality to the organisation, being a good member of the team in the belief that he helps to enlarge the range of choice of individual consumers. This then affords great protection to the autonomy of the technostructure and great immunity to its techniques of managing demand.

The recognition of this deception is the first step in controlling the technocracy and redirecting it to more humane goals.

Aesthetic Goals in a Technocracy

The technocracy itself according to Galbraith is inescapable: in an emergent superscientific culture long-range decision making and implementation become more difficult and necessary. Judgment demands precise socio-technical models and thus a structure incorporating central storage of information, decision-making autonomy and adequate techniques for implementing social change is required to make these decisions.

Galbraith however emphasises the role of aesthetic criteria in the decision-making process of the future technocracy. At present, aesthetic goals are beyond the reach of the technostructure, i.e. it cannot identify itself with them and thus if they are strongly asserted, they are viewed as constraints.

Aesthetic goals contest the claims of power lines over landscape, of power development over natural streams or national parks, of highways over natural streams, strip mining over virgin mountains and shopping centres over antique squares. To assert these goals is to interfere seriously with the management of the consumer and thus economic advantage in its effect on output, income and cost.

Because of this, the state (i.e. the government sector) is the only means possible for asserting aesthetic priorities and providing the essential framework for artistic effort. The nature of this aesthetic sensibility which is to be used in the technocracy, however is not characterised by Galbraith.

3. LIBERATION FROM THE CORPORATE STATE

Political and social theorists Herbert Marcuse and Norman Brown while differing in their emphasis on the nature of man's alienation and how it can be alleviated are both united against Marx on the primacy of consciousness in social change. For Marx "it was not consciousness of men that determines their social being, but on the contrary, their social being that determines their consciousness".[26] For Marcuse, liberation is also related to social domination but for Brown there is the further condition that liberation from the scientific world view must also take place (i.e. a reductionist view to which Marx, Freud and even Marcuse subscribes, to an extent).

Quantitative Changes

Marcuse unlike Galbraith (who sees the present consequences as a result of a misinterpretation of the system) sees the consequences inseparable from the system.

In his Essay on Liberation, Marcuse devotes an entire chapter to the role of the new sensibility in the impending revolution. Thus while quantitative changes can mean and can lead to revolution only in conjunction with qualitative changes can the system as a whole change.

Marcuse sees this qualitative change as being based on "a sensitivity receptive to the forms and modes of reality which thus far have been projected only by the aesthetic imagination",[27] only in this way, can we be freed from the repressive satisfactions[28] of the unfree society.

The Role of Art

Since aesthetic form is to emerge in the social process of production, art has to change its traditional locus and function. It would become an integral factor in shaping reality and the way of life, this however, he says would involve a transcendence of Art, the end of the segregation of the aesthetic from the real—the end of the commercial unification of business and beauty, exploitation and pleasure. Art would have to recapture its more primitive 'technical' connotations as the art of preparing (cooking!) cultivating, growing things and giving them a form which neither violates their matter nor the sensitivity of the individual.[29]

Marcuse sees art in its present form as the example of liberation but not as a tool for liberation. He notes that much art of this century has continually declared itself as anti-art, as a necessary mechanism for preserving itself from sublimation (repressive tolerance) by the forces of exploitation and consumerism. Only by this desublimation can art keep itself pure and alive and maintain its capacity for a deep response to the "in-itself" qualities of people and things. It is this knowledge and this aesthetic sensibility which will be needed after the revolution, as for art's actual liberation potential it is minor because it is art (i.e. a representation or metaphor of reality) and not reality itself.

Marcuse doesn't characterise the nature of this aesthetic sensibility—however he senses that the basic qualities of art are essential to the kind of man that the revolution wants to produce.

***

4. THE COUNTER CULTURE

Galbraith and Marcuse while differing in the radicality of their propositions for change both underline the role of an aesthetic sensibility in their theories. However they both see the inevitability of a technological state; Marcuse still speaks of the "social process of production" and Galbraith of the "super-scientific culture", the counter culture for better or worse denies the necessity of technological directives. Thus both Reich[30] and Roszak[31] see the evolution of the new consciousness in the youth movements in America as not merely "the age-old process of generational disaffection" but genuinely radical discontent significantly different to other sources of radical discontent.

Radical Discontent

Roszak[32] demonstrates that the discontent coming from questions of social justice in the black power movement and the working class is quite different to that of the student movements.

"What after all, does social justice mean to the outcast and dispossessed. Most obviously it means gaining admission to everything from which middle-class selfishness excludes them".[33] Thus black power, black culture and black consciousness could conceivably be steps merely to black consumption, black conformity, black affluence. Similarly for example in the May 1968 General Strike in France if the workers had taken control of French industry it is doubtful whether they would set technocratic priorities aside in favour of a new life style.

Thus New Left activists such as the Students for a Democratic Society have little in common with "older" generation Marxist guardians of social justice, who see these activists as decadent, spoiled, middle class young, who cannot settle down gracefully to the responsibilities of life in an advanced industrial order.[34]

The new discontent is not merely against social injustice, domination of one culture over another, not merely against capitalism and imperialism, not merely against what Marcuse calls surplus repression but challenges also "the nature of education, the validity of institutionalism and the legal system, the nature and purposes of work, the course of man's dealings with the environment, the relationship of self to technology and society".[35] This discontent seems to be challenging not just any one aspect of the corporate state or technocracy but rather the entire system and its premises.

This is particularly evident in the S.D.S. questioning of the fashionable thesis that we have reached the "end of ideology" in the Great Society. This is in part Galbraith's thesis that ideology is absent in the technocracy (as outlined before), however, it has simply blended itself into the indisputable truth of the scientific world view.

Bertalanffy[36] suggests that scientific world views are by no means objective and in his formulation of the General Systems Theory shows that the categories of thinking in science are determined by biological, cultural and linguistic factors. While science can come to a closer correspondence to 'reality' by a process of de-anthropomorphisation[37] it can only mirror reality and each aspect has thus only relative truth. This view is quite different to the reductionist thesis on which the current scientific world view is based—in that physical theory is the only one to which all possible science and all aspects of reality can be reduced.

Thus the technocrats deal in 'rationality', 'efficiency' and 'progress' and in the 'value-free' language of statistics and convince themselves that they have no ideological orientation. "The most effective ideologies are always those that are congruent with the limits of consciousness, for then they work subliminally."[38]

A New Life Style

The youth movement emphasises the importance of choosing a new life style (this is where the difference in generations lies), one based on satisfying the self rather than assuming one of the roles which the technocracy or corporate state offers. This preservation of the self against the state is not anti-social but rather of vital importance to the human community.

"Protection of nature and man from the machine is logical because of the power of the machine to dominate nature. A personal moral code that transcends law is necessary where law has ceased to express a balance set of values. In addition the new consciousness seeks the restoration of the non-material elements of man's existence, the elements like the natural environment and the spiritual that were passed by in the rush of material development."[39]

It also seeks the emergence of the non-intellective capacities in response to the dehumanised rationality of the technocracy—"those capacities that take fire from the visionary splendour and experience of human communion—become the arbiters of the good, the true and the beautiful".[40] The new consciousness also seeks to transcend science and technology, to restore them to their proper place as tools of man rather than as determinants of man's existence.

Both Roszak and Reich are very poetic and convey the impression of subjectivity in their writings on the counter-culture but appropriately so, if we consider "objectivity" within the current scientific world view as a manifestation of the technocratic ideology. The point of this digression on the counter-culture is that a spontaneous movement based on a new set of goals and values accompanied by a new sensibility that isn't based on economic or technological premises is in the process of developing.

The People's Park

That this new sensibility has an aesthetic basis is evident if we consider for example the People's Park—the muddy vacant lot near Berkeley campus owned by the University of California which was turned into a park by a group of 'street' people and students. They saw the plot of land in terms of the human and ecological situation of the city rather than in legal terms as private property. And in placing human needs and ecology (their understanding of what it is) ahead of law they proposed something of a new social order. They proposed a society in which aesthetics, ecology and human requirements would be paramount and in which decisions concerning these matters would be made not by persons designated by law in our society but by self-constituted local groups whose legitimacy came only from their proximity and concern. Jack Burnham goes as far as to characterise the People's Park as a "real-time work of art".[41]

By "real-time" Burnham means that the activity happened within the day-to-day flow of normal experience. As a contrast, appreciation of art objects usually happens in ideal, non-existential time in the sense that the art object is not necessarily dependant on the persons real experience of time.[42]

Ideal time and "experimental idealism" are furthermore both outgrowths of the classical frame of reference. That is to say that they stem from the intuition that location and proportion transcend the illusion of time—in science then, the emphasis is on strict control over isolated formal relationships—it is the reductionist hypothesis of the world.

5.THE AESTHETIC SENSIBILITY

The aim then in presenting the viewpoints of Marcuse, Galbraith and the attitudes of the counter-culture is that they all enlist that amorphous quality "the aesthetic sensibility" in active roles to rectify the problems of man and man, man and society, man and technology. The validity and relevance of their approaches is not of particular interest, rather it is the nature, function and definition of this 'aesthetic sensibility.'

Marcuse and Galbraith attribute it as something similar to the sensibility of artists and poets but this view is by no means adequate since the range of artistic response and sensibility is large and it would seem that some types of sensibility would be more adequate for their purposes than others.

In Chapter 6 a fundamental change in aesthetic sensibility from an object-orientated aesthetic to a systems-orientated aesthetic in an 'art' context will be discussed but whether this aesthetic is the same as the one envisaged by Marcuse or Galbraith or whether it forms the basis of the counter-culture's sensibilities or whether it is in fact a step beyond all these and whether it is a practical aesthetic in the light of society's problems cannot be proved within the limits of this thesis, however these are questions posed for future investigations.

The next chapter considers an ecological approach to problems of the environment and man's relationship to it and what can be described as the systems approach implicit in it. From this approach emerges an attitude which could also be described as a new (in the context of recent Western man) "aesthetic sensibility" which is very much a systems-orientated aesthetic. The nature moreover of this sensibility can be more readily identified and some of its components will be analysed in Chapter 5.

CHAPTER 4: SETTING THE PALETTE

1. ANTHROPOCENTRIC VIEW OF THE WORLD.

"Western society at large, believes that the world, if not the universe, consists of a dialogue between men, or between men and anthropocentric God: the result of this view is that man, exclusively is thought divine—given dominion over all life, enjoined among all creatures to subdue the earth. Nature is then an irrelevant backdrop to the human play called progress, or profit. If nature is to be brought to the foreground, it is only to be conquered—man versus nature."[43]

As a society our model of reality is one based on economics—the world is seen as a commodity, not as a series of interrelationships which incorporate physical and biological processes. We knew how to exploit the seashore for profit, sterilise the landscape for profit, fell the great forests for profit, fill protective marshes for profit. But we do not know or value the chemical elements and compounds that constitute life and their cycles, the importance of the photosynthetic plant, the essential decomposers, the ecosystems, their constituent organisms, their roles and co-operative mechanisms, the prodigality of life forms, or the genetic rod with which we confront the future."[44]

2. HISTORICAL ORIGINS OF THE ANTHROPOCENTRIC WORLD VIEW

Genesis

Whatever were the earliest roots of the western attitude to nature it seems that they were confirmed in Judaism. The story of Genesis which is the source of most generally accepted description of man's roles and powers insists upon dominion and subjugation in nature, encouraging the most exploitative and destructive instincts in man rather than those that are deferential and creative.

"Then God said 'Let us make man in our image, after our likeness: and let them have dominion over the fish of the sea, and over the birds of the air, and over the cattle, and over all the earth, and over every creeping thing that creeps upon the earth".[45]

While the literalness of Genesis has been rejected[46] it is evident that it is the literal belief and not the allegory which permeates the Western view of man and nature. Implicit in the story of Genesis is also the concept of time as non-repetitive and linear. The Greco-Roman conception of time was a cyclical notion and thus the idea of a beginning was impossible in this framework. The expression of this idea today (despite the fact that we consider ourselves in a "post-Christian age" we still live under its values) is in our implicit faith in perpetual progress which was unknown either to Greco-Roman antiquity or in the Orient.

Guardian Spirits

Christianity in contrast to ancient paganism and Asia's religions not only established a dualism of man and nature but also insisted that it is God's will that man exploit nature for his proper ends. In antiquity every tree, every spring, every stream had its own genius loci: its guardian spirit. These sprits were accessible to men and before one cut a tree, mined a mountain or dammed a brook it was important to placate the spirit in charge of that particular situation.

By destroying pagan animism, Christianity made it possible to exploit nature in a mood of indifference to the feelings of natural objects.[47]

What has been said must be qualified, in that Christianity is a complex faith and its consequences differ in different contexts. Only in a situation where technological advances made such spectacular advances could these values be so destructive. It seems that the change in Medieval times from the scratch plough (which required cross-plowing) to the 8 oxen plough which was more efficient but also required the pooling of resources (for no family had 8 oxen) vastly changed man's relation to the soil. Distribution of land was no longer based on needs of the family but rather on the capacity of a power machine to till the earth, and man now had the capacity to exploit nature in the context of the appropriate values.

Beliefs of Science

The origins of science in Western civilisation are tied to Christian theology. Since God had made nature, nature must also reveal the divine mentality—thus Friar Roger Bacon produced startlingly sophisticated work on the optics of the rainbow but as a venture in religious understanding

There seems then to be a relationship of modern science, in its origins, to the attitudes of Christian theology. Science and technology gave mankind the power to implement the values of dominion and subjugation of nature, since the values behind science were not incongruent to those of Christianity.

3. LANDSCAPE ARCHITECTURE

The Renaissance Tradition

McHarg points out that the Western tradition of landscape architecture (except for the eighteen century English tradition) has been identified with garden making.

In the Renaissance, the visual and symbolic expression of humanism upon the land typically expressed the authority of man by the imposition of a simple Euclidean geometry upon the landscape. "Man imposes his simple entertaining illusion of order, accomplished with great art, upon an unknowing and uncaring nature. The garden is offered as proof of man's superiority".

In France, Louis XIV lay transected by twin axes at Versailles, king by divine right, the ordered gardens below, testimony to the divinity of man and his supremacy over a base and subject nature. Typically this is a selected nature, decorative and tame whose order of array, unlike the complexity typical of nature, is reduced to a simple and comprehensible geometry.

The Japanese Tradition

In contrast is the traditional Japanese garden here there is also a very strict ordering of elements, however it is not the imposition of an overall scheme and fitting of parts into it without regard to their intimate interrelationship but rather a general principle which governs the relationships of the basic components at the most fundamental level—the order is created at the level of the moss and rocks not at the level of an overall scheme. Thus there is a perceptiveness to nature reflected in Japanese language, rich in descriptive power, in which subtle changes in natural processes (e.g. the tilth of soil and dryness of the wind) are precisely describable.

The Eighteenth Century English Landscape

This was a parallel development in Western culture. Its proponents, while lacking a science of ecology used native plant materials in interdependent communities with no imposed aesthetic—nature itself produced the aesthetic. (The exposure to Oriental principles of asymmetry had helped sustain this view). Form and process were indivisible aspects of a single phenomenon. It is obvious that the political socio-economic climate the time had much to do with this development (i.e. the absence of cities and the industrial revolution) while their views were adequate for the Eighteenth Century a more comprehensive theory is necessary now.

* * *

In this context it is interesting to examine superficially aspects of Richard Long's work and that of Michael Heizer—both are artists working in the natural environment in the late 60's and early 70's.

While it is not perhaps correct to examine their work outside an art context it is interesting nevertheless to compare the attitudes which their work expresses in relation to the environment, to what degree anthropocentric values are present. This is the type of re-orientation in values in art which will be discussed in Chapter 6.

Michael Heizer

Heizer works mainly on flat, arid desert areas[48] where there is little plant and animal life to respond to. His works up to 1970 ranged from huge rocks placed in depressions, dug into the desert (e.g. the 52 ton mass in a 51 x 10 x 9_' cement depression at Silver Springs, Nevada), ditches dug in the desert (the Five Conic Displacements—150 tons of earth was removed and the depression filled up with water after floods) to drawings made by trucks on the desert (Ground-incision/Loop Drawing), powder dispersals and metal installations in the environment which directly respond to the action of the environment (e.g. Dissipate).

The salient feature of his work seems to be an incorporation of natural processes in the work itself: the rain filling his depressions with colloidal matter "at a rate of 3-4 inches annually" and the use of the wind to create visual patterns "the wind carries away compositional difficulties and obliterates touch"[49] are examples.

In works such as Dissipate, the form of the work is dependent on the continuous processes of the environment—the 9 metal troughs (12' x 1' x 1') are fixed into the desert floor in a random pattern but due to expansion and contraction of the metal as a result of heat changes from day to night or due to the action of the wind (in filling the troughs with earth) or the action of floods, they change their fixed configurations and form patterns according to the effects of the environment.

However while Heizer's work embodies the recognition of interrelationships—it is more an interrelationship of the physical elements rather than those of more complex plant ecologies. Further, his expressed desire is in a sense still related to the anthropocentric man — he has chosen an area where he cannot upset the plant-animal relationships and this clouds our vision. One clue is in the scale of Hezier's work —it is huge and while his forms are minimal, pieces like Ground/Incision Loop Drawing begin to look like a typically abstract drawing except taken off the canvas and enlarged (perhaps this is why he uses the desert—because it is a flat, neutral surface).

He says "Man will never create anything really large in relation to the world—only in relation to himself and his size. The greatest scale he understands is the distance between the earth and the moon."[50] In conjunction with the scale of gesture in Hezier's work this statement suggests Hezier is operating within the same tradition as the Renaissance humanist gardener although perhaps with greater sensitivity to certain processes of the natural environment.

Richard Long

Long's pieces are both lyrical and pictorial—he conveys a strong feeling for the landscape. Long's geography is felt rather than treated as an abstraction—instead of subjecting nature to his will, he personifies it through a series of photographs and statements—emphasising existing relationships rather than imposing new man-centred ones.

His 2 mile walk sculpture, where lines are formed in the grass as he walks along four different imaginary lines 64, 32, 16 and 8 times, his presence in the environment is asserted perhaps not constructively but not destructively either—the trampled grass will grow back again.

His compositional devices are as simple as possible: lines, the intersection of lines and squares where he encloses some area by walking. Particular locations in England, Scotland and Ireland are important to Long whereas Hezier's work is not particular in the sense that the desert is generally invariant (or at least he views it as such) and the works could be placed anywhere within this general context. While Long's work doesn't show a particularly acute awareness of the interrelationships of nature it is close to an animistic relationship to nature; Long may in fact be placating the genius loci of specific places in his travels—he certainly isn't exploiting nature in a "mood of indifference to the feelings of natural objects".

While the full implications of these artists work will be developed later it is of interest that the traditional man-nature view has been somewhat modified. We are not however prepared to argue at this present point that the work embodies an ecological view of the man-nature relationship.

4. THE ECOLOGICAL VIEW OF THE WORLD

Mans' Dependence

We have implied what the ecological view is by stating what its antithesis appears to be, however, this will not suffice. An ecological view considers the world in terms of interrelationships, cycles and processes, all interdependent and man in this context (i.e. of the world) is not divine, perhaps he is the current, latest dominant species but in no sense is he outside these natural system.

McHarg gives the example of a simple capsule experiment[51] which demonstrates some of the cycles which man depends on. The capsule contains an energy source (the sun), some air, some water, some algae, growing in the water, some bacteria and man.

"The system depends first upon the sun, the net production of photosynthesis after respiration, upon the water and upon the cycling and recycling of the materials in the system by decomposers. The process requires that the substances or wastes, the output of one creature are the inputs to the others. The oxygen wastes of the plant were input to the man, the carbon dioxide of the man input to the plant; the substance of the plant input to the man, the wastes of the man input to the plant, the wastes of the man and plant input to the decomposers, the wastes of these the input to the decomposers, the wastes of these the input to the plant: and the water cycles continuously."[52]

In a sense the most important organism to man is the plant, algae—its chloroplasts are the dominant mechanism by which the light of the sun is transformed into the substances supporting all life, the sugar and carbohydrates. Plants may have in fact produced all the free oxygen, indeed all food, fossil fuels, the stabilization of the earth's surface and the terrestrial water systems, temperatures of climate and microclimate have been accomplished by plants. Man is the parasite of plants since plants are hardly dependent on man at all. In the light of man's dependence it logically is difficult to hold an anthropocentric view of the world.

Vital Cycles

The cycle discussed so far is only one of several cycles on which life and thus man depend. While energy from the sun is constantly entering and passing through the Earth's ecosystems, the ecosystems themselves have no similar extraterrestrial source of carbon, nitrogen, potassium, sulphur, oxygen and hydrogen. These substances must be continually recycled through the ecosystem if the ecosystem is to persist. The 3 cycles shown below are the carbon cycle, nitrogen cycle and phosphorous cycles.

Concept Of Fitness

While Darwin advanced the conception of biological evolution with natural selection as its primary mechanism Henderson observed that the earth was peculiarly suited to the evolution of matter, of life, of creatures and of man. Biological evolution still continues but does not respond easily to voluntary manipulation while the environment, because it is in a constant flux can be changed by the presence of organisms. The point is that the environment can be changed to produce a better fit but this is dependent on a knowledge of the environment and its interactions.

Creativity

Another aspect of the ecological view is the perception of the world and its evolution as a creative process.[53] While entropy or degraded energy in any system must increase according to the second law of thermodynamics, in life systems and the orderings that they accomplish there is evidence, not of degradation but of upgrading.

"Energy impinging on living communities and stored in carbon compounds sustains a variety of forms of life promoting their individual and group organisation, enhancing the capacity of the habitat to sustain life; regulating the economy of water movement and chemical transformation—in short doing work."[54]

This tendency of living organisms to raise matter to a higher order by entrapping energy from outside the organism and forcing it to do work is called negentropy or creation. Absolute entropy is destructive in that it is the condition when all energy would be degraded, random, simple, uniform, disordered, unable to perform any further work. In contrast idealized negentropy would exhibit high order, complexity, diversity, uniqueness and ability to perform work.

5. THE ECOLOGICAL SENSIBILITY

Thus the antithesis of the exploitative view of nature is the ecological view of man's dependence on nature not as a separate entity but as part of many interdependent systems. The complexity and holistic organisation of a system is in direct contrast to the simple relational man-nature dualism of the anthropocentric world view.

Insensitive exploitation of nature corresponds often to the degradation of energy and as such is a violation of the general principles of living systems. Also, the similarity of some systems (oceans and organisms)[55] points to the functional similarities of many organic (including man) and inorganic systems; thus from an ecological point of view, a man-nature dualism is untenable.

The point then is that the present crisis is largely due to values held towards nature, values whose origins are in Judeo-Christian theology and which are in many respects contradictory to the facts of the world.

The values expounded by McHarg,[56] then amount to a changed sensibility, one which emphasises interdependences, processes, isomorphisms, environments, concepts of fitness, continuous exchanges of energy, development of higher levels of order and energy states—in other words he is advocating a view where what can be termed as systems are of primary importance.

The ecological view however is part of a wider conceptual framework developed by Bertalanffy in his General Systems Theory. This is the subject of the next chapter.

CHAPTER 5 USEFUL COLOUR CHARTS

1. SYSTEMS

Approach to Analysis

There are two arguments for a systems approach to analysis of living phenomena.

1) that such an approach will reveal the 'Gestalten' properties that characterise the higher levels of organisation which we call 'living systems'.

2) that many of these Gestalten properties are common to the different levels of organisation of living matter (from bacteria to human societies) and thus provide a valid and powerful form of generalisation.

3) that while the properties can be generalised to the 'species', it need not necessarily claim generality to all living systems because systems analysis presupposes a knowledge of what functions the part system can undertake.

The approach however in this thesis is the second one, that a systems approach is a valid form of generalisation for many types of phenomena.

Defining a System

Angyal writing in the context of gestalt psychology[57] on the structure of wholes, states that those holistic connexions which cannot be resolved into relationships are systems. Bertalanffy[58] notes that three different kinds of distinctions can be made between any 3 elements: (a) according to their <u>number</u>, (b) according to their <u>species</u>, (c) according to the <u>relations</u> of the elements. Angyal[59] draws 4 distinctions between relations and systems.

1) Relationships involve two and only two members. Complex relationships can always be analysed into pairs of relata. Systems may involve an unspecified number of components not analysable in certain respects into pairs of relata.

2) Relata enter into a relationship by virtue of their immanent attributes while constituents enter a system through their positional values in the system.

3) The concept of a dimensional domain is necessary for systems. An example of such a domain is time or space—it is not necessarily important to have such a domain to make relationships. For example two colours which exist at separate points in space need not be compared with reference to that space, however in a system there is a specific form of distribution of members in that space.

4) Systems cannot be deduced from relations while deduction of relations from a system still remains a possibility.

Another way of looking at it, is that relationships are always summative i.e. the elements are the same within and outside the complex summation of characteristics and the behaviour of elements is as known in isolation. The elements in a system are always constitutive i.e. they are dependent on specific relations within the complex—you have to know not only the parts but also how they are put together.

Further, a sum can be considered as being gradually and thus linearly in time whereas a system has to be conceived of as being composed instantly in time.

Angyal concludes that causal thinking which has been the basis of thinking in science for a long time is an example of relational thinking and he conjectures that the change to systems thinking "may be as difficult as the transition from a 3-dimensional to a 4-dimensional geometry".[60]

2. OPEN SYSTEMS

Open and Closed Systems

Bertalanffy derives the general properties of all systems mathematically—finding that systems manifest behaviour such as growth, competition between parts, wholeness, progressive segregation, progressive mechanisation, centralisation, hierarchical order and finality.[61] These properties of systems while relevant have not been discussed. Our more immediate aim is to differentiate between the behaviour of closed and open systems.

"A closed system must according to the second law of thermodynamics eventually attain a time-equilibrium state with maximum entropy and minimum free energy, where the ratio between its phases remains constant. An open system may attain a time-independent state where the system remains constant as a whole and in its phases, though there is a continuous flow of component material. This is called the steady state."[62]

By definition then closed systems are systems which are considered to be isolated from their environments.[63] A further implication is that entropy can be expressed as a measure of probability and so a closed system tends to a state of most probable distribution. For example in a box of green and yellow marbles, it is highly improbable that all green marbles and all yellow ones align themselves on the left and right sides respectively. In open systems, since there is a steady import of energy from the environment the operation of entropy is counteracted and the open system is characterised by negative entropy (negentropy) rather than positive entropy. Thus open systems tend to states of most improbable distribution i.e. states of increased order and organisation.

On a large scale this is the observation that the ecologist makes (McHarg) through Darwin's theory of evolution. Before we list the common characteristics of Open Systems it is useful to note the similarity between information and entropy.

Information and Entropy

The theory of communication states that information in general cannot be interpreted as energy. The flow of information can sometimes correspond to the flow of energy (e.g. when light waves emitted by some objects reach the eye and elicit some reaction from the organism): sometimes it flows opposite to the flow of energy (e.g. in a telegraph cable the current flows in one direction and information is sent in either direction by interrupting the current at a point); sometimes information can be transmitted without a flow of energy or matter (e.g. in photoelectric doors, the interruption of light informs the photocell that someone is entering).

Information however can be measured in terms of decisions. For example in a game of 20 questions where we are supposed to find out an object by receiving yes/no answers to a question:

The information in one question is the decision between two alternatives, e.g. animal (non-animal). With two questions we can decide between four alternatives. Thus a measure of information can be expressed in terms of logarithm to base 2.

Entropy can also be expressed in these terms[64] (i.e. as a logarithm of probability). Thus negative entropy or information is a measure of order or of organisation since information is also an improbable state. This correspondence relates to the Naturalists view[65] that apperception of the system was potentially an ordering process and thus negentropic. Thus a man living in the forest would learn of its operation and while his presence would constitute a reduction of creation, the potential for its increase would be latent in the apperception of the forest by the observing man. Thus the man would, by intervention, be able to increase the forest's thermodynamic creativity. Thus the role of man in apperception and communication is thought to be dominant as the basis for creative expression.[66]

There is another strong similarity between the theory of communication and open systems in the concept of self-regulation. Ashby[67] shows logically that the use of a regulator to achieve homeostasis (i.e. the maintenance of a steady state) and the use of a correction channel to suppress noise in an information transference are homologous. For the full argument refer to Ashby's study.

Common Characteristics of Open Systems

Katz and Kahn[68] have listed these properties in general terms and we will refer to their classifications in analysing the work of artists considered in Chapter 6.

1. Importation of energy from the environment.. No open system (including a social structure) is self-sufficient or self-contained.
2. There is a through-put. Open systems transform the energy available to them, in other words the system does work.
3. Open systems export some product into the environment.
4. The pattern of activities of energy exchange has a cyclic character and the product exported into the environment provides sources of energy for repetition of the cycle of activities.
   For example, an industrial concern utilises raw materials and human labour to turn out a product which is marketed and monetary return is used to obtain more raw materials and labour to perpetuate the cycle of activities. In a social system, the structure is an interrelated set of events that return upon themselves to complete and renew the cycle of activities.
5. Negative entropy—open systems survive and maintain their characteristic internal order only so long as they import from the environment more energy than they expend in the process of transformation and exportation.
6. Open systems receive inputs that are informative and furnish signals to the structure, about the environment and about its own functioning in relation to the environment. This information, received as negative feedback, corrects the system's deviation from its course.
   A coding process for the given system simplifies the world into a few meaningful. and simplified categories.
7. The system corrects malfunctioning so that it maintains a steady state or homeostasis. The basic principle is the preservation of the character of the system and when there are unrestricted amounts of energy for input the system preserves its character through growth and expansion.
8. There is a tendency in open systems in the direction of differentiation and elaboration.
9. The principle of equifinality states that systems can reach the same final state from different initial conditions and by different paths of development.

3. ENVIRONMENTS OF OPEN SYSTEMS.

Part of the problem in treating living systems as open systems is the difficulty of characterising their environments. Bertalanffy's formulations do not include the processes of the environment itself which are among the determining conditions of the exchanges. In this section we will consider two approaches where the specific nature of the environment of the system is a prime consideration.

Causal Texture of the Environment

Emery and Trist[69] have analysed the concept of causal texture of the environment in relation to organisations. They list four ideal types.

1. **Placid, randomized environment**. This is the simplest type where goals and noxiants are relatively unchanging in themselves and randomly distributed. This means that there is no difference between tactics and strategy and the organization can exist adaptively as small units.
2. **Placid, clustered environment**.This is a static type where the goals and noxiants are not randomly distributed but rather, hang together in certain ways. Under these conditions organisations develop strategies as distinct from tactics and also grow in size, tending to centralised control and co-ordination.
3. **Disturbed-reactive environment**. This is a dynamic rather than a static environment. It is a clustered environment where there is more than one system of the same kind, i.e. the objects of one organisation are the same as others like it. These competitors seek to improve each others chances by hindering each other, each knowing that the others are playing the same game. Between strategy and tactics there is an intermediate response—i.e. operations.
4. **Turbulent fields**. Here the dynamic properties arise not simply from the interaction of identifiable component systems but from the field itself. Turbulence results from the complexity and multiple character of the interconnections. Individual organisations cannot adapt successfully simply through their direct interactions since they cannot predict the size or consequences of the actions they set into train. We could describe the field in western society as a turbulent one. The reasons for this are implied in Chapter 2 where the interconnections of the corporate state were described and the pervasiveness of its control noted. The turbulent field is caused by four basic factors:

   (i) Growth to meet old style competition, however the organisations are so large that their actions are persistent and strong enough to induce autotoxinous processes in the environment.

   (ii) The deepening interdependence between economic and other facets of society make it more difficult to predict the effects of corporations' actions.

   (iii) The increasing reliance on scientific research and development to meet the challenge of competition emphasises the need to manipulate needs because otherwise it is difficult to know whether the scientific research done years beforehand will be useful or useless when it is applied in the market situation.

   (iv) The radical increase in speed, scope and capacity for communication results in a quantity of information received at such a rate that it can scarcely be processed, not to speak of making decisions on its basis.

The contribution of these factors results in a field which is so complex and unpredictable that the corporations have no way of judging whether an action will be amplified beyond all expectations or will be completely ineffective. Emery suggests that it is only through social values that have overriding significance for all members of the field is it possible to reduce the turbulent environment to a simpler type. With such values the relevance of large classes of events no longer has to be sought in an intricate mesh of causal strands but is given directly by the ethical code.

Thus the type of system responses made must be linked to the nature of the causal texture of the environment. For a turbulent field organisations must make different responses and have different structures to those required in placid environments. In other words it is necessary to specify the properties of environments that are relevant to adaptive behaviour.

Perceptual Systems and their Environments

J.J. Gibson[70] has stressed that living systems learn and adapt because of their ability to react to general and less variable properties of the environment (invariants) rather than because of their sensitivity to the concrete events and objects which do after all yield a constant flux of stimulation.

1.Sources of Stimulation.

Gibson's hypothesis is that the environment consists of opportunities for perception, of available information, of potential stimuli. Further, the environment in relation to the organism exhibits certain invariant properties; for example for terrestrial man the earth is below, the air above, the waters are under the earth, the ground is level and a rigid surface of support. Thus it is the organism's ability to perceive these invariants of the environment which have resulted according to Gibson through natural selection in a perceptual system which is an active information-seeking perceptual system. The opposing view of perception is that the organism is passive in the perceptual process—stimuli from the environment excites his receptors and his brain organises these stimuli into patterns—this is a sensation based theory of perception. Gibson's view is that perceptual experience can take place without underlying sensory qualities specific to receptors—an information based theory of perception.[71] Thus Gibson's view is that the neural inputs of a perceptual system are already organized and therefore do not have organisation imposed on them. "The evidence of these chapters shows that the available stimulation surrounding an organism has structure, both simultaneous and successive and that this structure depends on sources in the outer environment. If the invariants can be registered by a perceptual system, the constants of neural input will correspond to the constants of stimulus energy, although the one will not copy the other. Then meaningful information can be said to exist inside the nervous system as well as outside".[72] He goes on to postulate that rather than the brain constructing information from the input of a sensory nerve, that the centres of the nervous system, including the brain, resonate to information.

2. Perceptual Systems.

Thus instead of studying specific sensory organs he examines perceptual systems. There are several ways higher animals have of orienting the perceptual apparatus of the body: listening, touching, smelling, tasting and looking. These kinds of attention involve adjustments and exploratory movements of the eye-head systems, ear-hand systems, hand-body systems, nose-head system and the mouth-hand system.

The implications of this theory on the interpretation of some recent art will be discussed in Chapter 6.

* * *

At the present stage it is sufficient to stress the importance of understanding the structure of the environment (as a source of stimulation in a perception theory or as a causal texture in social theory) for understanding the adaptive behaviour of an open system.

The approach of characterising the environment for the art system is the logic behind chapters 2, 3 and 4. To a degree Emery's and Gibson's analyses also characterise aspects of the environment of ideas about society and perception to which many of the recent contemporary artists are reacting.

4. A NEW CONCEPTUAL FRAMEWORK

Guiding Metaphors

There has been criticism that the systems theory cannot predict and hence cannot be experimentally confirmed or disconfirmed and thus that it is not a scientific theory. However it is the author's view that if systems theorising improves the comprehensiveness of the maps we make of human organisation then it must be considered as an advance.

Also Kuhn[73] stresses the all important role in scientific development of our guiding metaphors and principles for mapping the real world. He sees science at any given period dominated by a single "major paradigm", that is a scientific conception of the natural order so pervasive and intellectually powerful that it dominates all ensuing scientific discovery.

Rapoport elaborates: "the change in intellectual climate which allows one to see how problems which were overlooked previously is in a way more important than any single and special application. The 'Copernican Revolution' was more than the possibility somewhat better to calculate the movement of the planets, general relativity more than an explanation of a very small number of recalcitrant phenomena in physics; Darwinism more than a hypothetical answer to zoological problems; it was the changes in general frame of reference that mattered."[74]

Bertalanffy then sees the significance of the systems view as a reorientation of our conceptual framework at least in science from a mechanistic to an open system view.

The Open Systems World View

The mechanistic view resolved happenings into linear causal chains; conceived the world as a result of chance events and a Darwinistic `play of dice' and reduced all biological processes to laws known from inanimate nature.

The open systems view is that the world is based on principles of multivariable interaction (e.g. reaction kinetics, fluxes and forces in irreversible thermodynamics) and a dynamic expansion of physical laws in light of biological laws. An open systems view is not chaotic but states that teleological aspects exist in open systems in adaptiveness, purposiveness and goal-seeking behaviour. The unifying principle of the world is that there is organisation at all levels.

Furthermore the model of the world as a great organisation helps to reinforce the reverence for living which seems lost and this seems to be analogous to the reverence for living which both McHarg and Marcuse advocate.

In fact the mechanistic world view (in which the only organisation of reality is that which is imposed on the chaos by human minds) is a view related to the anthropocentric view of the world. This correlation is even more striking if we consider Newton's religious motivations in his scientific work.

Marcuse while he appears to reject the current sensibility (i.e. the mechanistic world view) cannot conceive of the alternative, however in the social sciences, the science of man we can nevertheless see a trend to the open-systems world view.

The Image of Man

The mechanistic and open systems world views in science are also influential in determining what can be described as the `image of man' in the sciences of man.

Many psychological theories are mechanistic in the sense that they support 'robot' models of human behaviour. An example is the behaviouristic theory which finds no differences between human behaviour and laboratory rats, with engineers subsequently patterning human behaviour after the model of rat behaviour.

There are four major principles in psychology which seem to derive from the mechanistic view.[75]

1. Stimulus Responses.

   The stimulus-response theory proposes that the behaviour of an animal and a human is a response to stimuli coming from outside, (for example conditioning by way of repetition of a sequence of conditional and unconditional stimuli according to Pavlov; conditioning by reinforcement of successful responses by Skinner and childhood experience according to Freud whereby socially acceptable behaviour is reinforced and psycho-pathological complexes are formed).

   Thus we have psychological engineering, advertising, motivation research, radio and T.V. as ways of conditioning or programming the human machine so that it buys what it should: washing powder wrapped in brilliant color, the biggest car as the symbol of the phallus and the refrigerator as symbol of the maternal womb.

2. Environmentalism.

   The environmentalism theory proposes that behaviour and personality are shaped by outside influences. This is the "give me a bunch of kids taken as they come and I will make them doctors, lawyers, beggars and thieves by the power of conditioning" theory. It is also linked to the belief that money buys everything—the Russians build better space vehicles, so more billions spent on education will produce the Einsteins to bridge the gap.

3. Equilibrium.

   The equilibrium theory proposes that behaviour is the reduction of tensions—the sexual ones in particular (Freud). Allied to this is the `principle of stability' which states that the basic function of the mental apparatus consists in maintaining homeostatic equilibrium.

4. Economy.

   The principle of economy, or the utilitarian principle, proposes that the expenditure of mental or vital energy is reduced to a minimum by the organism. This theory however overlooks the importance of stress in producing higher life forms, if indeed this principle were true, life forms would not have developed past the amoeba.

Man as Robot underlines all these approaches, and furthermore man as robot is the motor force of a mechanised and commercialised society. The goal of manipulating psychology is to make humans ever more into robots engineered by mechanised learning, advertising techniques, mass media, motivation research and brainwashing.

Recently however there has been a tendency for a holistic reorientation in psychology—the model of man is now seen as an active personality system. Manifestations of this reorientation can be seen in the theories of Piaget, Werner, Maslow, Allport; the neo-Freudian schools; egopsychology; the new look in perception (Gibson); and in theory of cognition, etc.

The psychological organism is no longer thought of as passive but rather as a primarily active system. The new image of man as a systems concept emphasises "immanent activity instead of outer directed reactivity and recognises the specificity of human culture compared to animal behaviour".[76] Man is not only surrounded by a physical environment but also by a symbolic universe and thus must be treated accordingly.

Perspectivism

Thus the open systems world view presents not only a different conceptual framework to the mechanistic view but also different values, since values are in fact different models of the way people act in and resolve the real world. It has been continually implied that our world would be a better one if and when these values are expressed by our culture as ideologies. It will, if the correspondence of the open systems model of the real world is correct, for then our values will correspond closer to the biological world of which we are a part.

However, one of the main difficulties in grasping this new conceptual framework is in the fact that Western thinking has been essentially in terms of opposites (e.g. thinking in terms of hot and cold, black and white, day and night, life and death), and thus is not suitable for dealing with holistic problems.

Bertalanffy suggests that the term 'perspectivist' view to describe the philosophical attitude underlying the open systems approach to science and contrasts it to the reductionist view, that physical theory is the only one to which all possible science and all aspects of reality eventually should be reduced—a perspectivist view stresses the relativity of the categories of experience and thus the relative nature of any `truth'.

CHAPTER 6: PAINTING A PICTURE

1. INTRODUCTION

Ideas in science have often manifested themselves in art. Naum Gabo speaks of the relationship of ideas in science to his own art.

"I would say that the philosophic events and the events in science at the beginning of this century have definitely made a crucial impact on the mentality of my generation. Whether many of us knew exactly what was going on in science or not, does not really matter. The fact was that it was in the air and an artist, with his sensitiveness acts like a sponge. He may not know about it but he sucks in ideas and they work on him."[77]

Thus it is not surprising to see the beginnings of a radical change in art, parallel to the re-orientation in science to a perspectivist or open-system orientated world view. Further, this change from a reductionist-mechanistic world view to a perspectivist open-systems view can be seen as a shift in "major paradigms"[78] in art as well as in science.

In the world, the transition to open-systems thinking is seen in the growing importance of ecology (note that systems concepts are integral to ecology) and the questioning of the mechanistic world-view by social, political theorists, the counter culture and the growth of perspectivist viewpoints in many disciplines, including biology and social sciences. In art the transition can be seen in ecological art works, in the equation of art with information (this conforms to the equation of creativity with higher levels of order due to negentropy and the equation of negentropy with information),[79] the general emphasis on processes rather than end-products and concern with characterising the nature of environments of the art-system and consequently extending the boundaries which concern the artist.

Harold Szeeman[80] comments on some of the characteristics of this new work: "the obvious opposition to form, the high degree of personal and emotional engagement; the pronouncement that certain objects are art although they have not previously been identified as such; the shift away from the result towards the artistic process; the use of mundane materials; the interaction of work and material; Mother Earth as medium, work-place, the desert as concept."

He goes on to say that "the artists represented in this exhibition are in no way object-makers. On the contrary they aspire to freedom from the object, and in this way deepen the levels of meaning of the object, reveal the meaning of those levels beyond the object. They want the artistic process itself to remain visible in the end product and in the "exhibition". It is significant that the mass of their body, the power of human movement plays an important role for these artists and creates the new alphabet of form and material".

Some of the artists (such as the earth artists) are not represented by works at all but with information—the conceptual artists are represented by working plans, which no longer require further realisation. This type of art is a far cry from formalist color painting (such as Noland, Olitski and Ellsworth Kelly) where discoveries of new visual formats and visual manipulations have a close relationship to the annual changes in automobile styling and are obviously consumer-product orientated, however these are consumer goods available only to the richest people. These are high status consumer products.

In part the reaction against an object-oriented aesthetic is an outcome of the artist's recognition of art having a different role in society to the economic one which is often assigned to it and thus it is also an outcome of the artist's recognition to avoid sublimation[81] of his art. Thus it becomes difficult to assign economic value to a pile of dirt, some photographs, holes in the desert, a work consisting of a 2 mile walk or a person cutting himself. It also becomes difficult to consider the presentation of these items as objects or things in themselves, it becomes necessary to consider them within some system—the meaning of these items is not in their intrinsic worth (which is how those unacquainted with this art tend to judge it) but in their positional value in some system.

In the context of a system, the concept of boundary becomes important—the artist considers the social environment outside art and art's position in this; considers art in relation to the corporate state; in relation to politics and the natural environment. The material limits are defined after considering these factors—to assume material limits is to work within a conventional mode and thus to accept a restricted context and the going concept of art and its role.

The consideration of art as a system necessarily questions the function of art in relation to a wide context—a wide environment. We have noted previously the necessity for a system to characterise its environment[82] and many of these artists have accepted Marcuse's and Reich's critiques of society as the environments for the art-system.

The implication of all these factors is that this art necessarily has a conceptual focus—art is not merely making objects and making judgments about them but it is about making judgments on the complex interrelationships and systems which affect the artist.[83]

The aim then of the following sections is to show more clearly the nature and development of a system-aesthetic in recent art and to show that it is a major re-orientation in art comparable to that in science. It must be emphasised that the present period is a transitional state between "major paradigms" in art and so inconsistencies do occur[84]—these will be outlined in the last chapter when we consider some consequences of the changed sensibility in art to the possible roles given to art in the future by Galbraith[85] and Marcuse.[86]

2. DEFINITION OF ART

Kustom City

Before we go on to show some of the historical development of the systems aesthetic in art, it is useful to state what we in fact mean when we say art and then to show the implications of this on the transition to a systems aesthetic. What is it that distinguishes the Kandy Kolored Hot Rods from Kustom City[87] from a Lichtenstein comic-strip and the Duchamp ready-made spade?

Tom Wolfe in his visit to Kustom City says "pretty soon you realise you're in a gallery .. half of them will never touch the road .. they're carted all over the country to be exhibited at hot-rod and custom-car shows .. they're full of big powerful, hopped-up chrome plated motors, because all that speed and all that lovely apparatus .. its like one of those Picasso or Miro rugs .. you hang them on the wall .. in effect they're sculpture."[88]

The Hot-Rod looks like art, it is used like art, the person who made it claims he is an artist and it produces an effect far surpassing a painting or a sculpture yet there is still doubt at the present time whether it is art or not.

The Lichtenstein painting uses "enlarged Ben-Day dots, raw primary colors and printers ink colors inspired by the crassest techniques of commercial illustration exploring the pictorial vocabulary of comic books"[89]—not even changing the composition but taking it as found. It may not look like art, it may not produce any aesthetic emotion but we know it is art.

The Duchamp Spade is an ordinary spade in its original state yet we are now sure that it is a work of art yet there are a million other spades identical to it and we don't consider these to be works of art. The Spade does not produce an aesthetic emotion in us any different to any other spade, it does not look like art, apart from the particular gallery it is exhibited, in its function is as a utensil for digging. If we didn't know that an artist had done it we would not know it was art yet there is no doubt in the minds of anyone associated with the art world that it is art.

Criteria

Donald Brook[90] has drawn 4 possible categories by which we judge something to be a work of art:

1) Genetic Criteria (this involves only the nature of the originating agent—the test may be not only that the man is known to be an artist but may also lie in the mode, style, purpose or intention of the generating process).
2) Objective Criteria (this involves what we perceive in looking, touching, smelling and whether this information corresponds to what we know a work of art to be).
3) Affective Criteria (this involves the effect it has on us—i.e. that it affects us with an `aesthetic' emotion).
4.) Functional Criteria (this involves how it is used—i.e. it is put in a gallery or in the foyer of an insurance block to be admired as a work of art).

All of these categories moreover should be used in conjunction with one another to determine an object's status as art. However, it is even more illuminating if we consider the problem from a systems viewpoint.

It is obvious that the effectiveness with which we can apply these categories depends on our understanding of the art context—i.e. our knowledge of artists, exhibitions, galleries, art-dealers, art museums, art-collectors, art-critics, our acquaintance with magazines on art, books on art, history of art, films on art, essays on art, etc. The Genetic criteria is proved if we have evidence of this man's activities as an artist (exhibitions in galleries), critic's confirmation that he is an artist (essays on his work)[91] the Objective criteria is then that the object resembles so many other things seen in the art context, in books, magazines, galleries, etc., the Affective criteria is that it produces a response in us which we known is an `aesthetic' one from our experience of such responses in an art context, or from our knowledge about such responses in books on art, magazine articles or discussions in an art context and the Functional criteria is whether the object is displayed in a gallery, bought by an art collector, etc.

The point then is that the art context provides us with information about the object's or situation's status as art. In other words the object obtains its meaning from its positional value in the art-system.[92]

"The recognition of art relies upon the recognition of cues (i.e. genetic, objective, affective or functional) which signal that the type of behaviour termed aesthetic appreciation is to be adopted. These cues form a context which reveals the art object".[93] Burgin goes on to say that an object becomes or fails to become a work of art in direct response to the inclination of the perceiver to assume an appreciative role.

Thus the hot-rod is potentially a work of art, it is as soon as it is placed in the art-system i.e. that art critics write about it as art and its maker as an artist, or it is exhibited in an art gallery (or the concept of an art gallery is extended to include the hot-rod factory). Wolfe, in writing his essay is in fact helping to make the hot-rod a work of art.

The status of Duchamp's Spade as art is totally dependent on its context—there are almost no intrinsic qualities in the spade to make it art—the spade depends totally on its value in the art system.

As a social system the art system has the same type of behaviour as any other open system,[94] furthermore it is useful to analyse closely what the artist's position is in this system if we are to understand how the artist can possibly change the system.

3. THE ART SYSTEM

The Changing Metaprogram

"Programming the art system involves some of the same features found in human brains and large computer systems."[95] Burnham notes that artists are the equivalent in their position in the system to that of programs and subroutines in a computer, i.e. they prepare new codes and analyse data in making works of art.

Their activities are supervised by metaprograms which consist of instructions, descriptions and the organisational structures of programs. Metaprograms include art movements, significant stylistic trends and the business, promotional and archival structures of the art world.

At a higher level art contains a self-metaprogram which reorganises the art impulse on a long term basis—it operates in establishing strategies on lower levels in terms of societal needs. However, there are many pictures of human life due to the relativity of the categories of human experience[96] and thus the nature of the self-metaprogram is rather vague and obscure. Nevertheless, it is an aim of this thesis to show that what Burnham calls the 'self-metaprogram' of art is in fact changing now.

Society's needs are such at the moment that consideration of the environment and man's actions in relation to it are of prime importance[97] and that an understanding of the inter-actions of economics, politics and social factors is integral to this consideration.[98] According to Bertalanffy the need is for a greater awareness of the interrelationship of all phenomena in the form of systems.[99]

That the "self-metaprogram of art is in fact changing, can be seen, in the loss of interest in the gallery scene by the informal public, the support for street art by several important critics, the newsreels of underground cinema, the fact that museums of modern art are closing the circuit on modernising and responses to politically inept groups such as the Art Worker's Coalition".[100] The reaction against object-based art because it lends itself to exploitation is a realisation by the artist (holding certain values of the nature of the specific art system (with contradictory values) of which he is a part). This argument will be discussed later.

Values

Values in the art system are merely information, preferences controlled by museums and art historians. The importance of values in art is similar to their importance in society in general in that they reduce the complexity of the environment of both the art and social systems.

In a society the only way a turbulent field[101] can be simplified is by common values—so that "large classes of events no longer have to be sought in an intricate mess of causal strands but are given directly by the ethical code".[102]

In art there is also a complex field—a vast assortment of possible art media, styles, ideas. Art like society is fragmented—a list of styles from any book on modern art would show the diversity of available art (most of the abstract styles from the beginning of the twentieth century are still painted and repainted not to speak of realism and traditional painting). The historian however imposes preferences (thus Greenberg develops a mainstream theory of avant-garde art—which holds that only the art in his definition of the mainstream is considered to be of any quality) to reduce the complexity of this field.

The Artist's Role

In a sense the artist produces the raw data and critics, magazines, galleries, museums, collectors and historians all exist to create information out of the unprocessed art data. Thus all the artists and art works in the world are potential art information. Some people, like the hot-rod designer are potential artists in the sense that when his data is recognised as potential art information he is an artist.

Thus the institutions which process art data are as important components of the system as the producer of data. Without the support system the object ceases to have definition, but without the object the support system can still sustain the notion of an object."[103]

The realisation of this relationship is in a sense a major cause of the radical changes in art at the moment, particularly in relation to much conceptual art.

The encoding process for information in cybernetics[104] always involves some definite process—typically this process can be broken down into hardware and software components. The hardware is the actual physical means used to code the information and the software is the program or procedure used to encode it. Different programs then can change the information resulting from the same data i.e. different art information results when the art data is encoded by books, catalogs, interview, reviews, advertisements, sales or contracts. Thus all these forms legitimately embody the work of art. The art-object then is merely an information `trigger' for mobilising the information cycle. Les Levine[105] stresses the importance of the mass media as an encoding process and the consequences for artists in not recognising its effect.

Inconsistencies[106] in some art which shows a systems-aesthetic is often a result of the failure of the artist to see or acknowledge his place in the art system. Thus the artist who is against consumer goods because of his political beliefs 'dematerialises' his objects so they cannot contribute to the economic system—he does not however recognise all the software extensions (i.e. magazines, books etc.) and the actual functioning of the art world as a system which continues to turn his dematerialised works into a commodity and the humble artist into a sought after star. This artist does not realise that he is simply producing raw data—to change the art information which is subsequently produced he has to alter the entire system. The simultaneous realisation of the art system and the need to change it are the reason many artists are shifting their emphasis from the production of data (which is not art information) to actual encoding of data (merely chosen from the real world) thus fulfilling the role previously executed by critics, curators, essayists and feeling that this way they can exert greater influence in changing the art system.[107] The actual consequences of this approach will be mentioned in the last chapter.

* * *

This section then has shown the usefulness of a systems approach as a tool to define what art is. The subsequent recognition of the possible irrelevance of the artist's work in a sense can be seen in an article on American grid-iron uniforms—in both Studio International and Art International by Peter Plagens where non-artist produced data is processed to produce art information. Thus when we consider the development of a Systems-oriented aesthetic it is quite reasonable to use critics interpretations of the new work because they are the ones who are actually producing the art information. The next sections will discuss the development of the systems oriented aesthetic from 2 aspects:

1) An examination of the actual objects or situations produced as art data, whether the actual morphology of the object or situation is a closed or open system (if it is a system at all) ignoring all the wider implications of the work.
2) An examination of the values and world views implied in the works or stated by the artists—to see whether their responses to the art- system, the social, political economic and environmental systems embodies what could be described as a perspectivist approach.[108]

It is expected that a systems-oriented aesthetic will also embody a perspectivist approach if a lack of correlation between the two is noticed it could be taken to indicate that art at the moment is in a state of transition between the object-oriented and systems-oriented aesthetic.

4. OBJECT-ORIENTED AESTHETICS

Op Art Objects

Op Art incorporates aspects of light sculpture, construction and painting with the common concern with illusion, perception and the physical and psychological impact of colour. Vasarely, the dominant figure in optical art, utilises various devices to create the illusion of movement and metamorphosis within the abstract organisation. Moreover, all his works are aimed at producing an end-product whose only function is to stimulate the eye—not to provide information through perception but rather to produce sensations on the optical nerve. The basis of his work is a sensation theory of perception and the mechanistic implications of this theory have already been noted by Bertalanffy.[109]

While his format varies from murals, books, tapestries, glass mosaic, slides, film or television his actual content is static in its actual form and when considered as objects out of their context they do not fulfil any of the criteria for an open system. Like any static object they make no response to the environment—no input passes through the object and no output results. Furthermore the object exists in an ideal time, i.e. it is conceived outside the influences of real-time ageing processes, deterioration effects and actual environmental effects on the object. The object of course does exist in real-time and when the object becomes covered in dust or begins to decay it is cleaned and restored to its ideal state.[110]

The processes of conception, production are separated from the object itself—there is no attempt to incorporate these as part of the object—nor is the object considered as a residue or evidence of some process (which it is of course). This is the same separation of end-product from the production process which occurs in consumer goods.

Also if we consider the connection between the object and the spectator, when the spectator is viewing the work because of the intrinsic qualities of the Op art object in relation to his perceptual apparatus, his eyes respond with a particular predictable sensation.

If we consider our definitions of systems and relationships[111] we see that this particular situation is a relationship and not a system. Here the relata (the object and the viewer's eye) enter a relationship due to their immanent qualities and not because of "positional values in a system". (i.e. what occurs in this perceptual situation is due to the intrinsic qualities of both the eye and the object.)

Typically even the formal elements of the design are built up part by part and exist only in relationships to each other—there is no holistic organisation of form as there is in minimal art.

Much kinetic art springs from Op and while the fact that most open systems move (i.e. change their nature, readjust themselves, grow etc) kinetic art should have been one of the more radical alternatives to a static formalist aesthetic, in most cases.[112] these have been merely modifications of static formalist sculpture—movement merely changes the internal compositional relationships—it does not change the object itself. The motion is also presented for a purely visual (rather than kinaesthetic etc.) perception of it, much the same as Op.

The open systems concepts then do not seem to be at all embodied in Op art objects themselves although the methods of production and research could embody a systems approach. We might be even tempted to consider Op art as a paradigm of an object-oriented art especially after we consider its close relationships to concepts of consumerism, mass-production and the suitability of its images in the corporate state from consumer packaging to monumental statements in equally monumental office blocks which are themselves monuments to the corporate state.

Pop Art Objects

The Pop Art object is similar to an Op object in that it has the qualities of a static object in an idealised time, it is an object detached from its production process although it does indicate the source of its content. It has the same logic as a consumer good i.e. when its images have been worn out symbolically they can be replaced with others, of identical function but a more topical form. This is an example of the obsolescence principle which is the natural consequence of not treating the object as part of a process.

While the images of Pop art set up connections with the environment—these do not form systems but rather are relationships since the connections are due to the immanent attributes of the paintings and the image in the environment.

In a sense there is some conceptual focus in Pop in the fact that the selection of images is a large (if not most important) part of the artistic process and we recognise this aspect of the process in the end-product. For example Warhol's soup-cans, Brillo boxes and Coca-Cola bottles, Lichtenstein's comic book images and Rosenquist's composite images all moreover executed in industrial techniques of commercial illustration.

The intention to make art a real-time activity and thus take art out of an idealised frame of reference[113] is evident firstly in the choice of images but later in Pop in the use of actual objects in conjunction with a painted image. Tom Wesselman's still-life's and works by Jim Dine are examples. In some of Dine's works, paint-brushes, pots of paint, shoes and socks (which could be mistaken as accidentally left near the painting) are actually part of the work. While the works remain objects however it is obvious that they do not embody open systems concepts.

Happenings however, which sprang from Pop Art's concern with the real environment seem to embody a system concept and these will be considered later.

Relation of Op Art to Society

Vasarely in the 50s suggested mass art as a legitimate function of industrial society and in one respect his contribution is valuable in that he helped to break down the naive yet long held idea that a tiny output of art objects could somehow beautify or even significantly alter the environment. Another illusion it tried to breakdown was that `artistic influence prevails by a physic osmosis given off by such objects' manifested in the fact that public beauty is the exclusive province of well-guarded museums.

However Vasarely's attempts to utilise technology is in some ways a failure—for while he produced vast quantities of works, available to the public as cheap multiples and thus had enlarged the art market his activity was still at the periphery of the industrial system. Also the substitution of a large quantity of useless art objects rather than making quality available to a large number of people is absurd. Vasarely has expanded the art market from an elitist consumer group to a mass market, however in the process—(because of the trivial nature of objects whose only function is to produce sensations on the retina) his objects start to resemble the other useless commodities already present in the American consumer market such as retractable headlights and such items as the Nothing Box (a little black box with a light that flickers on and off retailing for about the same price as a Vasarely multiple—designed to be used as a gift for those who already have everything).

In contrast to Vasarely while his production methods could use some systems concepts—a systems aesthetic is literal in that all phases of the life cycle are relevant. There is furthermore no primarily visual end product—the systems aesthetic resists functioning as an applied aesthetic but rather functions in revealing the progressive reorganisation of the natural environment. Thus it holds the means for improving the quality of life not merely enlarging its quantity.

Relation of Pop Art to Society

Pop Art made a similar contribution as Op Art destroying the concept of a precious, exalted and exclusive art object. Pop's significance to a great extent was its recognition of the actual popular culture as a source for the images of art. It was a reaction to the new continuum of consumer society at a time when the undesirable consequences of the misuse of technology and the consumer mentality were not evident as they are now. Furthermore, the recognition that the entire environment could become the work of art is important as a step in the development of a systems-oriented aesthetic. Art increasingly began to take a life-like format overlapping with the environment and blurring the distinctions between art and daily life. Thus it was taking on certain process-oriented characteristics: "the new problems for art concern constant redefinition of its boundaries and more process oriented distribution of energy".[114]

Commonplace images in Pop Art are in part a reaction to the usage of 'fine-art avant garde paintings' in a mass context. The advertising-packaging industry would endow its goods with some of the aesthetic excellence attributed to fine art. Thus 'A New Trend in Furnishing' provides sample interiors complete with an abstract expressionist painting on the wall—i.e. the latest avant garde artwork is lending character to a mass product. However while Pop Art reacted against this type of exploitation by producing the banal aspects of commercial advertising as art, because it remained in the same relationship to the economic context it too is exploited so that nowadays the same furniture interior features a painting of Campbell's Soup Tins.

Pop allies itself closely to the economics of plenty, it bears a generally sympathetic relationship to consumer society and thus appears to have a mechanistic world view underlying it. Andy Warhol when interviewed made the following comments:[115]

"...I think everybody should be a machine
I think everybody should like everybody."
Q. Is that what Pop Art is all about?
A. "Yes its liking things."
Q. And liking things is like being a machine?
A. "Yes because you do the same thing every time. You do it over and over again."

Furthermore, Warhol claims he likes monotony and demonstrates it by painting 200 cans of Campbell's soup. In addition Warhol's public personality has been projected through the media as a commodity in the same way movie idols are consumer commodities.

This same robot-model[116] of human behaviour is the basis on which advertising of consumer goods operates. As we have shown, a continuous demand for a corporation's product is necessary for it to maintain its autonomy.[117] Consequently it creates and maintains the demand for its goods typically by manipulation of people's symbolic needs through advertising.

The emphasis is on manipulation—the more predictable or more machine-like the individual[118] the easier it is for the corporation to maintain the continuous demand for its products. The techniques used typically exploit man's symbolic and psychological needs:

"People feel that if you jump from a Ford to a Cadillac, you must have stolen some money."

"You have to have a carton that attracts and hypnotizes this woman, like waving a flashlight in front of her eyes."

"The home freezer becomes a frozen island of security."

"One of the main jobs of the advertiser in this conflict between pleasure and guilt is not so much to sell the product as to give moral permission to have fun without guilt."[119]

Vance Packard states the obvious: "Much of this advertising seems to represent regress rather than progress for man in his long struggle to become a rational and self-guiding being". While Pop Art does sometimes express explicitly a judgment on the consumer society, more often it celebrates it. A local exception to this rule is Richard Larter, whose juxtaposed images of political figures and erotic images gives visual expression to Marcuse's theory on the connection between political and sexual repression in society.[120]

Nevertheless, Pop Art of this nature is criticism which still remains within the framework of a mechanistic world view. Even the use of collage, as a pictorial device—i.e. disparate, random images, presents a concept of the world incorporating chance causal chains—an unstructured, unorganised world unlike the perspectivist's model of the world.

The Consumer Object

To state that the consumer product is considered normally as a closed system seems obvious but it is necessary to point this out because of the close relationship of both Op Art and Pop Art to the consumer product. To illustrate this we need only consider that when the advertiser promotes it he is selling the end-product not the resource depletion, or the production process and not its consequences (polluting by-products or alienation of the factory's employees), nor is he selling it as potential waste (when its uses have been exhausted).

The failure to see objects as merely particular configurations of matter at a particular point in time (i.e. with a past history as well as a future history), as part of continuous transformation of energy, results in blindness to the relationship between phenomena. Thus many people are concerned about pollution but see it merely as a need for backyard cleanliness on a larger scale, not as being related to the entire network of political, economic and social systems.

We habitually attribute values to entities—thus pollution is bad and maintaining our growth of Gross National Product is good. From a systems viewpoint, however, entities do not have any intrinsic `goodness' or `badness' merely a position in a system. Pollution thus belongs to the system which includes: the consumer good, the corporation, the increasing scarcity of time, decreased public services, debasement of culture, advertising, etc.

The problem of pollution, then cannot be solved outside the context of the entire system, its symptoms can be merely hidden.

5. THE TRANSITION

Minimal Art

The beginnings of a systems-oriented aesthetic seems to appear in much of Minimal Art. Minimal artists tried to produce objects which were `wholes'[121] in other words that they constituted perceptually a single 'gestalt'. Consequently their forms were not constructed visually as a summation of parts but rather consisted of a single indivisible form.

This aim of Minimal art comes from its phenomenological basis: it is based on the philosophical idea that experience through our senses is the only reality—in other words that experience has to be dealt with directly. Thus the object and perceiver are both conceived as necessary constituents of a specific situation—the perceiver is supposed to experience the phenomena before him operationally—not by a mere casual observance "to clear one's presuppositions about it".[122] Furthermore the perceptual experience in this case was contrived as a real-time activity not an ideal-time activity in the case of Op Art object situation,[123] because in this case the experience of 'gestalt' depends primarily on movement in space and time around the object.

Burgin notes that the experience of time and space in perception are linked: "time in the perception of exterior events involves the observation of a succession linked with muscular-navigational memories—a visceral identification with change. Similarly kinaesthetic modes of appreciation are applied to the subjective transformation of these events in interior time and in recollection.[124] He concludes that to distinguish between the `arts of space' and the `arts of time' is a misconception based on materialism from a focus on the object rather than upon the behaviour of the perceiver.

The distinction between real-time and ideal-time perception can be seen in the modes of attention employed by the perceiver in relation to the Op Art object and the Minimal object.

In relation to the Op Art object the sensation on the retina can be considered to occur at a single point in time—there is little additional information (or rather sensation) to be obtained by moving in space relative to it whereas in relation to the minimal object to obtain the available information employment of many perceptual systems[125] is required—the Minimalist work can be best interpreted from the viewpoint of an information seeking theory of perception. In addition the Minimal object and viewer connection seems more dependent on a common dimensional domain[126] than the Op Art object and viewer relationship. Also the aspect of space-time seems more crucial to the dimensional domain of the Minimal object than it does to the Op object. Thus in a sense the current occupation with time and consequently ecology and consciousness of process has its origins in Minimal art.[127]

Donald Judd

The method of Minimalist art was often highly conceptualised. Donald Judd in his writings would compile in relation to his `specific objects' what he would call an entity's `list structure' i.e. all the enumerated properties needed to physically build the object. The art object's list structures also included its phenomenal qualities which did not show up in the fabricator's plans but proved necessary for 'seeing' the object. This rationalisation of the aesthetic process of art objects and their conceptual origins is thus a pre-requisite to the emergence of a systems aesthetic. The object both in its parts and its perceptual qualities becomes a holistic object.

Most importantly the object itself is no longer as important as the information about it. Thus an artist such as Robert Morris can order a copy of a piece by telephone and have it privately fabricated. His later works are focused on material forming techniques and arranging these results so that they no longer form specific objects but remain uncomposed. The precedence of process becomes increasingly obvious in works of this nature.

Morris leads into a vast range of materials, earth sculptures, air and steam works where the specific material determines the sculptural responses made to it.

Carl Andre

Carl Andre's works are typically within a strict self-imposed modular system. He uses convenient commercially available objects, like bricks, styrofoam planks, ceramic magnets, cement blocks and wooden beams.

Individual pieces are specifically conceived in the conditions of the place in which they are to occur. The component units are arranged (this implied the fixed nature of the parts and a preconceived notion of the whole). Furthermore, the parts are held together by gravity and when the component parts are removed from the particular site the artwork ceases to exist.

Andre's pieces are typically flat on the ground and impinge only slightly into the spectator's common space, Bochner[128] says of them "their persistent slightness is unavoidable and gives them their presence". Not only then is Andre systematic in his methodology but the connection of his work (consisting of a specific arrangement) to a specific location and to a specific perceiver can be described as a system—though not an open system under our terminology.[129]

Moreover while the beginnings of a systems-aesthetic appear in Minimal art the system is still closely related to the nature of the material or object used to display it—whereas the art discussed under systems-oriented art in its dematerialisation tends to be independent of particular material qualities.

Little Bay Wrap-Up

Many environmental works and events which are process works and thus often real-time activities also exhibit a transition towards a systems-oriented aesthetic.

Christo's Little Bay Wrap-Up in Sydney 1969 is such an example. One million square feet of coastline was wrapped up with a cream colored sarlon plastic and fixed with orange polypropalene rope. In a sense this was still a concern with formal sculpture in that the volumes of the wrapped coastline were highlighted by a single uniform surface. There was a modification of one's information about the site, and the visual element after the initial impression (because of the uniformity of texture and colour) was somewhat replaced by other sorts of perceptual information obtained through listening (as people moved over the site, the ocean, seagulls) touching (the altered surface of rocks, plastic stretched over solid and void) smelling (the ocean, etc.) and the wealth of information from one's bodily movements over the irregular surface.

The coastline remained packaged for a few weeks and once the plastic coating was removed there was no evidence at all on the actual site of the event having taken place. In addition, Christo's process orientation can be seen in the fact of planning, negotiating, obtaining information about weather, materials, etc. as well as the process of actually creating the work, adjusting his strategy as problems arose due to the nature of the environment on the site and the changing experiences in the changing environment,[130] were all part of the work. The residue of all this activity is a book which records its various aspects of planning and making. Initially it was intended that the coast remain covered in plastic until ultraviolet light finally caused the deterioration of the plastic.

Thus the work itself is only obtainable through a photographic record—it avoids the gallery situation in that it is beyond the scope of most collectors to buy the coastline or for that matter pay the huge cost of materials[131] and maintenance. The scale of the gesture is important for enormous resources have been mobilised in the production of a work which is physically ephemeral—leaving practically no residue (merely proof of its existence).

Furthermore, this work satisfies many of the criteria for an open system[132]—it takes energy from the environment (materials, manpower, physical rock structure): there is a transformation of the energy (i.e. the making, planning process) and it exports some product into the environment (information about the modified environment). The system grows (i.e. the quantity of wrapped coastline increases) as more inputs are absorbed however the source of these inputs is not really dependent on the output (unless the output is the artist's fame which results in his ability to procure more resources). In the process of making—there is a feedback relationship between problems in the transformation of the energy in the situation and the progressive solutions. The system is temporary and cannot maintain itself indefinitely, also it merely expands in size—it does not increase in the complexity of its organisation in the way an open system behaves. Also it is bounded within the limits of its initial conception and materials.

Eventstructure Research Group

As the name implies this group organises events using different types of inflatables as their media. Their work is similar in its process aspects to Christo's work. There is no real product—the plastic tube is merely a method for structuring an activity—i.e. it inflates and deflates and is modified by its specific relation to the external environment—people, landscape, projected film, sound, etc. All aspects of the process are relevant.

Again while the events embody some open system concepts—input, output and transformation, the growth limits are always determined by the initial boundary conditions (i.e. the form of the plastic tube). Thus their conception of open systems seems intrinsically bounded by their material limits (plastic inflatables)—similarly Christo's system concepts are bounded by the physical limitations of his media. As a contrast much of recent systems—oriented art seems media-independent[133] and thus is a more radical stance. Because the systems orientation is intrinsic in the qualities of the media used the system is not the main concern of this art but rather a by-product of other concerns.

ERG adopt the relationship suggested by Galbraith[134] in relation to industrial society—i.e. that sensitive individuals should be able to determine the uses of technology for non-consumer reasons. In this way they seem to be undermining the values of the technocracy. The possible continued use of each work contradicts in a sense the continuous stream of outputs necessary to maintain the growth economy. "What is needed now are more and more demonstrations of technological application outside the dictates of the institutionalised program. Such an open-ended exploitation of technology's resources becomes the evidence for all people that there is an extension of their individual wills and freedom."[135]

Christo's employment of technology implies a similar attitude—also both Christo and ERG emphasise the importance of contact between the artist and ordinary people as a means for changing their individual possibilities (i.e. changing their consciousness). In this contact the environment or event is not imposed in a mechanistic way for the production of specific predictable sensations but rather the participants can relate spontaneously to various kinds of information available to them.

6. SYSTEMS ORIENTED AESTHETICS

Ecological Art

In a sense the open systems concepts in the works of Hans Haacke and Alan Sonfist are also dependent on their materials. However while the boundary conditions for a Christo or ERG event is synonymous with the natural process in relationship of a specific material to a process, the choice of natural organic and inorganic processes in ecological art as the boundary conditions of the system enlarges it enormously. Also the fact that the medium used is nature which is the paradigm example of an open system[136] it is then to be expected that their works embody the characteristics of open systems.

Sonfist uses natural mineral crystals within a hollow glass sphere sealed at its cylindrical base. The configurations formed within it are never twice the same, following a self-generating cycle.

1) The crystals fall to the base through gravity.
2) With an application of heat or light the crystals are vaporised into a purplish gas which migrates upwards through the spherical space.
3) The vapour crystallises and the crystals adhere to the inside surface of the glass.

The analysis of Sonfist's work in terms of open systems characteristics reveals that it satisfies many of the criteria but not all: the system imports energy from the environment (heat and light) which transforms crystals into gas. The pattern of activities is furthermore cyclical. The system cannot however grow into more complex states (i.e. the principle of negentropy) and its final states are determined by the initial conditions—i.e. properties of the crystals, volume enclosed and enclosing surfaces of the sphere. This system while acting as a metaphor of larger ecological systems is potentially creative[137] in the sense that it is information about the physical environment which if used could result in a higher ordering of natural processes by man.

Hans Haacke

Hans Haacke's work has developed from works using water, emulsions, steam and air, initially within a strong geometric framework. However his later works reveal his decision to allow natural entities to organise themselves which is in direct contrast to Sonfist who has organised his process with an artificial boundary—artificial despite the fact that the process is dependent on this boundary—in condensing the vapour and supporting the crystals.

'A 150 foot plastic hose, tightly inflated with helium will fly high above the beach or sea ... And also I would like to lure 1000 sea gulls to a certain spot (in the air) by some delicious food so as to construct an air sculpture from their combined mass."[138]

Similarly Haacke's 'Spray of Ithaca Falls'—the freezing and melting of a rope depended on environmental conditions. A nylon rope was wrapped in screening and suspended across the falls. Flowing water and freezing cycles quickly built a snow and ice configuration over a four day period.

The similarities to Sonfist's work in its operation is obvious, however by the physical boundaries of Sonfist's work it could be considered as an object in an ideal-time framework[139] (except that its internal composition changes) however because Haacke's works are in the environment and are unable to be stored and can only be experienced by being present where the passing of time is simultaneous with the experience of viewing it.

Some of his works cause disturbances of an ecological or social system.[140] For example when he imported artificial rain and moss into an area of dry forest, he changed its vegetation for a short period.

Further extensions of the systems concept in Haacke's work lie in his willingness to use all forms of organic life and in some works is content not to structure them at all (i.e. total non-interaction) but merely witnesses such things as the hatching of chickens or exhibits a meteorological chart. The importance of the systems concept and not of the materials used is also evident where `invisible' components such as air, water and steam are used in a system.

It must be emphasized that because no artificial boundary is imposed by man the system can obviously continue to function as an open system in nature indefinitely—it has been noted that the containment of phenomena actually restricted its creative functioning because it was always dependent on its enclosure.

Real-time Art

The similarity of Richard Long's[141] work to Haacke's seems obvious; where Haacke responds to the information potential in animal ecologies[142], Long responds to the information potential in the landscape, Long is putting the landscape and his aesthetic response to it on display in a real-time situation—his response to the English countryside is typically sympathetic, without imposition and attentive to its subtleties. Paintings of landscapes act in a completely different way—the image becomes the important aspect and typically is contained in a finite pictorial frame by an anthropocentric man who admires the landscape but continues to exploit and destroy it. The extensions of the landscape painting, its anthropocentric character and ecological naivety can be seen in the example of the company director whose company destroys nature (either directly or by being part of a growth economy), increases entropy and generally acts in contradiction to biological and ecological principles. Like the painting "Nature" is considered as an ideal time state and has nothing to do with the entity he is despoiling. Thus with his profits he buys a house in picturesque natural surroundings just like his landscape painting.

When we speak of the distinction between Art and Life this is what we mean—that our responses to art conventionally have been idealised and symbolic (in this context they still may be also) and thus many of our attitudes to the real world are idealised too.[143]

Bertalanffy writes of a growing schism between biological drives and symbolic values. Thus while one of the reasons for rapid technological change is increased proficiency in symbol manipulation in philosophy, art, religion, literature, mathematics and various forms of scientific logic. But belief in symbols and ideologies often compels man to commit acts ordinarily against his biological well-being,[144] "the symbolic world of culture is basically unnature, far transcending and often negating biological nature, drives, usefulness and adaption".[145]

It seems from this that Marcuse's criticism of art as being an ineffective agent of social or environmental change stems from it being a condition of idealised time and not a real-time activity.[146] Thus when the artist consciously makes art a Life or real-time activity[147] it can start to have actual social and political consequences. Whether art should have this role is of course a different question—we may be in fact satisfied with its metaphorical roles.

Dennis Oppenheim

Oppenheim is an interesting figure because he is an Earth artist whose activities have become more and more focused on his own body. In a sense he is useful as a link between 2 different categories of recent art—Earth Art and Body Art and Performance Art.

Before we go on to discuss his work it is important to note that a distinctive feature of much recent art is the movement away from the gallery—Earth Art.[148] in fact makes this unavoidable whereas Body art and Performances can conceivably still occur in a gallery. The important point is that this enlargement of boundaries is important in that the artist becomes exposed to a new potential source for art information. Just as acceptance of the picture frame imposed certain finite possible modes of expression so too the gallery imposes certain limits to expression. Similarly the artist's reliance on consumer society (although this is perhaps unavoidable) similarly limits the range of expression—the art system offers the artist money and fame to conform.

As an Earth artist Oppenheim mowed fields of crops in geometrical configurations which usually contradicted the normal contours of the land. His works had similar qualities to Heizer's—i.e. an imposed gesture on the landscape and where Heizer's holes interact with environmental forces by filling up with water, Oppenheim's fields grow back to their former length. (An interesting aspect is that both the cut and uncut grass grows at a similar rate so that the difference in length between them remains constant—the work maintains its form despite the interaction with natural processes).

Oppenheim moved on from 'ground systems' to use of interacting ecologies. In July 1968 he directed the harvest of a 300 x 900 foot oat field. Cutting, gathering, baling and trucking of bales were stages of the art process documented. At that time the artist planned a work for the summer of 1969 in which "isolated episodes will be directed towards a core network involving every permutation (from planting to distributing the product)".[149] A portion of the crop is to be selected by the artist and sold in 25 lb. sacks. Also four carloads of wheat will be purchased from the Dutch commodity exchange in Amsterdam and sold short in the U.S.

The significance of this project is that Oppenheim is using the untapped energy and information network of the day-to-day environment with a minimum of reorganisation. It is also interesting to note that the art commodity system is undermined in a sense by the unsaleability of the process (it is a `ready made' process taken from the real environment) or by the fact that what is sold is some sort of residue which the art-consumer society snaps up, its art value being far in excess of its normally attributed economic value.

Isomorphisms

Oppenheim's work recently has shifted focus to his own body. This is an attempt to come in closer contact with systems as they affect the artist (i.e. the connection of his body to his mind). Here the material used to display the systems relationship impinges only on the artist himself—and the principle of withdrawing from imposition on the external environment and still yielding art information applies in an even more extreme way.

Oppenheim's body art also tries to set up morphological connections between his body processes and the land's processes. A film made in conjunction with Bob Fiore correlates an incision on Oppenheim's wrist and the subsequently slow healing process with a cut or a large ditch in natural terrain.

In a work called Backtrack he compares the evidence of past wounds or scars on his body to the characteristics of land in also manifesting its past in tangible forms. Oppenheim comments: "For me activity on land is charged, not passive like processed steel, the land holds traces of a dynamic past which the artist may allow to enter his work if he so wishes...I am creating a system that allows the artist to become the material, to consider himself as the sole vehicle of art—the distributor, initiator and receiver simultaneously".[150]

Another piece, "Material Interchange for Joe Stranard" consists of a jar containing a mosquito placed over a friend's arm, which eventually bites him. Out of this present context a mosquito biting someone yields very little information—in the context of Oppenheim's art concerns, the information is of a different nature to that expected.

"Think what's happening here. The mosquito is filling its body with a material lying below the surface on which it is standing and then becoming airborne. This involves an incredible material displacement. This foreign body is now carrying your blood around. Your blood now conforms to the interior configuration of an insect, it places a part of you in a state of material suspension."[151]

The point is that Oppenheim is presenting data which is accessible to everyone but by placing it in the context of his art works it becomes information about structural similarities between organic (including man) and inorganic systems. A viewpoint such as this cannot imply either an anthropocentric universe nor a chaotic one—there is structure at every level of the universe. This point of view moreover has been already presented to us by ecologists.[152] Oppenheim's work thus embraces a perspectivist philosophy—it also illustrates that underlying concerns of artists working within a real-time context are similar despite differences in media—thus Body artists are really dealing with processes, change and systems as too are Earth artists.

Another artist who has dealt vividly with isomorphisms between different phenomena is the musician John Cage.

"I have spent many pleasant hours in the woods conducting performances of my silent pieces, transcriptions, that is for an audience of myself, since they were much longer than the popular length which I have had published. At one performance I passed the first movement by attempting the identification of a mushroom which remained unsuccessfully unidentified. The second movement was extremely dramatic beginning with the sounds of a buck and doe leaping up to within ten feet of my rocky podium. The expressivity of this movement was not only dramatic but unusually sad from my point of view, for the animals were frightened simply because I was a human being. However, they left hesitatingly and fittingly within the structure of the work. The third movement was a return to the first, but with all those profound, so-well known alterations of world feeling associated by German tradition with the A-B-A".[153]

Real-Time Artists

When an artist acts in a real-time situation all the time and specifically is concerned with the causal links in a social system, it often becomes difficult to know when the artist is doing a piece (i.e. specifically processing art data into information).

For example Vito Acconci had an exhibition in a gallery over a period of some weeks. During this time he progressively moved all the furniture, clothing and utensils on which he was dependent from his flat 2 blocks down to the gallery where it was stored. As more of his belongings were removed from his flat, Acconci began to realise the extent to which he was dependent on certain items.

In this situation it is not only Acconci's belongings which are on exhibition at the gallery but Acconci's day-to-day real-time existence. One cannot contemplate this artwork in an idealised time situation.

Similarly with Gilbert and George, the sculptors, "You know as soon as they walk in, you don't have to ask whether they are doing a piece."[154]

Their performance of the Nerve Sculpture at an open-air concert by Blind Faith in Hyde Park involved walking completely unrelaxed, zombie-like twice around the audience. At one stage a group of skinheads started to jeer and throw things and police had to form a cordon to protect them.

"It was really a very impressive sculpture" says George "with cameras clicking and teenagers asking us questions about sex, drugs, religion and politics. We had prepared answers, mostly 'Yes' or 'No'. We wore dark suits, 'collar and tie' and when they asked 'Why are you dressed like that we said 'Only to be normal!'"[155]

7. ART AS INFORMATION—PROCESSING

Conceptual Art[156]

The recognition that art is really concerned with information processing and not necessarily working from data in the form of objects was confirmed by the emergence of conceptual art. Sol Le Witt has stated "since no form is intrinsically superior to another, the artist may use any form, from an expression of words (written or spoken) to physical reality, equally."[157]

Douglas Huebler's work can be broken up to fit into one of three categories: Duration, Location, or Variable Pieces. The artist specifies that all geographical, temporal and process lines of demarcation limit the conceptual boundaries of the piece but since most of Huebler's art is embedded in a real-time situation he places no physical boundaries around a work's beginning and end on its actual location.

Duration Piece 9 consists of a 1" x 1" x 3/4" plastic box which was enclosed within a larger cardboard container and sent by registered mail to an address in California, on being returned as undeliverable it was left altogether intact, enclosed in a slightly larger container and sent to Utah. When it was returned again he continued the same process, selecting addresses which marked off a line joining the two coasts of the United States.

Huebler's awareness of systems is quite substantial—he is drawing attention to the existence of various energy systems in the world which can be `plugged into', thus he utilises the U.S. postal service to describe over 10,000 miles of space in six weeks. It is significant that Huebler does not produce any art data, he selects a system already in the world (the U.S. postal service)and turns this data into art information (by simply posting a package in the mail).

Robert Barry is concerned about what we know about an environment without seeing or experiencing it. An exhibition in his bare studio consisted of 1) 1400 KH2 Carrier Wave (AM) 1968, 2) 1100 KH2 Carrier Wave (AM) 1968, 3) 98 MH2 Carrier Wave (FM) 1968, 4) KH2, 8.25 MM Ultrasonic installation, 5) Phosphorous-32 Radiation Piece, 1969, 6) Cesium-137 Radiation Piece 1969, 7) Electro-Magnetic Energy Field E = 110V, 6.2 metres 2, 1969.

Some of his recent proposals are statements such as "something which is very near in place and time but not yet known to me" or "something which affects me and my world but is unknown to me".

As far as the receiver is concerned the newer works involve a conceptual process which triggers off a dilemma known in philosophy as logical regression or a series of propositions that have no beginning and thus provoke circularity.

Again there is no data presented as such by Barry—the things used as his data exist in the real world—he merely selects them for art processing.

As Burnham states: "One of the transcending realisations of conceptualism is that any form of energy can or may be used to convey information, that the sender or carrier is in fact a secondary problem to that of formulating a significant reason for its use."[158] What the conceptual artist does is formulate reasons for using certain aspects of the real world.

Information and Creativity

It is interesting to reiterate at this point the relationship between information and entropy.

Bertalanffy[159] has shown the actual mathematical correlation between these two quantities and McHarg[160] has pointed out that man's creative role in nature should be considered thermodynamically as increasing the complexity, diversity, stability, quantity of species, number of symbioses[161] and lowering entropy in the biosphere.

We can consider information about the environment as being equivalent to entropy. The application of this equation is evident if we consider the information about the environment which is present in the genes of an organism. This information is the result of natural selection and is the means by which the organism has adapted to the environment. Those species whose genes contained inadequate information about the environment were unable to adapt and thus became extinct. Thus the maintenance of a high energy level of an organism is dependent on the adaptive usefulness of its information.

Man can be creative if through his apperception of the biosphere he can obtain information about the biosphere and can then intervene to produce changes which raise the energy levels of the biosphere. At the moment man is steadily lowering the energy levels of the biosphere.[162]

A first step to a creative role is a recognition of the systems underlying nature, thus the information which artists such as Haacke, Long, Oppenheim, Huebler are producing (i.e. the pervasiveness of organisation at all levels of nature, the perspectivist approach to the world, a systems-oriented aesthetic) is potentially creative in the natural world in that the information could lead to people changing their attitudes and actually intervening with nature to raise her complexity rather than reduce it.

However, until this information is used in this way, their work outside an art context remains only potentially creative.

The obvious point to make is that the ecologist presents the same information more precisely and clearly than any of these artists. The specific attribute of the artist could be that he expresses this same aesthetic[163] in a more striking fashion, or that he applies it practically to his own lifestyle (particularly those artists whose art activities are synonymous with their day-to-day activities in real-time) or he makes contradictory cultural values available (to the prevailing ones) for possible use by society when socio-political circumstances have changed.[164]

However the unimpaired survival of these values may be difficult: Seth Siegelaub who exhibits works by conceptualists Barry, Weiner, Kosuth and Huebler admits "my interest as a businessman isn't in circumventing the commercial system. I've just made pages of a book comparable to space (art situational space). Artists having their work go out as printed matter can be just as viable as selling Nolands."[165]

The difference is of course the nature of information in the two works (object-aesthetic vs systems-aesthetic) while their sale conveys the same art information.

Nevertheless the sale of a systems-oriented art (of which conceptual art is a subject), does pose certain questions in relation to the art-system, consumer society and the corporate state.

Consequences of Dematerialisation

Through the history of art there has been a certain tacit relationship between dealer, audience, collector and artist establishing control over the production and dissemination of a work of art. With the art discussed all previous notions of an object's intrinsic qualities have been challenged to the point where it would be a simple matter to reproduce some recent works with or without the artist's consent.

The dilemma in the present situation occurs when the collector obtains ownership of information which is available in the public domain in any case. It is the same kind of irony of the consumer society when a collector (disconcertingly?) buys a pile of earth, vegetables or any of the other 'poverty' materials which are the residue of some artist's process at 'art' prices which are considerably higher than the generally accepted economic value of these materials. A more subtle irony is that the artist is unwittingly predicting the future when we may in fact pay a high price for a clean pile of earth or for green plants outside an art context—already peace and quiet, time and natural beauty are becoming scarce commodities and consequently expensive.

While the 'dematerialised' art still assumes the form of a commodity particularly as printed material it is quite likely that the traditional art market will change for a new audience. The collector of carefully crafted, high quality decorative paintings will obviously become disenchanted in an art lacking visual sensual appeal and questioning his materialistic values so that the promoter of this art (dealers such as Siegelaub) will look for new markets and possibly find them in a more radical and politically motivated audience. Systems-oriented art could then articulate the necessary; 'aesthetic sensibility' which is a necessary basis for political and social changes which could be effected by this audience.

Art as information processing also leaves little in the way of protection for the artist. Style used to be the equivalent to patent rights. In the current situation where the artist's output is based on non-sequential ideas, it becomes difficult to support the notion of ownership. Ownership amounts to who amplifies the original data (which is available to all) so that it becomes information.

Bertalanffy[166] has noted that one characteristic of a system is competition between parts: every whole is based upon the competition of its elements as one part becomes dominant or is better organised to gain more information and energy from less organised systems (this principle accounts for the widening gap between the overdeveloped economics and the underdeveloped economics).

In an art system it means that as the fame of a living artist grows he simply ceases to make data. His subsequent output is information since it is already art history. Also the famous artist as a better organised system has greater access to museums and media and while he can plagiarise ideas from lesser known artists the reverse cannot occur.

Burnham however notes that the implications of this total art processing system are quite radical—"As information processing becomes better understood, institutions and persons other than artists will insist on creating their own art information, specifically in projects which demand money, planning and technical support beyond the artist's means."[167]

There are two possible consequences here that 1) the systems-aesthetic implicit in this art-information will be used by non-artists in which case this could be the foundations for liberation according to Marcuse[168] or that 2) the systems-aesthetic will provide aesthetic guidance to the technocracy when the technocracy participates in projects concerned with this type of art information.[169]

This is however only conjecture—there is no evidence that this will occur—the point is though to outline the radical potential of this dematerialised art.

8. POLITICAL IMPLICATIONS

Because systems-oriented art is typically a real-time activity it is not surprising to find it impinging on other systems beyond an art context. A perspectivist approach typically tries to extend the boundaries of the environment of the art system. Where Op and Pop Art condone the industrial process and thus the corporate state, systems oriented art questions it and comes into actual conflict with the corporate state's values.

Haacke's Cancelled Show

Hans Haacke's cancelled show at the Guggenheim is an obvious example of a conflict of values.

Haacke's interest in systems has been discussed already.[170] It is in this context of systems that we must see the offending work. The work, dealing with interactions between human organisms or more specifically with social systems consisted of photographs of real estate in New York and the captions to these had business information collected from the public records of the County Clerk's office which gave details of the owners, previous owners, landlords, mortgages and other business transactions.

"The works contain no evaluative comment. One set of holdings are mainly slum located properties owned by a group of people related by family and business ties. The other system is extensive real estate interests owned largely in commercial interests, held by 2 partners".[171]

The show was cancelled by the Director of the Museum because Haacke's work in correlating physical decay with specific financial transactions seemed to be too politically loaded.

The Director wrote: "We are pursuing aesthetic and educational objectives that are self-sufficient and without ulterior motives. On these grounds the trustees have established policies that exclude active engagement towards social and political ends."[172]

The point of course is that the Guggenheim Foundation itself represents and propagates certain attitudes contradictory to Haacke's. This can be seen in the functions of the Foundation—it dispenses thousands of dollars in grants every year; induces wealthy patrons to contribute to it; it holds spectacular social events and as a public or semi-public institution it is a priori a political symbol. Thus Haacke's exhibit is seen to be attacking 'the holy institution of private property in a capitalist society'. In relation to the art gallery (whose function is the selection of the superior objects of our culture) Haacke is implying that there is no difference between the power of money to control the direction of art and the power of money to keep rotten slums in existence.

Systems-Aesthetics as Values

The relevant point which arises from this cancellation for the systems-oriented aesthetic is that mere analysis of any environment using this approach 'objectively' (i.e. considering phenomena as inputs, transformation of energy, outputs, etc.) implies automatically a set of values.

We have seen that in nature a systems approach contradicts an anthropocentric man, in society it contradicts the corporate values. This is further evidence of Bertalanffy's implications of a systems approach in relation to the 'image of man'.[173]

Thus values on specific issues are closely tied to world views—an anthropocentric man is also subject to the corporate state's values—Haacke quite possibly in the context of his other systems (inorganic, organic and human) presented these without judgment, however to merely take a systems approach is, a priori a judgment.

Thus it is not surprising that other artists with developing sensitivity to systems (and thus perspectivist world views) are also in conflict with the aspects of the art-system, such as institutionalised galleries which represent contradictory values. Daniel Buren's refusal to exhibit at the Guggenheim and Robert Morris' cancelled show at the Tate are further examples.

Joseph Beuys

The political activities of Joseph Beuys stem directly from his art. While his systems-aesthetic is not as clearly defined as Haacke's a perspectivist viewpoint is nevertheless present.

Beuys' universe is typically structured, not chaotic, he has furthermore rejected the objectiveness associated with reductionist scientific theories which underlie our society's uncritical acceptance of all that technology has to offer.

He sees art as being a real-time activity and thus a political action. "Freedom is the creative capacity to introduce new causes into the course of history".[174] Thus it is not surprising that Beuys sees his most creative role as an educator. His political actions have been quite direct- from the founding of an Organisation of Non-Voters to interviews with Chancellor Willy Brandt on 'freedom of information'.

* * *

To reiterate the point of this section then, a systems oriented aesthetic a priori incorporates values which conflict with those of the corporate state and the scientific premises underlying the technocracy because both were formed on object-oriented, mechanistic and reductionist attitudes. While this was implied in the development of a General Systems Theory by Bertalanffy—the social and political conflicts with the Establishment, of art based on a systems aesthetic illustrates his point.

CHAPTER 7: CLEANING UP

A General Perspective

We have established then, a shift or tendencies towards a shift in the major paradigm in art from an object-oriented aesthetic to a systems-oriented aesthetic. Furthermore the metaprogram of art seems to be changing in response to the changing needs of society in relation to man, the environment and technology. This change moreover, is by no means without inconsistencies within its internal logic.

A systems approach reveals the interrelationship of dealers, galleries, collectors, artists and both their works and the software extensions of their works. (i.e. in magazines, books, etc.). Such an approach shows that each component has an effect on the total art information produced and that more frequently writers, critics and historians rather than artists generate actual art information. Typically, the artist merely produced the raw data and thus to a great extent factors outside the control of the artist determined the nature of the information produced. This realisation resulted in a shift in the role of the artist from the producer of data to the amplifier of existing data or as an art information processor.

This art information is increasingly about various types of systems rather than objects (which are merely components of systems) and this accounts for the general observation that art has become 'dematerialised'. It seems, also that the systems-oriented aesthetic exhibits in the responses it makes to data in the real world the same type of sensibility as the one expounded by McHarg in an environmental context and implied by Galbraith and Marcuse in a socio-economic context, and thus could conceivably play some role in social change.

The problem in its effectiveness, however, lies with the limitations the artist is subject to within the art-system, before we even consider its limitations in relation to the rest of society.

Where the artist has a commodity—a thing of limited supply to offer, his problems are merely those of demand (which it is the dealer's duty to stimulate). Where, however the art by its very nature offers no transferable rare physical product, the artist attempting to work and earn as an artist within a system which is geared to sale (in so far as it is in any way adjusted to art in the context of economics) must either starve or fabricate criteria of rarity for what is intrinsically not rare—for what may indeed "depend for its very identity as an endeavour within the domain of art upon the irrelevance of such criteria. In these circumstances distinctions between those artists who will permit their work to be 'dealt' with and those who will not, become distinctions with potentially critical overtones."[175]

If an artist is to allow his art (even if it is dematerialised) to become a commodity when his beliefs are apparently radically contradictory to the assumptions or beliefs formative in the socio-political structure of the Corporate State (whose smooth functioning depends on a continuous and predictable production-consumption cycle) is to defeat his intentions. For the information then contained in his art may be information about social change but it is also information about condoning the economic system he is trying to subvert. Furthermore, it must be stressed that this is only a problem if the artist is concerned with social change.

Art-Language

This is the criticism which the Art-Language Group offer in reference to many of the recent projects and performances. "Radical works are absorbed by the consumer capitalist system, the same as objects; instead of objects, it is now processes, photos of processes (signed), interviews, personalities and statements that are sold".[176] Lucy Lippard has recently expressed a similar disillusionment with an art mode whose great promise as an agent of social change seems to have been sublimated by consumerism.

Art-Language see this as an outcome of the fact that the 'new art' is still working within "imposed paradigms and a formalist superstructure." Art-Language aims to examine these premises and assumptions on which art has been based, to create new promises, new theories of art, new methodologies and alternatives to art making. This is done with the aim to ultimately propose ways that art can be effective in contributing to social change.

Kosuth sees the function of art as that of a question, to extend the concept of what art is. "The value of a particular artist after Duchamp can be weighed according to how much they questioned the nature of art",[177] i.e. what they added to the conception of art.

Thus the art process is seen as framing propositions as to what art is. Furthermore, Kosuth insists that art is relevant only to itself as a tautology—"art shares similarities with logic, mathematics as well as science."[178]

The Art-Language Group thus uses analytical theory in an attempt to formulate a system[179] similar to a transformational grammar to make propositions about art. There has been however some criticism of their method from philosophical viewpoints as well as for its communicative value.

It has been implied that the radicality of the new art is not necessarily its dematerialisation but rather the change to a systems type of thinking and within this framework many kinds of work can be placed including some of that criticised by Art-Language.

The works, of course, vary in the definition of the boundaries of the environments with which the particular art-system is placed. While Kosuth and Art-Language in a sense seem to have the narrowest boundary conditions (i.e. of art's relevance only to itself) they nevertheless exhibit a well-developed systems aesthetic. Kosuth's definition of art's function as being to increase the complexity of the concept of art is describing art's function in open systems terms. As in the thermodynamic sense creativity is negentropy or ordering of an organism to a higher energy or information level, which is what Kosuth is saying art should do, i.e. the function of art is to increase the creativity of art.

Modes of Behaviour

Furthermore, it is apparent that Kosuth and Art-Language can be seen to be fulfilling one of the possible modes of behaviour listed by Charles Harrison[180], to avoid sublimation, by the functioning of the art-system within the corporate state.

Harrison has characterised this mode as "the pursuit and analysis of the implications of the art work as such (the 'theory of art') in consciousness of the fact that those implications may/will have relevance in the long term in the cultural/political context."[181]

Another way to avoid sublimation and thus maintain the autonomy of expression is by "detachment, natural or self-imposed, from all broad considerations of context so far as possible, to protect the work from contamination".[182] This is the mode adopted by Richard Long[183] in his walks through the countryside.

A third mode of behaviour is "the self-conscious exposure of the discomfort inherent in the context—this might take the form of either ironic self-assertion with reference to the art context (Les Levine) or of anarchic self-assertion with reference to the social/political context. This last approach is usually limited in its effectiveness and usually is a means to much bad art."[184]

Les Levine

Les Levine's is perhaps the most advanced systems-aesthetic in art at present. He avoids the problem of working in the art-context and thus making money, by working with the art-context and using money as his medium. Where the industrialists think of art as a good tax dodge or as a kind of pastoral retreat, Levine considers business and industry as art in its most essential form.

Levine has set out to vindicate the art-system, his logic being that anything can be sold with public relations energy behind it. His "Plastic Disposables" challenge the market mechanisms which restrict the supply of certain art works making it clear that this restriction is not rarity or scarcity but economic strategy. He sees that Noland's stripe paintings could easily be mass-produced. It is in relation to this mass-production economic that Levine signed contracts with department stores for the sale of millions of Disposables at $1.25—through these he may make more money than Noland.

Levine admits that he's a corporate type with interests in all types of management and even intends moving into legitimate art "a business based on all the tried and true items of American consumerism: pop, colorfield and all the rest..."[185] One of the major functions of his gallery would be to create artists and art groups, re-image them where necessary.

Levine typically uses press releases, publicity getting strategies and shrewd advertising. "Basically it is business that supports art. Who else buys full page color advertisements? All good art, like any other product is packaged for a specific market. This is one of the reasons art usually approximates the size of furniture; art works increase in size directly in proportion to the prospective owner's status and apartment size."[186]

Levine has used other aspects of the art-system to create other works. Opening a restaurant as a work of art was done in relation to the sociology of New York's more frequented artists' bars. Burnham comments: "On the art level it has to be accepted for what it is: a self-organising, data generating system. This is a real-time art work—its gallery is open 14 hours a day, 7 days a week, always changing, charging no admission and allowing him to eat free."[187]

In other works, Levine again utilises aspects of the art-system: a work in relation to the Cornell Earth Art Show, a paint work in relation to the "So and So paints a Picture" series of Art News, a work making money on the Stock Exchange and a "Your Worst Work" Show in relation to the "New York Painting and Sculpture: 1940-70".

Levine's works not only operate as systems outside an art-context (i.e. processing of data from real world into art information) but also within the art context—each work is intrinsically tied to the phenomena of the art-system, amplifying what he sees as the essence of the art world in its actually functioning—i.e. money.

In all his work Levine employs the media to sell his work. He understands that in a technological society there are no real choices for people, only selections out of a number of pre-coded choices already made by society.[188] This is due in part to the monopoly certain power groups have to the media—for the information environment he sees as being as potent as the technological environment.

Furthermore, if the functioning of this environment is to become an open system, everyone needs to be able to plug into it, i.e. everyone should be capable of influencing everyone through it. At present the situation is a 1-way process—for technology to be 'supportive' in a biological sense this process should be a 2-way process. In the light of this aim, Levine sees the recent systems-oriented art (especially in its emphasis on art information) as being an attempt to influence the media environment and thus its role in fact is merely making us aware of the fact that to effect any sort of social change we have to deal directly with the information environment.

Conclusion

What this thesis proposes then, is that the systems-oriented aesthetic is evolving as the new major paradigm[189] in art as a response to the real needs of our society,[190] in a development parallel to the systems re-orientation in the sciences as outlined by Bertalanffy.[191]

It has been suggested that this systems-oriented art presents itself potentially as the most potent aesthetic consciousness in terms of effecting social change, especially since a systems aesthetic necessitates real-time activity.[192] An ideal-time art because of its unreal framework (i.e. separateness from reality) lends itself to being easily defined by the corporate state as an "inoffensive, marginal, decorative activity, a game, a pastime or a confessional, the past tense of creativity: something which is to be entered almost at birth in the immemorial narrative of art history."[193]

Systems-oriented art then has the aesthetics of social and environmental change[194] in it—however whether any art at the present time can actually directly <u>effect</u> radical social, political and environmental change is probably doubtful and whether it is in fact a function of art rather than other areas of human learning[195] to try, seems also doubtful.

The role of the artist according to Jack Burnham is a little more modest: artists are "deviation-amplifying systems or individuals who, because of psychological make-up are compelled to reveal psychic truths at the expense of the existing societal homeostasis".

If art however does have a specific revolutionary role it is according to Marcuse[196] that it `waits in the wings' until after the revolution has occurred and there provides the necessary sensibility to creatively (explicitly in thermodynamic terms—i.e. raising the complexity of the environment) reconstruct not only the physical environment but the social one as well.

BIBLIOGRAPHY

BOOKS

Angyal, A. <u>Foundations for a Science of Personality,</u> Cambridge: Harvard University Press, 1941.

Arnason, H. H. <u>A History of Modern Art</u>, London: Thames and Hudson, 1969.

Ashby, W. R. <u>Introduction to Cybernetics</u>, Wiley, 1956.

Avon, R. <u>The Industrial Society</u>, London: Weidenfield and Nicholson, 1966.

Battcock, G. <u>Minimal Art</u>, London: Studio Vista Ltd., 1969.

Berger, J. <u>Art and Revolution</u>, Baltimore: Penguin Books Inc., 1969.

Von Bertalanffy, L. "The Theory of Open Systems in Physics and Biology", <u>Science</u> vol. 111, 1950.

Von Bertalanffy, L. <u>General Systems Theory</u>, New York: Ludwig. George Braziller, 1968.

Burnham, Jack. Beyond Modern Sculpture; The Effects of Science and Technology on the Sculpture of This Century. New York: G. Braziller, 1968.

Cabanne, Pierre. 1971. <u>Dialogues with Marcel Duchamp</u>. London,: Thames and Hudson.

Cage, John. 1968. Silence: lectures and writings. London: Calder and Boyars.

Celant, Germano. Art povera. New York: Praeger Publishers, 1969.

Christo<u>, Wrapped Coast One Million Sq. Ft.</u> Minneapolis: Contemporary Art Lithographers.

COMPTON, M. <u>Robert Morris</u>, London: Tate Gallery, 1971.

Ehrlich, P. R. <u>Population, Resources, Environment</u> San Francisco: W.H. Freeman and Company 1970.

EHRLICH, P. R. <u>How to be a Survivor</u> London: Ballantine Books, Ltd., 1971.

Emery, F. E. <u>Systems Thinking (selected Readings)</u> Baltimore: Penguin Books Inc., 1969.

EMERY, F. E. and TRIST, E. L. "The Causal Texture of Organizational Environments", <u>Human Relations</u> vol. 18, 1965.

FISCHER, E. <u>The Necessity of Art</u>, Middlesex: Penguin Books Ltd. 1970.

GALBRAITH, J.K. <u>The New Industrial State</u>, London: Hamish Hamilton Ltd., 1967.

GIBSON, J.J. <u>The Senses Considered as Perceptual Systems,</u> London: George Allen and Unwin Ltd., 1966.

HENDERSON, <u>The Fitness of the Environment</u>, Lawrence J. Boston: Beacon Press, 1958.

KAPROW, Allan <u>Assemblage, Environments and Happenings</u> New York: Harry N. Abrams Inc., 1966.

KATZ, D. and KAHN, R.L., <u>The Social Psychology of Organisations</u> Wiley, 1966.

KOEHLER W. <u>The Place of Values in the World of Fact</u> Liveright, 1938.

KUHN, T. <u>The Structure of Scientific Revolutions</u> Chicago: University of Chicago Press, 1962.

LINDER, S.B. <u>The Harried Leisure Class</u>, New York: Columbia University Press, 1970.

LIPPARD, Lucy R. <u>Pop Art</u>, London: Thames and Hudson, 1967.

MARCUSE, Herbert "Liberation from the Affluent Society" <u>The Dialectics of Liberation</u>, Baltimore: Penguin Books Ltd., 1968.

MARCUSE, Herbert <u>An Essay on Liberation</u>, Baltimore: Penguin Books Inc., 1970.

McHARG, Ian L. <u>Design with Nature</u>, New York: The Natural History Press, 1969.

McLUHAN, Marshall <u>The Medium is the Message</u>, New York: Random House, 1967.

PACKARD, Vance. <u>The Hidden Persuaders</u>, London: Longmans, Green and Co., 1958.

PACKARD, Vance <u>The Waste Makers</u>, Middlesex: Penguin Books Ltd., 1967.

RAPPOPORT, A. "Critiques of Game Theory", <u>Behavioural Science</u> 4 (1959)

REICH, Charles <u>The Greening of America</u>, London: Allan Lane, The Penguin Press, 1970.

ROSENBERG, Harold Artworks and Packages, London: Thames and Hudson, 1969.
ROSZAK, Theodore The Making of a Counter Culture, New York: Doubleday and Co. Inc., 1969.
RUSSELL, John Pop Art Redefined
WHITE, L. "The Historical Roots of our Ecological Crises", Science vol. 155, 1967.
WHYTE, William H. The Organisation Man, London: Jonathan Cape, 1958.
WILLENER, Alfred The Action-Image of Society, London: Tavistock Publications, 1970.
WOLFE, Tom The Kandy-Kolored Tangerine-Flake Streamline Baby London: Jonathan Cape, 1968.

MAGAZINES

ATKINSON, Terry "Status and Priority", Studio International, January, 1970.
BAINBRIDGE, David "Status and Priority", Studio International, January, 1970.
BAKER, Kenneth "Keith Sonnier at the Modern", Artforum, October 1971.
BAKER, Kenneth. "London: Roeluf Louw", Artforum, May 1972.
BALDWIN, Michael "Status and Priority"Studio International, January 1970.
BENTHALL, Jonathan "Haacke, Sonfist and Nature", Studio International, March 1971.
BOCHNER, Mel "Excerpts from Speculation (1967-1970)", Artforum, May 1970.
BORDEN, Lizzie "Three Modes of Conceptual Art", Artforum, June 1972.
BOYDEN, Stephen "Man in a Changing Environment", Architecture in Australia, August, 1971.
BRISLEY, Stuart "Environments", Studio International June 1969.
BUREN, Daniel "Beware!" Studio International, March, 1970.
BURGIN, Victor "Rules of Thumb", Studio International May 1971.
BURNHAM, Jack "Systems Esthetics", Artforum, September 1968.
BURNHAM, Jack "Real Time Systems" Artforum, September 1969.
BURNHAM, Jack "Alice's head: Reflections on Conceptual Art", Artforum, February 1970.
BURNHAM, Jack "A Robert Morris Retrospective in Detroit" Artforum, March 1970.
BURNHAM, Jack "Les Levine: Business as Usual" Artforum, April 1970.
BURNHAM, Jack "Hans Haacke's Cancelled Show at the Guggenheim", Artforum, June 1971.
CLAY, Jean "Some aspects of bourgeois art", Studio International, June 1970.
COPLANS, John "An Interview with Don Judd", Artforum, June 1971.
EMERY, Fred "Man as Individual", Architecture in Australia, August, 1971.
EVENTSTRUCTURE RESEARCH CENTRE "Air Art. Two Concepts for an Operational Art". Art and Artists, January, 1969.
FORGE, Andrew "Forces against object-based art" Studio International, June 1969.
GRAHAM, Dan "Eight pieces by Dan Graham", Studio International, May 1972.
HARRISON, Charles "Virgin Soils and old land", Studio International, May 1971
HARRISON, Charles "Art and Language Press", Studio International, June 1972.
Heizer, Michael "The Art of Michael Heizer", Artforum, December 1969.
Higgens, Andrew "Clement Greenberg and the Idea of the Avant Garde", Studio International, October, 1971.
HURRELL, Harold "Status and Priority", Studio International, January 1970
JAPPE, Georg "A Joseph Beuys Primer", Studio International, September 1971.
KAPROW, Allan "Education of the Un-artist", Art News February, 1971.
KINGSLEY, April "Douglas Huebler", Artforum, May 1972.
KOSUTH, Joseph "Art after Philosophy", Studio International October, November, December, 1969.
LEVINE, Les "The Information Fall-Out" Studio International, June 1971.
LINVILLE Kasha "Sonsbeek: Speculations, Impressions" Artforum, October 1971.
LOVELL, Anthony "Lawrence Weiner", Studio International March, 1971.
MICHELSON, Annette "Three Notes on an Exhibition as a Work" Artforum, June 1970.
MORRIS, Robert "Some Notes on Phenomenology of Making" Artforum, April 1970.
MOYNIHAN, Michael "Gilbert and George", Studio International May, 1970.
NEMSER, Cindy "An Interview with Stephen Kaltenbach" Artforum, November 1970.
PINCUS-WITTEN, Robert "Keith Sonnier: Video and Film as Color-Field", Artforum, May 1970.
PINCUS-WITTEN, Robert "Fining it Down: Don Judd at Castelli" Artforum, June 1970.
PINCUS-WITTEN, Robert "Anglo-American Standard Reference Works: Acute Conceptualism", Artforum, October 1971.
PINCUS-WITTEN, Robert "Bochner at MOMA: Three Ideas and Seven Procedures", Artforum, December 1971.
PINCUS-WITTEN, Robert "Vito Acconci and the Conceptual Performance" Artforum, April 1972.
PLAGENS, Peter "Michael Asher: The Thing of It is", Artforum, April 1972.
REISE, Barbara "Sol Le Witt drawings 1968-69" Studio International, December 1969
REISE, Barbara "A Tail of Two Exhibition: The aborted Haacke and Robert Morris shows" Studio International, July-August 1971.
SHARP, Willoughby "An Interview with Joseph Beuys" Artforum, December, 1969.
SHARP, Willoughby "Dennis Oppenheim", Studio International November, 1971.
SMITHSON, Robert "Incidents of Mirror-Travel in the Yucatan" Artforum, September, 1969.
TILLIM, Sidney "Earth Works and the New Picturesque" Artforum, December 1968.
TOWNSEND, Charlotte "N.E. Thing Col and Les Levine" Studio International, April 1970.
TUCHMAN, Phyllis "An Interview with Robert Ryman" Artforum, May 1970.
TUCHMAN, Phyllis "An Interview with Carl Andre" Artforum, June 1970.
WASSERMAN, Emily "Alan Saret's Studio Exhibition" Artforum, March 1970.
WASSERMAN, Emily "This is Not Here", Artforum, January 1972
WEAVER, J.H. "The results of the Pursuit of Economic Growth" ,Architecture in Australia, August 1971.

CATALOGUES, INTERVIEWS, MANUSCRIPTS, ETC.

BROOK, Donald Art, Technology and Society,paper given for "Human Consequences of Technological Change", University of Sydney, 1972.
BROOK, Donald Flight from the Object, John Power Lecture on Contemporary Art, 1969.
BROOK, Donald The Definition of Art unpublished manuscript.
SMITH, Terry Art, Politics and Ideology, unpublished manuscript.
TAYLOR, Jennifer Recent Unorthodox Trends in Architecture M.A. Thesis, 1969.
SMITH, Terry, McGILLICK, Tony. The Situation Now, Central Street Gallery, Sydney.
Gallery, Sydney 1971.
VAN DER MARCK, Jan. Christo, Central Street Gallery, Sydney 1969.
VAN DER MARCK, Jan When Attitudes become Form, Institute of Contemporary Arts, London 1969.
VAN DER MARCK, Jan The Information Catalogue, Museum of Modern

Art, New York, 1970.

VAN DER MARCK, Jan Interview and Files on Evenstructures Research Group, March, 1972.

VAN DER MARCK, Jan Interview with Ian Burn (Art-Language) October, 1972.

VAN DER MARCK, Jan The Consequences of Today—papers given at the R.A.I.A. Centenary Convention, 1971.APPENDIX: Image-Frame Transformation

NOTES

1 There has been direct contact with some artists—Christo, Jeffrey Shaw and Theo Botschuyver (ERG) and Ian Burn (Art Language)

2 "The Medium is the Message" Marshall McLuhan.

3 Ibid. p. 24

4 "Population, Resources, Environment", Paul R. Ehrlich.

5 Maxwell S. McKnight, security adviser of Socony Mobil Oil Company.

6 "The Greening of America", Charles Reich.

7 "The New Industrial State", Kenneth Galbraith.

8 Charles Reich, op. cit. p. 64-95

9 How do voters enforce their will on pollution, the supersonic plane, mass transportation, the arms race or the Vietnam war?

10 As Galbraith notes op. cit. p. 170 "high technology and heavy capital use cannot be subordinate to the ebb and flow of market demand. They require planning; it is the essence of planning that public behaviour be made predictable—that is, subject to control". Thus corporations create their own demand for products via advertising—snowmobiles being more popular than hospitals.

11 Since the government does not represent all interests including minority ones such as agnostics, the poor, youth, radicals but rather organised interests only.

12 Charles Reich op. cit. p. 79

13 Charles Reich op. cit. p. 86

14 Kenneth Galbraith op. cit. p 176.

15 Ludwig von Bertalanffy "General Systems Theory", p. 60.

16 James Weaver "The results of the Pursuit of Economic Growth", Architecture in Australia, August 1971 p. 669.

17 Ibid. p. 672

18 Ian McHarg "Design with Nature" p. 189-195.

19 Stephen Boyden "Man in a Changing Environment", Architecture in Australia, August 1971, p. 655.

20 Herbert Marcuse "An Essay on Liberation", p. 17, chapter on the Biological Foundation for Socialism.

21 Stephen Boyden op. cit. p. 657

22 The presentation of only some views is obviously a bias but the aim is not to be didactic but rather to show the sources of ideas that influence these artists.

23 Kenneth Galbraith "The New Industrial State".

24 Theodore Roszak "The Making of a Counter Culture", p. 100

25 Kenneth Galbraith op. cit. p. 211

26 Theodore Roszak op. cit. p. 27.

27 Herbert Marcuse "An Essay on Liberation", p. 35.

28 An example cited by Roszak is the repression of sexuality (op. cit. p. 15). He states that to liberate sexuality would be to create a society in which technocratic discipline would be impossible—the strategy therefore chosen is not harsh repression but rather the Playboy version of total permissiveness. However while we are led to believe there is sex and sex galore, it has been assimilated to an income level and social status available only to "well-heeled junior executives and the jet set". Real sex we are led to believe is something that goes with the best Scotch, twenty seven dollar sunglasses and platinum-tipped shoelaces. It is sex which creates no binding loyalties, no personal attachments, no distractions from one's career, social position and to the system generally."

29 Marcuse suggests that there may be some primary distinction between beautiful and ugly; good and bad (in addition to the space and time suggested by Kant as pure forms of sensibility common to all human beings), prior to all rationalisation and ideology, a distinction made by the senses in distinguishing that which violates sensibility from that which gratifies it.

30 Charles Reich "The Greening of America"

31 Theodore Roszak "The Making of a Counter Culture"

32 Ibid. p. 67

33 Ibid. p. 68

34 Daniel and Gabriel Cohn-Bendit speaking after the French General Strike:

"The differences between the revolutionary students and workers spring directly from their distinct social position. Thus far students have had no real experience of grinding poverty—their struggle is about the hierarchical structure of society, about oppression in comfort. The workers on the other hand suffer from direct economic oppression and misery."

35 Charles Reich op. cit. p. 255.

36 Ludwig von Bertalanffy "General Systems Theory" p. 223

37 A progressive elimination of traits specific to human experience by a convergence of research, so that many methods are used to show the same aspect of reality and progressive elimination of human experience in a system of mathematical relations.

38 Theodore Roszak op. cit. p. 56

39 Charles Reich op. cit. p. 257

40 Theodore Reszak op. cit. p. 50.

41 Jack Burnham "Real-Time Systems" Artforum Sept.1969 p. 55.

42 The real-time, ideal time dichotomy is a parallel one to the life-art dilemma which is a problem for many artists today.

43 Ian McHarg "Design with Nature" p. 44.

44 Ibid.

45 The Bible, Genesis, verse 24.

46 By Theologians, Abraham Heschel, Gustave Weigel, Teilhard de Chardin and Paul Tillich.

47 While the cult of saints is purported to have replaced animism-the saint is functionally different from natural objects and remains a man approachable only in human terms.

48 Typically in Nevada, Silver Springs, Black Rock Desert, Coyote Dry Lake, Massacre Dry Lake, Mojave Desert.

49 Michael Heizer, Artforum, December 1969. p. 32.

50 Ibid., p. 36.

51 Ian McHarg op. cit. p. 44.

52 Ibid., p. 45.

53 Bertalanffy's argument encompasses all aspects of the ecological view including this one—see Chapter 5.

54 Ian McHarg op. cit. p. 53.

55 Ian McHarg ibid., p. 51.

56 Ian McHarg ibid., p. 32-33.

The crucial role of values is vividly demonstrated in McHarg's example of highway planning. Instead of reducing the problem to the simplest and most commonplace terms (with a profit and progress emphasis) i.e. the traffic volume, design speed, capacity, pavements, structures, horizontal and vertical alignments in the context of economic cost-benefit formula, he proposes that any cost-benefit analysis includes resource values, social values, and aesthetic values as well.

The maximum economic benefit should be replaced by the maximum social benefit at the least social cost. Also, in light of the ecological view, social benefit is measured in terms of the interdependence of many factors such as fitness of environment for the highway and for its potential creative effects (i.e. in contributing to public and private objectives of urban renewal).

57 A. Angyal "Foundations for a Science of Personality" Chapter 8.

58 Ludwig von Bertalanffy, op. cit., p. 54.

59 A. Angyal op. cit.

60 Ibid.

61 For a full mathematical derivation see L. von Bertalanffy op. cit. p. 60-77

62 Ludwig von Bertalanffy "The Theory of Open Systems in Physics and Biology", Science Vol. 111 (1950) pp 23-9.

63 Conventionally, chemical reactions are considered as closed systems but Kohler, ("The Place of Values in the World of Fact" pp. 314-28) analyses the flame of a candle as (a chemical reaction) an open system—the burning process is typically dependent on a continuous supply of inputs from the environment (oxygen) and continuous export of outputs to the environment (carbon dioxide).

64 Ludwig von Bertalanffy "General Systems Theory" p. 42.

65 Ian McHarg, op. cit. pp. 117-127.

66 The implication of thermodynamic creativity on "Art" will be considered in Chapter 6.

67 W.R. Ashby "Introduction to Cybernetics", pp. 202-18.

68 D. Katz and R.L. Kahn "The Social Psychology of Organisations", pp. 14-29.

69 F.E. Emery and E.L. Trist "The Causal Texture of Organizational Environments" Human Relations vol. 18 (1965) pp. 21-32.

70 J.J. Gibson "The Senses Considered as Perceptual Systems".

71 An information based theory of perception, because it sees stimulation as being obtained by the organism, not imposed on it, emphasises the goal-directedness of the organism's behaviour which we have already noted as a general property of open systems.

72 J.J. Gibson op. cit. p. 267.

73 Thomas Kuhn "The Structure of Scientific Revolutions".

74 A. Rapoport "Critiques of Game Theory" Behavioural Science 4 (1959) p. 49.

75 Ludwig von Bertalanffy op. cit. pp188-191.

76 Ibid.

77 Gabo interviewed by Abram Lasaw and Ilya Bolotowsky p. 159.

78 See Chapter 5 section 4—Guiding Metaphors.

79 See Chapter 5, Section 2—Information and Entropy.

80 Exhibition Catalogue for "When Attitudes become Form (Works-Concepts-Process-Situations-Information)", I.C.A., 1969.

81 i.e. repressive tolerance by society. See Chapter 3, Section 3—Role of Art.

82 See Chapter 5, Section 3—Causal Texture of Environment.

83 The artist is then a "perspectivist considering goals, boundaries, structure, input, output and related activity inside and outside the system". Jack Burnham , Artforum, September 1968, p. 32.

84 The Art-Language group are trying to accelerate this change by examining the premises on which art is based (often linguistic ones) rather than its forms—they in fact see their role as showing the fallacy or irrelevance of the paradigm underlying object-oriented art—whether their position is justifiable or their methods adequate is the subject of some debate at present.

85 See Chapter 3, Section 2—Aesthetic Goals in a Technocracy.

86 See Chapter 3, Section 3—Role of Art.

87 Tom Wolfe "The Kandy-Kolored Tangerine-Flake Streamline Baby" p. 63-87.

88 Ibid.

89 Robert Rosenblum "Pop Art and Non-Pop Art" an essay in "Pop Art Redefined" by John Russell.

90 Unpublished manuscript on Definition of Art.

91 This is what makes the Duchamp Spade such a convincing work of art—the quantity of information it has generated in an art context in books, magazines, galleries, etc.

92 If we considered the object or situation outside the context of art ideas, responses, processes (i.e. artist's, dealers, critics, curators) then by definition we could not conceive of it as art. The object's value as art exists only by virtue of its position in an art context. This was the definition (in Chapter 5 Section 1 Defining a System) of a system.

The Balinese say: "We have no art. We do everything as well as we can." However Balinese objects find their way into our museums and are exhibited as art or as "religious magical and household utensils exquisitely and lovingly made". Thus these objects become art once they are placed in our art system and thus our value system—our conception of high art is imposed on their objects. This again demonstrates that an object is art by virtue of its position in an art system.

93 Victor Burgin, Studio International, October 1969, p. 119.

94 See Chapter 5, Section 2, Common Characteristics of Open Systems.

95 Jack Burnham—Artforum September, 1969 p. 49

96 See Chapter 5 Section 4.

97 See Chapter 2 Section 1, 2

98 See Chapter 2 Section 3, 4.
99 See Chapter 5.
100 Jack Burnham op. cit.
101 See Chapter 5 Section 3—Causal Texture of the Environment.
102 Ibid.
103 Jack Burnham op. cit.
104 John Cunningham Lilly (1967)—Programming and Metaprogramming in the Human Biocomputer; Theory and Experiment.
105 Les Levine, "The information fall-out", Studio International, June 1971.
106 i.e. between the artist's stated aims and the actual results.
107 This seems to be the impulse behind Joseph Kosuth and the Art-Language Press.
108 See Chapter 5 Section 4.
109 See Chapter 5 Section 3 Perceptual Systems and Environments.
Section 4 Image of Man.
110 Jack Burnham—Artforum September, 1969 p. 50.
"Ideal time and 'experimental idealism' are both out-growths of the classical frame of reference. They stem from the intuition that location and proportion transcend the illusion of time. In both classical artistic and scientific experimentation the strictest control is exacted over formal relationships.
Reduction, isolation and manipulation are the foundations of the classic inventive structure in art or technology. The problem of form and anti-form represent polarities of this structure not an alternative. Paralleling experiments in classic science, works of art are simplified models of complex unmanageable situations.
Experimental idealism rests on the intellectual and physical isolation of the aesthetic experience. Its tools are picture frames, bases, spotlights, guards, galleries, hypostatic objects, and the concept of high art itself. It suggests that sensually the world is impossible as experience and must be broken down into palatable sanctuaries."
111 See Chapter 5 Section 1—Defining a System.
112 An exception which comes to mind is Tinguely's self-destructing machine "The Homage to New York".
113 The references to the Art-Life dichotomy which are so frequent these days are really the distinctions between ideal time and real time.
114 John Russell "Pop Art Redefined".
115 "What is Pop Art?" Art News, November 1963.
116 See Chapter 5, Section 4, Image of Man.
117 See Chapter 2, Section 3, Goals of Corporations.
118 The human being is reduced to making similar responses to those of Pavlov's conditioned dog.
119. Vance Packard, The Hidden Persuaders, 1958.
120 Marcuse's argument is that the repression of guilt caused by obscene behaviour in the political sphere is accomplished by `liberation' from guilt in the sexual sphere, i.e. by the encouragement of permissiveness in society, however as we have already pointed out this liberation is the Playboy version of sex and thus it is still within the framework of the corporate state's goals and thus not really liberating.
121 See Chapter 5, Section 1, Defining a System.
122 Allen Leepa "Minimal Art and Primary Meanings" from G. Battcock's "Minimal Art".
123 See Chapter 6, Section 4, Op Art Objects.
124 Victor Burgin Studio International, October 1969.
125 See Chapter 5, Section 3, Perceptual Systems and the Environment.
126 See Chapter 5, Section 1, Defining a System.
127 There is a historical link also in that many conceptual artists started out as second generation minimalists.
128 Mel Bochner "Serial Art, Systems, Solipsism" from G. Battcock's "Minimal Art".
129 See Chapter 5, Section 2, Differences between open and closed systems.
130 The plastic was particularly sensitive to changes in lighting conditions.
131 The project was sponsored by Alcorso-Sekers and the Aspen Centre of Contemporary Art.
132 See Chapter 5, Section 2.
133 It is not intended to take up the debate as to whether the photographs and written material are the media of the conceptual work—however it is the author's opinion that this is merely processed information about the work—and not the actual art data itself.
134 See Chapter 3, Section 2, Aesthetic Goals in a Technocracy.
135 Statement by ERG in Art and Artists, January, 1969.
136 General Systems Theory was developed primarily to explain biological phenomena.
137 It is the thermodynamic use of the word creative here—see Chapter 4, Section 4, Creativity.
138 From a letter by Haacke to Jack Burnham.
139 Jack Burnham op. cit.
140 The implications of the incident over the cancellation of Haacke's Guggenheim show will be referred to later.
141 See Chapter 4, Section 3, Richard Long.
142 It is obvious that Haacke's systems have a limited life as an "art experience" because his systems exist as "on-going entities" away from the viewer. However if we consider that Haacke is in fact not producing art data (see Chapter 6 Section 3) to be processed to produce art information but that his activity is the selection and processing of already available data then the relevance of his activity becomes more obvious. This concern of recent art in the processing of art information from already existing data is a recognition of the art-world as a system and the desire of the artist to be more effective in implementing changes through art information. This matter will be discussed in the last chapter.
143 Idealism in science has been mentioned already and is the basis of reductionist methods of analysis (e.g. laboratory rat experiments to determine human behaviour) and which typically produce oversimplified models of complex, unmanageable situations.
144 See Chapter 2.
145 Ludwig von Bertalanffy "Robots, Men and Minds" p. 27.
146 See Chapter 3, Section 3.
147 They have to avoid the idealisation of their activities through one of the software extensions (i.e. magazines, books etc.) The failure to do this may prove to be the ineffectiveness of this type of art. This problem is discussed further in the last chapter.
148 See Chapter 4, Section 3, Michael Heizer.
149 Letter from Dennis Oppenheim to Jack Burnham 1969.
150 Dennis Oppenheim interviewed by Willoughby Sharp Studio International, November, 1971.
151 Ibid.
152 Note: Henderson compares the regulation of alkalinity in the ocean to regulation of alkalinity in human blood, see McHarg "Design with Nature" p. 51.
153 John Cage "Silence"
154 Dennis Oppenheim, op. cit.
155 "Gilbert and George" Michael Moynihan, Studio International, May 1970.
156 The Art-Language-Group—the `purest' conceptualists are discussed in Chapter 7.
157 Sol Le Witt January 1969—"Sentences on Conceptual Art".
158 Jack Burnham Artforum, February, 1970.
159 See Chapter 5, Section 2, Information and Entropy.
160 See Chapter 4, Section 4, Creativity.
161 i.e. the interrelationships between organisms.
162 See Chapter 2, Section 2.
163 McHarg and Bertalanffy are both in fact presenting a new aesthetic.
164 See Chapter 3, Section 3, Role of Art.
165 Seth Siegelaub quoted by Jack Burnham op. cit.
166 Ludwig von Bertalanffy "General Systems Theory" p. 63.
167 Jack Burnham, Artforum, September, 1969.
168 See Chapter 3, Section 3.

169 See Chapter 3, Section 2.
170 See Chapter 6, Section 6, Hans Haacke.
171 From press release by the artist. April 3, 1971.
172 From a letter by Thomas Messer to the artist, dated March 19, 1971.
173 See Chapter 5, Section 4, Image of Man.
174 From an interview with Joseph Beuys by George Jappe Studio International, September 1971.
175 Charles Harrison, Studio International, May 1971.
176 Ian Burn from interview with author, October, 1972.
177 Joseph Kosuth, "Art after Philosophy", Studio International.
178 Ibid.
179 This involves the construction of a number of alternative frameworks (frameworks are isomorphic to systems in science) in which to put clusters of ideas related to art.
180 Charles Harrison, op. cit.
181 Ibid.
182 Ibid.
183 See Chapter 4, Section 3, Richard Long and also Chapter 6, Section 6, Real-time Art.
184 Charles Harrison, op. cit.
185 Les Levine, Artforum, April 1970.
186 Ibid.
187 Ibid.
188 Galbraith and Reich in their analysis of the Corporate State (see Chapter 2, Section 3 and Chapter 3, Section 2) confirm this view.
189 See Chapter 5, Section 4, Guiding Metaphors.
190 Which are non-materialistic in nature, embracing man's relations with man, man's relation to technology and man's relations to nature.
191 See Chapter 5, Section 4.
192 i.e. art taking place in the context of day-to-day life as a continuous process in actual experiential time while still remaining art. (The activity becomes art information when the artist formulates significant reasons for using the activity as art data).
193 Jean Clay, Studio International, June 1970.
194 Changes in society according to Marcuse must be preceded by changed values which this art seems to provide—i.e. qualitative as well as quantitative changes must be present if the new society is to be significantly different.
195 Meteorologists, geologists, geomorphologists, hydrologists, soil scientists, plant ecologists, animal ecologists, limnologists, cleanographers, ethologists, ethnographers, cultural anthropologists, political scientists, sociologists, economists, etc. seem to be in a better position to do this than artists considering their greater understanding of the physical and social environments.
196 See Chapter 3, Section 3, Liberation from the Corporate State.

Appendix: Image-Frame Transformation

"To put the final touch to your painting a frame is necessary".

Input = Image: Likeness a status, an idol; a picture or representation (not necessarily visual) in the imagination or memory; that which very closely resembles anything.

Tranformation: change of form, constitution or substance; metamorphosis; transmutation.

Output = Frame: the body; a putting together of parts; structure; a case made to enclose; border or support anything; the skeleton of anything.
Joan Grounds, Imants Tillers, Alec Tzannes.

APPENDIX B

ARTIST BIOGRAPHY

Born 1950, Sydney, Australia
Lives and works in Cooma, New South Wales.

STUDIES

1969-72 Bachelor of Science in Architecture (Honours), The University of Sydney. Awarded University Medal.

SOLO EXHIBITIONS

1973
Still Life 2, Watters Gallery, Sydney
1974
Moments of Inertia, Watters Gallery, Sydney
1974
Link Exhibition (No. 1): Still Life 2, Art Gallery of South Australia, Adelaide
1975
Conversations with The Bride, Watters Gallery, Sydney
1977
The Property of Being Found, Watters Gallery, Sydney
1978
Have you ever been taken the same way?, Royal Melbourne Institute of Technology, Melbourne
1979
52 Displacements, Watters Gallery; Sydney
1980
Other Realities, Melbourne Institute of Modern Art, Brisbane
Survey 13: Imants Tillers, National Gallery of Victoria, Melbourne
Q Space Annex, Brisbane
1981
Q Space Annex, Brisbane
Visible Suspension, n-space, Sydney
The Triangle, The Door, Watters Gallery, Sydney
Two Maps (A Local Mirage), Art Projects, Melbourne Q Space Annex, Brisbane
1982
One Painting, One Horizon, Institute of Modern Art, Brisbane
The Church + The Cross (with John Nixon), n-space, Kassel, Germany
The Church + The Cross (with John Nixon), V Space, Melbourne
Documenta 7 (with John Nixon), Art Projects, Melbourne
A Painting which is a souvenir (with John Nixon), Q.E.D., Central Street Gallery, Sydney
The Field, Art Projects, Melbourne
Composition with Three Equal and Parallel Rectangles (with John Nixon), Yuill/Crowley, Sydney
1983
White Aborigines, Matts Gallery, London
Yuill/Crowley, Sydney
Reconnaissance, Melbourne
1984
Bess Cutler Gallery, New York
Pandemonium, Yuill/Crowley, Sydney
1985
Bess Cutler Gallery, New York
Yuill/Crowley, Sydney
1986
42nd Venice Biennale, Australian Pavilion, Corderie at the Arsenale, Venice
Yuill/Crowley, Sydney
1987
Paintings for Venice: Australia at the 42nd Venice Biennale, Queensland Art Gallery, Brisbane; Australian Centre for Contemporary Art, Melbourne; Art Gallery of South Australia, Adelaide
Australian Appropriations: The Recent Paintings of Imants Tillers, Vollum Center Gallery, Reed College, Portland, Oregon
Bess Cutler Gallery, New York
Galerie Susan Wyss, Zurich
Yuill/Crowley, Sydney
1988
Imants Tillers: 1978-1988, Institute of Contemporary Arts, London; The Third Eye Gallery, Glasgow; Orchard Gallery, Derry, Northern Ireland
To the Fatherland (with Marianne Baillieu), Yuill/Crowley, Sydney
1989
Imants Tillers: 19301, National Art Gallery, Wellington; Govett-Brewster Gallery, New Plymouth, New Zealand; Bess Cutler Gallery, New York
Tomorrow will be the same but not as this is, Yuill/Crowley, Sydney
1990
Poem of Ecstasy, Deutscher Brunswick Street, Melbourne
One Painting, Cleaving, Wollongong City Art Gallery, Wollongong

The Shining Cuckoo, Yuill/Crowley, Sydney
Imants Tillers — Recent Paintings, Peter McLeavey Gallery, Wellington
The Bridge of Reversible Destiny, Yuill/Crowley, Sydney

1991

Action Paintings, Yuill/Crowley, Sydney
Imants Tillers, Peter McLeavey Gallery, Wellington
Journey: 33486, Deutscher Brunswick Street, Melbourne

1992

A Life of Blank, Plimsoll Gallery, Hobart; Monash University Gallery, Melbourne; Orange Regional Gallery, Orange; Queen Victoria Museum and Art Gallery, Launceston; Karyn Lovegrove, Melbourne; Michael Milburn Gallery, Brisbane

1993

Diaspora, National Museum of Art, Riga
Five Pollock Paintings, Peter McLeavey Gallery, Wellington
Within the Cleft, Michael Milburn Gallery, Brisbane

1994

Diaspora, Institute of Modern Art, Brisbane
Telepathic Music, Michael Milburn Gallery, Brisbane Jump, Sherman Galleries Goodhope, Sydney

1995

Via Paradiso, Karyn Lovegrove Gallery, Melbourne
Diaspora in Context: Connections in a Fragmented World. lmants Tillers makes a painting by Georg Baselitz, Joseph Beuys, Bernhard Blume, Carlo Carra, Giorgio de Chirico, Mike Kelley, Vytautas Landshergis, Cohn McCahon, Arnulf Rainer, Nicholas Roerich and Isidore Tillers, Pori Art Museum, Pori, Finland; Museum of Contemporary Art, Sydney; Govett Brewster Art Gallery, New Plymouth; Waikato Museum and Art Gallery, Hamilton, New Zealand

1996

Imants Tillers, Gow Langsford Gallery, Auckland

1997

The Enigma of Arrival, Sherman Galleries Goodhope, Sydney
Karyn Lovegrove, Melbourne
Michael Milburn Gallery, Brisbane

1998

Prayer for Rain, Raglan Gallery and Cultural Centre, Cooma
Monaro, 1998: Imants Tillers 1997 Lowenstein Sharp Arts 31 Fellow, Museum of Modern Art, Heide, Melbourne

1999

Not yet post-Aboriginal, Span Galleries, Melbourne
Nature Speaks, Sherman Galleries Goodhope, Sydney
Home Visitation, Chapman Gall try, Canberra
Towards Infinity: Works by Imants Tillers, MARCO Museum of Contemporary Art, Monterrey, Mexico

2000

Sherman Galleries Hargrave, Sydney
Greenaway Art Gallery, Adelaide

2002

Not yet Post-Aboriginal, Hazelhurst Regional Gallery and Arts Centre, Gymea, Sydney.

GROUP EXHIBITIONS

1969

Wrapped Coast (with Christo and Jeanne-Claude), Little Bay, Sydney

1970

Contemporary Art Society Annual Exhibition, The Blaxhand Gallery, Sydney

1971

Young Contemporaries Exhibition, The Blaxland Gallery, Sydney
Open Wide, Contemporary Art Society, Central Street Gallery, Sydney

1972

Young Contemporaries Exhibition, Central Street Gallery, Sydney
Contemporary Art Society Annual Exhibition, The Blaxhand Gallery, Sydney
The Joe Bonomo Story, Watters Gallery, Sydney

1973

Object and Idea, National Gallery of Victoria, Melbourne
Sculpturescape 73, Fifth Mildura Sculpture Triennial, Mildura
Recent Australian Art, Art Gallery of New South Wales, Sydney

1974

The Wynne Prize, Art Gallery of New South Wales, Sydney
Gifts from Patrick White, Art Gallery of New South Wales, Sydney
Boxes, Ewing and George Paton Gallery, The University of Melbourne, Melbourne
Artists for Whitlam, Hogarth Galleries, Sydney
Ten Years, Watters Gallery, Sydney

1975

The Phillip Morris Arts Grant, National Gallery of Victoria, Melbourne
13th Bienal de São Paulo, Brazil
Conversations with The Bride, South American Tour of Australian Works in Bienal de São Paulo

1976

Post-Object Art in Australia and New Zealand, Experimental Art Foundation, Adelaide

1977

Watters at Pinacotheca, Pinacotheca Gallery, Melbourne

1978

Artist's Books: Book Works, Ewing and George Paton Gallery, The University of Melbourne, Melbourne; Experimental Art Foundation, Adelaide; Institute of Modern Art, Brisbane; Franklin Furnace, New York

Roads how Exhibition 1: Works on Paper, Regional Development Program touring regional galleries in New South Wales

1979

The Work and its Context, Australian Embassy, Paris

3rd Biennale of Sydney: European Dialogue, Art Gallery of New South Wales, Sydney

1981

Australian Perspecta 1981: A Biennial Survey of Contemporary Australian Art, Art Gallery of New South Wales, Sydney

John McCaughey Memorial Prize, National Gallery of Victoria, Melbourne (winner)

Three Rejected Entries: Wynne, Sulman and Archibald Prizes, Art Projects, Melbourne

The Beacon, *n*-space at Cremorne Point, Sydney

Frankfurt Book Fair, Frankfurt

1982

Eureka! Artists from Australia, Serpentine Gallery, London; Institute of Contemporary Arts, London

Popism, National Gallery of Victoria, Melbourne

Documenta 7, Kassel

The Temple of the Winds, *n*-space at The Temple of the Winds, Royal Botanic Gardens, Melbourne

Art in the Age of Mechanical Reproduction, Ewing and George Paton Gallery, The University of Melbourne, Melbourne

1983

Project 40: Australian Artists at Venice and Kassel, Art Gallery of New South Wales, Sydney

Masterpieces: Out of the Seventies, Monash University Gallery, Melbourne

Tall Poppies: An Exhibition of Five Pictures, Melbourne University Gallery, Melbourne

Recent Australian Painting: A Survey 1970-1983, Art Gallery of South Australia, Adelaide

VOX POP: Into the Eighties, National Gallery of Victoria, Melbourne

George Baldessin: Sculpture and Etchings: A Memorial Exhibition, National Gallery of Victoria, Melbourne

Tribute to Mervyn Horton, Art Gallery of New South Wales, Sydney

Minimalism x Six, Institute of Modern Art, Brisbane

The Life of Energies, Artspace, Sydney

1984

Form>Image<Sign: Survey of Contemporary Australian Art, No. 3, Art Gallery of Western Australia, Perth

An Australian Accent, P.S.l., New York; Art Gallery of Western Australia, Perth; Art Gallery of New South Wales, Sydney

Accents/Expressions, The Corcoran Gallery of Art, Washington DC

Synthetic Art, Harm Bouckaert Gallery, New York New Work, Bess Cutler Gallery, New York Architectura Picta, Ewing and George Paton Gallery, tie University of Melbourne, Melbourne; Artspace, Sydney

1985

Production: Re-Production, Gallery 345, New York

Two Worlds Collide: Cultural Convergence in Aboriginal and White Australian Art, Artspace, Sydney

Dot and Circle: A Retrospective Survey of the Aboriginal Acrylic Paintings of the Western Desert, Royal Melbourne Institute of Technology Gallery, Melbourne

Group Show, Svetlana Achatz, Munich Little

Works by Big Thinkers, Bess Cutler Gallery, New York

Still Life, Art Gallery of New South Wales, Sydney

Seeing is Believing; Travelling Art Exhibition 1985, Art Gallery of New South Wales, Sydney

Visual Tension, Australian Centre for Contemporary Art, Melbourne

1986

Contemporary Issues 111: Works from the Collection of Robert and Nancy Kaye, Holman Hall Art Gallery, Trenton State College, New Jersey

6th Biennale of Sydney: Origins, Originality and Beyond, Art Gallery of New South Wales, Sydney

Investigations, Mclntosh-Drysdale, Washington DC

When Attitudes Become Form, Bess Cutler Gallery, New York

Group Show, Stavaridis Gallery, Boston

How Much Beauty Can I Stand?, Australian Centre for Contemporary Art, Melbourne

1987

Modern Art since 1984, Nexus Contemporary Art Center, Atlanta, Georgia

Avant Garde in the Eighties, Los Angeles County Museum, Los Angeles

Australia: Art and the West, Art Gallery of New South Wales, Sydney

Painters and Sculptors: Diversity in Australian Art, Queensland Art Gallery, Brisbane

Contemporary Australian Art, Museum of Modern Art, Saitama, Japan

Field to Figuration: Australian Art 1960-1986, National Gallery of Victoria, Melbourne

The Australian Bicentennial Perspecta, Art Gallery of New South Wales, Sydney; Art Gallery of Western Australia,

Perth; Frankfurter Kunstverein, Frankfurt; Wurttembergische Kunstverein, Stuttgart
Hybrid Products, S. L. Simpson Gallery, Toronto
Heroics, Walter Philips Gallery, The Banff Centre, School of Fine Arts, Banff, Alberta
State of the Art, Institute of Contemporary Arts, London
What is this Thing called Science?, Melbourne University Gallery, Melbourne
In Print Vol. Artists Books, Power Gallery of Contemporary Art, The University of Sydney, Sydney

1988

Creating Australia: 200 Years of Art 1788-1988, Queensland Art Gallery, Brisbane; Art Gallery of Western Australia, Perth; Art Gallery of New South Wales, Sydney; Tasmanian Museum and Art Gallery, Hobart; National Gallery of Victoria, Melbourne; Art Gallery of South Australia, Adelaide
Edge to Edge: Australian Contemporary Art to Japan, Museum of Art, Osaka; Hara Museum of Contemporary Art, Tokyo; Nagoya City Art Museum, Nagoya; Hokkaido Museum of Modern Art, Sapporo
Advance Australian Painting, Auckland City Art Gallery, Auckland
Stories of Australian Art, Commonwealth Institute, London
Australian Biennale, Art Gallery of New South Wales, Sydney; National Gallery of Victoria, Melbourne Redux: Michael Bidlo, Sherrie Levine, Doug Huebler, Phillip Taaffe, Richard Pettibone, Imants Tillers, Maloney Gallery, Los Angeles
A Changing Relationship—Aboriginal lhemes in Australian Art 1938-1988, S. H. Ervin Gallery, Sydney
Italo Scanga, Imants Tillers, Robin Winters, Dorothy Goldeen Gallery, Los Angeles
Pro Museum of Contemporary Art Collection in Finland, Vanhan Galleries, Helsinki Archibald Prize, Art Gallery of New South Wales, Sydney; Westpac Gallery, Melbourne
Images of Religion in Australian Art, National Gallery of Victoria, Melbourne

1989

After McCahon, Auckland City Art Gallery, Auckland American Pi(e), Bess Cutler Gallery, New York Archibald Prize, Art Gallery of New South Wales, Sydney
Freestyle: Australian Art 1960s to Now, National Gallery of Victoria, Melbourne
Porkkana Collection, The Old Student House, Helsinki; Titanik Galeria, Turku; The Art Museum of Hyvinkaa; The Art Museum of Mikkeli; The Art Museum of Kuopio

1990

Infbrmation, Terrain Gallery, San Francisco
Balance 1990, Queensland Art Gallery, Brisbane
Institute of Contemporary Arts Sothebys Benefit Auction, Nigel Greenwood Gallery, Marlene Eleni, Nieola Jacobs, Victoria Miro, London
Fluctua, Art Dock, Noumea, New Caledonia
L'été Australien à Montpellier, Musée Fabre, Montpellier
The Complex Picture, College Gallery, South Australian College of Advanced Education, Adelaide
Art From Australia: Eight Contemporary Views, Gedung Seni Rupa Nasional, Jakarta; National Art Gallery, Bangkok; Metropolitan Museum of Manila; National Art Gallery, Kuala Lumpa; National Gallery, Singapore
Shifting Parameters, Queensland Art Gallery, Brisbane
Inland, Australian Centre for Contemporary Art, Melbourne
Osaka Painting Triennale 90, Mydonie Osaka, Osaka
Archibald Prize, Art Gallery of New South Wales, Sydney; Blaxland Gallery, Melbourne
International Survey of Latvian Art, National Museuni of Art, Riga
Latvian Artists: Side by Side, High Court of Australia, Canberra
Strange Harmony of Contrasts, Roslyn Oxley9, Sydney;
Canberra School of Art, Canberra; Institute of Modern Art, Brisbane
Artists for Greenpeace, Linden Gallery, Melbourne
Art with Text, Monash University Gallery, Melbourne
A Rebours, Yuill/Crowley, Sydney
Conventional Practice: Still Life and the Model—from the Twenties to Tillers, Robyn Brady Pty Ltd at DC Art, Sydney

1991

Tokyo International Art Show, Tokyo
Porkkana Collection, The Museum of Contemporary Art, Helsinki
Preview Exhibition, Bess Cutler Gallery, Santa Monica
Opening Transformations, Museum of Contemporary Art, Sydney
Cologne Art Fair, Cologne
Aberdare Art Prize, Ipswich City Council Regional Gallery, Ipswich (winner)
Off the Wall/In the Air: A Seventies Selection, Monash University Gallery, Melbourne
Contemporary Landscapes, Institute of the Arts, Deakin University, Geelong
Contemporary Art Archive Exhibition, Museum of Contemporary Art, Sydney
41st Latvian Cultural Festival Art Exhibition, RSAS Gallery, Kintore, Adelaide

1992

Light Sensitive, Artspace, Auckland
Imants Tillers, Cohn McCahon, Charles Tole, Peter MeLeavey Gallery, Wellington

The Living Mandala, Access Gallery, National Gallery of Victoria, Melbourne
Distraction, Yuill/Crowley, Sydney
The Selective Eye, Peter McLeavey Gallery, Wellington
Domino 1: Collaborations between Artists, Melbourne, University Gallery, Melbourne
20th Century Australian and New Zealand Painting, Martin Browne Fine Art at Macdonald Street Galleries, Sydney
Inherited Absolute: Artists with Children, Australian Centre for Contemporary Art, Melbourne
Sight Regained: Collaborations between Artists and Architecrs, Westpac Gallery, Melbourne
A Selection of Nineteenth and Twentieth Century Australian Art, Deutscher Fine Art, Melbourne

1993

Installation and Objecthood, Martin Browne Fine Art, Sydney; Michael Milburn, Brisbane; Perc Tucker Regional Gallery, Townsville
Looking at Seeing and Reading, Ivan Dougherty Gallery, Sydney; Institute of Modern Art, Brisbane
Imants Tillers, John Young, Dale Frank, Sherman Galleries Goodhope, Sydney
Commitments, Institute of Modern Art, Brisbane; Artspace, Sydney
The Eye, Art Gallery of New South Wales, Sydney Shaman Summer in Finland, Aineen Thaidemuseo, Tornio
Osaka Painting Triennale, Osaka, Japan (awarded Grand Prize)
Identities: Art from Australia, Taiwan Museum of Art, Taipei, Taiwan;
Wollongong City Art Gallery, Wollongong

1994

25 Years of Performance Art in Australia, Ivan Dougherty Gallery, Sydney
Valsts, Soros Centre for Contemporary Arts, Riga
Virtual Reality, National Gallery of Australia, Canberra
Un/Peeled Art, Ballarat Fine Art Gallery, Ballarat
Humanism and Technology: The Human Figure in Industrial Society, National Art Museum, Seoul
Osaka Print Triennale, Mydome, Osaka
Sweet Damper and Gossip—Colonial Sightings from the Goulburn and North East, Benalla Art Gallery, Benalla
Looking at Seeing and Reading, Monash University Gallery, Melbourne
Faces of Hope Amnesty International, Australia, Art Gallery of New South Wales, Sydney
Prime TV Painting Prize, Newcastle Region Art Gallery, Newcastle (winner)
Photosynthesis, Roslyn Oxley9 Gallery, Sydney
Power Works: From the MCA Collection, Museum of New Zealand, Wellington; Govett-Brewster Art Gallery, New Plymouth; Waikato Museum of Art and History, Hamilton; Dunedin Public Ait Gallery, Dunedin
Virtuosi, Sherman Galleries Flargrave, Sydney; Christine Abrahams Gallery, Melbourne; Solander Gallery, Canberra

1995

Antipodean Currents: Ten Contemporary Artists from Australia, Guggenheim Museum SoHo, New York; John E Kennedy Center for Performing Arts, Washington DC
Australian Art 1940-1990. From the Collection of the National Gallery of Australia, The Museum of Fine Arts, Gifu, Japan
Smorgon Collection of Contemporary Art, Museum of Contemporary Art, Sydney
Text and Art, Logan Art Gallery, Logan City, Queensland
Baltic Presence, Latvian Centre, Strathfield, Sydney
In Tandem, Sherman Galleries Goodhope, Sydney
Patrick Pound, Jacky Redgate, Imants Tillers, Michael Milburn Gallery, Brisbane

1996

Systems End: Contemporary Art in Australia, OXY Gallery, Osaka; Hakone Open-Air Museum, Tokyo; Dong-Ah Gallery, Seoul; Kaohsiung Museum of Fine Arts, Taiwan
The John Kaldor Collection, Museum of Contemporary Art, Sydney Colonial Post Colonial, Museum of Modern Art, Heide, Melbourne
The World Over/Under Capricorn: Art in the Age of Globalisation, City Gallery, Wellington; Stedelijk Museum, Amsterdam
Perception and Perspective, Next Wave Festival, National Gallery of Victoria, Melbourne
Rosalie Gascoigne, Robert MacPherson, Jacky Redgate, Rover Thomas, Imants Tillers—Some Works from their Present and their Past, National Gallery of Australia, Canberra
Osaka Painting Triennale, Osaka Mydome, Osaka
Imants Tillers, Tracey Moffatt, Dale Frank, Geoff Lowe, Karyn Lovegrove Gallery, Melbourne

1996-97

The Century in Art. The Spirit in Australia 1880-1996, Museum of Contemporary Art, Sydney

1997

Anon, Sherman Galleries Goodhope, Sydney
Mike Parr, lmants Tillers, John Young, Sherman Galleries Goodhope, Sydney
A Thing of Beauty Is, Museum of Contemporary Art, London
In Place (Out of Time): Contemporary Art in Australia, Museum of Modern Art, Oxford
Visions of Reason: Five Artists and Complexity, US and European venues

Archibald Prize, Art Gallery of New South Wales Sydney; Victorian Arts Centre, Melbourne

Tokyo International Art Fair, Tokyo

Power, Corruption and Lies, Institute of Modern Art, Brisbane

Visy Board Art Prize, Barossa Vintage Festival, South Australia

Coded, Waikato Museum and Art Gallery, Hamilton, New Zealand

The Real Thing, Museum of Modern Art at Heide, Melbourne

1998

Expanse: Aboriginalities, Spatialities and the Politics of Ecstasy, University of South Australia Art Museum, Adelaide.

On the Ashes of the Stars ... STÉPHANE MALLARMÉ a celebration, Monash University Gallery, Melbourne

Remanence: Melbourne Festival 1998, Former Melbourne Magistrates Court and City Watch House, Melbourne

Ways of Being, Ivan Dougherty Gallery, Sydney (touring NSW regional galleries and Gold Coast Art Gallery)

Five Continents and a City, Mexico City Museum, Mexico city

Proscenium Artspace, Auckland

1999

Cinderellas Gems: Art and the Intellectual Mission: 20th Century Australian Art selected from University Collections in New South Wales, Macquaire University, Sydney. (touring regional galleries in Queensland, New South Wales and Victoria)

The Rose Crossing: Contemporary Art in Australia, Brisbane City Gallery; Hong Kong Arts Centre, Singapore Art Museum:

WORD, Museum of Contemporary Art, Sydney

Home and Away: Contemporary Australian and New Zealand Art from the Chartwell Collection, Auckland City Gallery

Snowy! Power of a Nation: 50 Years of the Snowy Mountains Scheme, Powerhouse Museum, Sydney.

2000

From Appreciation to Appropriation: Indigenous Influences and Images in Australian Visual Art, Flinders Art Museum, Adelaide

Australian Latvian Artists Society, Latvian House, Strathfield, Sydney.

Restricting the Palette: Colour and Land, Canberra School of Art Gallery, Canberra.

Artists in Focus—Iconography, Traditions and Influence, Homes à Court Gallery, Perth.

Spitting and Biting: Ten Contemporary Artists and the Print, Monash University Gallery, Melbourne.

2001

A Studio in Paris: Australian Artists at the Cité Internationale des Arts 1967-2000, S.H. Ervin Gallery, Sydney.

Colin McCahon: A Time for Messages, National Gallery of Victoria, Melbourne.

Southern Exposure: Centenary of Federation, Hazelhurst Regional Gallery and Arts Centre, Gymea, Sydney.

Greenaway Art Gallery at ARCO, 2001, Madrid

Sherman Galleries in Tokyo, Nicaf 2001, Tokyo

MCA Unpacked, Museum of Contemporary Art, Sydney.

Empathy: Beyond the Horizon, Pori Art Museum, Pori, Finland.

Osaka Triennale 2001: 10th International Contemporary Art Competition (awarded Silver Prize), Contemporary Art Space, Osaka.

2002

Art after Art, Neues Museum Weserburg Bremen, Carl Andre, John Armleder, Art & Language, John Baldessari, Jimmie Durham, General Idea, Rodney Graham, Robert Indiana, Bertrand Lavier, Jonathon Monk, Christian Phillip Muller, Albert Oehlen, Sigmar Polke, Jackson Pollock, Susi Pop, Stephen Prina, Robert Rauschenberg, C. Schneyder, Bob and Roberta Smith, Elaine Sturtevant, Yuji Takeoka, Tony Tasset, Imants Tillers, Piotr Uklanski, Andy Warhol, Heimo Zobernig.

COLLECTIONS

National Gallery of Australia, Canberra

Metropolitan Museum of Art, New York

National Gallery of New Zealand, Wellington

Osaka Cultural Foundation, Osaka

Museum of Contemporary Art, Sydney

National Museum of Art, Riga

National Gallery of Victoria, Melbourne

Art Gallery of New South Wales, Sydney

Art Gallery of South Australia, Adelaide

Art Gallery of Western Australia, Perth

Art Gallery of Queensland, Brisbane

High Court of Australia Collection, Canberra

Wollongong City Art Gallery, New South Wales

Monash University Collection, Melbourne

Australian Embassy, Paris

Museum of Contemporary Art, Helsinki

Museum of Modern Art at Heide Collection, Melbourne

Auckland City Art Gallery, New Zealand

Chase Manhattan Bank Collection, New York

Bell Resources Collection, New York

Westpac Corporate Art Collection, Sydney

Prudential Insurance Company Collection, New York

The Loti and Victor Smorgon Collection, Melbourne
Sussan Corporation Collection, Melbourne
Michael Darling Collection, Sydney
Lila and Gilbert Silverman Collection, Detroit
Pori Art Museum, Pori, Finland
John Kaldor Collection, Sydney
The Chartwell Collection, Hamilton, New Zealand
James Wolfensohn Collection, New York
Sakai City Collection, Osaka
MARCO Museum of Contemporary Art, Monterrey, Mexico
Plus numerous private and corporate collections in Australia and overseas.